Lecture Notes in Artificial Intelligence   11175

Subseries of Lecture Notes in Computer Science

More information about this series at http://www.springer.com/series/1244

Hidehisa Akiyama · Oliver Obst
Claude Sammut · Flavio Tonidandel (Eds.)

RoboCup 2017:
Robot World Cup XXI

 Springer

Editors
Hidehisa Akiyama (iD)
Fukuoka University
Fukuoka
Japan

Oliver Obst (iD)
Center for Research in Mathematics
Western Sydney University
Penrith, NSW
Australia

Claude Sammut (iD)
School of Computer Science and
    Engineering
University of New South Wales
Sydney, NSW
Australia

Flavio Tonidandel (iD)
Department of Computer Science
Centro Universitario da FEI
São Bernardo do Campo, São Paulo
Brazil

ISSN 0302-9743   ISSN 1611-3349   (electronic)
Lecture Notes in Artificial Intelligence
ISBN 978-3-030-00307-4   ISBN 978-3-030-00308-1   (eBook)
https://doi.org/10.1007/978-3-030-00308-1

Library of Congress Control Number: 2018953822

LNCS Sublibrary: SL7 – Artificial Intelligence

This Springer imprint is published by the registered company Springer Nature Switzerland AG
The registered company address is: Gewerbestrasse 11, 6330 Cham, Switzerland

Preface

RoboCup aims to promote robotics and AI by stimulating research and innovative technologies through annual competitions and scientific meetings. RoboCup 2017 was held at the Nagoya International Exhibition Hall in Nagoya, Japan, the same city that proudly hosted the first RoboCup in 1997. From July 27 to July 31, the event received more than 130,000 visitors to watch and cheer for 3,000 participants from 42 countries competing in RoboCupJunior and Major leagues.

Together with the competitions and challenges, RoboCup 2017 also hosted the 21st annual RoboCup International Symposium at the Aichi University Nagoya Campus, on July 31st. The RoboCup International Symposium provides an excellent opportunity for the scientific community to present their advances in Robotics and Artificial Intelligence, stimulated by the RoboCup competitions that encourage practical innovations in science, technology, and engineering. For the RoboCup International Symposium, we received a total of 58 regular paper submissions, which were reviewed by an international Program Committee. Each paper was reviewed and scored by three reviewers. Overall, we accepted 33 papers (57%), of which ten were chosen for oral presentation. Besides the regular papers, this book also includes nine Champion Team Papers, written by the teams who won the competitions. These papers represent the state of the art in each League and are intended to foster discussion on the future of RoboCup by introducing new promising ideas and technologies.

In addition to the accepted papers, the event was fortunate to have two invited keynote speakers. Prof. Hajime Asama (University of Tokyo) presented a talk on robots in real rescue environments and remote-control technology. Prof. Asama's distinguished career includes work on advanced robots for the Fukushima Power Plant damaged by the 2011 earthquake and tsunami. Prof. Maya Cakmak (University of Washington), presented her work on "End-User Programming for General Purpose Robots", which demonstrated how robots can be successfully programmed by a diverse group of users with different needs.

Two papers, presented at the symposium, were selected for special awards:

- Real-Time Online Adaptive Feedforward Velocity Control for Unmanned Ground Vehicles, by Nicolai Ommer, Alexander Stumpf, and Oskar von Stryk, was granted The Best paper Award for its Scientific Contribution.
- Using Convolutional Neural Networks in Robots with Limited Computational Resources: Detecting NAO Robots while Playing Soccer, by Nicolas Cruz, Kenzo Lobos-Tsunekawa, and Javier Ruiz-Del-Solar, was granted The Best paper Award for its Engineering Contribution.

These papers appear in this book.

Finally, we would like to thank the chairs of RoboCup 2017, Takeshi Ohashi, Hiroyuki Okada, Tomoichi Takahashi, Komei Sugiura, and all the members of the Organizing Committee, who managed this exceptional event. We would like to thank all members of the Program Committee and our additional reviewers for their time and expertise in reviewing the papers and ensuring the quality of the technical program. We also thank all the authors, participants and staff for their contributions in making this event a huge success. Our sincerest thanks to the entire RoboCup community for their enthusiasm, friendship, and successful work on intelligent robots for our future society.

July 2018

Hidehisa Akiyama
Oliver Obst
Claude Sammut
Flavio Tonidandel

Organization

Symposium Co-chairs

Hidehisa Akiyama	Fukuoka University, Japan
Oliver Obst	Western Sydney University, Australia
Sammut Claude	University of New South Wales, Australia
Flavio Tonidandel	Centro Universitario FEI, Brazil

Program Committee

H. Levent Akin	Bogazici University, Turkey
Minoru Asada	Osaka University, Japan
Bikramjit Banerjee	The University of Southern Mississippi, USA
Sven Behnke	University of Bonn, Germany
Heni Ben Amor	Arizona State University, USA
Reinaldo A. C. Bianchi	Centro Universitario FEI, Brazil
Joydeep Biswas	University of Massachusetts Amherst, USA
Joschka Boedecker	University of Freiburg, Germany
Ansgar Bredenfeld	Dr. Bredenfeld UG, Germany
Stephan Chalup	The University of Newcastle, Australia
Xiaoping Chen	University of Science and Technology of China, China
Esther Colombini	Unicamp, Brazil
Anna Helena Reali Costa	University of Sao Paulo, Brazil
Bernardo Cunha	University of Aveiro, Portugal
Klaus Dorer	Hochschule Offenburg, Germany
Alexander Ferrein	FH Aachen University of Applied Sciences, Germany
Thomas Gabel	Frankfurt University of Applied Sciences, Germany
Fredrik Heintz	Linköping University, Sweden
Luca Iocchi	Sapienza University of Rome, Italy
Jianmin Ji	University of Science and Technology of China, China
Gerhard Lakemeyer	RWTH Aachen University, Germany
Nuno Lau	University of Aveiro, Portugal
Olivier Ly	University of Bordeaux, France
Patrick MacAlpine	The University of Texas at Austin, USA
Eric Matson	Purdue University, USA
Tekin Meriçli	Carnegie Mellon University, USA
Çetin Meriçli	Carnegie Mellon University, USA
Elena Messina	National Institute of Standards and Technology, USA
Tomoharu Nakashima	Osaka Prefecture University, Japan
Daniele Nardi	Sapienza University of Rome, Italy
Paul G. Plöger	Bonn-Rhein-Sieg University of Applied Science, Germany

Mikhail Prokopenko	The University of Sydney, Australia
Luis Paulo Reis	University of Porto, Portugal
Thomas Röfer	German Research Center for Artificial Intelligence, Germany
Javier Ruiz-Del-Solar	Universidad de Chile, Chile
Raymond Sheh	Curtin University, Australia
Saeed Shiry	Amirkabir University of Technology, Iran
Gerald Steinbauer	Graz University of Technology, Austria
Frieder Stolzenburg	Harz University of Applied Sciences, Germany
Luis Enrique Sucar	INAOE, Mexico
Komei Sugiura	National Institute of Information and Communications Technology, Japan
Yasutake Takahashi	University of Fukui, Japan
Ubbo Visser	University of Miami, USA
Arnoud Visser	University of Amsterdam, Netherlands
Alfredo Weitzenfeld	University of South Florida, USA
Timothy Wiley	The University of New South Wales, Australia
Aaron Wong	The University of Newcastle, Australia

Additional Reviewers

Eduardo Alves	University of Sao Paulo, Brazil
Chloe Arluck	University of Miami, USA
Okan Aşık	Bogaziçi University, Turkey
Bruno Augusto Angelico	University of Sao Paulo, Brazil
Roberto Capobianco	Sapienza University of Rome, Italy
Jonathan Gerbscheid	Strangelove Amsterdam, Netherlands
Baris Gokce	Bogaziçi University, Turkey
Till Hofmann	RWTH Aachen University, Germany
Trent Houliston	The University of Newcastle, Australia
Tobias Klamt	University of Bonn, Germany
Seongyong Koo	University of Bonn, Germany
Eduardo Lorenzetti Pellini	University of Sao Paulo, Brazil
German Martin Garcia	University of Bonn, Germany
Brigida Mónica Faria	Instituto Politecnico do Porto, Portugal
Yuji Onuma	National Institute of Information and Communications Technology, Japan
İbrahim Özcan	Bogaziçi University, Turkey
Stefan Schiffer	RWTH Aachen University, Germany
Dominik Schlegel	Sapienza University of Rome, Italy
Falk Schmidsberger	Harz University of Applied Science, Germany
Geoff Skinner	The University of Newcastle, Australia
Alaa Tharwat	Frankfurt University of Applied Science, Germany
Daniel Thompson	The University of Southern Mississippi, USA
Mark Wallis	The University of Newcastle, Australia
Shuai Wei	University of Science and Technology of China, China
Zekun Zhang	University of Science and Technology of China, China

Contents

Champion Papers

Best Paper Award for Scientific Contribution

Real-Time Online Adaptive Feedforward Velocity Control for Unmanned Ground Vehicles

Nicolai Ommer$^{(\boxtimes)}$, Alexander Stumpf$^{(\boxtimes)}$, and Oskar von Stryk$^{(\boxtimes)}$

Department of Computer Science, TU Darmstadt, Darmstadt, Germany
nicolai.ommer@gmail.com, {stumpf,stryk}@sim.tu-darmstadt.de

Abstract. Online adaptation of motion models enables autonomous robots to move more accurate in case of unknown disturbances. This paper proposes a new adaptive compensation feedforward controller capable of online learning a compensation motion model without any prior knowledge to counteract non-modeled disturbance such as slippage or hardware malfunctions. The controller is able to prevent motion errors a priori and is well suited for real hardware due to high adaptation rate. It can be used in conjunction with any motion model as only motion errors are compensated. A simple interface enables quick deployment of other robot systems as demonstrated in Small Size and Rescue Robot RoboCup leagues.

1 Introduction

Precise control in an unknown, unstructured or dynamic environment is a crucial ability for autonomous robots to move safely among obstacles. Here, navigation, path planning, and controllers rely on a reliable motion model that cannot consider detailed knowledge about unknown external disturbances such as friction, slippage or even hardware malfunctions. These unmodeled disturbances may be counteracted by appropriate feedback controllers but will always decrease locomotion performance of the robot system as any deviation from a planned path requires continuous correction movements or in case of nonholonomic systems such as tracked robots even trajectory replanning.

The used motion model as well as the controllers are often derived directly from robot structure but can neither automatically adapt to changes in structure nor in the environment. In order to overcome such problems, model based agents have become popular in the fields of robotics which can infer characteristics of its structure and the surrounding world.

On the other side, learning approaches often require an unreasonable amount of training data in order to generalize well. In this work we have investigated a way to benefit from both worlds: instead of learning the entire motion model we figure out how to fix the performance errors of the existing model.

This motivates our contribution of an adaptive compensation feedforward controller which is capable of adapting online to motion errors caused by

© Springer Nature Switzerland AG 2018
H. Akiyama et al. (Eds.): RoboCup 2017, LNAI 11175, pp. 3–16, 2018.
https://doi.org/10.1007/978-3-030-00308-1_1

unknown disturbances. For this purpose, multiple learning approaches have been evaluated in terms of applicability, real-time performance, motion precision and motion error adaptation time. While learning approaches have been widely investigated in motor and multi-joint trajectory control, the application to locomotion trajectory control has not received much attention yet to the best of the author's knowledge.

The proposed controller has been evaluated with two robot platforms with distinct motion capabilities used in different RoboCup leagues: Small Size and Robot Rescue League. The adaptation is performed without any prior knowledge of any underlying motion model which demonstrates that the method can be applied to a wide range of systems.

2   Related Work

The RoboCup Small Size League (SSL) has to tackle with large robot control delays with at least 100 ms due to off-board processing. This problem can be bypassed by capable feedforward controllers, reducing all feedback error terms significantly. An early attempt was done by Gloye et al. using neuronal networks to predict the behavior of the robots based on the current state and motion command to overcome the system delay [1]. Based on the first trained neural network a second network has been trained to predict appropriate motion commands leading into the desired robot behavior. They demonstrated how the neural network is able to learn a model compensating for a disconnected motor. However, these networks can only be trained offline and require uniformly distributed data sets to cover the whole function space.

In order to use neural networks in adaptive control tasks, the concept of Feedback Error Learning has been applied in [2]. The online trained artificial neural network using an expanded version of the traditional back-propagation algorithm outperformed a standalone PD controller applied to a SCARA robot arm but the learning rate has to be adapted manually during training. Although the neural network compensated general deviations, the feedback controller was still active to capture irregularities.

The application of neural networks needs a lot of manual structural tuning such as determining the optimal number of layers and neurons. A more convenient class of learning approaches are function approximators which can directly infer from data. Locally Weighted Learning (LWL) categorizes a class of nonlinear function learners based on locally linear approximations. This type of function approximation can be even used to learn forward or inverse robot models [3]. In general, LWL methods can be split into two categories: Memory-based and incremental LWL.

A memory-based LWL method is Locally Weighted Regression (LWR) that stores all training data in memory in order to calculate the prediction at a query point [4]. For this purpose, all data is accumulated into a matrix from which the locally weighted regression coefficient must be determined via matrix inversion for each prediction. Obviously, this method is not suitable for online learning and real-time control as LWR suffers from intensive computations increasing quadratically by the number of data samples.

Locally Weighted Projection Regression (LWPR) instead is keeping and updating multiple locally weighted linear models to approximate non-linear functions [5,6]. This method enables incremental updates as the existing local model is just updated or a new one is created if there is no trustworthy model available. This is achieved by keeping a set of Receptive Fields (RF) with activation terms. Training data is then only added to a model if the RF provides sufficient activation. A forgetting rate weights training points gathered earlier down which is useful for systems that change over time. Furthermore, LWPR takes use of the online dimensionality reduction method Partial Least Squares (PLS) to handle redundant and irrelevant input data. As the method works incremental by design, it is well suited for our proposed approach. In this work the LWPR implementation by Klanke et al. [7] has been adopted.

Another interesting class of non-linear function approximators is Gaussian Process Regression (GPR) which is a non-parametric regression method that can approximate (multivariate) non-linear functions [8]. However, the complexity of prediction is cubic in the number of training samples [9] as all training data is put into a single kernel. For this reason Csato et al. proposed Sparse Online Gaussian Process (SOGP) [10] building a sparse kernel by using a Bayesian online algorithm and subsampling relevant data from sequentially arriving training data. In this way, the processing time has been reduced significantly and therefore makes it suitable for online processing. An implementation of SOGP is available in the Online Temporal Learning (OTL) library[1] which has been used in this work.

Recursive Least Squares (RLS) is an iterative approach of Linear Least Squares Regression (LLSR) [11]. The RLS algorithm minimizes the squared error of incrementally arriving samples by updating the internal weight vector instead of computing a full matrix inversion as LLRS does. This results in a constant prediction and update time but the model can only cover linear dependencies between inputs and output variables. Again the OTL library provides an implementation of RLS which is used in this work as well.

3   Adaptive Compensation Feedforward Controller

The proposed adaptive compensation feedforward control approach in Fig. 1 can be categorized as Direct Modeling [12] which learns a motion error compensation model based on all previously observed errors during robot movements. The basic idea is not to learn the entire motion model determining a transferring action between two consecutive states but the required compensating action to nullify all motion errors produced by feedforward commands. This approach reduces model complexity significantly and enables to focus on training of motion error compensations rather than the complete motion model of the robot. As the presented adaptive compensation feedforward controller does only predict compensating actions, it can be used in combination with any existing controller

---

[1] https://bitbucket.org/haroldsoh/otl.

such as feedback controllers. Additionally, the used compensation model and learning method can be initialized to return neutral (e.g. zero-valued) compensating actions when no prior training data is available. This reduces undesirable behaviors due to insufficient training or bad generalization capability of the used learner to a minimum.

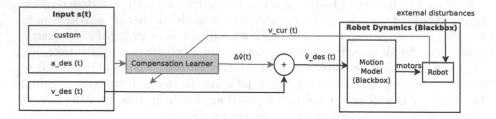

Fig. 1. Basic schema of the adaptive compensation feedforward controller

The input state vector $s(t)$ used by the proposed controller is composed of the desired velocity $v_{des}(t)$, the desired acceleration $a_{des}(t)$ and optional user selectable input values. The optional input values, for example IMU angles, can be selected by an expert in order to improve the inference from observed data.

In this work, the controller tracks the velocity of the robot base rather than single motor commands. Thus, the learning part tries to estimate a compensating velocity $\Delta\hat{v}$ to be added up to the target robot base velocity v_{des} in order to achieve the target velocity in real world while using feedforward control only.

The adaptive compensation controller works in two steps: Compensation model learning and error compensation prediction which are both explained next.

3.1 Compensation Model Learning

An ideal feedforward controller should be able to replace any feedback controllers. Indeed, we can learn from feedback errors in a way the adaptive compensation feedforward controller can prevent motion errors a priori instead of performing corrections in the feedback control loop afterwards.

This problem can be stated in a mathematical way. The robot will move in the next time step with a certain speed $v_{cur}(t+1)$ resulted from a previously commanded speed $v_{des}(t)$ and an execution error $\epsilon(t)$ caused by unmodeled disturbances:

$$v_{cur}(t+1) = v_{des}(t) + \epsilon(t). \tag{1}$$

The motion error $\epsilon(t)$ is often compensated by feedback controllers in robotic systems and can be determined by computing the difference between the commanded and resulting velocities:

$$\epsilon(t) = v_{des}(t) - v_{cur}(t+1). \tag{2}$$

On the other side, $\epsilon(t)$ can be minimized by adapting $v_{des}(t)$ properly which results in the velocity compensation rule:

$$\hat{v}_{des}(t) = v_{des}(t) - \epsilon(t) \tag{3}$$

$$\Rightarrow \quad 0 = \hat{v}_{des}(t) - v_{cur}(t+1) \tag{4}$$

with $\hat{v}_{des}(t)$ as adapted control output. As a result, we require a compensation policy $\pi(s(t))$ that must be able to predict a compensating action $\Delta\hat{v}$ to overcome the expected motion error ϵ based on the current state $s(t)$:

$$\pi(s(t)) \mapsto \Delta\hat{v}. \tag{5}$$

In this work, the labels $\Delta\hat{v}$ for the input state $s(t)$ are updated iteratively based on the current prediction and observed motion error:

$$\Delta\hat{v}^{(k+1)} = \underbrace{\Delta\hat{v}^{(k)}}_{\hat{=}\pi(s(t))^{(k)}} - k\epsilon \tag{6}$$

where k controls the adaption rate and the initial value $\Delta\hat{v}^{(0)}$ is usually zero. The resulting updated mapping $s(t) \mapsto \Delta\hat{v}^{(k+1)}$ is then given to the learner to update the compensation policy:

$$\pi(s(t))^{(k+1)} \mapsto \Delta\hat{v}^{(k+1)} \ (= \pi(s(t))^{(k)} - k\epsilon). \tag{7}$$

Non-modeled disturbance such as terrain (slippage) will affect execution errors as well. Therefore, it is highly desirable to add all available informative data to the state vector $s(t)$. Modern learning approaches are well suited for such kind of mapping problems as demonstrated later.

3.2 Error Compensation Prediction

In each control loop cycle the controller estimates a compensating action $\Delta\hat{v}$ based on the previously learned model. The compensation step can be expressed as:

$$\hat{v}_{des}(t) = v_{des}(t) + \Delta\hat{v} = v_{des}(t) + \pi(s(t)). \tag{8}$$

The resulting compensated velocity command $\hat{v}_{des}(t)$ can be directly forwarded to the robot controllers using a motion model internally that maps the velocity commands to motor commands. The measured velocity in the next time frame $v_{cur}(t+1)$ is back-propagated to the proposed adaptive compensation feedforward controller in order to update the compensation policy as described above.

4 Experiments

Multiple evaluation criteria and scenarios have been evaluated during this work. Especially runtime performance is crucial for robot controllers as computational time must comply with the control loop timing. Furthermore, the presented framework has been tested in simulation first and applied on real robots afterwards. During this experiments, error correction capabilities and adaptation speed have been investigated which is summarized next.

In the following sections, an iteration refers to a reproducible movement based on predefined trajectories. These iterations are repeated in order to compare the performance of the used learners over time.

4.1 Runtime Performance

The processing time can be split into two parts: Compensation model update and prediction. While the update time is negligible for the control loop as it can be performed asynchronously, the prediction time determines the maximum possible control loop frequency. During all experiments, the update rate for the rescue robot was 40 Hz, for the soccer robot 100 Hz and the prediction rate 100 Hz.

The experiments have been performed on the real robots and with a simulated SSL Robot within the software framework from TIGERs Mannheim [13] running on Intel i7 CPU with 2.6 GHz. Three different trajectories were specified while keeping the head orientation fixed (see Fig. 4): A circle, a curved rectangle, and a star, each about 2 m in diameter and between 8 s and 60 s long.

The robot receives velocity commands from our feedforward controller and uses an internal kinematics model to calculate wheel velocities. As the simulated robot would obviously behave perfectly, the low-level wheels commands have been artificially disturbed by a constant error while turning off all feedback controllers to simulate a non-calibrated system.

Table 1. Average processing timings of 1st, 2nd and 5th iteration for all evaluated learning approaches given in milliseconds.

	#	LWPR		SOGP		RLS	
		Prediction	Update	Prediction	Update	Prediction	Update
Rectangle	1	0.0310	0.0278	0.1700	1.1209	0.0490	0.2183
	2	0.0488	0.0423	0.2741	1.7781	0.0485	0.2111
	5	0.0479	0.0432	0.2704	1.6948	0.0479	0.2184
Circle	1	0.0271	0.0237	0.1477	0.9327	0.0524	0.2132
	2	0.0349	0.0317	0.1804	1.1189	0.0528	0.2198
	5	0.0360	0.0355	0.1899	1.2149	0.0519	0.2156
Star	1	0.0948	0.0845	0.8102	3.9831	0.0496	0.2293
	2	0.1317	0.1221	0.8146	4.1630	0.0490	0.2191
	5	0.1395	0.1315	0.8191	4.1901	0.0474	0.2202

Table 1 shows that LWPR and SOGP take more processing time when performing star trajectory due to input diversity provided by this movement pattern. This behavior can be explained as LWPR uses local models whose number is increasing over time when additional input space has been covered while in case of SOGP the number of basis vectors increases over time.

The noticeable update time of SOGP is caused by large matrix inversions. Although the prediction time of SOGP requires only a simple matrix multiplication, it suffers from the high matrix dimension and therefore underperforms LWPR and RLS. As expected, RLS runs with constant processing timings in every scenario.

All methods can be considered sufficiently fast for real-time control. The prediction time allows theoretical control rates beyond 1 kHz for all approaches, but SOGP can only be updated in a much slower rate. As prediction and update is done asynchronously, SOGP is still feasible for real-time control.

(a) SSL Robot by TIGERs Mannheim

(b) Rescue Robot by Team Hector

Fig. 2. Robots from different RoboCup leagues have been used for evaluation.

4.2   RoboCup Small Size Soccer Robot

The real soccer robot (see Fig. 2(a)) was driven with a kinematics model that maps velocity commands to motor commands [14]. The evaluation has been carried out with the trajectories introduced previously.

Running these experiments on the real soccer robot reveals another motivation for using adaptive feedforward controls. SSL robots are performing off-board processing due to limited space on the robot. This system setup introduces a delay time of about 100 ms to the control loop from which feedback controllers are suffering.

Comparison of Learning Methods. The next experiment has been performed with previously used learning approaches, compared with a PD feedback controller in addition. Figure 3 illustrates the evolution of all approaches after each iteration.

The most exciting result is the bad performance of the PD feedback controller caused by high control loop time leading to late and overcompensating reactions. This emphasizes the use of adaptive feedforward control proposed in this work.

RLS has performed very bad as well due to used linear compensation model. This linear model cannot capture non-linearities as required for controlling the

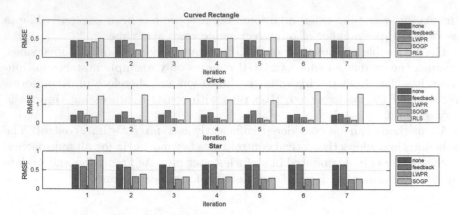

Fig. 3. Evolution of velocity RMSE for different control approaches applied at the real soccer robot. The 6th and 7th iteration have been performed without model updates to evaluate stability of the controller.

robot orientation. This resulted in non-converging model updates and continuous overcompensation leading to oscillatory motions in the rotational axis. For this reason, RLS could not be applied to the star shape due to the lack of controller equilibrium. From this point on, RLS has been rejected from all future experiments due to stability issues.

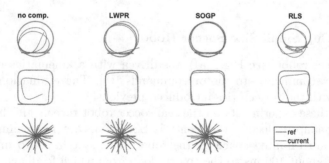

Fig. 4. Plot from the resulted movement of the fifth iteration for each learning approach. The green line shows the reference trajectory and blue the feedforward executed trajectory. (Color figure online)

Throughout all experiments, LWPR and SOGP performed similar well. After the first three iterations, all approaches were able to reduce the overall pose error significantly by feedforward motion error compensation which is visualized in Fig. 4. It shows the pose tracking improvement when using LWPR or SOGP.

Evaluation of Compensation Commands Using LWPR. Each deviation from the commanded velocity accumulates to a pose error which is typically compensated by feedback pose controllers that have been disabled throughout all experiments. As stated before the goal of our approach is to reduce the required pose adjustments. Hence, the velocity deviation is analyzed next using LWPR as example as it has performed best.

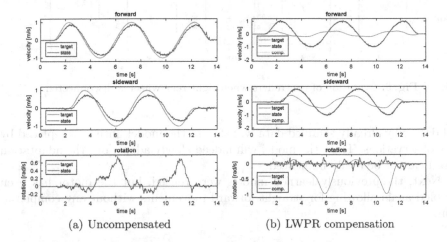

(a) Uncompensated   (b) LWPR compensation

Fig. 5. Comparison of circle trajectory execution without (left) and with LWPR compensation after five iterations (right) using the real soccer robot.

The uncompensated robot system shows a phase shift in transverse plane leading to reduced amplitudes (Fig. 5(a)) and is affected by an undesired rotational velocity accumulating to a rotational drift up to 90° after each iteration. This can be explained by the use of omni wheels causing a lot of non-modeled slippage.

Figure 5(b) shows how the LWPR feedforward controller is able to compensate successfully the phase shift and reduces even significantly the rotational drift of the system. The magenta line shows the compensating actions that the controller predicts at the corresponding states given the execution errors that have been observed in the five previous iterations. A full video of this experiment is available online at https://youtu.be/3_shNa66oA.

Evaluation of Performance on a Major Malfunction. The ability to adapt towards hardware wear and malfunctions is a major motivation for adaptive feedforward control. In the next experiment, the right rear wheel has been disabled causing the robot to drive a curve, although a forward movement is commanded.

This experiment should evaluate how well LWPR and SOGP can adapt to such situations. The first step was to drive in a straight line back and forth, starting with an empty model.

Figure 6 shows that SOGP converges much slower than LWPR during this experiment. In case of LWPR, the quick convergence has been achieved by tuning the integrated forgetting factor. But in contrast SOGP has no notion of forgetting

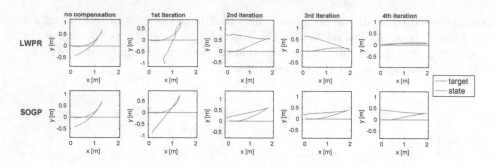

Fig. 6. Evolution of controllers when right rear wheel is disconnected.

old data why already sampled data will stay in the model until it is replaced by new observations. Thus, the model will indeed slowly adapt, but the adaptation speed cannot be easily influenced.

Next, the previously learned models were reused, but the motor has been enabled again allowing for straight forward movements without any compensation.

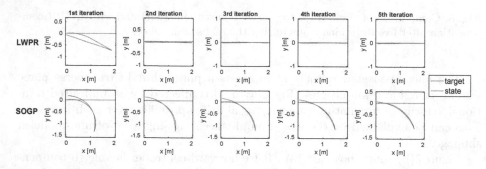

Fig. 7. Robot trajectory when right rear wheel is reconnected after a compensation model has been learned with disconnected wheel.

In the first iteration all controllers performing an expected overcompensation (Fig. 7). While LWPR can adapt to this new situation after the first iteration quickly, SOGP converges only slowly back to a zero compensation policy. As result LWPR shows clearly a better adaption capability.

4.3   RoboCup Rescue Tracked Robot

The second used robot platform for experiments is a tracked robot from the RoboCup Robot Rescue League by Team Hector [15]. This nonholonomic platform is based on a tracked differential drive and cannot move sidewards, which is why lateral drifts have devastating influence on locomotion performance. Furthermore, the rubber chains cause downhill sliding on inclined terrain during movements, no matter which orientation the robot has.

The robot world pose is estimated using Hector Slam [16] and the data from the integrated IMU is added to the input state of our adaptive compensation feedforward controller as discussed in Sect. 3. All compensating actions become dependent on the robot's three-axis-orientation, especially roll and pitch.

Rotation on a Ramp. Movements on even terrain can be executed precisely by the existing controllers, but the discussed slippage on inclined terrain is an interesting application for the presented controller. In the following experiment the robot should perform a full 360° rotation on a ramp. An ideal system would just rotate in place and stop exactly on its initial position (see Fig. 8(a)).

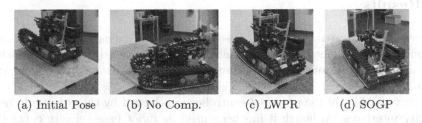

(a) Initial Pose   (b) No Comp.   (c) LWPR   (d) SOGP

Fig. 8. 360° rotation on a ramp using LWPR and SOGP after three iterations.

But the real robot system slides downhill ending off the ramp (see Fig. 8(b)). Both approaches, LWPR and SOGP, cannot prevent sliding downwards at all but reduce it as illustrated in Fig. 8. Only LWPR was even able to stabilize the rotatory velocity resulting in nearly zero orientation offset after each iteration.

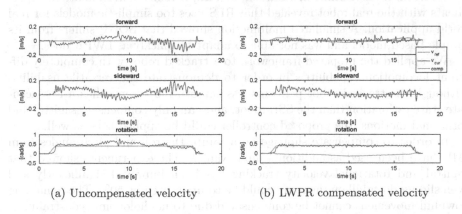

(a) Uncompensated velocity   (b) LWPR compensated velocity

Fig. 9. Velocity plot during the 360° rotation on a ramp with LWPR compensation.

The plots in Fig. 9(a) illustrates how the robot is sliding downhill, observable as non-zero velocities in transverse plane depending on current robot orientation. The LWPR controller is able to reduce successfully deviations by adapting the speed of each single track indirectly. In Fig. 9(b) the compensating actions are plotted in magenta demonstrating how the LWPR predictor does influence the track speeds by predicting appropriate compensating actions. This adaptive behavior can be watched in the video at https://youtu.be/cW20_JsZCzg.

All compensating actions are predicted reasonably based on motion errors observed previously. However, velocity deviations in lateral direction cannot be compensated directly due to nonholonomic constraints. Thus, the LWPR and SOGP feedforward controllers are able to reduce but not nullify sliding downhill the ramp.

5   Results

We have demonstrated that our proposed adaptive feedforward controller is able to compensate non-modeled disturbance online. All used learning approaches can run using state of the art consumer computer hardware in control rates beyond 1 kHz.

The versatility of the proposed controller is achieved by the commonly used velocity interfaces. Although it has been used as robot base velocity controller throughout this work, it can be considered as generic velocity controller which would even work on motor level. But it should be noted that velocity estimation accuracy is crucial for training the learner effectively.

While the SSL robot showed undesirable motion errors, the proposed controller is able to improve the movement accuracy significantly. Especially the robot orientation is suffering from major deviations depending on multidimensional input but could be stabilized as well by the implemented control policy.

While all three learning methods showed improvements in simulation, experiments with the real robot revealed that RLS uses too simplistic models for real world application. A simulated malfunction showed that SOGP suffers from its sample based model and was not able to adapt as quickly as LWPR does.

We applied the proposed framework to a tracked robot with completely different locomotion capabilities in order to demonstrate the versatile usability. Although the tracked robot performs less smooth movements, has a less accurate state estimation than the SSL robot, and can only compensate sagittal and rotational motions, the proposed controller could be applied here as well.

In order to compensate slippage on a ramp, the roll and pitch angles from IMU have been used as additional input values. The experiments showed that sagittal and rotational velocity tracking has been improved significantly and even sliding downhill on the ramp could be compensated by 50%. The remaining downhill movement cannot be compensated due to nonholonomic constraints.

All experiments have been performed under controlled conditions. As soon as there are non-consistent external influences that cannot be captured as input state for the learner such as changing traction, the adaptive feedforward controller may infer wrong, but the model will be adapted continuously. In such scenarios, the forgetting factor of LWPR is a crucial mechanism to control adaptation speed towards structural and environmental changes. However, the experiments demonstrated the high adaptation rate of the LWPR controller making it suitable for real hardware.

6   Conclusion

In this paper, an adaptive compensation feedforward controller framework based on a compensation model has been presented that can be used in conjunction with any existing motion model. While commonly used motion learning approaches are dependent on training the whole robot motion model, the presented compensation controller can be deployed without any pre-training.

A selection of different learning approaches has been analyzed for their capability as adaptive compensation feedforward controller. Only LWPR proved to comply with required computational speed, prediction accuracy, and model adaptability during the experiments. The proposed controller is able to compensate unmodeled disturbances such as robot decalibration or slippage. It can even improve the system's fault tolerance against hardware malfunctions due to online adaptability.

The framework has been applied to two very different robot systems across the RoboCup Leagues. Although those robots are underlying distinct mobility challenges, the controller was able to improve locomotion performance for each system.

References

1. Gloye, A., Wiesel, F., Tenchio, O., Simon, M., Rojas, R.: Robot heal thyself - precise and fault-tolerant control of imprecise or malfunctioning robots. In: International Symposium on RoboCup 2005, Osaka, Japan (2005)
2. Passold, F., Stemmer, M.R.: Feedback error learning neural network applied to a scara robot. In: 4th International Workshop on Robot Motion and Control, pp. 197–202 (2004)
3. Atkeson, C.G., Moore, A.W., Schaal, S.: Locally weighted learning for control. Artif. Intell. Rev. 11(1), 75–113 (1997)
4. Christopher, A., Andrew, M., Stefan, S.: Locally weighted learning. Artif. Intell. Rev. 11(1–5), 11–73 (1997)
5. Vijayakumar, S., Schaal, S.: Locally weighted projection regression: an O(n) algorithm for incremental real time learning in high dimensional space. In: Proceedings of the 17th International Conference on Machine Learning, ICML, vol. 1, pp. 288–293 (2000)
6. Vijayakumar, S., D'Souza, A., Schaal, S.: Incremental online learning in high dimensions. Neural Comput. 17(12), 2602–2634 (2005)
7. Klanke, S., Vijayakumar, S., Schaal, S.: A library for locally weighted projection regression. J. Mach. Learn. Res. 9(1), 623–626 (2008)

8. Rasmussen, C.E.: Gaussian Processes for Machine Learning. The MIT Press, Cambridge (2006). Chap. 2
9. Barber, D.: Bayesian Reasoning and Machine Learning. Cambridge University Press, Cambridge (2012)
10. Csató, L., Opper, M.: Sparse on-line Gaussian processes. Neural Comput. **14**, 641–668 (2002)
11. Benesty, J., Paleologu, C., Gänsler, T., Ciochina, S.: Recursive least-squares algorithms. In: A Perspective on Stereophonic Acoustic Echo Cancellation. STSP, vol. 4, pp. 63–69. Springer, Heidelberg (2011). https://doi.org/10.1007/978-3-642-22574-1_6
12. Nguyen-Tuong, D., Peters, J.: Model learning for robot control: a survey. Cogn. Process. **12**(4), 319–340 (2011)
13. Ryll, A., Geiger, M., Ommer, N., Sachtler, A., Magel, L.: TIGERs Mannheim - Extended Team Description for RoboCup 2016 (2016)
14. Rojas, R., Förster, A.: Holonomic control of a robot with an omnidirectional drive. KI-Künstliche Intelligenz **7** (2006)
15. Kohlbrecher, S., et al.: RoboCup Rescue 2016 team description paper hector Darmstadt. Technical report. Technische Universitaet Darmstadt (2016)
16. Kohlbrecher, S., Meyer, J., von Stryk, O., Klingauf, U.: A flexible and scalable SLAM system with full 3D motion estimation. In: Proceedings of the IEEE International Symposium on Safety, Security and Rescue Robotics, SSRR, Kyoto, Japan, pp. 155–160. IEEE (2011)

Best Paper Award for Engineering Contribution

Using Convolutional Neural Networks in Robots with Limited Computational Resources: Detecting NAO Robots While Playing Soccer

Nicolás Cruz[✉], Kenzo Lobos-Tsunekawa, and Javier Ruiz-del-Solar

Advanced Mining Technology Center and Department of Electrical Engineering,
Universidad de Chile, Santiago, Chile
{nicolas.cruz,kenzo.lobos,jruizd}@ing.uchile.cl

Abstract. The main goal of this paper is to analyze the general problem of using Convolutional Neural Networks (CNNs) in robots with limited computational capabilities, and to propose general design guidelines for their use. In addition, two different CNN based NAO robot detectors that are able to run in real-time while playing soccer are proposed. One of the detectors is based on the XNOR-Net and the other on the SqueezeNet. Each detector is able to process a robot object-proposal in ~1 ms, with an average number of 1.5 proposals per frame obtained by the upper camera of the NAO. The obtained detection rate is ~97%.

Keywords: Deep learning · Convolutional Neural Networks · Robot detection

1 Introduction

Deep learning has allowed a paradigm shift in pattern recognition, from using hand-crafted features together with statistical classifiers, to using general-purpose learning procedures to learn data-driven representations, features, and classifiers together. The application of this new paradigm has been particularly successful in computer vision, in which the development of deep learning methods for vision applications has become a hot research topic. This new paradigm has already attracted the attention of the robot vision community. However, the question is whether or not new deep learning solutions to computer vision and recognition problems can be directly transferred to robot vision applications. We believe that this transfer is not straightforward considering the multiple requirements of current deep learning solutions in terms of memory and computational resources, which in many cases include the use of GPUs. Furthermore, we believe that this transfer must consider that robot vision applications have different requirements than standard computer vision applications, such as real-time operation with limited on-board computational resources, and the constraining observational conditions derived from the robot geometry, limited camera resolution, and sensor/object relative pose.

One of the main application areas of deep learning in robot vision is object detection and categorization. These are fundamental abilities in robotics, because they enable a robot to execute tasks that require interaction with object instances in the real-world. State-of-the-art methods used for object detection and categorization are based on

© Springer Nature Switzerland AG 2018
H. Akiyama et al. (Eds.): RoboCup 2017, LNAI 11175, pp. 19–30, 2018.
https://doi.org/10.1007/978-3-030-00308-1_2

generating object proposals, and then classifying them using a Convolutional Neural Network (CNN), enabling systems to detect thousands of different object categories. But as already mentioned, one of the main challenges for the application of CNNs for object detection and characterization in robotics is real-time operation. On the one hand, obtaining the required object proposals for feeding a CNN is not real-time in the general case, and on the other hand, general-purpose object detection and categorization CNN based methods are not able to run in real-time in most robotics platforms. These challenges can be addressed by using task-dependent methods for generating few, fast and high quality proposals for a limited number of possible object categories. These methods are based on using other information sources for segmenting the objects (depth information, motion, color, etc.), and/or by using non general-purpose, but object specific weak detectors for generating the required proposals. In addition, fast and/or lightweight CNN architectures can be used when dealing with a limited number of object categories.

Preliminary CNN based object detection systems have been already proposed in the context of robotic soccer. In [1], a CNN system is proposed for detecting players in RGB images. Player proposals are computed by using color-segmentation based techniques. Then, a CNN is used for validating the player detections. Different architectures with 3, 4, and 5 layers are explored, all of them using ReLU. In the reported experiments, the 5-layer architecture is able to obtain 100% accuracy when processing images at 11–19 fps on a NAO robot, when all non-related processes such as self-localization, decision-making, and body control are disabled. In [2], a CNN-based system for detecting balls inside an image is proposed. Two CNNs are used, consisting of three shared convolutional layers, and two independent fully-connected layers. Both CNNs are able to obtain a localization probability distribution for the ball over the horizontal and vertical image axes respectively. Several nonlinearities were tested, with the soft-sign activation function generating the best results. Processing times in NAO platforms are not reported in that work. From the results reported in [1, 2], it can be concluded that these object detectors cannot be used in real-time by a robot with limited computational resources (e.g. a NAO robot) while playing soccer, without disturbing other fundamental processes (walk engine, self-localization, etc.).

In this context the main goal of this paper is to analyze the general problem of using CNNs in robots with limited computational capabilities and to propose general design guidelines for their use. In addition, two different CNN based NAO robot detectors that are able to run in real-time while playing soccer are proposed. Each of these detectors is able to analyze a robot object-proposal in ~1 ms, and the average number of proposals to analyze in the presented system is 1.5 per frame obtained by the upper camera of the NAO. The obtained detection rate is ~97%.

2   Deep Learning in Robots with Limited Computational Resources

The use of deep learning in robot platforms with limited computational resources requires to select fast and lightweight neural models, and to have a procedure for their design and training. These two aspects are addressed in this section.

2.1   Neural Network Models

State-of-the-art computer vision systems based on CNNs require large memory and computational resources, such as those provided by high-end GPUs. For this reason, CNN-based methods are unable to run on devices with low resources, such as smartphones or mobile robots, limiting their use in real-world applications. Thus, the development of mechanisms that allow CNNs to work using less memory and fewer computational resources, such as compression and quantization of the networks, is an important research area.

Different approaches have been proposed for the compression and quantization of CNNs. Among them, methods that compute the required convolutions using FFT [15], methods that use sparse representation of the convolutions such as [16, 17], methods that compress the parameters of the network [18], and binary approximations of the filters [5]. This last option has shown very promising results. In [5], two binary-based network architectures are proposed: Binary-Weight-Networks and XNOR-Networks. In Binary-Weight-Networks, the filters are approximated with binary values in closed form, resulting in a 32x memory saving. In XNOR-Networks, both the filters and the input of convolutional layers are binary, but non-binary non-linearities like ReLU can still be used. This results in 58x faster convolutional operations on a CPU, by using mostly XNOR and bit-counting operations. The classification accuracy with a Binary-Weight-Network version of AlexNet is only 2.9% less than the full-precision AlexNet (in top-1 measure); while XNOR-Networks have a larger, 12.4%, drop in accuracy. An alternative to compression and quantization is to use networks with a low number of parameters in a non-standard CNN structure, such as the case of SqueezeNet [3]. Vanilla SqueezeNet achieves AlexNet accuracy using 50 times fewer parameters. This allows for more efficient distributed training and feasible deployment in low-memory systems such as FPGA and embedded systems such as robots. In this work, we select XNOR-Net and SqueezeNet for implementing NAO robot detectors, and to validate the guidelines being proposed.

2.2   Design and Training Guidelines

We propose general design guidelines for CNNs to achieve real-time operation and still maintain acceptable performances. These guidelines consist on an *initialization step*, which sets a starting point in the design process by selecting an existing state-of-the-art base network, and by including the nature of the problem to be solved for selecting the objects proposal method and size, and an *iterative design step*, in which the base network is modified to achieve an optimal operating point under a Pareto optimization criterion that takes into account inference time and the classification performance.

Initialization

– Object Proposals Method Selection: A fast method for obtaining the object proposals must be selected. This selection will depend on the nature of the problem being solved, and on the available information sources (e.g., depth data obtained by a range sensor). In problems with no additional information sources, color-based proposals are a good alternative (e.g., in [11]).

- Base Network Selection: As base network a fast and/or lightweight neural model, as the ones described in Subsect. 2.1 must be selected. As a general principle, networks already applied in similar problems are preferred.
- Image/Proposal Size Selection: The image/proposal size must be set accordingly to the problem's nature and complexity. Large image sizes can produce small or no increases in classification performance, while increasing the inference times. The image size must be small, but still large enough to capture the problem's complexity. For example, in face detection, an image/window size of 20×20 pixels is enough in most state-of-the-art detection systems.

Sequential Iteration

A Pareto optimization criterion is needed to select among different network's configurations with different classification performances and inference times. The design of this criterion must reflect the importance of the real-time needs of the solution, and consider a threshold, i.e. a maximum allowed value, in the inference time from which solutions are feasible. By using this criterion, the design process iterates for finding the Pareto's optimal number of layers and filters:

- Number of layers: Same as in the image size case, the needed number of layers depends on the problem complexity. For some classification problems with a high number of classes, a large number of layers is needed, while for two-class classification, high performances can be obtaining with a small number of layers (e.g. as small as 3). One should explore the trade-off produced with the number of layers, but this selection must also consider the number of filters in each layer. In the early stages of the optimization, the removal of layers can largely reduce the inference time without hindering the network's accuracy.
- Number of filters: The number of filters in each convolutional layer is the last parameter to be set, since it involves a high number of correlated parameters. The variations in the number of filters must be done iteratively with slight changes in each step, along the different layers, to evaluate small variations in the Pareto criterion.

The proposed guidelines are general, and adaptations must be done when applying them to specific deep models and problems. Examples of the required adaptations are presented in Sects. 3.1 and 3.2 for the SqueezeNet and XNOR-Net, respectively.

3 Case Study: Real-Time NAO Detection While Playing Soccer

The detection of other robots is a critical task in robotic soccer, since it enables players to perceive both teammates and opponents. In order to detect NAO robots in real-time while playing soccer, we propose the use of CNNs as image classifiers, turning the robot detection problem into a binary classification task, with a focus on real-time, in-game use. Under this modeling, the CNN based detector will be fed by object proposals obtained using a fast robot detector (e.g. the one proposed in [11]).

Since the main limitation for the use of CNNs in robotic applications is the memory consumption and the execution time, we select two state-of-the-art CNNs to address the NAO robot detection problem: SqueezeNet [3], which generates lightweight models, and XNOR-Nets [5], which produces fast convolutions. NAO robot detectors using each of those networks are designed, implemented and validated. In both cases, the proposed design guidelines are followed, using the same Pareto criterion, with a maximum processing time of 2 ms to ensure real-time operation while playing soccer.

One important decision when designing and training deep learning systems is the learning framework to be used. We analyzed the use of three frameworks with focus on deployment in embedded systems: Caffe [12], TensorFlow [13], and Darknet [14]. Even though Caffe is implemented in C++, its many dependencies make the compatibility in 32-bit systems highly difficult. Tensorflow is also written in C++ (the computational core), but it offers a limited C++ API. Hence, we chose Darknet, which is a small C library with not many dependencies, which allows an easy deployment in the NAO, and the implementation of state-of-the-art algorithms [5].

For the training and validation of the proposed networks we use the NAO robot database published in [1], which includes images taken in various game situations and under different illumination conditions.

3.1 Detection of NAO Robots Using SqueezeNet

In the context of implementing deep neural networks in systems with limited hardware, such as the NAO robot, SqueezeNet [3] appears as a natural candidate. First of all, the small model size allows for network deployment in embedded systems without requiring large portions of the memory to store the network parameters. Second, the reduced

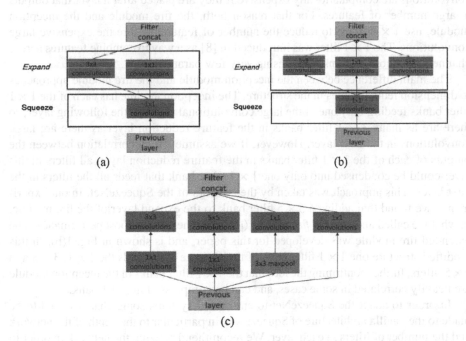

Fig. 1. (a) Fire module from SqueezeNet [3]. (b) Extended fire module (proposed here). (c) Inception module from GoogLeNet [7].

number of parameters can lead to faster inference times, which is fundamental for the real-time operation of the network.

These two fundamental advantages of the SqueezeNet arise from what the authors call a *fire module* (see Fig. 1(a)). The fire module is composed of three main stages. First, a squeeze layer composed of 1×1 filters, followed by an *expand layer* composed of 1×1 and 3×3 filters. Finally, the outputs of the *expand layer* are concatenated to form the final output of the fire module.

The practice of using filters of different sizes and then concatenating their outputs is not new, and has been used in several networks, most notably in GoogLeNet [7], with its *inception module* (see Fig. 1(c)). This module is based on the idea that sparse neural networks are less prone to overfitting due to the reduced number of parameters and are theoretically less computationally expensive. The problem with creating a sparse neural network arises due to the inefficiency of sparse data structures. This was overcome in GoogLeNet by approximating local sparse structures with dense components as suggested in [6], giving birth to the *naïve inception module*. This module uses a concatenation of 1×1, 3×3, and 5×5 filters; 1×1 filters are used to detect correlation in certain clusters between channels, while the larger 3×3 and 5×5 filters detect more spatially spread out of the clusters. Since an approximation of sparseness is the goal, ReLu activation functions are used to set most parameters to zero after training. The same principle is at the core of the fire module, which concatenates the outputs of 1×1 and 3×3 filters, but eliminating the expensive 5×5 filter. While concatenating the results of several filter's sizes boost performance, it has a serious drawback: large convolutions are computationally expensive if they are placed after a layer that outputs a large number of features. For that reason both, the fire module and the inception module, use 1×1 filters to reduce the number of features before the expensive large convolutions. The 1×1 filter was introduced in [8] as a way to combine features across channels after convolutions, while using very few parameters.

The main difference between the inception module and the fire module approaches to dimension reduction lies in the structure. The inception module has each of the 1×1 filter banks feeding only one of the large convolutional filters of the following layer, so there are as many 1×1 filter banks in the feature reduction layer as there are large convolutions in the next layer. However, if we assume a high correlation between the outputs of each of the 1×1 filter banks in the feature reduction layer, all filters in this layer could be condensed into only one 1×1 filter bank that feeds all the filters in the next layer. This approach was taken by the creators of the SqueezeNet. In our experiments, we found that adding a 5×5 filter bank to the expand layer of the fire module, in what we called an *extended fire module* (proposed here), can boost performance. The extended fire module was developed for this paper, and is shown in Fig. 1(b). In this modified structure one 1×1 filter bank of the squeeze layer feeds the 1×1, 3×3 and 5×5 filters, further confirming the idea that the 1×1 filter banks of the inception module are heavily correlated in some cases, and can be compressed in just 1 bank.

In order to adapt the SqueezeNet to embedded systems some changes need to be made to the vanilla architecture of SqueezeNet, in particular to the depth of the network and the number of filters in each layer. We recommend resizing the network in order to achieve optimal inference time by following the guidelines postulated in Sect. 2.

However, the size reduction usually comes with reduced network accuracy. To solve this problem, we propose to use the following two strategies. First, in case of reduced accuracy due to network resizing, we propose replacing the ReLu activation function with a PreLu activation function in early layers as suggested in [9]. If this approach fails to deliver extra accuracy, then replacing standard fire modules with extended fire modules can increase the quality of the network. The overall inference time can be further diminished without reducing accuracy by implementing all maxpool operations using non-overlapping windows as suggested in [10]. The proposed iterative algorithm to produce an optimal network is presented in Fig. 2.

---

reduce image size
make maxpool windows non-overlapping
while *network can be improved according to a Pareto criteria* **do**
    resize the network in term of layers and filters following the guidelines in Section 2
    if *the accuracy is lower than desired* **do**
        replace the ReLu activation functions of initial layers by PreLu
    end if
    if *the accuracy is lower than desired and using PreLu doesn't improve accuracy* **do**
        replace fire modules by extended fire modules
    end if
end while
end optimization

Fig. 2. Guidelines for real-time SqueezeNet implementation in embedded systems.

Table 1 presents execution times and classification performances achieved by different variants of the Squeeze network obtained by following the design procedure shown in Fig. 2. First, the SqueezeNet, designed originally for the ImageNet database, was modified (*NAO adapted SqueezeNet*) to provide the correct number of output classes, and the size of the input was changed to match the size of the used region proposals. This network was further changed by reducing the number of filters and layers according to the guidelines in Sect. 2, substituting ReLu with PreLu activation function in the first convolutional layer of the network, and using maxpool operations with non-overlapping windows, giving birth to the *miniSqueezeNet2* variant. For *miniSquee-zeNet3* several image input sizes were tested and 24 × 24 was found to have the right dimensions to achieve low inference time while preserving accuracy. To further reduce inference time, the number of filters was also diminished. Finally, in the *miniSquee-zeNet4* variant the number of layers and filters was further reduced, and the remaining

Table 1. Inference times and classification results for different SqueezeNet networks.

Name of the network	Inference time on the NAO [ms]	Classification rate [%]
NAO adapted SqueezeNet	68.4	51.25
miniSqueezeNet2	3.5	92.5
miniSqueezeNet3	1.55	96.33
miniSqueezeNet4	1.05	98.30

fire module was replaced by the newly developed extended fire module. The structure of *miniSqueezeNet4* is shown in Fig. 3.

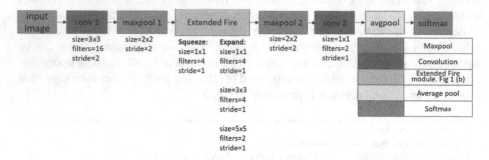

Fig. 3. Diagram of the miniSqueezeNet4 network designed in Sect. 3.1.

Interestingly as the inference time and number of free parameters decreases the network becomes more accurate. It is important to note that simply reducing the number of filters and layers is not a good method to achieve real-time inference, since following this simple approach will result in very poor network accuracy. Instead, by methodically and iteratively applying the proposed guidelines and testing the network, one can achieve very low inference time while retaining or even increasing accuracy. Another factor to take into account is that the network's size reduction can lead to a higher accuracy for small datasets due to the overfitting reduction, given the smaller number of tunable parameters. In the context of the RoboCup this characteristic becomes extremely relevant since datasets are small, because the building process is slow.

3.2 Detection of NAO Robots Using XNOR-Net

Since the use of deep learning approaches in robotic applications becomes limited by memory consumption and processing time, many studies have been conducted trying to compress models or approximate them using various techniques. In [4] it is stated that 70–90% of the execution time of a typical convolutional network is used in the convolution layers, so it is natural to focus the study in how to optimize or approximate those layers. From the many options that have been proposed in the last few years, XNOR-Nets [5] becomes an attractive option due to its claim to achieve a 58x speedup in convolutional operations. This speedup is produced since both the input representation in each layer, and the associated weights, are binarized. Hence, a single binary operation can replace up to 64 floating point operation (in a 64-bit architecture). However, since not all operations are binary, the theoretical speedup is around 62x, and in [5] a practical 58x speedup is achieved.

However, even if these results are promising, implementations on embedded systems need to consider the target architecture, which affects directly the speedup obtained by the binary convolutions. For example, in CPU implementations, two critical aspects are the word length and the available instruction set. In the specific case of the NAO, which uses an Intel Atom Z530, the word length is 32-bits, which halves the theoretical speedup, and the instruction set does not support hardware bit-counting operations, which are needed for an optimal implementation, since counting bits is an important factor in XNOR layers, as they replace sums in convolutions.

Since the authors of [5] do not release their optimized CPU version of XNOR-Nets, we use our own, by implementing the binary counterparts of the popular *gemm* and *im2col* algorithms, obtaining an asymptotic speedup of 15x in the convolutional operations, with the bottleneck being the bit counting operations, which are computed by software algorithms.

The design of convolutional networks using XNOR layers for specific, real-time applications must follow the design procedure explained in Sect. 2. However, since the XNOR layers are approximations of normal convolutions, in each design step, both the XNOR and the full precision versions of the used CNN architecture must be considered, in order to perform the next step, since some architectures take more advantage than others of the binarization. Furthermore, it is important to remark that even though XNOR layers can substitute any convolutional layers, it is not convenient to replace the first and the last convolution layers, since binarization in those layers produces high information losses.

To validate the proposed design methodology for the specific XNOR-Net architecture, we consider as base networks the following three, as well as their binarized versions: AlexNet, the convolutional network proposed in [14] for the CIFAR-10 database (here called *Darknet-CIFAR10*), and another network for the CIFAR-10 database, also proposed in [14] (here called *Darknet-CIFAR10-v2*). The performances of these three base networks, and their binarized counterparts, are shown in Table 2. We chose *Darknet-CIFAR10-v2* for applying our design guidelines, since it achieves high classification performance, using much less computation resources than the other two networks. As a result of applying the proposed design guidelines, the *miniDarknet-CIFAR10* network shown in Fig. 4 is obtained, which achieves a slightly lower classification performance than Darknet-CIFAR10-v2, but has an inference times of less than one millisecond (see last two rows in Table 2).

Table 2. Inference times and classification results for XNOR-Networks

Name of the network		Inference time on the NAO [ms]	Classification performance [%]
AlexNet	Full precision	7400	97.2
	XNOR	1500	97.8
Darknet-CIFAR10	Full precision	4400	99.2
	XNOR	400	93.8
Darknet-CIFAR10-v2	Full precision	48	98.6
	XNOR	11.5	98.1
miniDarknet-CIFAR10	Full precision	0.9	97.6
	XNOR	0.95	96.6

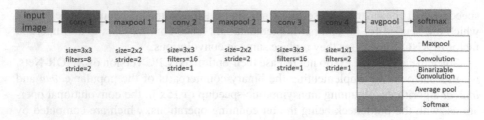

Fig. 4. Diagram of the miniDarknet-CIFAR10 network designed in Sect. 3.2.

3.3 Robot Detection While Playing Soccer

The two deep learning based detectors described in the two former sub-sections need to be fed using region proposals. As region proposals generator we choose the algorithm described in [11]. This algorithm scans the NAO image using vertical scanlines, where non-green spots are detected and merged into a bounding-box, which constitutes a region proposal. This algorithm runs in less than 2 ms in the NAO [11], and although it shows excellent results on simulated environments, it fails under wrong color calibration and challenging light conditions, generating false detections, which is why a further classification step is needed.

The computation time of the whole NAO robot detection system (proposal generation + deep based robot detector) is calculated by adding the execution time of the region proposal algorithm, and the convolutional network inference time multiplied by the expected number of proposals. To estimate the expected number of proposals, several realistic game simulations where run using the SimRobot simulator [11], and then the number of possible robot proposals was calculated for each of the cameras. The final execution times are presented in Table 3. It is important to note that we use the average number of proposals in the upper camera, since the lower camera rarely finds a robot proposal.

Table 3. Execution time of the robot detection system.

Regions proposal time	0.85 [ms]
Selected network inference time (XNOR-Net)	0.95 [ms]
Average number of proposals (in the upper NAO camera)	1.5
Average total detection time	2.275 [ms]

3.4 Discussion

The XNOR-Net and SqueezeNet design methodologies have been validated, obtaining inference times and classification performances that allow deployment in real robotic platforms with limited computational resources, such as the NAO robot. The main common principles derived from the proposed methodologies are:

1. To select a base network taking as starting point fast and/or lightweight deep models used in problems of similar complexity - XNOR-Net and SqueezeNet seems to be

good alternatives for object detection problems of a similar complexity than the robot detection problem described here.

2. To select an image/proposal size according to the problem's complexity (24 × 24 pixels was the choice in the described application).
3. To follow an iterative design process by reducing the number of layers and filters, following a Pareto optimization criterion that considers classification performance and inference time.

In the described NAO robot detection problem, the best detectors for each network type (XNOR-Net and SqueezeNet) are comparable, obtaining a very similar performance. While the XNOR-Net based detector achieves a marginally lower inference time (0.95 ms against 1.05 ms), the SqueezeNet based detector gives a better classification performance (98.30% against 96.6%). We also validate the hypothesis that hybrid systems that use handcrafted region proposals that feed CNN classifiers are a competitive choice against end-to-end methods, which integrate proposal generation and classification in a single network such as Faster R-CNN, since the use of the first kind of methods (handcrafted proposals + deep networks) make possible the application of the final detector in real-time.

It must be noted that while the reported network inference times are the ones of a network running in a real NAO robot, the reported classification performances correspond to the test results when using the SPQR database [1]. The performance using this database may differ from the performance in real-world conditions, since the data distribution in this database might be different from the one expected in real games.

4 Conclusions

In this paper two deep neural networks suited for deployment in embedded systems were analyzed and validated. The first one, XNOR consists on the binarization of a CNN network, while the second one, SqueezeNet, is based on a lightweight architecture with a reduced number of parameters. Both networks were used for the detection of NAO robots in the context of robotic soccer, and obtained state-of-the-art results (~97% detection rate), while having very low computational cost (~1 ms for analyzing each robot proposal, with an average of 1.5 proposal per image).

With this work, we show that using deep learning in NAO robots is indeed feasible, and that it is possible to achieve state-of-the-art robot detection while playing soccer. Similar neural network structures to the ones proposed in this paper can be used to perform other detections tasks, such as ball detection or goal post detection in this same context. Moreover, since the methodologies presented in this work to achieve real-time capabilities are generic, it is possible to implement the same strategies in applications with similar hardware restrictions such as smartphones, x-rotors and low-end robot systems.

Acknowledgements. This work was partially funded by FONDECYT Project 1161500.

References

1. Albani, D., Youssef, A., Suriani, V., Nardi, D., Bloisi, D.D.: A deep learning approach for object recognition with NAO soccer robots. In: Behnke, S., Sheh, R., Sarıel, S., Lee, D.D. (eds.) RoboCup 2016. LNCS, vol. 9776, pp. 392–403. Springer, Cham (2017). https://doi.org/10.1007/978-3-319-68792-6_33

2. Speck, D., Barros, P., Weber, C., Wermter, S.: Ball localization for Robocup soccer using convolutional neural networks. In: Behnke, S., Sheh, R., Sarıel, S., Lee, D.D. (eds.) RoboCup 2016. LNCS, vol. 9776, pp. 19–30. Springer, Cham (2017). https://doi.org/10.1007/978-3-319-68792-6_2

3. Iandola, F.N., Moskewicz, M.W., Ashraf, K., Han, S., Dally, W.J., Keutzer, K.: SqueezeNet: AlexNet-level accuracy with 50x fewer parameters and <1 mb modelsize. CoRR (2016). http://arxiv.org/abs/1602.07360

4. Hadjis, S., Abuzaid, F., Zhang, C., Ré, C.: Caffe con Troll: shallow ideas to speed up deep learning. In: Proceedings of the Fourth Workshop on Data Analytics in the Cloud (2015)

5. Rastegari, M., Ordonez, V., Redmon, J., Farhadi, A.: XNOR-Net: ImageNet classification using binary convolutional neural networks. In: Leibe, B., Matas, J., Sebe, N., Welling, M. (eds.) ECCV 2016. LNCS, vol. 9908, pp. 525–542. Springer, Cham (2016). https://doi.org/10.1007/978-3-319-46493-0_32

6. Çatalyürek, U.V., Aykanat, C., Uçar, B.: On two-dimensional sparse matrix partitioning: models, methods, and a recipe. SIAM J. Sci. Comput. **32**(2), 656–683 (2010)

7. Szegedy, C., et al.: Going deeper with convolutions. In: Proceedings of the IEEE Conference on Computer Vision and Pattern Recognition, pp. 1–9 (2015)

8. Lin, M., Chen, Q., Yan, S.: Network in network. CoRR (2013). http://arxiv.org/abs/1312.4400

9. Paszke, A., Chaurasia, A., Kim, S., Culurciello, E.: ENet: a deep neural network architecture for real-time semantic segmentation. CoRR (2016). http://arxiv.org/abs/1606.02147

10. Scherer, D., Müller, A., Behnke, S.: Evaluation of pooling operations in convolutional architectures for object recognition. In: Diamantaras, K., Duch, W., Iliadis, L.S. (eds.) ICANN 2010. LNCS, vol. 6354, pp. 92–101. Springer, Heidelberg (2010). https://doi.org/10.1007/978-3-642-15825-4_10

11. Röfer, T., et al.: B-Human team report and code release 2016 (2016). http://www.b-human.de/downloads/publications/2016/coderelease2016.pdf

12. Jia, Y., et al.: Caffe: convolutional architecture for fast feature embedding. arXiv preprint arXiv:1408.5093 (2014)

13. Abadi, M., Agarwal, A., et al.: TensorFlow: large-scale machine learning on heterogeneous systems (2015). http://tensorflow.org/

14. Redmon, J.: Darknet: open source neural networks in C (2013–2016). http://pjreddie.com/darknet/

15. Mathieu, M., Henaff, M., LeCun, Y.: Fast training of convolutional networks through FFTs. arXiv preprint arXiv:1312.5851 (2013)

16. Jaderberg, M., Vedaldi, A., Zisserman, A.: Speeding up convolutional neural networks with low rank expansions. arXiv:1405.3866 [cs.CV] (2014)

17. Liu, B., Wang, M., Foroosh, H., Tappen, M., Penksy, M.: Sparse convolutional neural networks. In: 2015 IEEE Conference on Computer Vision and Pattern Recognition, CVPR, Boston, MA, pp. 806–814 (2015)

18. Han, S., Mao, H., Dally, W.J.: Deep compression: compressing deep neural networks with pruning, trained quantization and Huffman coding. In: ICLR 2016 (2016). Best paper award

Oral Presentations

Large-Scale Stochastic Scene Generation and Semantic Annotation for Deep Convolutional Neural Network Training in the RoboCup SPL

Timm Hess[1(✉)], Martin Mundt[1,2], Tobias Weis[1], and Visvanathan Ramesh[1,2]

[1] Software Engineering for Computer Vision, Bembelbots, Goethe University Frankfurt, Frankfurt am Main, Germany
{hess,weis}@ccc.cs.uni-frankfurt.de
[2] Frankfurt Institute for Advanced Studies (FIAS), Frankfurt am Main, Germany
{mundt,ramesh}@fias.uni-frankfurt.de

Abstract. Object detection and classification are essential tasks for any robotics scenario, where data-driven approaches, specifically deep learning techniques, have been widely adopted in recent years. However, in the context of the RoboCup standard platform league these methods have not yet gained comparable popularity in large part due to the lack of (publicly) available large enough data sets that involve a tedious gathering and error-prone manual annotation process. We propose a framework for stochastic scene generation, rendering and automatic creation of semantically annotated ground truth masks. Used as training data in conjunction with deep convolutional neural networks we demonstrate compelling classification accuracy on real-world data in a multi-class setting. An evaluation on multiple neural network architectures with varying depth and representational capacity, corresponding run-times on current NAO-H25 hardware, and required sampled training data is provided.

1 Introduction

By the middle of the 21st century artificial intelligence based humanoid soccer robots are envisioned to win against a human team in a football game complying with official FIFA rules. At all times an instance model of the current situation is required to enable the complex interplay of sensing, control and prediction. Detection and classification of the agent's surroundings are essential constituents in the visual component of such a world model. By successively alleviating environmental constraints, e.g. illumination and color cues, the RoboCup challenge strives to capture real-world complexity. This results in greater need for efficient, robust real-time computer vision systems. The contemporary landscape of RoboCup research is at large dominated by model-driven approaches relying heavily on human engineered vision pipelines [1–4] that require substantial

---

T. Hess and M. Mundt have contributed equally.

© Springer Nature Switzerland AG 2018
H. Akiyama et al. (Eds.): RoboCup 2017, LNAI 11175, pp. 33–44, 2018.
https://doi.org/10.1007/978-3-030-00308-1_3

amounts of domain expertise to construct. Due to the rise of computational power and availability of large data sets deep convolutional neural networks (CNNs) have increased in popularity in both academia and industry and have been shown to perform exceptionally well on many vision tasks in the course of the last years [5–7]. With [8,9], only recently some of these advances have been applied to the Standard Platform League (SPL). Both of these works focus on binary classification of (NAO) robots and balls alone.

However, the successful training of deep neural networks depends on extensive, tediously gathered, curated and annotated data sets. To generalize well these data sets need to span the space of potential inputs as thoroughly as possible, oftentimes rendering deep neural network approaches infeasible. Building on advances in computer graphics and respective publicly available graphics-/game-engines (e.g. [10,11]) this issue can in principle be addressed by resorting to generated synthetic instances of the domain in question. Practicality in several domains has been demonstrated in the context of deep learning [12–16], although a careful consideration of the underlying assumptions in the generative model with respect to the task is crucial to avoid statistical mismatches in the data distributions that ultimately determine the overall viability of data driven approaches.

In this work we develop an automated framework, using a state of the art real-time rendering engine [11], for the generation of semantically annotated images of simulated SPL scenes through systematic mapping of geometric and photometric priors derived from specifications (e.g. [17]). In a series of experiments we demonstrate compelling results, evaluate tradeoffs in choice of different CNN architectures with respect to accuracy and runtime performance on the NAO-H25 robot and present insights in terms of required sampling density. Due to the modular nature of the simulation framework it is readily extensible to novel conditions coinciding with the goal of the RoboCup. To promote transparency and reproducibility in research, we open-source our contributions at https://github.com/TimmHess/UERoboCup.

2   Generative Scene Model

First, objects and their relative pose expressed in the form of meshes are assigned to geometrical parameters, whereas properties related to lighting and respectively the scattering, transmission and reflection thereof fall into the category of photometric parameters. We formalize the priors known from specifications in form of distributions and formulate the scene generation process in terms of stochastic sampling.

2.1   Geometric Parameters

A typical scene in a SPL match is comprised of a limited set of objects, that is one ball, a maximum of ten robots, two goals and the playing field, as well as a set of light sources. Being entirely static in nature, the playing field $\mathbf{F}$, with a spatial extent of $\mathbf{F}_w \times \mathbf{F}_h = 9\,\text{m} \times 6\,\text{m}$ [17], defines the geometrical boundaries for the placement of the other objects in a two-dimensional Cartesian coordinate system. To ensure approximately equal numbers of objects in the camera field of view for the later sampling of photometric parameters, the ball $\mathbf{B}$ is chosen as the central component in the stochastic scene generation process. We define the distribution on its spatial position to stem from two independent uniform distributions:

$$p(\mathbf{B}_{x,y}) = (\mathcal{U}(0, \mathbf{F}_w), \mathcal{U}(0, \mathbf{F}_h)). \tag{1}$$

A first robot $\mathbf{R}^{\text{cam}}_{x,y,\alpha}$, parametrized by its spatial position x, y and angle α from whose viewpoint the scene will later be rendered, is sampled such that it has a distance d to the ball and is placed randomly on the circle defined by above radius:

$$p(\mathbf{R}^{\text{cam}}_{x,y}|\mathbf{B}_{x,y}) = \mathbf{B}_{x,y} + \begin{bmatrix} \cos(\phi) & -\sin(\phi) \\ \sin(\phi) & \cos(\phi) \end{bmatrix} \begin{bmatrix} 0 & d \end{bmatrix}^{\mathsf{T}}. \tag{2}$$

Here distance $d \sim \mathcal{U}$ (0.3 m, 1.5 m), matched to the robots' static head pose with lowest pitch (spanning the vertical field of view), and angle $\phi \sim \mathcal{U}(0, 2\pi)$ are also chosen to be uniformly distributed. In order to vary the horizontal position of the ball in the camera's field of view, an angular offset $\gamma \sim \mathcal{U}(-30.5, +30.5)\pi(180)^{-1}$ is uniformly sampled corresponding to the horizontal field of view of current NAO hardware [18]. Letting β be the angle between $\mathbf{R}^{\text{cam}}_{x,y}$ and $\mathbf{B}_{x,y}$ in the field's coordinate system, then the angle of the robot is given by

$$p(\mathbf{R}^{\text{cam}}_{\alpha}|\beta) = \beta + \gamma. \tag{3}$$

N_R (in a typical game $N_R = 9$) other robots are uniformly placed on the field according to

$$p(\mathbf{R}^i_{x,y,\alpha}) = (\mathcal{U}(0, \mathbf{F}_w), \mathcal{U}(0, \mathbf{F}_h), \mathcal{U}(0, 2\pi)), \; i \in \{0, .., N_R\}. \tag{4}$$

Three different types of robots are considered (standing, sitting and lying), which we model using a categorical distribution with probabilities 0.8, 0.1 and 0.1, that have not been denoted in equations for the sake of simplicity.

Currently light sources are placed in an evenly spaced 3×2 grid 3 m above the field. The arrangement and quantity can in principle also be sampled from any distribution but has not yet been included in the current model.

2.2   Photometric Parameters

Consistent with a physics based model, light sources $\mathbf{L}$ are characterized through intensity $\mathbf{L}_I$ and temperature $\mathbf{L}_T$ [19], the latter effectively defining the illuminants' color. Given a set of N_I intensities, each represented by a normal distribution, we sample a light intensity according to

$$p(\mathbf{L}_I|k) = \mathcal{N}(\mu_k, \sigma_k), \quad k \sim \mathcal{U}(1, N_I), \tag{5}$$

assuming a range from 1700 lm, corresponding to a 100 W light-bulb [20], to 4000 lm approximating an upper limit of current consumer LED flood lights. The intensity value $\mathbf{L}_I$ in Eq. 5 is applied to all light sources in the scene, expressing the belief that venues are constructed in a self-consistent manner. The variance parameter σ_k models small perturbations as consequence of wear, current fluctuations and other forms of minor but non-negligible deviations and is thus assumed to be a small constant.

We restrict illuminant colors to follow the black body locus with D_{65} standard illuminant between temperatures of T_{low} and T_{high}, and sample uniformly from this space:

$$p(\mathbf{L}_T) = \mathcal{U}(T_{\text{low}}, T_{\text{high}}). \tag{6}$$

Reasonable temperatures range from 3000 K to 12000 K, spanning light-colors from yellow to white to blue.

As noted in the specifications of the SPL league, the playing field is restricted to be of green color. For ease of notation, we use the HSV colorspace and sample uniformly from

$$p(\mathbf{F}_{H,S,V}) = \big(\mathcal{U}(H_{\text{low}}, H_{\text{high}}), \mathcal{U}(S_{\text{low}}, S_{\text{high}}), \mathcal{U}(V_{\text{low}}, V_{\text{high}})\big), \tag{7}$$

where the hue is set to be between $H_{\text{low}} = 100°$ and $H_{\text{high}} = 140°$ resembling shades of green. $S_{\text{low}} = 0.5$, $S_{\text{high}} = 1.0$ and $V_{\text{low}} = 0.25$, $V_{\text{high}} = 1.0$ determine saturation and brightness. Lower limits of S and V have been chosen to exclude under-saturated and too dark colors.

3   Rendering and Semantic Annotation Workflow

Even though sophisticated ray-tracing rendering engines are capable of producing highly photo-realistic images [10], the use of intricate sampling techniques usually comes at the expense of high computational complexity. At the same time, modern deep learning methods require tremendous amounts of data to achieve state-of-the-art results.

The combination of former factors determines the speed at which new data in sufficient quantity can be produced whenever the need to adapt to novel conditions in either the generative model or the deep neural architecture arises. Accordingly, a crucial step is to identify a reasonable compromise between resource consumption and rendering fidelity. While a detailed analysis of the latter is out of scope of this work, we decided to use Epic Games' Unreal Engine 4 (UE4) [11] amongst other alternatives as it satisfies above mentioned requirements to the best of the authors' knowledge. A further aspect taken into consideration was the usability of the rendering software, specifically the open-source nature and underlying coding framework and interfaces, that permit modification of source code (For UE4 this is C++ code). While providing visually plausible images resulting from the underlying physically based shading [19], the real-time capabilities on current graphics processing units (GPU) are considered a substantial benefit.

We develop a rendering workflow, illustrated in Fig. 1, in consolidation with the priors derived in Sect. 2. Due to their constancy in placement and geometry,

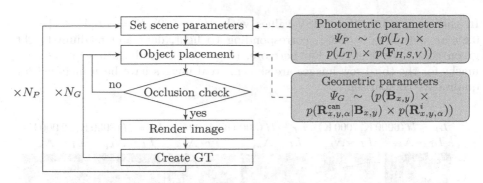

Fig. 1. The rendering workflow including the sampling processes of parameters. First, photometric parameters are used to set the scene, for which N_G different geometric configurations of objects are stochastically simulated. For each configuration an occlusion check is performed to ensure visibility of the ball before an image is rendered and the corresponding semantic ground truth segmentation mask is obtained. An overall amount of N_P scene configurations are sampled in this fashion.

the playing field as well as the goals are placed in a first step. A set of photometric parameters Ψ_P is sampled from the distributions described in Eqs. 5, 6 and 7 and corresponding scene attributes are set. For a given scene, N_G geometric configurations Ψ_G are drawn from the joint distribution of the probabilities given in Eqs. 1, 2, 3 and 4. For each such configuration, we cast a ray to perform a collision check to determine whether the ball is occluded by more than 50% by another object. If this occurs, sampling of Ψ_G is repeated. Otherwise the image is rendered and a semantically annotated ground-truth mask (GT) is created as explained below. This procedure is repeated for N_P distinct scene settings, each with N_G varying geometric configurations, resulting in an overall amount of $N_P \times N_G$ annotated images. The respective object meshes were created using Blender [10], excluding the NAO robot which is provided by [21]. The full pipeline including parameters and their distributions has been exposed and can be modified by the user through UE4's Blueprint framework (graphical user interface).

Apart from the evident benefit of saving time by making manual image annotation obsolete, automatic segmentation further guarantees bias- and error-free ground truth data. Objects of interest are selected from the list of entities present in the scene. For each pixel in the rendered image, we perform a ray-cast. If the first collision of the ray is with an object of interest, the respective index is written to the corresponding pixel in the segmentation mask. A file containing the mapping between indices and objects is generated.

Figure 2 showcases several example images using a discretized parameter set for ease of visualization. Three ranges of temperatures, reflecting white (6000–7000 K), yellow (3000–4500 K) and blue (8000–12000 K) tints that have empirically been observed to be most common in competition venues, are illustrated. Furthermore, two intensity-distributions $\mathcal{N}_{k_1}$ and $\mathcal{N}_{k_2}$ ($\mu_{k_1} < \mu_{k_2}$) are depicted.

In the same spirit, three HSV-values with $H = 120°, S = 1.0, V \in \{v_1 = 0.85, v_2 = 0.45, v_3 = 0.65\}$, corresponding to light, dark and medium bright green colors are depicted. Furthermore, respective ground truth segmentation masks for the third row images are shown. Real images have been included for qualitative comparison.

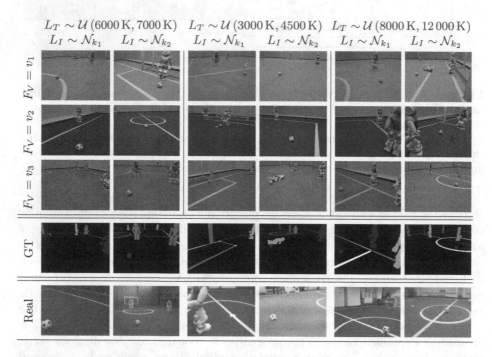

Fig. 2. Top three rows present a subset of rendered images drawn from the generative model. For ease of visualization, we chose images that correspond to discretized model parameters for the distributions of L_T, L_I and F_V. Ranges for L_T reflect white, yellow and blue color casts, the selected means of the intensity-distributions are equal to $\mu_{k_1} = 1700\,\mathrm{lm}$ and $\mu_{k_2} = 3600\,\mathrm{lm}$ with $\sigma_{k_1} = \sigma_{k_2} = 50$. The shown field colors represent green $(H = 120°, S = 1.0)$ with different brightness values $v_1 = 0.85, v_2 = 0.45$ and $v_3 = 0.65$. Semantic segmentation masks (GT) are visualized for the images in the third row. The bottom row shows real images for qualitative comparison. (Color figure online)

4   Deep Learning from Synthetic Images

To demonstrate the potential of our approach we evaluate deep convolutional neural networks in a classification context, where the training process is performed using synthetic images from our rendering workflow and accuracy is measured exclusively on real data. We consider a multi-class categorization comprised of the classes: robot, ball, goal post and field. The reason we do not include backgrounds outside the field boundaries stems from the assumption that common pre-processing steps are readily capable of identifying field boundaries.

Deep convolutional neural networks are typically trained using some form of stochastic gradient descent algorithms where the parameters Θ of a (deep) neural network are optimized such that a loss function $\mathcal{L}$ is minimized:

$$\Theta = \arg\min_{\Theta} \frac{1}{N} \sum_{n=1}^{N} \mathcal{L}(x_n, \Theta). \tag{8}$$

Here $x_{1,2\ldots N}$ denotes the training data set, and the optimization process is split into steps involving mini-batches $x_{1,2\ldots m}$ using estimates of the loss function's gradient with respect to the network's parameters. Using mini-batches is an often employed technique to speed up the optimization process and to introduce stochasticity into the gradient in order to let our network escape local minima [22]. In addition to mini-batches we apply momentum and weight decay term. The former in principle quickens learning convergence when gradients are aligned in subsequent steps, whereas the latter is a L_2 regularization term. The interested reader is pointed to [23] for a detailed description of optimization methods and their subtleties.

4.1   Data and Training Hyper-parameters

We derive a dataset of 25000 patches per class coming from an equivalent amount of unique scene configurations, without further augmentation. Here, a patch is defined as a rectangular image region spanning the area of an object and is extracted based on the semantically annotated mask, see Sect. 3 for details on how the mask is generated. A test set containing 780 patches per class has manually been extracted and annotated from real images taken in regular SPL game scenarios[1]. The training and evaluation of convolutional neural networks has been conducted using torch7 [24] on a single NVIDIA GTX 1080 GPU, deployment on the NAO robot has been realized by loading our trained networks with tiny-dnn [25] for optimized CPU usage. For our experimental evaluation of the neural networks we determine four suitable network structures with varying depths inspired by the works of [5,6] and chose a set of possible feature amounts in conjunction with runtime considerations on the current NAO hardware. For each of the four network structures the amount of features is determined by a parameter C_f, where C_f effectively represents a network's representational capacity as the layers are defined to contain an amount of features equivalent to either 2^{C_f} or 2^{C_f+1} and $C_f \in \{1, 2, \ldots, 6\}$. Consistent with [6] we express all "fully-connected" layers in the classifier through convolutions with spatial filter size 1×1 both due to efficiency in computational implementation and accuracy [26]. All pooling layers compute a conventional max pooling operation. Each layer is furthermore followed by a Dropout [27] where 25% of a layer's output units, or respectively 50% in fully-connected layers, is stochastically dropped. Activation functions are chosen to be Rectified Linear Units (ReLUs) [28], initialization

---

[1] We acknowledge contributions of parts of the real data generously provided by the following teams: HULKs, HTWK and SPQR.

follows the scheme proposed in [29] and cross-entropy has been used as a loss-function. One of the networks (BBN-M-C) replaces the fully-connected structure with a single convolutional layer without an activation function to map directly onto the classes similar to [6].

Table 1. CNN architectures with number of layers, spatial feature sizes and quantities, pooling dimensionality and added zero-padding. Architectures BBN-S and BBN-M are conceptually equal with the later having an extra layer and thus more representational complexity. BBN-M-C replaces the fully-connected structure with a single convolutional layer without an activation function to map directly onto the classes. BBN-L increases representational capacity through features with increased spatial size.

		BBN-S	BBN-M	BBN-M-C	BBN-L
Conv 1	No. features | Size	2^{C_f} | 5×5	2^{C_f} | 5×5	2^{C_f} | 5×5	2^{C_f} | 8×8
	Zero-padding	2	2	1	4
	Pooling size | Stride	2×2 | 2	2×2 | 2	2×2 | 2	4×4 | 2
Conv 2	No. features | Size	2^{C_f+1} | 3×3	2^{C_f+1} | 3×3	2^{C_f+1} | 3×3	2^{C_f+1} | 8×8
	Zero-padding	1	1	1	3
	Pooling size | Stride	2×2 | 2	2×2 | 2	2×2 | 2	4×4 | 2
Conv 3	No. features | Size	-	2^{C_f+1} | 3×3	2^{C_f+1} | 3×3	2^{C_f+1} | 5×5
	Zero-padding	-	1	1	3
	Pooling size | Stride	-	2×2 | 2	2×2 | 2	2×2 | 2
F-Conv 1	No. features | Size	256 | 1×1	256 | 1×1	-	512 | 1×1
	Stride, Padding	1 | 0	1 | 0	-	1 | 0
F-Conv 2	No. features | Size	128 | 1×1	128 | 1×1	-	-
	Stride | Padding	1 | 0	1 | 0	-	-
Output	No. features | Size	4 | 1×1	4 | 1×1	4 | 3×3	4 | 1×1

Hyper-parameters have been determined using a random search as presented in [30] on log-uniform scales with 20% of training data extracted uniformly and used for cross-validation. In particular the learning rate $(10^0, 10^{-1}, \ldots, 10^{-4})$, mini-batch size $(16, 32, \ldots, 128)$ and pre-processing methods (no pre-processing, zero-mean centering and global contrast normalization, see [23]) have been considered. Spatial input size of 32×32, a weight-decay of $5 \cdot 10^{-4}$ and a momentum term of 0.9 are kept constant. We determined the following set of parameters that are used in all subsequent experiments: an initial learning rate of 10^{-2}, a mini-batch size of 64 without any form of pre-processing. In addition to the initial learning rate we create a learning rate schedule, dividing the learning rate by a factor of 5 every 16 epochs, consistent with an observable plateau in our validation curve. With these parameters we trained for an overall of 40 epochs.

4.2 Network Accuracy, Capacity and Runtime Evaluation

We evaluate the influence of the representational capacity C_f on achieved accuracy and runtime for the previously determined hyper-parameters on the set

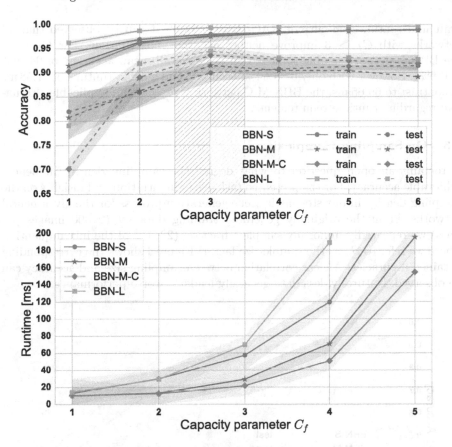

Fig. 3. Top panel: Train and test accuracies for the architectures defined in Table 1 in dependence on the capacity parameter C_f shown in a $\log_2$-uniform scale. Experiments were repeated five times for statistical consistency. Shaded regions represent minimum and maximum deviations from the obtained mean values. The hatched area depicts a (local) optimum of effective network capacity with under-fitting regimes for smaller and over-fitting present for larger C_f values. Bottom panel: Corresponding runtime on the NAO robot's hardware for different C_f, evaluated and averaged on a thousand forward passes. The range is constrained to ensure that the area of interest (low runtimes) is adequately resolved and the overall trend (power law behavior) is clear.

of proposed neural network architectures. For statistical consistency we repeat network training and evaluation processes five times and report runtimes as the mean of a thousand forward passes. In the top panel of Fig. 3 corresponding train and test accuracies are illustrated, whereas respective runtimes can be found in the bottom panel. $C_f < 3$ results in evident under-fitting, values greater than 3 seem to lie in a general over-fitting regime. While technically the test accuracy could plummet completely in this regime, the use of weight-decay counteracts this behavior resulting in only little loss in accuracy. In conjunction with the evaluated runtimes on current NAO-H25 hardware it can be observed that all networks with $C_f > 3$ improve neither accuracy nor runtime. For $C_f = 3$, the BBN-L network is able to achieve a best overall mean accuracy of 94.40% (± 0.6%). However with only 0.88% less accuracy and a mean runtime of 21.58 ms in contrast to 69.65 ms, the BBN-M-C network represents an applicable alternative regarding runtime requirements.

4.3 On Sampling Complexity

It remains an open question to what degree the sampling density influences achievable accuracy. For the presented task, we gain intuition and insights on the sampling density in our stochastic scene generation process for the given neural networks. From the originally generated training data set (25000 images per class) we repeatedly uniformly sample a fraction $(2^{S_n})^{-1}$ of the initial quantity, where we refer to S_n as the sample size factor. Figure 4 shows the corresponding obtained accuracies. A clear correlation between sampling size and accuracy can be observed. Naturally, less data generally leads to worse performance.

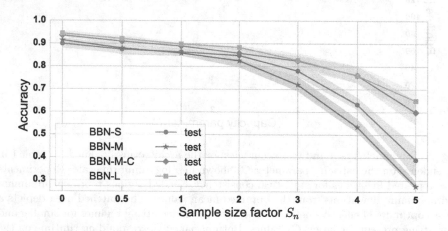

Fig. 4. Accuracy of the proposed networks with $C_f = 3$ on differently sized training sets. The sample size factor S_n determines a fraction $(2^{S_n})^{-1}$ of the original training set size (25000 per class). Consistent with previous experiments, the mean accuracy of five repetitions is visualized. Shaded regions represent the deviations.

5 Conclusion

We developed a stochastic scene generation process for the RoboCup SPL, consisting of a generative model and synthetic image and semantically enriched ground-truth creation employing a state-of-the-art physically based rendering engine [11]. Compelling multi-class classification results on real-world data have been demonstrated on a variety of deep convolutional neural network architectures that have been trained entirely from 3-D simulation. The space of neural network architectures, capacity, run-time and data quantity has systematically been probed, analyzed and insights have been shared. Our best network in terms of accuracy and speed is able to achieve approximately 94% accuracy in less than 22 ms per patch on current NAO-H25 hardware. Therefore the error-prone, tedious and time consuming manual human annotation and data gathering tasks have successfully been replaced.

Our approach provides the means for several future research prospects, that could include, but are not limited to: inferring the relative importance of individual scene parameters related to the image generation process (e.g. geometry, photometry, texture, etc.) for computer vision algorithms, the extension of the deep convolutional neural network based approach to detection approaches such as pixel-wise semantic image segmentation [16, 31] or the general inclusion of further available information such as depth. Being modular in nature, the rendering workflow is furthermore readily extensible to generation of temporally coherent scenes for potential use in localization, navigation and motion-estimation tasks.

References

1. Schwarz, I., Hofmann, M., Urbann, O., Tasse, S.: A robust and calibration-free vision system for humanoid soccer robots. In: Almeida, L., Ji, J., Steinbauer, G., Luke, S. (eds.) RoboCup 2015. LNAI, vol. 9513, pp. 239–250. Springer, Cham (2015). https://doi.org/10.1007/978-3-319-29339-4_20
2. Härtl, A., Visser, U., Röfer, T.: Robust and efficient object recognition for a humanoid soccer robot. In: Behnke, S., Veloso, M., Visser, A., Xiong, R. (eds.) RoboCup 2013. LNCS, vol. 8371, pp. 396–407. Springer, Heidelberg (2014). https://doi.org/10.1007/978-3-662-44468-9_35
3. Metzler, S., Nieuwenhuisen, M., Behnke, S.: Learning visual obstacle detection using color histogram features. In: Röfer, T., Mayer, N.M., Savage, J., Saranlı, U. (eds.) RoboCup 2011. LNCS, vol. 7416, pp. 149–161. Springer, Heidelberg (2012). https://doi.org/10.1007/978-3-642-32060-6_13
4. Qian, Y., Lee, D.D.: Adaptive field detection and localization in robot soccer. In: Behnke, S., Sheh, R., Sarıel, S., Lee, D.D. (eds.) RoboCup 2016. LNCS, vol. 9776, pp. 218–229. Springer, Cham (2017). https://doi.org/10.1007/978-3-319-68792-6_18
5. Goodfellow, I.J., Warde-Farley, D., Mirza, M., Courville, A.C., Bengio, Y.: Maxout networks. JMLR 28, 1319–1327 (2013)
6. Lin, M., Chen, Q., Yan, S.: Network in network. CoRR abs/1312.4400 (2013)
7. He, K., Zhang, X., Ren, S., Sun, J.: Deep residual learning for image recognition. In: CVPR, pp. 770–778 (2016). https://doi.org/10.1109/CVPR.2016.90
8. Albani, D., Youssef, A., Suriani, V., Nardi, D., Bloisi, D.D.: A deep learning approach for object recognition with NAO soccer robots. In: Behnke, S., Sheh, R., Sarıel, S., Lee, D.D. (eds.) RoboCup 2016. LNAI, vol. 9776, pp. 392–403. Springer, Cham (2017). https://doi.org/10.1007/978-3-319-68792-6_33
9. Speck, D., Barros, P., Weber, C., Wermter, S.: Ball localization for robocup soccer using convolutional neural networks. In: Behnke, S., Sheh, R., Sarıel, S., Lee, D.D. (eds.) RoboCup 2016. LNAI, vol. 9776, pp. 19–30. Springer, Cham (2017). https://doi.org/10.1007/978-3-319-68792-6_2
10. Blender.org: Blender. https://www.blender.org/. Accessed 12 Mar 2017

11. EpicGames: Unreal engine 4. https://www.unrealengine.com/. Accessed 12 Mar 2017
12. Butler, D.J., Wulff, J., Stanley, G.B., Black, M.J.: A naturalistic open source movie for optical flow evaluation. In: Fitzgibbon, A., Lazebnik, S., Perona, P., Sato, Y., Schmid, C. (eds.) ECCV 2012. LNCS, vol. 7577, pp. 611–625. Springer, Heidelberg (2012). https://doi.org/10.1007/978-3-642-33783-3_44
13. Fischer, P., et al.: FlowNet: learning optical flow with convolutional networks. In: ICCV (2015)
14. Richter, S.R., Vineet, V., Roth, S., Koltun, V.: Playing for data: ground truth from computer games. In: Leibe, B., Matas, J., Sebe, N., Welling, M. (eds.) ECCV 2016. LNCS, vol. 9906, pp. 102–118. Springer, Cham (2016). https://doi.org/10.1007/978-3-319-46475-6_7
15. Lerer, A., Gross, S., Fergus, R.: Learning physical intuition of block towers by example. In: ICML, vol. 48, pp. 430–438 (2016)
16. Veeravasarapu, V.S.R., Rothkopf, C.A., Ramesh, V.: Model-driven simulations for deep convolutional neural networks. CoRR abs/1605.09582 (2016)
17. RoboCup@Home Technical Committee: Robocup rulebook. http://www.tzi.de/spl/pub/Website/Downloads/Rules2016.pdf. Accessed 14 Mar 2017
18. SoftbankRobotics: NAO H25 technical specifications. http://doc.aldebaran.com/2-1/family/nao_h25/index_h25.html#nao-h25. Accessed 26 Mar 2017
19. Karis, B., Games, E.: Real shading in unreal engine 4. In: Physically Based Shading Theory and Practice, SIGGRAPH (2013)
20. docs.unrealengine.com: Lighting basics. https://docs.unrealengine.com/latest/INT/Engine/Rendering/LightingAndShadows/Basics/. Accessed 26 Mar 2017
21. SoftbankRobotics: NAOmodel. https://community.ald.softbankrobotics.com/en/resources/software/language/en-gb. Accessed 14 Mar 2017
22. Wilson, D., Martinez, T.R.: The general inefficiency of batch training for gradient descent learning. Neural Netw. **16**, 1429–1451 (2003). https://doi.org/10.1016/S0893-6080(03)00138-2
23. Goodfellow, I., Bengio, Y., Courville, A.: Deep Learning. MIT Press, Cambridge (2016)
24. Collobert, R., Kavukcuoglu, K., Farabet, C.: Torch7: a matlab-like environment for machine learning. In: BigLearn, NIPS Workshop (2011)
25. Zheltonozhskiy, E.: Tinydnn. https://github.com/tiny-dnn/tiny-dnn (2017). Accessed 12 Mar 2017
26. Springenberg, J., Dosovitskiy, A., Brox, T., Riedmiller, M.: Striving for simplicity: the all convolutional net. In: ICLR (Workshop Track) (2015)
27. Srivastava, N., Hinton, G.E., Krizhevsky, A., Sutskever, I., Salakhutdinov, R.: Dropout: a simple way to prevent neural networks from overfitting. JMLR **15**, 1929–1958 (2014)
28. Glorot, X., Bordes, A., Bengio, Y.: Deep sparse rectifier neural networks. In: JMLR, AISTATS 2011, vol. 15, pp. 315–323 (2011)
29. Glorot, X., Bengio, Y.: Understanding the difficulty of training deep feedforward neural networks. In: JMLR, AISTATS 2010, vol. 9, pp. 249–256 (2010)
30. Bergstra, J., Bengio, Y.: Random search for hyper-parameter optimization. JMLR **13**, 281–305 (2012)
31. Chen, L., Papandreou, G., Kokkinos, I., Murphy, K., Yuille, A.L.: DeepLab: semantic image segmentation with deep convolutional nets, atrous convolution, and fully connected CRFs. CoRR abs/1606.00915 (2016)

Fast and Precise Black and White Ball Detection for RoboCup Soccer

Jacob Menashe[✉], Josh Kelle, Katie Genter, Josiah Hanna, Elad Liebman, Sanmit Narvekar, Ruohan Zhang, and Peter Stone

The University of Texas at Austin, Austin, USA
{jmenashe,jkelle,katie,jphanna,eladlieb,sanmit,zharucs,
pstone}@cs.utexas.edu

Abstract. In 2016, UT Austin Villa claimed the Standard Platform League's second place position at the RoboCup International Robot Soccer Competition in Leipzig, Germany as well as first place at both the RoboCup US Open in Brunswick, USA and the World RoboCup Conference in Beijing, China. This paper describes some of the key contributions that led to the team's victories with a primary focus on our techniques for identifying and tracking black and white soccer balls. UT Austin Villa's ball detection system was overhauled in order to transition from the league's bright orange ball, used every year of the competition prior to 2016, to the truncated icosahedral pattern commonly associated with soccer balls.

We evaluated and applied a series of heuristic region-of-interest identification techniques and supervised machine learning methods to produce a ball detector capable of reliably detecting the ball's position with no prior knowledge of the ball's position. In 2016, UT Austin Villa suffered only a single loss which occurred after regulation time during a penalty kick shootout. We attribute much of UT Austin Villa's success in 2016 to our robots' effectiveness at quickly and consistently localizing the ball.

In this work we discuss the specifics of UT Austin Villa's ball detector implementation which are applicable to the specific problem of ball detection in RoboCup, as well as to the more general problem of fast and precise object detection in computationally constrained domains. Furthermore we provide empirical analyses of our approach to support the conclusion that modern deep learning techniques can enhance visual recognition tasks even in the face of these computational constraints.

Keywords: Machine learning · Deep learning · Classification Ball detection

© Springer Nature Switzerland AG 2018
H. Akiyama et al. (Eds.): RoboCup 2017, LNAI 11175, pp. 45–58, 2018.
https://doi.org/10.1007/978-3-030-00308-1_4

1   Introduction

RoboCup, or the International Robot Soccer World Cup, is an international robotics competition introduced in 1997 as a research initiative to advance the fields of robotics and artificial intelligence using soccer as a motivating challenge domain [5].

UT Austin Villa participates in the Standard Platform League (SPL) of the RoboCup competition. In 2016, the SPL league moved from a bright orange soccer ball, which had been used all previous years, to a classic truncated icosahedral black and white soccer ball.

This shift presented a significant challenge to the SPL teams; black and white are prominent colors throughout the field, whereas the previous orange ball could be easily distinguished from the surrounding environment using an RGB thresholding approach. With an accurate threshold it was a relatively simple matter to identify all of the "orange" pixels in the camera frame, and due to their sparseness, thoroughly evaluate each orange cluster to determine whether it was a ball. Since black, white, and gray are prominent colors on the soccer field, identifying a black and white soccer ball is a far more challenging task. The image is generally filled with clusters of black and white and thus it is too computationally expensive to scrutinize every cluster of black or white pixels. As described in Sect. 3, detecting a pattern is an involved process that is computationally expensive and thus great care must be taken to preserve computational capacity and maximize the payoff of investigating any particular ball candidate. This transition from orange to black and white thus rendered the problem of consistent ball detection significantly more difficult than in previous years. Ultimately, however, our new ball detection algorithm proved to be as good as or better than that of other teams at the competition and allowed UT Austin Villa to place second at the international RoboCup competition in Germany and first at the RoboCup US Open competition in Maine.

In this work we discuss UT Austin Villa's approach to solving the challenge of black and white ball detection with detailed analyses of the various components of our detection system. After we cover the necessary background work in Sect. 2 we proceed to Sect. 3 where we cover the main ball detection loop.

In Sect. 4 we provide empirical analyses of our ball detector and then summarize and conclude in Sect. 5.

2   Background

In this section, we first introduce RoboCup and the SPL, as well as the various challenges teams in the SPL have undertaken in recent years in order to stay competitive. Later in this section, we introduce heuristic approaches to this year's main challenge and briefly discuss Machine Learning as a possible complement to heuristics.

2.1 RoboCup Soccer Challenges

RoboCup has many leagues including multiple simulation leagues and various physical robot soccer leagues. Almost all of the leagues involve robot agents that must act autonomously in their environments.

UT Austin Villa has participated in a physical robot soccer league called the Standard Platform League since 2008. The SPL is different from other RoboCup leagues in that all teams must use the same robot platform, namely the Softbank NAO Robot. The NAO uses a single-core 1.6 GHz Intel x86 processor and a pair of 1280×960 non-stereoscopic cameras running at 30 Hz.

At RoboCup 2016, teams competed in 5 vs. 5 soccer games on a 9 m by 6 m soccer field. Each game consists of two 10-minute halves. Teams must play completely autonomously — no human input is allowed during games outside of game state signals sent by an official to communicate to the robots when a goal has been scored, when they have been penalized, etc. The robots on each team are additionally allowed to communicate with each other over a wireless network.

Historically, there have been many vision-related challenges since the SPL began using the NAO robots in 2008. In 2008, games were played with an orange street hockey ball on a 6 m by 4 meter field. This field had a blue goal and a yellow goal to allow teams to easily differentiate sides. Over time, the playing environment has become less and less color-coded. After a few changes in field size that eventually resulted in a 6 m by 4 m playing surface, in 2012 both goals became yellow. This change required teams to find ways other than goal color to differentiate the two sides of the field. The field size was increased again in 2013—to the current 9 m by 6 m—and then in 2015 white goals were introduced.

In 2016, the league removed the final color-coded landmark when they switched from playing with an orange street hockey ball to a black and white printed soccer ball. This paper discusses the research problems this change presented, as well as how we successfully handled these problems to finish 2nd at RoboCup 2016.

Due to the hardware constraints of the NAO and the characteristics of the SPL, the problem of visual object detection rests on two primary criteria:

1. Efficiency: Detectors process 1280×960 images faster than 30 Hz.
2. Precision: Detectors must minimize false positives.

The difficulty of completing the full sensing and action loop at 30 Hz is compounded by the fact that processing takes place sequentially on a single CPU core. UT Austin Villa's codebase in particular allocates approximately 10 ms for the entire ball detection pipeline. Even performing a full image read takes 14 ms, so care must be taken to minimize reads and isolate computations to the areas of the image most likely to yield results.

However, computational efficiency cannot come at the expense of precision. While a false negative may delay action for a short period of time, a single false ball detection can lead robots astray and cause the team to pursue a ball that doesn't exist. UT Austin Villa's detection system therefore aggressively prunes out false detections at the possible cost throwing out correct detections on occasion.

2.2 Heuristic Approaches

When deciding whether an object in the visual frame belongs to one class or another there are generally two possible approaches to take: hand-designed heuristic methods, and machine learning models.

Heuristic methods tend to be ad-hoc in nature, as finding the right combination of features involves a great deal of trial and error. For example, one might identify whether an object is a soccer ball by considering the patterns identified on the object and testing how close they are to the expected patterns of the ball. This general technique can be easy (i.e. computationally efficient) to compute and is common in the RoboCup domain.

Even though machine learning techniques have been very successful in object detection and recognition tasks [9], heuristic methods are still relevent because of their computational efficiency. Rather than apply a traditional "sliding window" approach, our algorithm incorporates machine learned models by first applying a high level heuristic search that quickly identifies ball candidates for further analysis, and progressively applies more rigorous filters to throw out candidates that are likely to be false positives. Finally the algorithm applies a more computationally expensive machine-learned ball classifier to verify that the selected candidate is indeed a soccer ball.

2.3 Machine Learning Approaches

Machine Learning (ML) is a more principled approach that is supported by a wide variety of algorithms in the computer vision literature. Examples of popular models are Support Vector Machines (SVMs) and Deep Neural Networks (DNNs) which map vectors of image pixels to discrete classifications. Many ML algorithms require anywhere from tens of thousands to millions of labeled samples for successful training. While these techniques are generally more accurate and robust than heuristic approaches, they must be provided with properly cropped input images that derive from either a sliding window or a region-of-interest (ROI) detection system. The latter of these has much greater potential for computational efficiency and, as we will describe below, is the most effective method of incorporating ML into RoboCup vision tasks such as soccer ball detection. Rather than using ML as a complete alternative to heuristics, in this work we show that ML can be combined with heuristics to strike an effective balance between generality, accuracy, and computational efficiency.

3   Ball Detection

In this section we describe the complete ball detection algorithm. Within the constraints of available space, we describe our approach with the goal of enabling full reimplementation. To complement our description, we also provide the complete source code from our implementation[1].

3.1   Ball Candidates

As shown in Algorithm 1, the ball detection algorithm can be broken down into six subroutines that are aimed at progressively refining an estimate of the ball's position. The first phase, seen on line 2, consumes a raw image and produces a set of regions with exceptionally high contrast. Line 3 of the algorithm iterates over these regions to identify dark blobs which intuitively correspond to the black pentagons on the soccer ball. This produces one set of blobs for each region. Line 4 organizes each set of blobs into one triplet per set; this triplet corresponds to a triangle formed by 3 pentagons. Line 5 of the algorithm selects the triangle whose characteristics most closely fit those of the soccer ball. Line 6 of the algorithm applies a Hough transform to estimate the ball's center and radius.

Finally a machine-learned classifier is used to filter out false positives in line 7. The remainder of this section describes these phases in further detail.

Algorithm 1. The ball detection algorithm described throughout Section 3.

1: **function** DETECTSOCCERBALL(RawImage i)
2:     $\mathcal{R}_{HC} \leftarrow$ DetectHighContrastROIs(i)
3:     $\mathcal{P} \leftarrow$ DetectBlackPentagons($\mathcal{R}_{HC}$)
4:     $\mathcal{T} \leftarrow$ ConstructTriangles($\mathcal{P}$)
5:     $t \leftarrow$ SelectBestTriangle($\mathcal{T}$)
6:     $b \leftarrow$ HoughCorrection(t)
7:     **return** b if Classify(b) **else return null**
8: **end function**

Line 2 [DetectHighContrastROIs]: The motivation behind computing regions of interest is speed. We cannot devote expensive image processing time to the whole image, so the algorithm first quickly narrows its focus to smaller subsets of the image. Compute time is then allocated to these smaller ROIs. Our ROI detector algorithm is based on the fact that the ball will produce regions of high contrast because it has black spots on a white surface. We identify areas of high contrast by using adaptive thresholding [1]. Adaptive thresholding requires two parameters - window size (measured in pixels) and a threshold value. Optimal window size depends on the size (in pixels) of the ball in the image, which in turn depends on the ball's position relative to the camera and the robot's orientation. A ball that is far away from the robot will appear smaller in the image and thus requires a smaller window size. To address this issue, the image is split into 3 parts - top, middle, and bottom, corresponding to far, medium, and close balls. Adaptive thresholding is applied to each part independently with different

---

[1] Source code is hosted at: https://github.com/LARG/spl-release.

window sizes and thresholds. Window sizes are selected to be approximately 1.6 times the projected ball size in that portion of the image.

Adaptive thresholding produces a set of response pixels - pixels that exceed the adaptive threshold. The algorithm ignores response pixels that are classified as green in the original color image because they are unlikely to have been captured from the ball. The algorithm clusters the non-green response pixels by Euclidean distance to one another. Any two pixels which have Euclidean distance at most 0.6 times the expected ball size are put into the same cluster. Each cluster is then converted to an ROI bounding box whose center is set to the cluster's centroid, and whose width and height is set to the expected ball diameter plus padding. ROIs whose projected world coordinates are greater than 20 m away are not returned.

Line 3 [DetectBlackPentagons]: In this phase, each ROI is evaluated independently with more computation to determine if a ball might be present. The first step is to identify the black pentagons of the ball. Blobs are computed by partitioning each row of pixels into either dark or light scanlines, and then merging scanlines into blobs based on the union find algorithm [2].

Scanlines are computed on the subsampled grayscale image, moving from left to right along a row of pixels. The first and last scanlines of the row are assumed to be white because the ROIs were padded to contain the entire ball. Because of imperfect lighting conditions, the black spots on the ball don't have a consistant grayscale value. Thus, the algorithm looks for pixel segments that are dark relative to their neighboring pixels. A color change is triggered when the percent difference between two adjacent pixels is more than 25% of their average color. We refer to this percentage as the *Blob Threshold* and examine alternative values in Sect. 4.1. A value of 25% enables the algorithm to be somewhat robust to varying lighting conditions. After every row of the ROI has been segmented into light and dark scanlines, they are then merged into blobs.

It is often the case that non-ball objects in the image will create blobs. We attempt to filter out these erroneous blobs according to the following heuristics:

1. The blob must cover at least some percentage of the area of its bounding box.
2. The blob cannot be too big or too small, relative to the expected ball size.
3. The blob's bounding box aspect ratio cannot be too narrow or too wide.
4. The blob cannot have too many green pixels.
5. The average intensity of the blob's constituent pixels must be below some threshold.

Line 4 [ConstructTriangles]: We make the assumption that at least 3 of the ball's black spots will be visible regardless of ball orientation, and that these 3 of the black spots will form a nearly-equilateral triangle. We group 3 blobs together into a "BlobTriangle" and apply the following series of heuristic tests to filter out BlobTriangles that probably aren't the result of a true ball. Thresholds and specific criteria can be found in our accompanying source code release.

1. Relative Size Test: The ratio between the areas of the smallest blob and largest blob cannot exceed some threshold.
2. Angle Test: The largest angle of the triangle formed by the three blob centroids cannot exceed some threshold. This angle is recorded as the BlobTriangle's score. A smaller score is considered better because smaller angels are more similar to the ideal equilateral triangle. We notice in practice that many false BlobTriangles are farther from equilateral than true BlobTriangles.
3. Float Test: The projected height of the ball must not be too far above or below the ground.
4. Intersecting Blob Test: No other blobs are allowed to be inside the triangle.

If the BlobTriangle passes all of these tests, then it proceeds to the next round of tests. If there are more than 3 blobs in the ROI, every combination of 3 is evaluated and the BlobTriangle with the largest score is chosen for its enclosing ROI.

Line 5 [SelectBestTriangle]: Next, the algorithm identifies the best ROI by computing the following real-valued heuristic features from the ROI's best Blob-Triangle. No single threshold is applied to any of these values because they are filtered in aggregate [8].

1. The percentage of green pixels in an imaginary box below the BlobTriangle. True balls usually have a large amount of green field directly below them, so a larger value here indicates higher likelihood.
2. Percentage of green pixels in the BlobTriangle's bounding box. True balls usually have very few green pixels on them, so a smaller number here indicates higher likelihood.
3. Projected Ball Height: Similar to the Float Test, but this time with a soft threshold.
4. Distance from the field. The center of the BlobTriangle in image coordinates is projected into world coordinates. The farther this projected position is from the field, the less likely it is to be a true ball.
5. Ball velocity, as measured by the difference in world distance coordinates between this BlobTraingle and the previously observed ball.
6. *KW Discrepancy*: The discrepancy between **K**inematics-based and **W**idth-based distance computations (see Menashe et al. [8]).

These values are fed through a multidimensional Gaussian estimator which has hard-coded means and standard deviations for each of the 6 features [8]. This gives a likelihood estimate for the BlobTriangle being the result of a true ball. If this likelihood estimate is below a certain threshold, we throw it out and no longer consider it to be a ball candidate. If multiple ROIs pass this test, then only the ROI with best BlobTriangle score will proceed to the next round. We refer to the precise threshold for the likelihood estimate as the *Gaussian Likelihood Threshold* and examine different settings of this variable in Sect. 4.1.

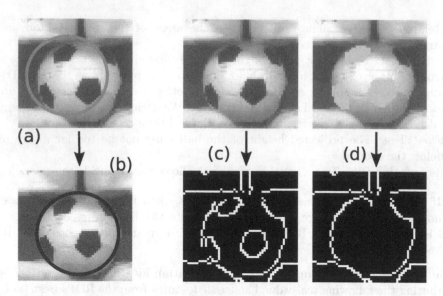

Fig. 1. (a) Ball localization based on BlobTriangle location. (b) Ball localization after Hough Transform. (c) Edge image without erasing dark blobs. (d) Edge image after erasing dark blobs.

Line 6 [HoughCorrection]: Before applying the final test, the algorithm uses a Hough transform to correct the estimated position and radius of the ball represented by the best triangle. This operation is only applied to the single best candidate due to being computationally expensive.

We want the resulting circle to conform to the ball's contour. However, the Hough transform sometimes "snaps" to the contours of the black spots on the ball due to their high contrast and similarity with normal edges. This problem is partially alleviated by overwriting the pixel values of these blobs to a ligher gray color; in this way the algorithm "erases" the dark blobs from the ROI, and is thus less likely to produce unwanted edges during the Hough transform. Figure 1 shows an example of this.

Line 7 [Classify]: In this final test, the ROI image is classified using a machine learned classifier with low false negative rate. If the classifier's prediction is positive, then we consider this ROI/BlobTriangle pair to be a ball, and we signal a ball observation to the rest of the system. Section 3.2 describes the classification step in further detail.

3.2   Classification

The last step of the filtering process described in Sect. 3.1 uses a general purpose machine learning technique to perform a final test on a potential ball detection. The algorithm uses a machine-learned classifier (MLC) - either a Deep Neural

Network (DNN) or a Support Vector Machine (SVM). In Sect. 4.2 we evaluate the relative effectiveness of these two approaches.

In this work, MLCs are trained with binary labels: 0 (or "negative") indicating that the input image does not contain a ball, and 1 (or "positive") indicating that the input image does contain a ball. Input images are taken from the ROI detection system described in Sect. 3.1, converted to the MLC's expected input format, and then processed by the MLC. Rather than evaluate every ROI, the computational complexity of our MLCs only allows for a single validation per image frame. Thus, we simply take the highest-scoring candidate and apply our MLC validation step to the candidate as a way to further reduce our false positive rate.

Support Vector Machines. One of the two MLCs we evaluate in this work is the Support Vector Machine. In order to train the SVM we collected our training dataset in two phases. In the first phase we used our candidate identification system to collect positive sample images of the ball, and manually removed false positives from the dataset. We were able to gather around 1,000 positive samples in this manner.

We collected negative samples by capturing images from the NAO's camera at various points on the field, taking care to ensure that none of the images had balls in their field of view. We then randomly divided these images into ROIs and supplied these ROIs as negative samples. We produced approximately 15,000 negative samples through this process.

We used OpenCV's Nu-SVM implementation with a linear kernel. Images were resized to 32-by-32 pixel grayscale and then transformed into a vector of 8-by-8 HoG descriptors. Training time generally ranged from 15 to 30 min on a modern laptop with an Intel i7 processor. Training time increased exponentially as more negative samples were added so in practice we were not able to go beyond the 15,000 noted above.

Deep Neural Networks. We also applied Deep Neural Networks to the binary ball classification problem using similar data collection techniques as with SVMs (Sect. 3.2), We used the Caffe Deep Neural Network implementation [4] on raw pixels with GPU training enabled. With this approach we were able to train the ball detector within about 2 hours on a typical laptop with GPU hardware.

In order to enable fast test-time processing on the NAO's hardware we used a simple DNN consisting of a single Gaussian convolutional layer. Even such a simple network required 3ms to test a single image, which was comparable with the test time for our SVM implementation. At the RoboCup competition we found that the SVM showed a lower false negative rate than the DNN, which was perhaps due to the simplicity of our DNN structure. Section 4.2 provides a complete comparison based on rigorous experiments.

4   Experiments

In this section we provide empirical analysis of different variable settings and MLC techniques to evaluate the options available when implementing the ball detection algorithm. In Sect. 4.1 we first look at the effect of varying one of the primary thresholds used in filtering out ball candidates. In Sect. 4.2 we examine the accuracy of both SVMs and DNNs to show the preferred technique to be used given one's computing and dataset constraints.

4.1   Ball Candidate Detection

Figure 2 shows the effect of altering the Gaussian likelihood threshold described in line 5 of Algorithm 1. This likelihood estimate threshold is described in detail by Menashe et al. [8] where it is also used for ball detection. The figure shows that recall is consistent except for very high threshold values, indicating that true positives consistently exhibit a high likelihood estimate and are seldom filtered by this step of the algorithm.

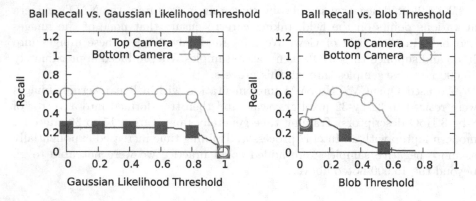

Fig. 2. A plot of Recall vs Gaussian Likelihood and Blob thresholds for ball candidates used in Algorithm 1.

4.2   SVM and Deep Classification

Deep Neural Network as Ball Classifier. Deep neural networks, and convolutional neural networks in particular [6,7], have demonstrated great success in visual recognition tasks. Due to the limited computational capacity of the robot, we design four simple neural network structures to perform ball classification. The first two networks are convolutional neural networks. They each have one convolution layer, a max-pooling layer, and a fully connected layer. The first network, which we will refer as Conv-1, learns 4 9×9 convolution filters with stride length 5. While the second one, Conv-2, has 32 7×7 convolution filters with stride length 4. The third network has a single fully connected layer. The fourth network has two fully connected layers, in which the hidden layer has 512 neurons. We will refer these two networks as Fc-1 and Fc-2. The dataset we use for evaluation was collected at two RoboCup competitions and has a total of 34,684 annotated images with 7,666 positives and 30,018 negatives. Table 1 shows the training times, model complexity, and efficacy results for each network.

Table 1. Classification results of neural network classifiers.

	Time	#Params	Precision	Recall	Accuracy
Conv-1	320 s	**1106**	.9797	.9746	.9907
Conv-2	213 s	5314	**.9948**	**.9941**	**.9977**
Fc-1	**12 s**	6146	.9251	.9341	.9712
Fc-2	116 s	1574402	.9914	.9772	.9936

We also test the transferability of the networks across different environments, since in RoboCup games could in different locations. We train the networks on a dataset collected in one environment and (1) test on some other data collected in the same environment; and (2) test on a dataset collected in a different environment, without any additional fine-tuning. The results are shown in Table 2a and b. Overall, the performance of all networks degrades considerably due to overfitting to a particular environment, especially the convolutional networks. This implies it is desirable to have deep networks fine-tuned or retrained when environment changes, which is practical given the training time in Table 1.

Table 2. (a) Transferability results of our DNN classifiers, using USopen 2016 dataset as source task and RoboCup 2016 dataset as target task. (b) Transferability results of our DNN classifiers, using RoboCup 2016 dataset as source task and USopen 2016 dataset as target task.

	USopen16 →		USopen16
	Precision	Recall	Accuracy
Conv-1	.9972	**1.000**	.9994
Conv-2	**.9991**	.9991	**.9996**
Fc-1	.9346	.9468	.9746
Fc-2	.9944	.9944	.9976

	USopen16 →		RoboCup16
	Precision	Recall	Accuracy
Conv-1	.1226	.1440	.6726
Conv-2	.4163	.8748	.7654
Fc-1	**.7349**	.8596	**.9218**
Fc-2	.7214	**.8923**	.9215

	RoboCup16 →		RoboCup16
	Precision	Recall	Accuracy
Conv-1	.9820	.9776	.9928
Conv-2	**1.000**	**.9910**	**.9984**
Fc-1	.9623	.9731	.9884
Fc-2	.9977	.9843	.9968

	RoboCup16 →		USopen16
	Precision	Recall	Accuracy
Conv-1	.6754	.2576	.8109
Conv-2	**.9890**	.3925	.8664
Fc-1	.8402	.5926	.8865
Fc-2	.9199	**.6064**	**.9026**

Support Vector Machine as Ball Classifier. Since their inception in the early 1990s, SVMs have proven to be a robust and powerful family of classifiers [3]. In these experiments we use the datasets from the DNN experiments to compare SVMs with three different kernels: linear, polynomial (degree 3), and radial basis function (RBF). The results are presented in Table 3a.

As we have done for deep nets, we also wish to measure the transferability, or generalization, of learning across domains. In these experiments we train the SVM models on a dataset collected in one environment and test on a dataset collected in a different one. These results are presented in Table 3b. Overall, the performance degrades dramatically, more so than in the neural networks case, due to overfitting to a particular environment, without the flexibility that the deep architectures offer. Again this implies that one must adjust or retrain the existing SVM models when presented with a new environment in order to maintain acceptable performance.

4.3 SVM versus DNN

There are two major lessons to take away from the SVM and DNN experiments of Sect. 4.2. First, transferred models perform poorly relative to models that are trained on datasets similar to their test sets. In the context of RoboCup, this means that it is highly beneficial to train models on-site at the competitions in order to train on data that will closely resemble what is seen in the official games.

Table 3. (a) Classification results of SVM classifiers. (b) Generalization results of our SVM classifiers. In the first stage we train a model on 80% of the source dataset and then test on the remaining 20%. We then test the trained model on the target (transfer) dataset.

SVM Kernel	Accuracy	AUC	Precision	Recall
SVM kernel	Accuracy	AUC	Precision	Recall
Linear	0.883	0.869	0.833	0.543
Polynomial	**0.970**	**0.990**	**0.972**	**0.881**
RBF	0.961	0.989	0.989	0.824

SVM Kernel	USOpen16				USOpen16→RoboCup16			
	Accuracy	AUC	Precision	Recall	Accuracy	AUC	Precision	Recall
Linear	0.893	0.923	0.807	0.655	**0.595**	**0.420**	**0.163**	**0.325**
Polynomial	**0.985**	0.997	0.962	**0.968**	0.363	0.140	0.098	0.027
RBF	0.982	**0.998**	**0.972**	0.944	0.421	0.134	0	0
	RoboCup16				RoboCup16→USOpen16			
Linear	0.992	0.997	0.995	0.960	0.781	0.387	0.200	0.001
Polynomial	0.998	0.999	**1.00**	0.987	**0.782**	**0.520**	1.00	**0.001**
RBF	**0.998**	**0.999**	0.998	**0.991**	0.782	0.337	1.00	0.001

Second, although complex multi-layer DNNs are too computationally expensive for constrained domains such as RoboCup, simpler networks can still provide an advantage over SVMs. In particular we see that the DNN recall observed in Table 1 is signifcantly higher than the SVM recall in Table 3a, while both techniques exhibit high accuracy.

To summarize, we find that a well-trained DNN can outperform a well-trained SVM on object classification tasks, even when the DNN's architecture is simplified to enable fast computation.

5   Conclusion and Future Work

In this work we have described UT Austin Villa's black and white soccer ball detection algorithm and discussed in detail the heuristic techniques applied as well as the machine-learned classification algorithms we incorporated for optimizing detector accuracy. In addition to our proven success at gameplay we provided empirical results indicating the benefits of applying a Deep Neural Network to the task of detecting false positives. We showed that a modest DNN architecture along with a heuristic ROI filtering pipeline can be combined to create a fast, precise object detection system that is suitable for computationally constrained environments such as RoboCup soccer.

As the RoboCup competition (and the SPL in particular) progresses toward more challenging and realistic requirements, lighting invariance will take on a greater role in vision algorithms in the coming years. Our work is designed to be robust to changes in lighting conditions, particularly in the area of geometric checks. However, improvements may still be possible with respect to adaptive thresholding and green detection in our color table. Improving these components will be the subject of future work.

References

1. Bernsen, J.: Dynamic thresholding of grey-level images. In: International conference on pattern recognition, vol. 2, pp. 1251–1255 (1986)
2. Bruce, J., Balch, T., Veloso, M.: Fast and inexpensive color image segmentation for interactive robots. In: Proceedings of the 2000 IEEE/RSJ International Conference on Intelligent Robots and Systems (IROS 2000), volume 3, pp. 2061–2066. IEEE (2000)
3. Cortes, C., Vapnik, V.: Support-vector networks. Mach. Learn. **20**(3), 273–297 (1995). https://doi.org/10.1007/BF00994018
4. Jia, Y., et al.: Caffe: Convolutional architecture for fast feature embedding. arXiv preprint arXiv:1408.5093 (2014)
5. Kitano, H., Asada, M., Kuniyoshi, Y., Noda, I., Osawa, E.: Robocup: The robot world cup initiative. In: Proceedings of the First International Conference on Autonomous Agents, AGENTS 1997, pp. 340–347. ACM, New York (1997)
6. Krizhevsky, A., Sutskever, I., Hinton, G.E.: ImageNet classification with deep convolutional neural networks. In: Advances in Neural Information Processing Systems, pp. 1097–1105 (2012)

7. LeCun, Y., Bengio, Y., Hinton, G.: Deep learning. Nature **521**(7553), 436–444 (2015)
8. Menashe, J., Barrett, S., Genter, K., Stone, P.: Ut Austin Villa, : advances in vision, kinematics, and strategy. In: The Eighth Workshop on Humanoid Soccer Robots at Humanoids (2013)
9. Russakovsky, O., et al.: Imagenet large scale visual recognition challenge. Int. J. Comput. Vis. **115**(3), 211–252 (2015)

Fear Learning for Flexible Decision Making in RoboCup: A Discussion

Caroline Rizzi[1]([✉]), Colin G. Johnson[1], and Patricia A. Vargas[2]

[1] School of Computing, University of Kent, Canterbury, UK
{cr519,C.G.Johnson}@kent.ac.uk
[2] Robotics Laboratory, School of Mathematical and Computer Sciences,
Heriot-Watt University, Edinburgh, UK
p.a.vargas@hw.ac.uk

Abstract. In this paper, we address the stagnation of RoboCup competitions in the fields of contextual perception, real-time adaptation and flexible decision-making, mainly in regards to the Standard Platform League (SPL). We argue that our Situation-Aware FEar Learning (SAFEL) model has the necessary tools to leverage the SPL competition in these fields of research, by allowing robot players to learn the behaviour profile of the opponent team at runtime. Later, players can use this knowledge to predict when an undesirable outcome is imminent, thus having the chance to act towards preventing it. We discuss specific scenarios where SAFEL's associative learning could help to increase the positive outcomes of a team during a soccer match by means of contextual adaptation.

Keywords: RoboCup · Cognitive learning
Contextual fear conditioning · Brain emotional model
Affective computing

1 Introduction

RoboCup is an important international scientific initiative with the goal to advance the state of the art of artificial intelligence for autonomous robots by proposing an ambitious challenge. The official challenge of the RoboCup initiative, established in 1997, states that "by the middle of the 21st century, a team of fully autonomous humanoid robot soccer players shall win a soccer game, complying with the official rules of FIFA, against the winner of the most recent World Cup." [4].

The relevance of the RoboCup competition is not on the challenge itself, but on the intrinsic gains from the journey to accomplish such a goal. RoboCup's initiative poses a challenge of high complexity that requires a significant body of research in the areas of artificial intelligence, sensor fusion, real-time planning and navigation, cooperation in multiagent robotics, context recognition, image processing, motor control, among others [7]. The RoboCup initiative has hosted

© Springer Nature Switzerland AG 2018
H. Akiyama et al. (Eds.): RoboCup 2017, LNAI 11175, pp. 59–70, 2018.
https://doi.org/10.1007/978-3-030-00308-1_5

annual competitions for more than 20 years now, a period over which significant advancements have been achieved towards autonomous robotics.

Despite RoboCup's many achievements in a number of research fields related to autonomous robotics, the development of contextual perception and flexible decision making has made modest progress. In this paper, we address RoboCup's stagnation in these areas, discussing the existing approaches and their limitations (Sect. 2). We propose in Sect. 3, as a potential approach to tackle these limitations, our artificial emotional model named SAFEL (Situation-Aware FEar Learning) [13,14,17], which consists of a hybrid architecture based on the fear-learning mechanisms of the brain. Finally, in Sect. 4, we suggest RoboCup scenarios where SAFEL could be useful to improve flexible decision making at both individual and multi-agent levels, followed by the conclusions in Sect. 5.

2   Intelligent Behaviour in RoboCup

Due to the inherent teamwork nature of soccer, most RoboCup-related works addressing intelligent behaviour and decision making tend to investigate techniques to optimise collaborative behaviour and pre-coordination [6,10,19]. These approaches are commonly based on pre-determined coordination strategies, such as predefined behaviour rules and pre-trained machine learning and/or evolutionary algorithms, which provide the robot players with a basis to decide when it is better to kick, dribble, pass, change roles, etc.

Although useful for training a team of robots to play collaboratively in most common soccer situations, these approaches lead to limited coordination strategies that are immutable and restricted to tactics stipulated prior to the actual soccer match. As a consequence, the same strategy is delivered against all opponent teams in the competition. However, different teams may use different tactics, and a specific pre-trained approach may fail against a particular opponent while being successful against another opponent team.

For example, suppose that strikers of a particular team may be more aggressive and negligent than normal, consequently causing more collisions and fouls, while another team's striker may be excessively cautious, which could slow it down. Therefore, the goalkeeper may need to take risky actions against the former team in order to avoid collisions and goals, which may not be necessary against the latter team.

If we consider the many aspects involved in a robot's action (e.g., the kick strength, the collision prevention strategy, the walking speed and the range and timing of vision perception), the final behaviour of a robot can be completely different from team to team, even when considering the same in-game situation (e.g., striker shooting to goal). Taking advantage of the behavioural variations among teams can be critical to winning a soccer match.

For this reason, a mechanism that allows the individuals of a team to learn and adapt at runtime to the playing behaviour of each opponent team is essential. The need for such a mechanism is accentuated by the ultimate goal of the RoboCup competition: a soccer match between a team of robots and a team of humans.

Usually, for a team of robots, the difference in behaviour is only meaningful when comparing two distinct teams. In other words, two different teams may have different approaches to how they implement their players under a particular role (e.g., striker, defender, goalkeeper). But it is uncommon for a team in the RoboCup competition to have two or more completely different implementations of the same role.

On the other hand, the behavioural difference goes further than just group level for a team of humans. This is because, not only different teams have different tactics, but also different individuals in a team may behave completely different under the same situation, even when assigned to the same role. Therefore, a team of human players entails even more complex behavioural differences if compared to a team of robots.

The need for real-time adaptation capabilities has been previously addressed using case-based reasoning [1,18]. In these works, case-based reasoning approaches are used for post-coordination as a mean to optimise players' positioning during the match. These works represent a great contribution towards post-coordination, flexible decision making and real-time adaptation.

Nevertheless, to the best of our knowledge, these works usually fall in one of the following limitations: (1) temporal information is not considered in the problem solving, (2) the approach is domain specific or (3) predictions' applicability is limited to the optimisation of players positioning. In addition, most of these approaches have been tested and applied only to RoboCup leagues based on simpler robots or on simulations. RoboCup leagues based on more complex robots, such as the Standard Platform League (SPL), still lack more robust real-time adaptation mechanisms. In the next section, we present a situation-aware fear-learning computational model, which is a real-time adaptation mechanism capable of overcoming the above-mentioned limitations.

3   SAFEL

SAFEL stands for *Situation-Aware FEar Learning*. It is a situation-aware computational system capable of providing robots with fear-learning skills in order to predict threatening situations to their own well-being or to their goals. SAFEL's model has been first proposed by us in [17], partially implemented and tested in [13] and improved in [14]. In this section, we briefly introduce SAFEL's biological inspiration and design. For a deeper understanding of SAFEL's model and further details on its implementation and performance analysis, we refer the reader to our previous publications [13,14,17].

SAFEL is a hybrid computational architecture inspired by the LeDoux's fear-learning model of the human brain [8,9]. According to LeDoux, fear learning greatly relies on two brain regions known as the *amygdala* and the *hippocampus*, as well as on a cognitive function known as the *working memory*.

Considerable evidence indicates the amygdala as an essential brain region for fear learning and memory [8,9]. It is responsible for processing the emotional significance of sensed stimuli by creating associations between neutral and aversive stimuli. On the other hand, the hippocampus is believed to be the main brain region involved in context processing [8]. In the hippocampus, sensory information is put together in order to form a unitary representation of the current state of affairs. Unlike information processed in the amygdala, representations formed in the hippocampus are not just visual, auditory or olfactory, but all of these at once, and includes the way these sensations relate to each other both in intensity and temporal order. Finally, the working memory creates associations between the contextual memory formed in the hippocampus with the emotional memory formed in the amygdala, giving emotional meaning to the contextual information acquired in past experiences.

SAFEL's architecture is based on the task division proposed by LeDoux. Therefore, analogous to the LeDoux model, SAFEL is divided into three modules that work in an integrated and parallel manner: the amygdala, the hippocampus and the working memory modules. Figure 1 depicts the SAFEL model, illustrating how the three modules of the architecture are interconnected.

Environmental stimuli detected by the robot (by means of sensors' input or direct user input) must first be normalized and categorised into aversive and neutral stimuli by the robot's controller before being delivered to the amygdala and hippocampal modules. The amygdala module is responsible for detecting threats by analysing the current values of aversive stimuli and associating them with simultaneously occurring neutral stimuli. This learning process is induced by means of a procedure analogous to *classical fear conditioning* [11].

In classical fear conditioning, associative learning is induced by pairing a neutral stimulus (i.e., a stimulus that initially elicits no specific response from the individual) with an aversive stimulus (i.e., a stimulus that naturally elicits fear or discomfort, such as pain and hunger). Eventually, the previously neutral stimulus acquires emotional meaning and becomes able to elicit the state of fear by itself, even in the absence of the aversive stimulus. When this happens, we say that the neutral stimulus is now a *conditioned stimulus*, which elicits fear as a *conditioned emotional response*.

In SAFEL's model, the amygdala module is also responsible for providing emotional feedback to the hippocampus module, which in parallel generates complex contextual representations of the sensed environmental stimuli. In the hippocampus, the amygdala emotional feedback and the generated contextual information are associated.

Finally, pieces of contextual information and their emotional significance are memorised in the working memory. Later, any previously experienced pattern of contextual information will trigger the retrieval of that stored memory and its emotional meaning. Consequently, if a particular situation preceded the occurrence of an aversive stimulus in a past experience, the working memory will retrieve the same state of fear triggered by that situation in the past, warning the individual that an undesirable situation is likely to happen in the near future.

SAFEL's amygdala module is based on a modified *artificial neural network* (ANN) proposed by us in [16], which allows robots to associate environmental stimuli at runtime based on the Pavlovian classical conditioning procedure [11]. In the amygdala module, this modified ANN is used to associate neutral and

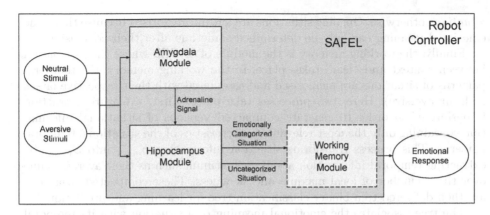

Fig. 1. The SAFEL model. Solid-border boxes represent areas of the brain whereas dotted-border boxes represent cognitive functions of the brain. The model receives neutral and aversive stimuli as input from the robot controller and outputs the corresponding emotional response back to the robot controller.

aversive stimuli at runtime. The ANN is pre-trained to generate a high output value whenever any aversive input is also high, and a low output otherwise, regardless of the value of neutral inputs. Associative learning takes place by adjusting the first-layer weights of the ANN according to the coincidence of input values. In other words, the association takes place whenever a high neutral stimulus input and a high aversive stimulus input co-occur. Eventually, the neutral stimulus is turned into a conditioned stimulus, becoming able to trigger by itself the same ANN output that the aversive stimulus would, even in its absence. The output of the ANN is said to be the *adrenaline signal*, which is a real value in the range [0,1] representing the current fear level of the system.

The hippocampus module is based on Dey's [3] conceptualization of situation awareness for expert systems. It is responsible for collecting, understanding and managing the states of the robot over time. To accomplish that, we have modelled and implemented the hippocampus module using SCENE [12,15], which is a powerful situation management platform that extends the JBoss Drools rule engine and its CEP (Complex Event Processing) platform [2].

The hippocampus module receives two inputs: *events*, which are sets of environmental stimuli at a given point in time, and the adrenaline signal relayed by the amygdala module. This module is responsible for assembling these events into pieces of information known as *situations*, which depict the robot's state of affair during a particular period of time. Situations are stored in the hippocampus module as matrices $S_{m \times n}$, where m is the number of time steps encompassed in a particular situation's duration and n is the number of stimuli being sensed by the robot.

Situations are later categorised in regards to their emotional meaning according to the subsequent emotional feedback from the amygdala. Situations are categorized as *aversive situations* if preceding high adrenaline signals, and *safe situations* otherwise. Ongoing situations are left uncategorised because their true emotional meaning can only be determined sometime after their conclusion.

Finally, the working memory is the module of SAFEL where the association between context and "fear" takes place. In the working memory, the temporal patterns of situations are memorised and associated with their respective labels (safe or aversive). Here, two processes take place. First, a feature extraction is performed in order to generate compacted versions of situational information containing only the most relevant characteristics of the situations' temporal patterns. This process transforms situation information $S_{m \times n}$ into $S'_{1 \times 3n}$, by extracting temporal information about each stimuli such as their average value over time, number of local maxima and skewness. These compacted situations are then delivered to a binary classification tree for learning and prediction.

The tree associates the emotional meaning of a situation with its temporal pattern. Then, whenever an emotionally uncategorised situation arrives, the tree attempts to predict its emotional meaning by comparing the temporal properties of this situation and of those previously learned. If the tree finds a match for that situation pattern, then it returns the emotional category linked to that pattern, which will be either safe or aversive. Ultimately, SAFEL's final output is the emotional category retrieved by the classification tree and indicates whether something aversive is likely to happen in the near future.

4   RoboCup Use Cases

Robot soccer poses a great challenge to robotics. It is real-time and takes place in a highly dynamic environment, perceived by means of the robots' sensors, which are in many cases susceptible to reading failures and noises. In such a challenging environment, advanced techniques and algorithms for flexible decision making, adaptation and fast reaction are essential. In this section, we discuss possible scenarios in the RoboCup SPL competition where a mechanism such as SAFEL, which provides flexible decision-making capabilities and real-time adaptation, would be desirable, if not essential.

4.1   Individuals' Adaptation

As mentioned in previous Sections, most research related to robot soccer focuses on improving teamwork and cooperative behaviour. Teamwork is undoubtedly crucial in soccer, but its effectiveness is limited to the level of skill of the team members. Good cooperation strategy is of little aid if the members of the team are unqualified. In addition, despite the intrinsic team-work nature of soccer, there are many situations in which individual players find themselves isolated from the rest of their team. In these cases, they have no choice but to rely on their own skills and decision-making capabilities. For this reason, we argue that mechanisms to improve the adaptation skills and flexible decision-making of individual players are also essential for robot soccer. This is, however, a neglected area of study in RoboCup.

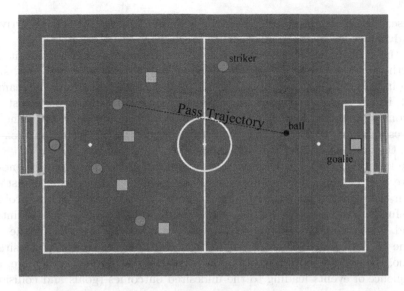

Fig. 2. Scenario example. Red squares represent players from team A, blue circles represent players from team B and the black circle represents the ball. The circle and square with thicker border line represent the respective team's goalkeeper. (Color figure online)

We propose the scenario exemplified in Fig. 2: suppose a match between team A and team B, where team A is currently attacking. Now suppose that a defender from team B manages to take possession of the ball and switch fields (i.e., pass the ball from one side of the field to the other in one shot). Because team A was fully engaged in the attack, all members of team A are in team B's side of the field, except the goalkeeper. Finally, also consider that, second by the goalkeeper from team A, the striker from team B is the closest player to the ball at this moment. The ball stops closer to the goalkeeper, but far enough so that the goalkeeper would have to leave the goal area vulnerable in order to reach it.

This hypothetical scenario is a clear example of a situation in which the goalkeeper is isolated from the rest of its team and is forced to rely only on its own judgement and skills. The striker from team B will certainly reach the ball before the other players of team A unless the goalkeeper intervenes in some way. The decision to be taken by the goalkeeper is, therefore, whether to intervene or not. Intervening would imply in leaving the goal area unattended and, consequently, vulnerable. On the other hand, not intervening would give an obvious advantage to the opponent striker for a clear shot to goal.

The answer to this question is not straightforward because it depends on the profile of the opponent team. If the opponent striker has weak shot, for instance, then it is likely to need more than one kick to attempt a goal, giving team A time to retreat and aid in the defence. Also, if the striker's first kick is not strong enough, then the ball will consequently be closer to the goalkeeper so that it does not need to leave the goal area unattended in order to reach the ball. Thus, in this case, staying in place, protecting the goal and waiting for help to arrive is more advantageous to the goalkeeper.

On the other hand, if the striker has a strong shot and a good aim, it may be worth to risk leaving the goal area and trying to reach the ball first, since staying in the goal area would likely result in a scoring opportunity for team B. At first, it may seem a trivial problem that depends only on whether the striker has strong kick or not. However, there are many factors involved, including the distances and angles between the elements of interest in this situation (i.e., the striker, the goalkeeper, the goal and the ball).

The kick that is weak from a particular position in the field, may be enough to score a goal from another position if we consider the angle and distance between the ball, the goal and the goalkeeper. The complexity of the problem can be further increased by the number of undesirable outcomes that we intend to avoid. For instance, in the above example, we defined that goals are the only outcome to be avoided. However, if we add collisions as another undesirable outcome, the behaviour profile of opponent teams will diverge even more, and the sequence of events leading to the undesired outcomes (goals and collisions) will become even more complex.

It is also worth mentioning that the sequence of events and their outcomes can only be analysed and associated after they occur at least once. Because it is not part of the pre-existing set of knowledge of team A, a learning process must take place at runtime. This means that the situation of interest must be experienced by the individuals first in order for them to acquire new knowledge about the world. Only then an association between environmental stimuli can be induced, leading to the necessary adaptations in behaviour.

We are currently working on a case study based on the scenario discussed above. In this case study, the goalkeeper is placed under the same isolated situation above described and tested against four different team behaviours, where both goals and collisions are considered to be undesirable outcomes. By using SAFEL's mechanism of fear learning, we expect the goalkeeper to learn when it is advantageous to leave the goal area vulnerable and go for the ball, considering the sequence of events and their outcome for each particular team behaviour and the positioning of the elements of interest in the field.

4.2   Cooperation and Team Work

In real-life soccer, human players commonly use both pre- and post- coordination strategies in conjunction. Soccer tactics usually involve the training of an agreed formation and strategy prior to the match, which is the pre-coordination phase. Nevertheless, unforeseen events may occur during the match, forcing teammates to communicate and adapt the team's strategy, which can be seen as a post-coordination phase. While pre-trained coordination is well developed and studied in the RoboCup competition (as discussed in Sect. 2), the development of post-coordination strategies is still overlooked.

Although SAFEL's adaptive learning is intended mainly for robots as individuals, we claim that it can be successfully applied to multi-robot tasks by improving collaborative behaviour and post-coordination. Among the varied methods with which post-coordination can be accomplished using SAFEL, we highlight two approaches, which are discussed below.

Anticipated Help Request. In many soccer situations, an undesirable outcome may be unavoidable, regardless of a player success in correctly predicting it and taking the appropriate actions. For instance, consider the example given in Sect. 4.1. The best way to avoid a goal when dealing with a particular opponent behaviour may be to leave the goal area and try to reach the ball first. However, this may also increase the chances of collision, since both striker and goalkeeper will attempt to reach the ball at the same time.

It may seem a dead-end situation, but using SAFEL's predictions to send an anticipated help request to the rest of the team is a valid and advantageous action in this case. By requesting help before it is actually needed, the goalkeeper allows its teammates to act with antecedence and, perhaps, aid in situations where help would be impracticable without the opportunity to anticipate their actions.

The goalkeeper, knowing that a particular sequence of events recurrently leads to an undesirable outcome, could message its teammates and warn them of its current situation. The teammates, in turn, could use SAFEL for learning to predict the goalkeeper's warning messages, by associating these messages with the sequence of events that recurrently precede them. Ideally, the teammates would become capable of predicting when the goalkeeper will be in trouble before the goalkeeper itself and have more options towards preventing undesirable outcomes. This cascade of predictions would not only improve the team's collaborative behaviour, but also potentially enhance the understanding among teammates to the point where they may be aware of each other's situation before any message is exchanged.

In the above discussion, we have instantiated the example of the goalkeeper, but the same approach could be used to any other playing role in a variety of situations. This is because SAFEL's approach for fear-learning is domain independent, thus applicable to any scenario where predictions based on temporal information are necessary for environmental adaptation, in and outside the RoboCup domain.

The Coordinator-Robot Approach. Similarly to SAFEL's proposal, the work of Ros et al. [18] is based on a fully distributed design, where each robot has an independent reasoning and perception of the world. Communication between teammate robots is allowed, but there is no global perception or control.

In order to solve coordination and collaborative behaviour using their decentralised model, Ros et al. propose an approach in which one single robot is selected as the "coordinator". The coordinator is responsible for reasoning over the current problem, given the state of the world, and messaging to the remaining teammates the sequence of actions that should be executed by the group in order to solve that problem.

This approach provides a simple solution to the post-coordination problem while preventing decision-making conflicts that could arise from a distributed system. Ros et al. also argue that this approach is useful for heterogeneous teams, where the role of coordinator could be assigned to the group of robots with higher computing power, while the remaining robots would only execute the actions calculated by the coordinators.

Like the work of Ros et al., SAFEL's adaptive fear learning is also based on decentralised perception and reasoning. For this reason, we argue that the approach of Ros et al. for coordination and collaboration could also be used with SAFEL. The inputs for SAFEL could be, for instance, the global state of the world (e.g., ball position, teammates positions, opponents positions, collisions, goals, etc.), estimated from the local state of affairs perceived by each teammate. Then, SAFEL's emotional response would indicate whether there is an imminent threat that the team should prioritise.

For instance, suppose that team A has used a machine learning algorithm to pre-train cooperative behaviour for defence purposes, which is based on the attacking behaviour of the other teams in the previous years of the RoboCup competition. Let's also suppose that team B has created a novel attack strategy, which is considerably distinct from those used by the other teams. Naturally, the pre-trained defence strategy of team A would be ineffective against team B.

In this scenario, SAFEL could be used with one or more coordinator robots. If there is a pattern in the attacking formation of team B that recurrently precedes goals from team B, then SAFEL would associate both and warn the coordinator robot whenever that formation pattern occurs again. This would give the coordinator the chance to act before another goal is scored, by adapting the defence strategy of the team. For example, instead of using the default pre-trained sequence of actions, the coordinator could change it to a more risky or aggressive defence, such as sending all teammates to defend the goal area, which should be used only in extreme situations. In this example, the adaptation capabilities provided by SAFEL go further than individuals' level, by adapting the behaviour of the team as a whole.

4.3 Drop-In Competition

The drop-in competition, introduced in 2013 [5], encourages the creation of agents capable of coordinating and co-operating with other teammates in an ad-hoc manner. In this competition, robots of different RoboCup teams collaborate as a single team towards a common goal: win the match with the highest goal difference possible.

The biggest challenge of the drop-in competition reside in the lack of pre-coordination, which affects the players' capability to properly communicate. Because of the limited and possibly misleading communication, many RoboCup teams do not completely trust their teammates' messages during the drop-in competition. Doing so could mislead their robots towards engaging in a disadvantageous or non-intelligent behaviour, which would negatively affect their score in the competition. According to Genter et al. [5], some RoboCup teams have developed strategies to determine the reliability of their teammates' messages and skills. Others, in turn, have solved the issue by simply not accepting any incoming messages, or even by not communicating at all with teammates. This has led RoboCup teams to converge to a single strategy in the drop-in competition that Genter et al. describe as "Play the ball if it is close and/or no other robot wants to play the ball. Take a supporting position otherwise".

This simplistic strategy clearly diverges from the main goal of the drop-in competition. Genter et al. argue that strategies for ad-hoc teamwork can be improved in many ways, among which they mention the creation of mechanisms to: (1) evaluate the reliability of each teammate's communication; (2) evaluate the relative skill of each teammate in particular roles and positions; and (3) identify when it is better to make or receive a pass. We argue that the fear-learning mechanism of SAFEL fulfils the exact needs indicated by Genter et al., since all the three above-listed real-time evaluations can be performed in terms of associations between sequences of events and their undesirable outcomes.

5   Conclusion

In this paper, we have discussed the current gaps in the areas of contextual perception, real-time adaptation and flexible decision-making within the RoboCup competitions, mainly in respect to the Standard Platform League (SPL). Later, we proposed SAFEL as a potential approach for tackling these gaps. SAFEL is an emotional model for artificial fear-learning, which is inspired by well-known neuroscience findings on the brain's mechanisms of fear learning. Ultimately, we discussed scenarios within the RoboCup SPL where real-time adaptation is essential at both individual and multi-agent levels and suggested approaches for addressing these situations using SAFEL's associative learning. Future work involves using SAFEL to implement the scenario discussed in Sect. 4.1.

Acknowledgments. The first author is financially supported by CAPES, a Brazilian research-support agency (process number 0648/13-2).

References

1. Ahmadi, M., Keighobadi-Lamjiri, A., Nevisi, M.M., Habibi, J., Badie, K.: Using a two-layered case-based reasoning for prediction in soccer coach. In: Proceedings of the International Conference of Machine Learning; Models, Technologies and Applications (MLMTA), pp. 181–185 (2003)
2. Bali, M.: Drools JBoss Rules 5.X Developer's Guide. Packt Publishing, Birmingham (2013)
3. Dey, A.K.: Understanding and Using Context. Pers. Ubiquit. Comput. 5(1), 4–7 (2001). https://doi.org/10.1007/s007790170019
4. Ferrein, A., Steinbauer, G.: 20 Years of RoboCup. Künstliche Intelligenz 30(3–4), 225–232 (2016). https://doi.org/10.1007/s13218-016-0449-5

5. Genter, K., Laue, T., Stone, P.: Benchmarking robot cooperation without pre-coordination in the RoboCup standard platform league drop-in player competition. In: 2015 IEEE/RSJ International Conference on Intelligent Robots and Systems (IROS), pp. 3415–3420 (2015). https://doi.org/10.1109/IROS.2015.7353853

6. Genter, K.: UT Austin Villa: project-driven research in AI and robotics. IEEE Intell. Syst. **31**(2), 94–101 (2016). https://doi.org/10.1109/MIS.2016.35

7. Kitano, H., Asada, M., Kuniyoshi, Y., Noda, I., Osawai, E., Matsubara, H.: RoboCup: a challenge problem for AI and robotics. In: Kitano, H. (ed.) RoboCup 1997. LNCS, vol. 1395, pp. 1–19. Springer, Heidelberg (1998). https://doi.org/10.1007/3-540-64473-3_46

8. LeDoux, J.: The Emotional Brain: The Mysterious Underpinnings of Emotional Life. Phoenix, London (1999)

9. LeDoux, J.: The emotional brain, fear, and the amygdala. Cell. Mol. Neurobiol. **23**(4–5), 727–738 (2003). https://doi.org/10.1023/a:1025048802629

10. Nitschke, G.: Emergent cooperation in RoboCup: a review. In: Bredenfeld, A., Jacoff, A., Noda, I., Takahashi, Y. (eds.) RoboCup 2005. LNCS (LNAI), vol. 4020, pp. 512–520. Springer, Heidelberg (2006). https://doi.org/10.1007/11780519_48

11. Pavlov, I.P.: Conditioned Reflexes: An Investigation of the Physiological Activity of the Cerebral Cortex. Oxford University Press, Oxford (1927)

12. Pereira, I., Costa, P., Almeida, J.: A rule-based platform for situation management. In: 2013 IEEE International Multi-Disciplinary Conference on Cognitive Methods in Situation Awareness and Decision Support (CogSIMA), pp. 83–90 (2013). https://doi.org/10.1109/CogSIMA.2013.6523827

13. Rizzi, C., Johnson, C.G., Fabris, F., Vargas, P.A.: A Situation-aware fear learning (SAFEL) model for robots. Neurocomputing **221**, 32–47 (2017). https://doi.org/10.1016/j.neucom.2016.09.035

14. Rizzi, C., Johnson, C.G., Vargas, P.A.: Improving the predictive performance of SAFEL: a situation-aware FEar learning model. In: 25th IEEE International Symposium on Robot and Human Interactive Communication (RO-MAN), pp. 736–742 (2016). https://doi.org/10.1109/ROMAN.2016.7745201

15. Raymundo, C.R., Costa, P.D., Almeida, J., Pereira, I.: An infrastructure for distributed rule-based situation management. In: 2014 IEEE International Inter-Disciplinary Conference on Cognitive Methods in Situation Awareness and Decision Support (CogSIMA), pp. 202–208 (2014). https://doi.org/10.1109/CogSIMA.2014.6816563

16. Raymundo, C.R., Johnson, C.G.: An artificial synaptic plasticity mechanism for classical conditioning with neural networks. In: Zeng, Z., Li, Y., King, I. (eds.) Advances in Neural Networks. LNCS, pp. 213–221. Springer, Cham (2014). https://doi.org/10.1007/978-3-319-12436-0_24

17. Raymundo, C.R., Johnson, C.G., Vargas, P.A.: An architecture for emotional and context-aware associative learning for robot companions. In: 24th IEEE International Symposium on Robot and Human Interactive Communication (RO-MAN), pp. 31–36 (2015). https://doi.org/10.1109/ROMAN.2015.7333699

18. Ros, R., Arcos, J.L., Lopez de Mantaras, R., Veloso, M.: A case-based approach for coordinated action selection in robot soccer. Artif. Intell. **173**(910), 1014–1039 (2009). https://doi.org/10.1016/j.artint.2009.02.004

19. Whiteson, S., Kohl, N., Miikkulainen, R., Stone, P.: Evolving keepaway soccer players through task decomposition. In: Cantú-Paz, E. (ed.) GECCO 2003. LNCS, vol. 2723, pp. 356–368. Springer, Heidelberg (2003). https://doi.org/10.1007/3-540-45105-6_41

Proposed Environment to Support Development and Experiment in RoboCupRescue Simulation

Shunki Takami[1]([⊠]), Kazuo Takayanagi[1], Shivashish Jaishy[1], Nobuhiro Ito[2], Kazunori Iwata[3], Yohsuke Murase[4], and Takeshi Uchitane[5]

[1] Graduate School of Business Administration and Computer Science, Aichi Institute of Technology, Toyota, Japan
takamin@maslab.aitech.ac.jp
[2] Department of Information Science, Aichi Institute of Technology, Toyota, Japan
[3] Department of Business Administration, Aichi University, Nagoya, Japan
[4] RIKEN Advanced Institute for Computational Science, Kobe, Japan
[5] Research Institute for Economics and Business Administration, Kobe University, Kobe, Japan

Abstract. The RoboCupRescue Simulation project is a test bed for multi-agent systems research for disaster relief. However, researchers have to implement many types of algorithm and require a complicated procedure for experiments, which places a heavy burden on them. Therefore, we propose an environment that integrates an agent-development framework and an experiment-management system to support researchers.

Keywords: Programming environment · Experiment management Rescue Simulation

1 Introduction

In recent years, the annual RoboCup international robotics competition has hosted the RoboCupRescue Simulation (RRS) project to confront large-scale natural disasters [1]. In particular, the Agent Competition is a platform for studying disaster-rescue agents and simulations. Our aim is to contribute to society by submitting results for this project.

However, in order to solve the disaster-relief problem targeted by the RRS, it is necessary to implement a combination of multiple algorithms such as those for path planning, information sharing, and resource allocation. In the experiment, numerous simulations are required for multiple disaster areas and changes in the various conditions of the area, such as fire, building collapse, and communication. Because these are burdensome for researchers, we propose an environment that integrates an agent-development framework and an experiment-management system. In the evaluation, we confirm that code re-usability and researcher burden were reduced in the experiment.

© Springer Nature Switzerland AG 2018
H. Akiyama et al. (Eds.): RoboCup 2017, LNAI 11175, pp. 71–83, 2018.
https://doi.org/10.1007/978-3-030-00308-1_6

2   Research and Development in RRS

2.1   Overview of RRS

The RRS is a research platform that simulates disaster situations and disaster-relief activities on a computer. It can handle disaster-relief activities over roughly five hours from the occurrence of a disaster.

Figure 1 shows the activities of agents in the RRS. In the disaster-relief activities, we control six types of agents, namely AmbulanceTeam, FireBrigade, Police-Force, and the headquarters of each of these units. In addition, there are agents to simulate disaster situations, namely Civilian agent.

- **AmbulanceTeam and AmbulanceCentre**
  These agents rescue other agents that cannot move by themselves.
- **FireBrigade and FireStation**
  These agents extinguish fires in buildings.
- **PoliceForce and PoliceOffice**
  These agents clear road blockages.
- **Civilian**
  In the competition, this agent moves automatically to evacuation centers.

By using the RRS, it is possible to research applications of artificial intelligence and information science to natural-disaster rescue problems. Researchers have been investigating algorithms for route searching, information sharing, and task allocation in a disaster situation. In the RRS project, five tasks are advocated especially, namely Group Formation, Path Planning, Search, Multi-Task Allocation, and Communication. Every year, competitions using agent programs are held for the purpose of technical exchange.

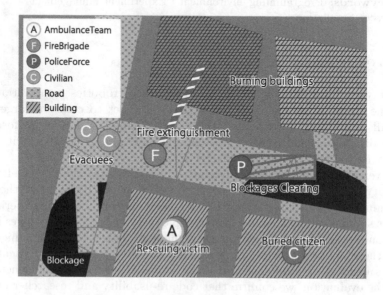

Fig. 1. Overview of RRS

2.2   Agent Development in RRS

The disaster-relief problem handled by the RRS is a complex problem as the damage situations, such as fire, building collapse, and the availability of wireless communication, change from moment to moment in afflicted areas. These changes are addressed by the disaster-relief strategies of teams of disaster-relief robotss that differ according to the disaster situation. To construct a disaster-relief strategy, it is necessary to prepare all the algorithms for tasks such as route searching, information sharing, and resource allocation in the disaster environment. Moreover, in activities such as the PoliceForce clearing blockages, it is necessary to use angles and coordinates to specify the direction for activity and the positions of the agents.

To promote research involving the RRS, it is necessary to clarify the structure of a complicated disaster-relief problem and subdivide it before solving it.

2.3   Experiments in RRS

To develop and evaluate RRS agents, it is necessary to conduct experiments on multiple disaster areas while considering various conditions such as the locations of fires, the rate at which buildings collapse, and communication situations. Also, the parameters of an agent may be set for each of these situations. All this requires numerous simulations.

In the RRS, each simulation takes around 20 min to execute. Thus, multiple computing hosts may be simulated simultaneously to improve the efficiency of the experiment. It is common to distribute the agent process to more computers in one simulation, so it is necessary to control all these computers simultaneously. However, since the time synchronization between the simulator components is based on the command transmission of the kernel, there is no need to externally control it. Therefore, we externally control just the activation and termination of components.

2.4   Related Work

OpenRTM-aist. OpenRTM-aist [2] is a framework for robot development that was developed by the National Institute of Advanced Industrial Science and Technology and whose implementation is based on the RT-Middleware standard [3]. This common platform standard divides robot elements such as actuator control, sensor input, and algorithms necessary for behavior control into single components (This is called RT-Component:RTC), and then constructs a robot by combining all such components. This makes it possible to subdivide the elements that are necessary for controlling the robot. Because each component can be exchanged as a module and existing modules can be included, it is possible to reduce the burden on developers in the development and improvement of robots.

Because RT-Middleware is applied mainly to real robots, it is suitable for developing robots that are controlled in real time. It is difficult to utilize existing code and knowledge when adopting RT-Middleware because RRS agents are programed mainly with a sequential structure.

Hinemos. Hinemos is software that was developed by NTT Data Corporation to monitor and manage the job execution of multiple computing hosts [4]. We can automate the execution of an experiment by treating the experiment as each process, and it is also possible to manage the execution on multiple calculation hosts. Hinemos allows the management of issues such as job exit codes, job stylization, advanced experiment scheduling, and GUI execution management. However, because Hinemos is high-function general-purpose software used for various computer-based business tasks, it has a high operational cost if used for RRS experiments.

OACIS. OACIS is a simulation-execution management framework developed by the discrete-event-simulation research team of the RIKEN Advanced Institute for Computational Science [5]. This software manages jobs in a similar way to Hinemos. In particular, it has a job-management function that specializes in the simulation and management of experiment results, and a function that specializes in the execution of simulations. It is possible to use OACIS to support numerous simulations and to perform analysis with various conditions by managing the experimental parameters and automatically managing the results.

However, because OACIS is a general-purpose system for various types of simulation software, complicated operations are required to execute RRS simulations. The creation of simulation scripts, the agent programs, and the map and scenario files must be managed by other methods, making OACIS complicated to use for the RRS.

3   Proposal and Implementation

3.1   Research Objective

In this paper, which is based on the current state of RRS agent development and experiments, we implement an agent development framework by introducing a modular structure to clarify and solve the complicated problems associated with disaster relief. We also propose the framework as our community standard, which makes it easy to reuse program code. Furthermore, to reduce the experimental burden, we implement an RRS experimental environment that is based on the OACIS simulation-execution management framework. We then combine the agent framework and the RRS experimental environment. Finally, we propose an environment that offers comprehensive support for agent development and experiments.

3.2   Proposal of Environment to Support Development

Design of Agent-Development Framework. In order for many researchers to clarify and solve complicated problems, we modularize part of the program code. To make it easier to reuse the program code and to reduce the burden on researchers, an agent-development framework is desired. A framework-design method based on OpenRTM-aist (mentioned in Sect. 2.4) would also be conceivable. However, RRS agents are programmed in a sequential structure, so we propose and design a unique Agent Development Framework (ADF) that makes it easier to utilize existing program code and knowledge.

Introduction of a Common Agent Architecture. By defining the overall behavior of an agent as a common architecture, we reduce the differences in combinations of components by each developer and ensure re-usability. This allows developers to implement modules based on this common architecture when developing agent programs.

Figure 2 shows the architecture before and after introducing this common architecture. The left-hand portion of the figure shows the existing agent structure, whereas the right-hand portion introduces the common architecture. The portability of the existing program is low because each researcher builds an agent program independently according to individual research agendas. We have commonized the agent-program structure, which is the shaded part of the figure, so that the program code can be re-used easily. Also, this unifies the communication protocol between agents and enables communication with agents developed by others.

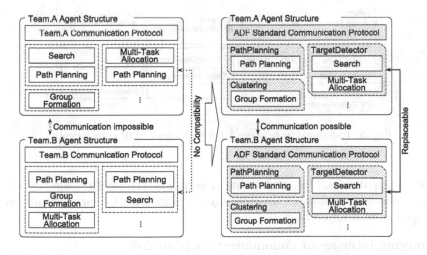

Fig. 2. Before and after introducing common architecture

Modularization of Program Code. As with the RT-Middleware discussed in Sect. 2.4, component modularization is introduced to reduce the burden on researchers and to make it possible to reuse the program code used in agent development.

- **Algorithm modularization**

  At the present stage of modularization, we divide as much as possible based on the five tasks presented in the RRS project. Figure 3 shows the relationship between RRS tasks and ADF components. The top portion of the figure contains five tasks, and the bottom portion contains the framework components. We classify algorithms for solving complex problems and algorithms for solving simple problems as Complex Modules and Algorithm Modules, respectively, thereby clarifying the directionality of each module. We view algorithms to solve complex problems (Complex Modules) as aggregates of simple problems. Thus, the modules should be programmed by dividing the structure inside the program code as much as possible. Moreover, if it is found empirically that the program can be divided in the future, we aim to clarify complicated problems as new modules.

- **Modularization of control program**

  As described in Sect. 2.2, it is necessary to control an agent by specifying such properties as its coordinates and angles. Low-level agent control is modularized as a control program. By separating macro algorithms such as decision making and micro algorithms such as control using the coordinates and angles, we reduce the burden on researchers who wish to study a single algorithm such as the decision-making one.

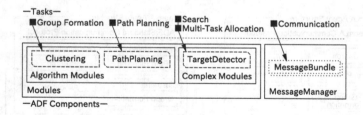

Fig. 3. Relationship between RRS tasks and ADF components

Other Approaches. By introducing a common architecture for agents, it becomes possible to manage the inter-agent communication protocol and various agent parameters collectively.

- **Unifying inter-agent communication protocols**

  In the RRS, the inter-agent communication protocols are currently not unified, which strengthens the dependency between components makes it difficult to modularize the algorithm. Therefore, with reference to the RRS inter-agent communication protocols proposed by Ota et al. [6] and Obashi et al. [7], we define a common inter-agent communication protocol. We define messages communicated under this protocol as members of either an information-sharing family or a command family. In the information-sharing family, information about agents, roads, and buildings is shared. In the command family, commands for relief, fire extinguishing, blockage clearing, and searching are ordered.

– **Collective management of parameters**
In the framework, we commonize the parameter-input interface by collectively managing the designation of modules and parameters in the algorithm that are to be changed at the time of the experiment. This makes it easy to input parameters from tools that support the experiments, such as OACIS described in Sect. 2.4.

3.3 Implementation of Agent-Development Framework

Implementation Overview. Figure 4 shows the structure of the agent-development framework that is implemented. The internal aspects of the agent, as represented by the shaded part in the figure, are implementations of the framework. The parts indicated by dotted lines are modules, which are the objects to be programmed at the time of agent development. In this section, we describe each implementation of the framework based on the design discussed in Sect. 3.2.

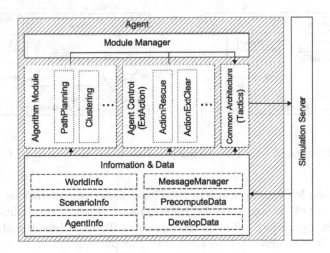

Fig. 4. Structure of framework

Common Agent Architecture. This component defines how agents invoke algorithm modules and control-program modules to determine behavior. This component is referred to as Tactics. Each agent determines its behavior by invoking elements such as task assignment, a route-search algorithm, and a control-program module within Tactics. In addition, each module is invoked by its alias name and can select the module to be attached by the agent-configuration file.

Modules. In Sect. 3.2 shows that each task is modularized as Clustering, Path-Planning, or TargetDetector. Also, the control program is modularized as ExtAction. An instance of the module is created and managed in a component called the ModuleManager. This further enables switching the module to be used by loading the module-configuration file (module.cfg) at agent startup.

Collective Management of Parameters. The settings of the module to be loaded are obtained from the aforementioned file module.cfg. In addition, parameters in algorithms can be obtained from the DevelopData component, and each value can be input by JSON [8] formatted text as an argument at agent startup.

3.4   Proposal of Environment to Support Experiments

To realize the RRS experimental-support environment, we introduce experiment management using the OACIS simulation-execution management framework.

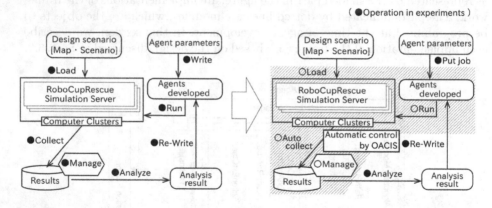

Fig. 5. Before and after introducing experimental management by OACIS

In Fig. 5, the left-hand portion of the figure shows the operations before the introduction of OACIS experimental management, whereas the right-hand portion shows the operations after its introduction. To experiment with an agent in the RRS, it was necessary to designate the parameters of various agents, control computer clusters to execute simulation, and collect and manage numerous results as indicated by the black points. By introducing experimental management by OACIS, the work shown in the shaded area in the figure is automated and the operation performed in experiments can be reduced. Moreover, by automating the experimental operation, it becomes easier to reproduce the experiment.

However, because OACIS is a general-purpose system, there are insufficient functions that can be applied to RRS experiments. Therefore, we develop functions to be supplemented when applying OACIS to RRS experiments as an extension to the RRS. This section describes these supplemental functions. This solves the complicated problem that OACIS to use for RRS described in Sect. 2.4.

- **Agent management**
  Although OACIS can manage simulators and experimental parameters, it cannot manage the agent program itself. Therefore, we develop an extension to manage the agent program.
- **Map and Scenario management**
  OACIS cannot manage maps and disaster scenarios as can agent programs. Therefore, we develop an extension to manage maps and disaster scenarios.
- **Computer cluster management**
  In the RRS, one simulation is executed in a computer cluster, combining many computers. Although OAICS supports job execution in computer clusters, it does not conform to the protocol of launching processes required by the RRS program. We developed a mechanism to adjust an interface to launch the RRS program using OACIS.
- **Simulation script**
  It is necessary to prepare a script that describes a series of actions in a simulation, which can be executed from OACIS. This script loads an agent and MapScenario, connects to each computer of the computer cluster, and executes the simulation. This enables it to treat experiments as a single job and enables management by OACIS.
- **Simulator management**
  In OACIS, a simulation script and a set of parameters that can be specified are known collectively as a Simulator. Parameters change depending on the purpose of the experiment, such as the agents to be used, the modules to be used, and the parameters of the algorithms. Therefore, we develop a mechanism to register Simulator with OACIS according to various experimental methods.

3.5   Extensions of OACIS for RRS

In implementing the extension to sustain maintainability, we did not modify the OACIS body program, which is controlled by the extension part through an API provided by OACIS. Figure 6 shows a conceptual image of the OACIS extensions. The shaded areas in the figure are extensions to the RRS.

- **Agent management**
  This extension unit enable to upload the agent program body in the directory under management. Then, we register and manage the agent's name and storage location, parameters, comments, and registration date and time in the database of the extension unit. This enables to manage the agent files in an integrated way.

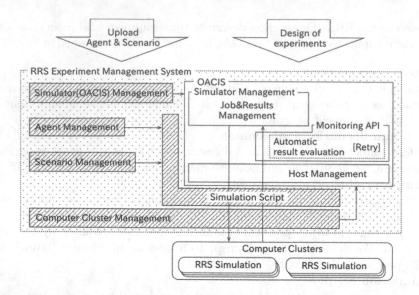

Fig. 6. Extensions of OACIS for RRS

- **Map and Scenario management**
  This extension unit enable to upload the map and scenarios in the directory
  under management, similarly as with the agents. Then, we register and manage the name and storage location, comments, and registration date and time
  in the database of the extension unit.
- **Computer cluster management**
  Information about the computer cluster is managed in the database of
  the extension unit. When executing the simulation, the simulation script is
  invoked on the local host and simulation is executed using each computer.
  The simulation script connects to each designated computer according to the
  configuration file of the computer cluster that is arranged in each working
  directory. Therefore, switching of computer clusters in the simulation script
  is enabled by changing the working directory of the OACIS computing host.
  This enables execution of the simulation using the computer cluster.
- **Simulation script**
  The agent program and the map and scenario used for the simulation are
  transferred to each computer using SSH. Then, after executing the agent's
  compilation script, the simulation is started. This script also controls the
  activation timing of simulators that are necessary for starting the simulation.
  If the script ends normally, exit code 0 is outputted. Otherwise, if abnormal
  termination occurs, an exit code other than 0 is output so that OACIS can
  judge whether the termination was normal. This enables RRS execution using
  OACIS.

- **Simulator management**
  Various kinds of parameters according to identifiers of agents, parameters of the agents, map, disaster scenarios and so on can be registered as Simulator in OACIS. A unique pattern of parameters according to OACIS Simulator can be registered as ParameterSet in OACIS. OACIS ParameterSet includes the following values which the simulation script and each agent can read.
  - Agent program code
  - Agent program code + Various modules
  - Parameters of algorithms

4 Evaluation

4.1 Purpose of Evaluation

With regard to the developmental and experimental support environment proposed in Sect. 3, we developed and tested the agent program at an actual workshop to evaluate whether the re-usability of the code and the burden of the experiment were improved.

4.2 Experimental Method

At the workshop of the RoboCup Simulation League held at Fukuoka University on October 22–23, 2016, roughly 30 people were divided into six teams to develop agents using ADF. We conducted an experiment to collaborate and work in combination with AmbulanceTeam, FireBrigade, and PoliceForce agents that were developed by each team. In doing so, we confirmed that it was possible to combine agents developed by different developers in this experiment. At the workshop, we experimented with only six combinations because of time restrictions. However, at a later date, we also experimented with a total of 216 combinations.

4.3 Results and Discussion

Table 1 gives the top eight results of the combined experiments of each team (A–F), those of a sample team, and the results for each team as a reference. From the results of the experiments, it can be seen that we arrived at good results even with different teams. In addition, this experiments was conducted easily because it is just changing modules designation that loading. Therefore, we find that agents developed using the framework proposed in this paper can work in cooperation even if they are combined separately.

Moreover, in experimental execution until now, when simulating experimentally in an environment such as a workshop, one operator has basically operated the simulator directly and has managed aspects such as the simulation results. In this case, because there were many steps to manipulate, there were cases in which the results were accidentally not saved. However, no trouble occurred

Table 1. Top eight results of combined experiments (* are reference values)

Rank	AT	FB	PF	Score
1	A	C	A	143.4091
2	A	B	A	141.4178
3	E	B	A	140.9280
4	A	B	F	136.5078
5	E	B	B	134.8257
6	B	B	D	134.3782
7	C	B	D	134.3404
8	B	B	E	133.8126
(*)	Sample	Sample	Sample	114.2580
	A	A	A	114.2574
	B	B	B	126.5861
	C	C	C	124.3933
	D	D	D	114.2580
	E	E	E	119.9167
	F	F	F	120.8222

despite many operators being involved in the operation because the operational content was simple and automated. This indicates that the burden on researchers at the time of the experiments can be reduced.

Furthermore, we are planning to hold workshops at universities in Italy, Spain, and France and we will introduce these results and claims to our proposal.

5   Conclusion

In this paper, we proposed an environment as RRS community standard that integrates an agent-development framework and an experiment-management system to support researchers. In the evaluation, we confirmed that code re-usability was improved and that the burden on researchers during the experiment was reduced. We are planning to hold workshops in each country to further confirm the effectiveness of our proposal. As mentioned in Sect. 3.2, the algorithms for solving complex problems (known as the Complex Modules) are aggregated from simpler problems. Thus, in the future, if it is found empirically that the program in question can be divided, we aim to clarify complicated problems as new modules. This will lead to the better resolution of disaster-relief problems. Eventually, we aim to return the research results of the RRS project to society by clarifying disaster-relief problems and proposing individual algorithms that are applicable to disaster relief.

Acknowledgment. This work was supported by JSPS KAKENHI Grant Number JP16K00310 and JP17K00317. Y. M. appreciates the support by JST CREST and by MEXT as "Exploratory Challenges on Post-K computer(Studies of multi-level spatiotemporal simulation of socioeconomic phenomena)".

Appendix: The Framework and Tools

The ADF and experiments support tools on this paper are available on the website (https://maslab.aitech.ac.jp/rrs/rcs17/).

References

1. RoboCupRescue Simulation. http://roborescue.sourceforge.net/
2. National Institute of Advanced Industrial Science and Technology. OpenRTM-aist. http://www.openrtm.org/
3. Ando, N., Suehiro, T., Kitagaki, K., Kotoku, T., Yoon, W.-K.: RT-middleware: distributed component middleware for RT (robot technology). In: IROS 2005 (2005)
4. NTT Data Corporation. Hinemos. https://ja.osdn.net/projects/hinemos/
5. Murase, Y., Uchitane, T., Ito, N.: A tool for parameter-space explorations. Phys. Procedia **57**, 73–76 (2014)
6. Ohta, T., Toriumi, F.: RoboCupRescue2011 rescue simulation league team description. In: RoboCup 2011 Istanbul (2011)
7. Obashi, D., Hayashi, T., Iwata, K., Ito, N.: An implementation of communication library among heterogenous agents NAITO-Rescue 2013 (Japan). In: RoboCup 2013 Eindhoven (2013)
8. ECMA: ECMA-404: JSON Data Interchange Format. European Association for Standardizing Information and Communication Systems (2013)

Competition Design to Evaluate Cognitive Functions in Human-Robot Interaction Based on Immersive VR

Tetsunari Inamura[1,2(✉)] and Yoshiaki Mizuchi[1]

[1] National Insititute of Informatics, 2-1-2 Hitotsubashi,
Chiyoda-ku, Tokyo 101-8430, Japan
inamura@nii.ac.jp
[2] SOKENDAI (The Graduate University for Advanced Studies), 2-1-2 Hitotsubashi,
Chiyoda-ku, Tokyo 101-8430, Japan

Abstract. While RoboCup Soccer and RoboCup Rescue have simulation leagues, RoboCup@Home does not. One reason for the difficulty of creating a RoboCup@Home simulation is that robot users must be present. Almost all existing tasks in RoboCup@Home depend on communication between humans and robots. For human-robot interaction in a simulator, a user model or avatar should be designed and implemented. Furthermore, behavior of real humans often lead to unfair conditions between participant teams. Since the one-shot trial is the standard evaluation style in the current RoboCup, human behavior is quite difficult to evaluate from a statistical point of view. We propose a novel software platform for statistically evaluating human-robot interaction in competitions. With the help of cloud computing and an immersive VR system, cognitive and social human-robot interaction can be carried out and measured as objective data in a VR environment. In this paper, we explain the novel platform and propose two kinds of competition design with the aim of evaluating social and cognitive human-robot interaction from a statistical point of view.

Keywords: RoboCup@Home · Immersive virtual reality
Human-robot interaction · Evaluation of social and cognitive behavior

1 Introduction

We have been developing an immersive virtual reality (VR) system for a RoboCup @Home simulation [1]. While RoboCup Soccer and RoboCup Rescue have simulation leagues, RoboCup@Home does not. One reason for the difficulty of realizing a RoboCup@Home simulation is that robot users must be present. Almost all existing tasks in RoboCup@Home[1] depend on communication between a robot and humans. For human-robot interaction in a simulator, a

---

[1] http://www.robocupathome.org/rules.

© Springer Nature Switzerland AG 2018
H. Akiyama et al. (Eds.): RoboCup 2017, LNAI 11175, pp. 84–94, 2018.
https://doi.org/10.1007/978-3-030-00308-1_7

user model or avatar should be designed and implemented. Although this problem could be solved by using our immersive VR system, another difficulty with evaluating the quality of human-robot interaction still remains.

Not only RoboCup@Home but also RoboCup Soccer, Robocop Rescue, and other leagues tend to evaluate physical actions such as grasping, navigation, object tracking, and object/speech recognition because it is easy to evaluate them with objective sensor signals or ground truth data. However, evaluating the quality of human-robot interaction, such as the impressions of an individual user and whether a robot utterance is easy to understand, involve dealing with cognitive events, which are difficult to observe as objective sensor signals. One of the ultimate aims of RoboCup@Home is to realize intelligent personal robots that operate in daily life. While evaluating such social and cognitive functions is important, tasks for real competitions with time and space limitations cannot be designed for such evaluation. For example, using questionnaires is one conventional method for evaluating the social and cognitive functions of robots; however, this is difficult in real competitions because the number of samples that can be obtained is quite small.

Therefore, we propose a novel platform for competition design that can be used to evaluate the social and cognitive functions of intelligent robots through VR simulation. In Sect. 2, we propose a novel software platform that integrates ROS and Unity middleware to realize a seamless development environment for VR interaction between humans and robots. After that, we propose two tasks as examples of task design for evaluating social and cognitive functions. In Sect. 3, we propose the Interactive CleanUp task, which is aimed for statistically evaluating human-robot interaction. In Sect. 4, the Human Navigation task is proposed to observe and evaluate human behavior in terms of the quality of robot utterances. In Sect. 5, we discuss the feasibility of social and cognitive evaluation based on our proposed software platform.

2 Integrating Cloud-Based Immersive VR and ROS

Software for a RoboCup@Home simulation should enable both a conventional robot simulation and a real-time and immersive VR system for human-robot interaction to be integrated. Table 1 shows software systems and their pros and cons. Since conventional robot simulators focus mainly on simulating the physical world and modeling environments, the presence of human users is not discussed and implemented. There is currently no platform that enables the conventional robot simulation based on ROS middleware to be integrated with immersive VR applications for real-time human-robot interaction.

Our previous software platform, SIGVerse (ver.2)[2], was adopted for the first RoboCup@Home simulation trial in JapanOpen 2013 [1]. It enables users to log in to a VR avatar that makes it possible to communicate with virtual robots; however, it was constrained in that a variety of VR devices could not be used due to there being exclusive APIs. The API design was also too limited to fully support ROS middleware.

Table 1. Systems for robot simulation and VR interfaces; functions and limitations.

Platform	Graphic fidelity	Physics performance	Scalability of environment	Robotic middleware	Human immersion	Multi-client simulation	Licensing
Gazebo [5]	Very good	Very good	Good	ROS	Unsupported	Unsupported	Open source
USARSim [6]	Very good	Excellent	Very good	ROS	Unsupported	Supported	Commercial
V-REP [9]	Very good	Very good	Good	ROS	Unsupported	Supported	Open source
Choreonoid [7]	Very good	Very good	Not good	OpenRTM	Unsupported	Unsupported	Open source
Open-HRP [8]	Very good	Very good	Not good	OpenRTM	Unsupported	Unsupported	Open source
Webots [10]	Excellent	Very good	Very good	ROS, NaoQI	Unsupported	Supported	Commercial
SIGVerse (Ver. 2) [2]	Very good	Good	Good	None	Supported	Supported	Open source
SIGVerse (Ver. 3)	Excellent	Excellent	Excellent	ROS	Supported	Supported	Open source

Thus, we developed a new version of the SIGVerse platform that integrates Unity and ROS middleware to support a variety of VR devices and software resources created by the ROS community. Figure 1 shows the architecture of SIGVerse (ver. 3) in detail. SIGVerse is a server/client system. An identical VR environment (scene), composed of 3D object models, such as user avatars, robots, and furniture, is shared among servers and clients. Events in the server and clients are synchronized with Unity's built-in networking technology.

Participants can log in to an avatar via a VR interface such as a head-mounted display (HMD), motion capture devices, and audio headsets. In accordance with the input from VR devices, the behavior of the participant is reflected in the avatar through scripts attached to objects. Perceptual information such as perspective visual feedback is provided to the participant. Thus, participants can interact with a virtual environment in a manner similar to a real environment.

The system has a bridging mechanism between the ROS and Unity middleware that is based on JSON, which is provided by a WebSocket, and BSON, which is provided by an exclusive TCP/IP connection. Several works have proposed connecting Unity and ROS middleware [3,4]; however, huge data such as image data is difficult to send from Unity to ROS middleware in real-time. We measured the frequency of sending successive pairs of 900-[KB] RGB images and 600-[KB] depth image frames from a desktop computer, which had an Intel Xeon E5-2687W CPU, to a virtual machine on the same computer. Although the average frequency with JSON-based bridging was only 0.55 [fps], the frequency with BSON-based bridging was 57.60 [fps]. According to the specifications of standard 1-[Gbps] network interface cards, our platform has the potential to send four raw RGB images with a resolution of 640 × 480 captured by seven cameras within 30 [ms]. Software for controlling virtual robots can be used in real robots as well without any modification and vice versa.

Information for reproducing multimodal interaction experiences is stored on a cloud server as a large-scale dataset of embodied and social information.

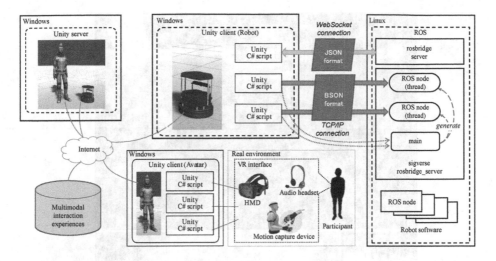

Fig. 1. Software architecture of SIGVerse

By sharing such information, users can reproduce and analyze multimodal interactions after an experiment.

From the next section, we propose two tasks as examples of statistically evaluating social and cognitive functions on the basis of the VR software platform.

3   Task I: Interactive Cleanup

3.1   Task

Human behavior is one of the most important factors in the RoboCup@Home tasks. In the FollowMe task, the walking behavior of a real human is the target of recognition. In the Restaurant task, the instructions given by a human (referee) are observed by robots. A common limitation with using real human behavior is that behavior cannot be repeated several times to achieve a uniform condition for all task sessions. Thus, unfair conditions between each participant team are sometimes indicated to be a problem.

We propose a new task named Interactive Cleanup to solve the above problem in a VR environment. This task evaluates the ability of a robot to understand pointing gestures made by humans. The robot has to select a target object, which is pointed at by a human, grasp the object, and put it into a trash can. The target trash can is also pointed at with a pointing gesture. Therefore, the robot always has to observe the human's gesture to understand the target object and target trash can. Figure 2 shows a picture of the VR task environment.

The procedure of the task is as follows.

- A human avatar points to one of the objects on a table. The human uses both right and left arms.

Fig. 2. VR environment for Interactive CleanUp

- After pointing to a target object, the human points to one of the trash cans.
- The robot should take the target object, move to the target trash can, and put the object into it.
- The procedure returns to step 1, and the task is repeated 36 times. A variety of pointing gestures made by the human avatar should be recorded beforehand. Different gestures should be reproduced in each session.

3.2   Evaluation Result

This task was carried out at RoboCup JapanOpen 2016. Three teams took part in this task. The score distribution of the teams is shown in Fig. 2 and Table 2.

The vertical axes in Fig. 3 indicate the score for each session; the horizontal axes correspond to the session index. The robot could get a point when it grasped

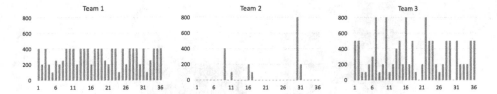

Fig. 3. Score distribution for Interactive CleanUp task

Table 2. Score stats for interactive CleanUp task

Team	Average	Standard error
Team 1	314	108
Team 2	50	152
Team 3	339	234

the correct target or completely put a target object into the correct trash can. If it failed to recognize/grasp the object, navigate to a destination, or throw away the object, a negative point was given as penalty to the total score.

As shown in Fig. 3 and Table 2, there was a wide distribution in the points acquired by the robot. If the evaluation had been a one-shot trial, team 2 might have won the competition. Our platform enabled the robot to take part in multiple sessions in a variety of conditions such with different types of objects, environmental lightning conditions, and furniture layouts. Human gestures and behavior in particular should be given to the robots as uniform and fair data. This result shows the advantage and feasibility of our platform from the viewpoint of a statistical evaluation of real human-robot interaction in the RoboCup competition.

4   Task II: Human Navigation

4.1   Task

This test was done to evaluate the ability of a robot to generate natural and friendly language expressions to explain how to get to a destination and where a target object is. The robot has to generate natural language expression in accordance with the location and gaze direction of the human avatar and layout of the environment. In this test, communication is done only through text messages and voice utterances. The robot cannot use any gestures or visual information.

A virtual environment for this task is shown in Fig. 4. The environment consists of four rooms, a kitchen, a bed room, a living room, and a lobby. The robot itself does not exist in the environment because communication is carried out using only text messages and voice utterances.

The procedure of the task is as follows.

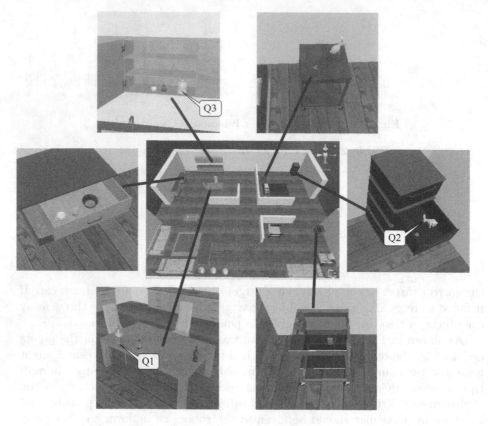

Fig. 4. Environment used in the Human Navigation task.

- The robot system receives the target object information (object ID, location)
- The robot can observe the status (position, posture, gaze direction, etc.) of a human avatar by using an exclusive API in the virtual environment.
- The robot generates appropriate sentences to explain where the target object is. The sentences can be displayed in the HMD or synthesized as voice sound.
- The participant reads or listens to the explanation and controls the human avatar. The robot cannot physically guide the participant such as by pointing.
- The time required to find the target object is measured. The time limitation for each session is 5 min. If a participant finds the target or gives up, the robot system proceeds to the next session.
- The session is repeated for several times per participant.

We asked 10 participants to take part in this task by using the immersive virtual reality system. The participants wore an HMD (Oculus Rift CV1) to log in to the human avatar. They controlled the avatar by using a handheld device (Oculus Touch). Three directions given by the robot, Q1, Q2, and Q3, are shown in Fig. 4. In this primitive investigation, we used the pre-defined utterances shown in Table 3.

Table 3. Instructions used in Human Navigation task

Q1	Please take a green PET bottle on the desk at the kitchen
Q2	There is a brown chest in the bedroom. Please take a toy bunny from the second drawer from the top
Q3	There is a cabinet above the kitchen sink. Please take a white sugar pot from the second cabinet from the right

4.2 Evaluation Result

Table 4 shows the result of the experiments for the 10 participants. Figure 5 shows a timeline of a certain session. As shown in the table, almost all of the sessions were completed within one minute. Even though the VR environment was hidden from the participants before the sessions, no one hesitated to go to the right location and successfully grasp the correct target object.

This means that we can manage a competition in which a general audience can take part. Such a competition would provide a fair and open evaluation against the problem for current RoboCup@Home tasks, which depend on just one-shot and non-uniform data. Additionally, another advantage is that the reactions and behavior of avatars can be easily recorded in the system. Quantitative evaluation after a real session can be performed. Objective observation of human behavior should be key in designing the social and cognitive tasks.

Table 4. Time required to complete task. (unit: [sec]) hint indicates time when subject used replay function.

	Q1	Hint	Q2	Hint	Q3	Hint
A	49		41		42	
B	17		44		32	
C	33		34		30	
D	19		35		34	
E	17	9	26	13	20	
F	27		48		34	
G	37		69		36	
H	35		41		37	
I	19		32		28	
J	40		48		36	
Ave	29.3		41.8		32.9	
Max	49		69		42	
Min	17		26		20	
Std	10.6		11.3		5.7	

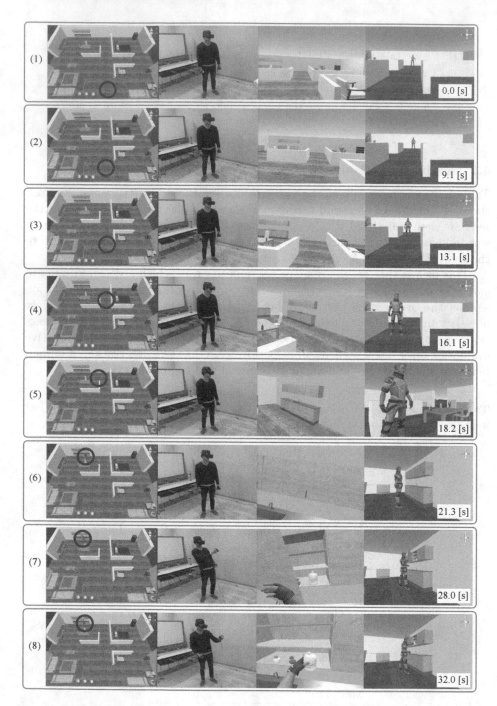

Fig. 5. Timeline of session of Human Navigation task. Four columns in each picture are, from left, whole environment and position of avatar, participant operating avatar, first-person view from avatar, avatar's behavior.

5   Discussion and Conclusion

We proposed a novel software platform and task design to evaluate high-level cognitive functions in human-robot interaction. The conventional RoboCup@Home tasks tend to focus on physical functions in the real world; however, user behavior and reactions are also an important target of evaluation. Such evaluation is available with the help of the proposed platform.

We carried out two tasks with the proposed platform. The results show that VR simulation can be used to evaluate the quality of human-robot interaction that includes social, physical, and cognitive interaction. Statistical evaluation is difficult in conventional physical human-robot interaction due to limitations in workable time, hardware durability, and provision of fair interaction data. The proposed platform can solved these problems by recording human-robot interaction and crowd-sourcing through immersive VR devices.

Interactive CleanUp and Human Navigation were done at RoboCup JapanOpen 2016 and 2017, respectively. Not only new tasks for cognitive HRI but also conventional tasks such as EGPSR using the proposed platform have been carried out at JapanOpen. This means that a variety of tasks required for RoboCup@Home are feasible on the proposed platform.

In the near future, we believe that the proposed software platform and task design should be carried out for the RoboCup@Home simulation league as well as other simulation leagues.

This system is open source software. Everyone can download the source code from GitHub repository[2] and get documentation from the SIGVerse wiki[3].

References

1. Inamura, T., Tan, J.T.C., Sugiura, K., Nagai, T., Okada, H.: Development of RoboCup@Home simulation towards long-term large scale HRI. In: Behnke, S., Veloso, M., Visser, A., Xiong, R. (eds.) RoboCup 2013. LNCS (LNAI), vol. 8371, pp. 672–680. Springer, Heidelberg (2014). https://doi.org/10.1007/978-3-662-44468-9_64
2. Inamura, T., et al.: Simulator platform that enables social interaction simulation - SIGVerse: SocioIntelliGenesis simulator. In: IEEE/SICE International Symposium on System Integration, pp. 212–217 (2010)
3. Codd-Downey, R., Forooshani, P.M., Speers, A., Wang, H., Jenkin, M.: From ROS to unity: leveraging robot and virtual environment middleware for immersive teleoperation. In: IEEE International Conference on Information and Automation, pp. 932–936 (2014)
4. Hu, Y., Meng, W.: ROSUnitySim: development of a low-cost experimental quadcopter testbed using an arduino controller and software. J. Simul. 92(10), 931–944 (2016)
5. Koenig, N., and Howard, A.: Design and use paradigms for Gazebo, an open-source multi-robot simulator. In: Proceedings of IEEE/RSJ International Conference on Intelligent Robots and Systems, pp. 2149–2154 (2004)

---

[2] https://github.com/SIGVerse.
[3] http://www.sigverse.org/wiki/en/.

6. Lewis, M., Wang, J., Hughes, S.: USARSim: simulation for the study of human-robot interaction. J. Cogn. Eng. Decis. Mak. **1**(1), 98–120 (2007)
7. Nakaoka, S.: Choreonoid: extensible virtual robot environment built on an integrated GUI framework. In: Proceedings of IEEE/SICE International Symposium on System Integration, pp. 79–85 (2012)
8. Kanehiro, F., Hirukawa, H., Kajita, S.: OpenHRP: open architecture humanoid robotics platform. Int. J. Robot. Res. **23**(2), 155–165 (2004)
9. Rohmer, E., Singh, S.P.N., and Freese, M.: V-REP: a versatile and scalable robot simulation framework. In: IEEE/RSJ International Conference on Intelligent Robots and Systems, pp. 1321–1326 (2013)
10. Michel, O.: Webots TM : professional mobile robot simulation. Int. J. Adv. Robot. Syst. **1**(1), 39–42 (2004)

Toward Real-Time Decentralized Reinforcement Learning Using Finite Support Basis Functions

Kenzo Lobos-Tsunekawa[✉], David L. Leottau,
and Javier Ruiz-del-Solar

Department of Electrical Engineering, Advanced Mining Technology Center,
Universidad de Chile, Santiago, Chile
{kenzo.lobos,dleottau,jruizd}@ing.uchile.cl

Abstract. This paper addresses the design and implementation of complex Reinforcement Learning (RL) behaviors where multi-dimensional action spaces are involved, as well as the need to execute the behaviors in real-time using robotic platforms with limited computational resources and training times. For this purpose, we propose the use of decentralized RL, in combination with finite support basis functions as alternatives to Gaussian RBF, in order to alleviate the effects of the curse of dimensionality on the action and state spaces respectively, and to reduce the computation time. As testbed, a RL based controller for the in-walk kick in NAO robots, a challenging and critical problem for soccer robotics, is used. The reported experiments show empirically that our solution saves up to 99.94% of execution time and 98.82% of memory consumption during execution, without diminishing performance compared to classical approaches.

Keywords: Reinforcement Learning · Decentralized control
Multi-agent systems · Robot soccer · RoboCup · Standard Platform League

1 Introduction

Reinforcement Learning (RL) has been applied in robotics for learning complex behaviors. However, even though successful implementation of RL in robotics have increased largely in the last few years [18], there are still many factors that limit the massive use of RL in general robotic problems, such as the high dimensionality of the state and action spaces, and the need of numerous real-world experiments.

The first factor is related to the inherent complexity of behaviors required by robots operating in the real world. Thus, when fine-grained RL controllers are required to achieve high performance, classic RL models scale exponentially their complexity, according to the dimensionality of the state and action spaces. This is undesirable since it causes two main effects: an unfeasible number of training episodes to achieve asymptotic convergence, and an impracticable computational cost for real-time execution, since the controller actions usually need to be executed in short time cycles to achieve high performance. In light of these issues, the RL approach becomes limited to those problems in which high computation resources are available, long experiment

© Springer Nature Switzerland AG 2018
H. Akiyama et al. (Eds.): RoboCup 2017, LNAI 11175, pp. 95–107, 2018.
https://doi.org/10.1007/978-3-030-00308-1_8

and training times are possible, and/or the design or modeling can be simplified without sacrificing performance.

In this work, we propose to deal with these issues, without oversimplifying the problem itself, by: (i) using Decentralized Reinforcement Learning (D-RL), which empirically accelerates convergence [4] and reduces considerably the effects of the curse of dimensionality on the action space; and (ii) applying Finite Support Basis Functions (FSBF) in the state representation of RL, which provides a representation similar as the one resulting from the use of Gaussian RBF (Radial Basis Functions), but with much reduced computation time.

To validate our approach, we consider the specific case of the in-walk kicks [12] in robotic soccer, where the robot must learn to push the ball toward a desired target, only by using the inertia of its own gait. This problem becomes an ideal testbed, since it is a challenging and relevant problem in robotic soccer, and both the state and action spaces must be sufficiently fine-grained to capture the complexity of the problem and achieve competitive performances. Moreover, the solution must run on real time, on an embedded device such as the NAO robot's CPU [19].

The proposed model for the in-walk kick problem is similar to the one presented in [6, 9], since this task can be considered as a particular case of the ball-pushing behavior. However, those works differ from ours, since for this case, all three axes of the gait velocity vector are learned autonomous and simultaneously through RL, and no human intervention is required during the learning process. In addition, we introduce a novel approach to adapt and synchronize the RL time step to the time step of the robot's gait.

The remainder of this paper is organized as follows: D-RL is reviewed shortly in Sect. 2. Section 3 presents a brief overview about FSBF for the proposed state representation. Then, the in-walk kick behavior and the proposed modeling are described in Sect. 4. Finally, Sect. 5 presents an experimental validation of the proposed methodology, and in Sect. 6 conclusions of this work are given.

2 Decentralized Reinforcement Learning

Two main limitations were previously remarked about the use of RL in complex behaviors performed with physical robots: the high number of training episodes to achieve asymptotic convergence, and the expensive computational cost for real-time execution. Under the presence of multi-dimensional action spaces, the standard RL solutions can be called Centralized RL (C-RL) systems, if each of those action subspaces are discretized (in a finite set of actions), combined, and computed as a single set of actions.

In C-RL, the number of possible actions grows exponentially with the action space dimensionality. This makes it hard exploring sufficiently the whole action-state space, producing a very slow convergence, and increasing exponentially the execution time. D-RL helps to alleviate both issues, by splitting the learning problem into multiple independent agents, each acting in a different action space dimension [4]. This allows the design of independent state models, reward functions, and learning agents for each action dimension. The benefits of the D-RL over C-RL in terms of computation time can be quantified as [2]:

$$DRL_{speedup} = \frac{\prod_{m=1}^{M} A^m}{\sum_{m=1}^{M} A^m} \tag{1}$$

where M is the number of agents (action space dimensionality), and A^m the number of possible discrete actions in the action dimension m.

In [2], a robotic application of D-RL is presented, where the individual action components are learned in parallel by independent learning agents. Moreover, [4] shows empirically that D-RL is not only capable of attain coordination among agents without any explicit mechanism of coordination, but that D-RL outperforms C-RL in two different problems: a modified version of the popular MountainCar3D testbed, and a physic robot tasked with a ball-pushing problem.

3 Finite Support Basis Functions

One important design component of a RL agent is how it deals with the state space. While for discrete state space problems the classic tabular representation is natural, other representations are preferred for continuous, or discrete but large, state spaces.

For real-time applications, linear parametric approximations are usually used, being among the most used tile coding [16] and Gaussian RBF [14]. Although Gaussian RBF have many desired mathematic properties, their use is usually restricted due to its high computation time, and therefore the fast tile coding is used, even when Gaussian RBF can achieve a better performance [15].

To deal with this issue we propose the use of FSBF, as replacements of Gaussian RBF to provide a similar state space representation, with a much-reduced computation time, due to the sparsity introduced by these FSBF in the feature vector. Although the approximation of Gaussian RBF has been addressed in [7, 17], mainly in the field of control systems, the computational benefits of this approximation have not been presented, and no previous applications of this kind of approximation have been presented in the context of RL, where the speedup produced by its use can be very large, due to the need to compute the Q-Values for every possible action.

Consider the case of a Gaussian RBF representation, in which Gaussians are placed in a uniform fashion over the state space S, with dimensionality $|S| = N$. In each dimension i, n_i 1D Gaussians are used, creating a total amount of $M = \prod_{i=1}^{N} n_i$ multivariate Gaussians. Then, the Q-Values needed for value iteration algorithms are computed as:

$$Q(s, a) = \frac{\sum_{j=1}^{M} \phi_i(s)\theta_j^a}{\sum_{j=1}^{M} \phi_i(s)} \tag{2}$$

where θ^a are the weights for action a, and ϕ is the M-dimensional feature vector.

The main issue with linear Gaussian RBF approximators, is that M grows exponentially with N, and since Gaussians are non-zero over the entire space, all the elements in the sum must be calculated explicitly, even if only a few of them actually contribute to the sum. However, if multivariate Gaussians are chosen with the same diagonal covariance matrix, Eq. (2) can be rewritten as:

$$Q(s,a) = \frac{\sum_{k \in A} \left(\prod_{n=1}^{N} \phi_{k_i}^i(s_i) \right) \theta_k^a}{\sum_{k \in A} \left(\prod_{n=1}^{N} \phi_{k_i}^i(s_i) \right)} \tag{3}$$

where $\phi_{k_i}^i$ are 1D Gaussians, and $A = \{(k_1, \ldots, k_N) | k_i = 1, \ldots, n_i \ i = 1, \ldots, N\}$.

From Eq. (3), it can be noted that the number of different 1D Gaussians $\sum_{i=1}^{N} n_i$ is much lower that the number the $\prod_{i=1}^{N} n_i$ multivariate Gaussians, and that the same 1D basis function appears many times in the sum.

It follows that if the unidimensional basis is chosen with finite support region, then the number of non-zero terms in the sum becomes strongly reduced, thus saving much computation time. Some examples of FSBF are 3-σ Gaussians approximations, and kernels like Epanechnikov, cosine and even triangular functions, as shown in Fig. 1.

Using this methodology, the computation cost depends only on the width chosen for the unidimensional basis functions, and their density in the state space, instead of the number of basis functions. This allows to place more basis functions over the state space without extra computation time, if their density and support region width are kept. Finally, the computation speedup from using this strategy can be expressed as:

$$state_{speedup} = \frac{\prod_{i=1}^{N} n_i}{\prod_{i=1}^{N} width_i} \tag{4}$$

where $width_i$ is the support region width of the basis functions in the dimension i, in terms of the distance among basis functions in the same dimension.

In Sect. 5, the proposed state representation is empirically validated with the in-walk kick problem by comparing it with the standard Gaussian RBF representation.

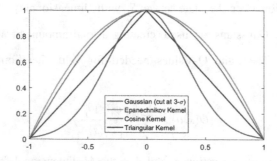

Fig. 1. Normalized finite support functions.

4 Validation Problem: The in-Walk Kick in Biped Robots

In the context of robotic soccer, kick motions can be considered the second most important robot motion after walking, due to their impact in the game performance. Given that, several methods have been developed for the design and implementation of kick motions [1, 10, 12, 13]. These methods can be classified in two groups: methods that create independent motions [1, 10, 13], and methods that make use or modify the robot gait to perform a kick (in-walk kicks) [11]. While the former methods are able to make full use of the hardware capabilities of the robot and can be studied independently, the later have the advantage of a much faster activation time, since they do not need to wait for the robot to finish the walking motion and to stabilize, saving critical time in challenging game situations. The in-walk kicks were originally introduced and implemented in [12], in which the gait phases are modified to create kick motions. To the best of our knowledge no other implementations have been reported. It must be noted that the in-walk kicks approach is not only limited by the hardware capabilities of the robot, but also by the gait design and implementation.

In this work, we propose a variant of the in-walk kick [12], which is commonly used in the Standard Platform League (SPL) of the RoboCup competition[1]. The proposed implementation consists of in-walk kicks that are performed using only the inertia of the gait, without any specially designed kick motion. Details of the modeling and implementation are presented below.

4.1 General Modeling

We propose an end to end implementation of the in-walk kicks, by designing a RL based controller over the omnidirectional gait developed in [5] as released in [11], i.e. designing a controller over the velocities commands v_x, v_y and v_θ.

The proposed in-walk implementation can be viewed as an instance of the ball-pushing behaviors proposed in [6, 9], and the same state and action models can be used. These models have been thoroughly validated in many implementations of the ball-dribbling behavior (another example of ball-pushing behavior), such as 2D simulators [6, 8], 3D simulators [3, 7, 9] and on physical robots [3, 9], obtaining excellent results in the RoboCup 2015 and 2016, in the SPL league.

The basic state model of the ball-pushing behaviors presented in [6] consists on the distance from the robot to the ball (ρ), the bearing of the robot with respect to the ball (γ), the angle formed between the robot, the ball and the target (φ), and the distance from the ball to the desired target (ψ). All these distances and angles are calculated from a foot coordinate frame, and the specific foot is chosen by a handcrafted foot selector. The angles and distances are shown in Fig. 2.

---

[1] RoboCup SPL official web site: http://www.tzi.de/spl/bin/view/Website/WebHome.

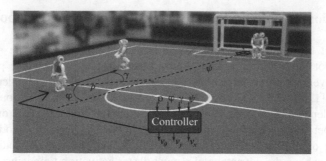

Fig. 2. Geometric state variables for the NAO using a magenta jersey. Obstacles, such as the NAO robots using cyan jerseys are not considered in the state formulation. (Color figure online)

4.2 Extended Ball-Pushing Modeling for Humanoid Biped Robots

Although several publications validate that the previous state model can obtain good performances [3, 6, 8], that modeling does not consider many aspects of the physical robot such as its biped nature and the used gait implementation [5]. We propose the following extensions to the previous model, since in the in-walk kick problem, as opposed to the ball-dribbling problem, the performance is the result of a single inter-action between the robot and the ball, thus needing as much precision as possible:

- **Gait Synchronization:** Previous implementations of RL controllers for the ball-dribbling use a fixed time step among actions. However, the implementation of the robotic gait in [5] is constantly planning its next step, and only reads velocity commands once in each phase (half-step). Neglecting this phenomenon derives in taking actions in different parts of the phases, producing a violation of the Markov property. To address this issue, we propose a model in which the controller's actions are taken once per half step, instead of using a fixed time step.
- **Phase Type:** Even if the agent actions are synchronized with the gait generator (walking engine), symmetric situations arise since at the end of each phase, the robot has one foot forward and the other foot backwards, and if this phenomenon is not included in the state model, precise time step planning becomes very difficult. To model this phenomenon, a binary state can be added to the state model to represent which foot is currently forward.
- **Foot Selector:** Even though the foot selector proposed in [9] works well, it can limit the performance, mainly in symmetric situations where the foot selector can arbitrarily assign the farthest foot from the ball. We propose to calculate the features ρ, γ and φ from the center of the robot, instead from the selected foot coordinate system, so the RL agent can learn its own foot selector.

4.3 Decentralized Reinforcement Learning Modeling

This work uses the results presented in [4, 8] which empirically validate the effectiveness of the decentralized approach in mobile robotics and common testbeds.

The design of the action space while critical, maintains the approach presented in [8]. Since the requested velocity vector of the omnidirectional biped walk engine is $[v_x, v_y, v_\theta]$, it is possible to decentralize this 3-Dimensional action space by using three separate learning agents, $Agent_x$, $Agent_y$, and $Agent_\theta$ acting in parallel in a multi-agent task. Careful considerations must be taken in the number of discrete actions for each agent. While larger numbers of actions produce more complex behaviors, it also increases the number of episodes needed for convergence, since not only the search space grows, but also coordination among agents is more difficult. The proposed action space is shown in Table 1, where the minimum and maximum values for each velocity component are the ones used in [11].

The proposed state model shared by the three independent agents is presented in Table 1, where the geometric state variables ρ_{center}, γ_{center} and φ_{center} are calculated from the center of the robot, *phaseType* represents which foot is currently forward, and the number of cores corresponds to the number of 1D basis functions placed uniform along each state dimension (the product of the number of cores becomes the dimensionality of the feature vector).

Table 1. State and action spaces for the D-RL modeling of the in-walk kick problem.

Joint state space: $S = [\rho, \gamma, \varphi]^T$				Action space: $A = [v_r, v_y, v_\theta]^T$			
Feature	Min	Max	N. Cores	Agent	Min	Max	N. Actions
ρ_{center}	0 mm	800 mm	15	v_x	0 mm/s	120 mm/s	16
γ_{center}	$-70°$	$70°$	11	v_y	-70 mm/s	70 mm/s	15
φ_{center}	$-90°$	$90°$	13	v_θ	$-30°/s$	$30°/s$	17
phaseType	–	–	Binary				

Finally, the reward is chosen the same for each independent agent, to ensure a full-cooperation task. Since the objective is to kick as strong and accurate as possible, a high positive reward must be given at the terminal state when the robot hits the ball, but decay depending on the ball trajectory deviation from the target, and the distance between the ball and the target. For non-terminal states, a reward similar to the ball-dribbling problem [6] is used to guide the robot towards the ball:

$$r = \begin{cases} K \exp\left(-\frac{\psi_{error}}{\psi_0}\right) \exp\left(-\frac{\alpha_{error}}{\alpha_0}\right) & \text{if ball touched} \\ -\left(\frac{\rho}{\rho_{max}} + \frac{|\varphi|}{\varphi_{max}} + \frac{|\gamma|}{\gamma_{max}}\right) & \text{otherwise} \end{cases} \quad (5)$$

where ψ_{error} is the distance that the ball still needs to travel to reach the target in its current trajectory, α_{error} is the angle deviation of the ball's trajectory from a straight line to the target, and the parameters ψ_0 and α_0 allow the design of rewards with more focus on kick strength or precision. Finally, the gain parameter K is used for convergence purposes, since the high positive reward can only be given once per episode.

5 Results

5.1 Experimental Set up

We present experiments that compare the proposed state model presented in Sect. 4 (gait synchronization, phase type and no foot selector) against the one presented in [8], as well as the use of the different basis functions presented in Sect. 3. It is worth mentioning that in these experiments we use just the proposed D-RL modeling and not C-RL, since in the in-walk kick with biped robots problem the action space is large enough to make the use of C-RL unfeasible (with more than a thousand discrete actions).

The experiments are performed in the SimRobot 3D simulator released in [11]. Since the objective of the training is to achieve fast yet powerful and accurate kicks, with the intent to score goals in as many situations as possible, the training conditions must be both challenging and general. In each episode, the ball is situated on a fixed position from the goal, with a distance of 1.5 m, which is the experimental maximum distance that a linear controller can achieve in the current environment. Furthermore, the robot starts in a random position, at 1 m from the ball and always facing it, but with a $|\varphi| < \varphi_{max}$, as shown in Fig. 3. This random initialization is designed so the learning agent can successfully learn many points of operation, and thus achieve a general kick behavior. The episode termination criterion is given by the following conditions: episode timeout of 200 s, the robot or the ball leaves the field, or the ball is pushed by the robot. Since episodes can finish in less than a few seconds and with unsuccessful kicks, a high number of episodes is needed. In the following experiments, the total number of training episodes is set to 1,500.

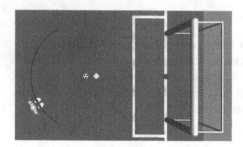

Fig. 3. Training environment. The red segment represents possible initial positions of the robot, and the red circle is the kick target. (Color figure online)

Table 2. Training parameters.

Parameter	Value
Learning rate	0.1
Discount factor	0.99
λ	0.9
σ	0.5 Δ
Width	3 Δ
Decay	15
K	50
ψ_0	300 mm
α_0	14°

The performance indexes considered for the experiments are defined as follows:

- **DistanceError** (ψ): The distance left to travel from the ball to the goal line, normalized by the initial 1.5 m distance. This measures the ability to perform strong kicks.

- **AngleError** (α): The angle deviation of the ball's trajectory from a straight line to the target, normalized by the maximum angle that would score a goal. This measures the accuracy of the kicks, and depends on the previous alignment.

The following experiments are performed using the popular $Sarsa(\lambda)$ algorithm for training each of the three agents, with an exponentially decaying ϵ-greedy exploration ($\epsilon = \exp(-decay * episode/maxEpisodes)$). Since the idea of using FSBF to save computation time needs to be validated, experiments are performed using the following functions as 1D basis functions: cosine kernel, Epanechnikov kernel, triangular kernel, and 3-σ Gaussian approximation. The parameters used in the experiments are shown in Table 2, where Δ is the distance between the centers of the basis functions in each dimension, and the parameters K, ψ_0 and α_0 correspond to the parameters of the reward in Eq. (5). The value of σ is a very common heuristic choice, and the support area of the other FSBF is set to match the 3-σ Gaussian approximation in terms of support area, to provide comparative results against fixed computation resources. For illustrative purposes, a video showing some episodes of the learning evolution is shown in [20], in which the proposed state model and the Epanechnikov basis functions are used.

5.2   State Model Comparison

The experiments in Fig. 4 show the learning evolution using the base state model for the ball-pushing behaviors [8] and the one proposed here. In both cases, the state representation is done using Gaussian RBF, and the rest of the parameters are taken from Table 2. The learning evolution results are plotted by averaging 15 trials, and error bars show the standard error.

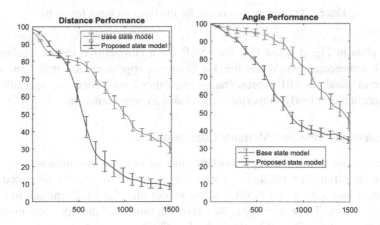

Fig. 4. Training performances for the different state models.

These results show a significant improvement when using the proposed model. The reason for the difference in the distance performance is explained by the fact that in the base model a precise step planning could not be performed, and thereby, the kicks lose strength. The differences in the angle performances are explained by the lack of foot selector and the inclusion of the *phaseType* in the proposed state model, which allows the robot to align itself correctly to kick the ball, even in symmetric conditions, where the previous foot selector choses arbitrarily foot assignments.

5.3 Basis Functions Comparison

To provide results for the proposed state representations, Fig. 5 presents the learning evolution of different finite basis functions, as well as the traditional Gaussian RBF representation. In the presented cases, the proposed state model is used, and the rest of the parameters were taken from Table 2. Again, the learning evolution results are plotted by averaging 15 trials, and error bars show the standard error.

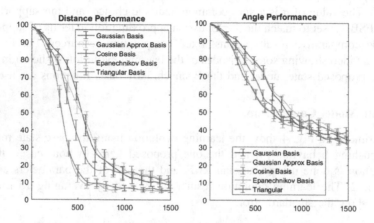

Fig. 5. Training performances for the different basis functions.

The plots in Fig. 5 show that the FSBF are a competitive choice against Gaussian RBF representations. While the 3-σ Gaussian approximation maintains the performance of standard RBF representation, the other basis functions, specially cosine and Epanechnikov clearly outperform the Gaussian representation.

5.4 Execution Time and Memory Consumption

Since the proposed methodology must run in real time on an embedded system, its execution time must be negligibly compared to the 17 ms cycles produced by the image acquisition rate in the NAO, and the model must be small enough to fit in the available memory. Table 3 presents the execution times and memory consumptions of different approaches. This table also considers C-RL to remark the importance of the proposed methodology in reducing computational resources. Memory consumption is measured from model's weights, and execution time is measured as the average execution time of a random policy, since the execution time does not depend on the learned policy, and using random policies allows the inclusion of the C-RL approach in the analysis, even if it was not trained. The FSBF used in Table 3 corresponds to the 3-σ Gaussian approximation, and the executions times for other FSBF are very similar, since the evaluation time of the 1D FSBF is negligibly compared to the feature vector calculation. To provide comparable results, in all cases the number of discrete actions per action dimension and cores are kept the same.

Table 3. Execution times for the different approaches.

Setting	Execution Time [ms]	Model Size [MB]
C-RL + Gaussian RBF	304.72	70
C-RL + FSBF	11.57	70
D-RL + Gaussian RBF	4.42	0.82
D-RL + FSBF	0.17	0.82

The results in Table 3 show that substantial computation resources can be saved by using the proposed methodology. The effective speedup produced by the D-RL against its C-RL counterpart comes close to the theoretical one expressed in Eq. (4) (an effective speed of x69 against the theoretical of x85), and the effective speedup from the state representation is x26 instead of x238, since memory access for FSBF is not contiguous, among other overheads. Finally, a x85 memory saving is achieved product of the D-RL scheme, with models using less than a megabyte of memory, fitting in most embedded systems.

6 Conclusions

In this paper, we presented a general methodology for achieving high performance and computationally cheap RL behaviors, for complex problems in which both, training times and computation resources are limited. In that sense, we presented the following solutions: first, to alleviate the effects of the curse of dimensionality on the action space, Decentralized RL was proposed, where each action dimension is controlled individually by independent learning agents acting in parallel in a multi-agent task. Second, the use of finite support basis functions, as alternatives to Gaussian RBF as linear approximators, were proposed to generalize the state space and reduce considerably computation time.

We considered the in-walk kick task from soccer robotics as a real-world validation problem. The proposed solution saves about 99.94% of execution time and 98.82% of memory consumption with respect to a centralized RL system implemented with standard Gaussian RBF, without sacrificing performance. Furthermore, basis functions like cosine and Epanechnikov empirically showed better performance and faster convergences than the Gaussian RBF representation.

We also presented a novel state model for the ball-pushing behaviors in which the RL agent actions are synchronized with the biped gait. This outperformed considerably the in-walk kick in terms of accuracy and effectiveness with respect to the former modeling for ball-pushing behaviors

Finally, it is interesting to mention that the behavior that arises through model-free RL makes intense use of the dynamics and geometry of the robot. In [20] some examples of the learned behaviors can be observed.

Acknowledgements. We would like to thank the BHuman SPL Team for sharing their code release, contributing the development of the Standard Platform League. This work was partially funded by FONDECYT Project 1161500.

References

1. Böckmann, A., Laue, T.: Kick motions for the NAO robot using dynamic movement primitives. In: Behnke, S., Sheh, R., Sarıel, S., Lee, Daniel D. (eds.) RoboCup 2016. LNCS (LNAI), vol. 9776, pp. 33–44. Springer, Cham (2017). https://doi.org/10.1007/978-3-319-68792-6_3
2. Busoniu, L., Schutter, B.D., Babuska, R.: Decentralized reinforcement learning control of a robotic manipulator. In: Ninth International Conference on Control, Automation, Robotics and Vision, ICARCV 2006, Singapore, 5–8 December 2006, pp. 1–6 (2006)
3. Celemin, C., Ruiz-del-Solar, J.: Interactive learning of continuous actions from corrective advice communicated by humans. In: Almeida, L., Ji, J., Steinbauer, G., Luke, S. (eds.) RoboCup 2015. LNCS (LNAI), vol. 9513, pp. 16–27. Springer, Cham (2015). https://doi.org/10.1007/978-3-319-29339-4_2
4. Leottau, D.L., Vatsyayan, A., Ruiz-del-Solar, J., Babuška, R.: Decentralized reinforcement learning applied to mobile robots. In: Behnke, S., Sheh, R., Sarıel, S., Lee, D.D. (eds.) RoboCup 2016. LNCS (LNAI), vol. 9776, pp. 368–379. Springer, Cham (2017). https://doi.org/10.1007/978-3-319-68792-6_31
5. Graf, C., Röfer, T.: A center of mass observing 3D-LIPM gait for the RoboCup standard platform league humanoid. In: Röfer, T., Mayer, N.M., Savage, J., Saranlı, U. (eds.) RoboCup 2011. LNCS (LNAI), vol. 7416, pp. 102–113. Springer, Heidelberg (2012). https://doi.org/10.1007/978-3-642-32060-6_9
6. Leottau, D.L., Ruiz-del-Solar, J., MacAlpine, P., Stone, P.: A study of layered learning strategies applied to individual behaviors in robot soccer. In: Almeida, L., Ji, J., Steinbauer, G., Luke, S. (eds.) RoboCup 2015. LNCS (LNAI), vol. 9513, pp. 290–302. Springer, Cham (2015). https://doi.org/10.1007/978-3-319-29339-4_24
7. Schilling, R.J., Member, S., Carroll, J.J., Al-ajlouni, A.F.: Approximation of nonlinear systems with RBF neural networks. In: IEEE Transactions on Neural Networks (2001)
8. Leottau, D.L., Ruiz-del-Solar, J.: An accelerated approach to decentralized reinforcement learning of the ball-dribbling behavior. In: AAAI Workshop: Knowledge, Skill, and Behavior Transfer in Autonomous Robots (2015)
9. Leottau, L., Celemin, C., Ruiz-del-Solar, J.: Ball dribbling for humanoid biped robots: a reinforcement learning and fuzzy control approach. In: Bianchi, R., Akin, H., Ramamoorthy, S., Sugiura, K. (eds.) RoboCup 2014. LNCS (LNAI), vol. 8992, pp. 549–561. Springer, Cham (2015). https://doi.org/10.1007/978-3-319-18615-3_45
10. Müller, J., Laue, T., Röfer, T.: Kicking a ball – modeling complex dynamic motions for humanoid robots. In: Ruiz-del-Solar, J., Chown, E., Plöger, Paul G. (eds.) RoboCup 2010. LNCS (LNAI), vol. 6556, pp. 109–120. Springer, Heidelberg (2011). https://doi.org/10.1007/978-3-642-20217-9_10
11. Röfer, T., et al.: B-Human team report and code release 2016 (2016). http://www.b-human.de/downloads/publications/2016/coderelease2016.pdf

12. Röfer, T., et al.: B-human team report and code release 2011 (2011). http://www.b-human. de/downloads/bhuman11_coderelease.pdf
13. Wenk, F., Röfer, T.: Online generated kick motions for the NAO balanced using inverse dynamics. In: Behnke, S., Veloso, M., Visser, A., Xiong, R. (eds.) RoboCup 2013. LNCS (LNAI), vol. 8371, pp. 25–36. Springer, Heidelberg (2014). https://doi.org/10.1007/978-3-662-44468-9_3
14. Busoniu, L., Babuska, R., Schutter, B.D., Ernst, D.: Reinforcement Learning and Dynamic Programming Using Function Approximators, 1st edn. CRC Press Inc, Boca Raton (2010)
15. Papierok, S., Pauli, J.: Application of reinforcement learning in a real environment using an RBF network. In: 1st International Workshop on Evolutionary and Reinforcement Learning for Autonomous Robot Systems. ERLARS 2008 (2008)
16. Sutton, R.S., Barto, A.G.: Introduction to Reinforcement Learning, 1st edn. MIT Press, Cambridge (1998)
17. Rudenko, O.G., Bezsonov, A.A., Liashenko, A.S., Sunna, R.A.: Approximation of gaussian basis functions in the problem of adaptive control of nonlinear objects. Cybern. Syst. Anal. **47**, 1–10 (2011)
18. Kober, J., Peters, J.: Reinforcement learning in robotics: a survey. In: Wiering, M., van Otterlo, M. (eds.) Reinforcement Learning. ALO, vol. 12, pp. 579–610. Springer, Heidelberg (2012). https://doi.org/10.1007/978-3-642-27645-3_18
19. Gouaillier, D., et al.: Mechatronic design of NAO humanoid. In: IEEE International Conference on Robotics and Automation, Kobe, Japan, pp. 769–774. IEEE (2009)
20. Lobos-Tsunekawa, K., Leottau, D.L., Ruiz-del-Solar, J.: Decentralized Reinforcement Learning In-Walk Kicks using Finite Basis Functions. https://youtu.be/3fp-r3xQeAQ. Accessed 5 June 2017

A Machine Learning System
for Controlling a Rescue Robot

Timothy Wiley[1], Ivan Bratko[2], and Claude Sammut[1(✉)]

[1] School of Computer Science and Engineering, The University of New South Wales,
Sydney, Australia
{t.wiley,c.sammut}@unsw.edu.au
[2] Faculty of Computer and Information Science, The University of Ljubljana,
Ljubljana, Slovenia
bratko@fri.uni-lj.si

Abstract. Many rescue robots are reconfigurable, having subtracks (or flippers) that can be adjusted to help the robot traverse different types of terrain. Knowing how to adjust them requires skill on the part of the operator. If the robot is intended to run autonomously, the control system must have an understanding of how the flippers affect the robot's interaction with the ground. We describe a system that first learns the effects of a robot's actions and then uses this knowledge to plan how to reconfigure the robot's tracks so that it can overcome different types of obstacles. The system is a hybrid of qualitative symbolic learning and reinforcement learning.

Keywords: Machine learning · Qualitative models · Rescue robots

1 Introduction

Driving a wheeled robot on flat ground is relatively straightforward once the robot has a map of its environment. The operator only needs to control the steering and speed. Driving a tracked vehicle over rough terrain is much more difficult, especially if the vehicle has subtracks, or flippers, because the operator must make decisions about the configuration of the flippers, as well as steering and speed. Thus, subtracks give the robot greater terrain traversal capabilities at the expense of greater control complexity. Reconfigurable robots are used commonly in urban search and rescue, but are mostly tele-operated. However, remote control is impossible when there is a loss of communication. Therefore, rescue robots need at least enough autonomy to be able to navigate out of a radio dropout zone. The goal of this research is to develop an autonomous driving system for reconfigurable robots. Since the interactions of the robot with the terrain in a disaster site are extremely difficulty to predict, we use a learning system to build a model of how control actions, including changing flipper angles, affect the robot's state. Once we have the model, the driving system can plan a sequence of actions to achieve the desired goal state.

© Springer Nature Switzerland AG 2018
H. Akiyama et al. (Eds.): RoboCup 2017, LNAI 11175, pp. 108–119, 2018.
https://doi.org/10.1007/978-3-030-00308-1_9

An important requirement is that the learning system must be able to acquire the model in a small number of trials. A naive application of reinforcement learning [22], which is commonly used for such tasks, may need thousands of trials, which would be very slow and eventually break the robot. Therefore, a more economical approach is required. When humans learn a new skill, they are almost always guided by some knowledge of the domain. For example, when learning to drive a car with a manual gear shift, an instructor tells the student something like, "gradually depress the clutch while releasing the accelerator, then shift the gear lever and depress the accelerator, at the same time releasing the clutch". If the student was required to deduce this sequence by trial and error, this would take a very long time. However, armed with the instructor's hints, the student only needs to learn how to make this plan operational, by learning how to synchronise the actions so as not to stall the car.

In this scenario, the student has been given a plan the describes the correct sequence of actions, but leaves out the numerical details, which must still be learned through trial and error. However, knowing what actions to perform greatly reduces the number of trials, as now the student only needs to refine a set of parameters within a given envelop. We adopt a similar approach to building a control system for driving a rescue robot. A planner produces a sequence of actions and reinforcement learning system performs the parameter refinement.

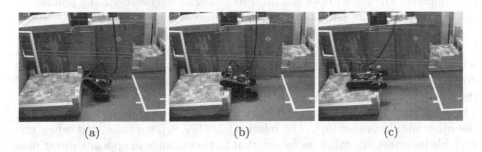

(a)   (b)   (c)

Fig. 1. The Negotiator robot reversing up a high step

The planner requires models of the actions the robot can perform. That is, it must know the preconditions and effects of each action. These may be given by an instructor, as above for learning to drive a car, or the models may, themselves, be learned. During a "pre-training" phase, the robot performs random actions, observing the robot's state before and after each action. These observations become training examples for a system that learns a qualitative model of the actions. A qualitative model is like the instructor's explanation. It describes each action at an abstract level but does not specify exact numerical values for any parameters. This two stage learning process, acquiring an approximate abstract model, followed by reinforcement learning to refine parameters, greatly reduces the overall search space, and therefore reduces the number of trial required to learn a new skill. However, it is possible that the learned qualitative model is incorrect, in the sense that it does not provide the constraints needed to learn an operational behaviour. In this case, system acquires more training data to refine the qualitative model. Thus, it is a *closed-loop* learning system that can continuously improve its behaviour. Closed-loop learning is the main focus of this paper, but we must first explain the qualitative representation of actions and how these are used for planning. We then describe how the qualitative models are acquired by a symbolic learning system and how reinforcement learning refines action parameters. Experimental results are presented that demonstrate that by closing the loop in the learning system, errors from a single pass can be corrected.

2   Qualitative Representation of a Rescue Robot

The experimental platform that we use is an iRobot Negotiator, shown in Fig. 1 climbing a step. In this case, the step is too high for the robot to climb with the flippers forward, since they are not long enough lift to robot over the step. Instead, the robot reverses up to the step and uses the flippers to raise the body, which is long enough to reach over the edge of the step. The robot's planning system should be able to reason about the geometry of the vehicle and make appropriate decisions about what sequence of actions will achieve it's goal. To do so, the planner must have a model of how actions affect the robot and its environment. The model does not need to be highly accurate for the planner to get the right sequence. An approximate qualitative model will suffice.

The qualitative model is based on Kuiper's QSIM [8] but is extended so that it can be used for planning. QSIM represents the dynamics of a system by a set of *qualitative differential equations* (QDE). An example of a model for this domain is shown in Fig. 2. The graph shows the relationship of the angles of the robot's body to the floor, θ_b, and the flipper angle, relative to the body, θ_f. The relation, $M^+(\theta_f, \theta_b)$, indicates that if one of the arguments increases (θ_f), the other also increases (θ_b). The relation, $M^-(\theta_f, \theta_b)$, says the that when one variable increases, the other decreases, that is, they change in opposite directions. The $const(\theta_b, 0)$ relation states that θ_b remains steady at 0.

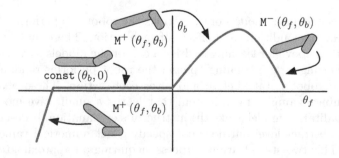

Fig. 2. Qualitative Models for the Negotiator Robot, describing the relationship between the angle of the flippers, θ_f, and base, θ_b, through four operating regions.

Each segment in the graph represents an *operating region*, that is, a region of the state space in which one model holds. As the flippers rotate clockwise through 360°, the body is raised and lowered, while the flippers are angled below the body, but have no effect when they are above the body. If the flippers are rotated anticlockwise, they can raise the body. To accommodate different operating regions, we extend the QSIM notation so that each QDE has an associate *guard*, which is the condition under which that QDE holds.

$$Guard \rightarrow Constraint \tag{1}$$

Since a QDE does not specify a numerical relationship between variables, we regard a QDE as a *constraint* on the possible values of the variables. For example, in a particular region, if the flipper angle decreases, the body angle increases. QSIM was originally intended to perform qualitative simulation. That is, given an initial condition, QSIM estimates how the system's state evolves over time. A state in QSIM is represented by the qualitative values of the variables. However, a qualitative variable does not take on a numerical value. Instead it's value is a pair: *magnitude/direction*, where the magnitude may be a fixed landmark value or an interval, and the direction is one of increasing, decreasing or steady. For example, the robot's position may be given by $x = 0..x_{step}/inc$, which states that the x position of the robot is between its initial position and the position of the step, and its value is increasing. A set of transition rules specifies how one state evolves into the next. For example, when the robot reaches the step, the position becomes $x = x_{step}/std$. A detailed explanation is given by Wiley [26].

3   Planning with Qualitative Models

QSIM has no concept of an action, which is needed for planning. We extend the QSIM representation by distinguishing certain variables as *control variables*, whose values can be changed by the planner. A change in a control variable corresponds to an action. For example, changing the flipper angle, θ_f, corresponds to the motor action that moves the flipper. Like classical planning, given an initial state and a goal state, the qualitative planner searches for a sequence of actions that leads to the goal state. We briefly describe the planner below, but details of the implementation are given elsewhere [27,28].

Qualitative planning differs from classical planning and numerical simulation because the variables can specify a range of values. Therefore, a qualitative state can be thought of as defining constraints on regions of valid quantitative states, that is, where the variables take on specific values. For example, a qualitative state may be $x = 0..x_{step}/inc, \theta_b = 0/std, v = 0..max/std, \theta_f = 0..90/std$, which describes the robot driving up to the step. To find a sequence of actions the qualitative planner must propagate the constraints from the initial to the final state. Therefore, planning can be seen as a constraint satisfaction problem. We take advantage of this, translating the planning problem into an Answer Set Programming (ASP) problem [4] and using the Clingo-4 solver [5] to generate the plan, described in [27].

The search space for the qualitative planner is considerably smaller than the search space for the corresponding continuous domain. This can be seen from the previous observation that one qualitative state covers a region of quantitative states. Thus, qualitative planning is reasonably efficient in finding a sequence of actions. However, these actions are only approximate, in the same sense as the driving instructor's plan for changing gears. In this case of the robot, as it approaches an obstacle, the plan may say that the flippers should be raised, but not by how much. We will see in Sect. 5, that "how much" can be found by reinforcement learning, but for this to be efficient, i.e. require only a small number of trials, the planner must pass on its constraints to the reinforcement learning system.

In addition to the sequence of actions, the planner generates the state transitions caused by those actions:

$$s_0 \xrightarrow{a_0} s_1 \xrightarrow{a_1} s_2 \rightarrow \ldots \xrightarrow{a_n} s_g$$

Thus, for each action, we have the preceding and succeeding states. As these are qualitative states, they effectively specify the preconditions and postconditions of the action. Thus, when the reinforcement learning system searches for the angle to set for the flippers, it must only search with the constraints of the pre and post conditions. In the following sections we explain how the qualitative model is learned and then how reinforcement learning is used to find operational parameters for the actions generated by the planner.

4   Learning a Qualitative Model

To learn a qualitative model of the robot, the system must acquire samples of the robot's interaction with its environment. In the experiments described in Sect. 6, a human operator drives the robot, performing random actions. This could equally be done by the robot "playing" by itself. Each time an action is performed, the before and after states are recorded so that the changed effected by the action can be determined. An example of flipper actions is shown in Fig. 3. The figure also shows qualitative relations induced by Padé [29]. This systems uses a form of regression, called *tubed-regression*, to find regions of a graph where neighbouring points have the same qualitative relation. In Fig. 3, Padé has identified regions where the body angle increases with the flipper angle, decreases, or remains steady. In this case, the binary relation between the angles has been rewritten in functional form so that the body angle is dependent on the flipper angle. Note that this plot corresponds to the graph in Fig. 2.

The data show that there are several operating regions where these relations apply. Recall that we express the qualitative model as a set of rules, whose left hand side specifies the operating region and the right hand side give the qualitative constraints (Eq. 1). These rules can be automatically generated from the graph by applying a symbolic rule learning system or decision tree learner. In this case, we use Quinlan's C4.5 [18]. A problem with this is that classifier learning systems usually require negative examples, as well as positive examples.

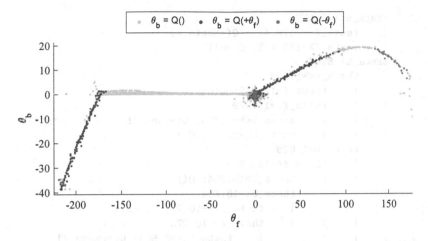

Fig. 3. Body angle versus flipper angle from actions

To accommodate this, we make a kind of closed world assumption where the space outside the sampled area is assumed to contain only negative examples. Thus, *null* values are randomly added to the C4.5's training data so that it can induce a decision tree in which the conditions in the intermediate nodes specify the operating region where the qualitative relation in the leaf node applies. Figure 4 shows the decision tree induced from the flipper data. Since the training data are noisy, the decision tree is not as clean as a model that a human might write.

With the qualitative model represented by the decision tree, the planner can determine the qualitative state of the system. QSIM's transition rules, mentioned in Sect. 2, tell the planner what possible next states are reachable depending on which action is applied in the current state. With this information, the planner can search for a sequence of actions that will achieve its goal.

5   Refining Actions by Reinforcement Learning

The actions generated by the planner are qualitative. For example, to climb a low step, the plan may indicate that the velocity should be forward, non-zero and the flipper angle should be between 0 and 90°. To find values of velocity and flipper angle that actually work, the robot must perform some trial and error learning. Figure 5 illustrates this process. For each action generated by the plan, the robot has many options for executing that action (e.g. selecting an angle between 0 and 90°). Through trial and error learning, it must discover the parameter settings that will result in the robot achieving its goal.

Parameter refinement is setup as a Semi-Markov Decision Process (SMDP) over Options [23]. In a SMDP, time is continuous and actions have a duration, which may be of variable length. The robot may try to select a set of options, that is, numerical control value settings, that will work, called a *satisficing* solution,

```
theta_b<=-5.072
|     theta_f<=-178.415: Q(+theta_f)
|     theta_f>-178.415: Q(null)
theta_b>-5.072
|     theta_b<=1.628
|     |     theta_f>17.279: Q(null)
|     |     theta_f<=17.279
|     |     |     theta_b<=-2.772: Q(+theta_f)
|     |     |     theta_b>-2.772: Q()
|     theta_b>1.628
|     |     theta_f<=133.524
|     |     |     theta_b>18.704: Q()
|     |     |     theta_b<=18.704
|     |     |     |     theta_f<=-10.273: Q(null)
|     |     |     |     theta_f>-10.273
|     |     |     |     |     theta_f<=98.500: Q(+theta_f)
|     |     |     |     |     theta_f>98.500: Q(null)
|     |     theta_f>133.524
|     |     |     theta_f<=154.558: Q(-theta_f)
|     |     |     theta_f>154.558: Q()
```

Fig. 4. The C4.5 decision tree

or it may try to find settings to achieve an optimal solution. Which type of solution is found depends on the reward function that is set. For a satisficing solution, the reward is simply 1 if the plan succeeds and 0 if it fails. To find an optimal solution, a cost function must be defined. Here, we only consider satisficing solutions, but optimal solutions are treated in [26]. The robot repeats trials, updating its policy according to its reward, until a solution is found.

The unique part of this process is how the SMDP is constructed from a plan. First, the ranges for all continuous variables must be discretised for the SMDP algorithm. This corresponds to the intervals in the qualitative model being split into a set of smaller intervals. So we know distinguish between a quantitative state description, where all the variables are continuous, a qualitative state description, as described in Sect. 2 and a *discretised* state representation, which is similar to the BOXES representation [11], commonly used in reinforcement learning. For each action, the qualitative states satisfying the pre-condition and post-condition are required. Options are formed from every combination of discretised states that are subsets of the qualitative states. QSIM constrains a variable's rate-of-change, as well as its magnitude. If the qualitative state satisfying the post-condition has an increasing rate-of-change, its quantitative value must increase during the option, likewise for decreasing or steady rates-of-change. Only options that satisfy the rates-of-change constraints are added to the SMDP.

Once the system has found the available options, it can perform its trial and error learning to turn the planning actions into operational motor commands.

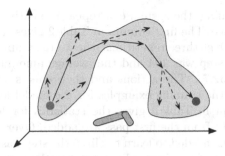

Fig. 5. The planner gives an approximation of actions, (yellow region) that must be refined by trial and error learning into precise motor actions (arrows). (Color figure online)

However, the quality of the plan depends on the quality of the model that was induced from the original training data, which was randomly sampled in the beginning. If the sampling does not yield sufficient training data in the regions of the state space relevant to the task, then the model may be poor, resulting in inefficient plans. This problem can be reduced by closed-loop learning.

6 Closed-Loop Learning and Experiments

The learning process begins with the collection of training examples for learning the qualitative model. In these experiments, the data were generated by a human operator instructing the robot to perform mostly random actions. Experiments were performed for several tasks using the Negotiator robot [26,28]. These included driving over different height steps and climbing a staircase. Of these, climbing a high step, which requires the reversing manoeuvre, was the most difficult and is the one we focus on in this discussion. The number of examples for each task is shown in Table 1. Because the high step requires a complex plan, we obtained one training set of random examples and one handcrafted set. As explained below, the handcrafted data set was created because the random set resulted in very long plans. However, closed-loop learning helps avoid sampling problems.

Table 1. Training data sets used in the experiments.

Data set	Number of examples	Duration (seconds)	Sampling frequency (seconds per sample)
Low step	1290	129.1	0.1
High step	2740	280.2	0.1
High step (Generated)	250	5.3	0.1
Staircase	765	160.1	0.2

In closed-loop learning, the system can repeat the entire learning process to improve its performance. The first column in Table 2 gives statistics for learning to climb a high step. Over three repetitions, the average number of trials needed to learn to climb the step was 104 and the average amount of time needed to complete the task is 32.7 s. The actions and their effects are recorded so that they can be added to the training examples for the model learner.

The second column in Table 2 gives the statistics for learning to climb a high step after the data from the first pass are added. Over five repetitions, the average number of trials needed to learn to climb the step has been reduced to 31 and the average amount of time needed to complete the task is 25.1 s, indicating that a better plan was produced.

Table 2. Results for climbing a high step

Climbing high step	1st pass	2nd pass
Repeats	3	5
Min. trials	102	22
Max. trials	105	41
Avg. trials	104	31
Avg. time	32.7 (s)	25.1 (s)

The systems performs better because the training data for closed-loop learning contains more training examples in areas that the human operator failed to properly sample. In fact, the difference is stronger than the table indicates. In the first pass, the planner was helped by using the handcrafted training examples. Had this not been done, the number of trials and times would have been significantly greater.

7   Related Work

Madani, Hanks and Condon [9] show that when deterministic planning is possible, it has the advantage of having lower computational complexity than non-deterministic or stochastic planning. When the domain is continuous or noisy, any plan generated by a classical planner can only be a rough approximation to an optimal solution. Stochastic planning is able to generate solutions that are robust and somewhat closer to optimal when uncertainty is present. However, to achieve high performance in both learning and execution, they are usually heavily engineered to suit a specific problem domain. Abbeel, *et al.* [1] and Stulp, *et al.* [21] are excellent examples of systems that achieve very impressive performance in their respective domains of helicopter flight and humanoid robot walking. In both cases, much of this performance is achieved by priming the learning system with models of helicopter dynamics or gait trajectories. Thus learning is largely a matter of tuning parameters.

Model-based reinforcement learning methods provide structure to a problem to reduce the search required in both learning and planning. Structure can also be provided in the form of algebraic decision diagrams as in SPUDD [7] or by performing dimensionality reduction [10]. Hierarchical learning systems reduce search complexity by breaking a problem into layers. In some cases, each layer employs the same learning mechanism applied to different levels of abstractions, such as Dietterich [3], and Hengst [6]. Others use different representations and algorithms for each layer. For example, Powers and Balch [17] have a layered architecture for controlling a vehicle in a simulated world. A deliberative layer represents the world as a grid and performs path planning. The actual control is performed by a lower, reactive layer, which handles uncertainty in a continuous world. Our approach is similar in spirit to Powers and Balch [17] except that we aim for greater domain independence by combining a general purpose planner, for constructing a sequence of abstract actions, with a parameter optimisation method to learn the implementation of those actions in a non-deterministic environment. The action models of the planner are extended to include qualitative models for reasoning about continuous variables and their qualitative relations, and are learned through active discovery by the robot.

This research builds on our own previous work on combining qualitative and quantitative methods in learning and planning. Potts [16] used machine learning to perform system identification. Ryan [19] created a planner that generates a sequence of actions whose implementation is not given but which can be learned by reinforcement learning. Ryan's method worked well in discrete domains but does not scale well to continuous domains. This problem was addressed by Sammut and Yik [20], who developed a system for learning the gait for a bipedal robot. Here, a planner produces a sequence of parameterised qualitative actions. Subsequent trial-and-error learning determines the values of those parameters so that the qualitative plan is made operational. Brown [2] used Inductive Logic Programming to learn action models for a robot planning system.

In work related to locomotion in rescue robots, Ohno et al. [14] manually specify control rules before learning precise actuator movements. Mihankhah [12] follow a similar pre-programmed approach with fuzzy controllers, and Tseng [24] explicitly model a robot slipping. Vincent and Sun [25] use reinforcement learning to teach a robot, in simulation, to climb over a box, and Mourikis [13] train multiple PID controllers to climb a staircase. These approaches all focus on learning the actuator movements. This is equivalent to only our parameter refinement stage, whereas, this work also builds a model of the robot and plans the robot's actions.

8   Conclusion

We have demonstrated a hybrid learning system that combines learning qualitative models with reinforcement learning. The result is a system that learns complex plans in a relatively small number of trials, supporting the claim that high-level knowledge about the task can reduce the attempts needed to learn a new skill.

There are several ways in which the present system can be improved. It relies on existing base learning methods, where Padé is used to induce qualitative relations that are then used by C4.5 to organise them by operating region. The use of these base learners has limitations. Padé can only induce M^+ and M^- relations for a limited number of variables. C4.5 requires the artificial introduction of negative training examples. In the future, we would like to explore different methods for learning qualitative models, such as [15]. It would also be preferable to find alternatives to C4.5 that can learn from positive only data or a form of model tree learning that can induce the qualitative model as it builds the classifier for the operating region.

Acknowledgements. We thank Jure Žabkar, the University of Ljubljana, for his help in using the Padé software, and Torsten Schaub and Max Ostrowski, the University of Potsdam, for their assistance with the Clingo-4 ASP solver, which are used in our symbolic planner. This research was supported by the Australian Research Council grant DP130102351 and an Australian Postgraduate Award.

References

1. Abbeel, P., Coates, A., Ng, A.Y.: Autonomous helicopter aerobatics through apprenticeship learning. Int. J. Robot. Res. **29**, 1608–1639 (2010)
2. Brown, S., Sammut, C.: Learning tool use in robots. In: Langley, P. (ed.) Advances in Cognitive Systems: Papers from the AAAI Fall Symposium, pp. 58–65. AAAI Press, Menlo Park (2011)
3. Dietterich, T.G.: The MAXQ method for hierarchical reinforcement learning. In: 15th International Conference on Machine Learning, pp. 118–126 (1998)
4. Gebser, M., Kaminski, R., Kaufmann, B., Schaub, T.: Answer set solving in practice. Synthesis Lectures of Artificial Intelligence and Machine Learning. Morgan & Claypool Publishers, San Rafael (2013)
5. Gebser, M., Kaufmann, B., Kaminski, R., Ostrowski, M., Schaub, T., Schneider, M.: Potassco: the Potsdam answer set solving collection. AI Commun. **24**(2), 107–124 (2011)
6. Hengst, B.: Discovering hierarchy in reinforcement learning with HEXQ. In: 19th International Conference on Machine Learning, pp. 243–250. Morgan Kaufmann (2002)
7. Hoey, J., St-Aubin, R., Hu, A., Boutilier, C.: SPUDD: stochastic planning using decision diagrams. In: Proceedings of the Fifteenth Conference on Uncertainty in Artificial Intelligence, pp. 279–288. Morgan Kaufmann (1999)
8. Kuipers, B.J.: Qualitative simulation. Artif. Intell. **29**(3), 289–338 (1986)
9. Madani, O., Hanks, S., Condon, A.: On the undecidability of probabilistic planning and related stochastic optimization problems. Artif. Intell. **147**(1–2), 5–34 (2003)
10. Mahadevan, S.: Learning representation and control in markov decision processes: new frontiers. Found. Trends Mach. Learn. **1**(4), 403–565 (2009)
11. Michie, D., Chambers, R.A.: BOXES: an experiment in adaptive control. Mach. Intell. **2**(2), 137–152 (1968)
12. Mihankhah, E., Kalantari, A., Aboosaeedan, E., Taghirad, H.D., Moosavian, S.A.A.: Autonomous staircase detection and stair climbing for a tracked mobile robot using fuzzy controller. In: Proceedings of the 2008 IEEE International Conference on Robotics and Biometrics, pp. 1980–1985 (2008)

13. Mourikis, A., Trawny, N., Roumeliotis, S.I., Helmick, D.M., Matthies, L.: Autonomous stair climbing for tracked vehicles **26**(7), 737–758 (2007)
14. Ohno, K., Morimura, S., Tadokoro, S., Koyanagi, E., Yoshida, T.: Semi-autonomous control system of rescue crawler robot having flippers for getting over unknown-steps. In: 2007 IEEE/RSJ International Conference on Intelligent Robots and Systems, pp. 3012–3018 (2007)
15. Pang, W., Coghill, G.M.: QML-Morven: a novel framework for learning qualitative differential equation models using both symbolic and evolutionary approaches. J. Comput. Sci. **5**(5), 795–808 (2014)
16. Potts, D., Sammut, C.: Incremental learning of linear model trees. Mach. Learn. **6**(1–3), 5–48 (2005)
17. Powers, M., Balch, T.: A learning approach to integration of layers of a hybrid control architecture. In: IEEE/RSJ International Conference on Intelligent Robots and Systems, IROS 2009, pp. 893–898 (2009)
18. Quinlan, J.R.: C4.5: Programs for Machine Learning. Morgan Kaufmann, San Manteo (1993)
19. Ryan, M.R.K.: Using abstract models of behaviours to automatically generate reinforcement learning hierarchies. In: Sammut, C., Hoffmann, A. (eds.) Proceedings of the Nineteenth International Conference on Machine Learning, pp. 522–529. Morgan Kaufmann Publishers Inc., Sydney (2002)
20. Sammut, C., Yik, T.F.: Multistrategy learning for robot behaviours. In: Koronacki, J., Raś, Z., Wierzchon, S., Kacprzyk, J. (eds.) Advances in Machine Learning I. SCI, vol. 262, pp. 457–476. Springer, Heidelberg (2010). https://doi.org/10.1007/978-3-642-05177-7_23
21. Stulp, F., Buchli, J., Theodorou, E., Schaal, S.: Reinforcement learning of full-body humanoid motor skills. In: IEEE-RAS International Conference on Humanoid Robots, pp. 405–410 (2010)
22. Sutton, R.S., Barto, A.G.: Reinforcement learning: An introduction, 1st edn. MIT Press, Cambridge (1998)
23. Sutton, R.S., Precup, D., Singh, S.P.: Between MDPs and semi-MDPs: a framework for temporal abstraction in reinforcement learning. Artif. Intell. **112**(1–2), 181–211 (1999)
24. Tseng, C.K., Li, I.H., Chien, Y.H., Chen, M.C., Wang, W.Y.: Autonomous stair detection and climbing systems for a tracked robot. In: IEEE International Conference on System Science and Engineering, pp. 201–204 (2013)
25. Vincent, I., Sun, Q.: A combined reactive and reinforcement learning controller for an autonomous tracked vehicle. Robot. Auton. Syst. **60**(4), 599–608 (2012)
26. Wiley, T.: A Planning and Learning Hierarchy for the Online Acquisition of Robot Behaviours. Ph.D. thesis, School of Computer Science and Engineering, University of New South Wales (2017)
27. Wiley, T., Sammut, C., Bratko, I.: Qualitative simulation with answer set programming. In: Schaub, T., Friedrich, G., O'Sullivan, B. (eds.) Proceedings of the Twenty-First European Conference on Artificial Intelligence, pp. 915–920. IOS Press, Prague, August 2014
28. Wiley, T., Sammut, C., Hengst, B., Bratko, I.: A planning and learning hierarchy using qualitative reasoning for the on-line acquisition of robotic behaviors. Adv. Cogn. Syst. **4**, 93–112 (2016)
29. Žabkar, J., Mozina, M., Bratko, I., Demsar, J.: Learning qualitative models from numerical data. Artif. Intell. **175**(9–10), 1604–1619 (2011)

Analysing Soccer Games with Clustering and Conceptors

Olivia Michael[1][(✉)], Oliver Obst[1][(✉)], Falk Schmidsberger[2],
and Frieder Stolzenburg[2][(✉)]

[1] Centre for Research in Mathematics, Western Sydney University,
Locked Bag 1797, Penrith, NSW 2751, Australia
17974761@student.westernsydney.edu.au, o.obst@westernsydney.edu.au
[2] Department of Automation and Computer Sciences, Harz University of Applied
Sciences, Friedrichstr. 57-59, 38855 Wernigerode, Germany
{fschmidsberger,fstolzenburg}@hs-harz.de

Abstract. We present a new approach for identifying situations and behaviours, which we call *moves*, from soccer games in the 2D simulation league. Being able to identify key situations and behaviours are useful capabilities for analysing soccer matches, anticipating opponent behaviours to aid selection of appropriate tactics, and also as a prerequisite for automatic learning of behaviours and policies. To support a wide set of strategies, our goal is to identify situations from data, in an unsupervised way without making use of pre-defined soccer specific concepts such as "pass" or "dribble". The recurrent neural networks we use in our approach act as a high-dimensional projection of the recent history of a situation on the field. Similar situations, i.e., with similar histories, are found by clustering of network states. The same networks are also used to learn so-called conceptors, that are lower- dimensional manifolds that describe trajectories through a high-dimensional state space that enable situation-specific predictions from the same neural network. With the proposed approach, we can segment games into sequences of situations that are learnt in an unsupervised way, and learn conceptors that are useful for the prediction of the near future of the respective situation.

Keywords: Robotic soccer · Logfile analysis · Clustering
Recurrent neural networks · Conceptors · Information retrieval

1   Introduction

Some of the recent achievements of AI systems [6,9,20,28] have in common that they use some form of machine learning as a key component, and that their performance can be immediately compared against the performance of a human player. Teams in the soccer simulation leagues play against each other,

© Springer Nature Switzerland AG 2018
H. Akiyama et al. (Eds.): RoboCup 2017, LNAI 11175, pp. 120–131, 2018.
https://doi.org/10.1007/978-3-030-00308-1_10

a comparison against humans is not a part of the competition.[1] As such, it is impossible to say how well simulation league teams play in terms of potential human performance. It is, however, possible to observe continuing progress in performance of champion teams [11,13]. In this paper, we propose a new method for automatically analysing soccer matches, a step we see as a prerequisite to learning behaviours and strategy for a team.

1.1 Motivation

A capability to model and describe possible situations and interactions in a game of autonomous robots has benefits for training or programming the team. With a meaningful vocabulary of situations, appropriate actions and strategies can be implemented, and together with a deeper analysis of past soccer matches, likely future situations can be better predicted.

In the context of RoboCup soccer, several efforts have been made to support the description of situations, interactions between players, or sequences of actions and situations. In [21,22], for example, UML statecharts are used to describe plans of individual agents and the team, with the goal to manually specify team behaviour. An information-theoretic approach for the analysis of interactions has been developed in [8]; this approach is able to identify dynamic relationships between players of a team and its opponents. In contrast to the UML statecharts approach, the information-theoretic analysis of interactions is model-free, and does not rely on predefined, soccer-specific concepts (e.g., pass or dribble). One possible output of this approach are interaction diagrams that can be used to analyse strengths of specific players in a given match. The approach for performance analysis in soccer in [1] also requires definition of events and situations, in this case based on a predefined ontology and rules that only use positions of objects to detect events in a game. A qualitative representation of time series has been introduced in [19] with the idea to use this representation for rule-based prediction of sequences.

To be able to analyse, communicate, and learn team behaviour, it would be beneficial to use an approach that also does not rely on predefined soccer knowledge, but for example is able to learn how to describe situations or plans from recorded logfiles of games. This way, the analysis will rely on behaviours frequently occurring in past games instead of behaviours that may be familiar to the developer from, e.g., human soccer matches, or similar prior knowledge that is required when using manually specified plans.

An obvious application of identifying frequent behaviours in games is the analysis of logfiles, to be used for programming to improve team performance, or for automated commentator systems. A challenge for the goal of identifying behaviours is to solve the apparently simple questions what constitutes a

---

[1] To our knowledge, experimental games in the earlier years of RoboCup against a team of humans using joysticks to control players were easily won by computer programs. It should be noted, however, that the soccer simulation was not designed to be played by humans, and how human players interface with the simulation will obviously affect performance to a large degree.

behaviour and what "situation" means in a soccer match. Even though the simulation naturally segments a game into steps of 100 ms, such a fine grained segmentation does not appear to be practical to compare longer sequences of actions, or "moves".

Being able to predict likely moves from a given situation is a useful first step towards learning behaviours for soccer players. While a few successful teams employed machine learning techniques, most notably reinforcement learning in e.g., [12,14,15,26], or planning with MDPs in [5], use of machine learning has been limited to components like individual skills or behaviours.

Learning most of the teams behaviour is quite challenging due to the large number of possible actions each player can choose from. The large number of possible moves is also a challenge for computer programs created to play the game of Go, and the recent success in this field [28], for example, is based on so-called "policy networks". A successful prediction of expert moves from a given situation on the Go board has been a first step in this success story. To take this first step in robotic soccer, the goal of our project is to eventually be able to identify both "actions" and "situations", with the application to learn probability distributions of the form $p(\text{action}|\text{situation})$.

1.2   Notions

Let us now clarify some terminology, e.g., what we mean by a situation or move. When we analyse time-series data by machine learning techniques, we shall distinguish the raw observed data from its reflection in a world model. In our case, on the one hand, we have the soccer simulation data given by logfiles representing more or less real-world data. On the other hand, we have a world model which will be loaded into an artificial recurrent neural network, explained later in some detail.

A soccer simulation game in the RoboCup 2D simulation league lasts 10 mins in total, divided into 6000 cycles where the length of each cycle is 100 ms. The central SoccerServer [7] controls every virtual game with built-in physics rules. Logfiles comprise information about the game, in particular about the current positions of all players and the ball including their velocity and orientation for each cycle, which we call *world state* in the following, corresponding to an actual situation.

The challenge in the simulation league is to derive for all possible world states, possibly including their state history, the best possible action to perform for each player, understood as intelligent agent in this context [27, Sect. 2]. An *action* in our case might be kick, dash (used to accelerate the player in direction of its body), turn (change the players body direction), and others more. Each action is executed in the actual cycle, but its effect may hold on for a longer period of time.

For modelling the time-series induced by the logfile, we use recurrent neural networks of a very simple form, namely echo state networks [17]. They consist of a number of input neurons, containing the world state information of a given cycle. The input neurons are connected with a reservoir usually consisting of hundreds of neurons in a hidden layer. All neurons in the reservoir are connected randomly among each other, at least initially. At each time point, an output signal is read out by further connections from the reservoir to one or more output neurons. By this procedure, each world state is reflected by a *reservoir state* corresponding to the same cycle time.

A fundamental condition for recurrent neural networks to be useful in learning tasks is the so-called echo state property: Any random initial state of a reservoir is forgotten, such that after a washout period the current network state simply is a function of the driver [18]. We can use the series of reservoir states for predicting future development of the game. Thus we implicitly compute a probability distribution for the next world state or action. In order to reach this goal, we partition the game into different moves by clustering methods [2, Sects. 6 and 7]. A *move* in this context means a pattern of similar states. It is derived from a sequence of consecutive reservoir states which might occur several times during the whole game but it means the respective series of world states.

The idea is that each move corresponds to a certain behaviour such as e.g. kicking a goal. When a recurrent neural network is actively generating or is passively being driven by different dynamical patterns, its reservoir states are located in different regions of the multi-dimensional neural state space, characteristic for that pattern. A move thus corresponds to a specific concept which can be captured by a *conceptor* [18]. They allows us to analyse and identify moves and finally to predict the development of the game. This is the main objective of this paper.

1.3 Overview

The rest of the paper is structured as follows: Next, we will describe the used methods in more detail, from data preparation to recurrent neural networks with conceptors and clustering algorithms (Sect. 2). After that, we state some results on clustering and prediction in soccer games (Sect. 3). Finally, we end up with conclusions and a brief outlook on future work (Sect. 4).

2 Methods

2.1 Data Preparation

In order to prepare the data needed, we use recorded logfiles from 2D soccer simulation matches between two teams. The main data set we will be using throughout this paper is a match between the teams Gliders2012 [24] and MarliK [29].[2] For more detailed experiments, we also created a data set of 101 games, run using the teams Helios2016 [3] and Gliders2016 [25]. Each logfile contains the "state of the world", ground truth information sampled every 100 ms,

---

[2] The logfile is taken from the site http://chaosscripting.net/, a backup of the official soccer simulation website.

which includes the positions of the players and the ball in x and y coordinates, as well as the speed and the stamina of the players.

The soccer simulator records games in a binary format, which we converted to text using the tool rcg2txt, from the librcsc library [4]. The resulting data were then converted from text to csv files (comma separated values) using a custom Python script. For the work in this paper, we only made use of player and ball positions (23 objects with x- and y-positions, i.e. 46 values for each step of the simulation). As already said, each match lasts 6000 steps (10 mins in real time), but in some situations game time may be stopped, which can lead to extra steps. On average, we recorded close to 6500 game states per match.

2.2   Recurrent Neural Networks with Conceptors

The world model of the time-series data, as created in the data preperation phase, is loaded into a recurrent neural network. Following the lines of [18, Sect. 3], a (discrete-time) *recurrent neural network* consists of (a) N^{in} input neurons, (b) a reservoir, that is a set of N recurrently connected neurons, and (c) N^{out} output neurons (cf. Fig. 1). The connections between neurons have weights which may be comprised in weight matrices: W^{in} is the $N \times N^{\text{in}}$ input weight matrix, W^{res} the $N \times N$ reservoir matrix, and W^{out} the $N^{\text{out}} \times N$ readout matrix. The network operates in discrete time steps $n = 0, 1, 2, \ldots$ according to the following update equations:

$$x(n + 1) = \tanh(W^{\text{res}} \cdot x(n) + W^{\text{in}} \cdot p(n + 1) + b)$$
$$y(n) = W^{\text{out}} \cdot x(n)$$

Here $p(n)$ denotes the input (training) signal (here: the logged data from the recorded soccer games), $x(n)$ the reservoir state, and $y(n)$ the target signal (here: the next input state). b is an $N \times 1$ bias vector. Like the input weights, it is fixed to random values. Due to the commonly used non-linear activation function tanh, the reservoir state space is reduced to the interval $(-1; +1)$. A time-series may represent a move, which can be learned by so-called conceptors as follows: The sequence of world states representing the move is stored into the reservoir such that it can generate the driven responses $x(n)$ even in the absence of the driving input. For this, ridge regression may be employed. Primarily, the output weights W^{out} are learned. Nevertheless, in order to retrieve the output pattern individually, the reservoir dynamics is restricted to the linear subspace characteristic for that pattern. This is done by special matrices called conceptors. These are lower-dimensional manifolds that describe trajectories through a high-dimensional state space that enable situation-specific predictions from the same neural network. For more details the reader is referred to [18].

For the analysis of soccer games, different moves are associated with conceptors. However, we usually do not know in advance which are the moves of the whole game. Thus we first have to establish a repertoire of moves that form the whole game. We want to identify and learn moves by clustering methods, which is explained in the next section. To support a wide set of strategies, our goal is

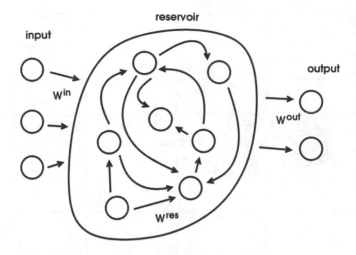

Fig. 1. Recurrent neural network capturing the world model.

to identify situations from data, in an unsupervised way without making use of pre-defined soccer specific concepts such as "pass" or "dribble".

2.3   Clustering of Games in Moves

As described above, we extract the positions of all players and the ball from logfiles, for each cycle of the game and store them as world states normalised to the range $(-1; +1)$ (because of the use of the tanh function, see above). In the example in Fig. 2, all world states from a logfile MarliK vs. Gliders2012 are drawn, here for the ball and the two goalies.

To identify the sequences of world states that represent moves leading to similar game situations, we use the actual world state $p(i)$ to compute the reservoir state $x(i)$ for each cycle of the game. A reservoir state represents the current state of the game, as well as the history that led to that state, therefore we can assume that similar reservoir states represent similar moves in a game. Clustering of all reservoir states $x(i)$ is able to identify such similar moves. Cluster members are close to each other in the reservoir state space; that is, for each member the current game situation and its short-term past are similar to other cluster members.

We use the X-means algorithm [23] to derive the clusters and the number of clusters. This algorithm extends the well-known k-means clustering method with an efficient estimation of the number of clusters. While the number of clusters has to be fixed in advance in the k-means methods, X-means clustering starts with $k = 2$ clusters and splits clusters, if their average squared distance to the centroid still can be improved.

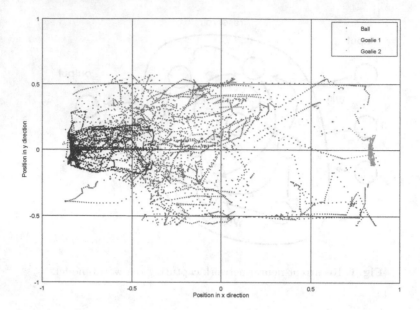

Fig. 2. Position visualization of the two goalies and the ball.

3   Results

To test our approach we extract the 6493 world states from the logfile MarliK_1-vs-Gliders2012_3 and store these states into a recurrent neural network with 46 input neurons, 600 neurons in the reservoir and 46 output neurons. We compute the reservoir states $x(i)$ for each world state and cluster them with the X-Means algorithm of the data mining tool WEKA 3.8 [10,16]. With the maximal number of clusters of 100 and a maximum of 5 iterations as presetting parameters, we get 64 clusters.

By this procedure, we achieved two main results: First, each resulting cluster can be associated with one or more sequences of world states, i.e. with moves. Each cluster consists of a set of similar reservoir states. The reservoir states in each cluster may come from different phases of the soccer game. Nevertheless in a cluster often several reservoir states stem from consecutive time steps. The reason for this is that the world state and hence the reservoir state does not change too much from one time step to the other according to the network dynamics. Each sequence of these consecutive reservoir states now belongs to a move. Note that in the figures only the final phases of the moves, strictly speaking the world states corresponding to the consecutive reservoirs states, are shown. Actually the moves start some time steps earlier.

Figure 3 shows all 5 moves of cluster 5 for all players and the ball, and Fig. 4 all moves of cluster 41. In the subfigures for each move, the part of the respective world state sequence is drawn, where the reservoir states $x(i)$ are in the actual cluster. With the now identified clusters and moves it is possible to compute the

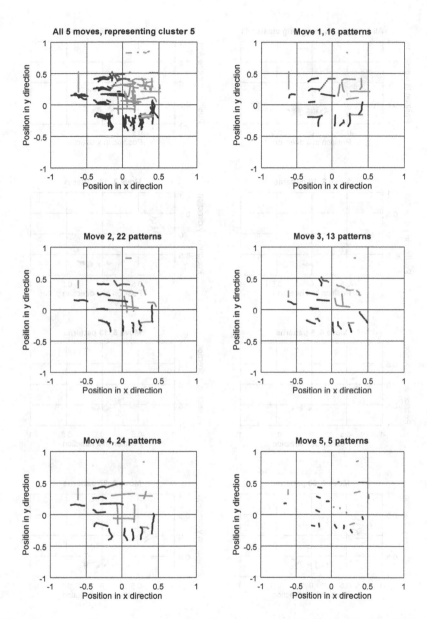

Fig. 3. All states referring to cluster 5. The trajectories of the ball (red), of the left team (blue), and of the right team (green) are shown (colours in online version).

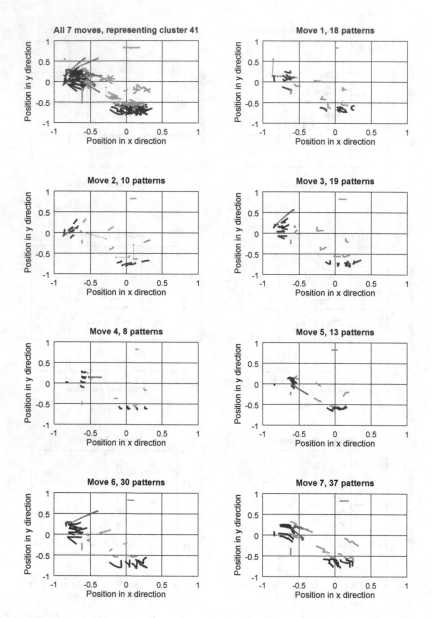

Fig. 4. All states referring to cluster 41. Again, the trajectories of the ball (red), of the left team (blue), and the right team (green) are shown (colours in online version).

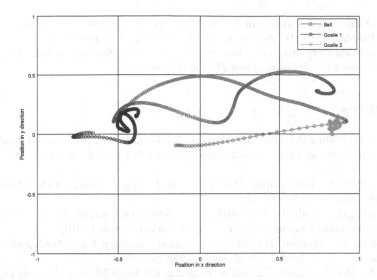

Fig. 5. Prediction of an entire game by the reservoir dynamics of the recurrent neural network.

conceptors for these moves in the respective game situations. These conceptors allow us to predict the next world states in similar situations in the game, e.g., whether the next action will be a kick to the goal.

As a second result, with the resulting conceptor of the reservoir filled with all world states, i.e. over all time steps of the whole game, we can also respresent a simplified picture of the entire game, i.e. a kind of replay. This is shown in Fig. 5. For the sake of simplicity, only goalies and ball are drawn here. As one can see, the figure shows that the goalies keep to the goal area and that the ball moves essentially back and forth from one goal to the other. This seems to be an absolutely plausible summary of the whole soccer game. Of course, this point needs further investigation.

4   Discussion and Final Remarks

We have shown how clustering methods in conjunction with conceptors in recurrent neural networks help to determine moves of soccer game. Conceptors allow us to make predictions of the whole game or the next move, e.g., whether there is a probability of kicking a goal.

Future work will concentrate on analysing more deeply different moves and their structure and the prediction accuracy of conceptors. The overall method shall be improved such that it is applicable in real-time and online. For this, the neural network model shall be simplified even further.

Acknowledgements. The research reported in this paper has been supported by the German Academic Exchange Service (DAAD) by funds of the German Federal

Ministry of Education and Research (BMBF) in the Programmes for Project-Related Personal Exchange (PPP) under grant no. 57319564 and Universities Australia (UA) in the Australia-Germany Joint Research Cooperation Scheme within the project *Deep Conceptors for Temporal Data Mining* (Decorating).

References

1. Abreu, P., Moura, J., Silva, D.C., Reis, L.P., Garganta, J.: Performance analysis in soccer: a Cartesian coordinates based approach using RoboCup data. Soft Comput. **16**, 47–61 (2012)
2. Aggarwal, C.C.: Data Mining–The Textbook. Springer, Cham (2015). https://doi. org/10.1007/978-3-319-14142-8
3. Akiyama, H., et al.: HELIOS2016: team description paper. In: RoboCup 2016 Symposium and Competitions: Team Description Papers (2016)
4. Akiyama, H., Shimora, H.: librcsc-4.1.0 library package for RoboCup simulation clients, May 2011. http://rctools.sourceforge.jp/
5. Bai, A., Wu, F., Chen, X.: Online planning for large Markov decision processes with hierarchical decomposition. ACM Trans. Intell. Syst. Technol. **6**(4), 45:1–45:28 (2015)
6. Brown, N., Sandholm, T.: Safe and nested endgame solving for imperfect-information games. In: Proceedings of the AAAI workshop on Computer Poker and Imperfect Information Games (2017)
7. Chen, M., et al.: Users Manual: RoboCup Soccer Server – for Soccer Server Version 7.07 and Later. The RoboCup Federation, February 2003. http://helios.hampshire. edu/jdavila/cs278/virtual_worlds/robocup_manual-20030211.pdf
8. Cliff, O.M., Lizier, J.T., Wang, X.R., Wang, P., Obst, O., Prokopenko, M.: Quantifying long-range interactions and coherent structure in multi-agent dynamics. Artif. Life **23**, 34–57 (2017)
9. Ferrucci, D.A., et al.: Building Watson: An overview of the DeepQA project. AI Magazine **31**(3), 59–79 (2010)
10. Frank, E., Hall, M.A., Witten, I.H.: The WEKA Workbench. Online Appendix for "Data Mining: Practical Machine Learning Tools and Techniques", 4th edn. Morgan Kaufmann, Burlington (2016)
11. Gabel, T., Falkenberg, E., Godehardt, E.: Progress in RoboCup revisited: the state of soccer simulation 2D. In: Behnke, S., Sheh, R., Sarıel, S., Lee, D.D. (eds.) RoboCup 2016. LNCS (LNAI), vol. 9776, pp. 144–156. Springer, Cham (2017). https://doi.org/10.1007/978-3-319-68792-6_12
12. Gabel, T., Riedmiller, M.: Learning a partial behavior for a competitive soccer agent. Künstliche Intelligenz **2**, 18–23 (2006)
13. Gabel, T., Riedmiller, M.: On progress in RoboCup: the simulation league showcase. In: Ruiz-del-Solar, J., Chown, E., Plöger, P.G. (eds.) RoboCup 2010. LNCS (LNAI), vol. 6556, pp. 36–47. Springer, Heidelberg (2011). https://doi.org/10. 1007/978-3-642-20217-9_4
14. Gabel, T., Riedmiller, M., Trost, F.: A case study on improving defense behavior in soccer simulation 2D: the NeuroHassle approach. In: Iocchi, L., Matsubara, H., Weitzenfeld, A., Zhou, C. (eds.) RoboCup 2008. LNCS (LNAI), vol. 5399, pp. 61–72. Springer, Heidelberg (2009). https://doi.org/10.1007/978-3-642-02921-9_6
15. Gabel, T., Roser, C.: FRA-UNIted – team description 2016. In: RoboCup 2016 Symposium and Competitions: Team Description Papers. Leipzig, Germany (2016)

16. Hall, M., Frank, E., Holmes, G., Pfahringer, B., Reutemann, P., Witten, I.H.: The WEKA data mining software: an update. SIGKDD Explor. **11**(1), 10–18 (2009)
17. Jaeger, H.: Echo state network. Scholarpedia **2**(9), 2330 (2007). Revision #151757
18. Jaeger, H.: Controlling recurrent neural networks by conceptors. CoRR - Computing Research Repository abs/1403.3369, Cornell University Library (2014). http://arxiv.org/abs/1403.3369
19. Lattner, A.D., Miene, A., Visser, U., Herzog, O.: Sequential pattern mining for situation and behavior prediction in simulated robotic soccer. In: Bredenfeld, A., Jacoff, A., Noda, I., Takahashi, Y. (eds.) RoboCup 2005. LNCS (LNAI), vol. 4020, pp. 118–129. Springer, Heidelberg (2006). https://doi.org/10.1007/11780519_11
20. Mnih, V., et al.: Human-level control through deep reinforcement learning. Nature **518**(7540), 529–533 (2015)
21. Murray, J.: Specifying agent behaviors with UML Statecharts and StatEdit. In: Polani, D., Browning, B., Bonarini, A., Yoshida, K. (eds.) RoboCup 2003. LNCS (LNAI), vol. 3020, pp. 145–156. Springer, Heidelberg (2004). https://doi.org/10.1007/978-3-540-25940-4_13
22. Murray, J., Obst, O., Stolzenburg, F.: Towards a logical approach for soccer agents engineering. In: Stone, P., Balch, T., Kraetzschmar, G. (eds.) RoboCup 2000. LNCS (LNAI), vol. 2019, pp. 199–208. Springer, Heidelberg (2001). https://doi.org/10.1007/3-540-45324-5_18
23. Pelleg, D., Moore, A.W.: X-means: extending k-means with efficient estimation of the number of clusters. In: Langley, P. (ed.) Proceedings of the Seventeenth International Conference on Machine Learning (ICML 2000), Stanford University, Stanford, 29 June–2 July 2000, pp. 727–734. Morgan Kaufmann (2000)
24. Prokopenko, M., Obst, O., Wang, P., Held, J.: Gliders 2012: tactics with action-dependent evaluation functions. In: RoboCup 2012 Symposium and Competitions: Team Description Papers (2012)
25. Prokopenko, M., Wang, P., Obst, O., Jaurgeui, V.: Gliders 2016: Integrating multi-agent approaches to tactical diversity. In: RoboCup 2016 Symposium and Competitions: Team Description Papers. Leipzig, Germany, July 2016
26. Riedmiller, M., Merke, A.: Using machine learning techniques in complex multi-agent domains. In: Kühn, R., Menzel, R., Menzel, W., Ratsch, U., Richter, M.M., Stamatescu, I.O. (eds.) Adaptivity and Learning: An Interdisciplinary Debate, pp. 311–328. Springer, Heidelberg (2003). https://doi.org/10.1007/978-3-662-05594-6_22
27. Russell, S., Norvig, P.: Artificial Intelligence – A Modern Approach, 3rd edn. Prentice Hall, Englewood Cliffs (2009)
28. Silver, D., et al.: Mastering the game of Go with deep neural networks and tree search. Nature **529**(7587), 484–489 (2016)
29. Tavafi, A., Nozari, N., Vatani, R., Yousefi, M.R., Rahmatinia, S., Pirdir, P.: MarliK 2012 soccer 2D simulation team description paper. In: RoboCup 2012 Symposium and Competitions: Team Description Papers (2012)

Poster Presentations

Poster Presentations

CABSL – C-Based Agent Behavior Specification Language

Thomas Röfer[1,2]([✉])

[1] Cyber-Physical Systems, Deutsches Forschungszentrum für Künstliche Intelligenz,
Enrique-Schmidt-Str. 5, 28359 Bremen, Germany
thomas.roefer@dfki.de
[2] Universität Bremen, Fachbereich 3 – Mathematik und Informatik,
Postfach 330 440, 28334 Bremen, Germany

Abstract. This paper describes the *C-based Agent Behavior Specification Language* (CABSL) that is available as open source [8]. It allows specifying the behavior of a robot or a software agent in C++11. Semantically, it follows the ideas of the *Extensible Agent Behavior Specification Language* (XABSL) developed by Lötzsch *et al.* [6], i.e. robot behavior is described as a hierarchy of finite state machines. However, its integration into a C++ program requires significantly less programming overhead than when using XABSL. CABSL has been part of all B-Human code releases since 2013 [9], but it is now also available as a standalone release that works without the B-Human base system.

1 Introduction

Modeling the behavior of a software agent or a robot is an important part of building autonomous systems. In the domain of RoboCup, real-time requirements and limited computational resources often prevent the use of planning-based approaches. Instead, the behavior is explicitly specified. In this context, hierarchical finite state machines have been proven to be a successful concept. They come in different forms, e.g. as Nilsson's *Teleo-Reactive programs* [7] or as *Hierarchical Task Networks* [3], although the latter are typically used to plan ahead. The *C-based Agent Behavior Specification Language* (CABSL) presented in this paper allows following the approach of modeling behavior as hierarchical finite state machines directly in C++, i.e. the language in which many robots are programmed anyway. As a result, CABSL avoids the programming overhead that usually comes from combining different programming languages.

The paper is organized as follows: First, Sect. 2 discusses behavior modeling languages and in particular CABSL's predecessor XABSL. Then, the language CABSL is presented in Sect. 3. In Sect. 4, CABSL is compared to XABSL. Section 5 discusses the impact CABSL had so far. Finally, the paper concludes in Sect. 6.

© Springer Nature Switzerland AG 2018
H. Akiyama et al. (Eds.): RoboCup 2017, LNAI 11175, pp. 135–142, 2018.
https://doi.org/10.1007/978-3-030-00308-1_11

2   XABSL

Many ways have been developed to specify the behavior of a software agent or a robot. Risler [12] gives a good overview of the different approaches in his PhD thesis. The approach that is most similar to the system presented in this paper is the *Extensible Agent Behavior Specification Language* (XABSL) developed by Lötzsch *et al.* [6]. It initially allowed specifying behavior using XML and used XML Schema to compile the source code to an intermediate representation that was interpreted by the *XABSL Engine* at runtime. Bastian Schmitz later developed a compiler in Ruby that understands a more C-like language and creates the same intermediate code [10]. It was later integrated into the official XABSL release. Risler later also integrated multi-agent features into the language [12]. The XABSL release [13] comes with an example behavior for the ASCII Soccer simulator by Balch [1], which was also used as an example for the CABSL release described in this paper (cf. Fig. 1).

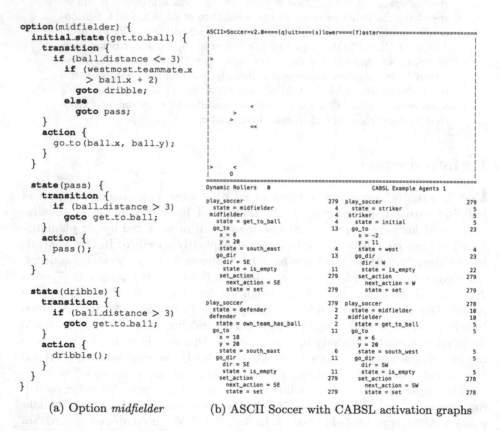

(a) Option *midfielder*   (b) ASCII Soccer with CABSL activation graphs

Fig. 1. Behavior originally developed by Lötzsch *et al.* [6] for the ASCII Soccer simulator by Balch [1] ported to CABSL

3   Approach

A robot control program is executed in cycles. In each cycle, the agent acquires new data from the environment, e.g. through sensors, runs its behavior, and then executes the commands the behavior has computed, i.e. the agent acts. This means that a robot control program is a big loop, but the behavior is just a mapping from the state of the world to actions that also considers what decisions it has made before.

3.1   Options

CABSL describes the behavior of an agent as a hierarchy of finite state machines, the so-called *options*. Each *option* consists of a number of *states*. Each state can define transitions to other states within the same option as well as the *actions* that will be executed if the option is in that state. One of the possible actions is to call another option, which lets all options form a directed acyclic graph (cf. Fig. 2a). In each execution cycle, a subset of all options is executed, i.e. the options that are reachable from the root option through the actions of their current states. This current set of options is called the *activation graph* (actually, it is a tree). Starting from the root option, each option switches its current state if necessary and then it executes the actions listed in the state that is then active. The actions can set output values or they can call other options, which again might switch their current state followed by the execution of actions. Per execution cycle, each option switches its current state at most once.

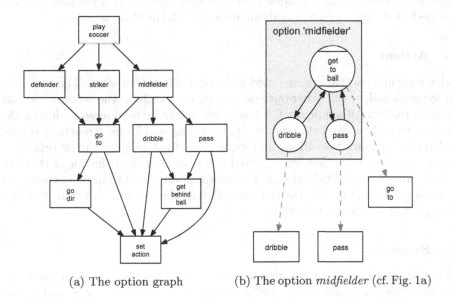

(a) The option graph   (b) The option *midfielder* (cf. Fig. 1a)

Fig. 2. The option graph

3.2 States

Options can have a number of states, e.g. *get_to_ball*, *pass*, and *dribble* in the example (cf. Figs. 1a, 2b). One of them is the *initial state*, in which the option starts when it is called for the first time and to which it falls back if it is executed again, but was not executed in the previous cycle, because no other option called it. There are two other kinds of special states, namely *target states* and *aborted states*. They are intended to signify to the calling option that the current option has either succeeded or failed. The calling option can determine, whether the last sub-option it called has reached one of these states. It is up to the programmer to define what succeeding or failing actually mean, i.e. under which conditions these states are reached.

3.3 Transitions

States can have *transitions* to other states, e.g. *get_to_ball* has transitions to *pass* and *dribble* (cf. Fig. 1a). They are basically decision trees, in which each leaf contains a `goto`-statement to another state. If none of these leafs is reached, the option stays in its current state.

An option can have a *common transition*. Its decision tree is executed before the decision tree in the current state. The decision tree of the current state functions as the `else`-branch of the decision tree in the common transition. If the common transition already results in a change of the current state, the transitions defined in the states are not checked anymore. In general, common transitions should be used sparsely, because they conflict with the general idea that each state has its own conditions under which the state is left.

3.4 Actions

States have *actions* that are executed if the option is in that state. They set output symbols and/or call other options, e.g. execute *go_to* in the state *get_to_ball* (cf. Figs. 1a, 2b). Although any C++ statements can be used in an action block, it is best to avoid control statements, i.e. branching and loops. Branching is better handled by state transitions and loops should not be used in the behavior, but rather in functions that are executed before or after the behavior or that are called from within the behavior. It is allowed to call more than one sub-option from a single state, but only the last one called can be checked for having reached a target state or an aborted state.

3.5 Symbols

All options have access to the member variables of the C++ class in the body of which they are included, e.g. *ball_distance*, *westmost_teammate_x*, *ball_x*, and *ball_y* (cf. Fig. 1a). These member variables function as *input symbols* and *output symbols*. Input symbols are usually used in the conditions for state transitions. Output symbols are set in actions.

There are four predefined symbols that can, e.g., be used in the conditions for state transitions:

option_time is the time the option was continuously active, i.e. the time since the first execution cycle it became active without being inactive afterwards. The unit of the time depends on the time values passed to the behavior engine. For instance, the time measure used in the ASCII Soccer behavior is just the number of execution cycles. The option times are shown behind the option names in Fig. 1b.

state_time is the time the option was continuously in the same state, i.e. the time since the first execution cycle it switched to that state without switching to another one afterwards. The state_time is also reset when the option becomes inactive, i.e. the state_time can never be bigger than the option_time. Again, the state times are shown behind the state names in Fig. 1b.

action_done is true if the last sub-option executed in the previous cycle was in a *target state*.

action_aborted is true if the last sub-option executed in the previous cycle was in an *aborted state*.

3.6 Parameters

Options can have *parameters*. From the perspective of the option, they are not different from input symbols. As in C++, parameters hide member variables of the surrounding class with the same name. When calling an option, its actual parameters are passed to it as they would be in C++.

However, parameters must be streamable into a standard *iostream* as text, because they are added to a data structure that allows visualizing the activation graph. Therefore, any parameter of a non-primitive datatype P must overload std::ostream& operator(std::ostream&, P). The visualization of options with parameters can be seen in Fig. 1b for the options go_to(int x, int y), go_dir(Action next_action), and set_action(Action next_action). Action is an enumeration type the values of which (mainly cardinal directions) can only be shown literally in the activation graph, because a specialized streaming operator was defined. As can be seen in the following section, the syntax of parameter definitions is different from the syntax C++ normally uses, because the C++ preprocessor must be able to extract them.

3.7 Grammar

In the following grammar, <C-ident> is a normal C++ identifier. <C-expr> is a normal C++ expression that can be used as default value for a parameter. <C-ifelse> is a decision tree. It should contain goto statements to other states (names of states are C++-labels). <C-statements> is a sequence of arbitrary C++ statements.

```
<cabsl>       = { <option> }

<option>      = option '(' <C-ident> { ',' <param-decl> } { ',' <param-dflt> } ')'
                '{'
                [ common_transition <transition> ]
                { <other-state> } initial_state <state> { <other-state> }
                '}'

<param-decl>  = '(' <type> ')' '_' <C-ident>

<param-dflt>  = '(' <type> ')' '(' <C-expr> ')' '_' <C-ident>

<other-state> = ( state | target_state | aborted_state ) <state>

<state>       = '(' C-ident ')'
                '{'
                [ transition <transition> ]
                [ action <action> ]
                '}'

<transition>  = '{' <C-ifelse> '}'

<action>      = '{' <C-statements> '}'
```

3.8   Code Generation

Technically, the C++ preprocessor translates each option to a member function (two for options with parameters) and a member variable of the surrounding class. The member variable stores the context of the option, e.g. which is its current state. The context is passed as a hidden parameter to each option with the help of a temporary wrapper object. Each state is translated to an if-statement that checks whether the state is the current one and that contains the transitions and actions. CABSL uses C++ labels as well as line numbers (__LINE__) to identify states. Therefore it is not allowed to write more than one state per line. Each state defines an unreachable goto statement to the label initial_state, which is defined by the initial state. Thereby, the C++ compiler will ensure that there is exactly one initial state if the option has at least one state. The compiler can also warn if there are unreachable states.

As all options are defined inside the same class body, where C++ supports total visibility, every option can call every other option and the sequence in which the options are defined is not important. In addition, each option has access to all member variables defined in the surrounding class. Each option sets a marker in its context whether its current state is a normal, target, or aborted state. It also preserves that marker of the last sub-option it called for the next execution cycle so that the symbols action_done and action_aborted can use it. The context also stores when the option was activated (again) and when the current state was entered to support the symbols option_time and state_time.

4   Comparison to XABSL

There are several advantages of CABSL over XABSL. The first is the very small coding overhead when using CABSL. In XABSL, all input symbols and output symbols need to be registered with the engine both on the C++ side and on the XABSL side. In CABSL, all members of the surrounding class can directly be used. XABSL only supports the datatypes *boolean*, *double*, and *enumeration*. In contrast, CABSL supports any datatype that can be used in C++. CABSL can also perform any kind of C++ computation, while XABSL requires moving computations that exceed its expressiveness to external C++ functions that again have to be registered with the engine. As CABSL is just C++, IDEs can offer auto-completion of identifiers, check the code while typing, and their integrated debuggers can be used. In addition, no custom build step is required.

However, there are also a number of drawbacks of using CABSL instead of XABSL. While XABSL has a fixed syntax and the XABSL compiler makes sure that the programmer follows it, CABSL is just a set of C++ macros that can also be used in ways that violate the intended grammar, but are still accepted by the C++ compiler. All further drawbacks listed here were never relevant for the author's team, because they concern features that were never used. CABSL is limited to C++, while XABSL also provides a Java implementation of the engine. XABSL can generate an extensive documentation in HTML. However, this feature was more useful when XABSL sources still used the XML format, which made them hard to read. For use in publications, CABSL comes with a script that can generate graphs as shown in Fig. 2. The XABSL engine supports replacing the behavior on the fly, i.e. it is possible to upload a new behavior specification to a robot while the code is running. This requires some external infrastructure for sending the code to the robot, but is in general easy to implement. CABSL does not offer a similar feature, but if desired, it would be possible to compile the CABSL behavior into a shared library, which could then be exchanged at runtime. In fact, de Haas *et al.* [4] follow a similar approach for their behavior specification language that was also compiled to native code.

5 Impact

The team B-Human has used CABSL since 2013 and has become world champion twice with behaviors written in it [9]. Some teams who base their robot control software on B-Human's yearly code releases also use it, e.g. [11,14]. For instance, the Nao Devils Dortmund state in their team report [5]: "Since 2013, we use CABSL which [...] implements XABSL as C++ macros allowing for easy access to all data structures...". The Bembelbots Frankfurt, who do not use B-Human's base system, write in their report [2]: "...later replaced by the commonly used XABSL language. Several drawbacks let us move further to the C-implementation published by B-Human [...]. Old behavior models could easily be reimplemented...". The standalone release of CABSL is exactly meant for such users, who just want to specify a robot behavior, but who do not want to use the whole B-Human system.

6 Conclusion

The paper presented the behavior specification language CABSL. It is an easy way to specify robot behavior in the form of hierarchical finite state machines in C++. It has already been used by several other RoboCup teams. It is now available as an open source standalone release that allows using its most recent version without using the B-Human framework [8].

References

1. Balch, T.: The ASCII robot soccer homepage (1995). https://www.cs.cmu.edu/~trb/soccer
2. Brast, J.C., et al.: Team report 2016 (2016). http://www.jrl.cs.uni-frankfurt.de/web/wp-content/uploads/2016/12/TeamReport_Bembelbots_2016.pdf
3. Georgievski, I., Aiello, M.: An overview of hierarchical task network planning. CoRR abs/1403.7426 (2014). http://arxiv.org/abs/1403.7426
4. de Haas, T.J., Laue, T., Röfer, T.: A scripting-based approach to robot behavior engineering using hierarchical generators. In: Proceedings of the 2012 IEEE International Conference on Robotics and Automation (ICRA). IEEE (2012)
5. Hofmann, M., et al.: Nao Devils Dortmund team report 2016. Technical report. Technische Universität Dortmund (2016). https://github.com/NaoDevils/CodeRelease2016/blob/master/TeamReportNaoDevils2016.pdf
6. Lötzsch, M., Risler, M., Jüngel, M.: XABSL - a pragmatic approach to behavior engineering. In: Proceedings of IEEE/RSJ International Conference of Intelligent Robots and Systems (IROS), pp. 5124–5129, Beijing, China (2006)
7. Nilsson, N.: Teleo-reactive programs for agent control. J. Artif. Intell. Res. 1, 139–158 (1994)
8. Röfer, T.: CABSL - C-based agent behavior specification language (2017). https://github.com/bhuman/CABSL
9. Röfer, T., et al.: B-Human team report and code release 2013 (2013). https://www.b-human.de/downloads/publications/2013/CodeRelease2013.pdf
10. Röfer, T., et al.: Germanteam robocup 2005 (2005). http://www.informatik.uni-bremen.de/kogrob/papers/GT2005.pdf
11. Riccio, F.: Programming NAO-robots (2014). http://www.dis.uniroma1.it/~nardi/Didattica/CAI/matdid/RobotProgrammingNao.pdf. Slides from a lecture at Sapienza Universitá di Roma
12. Risler, M.: Behavior control for single and multiple autonomous agents based on hierarchical finite state machines. Fortschritt-berichte vdi, Technische Universität Darmstadt, 15 May 2009. http://tuprints.ulb.tu-darmstadt.de/2046
13. Risler, M., Lötzsch, M., Jüngel, M., Krause, T.: XABSL - the extensible agent behavior specification language (2009). http://www.xabsl.de
14. Sterner, N.A.: Behavior programming of the goal keeper using CABSL, semester thesis, nomadZ project reports, ETH Zürich (2014). https://www1.ethz.ch/robocup/ProjectReports/2014_Nico_Behavior_Programming_of_the_Goalkeeper_Using_CABSL

Secured Offline Authentication on Industrial Mobile Robots Using Biometric Data

Sarah Haas[1](✉), Thomas Ulz[2], and Christian Steger[2]

[1] Development Center Graz, Infineon Technologies Austria AG, Graz, Austria
sarah.haas@infineon.com
[2] Institute for Technical Informatics, Graz University of Technology, Graz, Austria
{thomas.ulz,steger}@tugraz.at

Abstract. The increased usage of mobile robots in the industrial context entails higher safety risks for employees on the production floor. To enable safety, the usage of security concepts on industrial mobile robots is essential. One step towards security is authentication that is necessary to prevent unauthorized people from manipulating an industrial mobile robot's software or configuration. Traditional authentication schemes that utilize username and password are not feasible for industrial mobile robots as either (a) a remote connection would be necessary to check the credentials or (b) the credentials need to be checked locally on the robot. Remote connections are problematic due to connectivity problems similar to them at RoboCup Logistics League competitions. If the credentials need to be checked on the robot, the usernames and passwords of all authorized people need to be stored and maintained there. As both possibilities are not feasible for industrial mobile robots, we propose an offline authentication approach that uses biometric data to authenticate a user on a mobile robot. The approach uses expiring passwords and a smart card to authenticate authorized people on the mobile robot. The smart card is equipped with a fingerprint reader to check that only authorized people are allowed to authenticate at a mobile robot. To show that the approach is able to provide secured authentication, a threat analysis is performed.

1 Introduction

In the last decades, production facilities introduced automation to produce more products in less time and to increase the production efficiency and with that decrease costs. However, customer demands changed from traditional products to highly customized products. These customized products require the production of small batch sizes which cannot be achieved in traditional mass production facilities. This trend of customized products started with the beginning of the *fourth industrial revolution* [19]. In this context, movements such as *Industry 4.0* [2] try to develop concepts for future *smart factories* [22] to reinvent highly flexible production in industrial countries. One of the developments from the

© Springer Nature Switzerland AG 2018
H. Akiyama et al. (Eds.): RoboCup 2017, LNAI 11175, pp. 143–155, 2018.
https://doi.org/10.1007/978-3-030-00308-1_12

Industry 4.0 movement is the *cyber physical system* (CPS) [17]. A CPS is a physical process controlled and monitored by some software and can even be connected to the Internet.

The increased automation in factories entailed an increased usage of robots for industrial applications which are a form of CPSs as they use sensor and actuators to interact with the physical world and are controlled by a computer system. Industrial robots for automation are widely used in manufacturing nowadays, but the importance of Industrial Mobile Robots (IMR) also increased in the last years due to their flexibility [18]. This flexibility can be seen in the RoboCup Logistics League Sponsored by Festo [16] (RCLL) where a production floor is simulated where IMRs need to fulfill tasks in order to manufacture products. The tasks in the RCLL are limited to transportation of material between machines that manipulate the material. These transportation tasks are a very realistic scenario also in real production facilities. In real production facilities, humans will also move on the production floor together with the IMRs similar to the referees in the RCLL. Due to the fact that IMRs and humans share the same environment, safety risks arise that are not present when material is moved using static conveyor systems. As IMRs are controlled by computer systems, a precondition for safety is the security of the computer system [5, 12].

One major step towards security is authentication where humans or machines need to prove their identity in order to get authorized to access a system. In the context of IMRs, authentication is a crucial topic as it is possible that external staff such as custodial or maintenance staff are present on the production floor. As a precaution, the external staff is assumed to be not trustworthy and might manipulate an IMR's interface or change its configuration. These manipulations might lead to safety threats for employees on the production floor. Therefore, authentication on the IMRs is necessary to prevent unauthorized people from performing malicious actions on an IMR. However, traditional username and password based authentication schemes are not feasible in this scenario as it is either necessary to

(a) remotely connect to a server to check the user credentials or
(b) to store the credentials locally on the robot to check them.

The remote connection might suffer from connectivity problems due to the wireless connection as it can be seen in the RCLL. Storing the credentials locally on the robot poses a high maintenance effort as the credentials need to be updated each time a new user is authorized to access the robot and each time a user's authorization is taken away. Both of these problems show that a traditional credential-based authentication is nearly infeasible for this scenario. Therefore, we propose a mechanism using one-time passwords, a smart card, and biometrics in the form of a fingerprint to authenticate users on IMRs. The one-time passwords in combination with a time value are used to generate passwords that expire after one usage to avoid security problems regarding revealed passwords. The smart card is used to generate and store the one-time passwords securely. The fingerprint is used to authenticate the user on the smart card to overcome issues with stolen or lost smart cards. The mentioned time needs to be synchronized to enable the authentication. The synchronization is done by using the machines on the production floor as a gateway into the network to avoid the necessity of a direct wireless connection to a gateway.

To sum up, the contributions of this paper are:

- An authentication approach that allows users to authenticate on an IMR without the need for traditional credentials
- A method to synchronize the time using equipment on the production floor.

The remainder of this paper is structured as follows. Section 2 discusses the related work and background regarding topics such as authentication and one-time-passwords. In Sect. 3, the authentication approach is shown in detail. Furthermore, the synchronization of the time, as well as the recovery behavior in case of a not synchronized time, are shown. In Sect. 4, a security analysis was made to show that the proposed authentication approach prevents unauthorized people from accessing the system. Finally, the paper is concluded in Sect. 5.

2 Background and Related Work

2.1 Authentication on Mobile Robots

To the best knowledge of the authors, the only existing user authentication approach using biometric data on robots was proposed by Kim et al. [8]. Kim et al. use a vision-based method to authenticate users by recognizing users faces, clothes colors and body height. The recognized biometrics are combined to identify users, but the method is also able to identify users when only the body height is available. However, each user's data needs to be stored on each robot to be able to identify them.

A more lightweight approach addresses authentication of mobile agents on other mobile agents [9]. The main differences to the previous approach are the use of shared secret keys instead of biometrics for authentication and that agents authenticate on other agents. The authors state that public key cryptography cannot be used in such authentication scenarios due to the fact that they are slow and due to the occurring overhead. The shared key in combination with some other properties such as the agent ID is used to create a ticket that can be verified with the same shared key. A ticket created once does not become invalid which might make it more vulnerable to attacks.

A very interesting approach was proposed by Wael Adi where some kind of electronic DNA (eDNA) is generated for each robot for authentication [1]. The author uses physically unclonable functions to create a unique eDNA for each robot. The eDNA is generated initially by key derivation and hashing of some initial secret keying material. Then an eDNA chain is generated by creating so-called identity modules that are used to identify a specific part of the robot. Using those modules, anyone can validate the identity of the robot by challenging the module. Later, the robots eDNA changes with its interactions. To authenticate, the robot needs to prove that it participated in a particular event that is stored in its eDNA chain. This approach is very interesting but also very complex and requires knowledge of the whole domain a robot moves in to be able to verify the robot's identity.

2.2 Biometric Authentication

Clancy et al. [3] proposed a smart card based authentication algorithm that uses fingerprints to identify users. First, a fingerprint scanner on a terminal is used to capture a user's fingerprint. Then, a numeric template is generated from the fingerprint and sent to the smart card as well as a digit that should be signed. Afterward, the smart card verifies the template, generates a signature for the sent digit and sends it back to the terminal where the signature is verified, and the access is granted. The main contribution of this paper, however, was an efficient and more accurate algorithm to detect the fingerprints and decrease the number of false positives. Many approaches try to improve the quality of fingerprint checking such as [7,20] or [21] to overcome issues with performance, false positives or attacks such as template attacks.

Li et al. [11] proposed an approach for biometric-based remote authentication of users using smart cards where both smart card and server need to prove their identity. In their approach, the user has to register on a server with his identity (i.e. username), password and biometric data (i.e. fingerprint). Afterward, the user receives a smart card that can be used for authentication. Both smart card and server send messages to each other containing random numbers. Both try to verify the message and authenticate each other if the message is correct.

2.3 Secure Element

A secure element is a hardware device that is used to store confidential or cryptographic data securely, and provides tamper-resistance. Secure elements might also be able to perform operations such as computing cryptographic hashes or encrypting data. These secure elements are used to protect any kind of confidential data against physical attacks. Examples are chip cards used for banking applications or trusted platform modules [10] in laptops to protect passwords or the firmware.

2.4 One-Time Passwords

The one-time password (OTP) concept was invented by Haller [6] in 1994 to overcome the issues with usernames and passwords that are transmitted in plain text and are therefore prone to eavesdropping attacks. The idea was to compute a hash of the credentials to prevent adversaries from revealing the plain text passwords. OTPs were later also considered as a solution to prevent replay attacks where an attacker captures the hashed or encrypted login information and repeats to send it to the targeted system later in time to gain access to the targeted system without knowing the actual login information. Replay attacks were prevented by adding a moving factor to the hash such as a counter or time value.

M'Raihi et al. [13] proposed an HMAC-based one-time password algorithm (HOTP) that adds additional security to OTPs by introducing a counter to generate different OTPs even if the secret key or password is always the same. HMAC is a message authentication code that relies on cryptographic hash functions. To compute an OTP with HOTP, the secret key and the current counter are passed to the hash function of the HMAC. Afterward, the counter is increased by a specific value. The generated OTP is truncated and presented to the user on a token. The truncated OTP must then be typed into the system the user wants to authenticate on.

In contrast to HOTP that is an event-based algorithm where the counter changes with each newly generated OTP, TOTP is based on a time value instead of events [14]. The principle of TOTP is similar to HOTP which means that an HMAC using a secret key and a time value are used as parameters for the hash function. As already said, the moving factor for TOTP is a time value that increases continuously and does not depend on events. However, TOTP also requires a token that displays the truncated OTP to type it into the system a user wants to authenticate on.

3   Authentication Approach

The authentication approach proposed in this paper checks that only authorized people gain access to the IMRs. As traditional username and password based authentication approaches are not feasible in this scenario, the approach uses a smart card with an integrated fingerprint reader and a secure element on the IMR to authenticate a user. The proposed approach is based on TOTP [14] but does not use tokens and does not require the user to input a password into the IMR. To authenticate, the user only needs to place the smart card near the IMR's NFC module as it can be seen in Fig. 1.

Furthermore, several preconditions need to be met to perform an authentication:

- **Backend:** System holding the serial numbers, secret keys and time values of each IMR. The backend is able to generate and store a derived key for each IMR. This is done by providing the IMR's serial number and secret key as parameters for a strong cryptographic hash function such as SHA-256 [4]. The reason for derived keys is that one single cryptographically strong master key can be used to generate a bunch of cryptographically strong derived keys. It also increases the security of the whole approach by using individual keys on every robot.
- **User:** Staff that has access to the backend to store the time values and derived keys on the smart card.

- **IMR:** Robot equipped with an NFC module with an LED for notifications and a secure element holding the derived key of the robot and increasing the time value.
- **Smart Card:** A secure element that stores the derived key and time value capable of computing an OTP. It is equipped with a fingerprint reader and an NFC antenna. The time value stored on the smart card is one that lies within the time range Δt when the user tries to authenticate on the IMR. Δt can be a range of several hours.

Fig. 1. Authentication of a user on a robot using NFC and a fingerprint reader on a smart card.

3.1 Biometric Authentication Approach

The authentication approach consists of two steps. In step one the user needs to authenticate himself on the smart card to unlock the computation of the OTP. Step two is to send the computed OTP to the IMR and verify it. In the following passage, the authentication will be described in detail with references to the numbers in Fig. 2.

(1) Independent from any authentication or other operation, the IMR always computes batches of OTPs, meaning that the IMR computes a number of OTPs for a specific time range Δt that can be changed by authorized staff. The IMR might, for example, compute 36 OTPs for a Δt of 3 h where one OTP is computed for every 5 min. The computation of batches of OTPs is done to make the verification of an OTP from a smart card possible as the smart card is not able to increase the time due to the fact that it can only compute OTPs when in the range of an NFC field. To compute the OTPs, the time value and the derived key are provided as parameters to a strong cryptographic hash function such as SHA-256. The output of the hash function represents the OTP. (2) The authentication is initiated by the user who places his finger on the fingerprint sensor and brings the smart card in the NFC field provided by the IMR. (3) The smart card verifies the fingerprint by comparing the input fingerprint with the

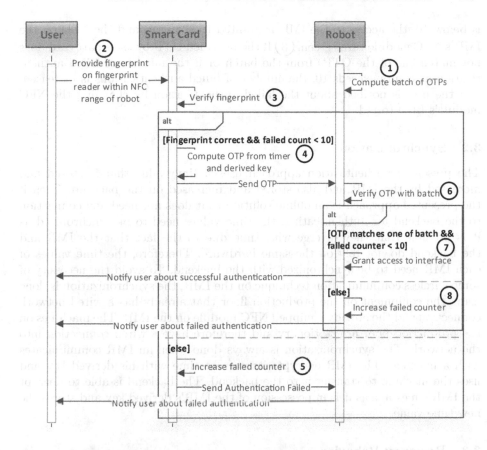

Fig. 2. Sequence diagram of the authentication approach.

one stored on the smart card's memory. ④ The smart card counts the authentication attempts that failed when users provided their fingerprint. If the number of failed authentication attempts is smaller than 10 and the provided fingerprint matches the one stored on the smart card, the OTP is computed. The OTP is computed by providing the IMR's derived key and the time value stored on the smart card as parameters for the hash function. The hash is computed by the smart card and then sent to the IMR for verification. ⑤ In the case that the number of failed attempts exceeds 10 or the provided fingerprint does not match the one stored on the smart card, the number of failed authentications is increased by 1 and the authentication is not performed. The notification of a failed authentication is sent to the IMR to inform the user about the failed authentication attempt by the IMR using an LED that turns red. ⑥ The IMR verifies the OTP by comparing it to the batch-generated OTPs of the last time period Δt. ⑦ The IMR also counts the failed authentication attempts where the provided OTP was not valid. If the OTP from the smart card matches one of the batch-generated OTPs and the number of failed authentication attempts is below 10, the access to the IMR is granted to the user, and the LED on the IMR's NFC module turns green. ⑧ If the provided OTP by the smart card does not match one of the OTPs from the batch or if the number of failed authentication attempts exceeds 10, the number of failed authentications is increased, and the user is notified about the failed authentication by changing the NFC module's LED to red.

3.2   Synchronization

The presented authentication approach uses a time value that is stored and increased by the IMR and also stored and increased on the backend. Even if the presented approach is an offline solution that does not need any connection to the backend for authenticating, the time values need to be synchronized as it is possible that they diverge with time due to the fact that the IMR and the backend do not rely on the same hardware. Therefore, the time values of each IMR need to be synchronized with the backend. To avoid the necessity of some wireless communication technique on the IMR, the synchronization is done using the equipment on the production floor that already has a wired network connection and the already equipped NFC module on the IMR. The machines on the production floor are stationary and therefore have a wired connection into the network. The synchronization is always done when an IMR communicates with a machine. The IMR encrypts its current time with his derived key and uses the machine to transfer it to the backend. The backend is able to decrypt the IMR's message as it is in possession of the IMR's derived key and stores the new time value.

3.3   Recovery Behavior

The synchronization behavior is necessary to ensure that the IMR's time and the backend's time are almost equal. However, it can happen that an IMR has a malfunction and is not able to synchronize. If the time values diverge in this case, it would not be possible to authenticate on the IMR anymore. Therefore, a recovery behavior is necessary to enable a user to authenticate on the IMR even if the times on the IMR and the backend diverge. The owner of the IMRs is provided with a recovery key that can be used to enable authentication even if the time values diverge. To recover the time value, the recovery key that is stored on a smart card is provided to the IMR. If the recovery key is correct, the LED on the NFC module turns green. Then the user must put the smart card holding the derived key of the IMR in the NFC range of the IMR. The IMR sends its current time value once to the provided smart card. With the value, the smart card can then perform the normal authentication steps. This recovery behavior is feasible as the user does not need to reinstall the time on the smart card over the backend. Furthermore, the recovery behavior is secured due to the fact that another smart card is necessary to reactivate the authentication. A condition, however, is that the user trying to gain access to the IMR is not the same user that holds the recovery key.

Another recovery needs to be done when the number of authentication attempts on the IMR is reached. This can also be done using the recovery key. The number of failed authentications is simply reset when the recovery key is provided to the IMR. Afterward, the normal authentication process can be performed.

It is not necessary to define a recovery behavior for the smart card as disabling the smart card after too many attempts is a security mechanism. Furthermore, the smart card can be reinstalled with a correct derived key and a correct time value.

4 Evaluation

4.1 Comparison to Other Approaches

Table 1 shows a feature comparison between the proposed approach and three state-of-the-art approaches described in Sect. 2. The table's cells are contain Ys and Ns. Y indicates the presence of the feature, N indicates the feature's absence. Furthermore, the cells are marked red or green to show whether this feature's presence or absence in the approach indicates a weakness. Red means that the feature is a weakness, green means that the feature is a strength. The chosen features indicate the security level of the approach as well as the approach's feasibility in real life when authenticating offline. Expiring passwords make it significantly harder for adversaries to hack the robot. Two-factor authentication adds another level of security as a correct fingerprint and smart card are necessary. A recovery behavior increases the approach's feasibility. Individual user data on the robot is accompanied by a high maintenance effort when adding or removing authorized people. Offline authentication overcomes issues with wireless communication regarding connectivity.

The table shows that there is no approach yet that satisfies as many features as the one proposed in this paper.

Table 1. Comparison of different state-of-the-art approaches with the proposed authentication approach.

	Kim et al. [9]	Kim et al. [8]	Li et al. [11]	This Paper
Expiring Password/Ticket	N	N	N	Y
Two-factor authentication	N	N	Y	Y
Recovery behavior	N	N	N	Y
Individual user data on robot	Y	Y	N	N
Offline authentication	Y	Y	N	Y

4.2   Threat Analysis

To show the security level of the proposed approach, a threat analysis [15] was performed. A threat analysis is used to list **Entities (E)**, **Assets (A)** that need protection, possible **Threats (T)**, necessary **Assumptions (As)** as well as **Countermeasures (C)** and **Residual Risks (R)** that occur in the approach.

In the beginning, it is necessary to identify the entities and make assumptions regarding their trustworthiness. The entity **(E1)** User is assumed to be not trustworthy and might be a possible adversary. The entity **(E2)** Smart Card is assumed to be trustworthy. The entity **(E3)** IMR is assumed to be curious. Entity (E4) secure element is assumed to be trustworthy. Entity **(E5)** malicious adversary is assumed to be not trustworthy and might be able to perform attacks on equipment.

Using the entities, the assets that need to be protected need to be discussed. **(A1)** Keys on the IMR and the smart card need to be protected. Loss of the keys might enable an adversary to reveal the time value and access an IMR. **(A2)** Time value should be protected as the loss might make attacks easier. **(A3)** Interfaces on the IMR need to be protected from unauthorized usage not to endanger employees.

Before discussing the threats, several assumptions regarding the authentication approach need to be stated. First, (As1) the IMR uses a secure element to store the derived key, and check and generate the OTPs. Second, (As2) the derived key was already stored on the IMR's secure element. Third, (As3) the time value is synchronized between IMR and backend. Fourth, (As4) it is assumed that the backend is sufficiently secured and therefore, the threat analysis will not address it.

For each threat, the assets and entities, as well as the possible countermeasures and residual risks, are listed. The residual risks are threats that cannot be mitigated by the proposed approach.

(T1) Intentional and unintentional backdoors in secure element and **(T2)** wrongly implemented/weak cryptography on the secure element both concern the entities (E2), (E3) and (E4) and threaten the assets (A1) and (A2). Both threats can be secured by (C1) as secure elements are certified for a specific security level. The certificate proves the correctness of the cryptographic implementation and that no undocumented backdoors exist.

(T2) Loss/theft of Smart Card concerns the entities (E1), (E2) and (E5) and threatens the assets (A1), (A2) and (A3). The smart card is protected (C2) due to the necessity to authenticate on the card using a fingerprint where an adversary cannot simply use the smart card for authentication on the IMR. The time value is (C3) as the data on the smart card expires, and the authentication cannot be performed afterward. (C4) Protects the derived key and time value as the smart card is tamper resistant. The limited authentication attempts are (C5) as it shuts down brute-force attacks.

(T4) Manipulation of the time value on smart card or IMR concerns entities (E1), (E2), (E3), (E4) and (E5), and threatens the asset (A2) and (A3). (C6) Protects the authentication as a wrong generates invalid OTPs. The time value is stored on a secure element that aims to protect the time value from any manipulations (C7).

(T6) Replay attacks with same OTP concern entities (E1), (E2), (E3), (E4) and (E5), and threatens the asset (A3). This threat is protected by (C8) as the OTP becomes invalid after the first usage due to the counter for several authentications with the same time value.

(T7) Physical attacks on IMR and smart card concerns entities (E2), (E3), (E4) and (E5) and threatens the assets (A1), (A2) and (A3). The secure elements on IMR and smart card provide tamper resistance which means that adversaries are hindered from revealing the key (C9).

(T8) DoS attack on an IMR concerns entities (E1), (E3) and (E5) and threatens the asset (A3). The limited number of authentication attempts mitigates DoS attacks (C10).

(T9) Remote attacks on the authentication process concerns entities (E1), (E2), (E3) and (E5) and threatens the asset (A3). The short communication range of NFC limits the possibilities for remote attacks significantly (C11).

The given threat analysis is not exhaustive and addresses the most important threats identified by the authors. However, the analysis shows that no residual risks remain for the proposed approach.

5 Conclusion

In this work, an offline authentication approach for industrial mobile robots using a smart card and biometric data was proposed. The approach is used to overcome the connectivity problems with remote authentication schemes and the maintenance issues with traditional username and password based schemes. The approach uses a derived key and a time value to generate one-time passwords that expire and do not rely on a specific user that reduces the maintenance effort significantly compared to user dependent passwords. The evaluation emphasizes the security features of the proposed approach and shows the feasibility compared to other approaches.

Acknowledgment. The work/A part of the work has been performed in the project Power Semiconductor and Electronics Manufacturing 4.0 (SemI40), under grant agreement No 692466. The project is co-funded by grants from Austria, Germany, Italy, France, Portugal and - Electronic Component Systems for European Leadership Joint Undertaking (ECSEL JU).

References

1. Adi, W.: Mechatronic security and robot authentication. In: 2009 Symposium on Bio-inspired Learning and Intelligent Systems for Security, pp. 77–82. IEEE (2009)
2. Bauernhansl, T., Ten Hompel, M., Vogel-Heuser, B.: Industrie 4.0 in Produktion, Automatisierung und Logistik: Anwendung · Technologien · Migration. Springer, Heidelberg (2014). https://doi.org/10.1007/978-3-658-04682-8

3. Clancy, T.C., Kiyavash, N., Lin, D.J.: Secure smartcardbased fingerprint authentication. In: Proceedings of the 2003 ACM SIGMM Workshop on Biometrics Methods and Applications WBMA 2003, pp. 45–52. ACM (2003)
4. Gilbert, H., Handschuh, H.: Security analysis of SHA-256 and sisters. In: Matsui, M., Zuccherato, R.J. (eds.) SAC 2003. LNCS, vol. 3006, pp. 175–193. Springer, Heidelberg (2004). https://doi.org/10.1007/978-3-540-24654-1_13
5. Grieco, L.A., et al.: IoT-aided robotics applications: technological implications, target domains and open issues. Comput. Commun. **54**, 32–47 (2014)
6. Haller, N.: The S/KEY one-time password system. In: Proceedings of the Internet Society Symposium on Network and Distributed Systems (1994)
7. Jin, A.T.B., Ling, D.N.C., Goh, A.: Biohashing: two factor authentication featuring fingerprint data and tokenised random number. Pattern Recogn. **37**(11), 2245–2255 (2004)
8. Kim, D., Lee, J., Yoon, H.S., Cha, E.Y.: A non-cooperative user authentication system in robot environments. IEEE Trans. Consum. Electron. **53**(2), 804–811 (2007)
9. Kim, J., Kim, G.S., Eom, Y.I.: Lightweight mobile agent authentication scheme for home network environments. In: Zhang, J., He, J.-H., Fu, Y. (eds.) CIS 2004. LNCS, vol. 3314, pp. 853–859. Springer, Heidelberg (2004). https://doi.org/10.1007/978-3-540-30497-5_132
10. Kinney, S.L.: Trusted Platform Module Basics: Using TPM in Embedded Systems. Newnes, Amsterdam (2006)
11. Li, C.T., Hwang, M.S.: An efficient biometrics-based remote user authentication scheme using smart cards. J. Netw. Comput. Appl. **33**(1), 1–5 (2010)
12. Line, M.B., Nordland, O., Røstad, L., Tøndel, I.A.: Safety vs security? In: Proceedings of the 8th International Conference on Probabilistic Safety Assessment and Management (PSAM 2006), New Orleans, USA (2006)
13. M'Raihi, D., Bellare, M., Hoornaert, F., Naccache, D., Ranen, O.: HOTP: an HMAC-based one-time password algorithm. Technical report, RFC4226 (2005)
14. M'Raihi, D., Machani, S., Pei, M., Rydell, J.: TOTP: time-based one-time password algorithm. Technical report, RFC6238 (2011)
15. Myagmar, S., Lee, A.J., Yurcik, W.: Threat modeling as a basis for security requirements. In: Symposium on Requirements Engineering for Information Security (SREIS), vol. 2005, pp. 1–8. Citeseer (2005)
16. Niemueller, T., Ewert, D., Reuter, S., Ferrein, A., Jeschke, S., Lakemeyer, G.: RoboCup Logistics league sponsored by festo: a competitive factory automation testbed. In: Jeschke, S., Isenhardt, I., Hees, F., Henning, K. (eds.) Automation, Communication and Cybernetics in Science and Engineering 2015/2016, pp. 605–618. Springer, Cham (2016). https://doi.org/10.1007/978-3-319-42620-4_45
17. Rajkumar, R.R., Lee, I., Sha, L., Stankovic, J.: Cyber-physical systems: the next computing revolution. In: Proceedings of the 47th Design Automation Conference, pp. 731–736. ACM (2010)
18. Schneider, S., et al.: Design and development of a benchmarking testbed for the factory of the future. In: 2015 IEEE 20th Conference on Emerging Technologies & Factory Automation (ETFA), pp. 1–7. IEEE (2015)
19. Schwab, K.: The Fourth Industrial Revolution. Penguin, London (2017)
20. Sutcu, Y., Sencar, H.T., Memon, N.: A secure biometric authentication scheme based on robust hashing. In: Proceedings of the 7th Workshop on Multimedia and Security, MM#38; Sec 2005, pp. 111–116. ACM (2005)

21. Tuyls, P., Akkermans, A.H.M., Kevenaar, T.A.M., Schrijen, G.-J., Bazen, A.M., Veldhuis, R.N.J.: Practical biometric authentication with template protection. In: Kanade, T., Jain, A., Ratha, N.K. (eds.) AVBPA 2005. LNCS, vol. 3546, pp. 436–446. Springer, Heidelberg (2005). https://doi.org/10.1007/11527923_45
22. Zuehlke, D.: SmartFactory - towards a factory-of-things. Ann. Rev. Control **34**(1), 129–138 (2010)

Follow Me: Real-Time in the Wild Person Tracking Application for Autonomous Robotics

Thomas Weber[✉], Sergey Triputen, Michael Danner, Sascha Braun,
Kristiaan Schreve, and Matthias Rätsch

Reutlingen University, 72762 Reutlingen, Germany
{thomas.weber,sergey.triputen}@reutlingen-university.de
https://www.reutlingen-university.de/home/

Abstract. In the last 20 years there have been major advances in autonomous robotics. In IoT (Industry 4.0), mobile robots require more intuitive interaction possibilities with humans in order to expand its field of applications. This paper describes a user-friendly setup, which enables a person to lead the robot in an unknown environment. The environment has to be perceived by means of sensory input. For realizing a cost and resource efficient *Follow Me* application we use a single monocular camera as low-cost sensor. For efficient scaling of our Simultaneous Localization and Mapping (SLAM) algorithm, we integrate an inertial measurement unit (IMU) sensor. With the camera input we detect and track a person. We propose combining state of the art deep learning with Convolutional Neural Network (CNN) and SLAM algorithms functionality on the same input camera image. Based on the output robot navigation is possible. This work presents the specification, workflow for an efficient development of the *Follow Me* application. Our application's delivered point clouds are also used for surface construction. For demonstration, we use our platform *SCITOS G5* equipped with the afore mentioned sensors. Preliminary tests show the system works robustly in the wild (This work is partially supported by a grant of the BMBF FHprofUnt program, no. 03FH049PX5).

Keywords: Mobile robotics · 3D perception · Navigation
Human-robot interaction · Person tracking · Machine learning · CNN
SLAM

1 Introduction

1.1 Motivation

Robotics navigation and control is a complex task to deal with. Robust detection and tracking of people in autonomous robotics applications is a key task nowadays. It is also essential to intuitive human machine interaction. Our aim is providing an easy to implement, flexible and adaptable application for this

H. Akiyama et al. (Eds.): RoboCup 2017, LNAI 11175, pp. 156–167, 2018.
https://doi.org/10.1007/978-3-030-00308-1_13

task. One of our main goals is a robust application for in the wild usage. For head detection, person tracking and robot navigation there are several projects providing great and useful solutions. This work combines them to an affordable complete system that performs very well. The paper is structured as follows: First, we describe in a broad overview how our application works. Next, we dive deeper into theory, our approaches and techniques used in the application and state further work and possible enhancements on these approaches. This is followed up by instructions for implementation, hardware and our robot platform *SCITOS G5*, produced by MetraLabs GmbH. Finally, we show our application in early experiments.

1.2   Related Work

Different approaches on person detection and tracking involving autonomous robotics were proposed over time, such as [2,18]. However, they often lack simplicity and require multiple sensory inputs. For sensory input, we opt for using only a single low-cost consumer monocular web cam, in our case the *Sony PlayStation Eye Camera* and a common IMU chip package, a *Bosch BNO055*. This way our application can be deployed on existing setups inexpensively. The approach of the head detector used in our work is inspired by the success of deep Convolutional Neural Networks (CNN). First successfully introduced by Krizhevsky [15] by winning the LSVRC-2012 ImageNet challenge, CNNs dominate in all vision task challenges today. Convolutional Neural Networks is a machine learning approach for computer vision tasks and were already used for head detection by [26]. Our detector is based on the Single Shot Detector (SSD) from Liu [16], which is more advanced than Faster R-CNN [21]. Our internal research group is involved in SLAM [22] and face recognition experiments, so we have knowledge transfer from our work to other projects.

1.3   Purposed Solution

The main steps in our workflow to realize the *Follow Me* application are shown in Fig. 1: First, we take a 2D camera image frame and use it for head detection via a CNN and create bounding boxes. We implement calibration and scaling to real-world dimensions for LSD-SLAM algorithm on embedded hardware *NVIDIA Jetson TK1 developer kit* by utilizing a *Bosch BNO055* IMU. This setup allows us to generate real-world scaled point clouds. The point cloud is reduced to a volume of interest including only the tracked head. To create a surface out of these points we use a Poisson surface reconstruction algorithm. We propose using the results of those processes to construct the points for the head and calculate the head position with respect to the current robot position. We transform the CNN based 2D head detection to 3D world space coordinates. To improve the world space coordinates, we show a workflow to fuse the SLAM and CNN estimated position and track a person. Finally, the positional data is sent to motion controller feedback algorithms. The main contribution of this work is a robust *Follow Me* application based on deep learning CNN, SLAM and a 3D morphable face model (3DMM) [11]. We observe that a fusion of 2D based and 3D SLAM based world space coordination improves the estimation between the robot and the person. The core novelties of the paper are: (1) *Follow Me* using a single monocular low-cost webcam (2) a CNN based surround head detection; this means the occiput is also recognized (3) Taking advantage of scaled SLAM with IMU to improve distance estimation and fusion (4) Robust tracking of person instances using 3D points and 2D transformation fused.

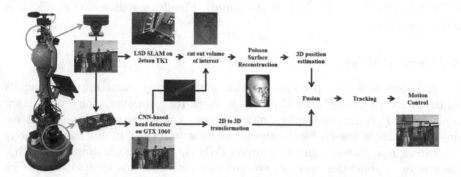

Fig. 1. Workflow of *Follow Me*: 2D image used for parallel CNN head detection and LSD-SLAM point cloud generation. Point cloud reduced to volume of head based on CNN bounding box. 3D surface reconstruction and 2D transformation for head world space coordinates. Fusion of SLAM and CNN head position. Tracking and motion control.

2   2D CNN-Based and 3D SLAM-Based Person Tracking

2.1   Single Shot MultiBox Convolutional Neural Network Based Head Detector

Our detector CNN uses an SSD approach from Liu [16], which needs only a single forward feed for detection of heads on a 2D RGB image, recorded with a low-cost webcam. Several feature maps with different scales are used. Each box predicts the shape and the confidence of the class. Based on this information the bounding boxes are estimated. The base for the network is a VGG-16 network [24]. The feature layers for the feature maps are connected to the end of the network. This results in a high improvement of the speed.

2.2   Training and Evaluation

For training the network the HollywoodHeads Dataset [1] is used. This dataset contains 224,740 video frames from Hollywood movies with annotations of bounding boxes of the heads. Some examples from the data set are shown in Fig. 2(a, b). The data set is split in a training set which contains 216,719 frames, a validation set which contains 6,719 frames and a test set, which contains 1,302 frames. This split is proposed in [26]. The *Caffe* framework [12] is used for training and deployment. The training was performed on a *GeForce GTX 1060 6* GB on *Ubuntu 14.04 LTS*. We achieve 59.7% Mean Average Precision (mPA). Field tests show, that the SSD detector is stable, even under harsh conditions, as Fig. 2(c, d) shows.

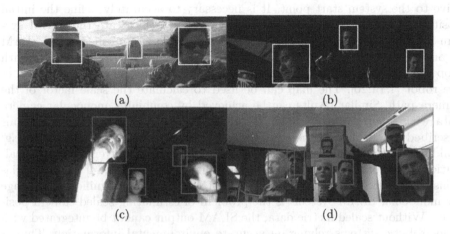

(a)   (b)

(c)   (d)

Fig. 2. Example frames from the HollywoodHeads data set [1] (a, b) and detections results of our trained SSD network (c, d)

2.3   Coordination Transformation

The CNN detection takes place in 2D. The position of the head in world space coordinates plays a major role in robust tracking. Persons crossing can cause problems e.g. when people cross each other at different distances from the camera. To avoid this, a transformation of the detection coordinates in the 2D image into 3D world space coordinates is done. This improves the tracking and enables differentiating between crossing tracks in 2D image coordinates when using 3D world space coordinates. The knowledge of the size of the bounding box from SSD is used to estimate the distance of the head in real world coordinates. Therefore, a data series is recorded representing the distance in relationship to the area of the bounding box. Based on this data a function is estimated which approximates the relationship between the *area* of the bounding box in *pixels* and the distance in world space *cm*: $z_{world} = 15022 \cdot area^{-0.525}$. For the estimation of the x and y in world space, z_{world} is used in calculations $x_{size} = 2 \cdot z_{world} \cdot arctan(\alpha_{FoV}/2)$ and likewise $y_{size} = 2 \cdot z_{world} \cdot arctan(\alpha_{FoV}/2) \cdot 2/3$, which are depended on the used camera sensor parameters. Based on the *area*, relations of pixels in the image to the size in real world in cm are $x_{relation} = x_{size}/x_{camRes}$ and $y_{relation} = y_{size}/y_{camRes}$. The real world coordinates are calculated based on relations between pixels in the image to the size in real world and the image coordinates:

$x_{world} = x_{relation} \cdot x_{imagePos} - x_{size}/2$ and $y_{world} = y_{relation} \cdot y_{imagePos} - y_{size}/2$. Finally, we have a world space position $[x_{world}, y_{world}, z_{world}]$ with the camera sensor centre-point as origin.

2.4 SLAM-Based 3D Head Extraction

Most positioning, orientation and odometry systems provide only pose data relative to the system start point. It is necessary to accurately define the initial position and scale before motion starts in order to integrate the SLAM system into other robot systems interacting with the environment. Several SLAM algorithms have been developed to build a map based on the key-frames with loop closure detection and to propose a way to identify the current location of the robot [4,19,20]. The map can be used to calculate the scale factor of the camera path. Similar results can be achieved by combining monocular camera data with other sensors [5,8,25]. There are many existing SLAM algorithms described today. Most of them are dealing with standard navigation tasks (e.g. building key-frame based maps, loop closure detecting or current position localization). One of the more popular approaches is PTAM [13,14] and its variations, such as LSD-SLAM [4,7] and ORB-SLAM [19,20]. A significant challenge for monocular SLAM systems is the problem of estimating scaled camera positions. Without scaled metric data, the SLAM output cannot be integrated with other robotic systems relying on accurate environmental information. That is why some approaches use RGB-D or stereo cameras [3,17]. Depth maps generated from RGB-D cameras can be used to find scaled metric camera positions. Additionally, RGB-D hardware makes 3D environment reconstruction possible [3]. This approach is more expensive than monocular systems. However, scaled environmental information can be obtained if the monocular camera data is combined with other sensors, e.g. laser scanners, etc. The PTAM algorithm uses an altimeter based solution [6]. PTAM does not provide scaled 3D environmental data, though. The authors are not aware of a monocular SLAM system that provides a scaled point cloud representation of the environment aligned to some global coordinate system.

2.5 Spaces Alignment Problem and Solution

The main steps of LSD-SLAM and real-world scale and orientation synchronization are taken during the LSD-SLAM algorithm initialization period. We should remember, that LSD-SLAM systems without spacial equipment (such as an external IMU sensor) have no information about the real-world camera position, orientation and surrounding object sizes. The LSD-SLAM camera position and orientation estimating process is based on tracking special points in a particular frame. It is necessary to have depth information for them. Initially, it uses random numbers for the depth hypotheses, i.e. $d \in [0, 1]$ random numbers for each feature point in the first frame. Also, for the first frame camera position and orientation the initial position vector $[0, 0, 0]$ and quaternion $[1, 0, 0, 0]$ are used. This random distance is used for camera tracking and for defining the estimated camera position and orientation. At the next step the calculated camera position and orientation error is used in the triangulation task to update the point cloud depth information. After some iterations, the calculation results converge into an optimal combination of depths and camera tracking data. It is obvious that after the initialization period the estimated point depths and camera position and orientation data have unpredictable values. The initialization time and final distance scale factor depend on a random distribution of initial hypothetical depths. Now the task can be formulated: we are looking for a combination of rotation, scaling and translation factors that will map LSD-SLAM estimated coordinate system space to the IMU sensor coordinate system. It is very important to have the transformation from LSD-SLAM space to the sensor space, because the IMU sensor coordinate system is aligned to the gravity vector. That means it is aligned to the world coordinate system. It makes it possible to use an octree optimized 3D model representation for the estimated point cloud. In order to find a solution, first of all, it is necessary to formally define the input data. LSD-SLAM estimates data as a set of key-frames which describe camera position and orientation with a set of points or coordinates (or estimated distance from the camera to each feature point). This will be denoted as $\mathbf{L} = \{T, \mathbf{P}\}$ where $T \in \mathbb{Sim}(3)$ such that: $T = (s\mathbf{R}\ \mathbf{t},\ 0\ 1)$ with $\mathbf{R} \in SO(3)$, $\mathbf{t} \in \mathbb{R}^3$, $s \in \mathbb{R}^+$. The $\mathbb{Sim}(3)$ group represents transformation and scaling in a three dimensional space. Here s is a scale factor and $\mathbf{t}$ a translation vector in 3D space. $\mathbf{R}$ is an element of the $SO(3)$ group that represents rotation. Each element of the $SO(3)$ group can be represented in several different forms (e.g. rotation matrix, quaternion or vector and angle combination). T represents the camera transformation estimated by LSD-SLAM. Furthermore $\mathbf{P} = \{\mathbf{p} = \langle\ u, v, d\ \rangle \mid u \in \mathbb{Z}^+,\ v \in \mathbb{Z}^+,\ d \in \mathbb{R}^+\}$ where $[u,\ v]$ are the pixel coordinates on the frame and d is a distance from the camera position to the point. In order to calculate 3D coordinates of the points in a key-frame point cloud, it is also necessary to have the intrinsic camera matrix: $M = [f_x\ 0\ c_x,\ 0\ f_y\ c_y,\ 0\ 0\ 1]$ where: $\mathbf{f} = [f_x,\ f_y]$ - camera focus distance per axis. $\mathbf{c} = [c_x,\ c_y]$ - image position of the principle axis in pixel coordinates. Let $\mathbf{X} = \{\mathbf{x} \mid \mathbf{x} \in \mathbb{R}^3\}$ represent $\mathbf{P}$ in the 3D space of the LSD-SLAM coordinate system. It can be calculated by mapping: $\delta: \mathbf{P} \to \mathbf{X}$. Where δ is: $\mathbf{X} = \delta(\ \mathbf{L}, M\ ) = T\,[(u - c_x) \cdot d/f_x,\ (v - c_y) \cdot d/f_y,\ d,\ 1,\ ]$. We are receiving additional information from an external sensor, in this case an IMU. For LSD-SLAM estimated data, we will use set $\mathbf{S}$, which describes sensor measured data $\mathbf{S} = \{T',\ \mathbf{P}'\}$. For IMU sensor measured data $T' \in \mathbb{Sim}(3)$ is a transformation into the real world metric coordinate system and $\mathbf{P}' \equiv \varnothing$ is an empty set, because the IMU model do not have any information about the 3D real world geometry. Because $\mathbf{P}'$ is empty, $\mathbf{X}'$ cannot be obtained. As described in the previous subsection, we are looking for a combination of rotation, translation and scale conversions from $\mathbf{L}$ to $\mathbf{S}$. Formally that conversion combination can be represented as an element of $\mathbb{Sim}(3)$: $\Lambda = (s\mathbf{R}\ \mathbf{t},\ 0\ 1)$ with $\mathbf{R} \in SO(3)$, $\mathbf{t} \in \mathbb{R}^3$, $s \in \mathbb{R}^+$. Finally, we can formalize our task as follows: we are looking for a mapping $\Lambda: \mathbf{L} \to \mathbf{S}$. In order to find Λ we can only use the LSD-SLAM camera position and orientation and then relate it to the IMU sensor measurements. As already mentioned $\mathbf{P}'$

(hence $\mathbf{X}'$ as well) is an empty set for the sensor coordinate system. Therefore the equation for finding Λ becomes: $\Lambda^* := argmin_{(s,\mathbf{R},t)} \left(\sum \left\| T' - \Lambda \times T \right\|^2 \right)$

The element usage is based on the fact that T and T' are part of the $\mathbb{S}\mathrm{im}(3)$. The solution to this equation is discussed in detail in [9,10]. And so, we are able to reconstruct the point cloud in the IMU sensor coordinate system. With the calculated Λ^*, we can transform the LSD-SLAM estimated point cloud to the IMU sensor coordinate system: $\mathbf{X}' \approx \Lambda^* \times \mathbf{X} \approx \Lambda^* \times \delta(\mathbf{L},\ M)$.

Inertial Measurement Unit Calibration. Integrated in our IMU there are three gyroscopes and three accelerometers that are orientated along the three axis. We need to calculate continually the current position, orientation and track the motion of the robot for each of the six degrees of freedom $x, y, z, \theta_x, \theta_y, \theta_z$. A disadvantage of an IMU in general is that they suffer from accumulated error. In our experiments, it is a problem to calculate a linear acceleration in a defined time period and additionally there is a misalignment and non-orthogonality error. To improve the results of IMU sensors and correct misalignment, we strap the IMU onto a stepper motor and calibrate it in relation to different angles from 0° to 360 ° by tracking the sensor values of each step.

Extracting Point Cloud of the Head. While moving we will get varying camera positions from where every frame is tracked. The first camera position defines a key frame; any further position delivers a current tracked frame. We extract feature points from the key frame to reconstruct the point cloud and identify the feature points on the tracked frame. This progress is supported by camera calibration parameters which are estimated by the camera position and orientation. These calibration parameters describe a calculated view of the frame, in which we use image and head detection for the current tracked frame. The whole camera volume is cropped to a volume of interest where the head is positioned and we use the z distance of each point to reduce the point cloud to an extraction of the head. In summary, we propose combining the camera calibration parameters, all the data from LSD SLAM (position and orientation) and the bounding box of head detection CNN to get our volume of interest in order to reduce unnecessary information and get an extracted point cloud, as shown in Fig. 3.

2.6   Poisson Triangulation Based Estimation of the Head Position

There are several methods for surface reconstruction. Some of these can be divided into global and local fitting procedures. Global fitting procedures are in implicit form and can be represented as the sum of radial basis functions (RBFs) at the centre of the points. The RBFs are not linked to the data points but to the surrounding space. Local fitting techniques use the distance from tangent planes to the next point. The Poisson surface reconstruction combines both methods. It uses the Poisson equation, which is also used in other applications

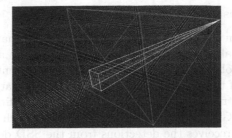

Fig. 3. Simplified example: camera frustum (red), volume of interest by CNN bounding box (yellow), points in volume of interest (green), other points in grey (Color figure online)

of physics. The algorithm used here aims to reconstruct a watertight model. Experiments shows a *search radius* of less than 2 generates dents in the surface from volume of interest. The optimum seems a radius of 4. Results of the Poisson Triangulation method are feasible. It is possible to produce a waterproof mesh. Large holes can be closed in the process, like in Fig. 4. We propose applying real-time 3D face fitting via the *Surrey face model*'s first component, the 3D morphable PCA shape model, and its landmark annotations onto the generated mesh. Further information are available in [11].

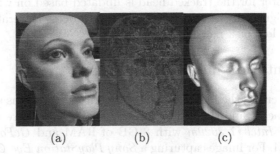

(a)   (b)   (c)

Fig. 4. Demonstration of a surface reconstruction (c) using the Poisson method on a point cloud (b) generated from a dummy head (a)

2.7 Fusion of Positional Data

From the fitted 3DMM, we select the nose tip landmark as coordinate for the tracking z position. In case the occiput is captured, in our first implementation we accept a suboptimal fitting, since the nose tip landmark is still on the surface and therefore a good estimate of the head position. We advocate a simple fusion of the SLAM 3D position from 3DMM fitting landmark P_{SLAM} and the CNN 2D transformed world space position P_{CNN} in form of: $P_{fused} = \alpha \cdot P_{SLAM} + \beta \cdot P_{CNN}$ with $P_i = [x, y, z]$ and $\alpha + \beta = 1$. P_{fused} is input to a Kalman filter described in Sect. 2.8. Optimal values for α and β depend on actual hardware implementation and should be determined in experiments.

2.8   Global Nearest Neighbour (GNN) Tracking

After the detection in 2D and 3D, the fused world coordinates of the head are input to a tracking algorithm. For single object tracking a combination of a Kalman filter and global nearest neighbour data assignment is used. This can extend it to a state of the art joint probabilistic data-association filter algorithm [23], which enables a robust multi-object tracking. In our first implementation, a single track of the GNN tracking algorithm is used, which is sufficient. Every iteration the tracker receives the detections from the SSD detector CNN transformed in 3D coordinates. First the tracker needs to be initialized. Therefore, a tracker object must be created. For this purpose, a detection is selected, which should be tracked. This can be externally requested from the user. The tracker object initializes a Kalman filter [27] with the coordinates of the selected detection. The state transition function of the Kalman filter is based on Newton's equations of motion with a constant acceleration of the system. For implementation *FilterPy*, a Kalman filtering and optimal estimation library in Python is used. The Kalman filter predicts the position of the tracked object at the next time step based on the process model. The Gaussian probability is calculated between the predicted position and the current detections. To limit this range a gating is applied. The size of the gate increases with increasing covariance of the Kalman filter. The detection with the highest probability inside the gate is assigned to the tracker. The tracker uses the detection to update the Kalman filter. A live counter for the tracked head is updated based on whether a detection could be assigned to the tracker or not. This process is iteratively repeated until the track is lost or a new track is requested.

3   Implementation and Testing

The following describes the hardware and software specifications and technology for the person tracker and their implementation. The hardware used in for the application is an *Intel i7 2620m* with 8 GB of RAM and *GeForce GTX 1060* with 6 GB VRAM. For image capturing a *Sony PlayStation Eye Camera* is used, with a framerate of 60 frames per seconds and low motion blur. The resolution of 640×480 satisfies the required resolution for the detector CNN. The software implementation is written completely in *Python* and takes place on *Ubuntu 14.04 LTS*. For array implementations and operations, we use *Numpy*. The SLAM part runs on a *NVIDIA Jetson TK1 developer kit* with a *Bosch BNO055* IMU.

User Interface: The user interface of the head tracker is implemented with *OpenCV*. The user interface shows the current captured scene. All detections are marked with bounding boxes and their position in world space coordinates. To trigger a tracking request, a user simply clicks inside the target bounding box. Alternative implementation may allow for voice or gesture based selection of a bounding box by ID. The tracked head is marked with a different colour, to distinguish the detection bounding boxes. Figure 5 shows the implemented user interface.

Fig. 5. User interface of the head tracker. Detection bounding boxes in green, tracking target in red. Displayed over each is the head position in world space coordinates in relation to the camera sensor. (Color figure online)

Fig. 6. Video image sequence of the *Follow Me* application

Robot Motion Control: The final positional data P from the Kalman filter prediction is sent to the robot's motion controller feedback algorithm, which calculates rotation angle and distance to point P with respect to the robot's coordinate space. The feedback algorithm is set to keep a fixed offset to the target.

Testing: Figure 6 depicts a video image sequence. In the upper left corner, the User Interface is overlaid. The scenery is shot in third person to provide a holistic view of the demonstration. In the image sequence, several persons cross and occlude the tracked person in front of the robot in between person and robot and behind the person. Notice the tracking stays on the target person.

4   Conclusion

We have implemented an early working *Follow Me* application with the potential to achieve better results than existing solutions which use more expensive sensors. Our system is still work in progress, though. Further tasks aim to improve stability in the wild, while keeping low budget hardware. With SLAM, we can create a map of the environment to improve navigation and obstacle avoidance. We suggest upgrading the workflow with the use of blend shapes in the 3D morphable face model. Blend shapes are simply described by the difference between two three dimensional objects. Those objects represent human faces with different expressions. After the registration of the face with the method of a 3D morphable model (3DMM) [11] we can do further normalization via blend shapes and eventually enable a more stable face recognition.

References

1. Hollywoodheads dataset. http://www.di.ens.fr/willow/research/headdetection/. Accessed 01 Feb 2017
2. Eisenbach, M., Vorndran, A., Sorge, S., Gross, H.M.: User recognition for guiding and following people with a mobile robot in a clinical environment. In: IEEE/RSJ International Conference on Intelligent Robots and Systems (IROS), pp. 3600–3607. IEEE (2015)
3. Endres, F., Hess, J., Engelhard, N., Sturm, J., Cremers, D., Burgard, W.: An evaluation of the RGB-D SLAM system. In: Robotics and Automation (2012)
4. Engel, J., Schöps, T., Cremers, D.: LSD-SLAM: large-scale direct monocular SLAM. In: Fleet, D., Pajdla, T., Schiele, B., Tuytelaars, T. (eds.) ECCV 2014. LNCS, vol. 8690, pp. 834–849. Springer, Cham (2014). https://doi.org/10.1007/978-3-319-10605-2_54
5. Engel, J., Stueckler, J., Cremers, D.: Large-scale direct SLAM with stereo cameras. In: International Conference on Intelligent Robots and Systems (IROS) (2015)
6. Engel, J., Sturm, J., Cremers, D.: Camera-based navigation of a low-cost quadrocopter. In: International Conference on Intelligent Robot Systems (IROS) (2012)
7. Engel, J., Sturm, J., Cremers, D.: Semi-dense visual odometry for a monocular camera. In: IEEE International Conference on Computer Vision (ICCV) (2013)
8. Engel, J., Sturm, J., Cremers, D.: Scale-aware navigation of a low-cost quadrocopter with a monocular camera. Robot. Auton. Syst. (RAS) **62**, 1646–1656 (2014)
9. Horn, B.: Closed-form solution of absolute orientation using unit quaternions. J. Opt. Soc. Am. **4**, 629–642 (1987)
10. Horn, B., Hilden, H., Negahdaripour, S.: Closed-form solution of absolute orientation using orthonormal matrices. J. Opt. Soc. Am. **5**, 1127–1135 (1988)
11. Huber, P., et al.: A multiresolution 3D morphable face model and fitting framework. http://www.patrikhuber.ch/files/3DMM_Framework_VISAPP_2016.pdf
12. Jia, Y., et al.: Convolutional architecture for fast feature embedding. arXiv preprint arXiv:1408.5093 (2014)
13. Klein, G., Murray, D.: Parallel tracking and mapping for small AR workspaces. In: Proceedings of the International Symposium on Mixed and Augmented Reality (ISMAR 2007, Nara) (2007)

14. Klein, G., Murray, D.: Parallel tracking and mapping on a camera phone. In: Proceedings of the International Symposium on Mixed and Augmented Reality (ISMAR 2009, Orlando) (2009)
15. Krizhevsky, A., Sutskever, I., Hinton, G.E.: Imagenet classification with deep convolutional neural networks. In: Pereira, F., Burges, C.J.C., Bottou, L., Weinberger, K.Q. (eds.) Advances in Neural Information Processing Systems 25, pp. 1097–1105. Curran Associates, Inc. (2012). http://papers.nips.cc/paper/4824-imagenet-classification-with-deep-convolutional-neural-networks.pdf
16. Liu, W., et al.: SSD: single shot multibox detector. In: Leibe, B., Matas, J., Sebe, N., Welling, M. (eds.) ECCV 2016. LNCS, vol. 9905, pp. 21–37. Springer, Cham (2016). https://doi.org/10.1007/978-3-319-46448-0_2
17. Maier, R., Sturm, J., Cremers, D.: Submap-based bundle adjustment for 3D reconstruction from RGB-D data. In: Jiang, X., Hornegger, J., Koch, R. (eds.) GCPR 2014. LNCS, vol. 8753, pp. 54–65. Springer, Cham (2014). https://doi.org/10.1007/978-3-319-11752-2_5
18. Mueller, S., Schaffernicht, E., Scheidig, A., Boehme, H.J., Gross, H.M.: Are you still following me? In: European Conference on Mobile Robots (ECMR), pp. 211–216. Albert-Ludwigs-Universitaet Freiburg - Universitaetsverlag (2007)
19. Mur-Artal, R., Tardos, J.: ORB-SLAM: tracking and mapping recognizable features. In: Robotics: Science and Systems (RSS) Workshop on Multi View Geometry in Robotics (MVIGRO) (2014)
20. Mur-Artal, R., Tardós, J.: Probabilistic semi-dense mapping from highly accurate feature-based monocular SLAM. In: Robotics, Science and Systems (2015)
21. Ren, S., He, K., Girshick, R., Sun, J.: Faster R-CNN: towards real-time object detection with region proposal networks. In: Advances in Neural Information Processing Systems (NIPS) (2015)
22. Triputen, S., Schreve, K., Tkachev, V., Rätsch, M.: Closed-form solution for IMU based LSD-SLAM point cloud conversion into the scaled 3D world environment. In: Submitted IEEE AIM (2017)
23. Shiry, S., Menhaj, M.B., Daronkolaei, A.G.: Multiple target tracking for mobile robots using the JPDAF algorithm. In: 2007 19th IEEE International Conference on Tools with Artificial Intelligence, vol. 01, pp. 137–145 (2007)
24. Simonyan, K., Zisserman, A.: Very deep convolutional networks for large-scale image recognition. CoRR abs/1409.1556 (2014). http://arxiv.org/abs/1409.1556
25. Usenko, V., Engel, J., Stückler, J., Cremers, D.: Direct visual-inertial odometry with stereo cameras. In: Robotics and Automation (ICRA) (2016)
26. Vu, T., Osokin, A., Laptev, I.: Context-aware CNNs for person head detection. CoRR abs/1511.07917 (2015). http://arxiv.org/abs/1511.07917
27. Welch, G., Bishop, G.: An introduction to the Kalman filter. Technical report, Chapel Hill, NC, USA (1995)

Learning to Use Toes in a Humanoid Robot

Klaus Dorer[✉]

Elektrotechnik-Informationstechnik, Hochschule Offenburg, Offenburg, Germany
klaus.dorer@fh-offenburg.de

Abstract. In this paper we show that a model-free approach to learn behaviors in joint space can be successfully used to utilize toes of a humanoid robot. Keeping the approach model-free makes it applicable to any kind of humanoid robot, or robot in general. Here we focus on the benefit on robots with toes which is otherwise more difficult to exploit. The task has been to learn different kick behaviors on simulated Nao robots with toes in the RoboCup 3D soccer simulator. As a result, the robot learned to step on its toe for a kick that performs 30% better than learning the same kick without toes.

1 Introduction

Evolution has spent the effort to equip humans with toes. Toes, among other advantages, allow humans to walk smoother and faster with longer steps. Naturally, this has been subject of much research in humanoid robotics.

Passive toe joints have been suggested and used since quite some time to consume and release energy in the toe-off phase of walking. Early examples are the Monroe [8], HRP-2 [15] or Wabian-2R [14] robots.

Active toe joints are less common, but also in use for several years. The H6 robot [11] used toes to reduce angular knee speeds when walking, to increase leg length when climbing and to kneel. The Toni robot [3] improved walking by over-extending the unloading leg using toes. Toyota presented a toed robot running at 7 km/h [16]. Lola [4] is equipped with active toe joints and active pelvis joints to research human-like walking. Active toe joints increase the difficulty of leg behaviors in a couple of ways:

- of course they add a degree of freedom (DoF).
- it makes the leg of the robot kinematically redundant. Inverse-kinematics will not find unique solutions which adds effort to deal with, but also offers room for optimization [5].
- moving the toe of a support leg in any case reduces the contact area of the foot, either by stepping on the toe or by lifting the toe off the ground.
- on real robots, they typically increase the complexity of construction and weight of the feet and consume energy.

© Springer Nature Switzerland AG 2018
H. Akiyama et al. (Eds.): RoboCup 2017, LNAI 11175, pp. 168–179, 2018.
https://doi.org/10.1007/978-3-030-00308-1_14

All examples above for passive or active toes are model-specific either in a sense to be specific to a robot model or to be behavior-specific in calculating desired toe angles.

A couple of more recently built robots avoid the complexity of actuating toes and the inflexibility of flat feet by wearing shoes. Examples are Petman, Poppy [9] or Durus [2,12] that is able to walk many times more energy-efficiently with this and other improvements. Shoes, or rounded feet in general, improve energy-efficiency of walking, but would not provide the benefits of active toes for any behavior like the kicking behavior demonstrated in this paper.

Learning in combination with toe movement has been employed by Ogura et al. [14]. They used genetic algorithms to optimize some parameters of the ZMP-based foot trajectory calculation for continuous and smooth foot motion. This approach optimizes parameters of an abstract parameter space defined by an underlying model. This has the advantage, that the dimension of the search space is kept relatively small, but it does not generalize to work for any behavior.

Learning to kick is common in many RoboCup leagues. A good overview can be found in [7]. However, none of these report on kicking with toed robots. MacAlpine et al. [10] use a layered learning approach to learn a set of behaviors in the RoboCup 3D soccer simulator used in this work. They learn keyframes for kicking behaviors and parameters for a model-based walking. Although the work is not focused on learning to use toes, they report on an up to 60% improvement in overall soccer game play using a Nao robot variation with toes (see Sect. 2). This demonstrates the ability of their approach to generalize to different robot models, but is still model-based for walking. Abdolmaleki et al. [1] use a keyframe based approach and CMA-ES, as we do, to learn a kick with controlled distance, which achieves longer kick distances than reported here, but also requires considerably longer preparation time. However, their approach is limited to two keyframes resulting in 25 learning parameters, while our approach is not limited to an upper number of keyframes (see Sect. 3). Also they do not make use of toes. It is interesting to see, that also in their kick, the robot moves to the tip of its support foot to lengthen the support leg. Not using toes, their kick results in a falling robot after each kick.

The work presented here generates raw output data during learning without using an underlying robot- or behavior-model. To demonstrate this, we present learning results on different robot models (focusing on a simulated Nao robot with toes) and two very different kick behaviors without an underlying model.

The remainder of the paper is organized as follows: In Sect. 2 we provide some details of the simulation environment used. Section 3 explains our model-free approach to learning behaviors using toes. It is followed by experimental results in Sect. 4 before we conclude and indicate future work in Sect. 5.

2 Domain

The robots used in this work are robots of the RoboCup 3D soccer simulation which is based on SimSpark[1] and initially initiated by [13]. It uses the ODE

---

[1] http://simspark.sourceforge.net/.

physics engine[2] and runs at a speed of 50 Hz. The simulator provides variations of Aldebaran Nao robots with 22 DoF for the robot types without toes and 24 DoF for the type with toes, NaoToe henceforth. More specifically, the robot has 6 (7) DoF in each leg, 4 in each arm and 2 in its neck. There are several simplifications in the simulation compared to the real Nao:

- all motors of the simulated Nao are of equal strength whereas the real Nao has weaker motors in the arms and different gears in the leg pitch motors.
- joints do not experience extensive backlash
- rotation axes of the hip yaw part of the hip are identical in both robots, but the simulated robot can move hip yaw for each leg independently, whereas for the real Nao, left and right hip yaw are coupled
- the simulated Naos do not have hands
- the touch model of the ground is softer and therefore more forgiving to stronger ground touches in the simulation
- energy consumption and heat is not simulated
- masses are assumed to be point masses in the center of each body part

The feet of NaoToe are modeled as rectangular body parts of size 8 cm × 12 cm × 2 cm for the foot and 8 cm × 4 cm × 1 cm for the toes (see Fig. 1). The two body parts are connected with a hinge joint that can move from $-1°$ (downward) to 70°.

All joints can move at an angular speed of at most 7.02° per 20 ms. The simulation server expects to get the desired speed at 50 Hz for each joint. If no speeds are sent to the server it will continue movement of the joint with the last speed received. Joint angles are noiselessly perceived at 50 Hz, but with a delay of 40 ms compared to sent actions. So only after two cycles the robot knows the result of a triggered action. A controller provided for each joint inside the server tries to achieve the requested speed, but is subject to maximum torque, maximum angular speed and maximum joint angles.

The simulator is able to run 22 simulated Naos in real-time on reasonable CPUs. It is used as competition platform for the RoboCup 3D soccer simulation league[3]. In this context, only a single agent was running in the simulator.

3 Approach

The guiding goal behind our approach is to create a framework that is model-free. With model-free we depict an approach that does not make any assumptions about a robot's architecture nor the task to be performed. Thus, from the viewpoint of learning, our model consists of a set of flat parameters. These parameters are later grounded inside the domain. In our case, the grounding would mean to create 50 joint angles or angular speed values per second for each of the 24 joints of NaoToe. This would result in 1200 values to learn for a behavior with

---

[2] http://www.ode.org/.

[3] http://www.robocup.org/robocup-soccer/simulation/.

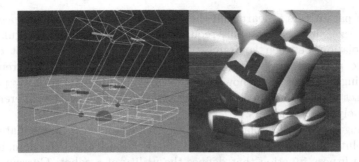

Fig. 1. Wire model of the Nao with toes (left) and how it is visualized (right).

one second duration assuming the 50 Hz frequency of the simulator. This seemed unreasonable for time being and led to some steps of relaxing the ultimate goal.

As a first step, the search space has been limited to the leg joints only. This effectively limits the current implementation of the approach to leg behaviors, excluding, for example, behaviors to get up. Also, instead of providing 50 values per second for each joint, we make use of the fact that output values of a joint over time are not independent. Therefore, we learn keyframes, i.e. all joint angles for discrete phases of movement together with the duration of the phase from keyframe to keyframe. The experiments described in this paper used two to eight of such phases. The number of phases is variable between learning runs, but not subject to learning for now, except for skipping phases by learning a zero duration for it.

The RoboCup server requires robots to send the actual angular speed of each joint as a command. So the first representation used in this work is to directly learn the speed values to be sent to the simulator. This requires to learn 15 parameters per phase (14 joints + 1 for the duration of the phase) resulting in 30, 60, 90 and 120 parameters for the 2, 4, 6, 8 phases worked with. The disadvantage of this approach is, that the speed will be constant during one phase and will especially not adapt to discrepancies of the commanded and the true motor movement.

The second representation therefore interpreted the parameters as angular values to reach at the end of a phase as is done in [10] for kicking behaviors. A simple controller divided the difference of the current angle and the goal angle of each joint by the duration and sent a speed accordingly. The two representations differ in cases, when the motor does not exactly follow the commanded speed. Using keyframes of angles will adjust the speeds to this situation.

A third representation used a combination of angular value and the maximum amount of angular speed each joint should have. The direction of movement is entirely encoded in the angular values, but the speed is a combination of representation one and two above. If the amount of angular speed does not allow to reach the angular value, the joint behaves like in version 1. If the amount of angular speed is bigger, the joint behaves like version 2. This almost doubles the amount of parameters to learn, but the co-domain of values for the speed values is half the size, since here we only require an absolute amount of angular speed.

Interpolation between keyframes of angles is linear for now. It could be changed to polynoms or splines, but we do not expect a big difference since the resulting behavior is anyhow smoothened by the inertia of body parts and since phases can be and are learned to be short in time if the difference from linear to polynomial matters.

Learning is done using plain genetic algorithms and covariance matrix adaptation evolutionary strategies (CMA-ES) [6]. Feedback from the domain is provided by a fitness function that defines the utility of a robot. Currently implemented fitness functions use ball position, robot orientation and position during or at the end of a run. The decision maker to trigger the behavior also uses foot force sensors.

To summarize, the following domain knowledge is built into our approach:

- the system has to provide values at 50 Hz (used as angular speeds of the joints)
- there are up to 232 free parameters for which we know the range of reasonable values (defined by minimum and maximum joint angles and angular speeds and maximum phase duration)
- a fitness function using domain information gives feedback about the utility of a parameter set
- a kicking behavior is made possible by moving the player near the vicinity of the ball.

The following domain knowledge is not required or built into the system:

- geometry, mass of body parts
- position or axis of joints
- the robot type (humanoid, four-legged, ...)

4   Results

The first behaviors to learn were kicks. Experiments have been conducted as follows. The robot connects to the server and is beamed to a position favorable for kicking. It then starts to step in place. Kicking without stepping is easier to achieve, but does not resemble typical situations during a real game. The step in place is a model-based, inverse-kinematic walk and is not subject to this learning for now. After 1.4 s, the agent is free to decide to kick. It will then decide to kick as soon as foot pressure sensors show a favorable condition. Here it means if kicking with the right leg, the left leg had to just touch the ground and the right leg had to leave the ground. After the kick behavior, the agent continues to step in place until the overall run took five seconds. A run is stopped earlier, if the agent falls (z component of torso's up-vector <0.5). This will typically be the case for most of the individuals of the initial random population.

Table 1 shows the influence of the three representations used for the learning parameters as well as the influence of using different amounts of phases. Each value in the table is the result of 400.000 kicks performed using genetic algorithms. The best kick has been learned using version 3 and 4 phases ending in a kick that is more than 8 m on average. Due to the long learning times, no oversampling for the results in the table has been used, so there is certainly some noise in the single values. However, in all of the runs the agent was able to learn at least a reasonable kick. Averaging over the four runs for different phases, version 3 (learning angular values and speeds) had the highest utility. The value for 8 phases just learning angular speeds is missing due to a problem with the simulator that lets the robot explode in some situations. This happened too often in the 8 phase angular speed scenario to create sensible learning data (see below).

Table 1. Influence of representation and number of phases.

Phases	2	4	6	8	Average
Just speed	6.4	3.5	5.4	-	5.1
Just angles	4.2	3.7	4.4	5.0	4.3
Angles and speed	4.1	8.1	7.2	5.3	6.2
Average	4.9	5.7	5.7	5.15	5.2

The result of the learning process for NaoToe learning angles and speeds with four phases is shown in Fig. 2. It was achieved using a plain genetic algorithm with

- population size: 200
- genders: 2
- parents per individual: 2
- individual mutation probability: 0.1
- gene mutation probability: 0.1
- selection: Monte-Carlo + take over best 10%
- recombination: Multi-Crossover.

Utility function is the kick distance (positive x-coordinate) minus the absolute amount of y-deviation of a straight kick minus a penalty of 2 for falling. The factor two has been chosen as a result of initial experiments. A much lower penalty resulted in better kick distances but the robot falling regularly. A much higher penalty did not result in good kicks, as if it is easier to learn to kick first and to then try keeping upright as opposed to the other way around.

The figure shows the average fitness of a generation and the best individual of 128 generations measured with 10-fold oversampling. It combines the results of $200 * 10 * 128 = 256,000$ kicks performed during learning in about two days of simulation. As can be seen, the learning resulted in a kick distance of more than 8 m.

The noise in the curve, especially points with decreasing utility compared to the predecessor generation, is partially due to mutation of the previous best

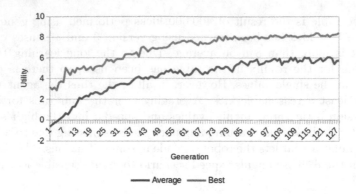

Fig. 2. Learning curve of plain genetic learning with NaoToe.

individual, but mainly it is the non-determinism of the simulator. It could be decreased by a higher number of oversampling runs, lengthening the learning process even more.

The resulting initial movement of the robot is shown in Fig. 6. The robot learned to improve the kick considerably by stepping on its toes of the support leg, seen especially in sub-images three and four. Not shown in the figure: after the kick, the robot also learned to get back into position to successfully continue stepping in place.

The overall kick takes eight simulation cycles, which takes 0.16 s to perform. A comparable hand-tuned kick reaching 8 m takes about 1 s, a kick reaching 15 m takes about 2 s. With a speed of approximately 1 m/s for the fastest teams, this means we can perform the new kick before opponents reach the ball in situations where opponents are almost one (two) meter(s) closer compared to comparable kicks in the league. Although the fitness function does not explicitly contain a preference for short times, implicitly quick kicks are preferred by the penalty for falling. The longer the robot is on one leg, the higher the likeliness of falling down. The detailed movement of the toes is shown in Fig. 3.

The same learning has been performed for the Nao without toes. As can be seen in Fig. 4, without the availability of toes, the learning curve flattens out at 5.5 m.

Table 2 shows a summary of the results for 10-fold and 50-fold oversampling. The difference of the two oversampling columns shows that there is still quite some noise in measuring utilities, even using 10-fold oversampling. NaoToe performs more than 30% better than Nao. It fell 3 out of 50 times, which is unfavorable and indicates that the penalty for falling should have been chosen slightly higher.

Most interesting are the cross-parameterization runs in row three and four. Using the kick learned by NaoToe on a Nao without toes (ignoring the toe parameters) results in falling 98% of the time and a kick utility of 1.275. Considering the fall penalty of the fitness function, the average kick distance would only be approximately 3.25 m. As can be seen in Fig. 6, the robot is able to lean

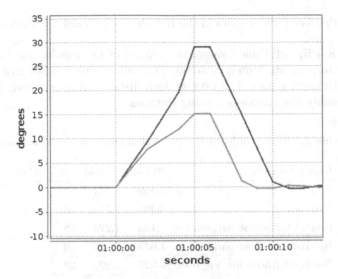

Fig. 3. Movement of the toes (support leg in dark).

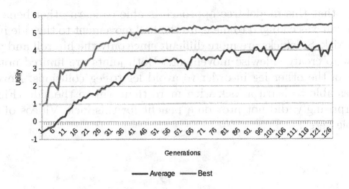

Fig. 4. Learning curve of plain genetic learning with Nao.

backwards considerably by stepping on its toe. Without the toe available in Nao, the robots falls backwards most of the time.

Similar results were measured when running the parameterization learned by Nao on NaoToe. Toe movement has been kept at zero in this run. Although the robot remains standing in all 50 tries, the result is a mere 1.5 m. Deeper analysis shows that the robot hits the ground with the heel of its kicking leg most of the time. This is surprising and not yet completely understood. One reason could be the slightly different mass distribution in the foot of NaoToe compared to Nao. Another reason could be that although the toes are not actively moving, they could be slightly bend by the force acting on them. However, the amount has been confirmed to be less than 0.01° and is therefore unlikely to cause such an effect. Also, foot force sensors are used to decide when to trigger the behavior.

It could be that the force sensors in the feet show zero values, while the toes still touch the ground.

Finally, row five of Table 2 shows the impact of not moving the toes for the NaoToe parameterization on a NaoToe. The robot is four times more likely to fall than with moving toes. The average kick distance of approximately 5.4 m is also considerably less than when using the toes.

Table 2. Utilities of learned kicks and of cross-parameterization.

Utility measures	10 fold	50 fold	falls (in %)
Nao	5.469	5.161	0
NaoToe	8.407	7.736	6
Nao with NaoToe parameters	1.135	1.275	98
NaoToe with Nao parameters	1.635	1.515	0
NaoToe without moving toes	5.627	5.226	24

To show that this model-free approach is able to learn other behaviors, the utility function was changed to measure the ball movement to the side in order to learn a sidekick. Sidekicks are more difficult since only the hip roll and yaw-pitch joints allow to create sidewise movements. Both joints are limited not to move to the side of the other leg in order to avoid leg-to-leg collisions. Nevertheless, NaoToe was able to learn a kick with more than 5 m to the side (Fig. 5). The toes, unsurprisingly, did not provide a benefit for this kick. Videos of the kicks are available here[4].

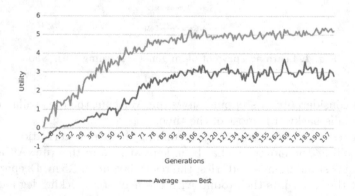

Fig. 5. Learning curve of learning a sidekick with NaoToe.

Initial experiments with learning to walk this way by performing a learned double step during model-based walking results in a walk that is up to now

---

[4] https://www.dropbox.com/s/u3k3117zc0ptg1m/RoboCupSymposium.mp4?dl=0.

86% the speed of pure model-based walking. Unfortunately, attempts to learn walking using NaoToe are hampered by a bug in the simulator that lets the robot explode in some cases of toe movement. For kick learning this did in most cases not exhibit a problem, since such parameter settings did not result in ball movement and were eliminated by the genetic search. For walking, however, the genetic algorithm does exploit this bug by learning to explode in situations were the torso fragment of the robot is boosting forward.

Fig. 6. Sequence of movement when kicking with NaoToe.

5   Conclusions and Future Work

With the model-free approach presented in this paper we were able to learn different behaviors on different robot type variations. In particular, the advantages of a robot with toes could be exploited in a quick forward-kick without the need to care for problems with, for example, inverse kinematics.

We have not been successful in transferring a learned kick on Nao to a useful kick on NaoToe so far using CMA-ES. All attempts ended in kicks of NaoToe with a distance of two to four meters only. The opposite, learning a kick on Nao from parameters learned for NaoToe did work. This deserves further investigations since learning times could hopefully be reduced considerably compared to learning from scratch each time. CMA-ES is, however, able to adjust a learned kick of e.g. NaoToe to different ball positions with respect to the robot.

The examples of learned behaviors in this paper are all kicks. The model-free approach, however, should allow to learn any behavior, at least for legs in its current implementation. We are currently investigating to learn a walk using toes. This is more difficult since the duration of a walk behavior before repeating itself is longer than for the kicks shown here, so the parameter space is increasing. First results are promising, but hampered by a problem of the currently used simulator.

Acknowledgment. Thanks to the magmaOffenburg team for providing the agent software and tools used in this paper, as well as to the contributors of the RoboCup 3D soccer simulator and RoboViz visualizer.

Appendix

Parameter values learned by Nao and NaoToe for the forward kick behavior. The abbreviations are L/R = left/right, H/K/F/T = hip/knee/foot/toe, Y/R/P = yaw/roll/pitch. Times are in cycles, angles in degrees, speeds in degrees per cycle of 50 Hz (Table 3).

Table 3. Parameter values learned by Nao and NaoToe.

	Nao								NaoToe							
Phase	1	2	3	4	1	2	3	4	1	2	3	4	1	2	3	4
TIME	3.3	1.5	0.2	1.5	-	-	-	-	2.2	2.3	0.7	0.9	-	-	-	-
	Angle				Speed				Angle				Speed			
LHYP	0.3	−21.3	−5.4	−22.7	5.8	0.0	5.2	3.0	−5.7	0.9	−43.6	−18.5	0.6	1.3	5.9	5.6
LHR	−7.0	−5.4	0.2	7.6	4.9	3.1	4.7	0.9	5.2	−10.0	0.6	12.0	4.3	3.4	4.9	4.0
LHP	−11.7	19.4	−36.3	−57.3	6.4	0.3	1.5	1.5	−28.6	−8.7	18.8	12.8	6.7	5.7	3.4	6.9
LKP	−12.6	−33.9	−71.1	−57.7	3.7	5.6	7.2	2.5	−74.0	−78.8	−61.7	−58.4	2.9	2.1	6.2	5.4
LFP	7.5	−12.3	−18.2	−11.2	0.1	5.1	0.6	7.1	18.8	−13.9	−11.0	−11.0	6.4	0.3	4.5	4.2
LFR	13.9	15.8	6.2	9.3	2.3	6.5	2.5	0.7	2.9	11.8	−3.1	−11.8	6.0	3.2	2.2	1.7
LTP	-	-	-	-	-	-	-	-	68.3	21.9	25.2	63.9	4.1	4.4	4.1	4.2
RHYP	−28.3	−25.7	−43.6	−31.9	6.6	1.2	6.9	3.1	−20.3	−26.7	−7.6	−40.5	0.9	6.0	3.3	3.6
RHR	16.8	9.8	−16.0	−3.0	6.1	5.6	3.9	3.9	−1.3	15.5	14.1	11.5	4.9	6.6	2.3	2.9
RHP	74.5	66.4	21.7	−38.8	6.5	2.8	1.0	5.1	48.0	57.0	−5.8	−34.1	1.7	6.2	6.4	0.1
RKP	−78.4	−45.0	−94.7	−79.7	0.3	0.1	1.0	4.7	−76.9	−53.3	−97.3	−25.2	5.2	5.3	6.8	6.9
RFP	30.9	31.1	−38.0	−7.6	6.8	0.6	2.6	2.5	−52.7	26.8	−16.2	−45.7	7.1	7.1	7.1	1.9
RFR	−17.8	−1.1	−10.3	4.8	4.2	6.1	1.0	7.1	−12.2	−13.0	14.1	−6.0	4.8	6.5	0.3	6.3
RTP	-	-	-	-	-	-	-	-	20.3	44.6	6.8	37.1	3.4	1.8	2.0	4.9

References

1. Abdolmaleki, A., Simões, D., Lau, N., Reis, L.P., Neumann, G.: Learning a humanoid kick with controlled distance. In: Behnke, S., Sheh, R., Sarıel, S., Lee, D.D. (eds.) RoboCup 2016. LNCS (LNAI), vol. 9776, pp. 45–57. Springer, Cham (2017). https://doi.org/10.1007/978-3-319-68792-6_4
2. Ackerman, E.: DURUS Brings Human-Like Gait (and Fancy Shoes) to Hyper-Efficient Robots (2016). http://spectrum.ieee.org/automaton/robotics/humanoids/durus-brings-humanlike-gait-and-fancy-shoes-to-hyperefficient-robots
3. Behnke, S.: Human-like walking using toes joint and straight stance leg. In: Proceedings of 3rd International Symposium on Adaptive Motion in Animals and Machines (AMAM), Ilmenau (2005)
4. Buschmann, T., Schwienbacher, M., Favot, V., Ewald, A., Ulbrich, H.: The biped walking robot lola - hardware design and walking control. J. Rob. Soc. Jpn. **30**, 363–366 (2012)
5. Buschmann, T.: Simulation and control of biped walking robots. Ph.D. dissertation, Technische Universität München (2010)
6. Hansen, N., Müller, S.D., Koumoutsakos, P.: Reducing the time complexity of the derandomized evolution strategy with covariance matrix adaptation (CMA-ES). Evol. Comput. **11**(1), 1–18 (2003)

7. Jouandeau, N., Hugel, V.: Optimization of parametrised kicking motion for humanoid soccer player. In: Autonomous Robot Systems and Competitions (ICARSC) (2014)
8. Kumagai, M., Emura, T.: Sensor-based walking of human type biped robot that has 14 degree of freedoms. In: Annual Conference on Mechatronics and Machine Vision in Practice (M2VIP 1997), p. 112 (1997)
9. Lapeyre, M., Rouanet, P., Oudeyer, P.: The poppy humanoid robot: leg design for biped locomotion. In: 2013 IEEE/RSJ International Conference on Intelligent Robots and Systems (IROS), Tokyo, Japan, 3–7 November 2013
10. MacAlpine, P., Depinet, M., Stone, P.: UT Austin villa 2014: RoboCup 3D simulation league champion via overlapping layered learning. In: Proceedings of the Twenty-Ninth AAAI Conference on Artificial Intelligence (AAAI), vol. 4, pp. 2842–2848 (2015)
11. Nishiwaki, K., Kagami, S., Kuniyoshi, Y., Inaba, M., Inoue, H.: Toe joints that enhance bipedal and fullbody motion of humanoid robots. In: Proceedings of the 2002 IEEE International Conference on Robotiks and Automation Washington, DC, May 2002
12. Reher, E.A., Cousineau, A., Hereid, C., Hubicki, M., Ames, A.D.: Realizing dynamic and efficient bipedal locomotion on the humanoid robot DURUS. In: International Conference on Robotics and Automation (ICRA) (2016, to appear)
13. Obst, O., Rollmann, M.: SPARK - a generic simulator for physical multiagent simulations. Comput. Syst. Sci. Eng. 20(5), 347–356 (2005)
14. Ogura, Y., et al.: Human-like walking with knee stretched, heel-contact and toe-off motion by a humanoid robot. In: Proceedings of the IEEE/RSJ International Conference Intelligent Robots System (IROS), pp. 3976–3981 (2006)
15. Sellaouti, R., Stasse, O., Kajita, S., Yokoi, K., Kheddar, A.: Faster and smoother walking of humanoid HRP-2 with passive toe joints. In: Proceedings of the 2006 IEEE/RSJ International Conference on Intelligent Robots and Systems, Beijing, China, 9–15 October 2006
16. Tajima, R., Honda, D., Suga, K.: Fast running experiments involving a humanoid robot. In: Proceedings of the IEEE International Conference on Robotics and Automation (ICRA), pp. 1571–1576 (2009)

Cloud Simulations for RoboCup

Enric Cervera[1(✉)], Gustavo Casañ[1], and Ricardo Tellez[2]

[1] Robotic Intelligence Lab, Universitat Jaume I, 12006 Castelló de la Plana, Spain
ecervera@uji.es
[2] The Construct Sim LTD., 08007 Barcelona, Spain

Abstract. Possibly the most appealing aspect of RoboCup is working with real robots, specially for young people. Yet as the complexity of the task increases, the effort in software development becomes higher, and a simulation testbed can be a valuable tool for prototyping and testing software solutions prior to their implementation on a real robot. In fact, several RoboCup leagues feature both real and virtual competitions. In addition, the RoboCup community could benefit from the cooperation and sharing of experiences among users in an online worldwide platform. We present a simulation tool based on the cloud, which can model complex robots off the shelf by using only a web browser as the base system for learning robotics, and running competitions. Such a platform minimizes costs and the troubles associated with different operating systems, while providing a rich experience of testing, with the possibility of a straightforward transfer to a real robot. Moreover, users can easily share their simulations for cooperative learning.

Keywords: Cloud robotics · Simulation

1 Introduction

With the advent of powerful computers and graphic cards, 3D realistic simulators are becoming popular in RoboCup leagues. Yet programming and maintaining a simulator is complex, hard, and time consuming. A prototypical example is the RoboCup Rescue Virtual Robot Competition, launched in 2006, which uses a simulation software, USARSim (Unified System for Automation and Robot Simulation) [2], built on top of the Unreal game engine[1]. This engine has evolved along several versions (2004, UT3, UDK) that required to rewrite the simulation software from scratch. Initially maintained by the National Institute of Standards and Technology (NIST), but no longer supported, it recently switched to a different platform developed by the Open Source Robotics Foundation (OSRF) [15].

Another example is the RoboCup Junior Rescue CoSpace [7], with a simulator built on top of the Microsoft Robotics Developer Studio. This framework has not been updated since 2014, as a result there are increasing difficulties in

---

[1] https://www.unrealengine.com/.

© Springer Nature Switzerland AG 2018
H. Akiyama et al. (Eds.): RoboCup 2017, LNAI 11175, pp. 180–189, 2018.
https://doi.org/10.1007/978-3-030-00308-1_15

fixing bugs, adding support for modern robots and sensors, or working with new versions of operating systems.

On the other hand, RoboCup Soccer uses an open source simulator, SimSpark [17], in the 3D simulation league. We can only wonder how much effort is replicated among those simulator platforms, which face similar problems (physical engine, graphical visualization) in different yet related domains.

In recent years we have been working on web-based laboratories for both real robots and simulators [4]. We have developed web interfaces for systems based on the ROS middleware [3,12], which provides a hardware abstraction layer, enabling the user to share the same code between a real robot and its simulated model. Our aim is the development of a common platform for robotic simulations, suitable for any RoboCup virtual competition, and even for replicating the leagues that right now only use physical robots. Such platform would be based on a cloud infrastructure, enabling the users to run their simulations from their browsers, and to share their experiences with other users throughout the world.

The rest of the paper is organized as follows: Sect. 2 outlines our cloud simulation platform, along with some demonstration examples in competitions and education; in Sect. 3, we advocate for the adoption of a common, open-source, cloud simulation platform in RoboCup leagues; finally, Sect. 4 draws some conclusions and outlines some future lines of work.

2   Cloud Simulation Platform

RDS² (ROS Development Studio) is a web application for the simulation of robots in the cloud. The platform consists of Virtual Machines (VMs) [16] running in the cloud infrastructure provided by Amazon Web Services (AWS) [8]. Each user connects to a single, dedicated VM, running a full-featured distribution of Ubuntu Linux with all the necessary software already installed and configured: ROS, simulators, and development tools.

An advantage of VMs is that they can be mapped to different physical machines based on the power and memory requirements, e.g., a low-complexity simulation can run in single CPU with low memory, but a high-fidelity complex environment may use a multi-CPU machine with one or several additional GPUs and a larger amount of RAM. In any case, the user connects to the VM through a client machine, with no special power or system requirements, since only a browser is needed.

The user interface consists of a web page with a login and password, which gives access to all the tools through the web browser: no other software is needed in the client computer. Different windows in the browser are used for the components of the platform (notebook, simulation view, file editor, shell) as depicted in Fig. 1.

This interface works on top of any WebGL [9] enabled browser, like Safari, Chrome or Firefox. It can be used with any computer or device running any

---

² http://env.theconstructsim.com/RDS.

Fig. 1. User interface: from left to right, notebook, simulator view, file editor (top) and shell (bottom).

of those browsers, in any operating system, including Linux, Windows, Mac, or even tablets and smartphones.

The Robot Operating System (ROS) has become a de-facto standard among robotics researchers as an open source framework for robot programming and control [12]. Currently, two simulators are supported in the cloud platform, Gazebo [10] and Webots [11].

ROS supports several client libraries in different programming languages. The main supported libraries are written in C++ and Python, but there is also active development in Lisp, C#, Go, Haskell, Java, Javascript, Julia, Lua, Matlab, Pharo, R, and Ruby.

The main programming interface of the cloud platform consists of the Jupyter Notebook, an open-source web application for creating and sharing documents that contain live code, data visualization and explanatory text [13], which supports over 40 programming languages, including most of the languages supported in ROS.

A cloud platform provides the user with the infrastructure for creating a social network that encourages the interaction between the community members [1]. Users can share their simulations and code, collaborate or compete against each other. Such communities, e.g. the Scratch platform [14], have an incredible educational potential in computer and engineering disciplines.

In the following we present some working applications of the cloud platform: two online competitions, and an online course.

2.1 Online Competitions

One way to encourage students and robotics research is by doing contests where the participants have to compete against each other. Two competitions have been organized using the cloud platform and simulations of humanoid robots: a NAO robot race, and sumo fighting between two Darwin robots.

In the racing competition (Fig. 2), a Nao humanoid has to be programmed to walk 10 m as fast as possible. Participants are given a standard walking controller, which can be modified and optimized for speed and robustness. Modifications are uploaded to each user's account, and the system performs the simulations and compares the results.

Fig. 2. Nao race: the robot is programmed for walking 10 m as fast as possible, the time is measured by an automatic chronometer at the finish line.

The Sumo Challenge (Fig. 3) was a worldwide contest, consisting of two simulated Darwin humanoid robots that must fight against each other in a simulated sumo dojo. Participants had to build a controller for their robot, trying to knock out the opponent. The controllers were automatically taken each day and made to fight against the rest of participants in a Bubble Sort style league.

2.2 Online Courses

We have recently used the cloud platform in a MOOC (Massive Open Online Course) on Autonomous Mobile Robots, where we designed a simulation environment inspired in the RoboCup Junior Rescue competition (Fig. 4). In this world, the robot must be programmed first to follow a line with obstacles and intersections, then to find and pick some balls scattered around the room, and carry them to a destination area.

The simulation platform was used in combination with a Learning Management System based on Moodle [5]. The students worked on the lessons and examples, developed the exercises on the simulators, and submitted their code

Fig. 3. Sumo challenge: the robots are programmed to fight each other according to the rules, with an automatic referee for scoring the matches.

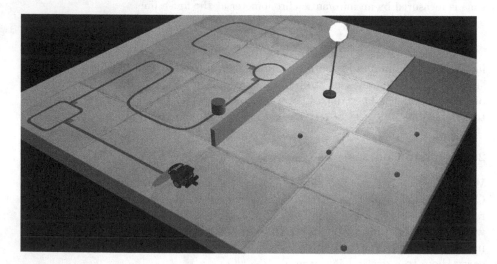

Fig. 4. MOOC simulation world inspired in the RoboCup Junior Rescue competition.

through Moodle workshops, with peer assessment activity, where students submit their own work and then receive a number of submissions from other students which they must assess according to the teacher's specifications [6].

3   A Proposal for RoboCup

From its initial challenge in soccer, RoboCup has expanded into a wide range of domains. Though initially focused on the development of real robots, the advantages of simulators for fast prototyping and cost reduction has led to many of the leagues having either physical or simulated robots sub-leagues.

Each league has developed its own simulation software: while adapting to a particular domain may be an advantage, an undesirable consequence is the need of more resources for the development of software that could share a common base.

We advocate for the convergence of all the RoboCup simulators in a common open-source cloud platform. The advantages would be the optimization of the development resources and the availability of a cross-platform, powerful simulation engine, which can be run efficiently, no matter what operating system or hardware is used. The only requirements are a WebGL-enabled browser and an Internet connection. The participants would also have an easier time taking part in different competitions.

Based on the recent history of the RoboCup simulation competitions, we believe that the community is moving towards such a common, open-source platform. An example of this is the evolution of the RoboCup Rescue Simulation Platform: its was based initially on the Unreal Engine, but recently was moved to the Gazebo platform, benefitting from the progress made by the Open Source Robotics Foundation [15]. The maintenance of the simulation environment is now in hands of the open source community, since the simulator is no longer actively supported by the National Institute of Standards and Technology (NIST).

Moving this league to the cloud platform would be straightforward, since the tools (Gazebo and ROS) are already supported.

Two other different simulators are being used in RoboCup leagues: SimSpark for RoboCup Soccer Simulation [17], and Microsoft Robotics Developer Studio (MRDS) for RoboCup Junior CoSpace [7].

In this case, there are two ways for implementing the leagues in the cloud: one possibility is importing the world simulation files into Webots or Gazebo, the cloud supported simulators; the other alternative is to develop the WebGL and ROS interfaces for those simulators, which should be feasible for SimSpark since it already works in Linux, but quite problematic for MRDS, which only works in Windows.

It should be noted that supporting a specific simulator is a heavy task; in fact, MRDS has not been updated or patched since version 4.0, which was released in early 2012. Moreover, the Robotics Division of Microsoft Research was suspended in September 2014.

Other leagues that only used hardware platforms could be candidates to activate their simulated counterpart: in RoboCup@Work, the KUKA youBot platform is one candidate system for use, and this platform is readily available in the Webots and Gazebo simulators (Fig. 5). Participants who can't afford such a costly physical robot would definitely benefit from the availability of a simulated environment.

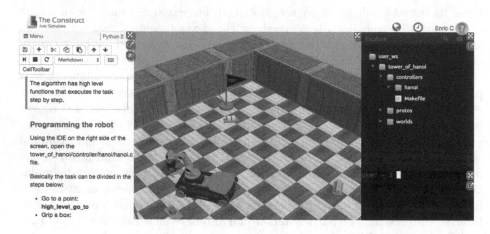

Fig. 5. Simulated environment of a KUKA youBot platform, a candidate system for the RoboCup@Work competition.

Competition based on low-cost platforms, like RoboCup Junior, can also benefit from the access to a simulation platform. It would allow the users to test their algorithms on standard platforms, or even simulate their own specific hardware design. We have already implemented the environment of the line sub-league of RoboCup Junior rescue (Fig. 6).

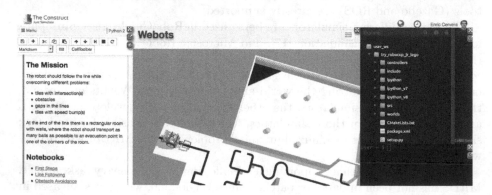

Fig. 6. Simulated environment for the RoboCup Junior Rescue competition.

3.1   Advantages of Cloud Simulators

These are the main advantages of using a web based simulator:

1. They do not need installation nor maintenance. Such operations are performed by the web portal that provides the simulator. Hence, neither the school nor the students have to deal with this unrelated task.
2. Students cannot break the simulation program by making errors or miss use of the simulation. If students make mistakes and something goes wrong crashing the simulation, they just can relaunch the web simulation again and start again from the initial conditions.
3. Different simulators available which allows entrance at different level of complexity. A web simulation system can provide different simulators at the same portal, each one with a different level of abstraction (for high school students, for university students, etc.).
4. Students can use any type of computer. Only a WebGL-enabled browser is needed.
5. Students and teachers can work from anywhere. Since the only requirement is to have access to internet, teachers and students can actually be anywhere while doing their simulations.
6. Students can cooperate with their mates while working on the simulation. Web simulation is by nature a collaborative thing, at the contrary of desktop simulations. Hence, differently from desktop simulators, web simulators allow the work of different people at the same time on the same simulation.

3.2   Drawbacks

As any system, web simulations have also drawbacks:

1. Users need a fast enough internet connection. Web simulations are run through an internet connection, and since the simulations tend to be complex, it is required to have an internet connection with fast speed.
2. By being on the cloud, web simulation inherits all the security problems that any cloud system has. It is very difficult to ensure that the data stored in the cloud will not be accessed by unauthorized people.

4   Conclusion and Future Work

We have presented a cloud simulation platform suitable for RoboCup Virtual Competitions. An open-source, common simulation platform has an important advantage over the current scattered development of specific simulators for each RoboCup league: programming and maintaining a simulator application is hard and time consuming. In addition, the cloud platform allows any user, anywhere, to run a simulation with any device equipped with a WebGL-enabled browser, be it a laptop, desktop, tablet, or even a smartphone.

Obviously, an Internet connection is needed, and the cost of the cloud infrastructure needs to be taken into account. We have presented a platform built on top of AWS, which can be used initially for free. More powerful computing configurations with an increasing number of CPUs and GPUs are available at an additional cost.

We expect that the RoboCup community opens a debate about the adoption of this or a similar platform for future editions of the virtual leagues. In the near future, we plan to offer cloud versions for all the leagues that currently use simulators, and develop simulation versions of some other leagues that use physical robots. The cloud allows to share simulations and code, enabling the development of a lively community of RoboCup users, which would become a complement and reinforcing tool for the successful RoboCup events throughout the world.

Acknowledgement. Support of IEEE RAS through the CEMRA program (Creation of Educational Material for Robotics and Automation) is gratefully acknowledged. This paper describes research done at the Robotic Intelligence Laboratory. Support for this laboratory is provided in part by Ministerio de Economia y Competitividad (DPI2015-69041-R), by Generalitat Valenciana (PROMETEOII/2014/028) and by Universitat Jaume I (P1-1B2014-52).

References

1. Beetham, H., Sharpe, R.: Rethinking Pedagogy for a Digital Age: Designing for 21st Century Learning. Routledge, Abingdon (2013)
2. Carpin, S., Lewis, M., Wang, J., Balakirsky, S., Scrapper, C.: USARSim: a robot simulator for research and education. In: 2007 IEEE International Conference on Robotics and Automation, pp. 1400–1405. IEEE (2007)
3. Casañ, G.A., Cervera, E., Moughlbay, A.A., Alemany, J., Martinet, P.: ROS-based online robot programming for remote education and training. In: 2015 IEEE International Conference on Robotics and Automation (ICRA), pp. 6101–6106. IEEE (2015)
4. Cervera, E., et al.: The robot programming network. J. Intell. Rob. Syst. **81**(1), 77 (2016)
5. Cole, J., Foster, H.: Using Moodle: Teaching with the Popular Open Source Course Management System. O'Reilly Media Inc., Newton (2007)
6. Dooley, J.F.: Peer assessments using the Moodle workshop tool. In: ACM SIGCSE Bulletin, vol. 41, pp. 344–344. ACM (2009)
7. Eguchi, A., Shen, J.: Student learning experience through CoSpace educational robotics: 3D simulation educational robotics tool. In: Cases on 3D Technology Application and Integration in Education, pp. 93–127. IGI Global (2013)
8. González-Martínez, J.A., Bote-Lorenzo, M.L., Gómez-Sánchez, E., Cano-Parra, R.: Cloud computing and education: a state-of-the-art survey. Comput. Educ. **80**, 132–151 (2015)
9. Hennig, M., Gaspers, D., Mertsching, B.: Interactive WebGL-based 3D visualizations for situated mathematics teaching. In: 2013 International Conference on Information Technology Based Higher Education and Training (ITHET), pp. 1–6. IEEE (2013)

10. Koenig, N., Howard, A.: Design and use paradigms for Gazebo, an open-source multi-robot simulator. In: Proceedings of the 2004 IEEE/RSJ International Conference on Intelligent Robots and Systems, (IROS 2004), vol. 3, pp. 2149–2154. IEEE (2004)
11. Michel, O.: Cyberbotics Ltd. Webots^{TM}: professional mobile robot simulation. Int. J. Adv. Rob. Syst. **1**(1), 5 (2004)
12. Quigley, M., et al.: ROS: an open-source robot operating system. In: ICRA Workshop on Open Source Software, pp. 1–6 (2009)
13. Ragan-Kelley, M., et al.: The Jupyter/IPython architecture: a unified view of computational research, from interactive exploration to communication and publication. In: AGU Fall Meeting Abstracts, H44D–07 (2014)
14. Resnick, M.: Scratch: programming for all. Commun. ACM **52**(11), 60–67 (2009)
15. Shimizu, M., Koenig, N., Visser, A., Takahashi, T.: A realistic robocup rescue simulation based on gazebo. In: Almeida, L., Ji, J., Steinbauer, G., Luke, S. (eds.) RoboCup 2015. LNCS (LNAI), vol. 9513, pp. 331–338. Springer, Cham (2015). https://doi.org/10.1007/978-3-319-29339-4_27
16. Xu, L., Huang, D., Tsai, W.T.: Cloud-based virtual laboratory for network security education. IEEE Trans. Educ. **57**(3), 145–150 (2014)
17. Xu, Y., Vatankhah, H.: SimSpark: an open source robot simulator developed by the RoboCup community. In: Behnke, S., Veloso, M., Visser, A., Xiong, R. (eds.) RoboCup 2013. LNCS (LNAI), vol. 8371, pp. 632–639. Springer, Heidelberg (2014). https://doi.org/10.1007/978-3-662-44468-9_59

Concurrent Hierarchical Reinforcement Learning for RoboCup Keepaway

Aijun Bai[1][(✉)], Stuart Russell[1], and Xiaoping Chen[2]

[1] Computer Science Division, Univerisity of California at Berkeley, Berkeley, USA
{aijunbai,russell}@berkeley.edu
[2] Department of Computer Science, University of Science and Technology of China,
Hefei, China
xpchen@ustc.edu.cn

Abstract. RoboCup Keepaway, originated from the RoboCup soccer simulation 2D challenge, has been widely used as a machine learning benchmark. In this paper, we present a concurrent hierarchical reinforcement learning approach to RoboCup Keepaway. Following the idea of *hierarchies of abstract machines* (HAMs), we write a partial policy as a HAM from the perspective of a single keeper, run multiple instances of the HAM, and use reinforcement learning to learn the optimal completion of the resulting joint HAM. Furthermore, we apply the idea of exploiting the intrinsic internal transitions within the HAM structure for more efficient learning. Experimental results confirm that the concurrent HAM approaches outperform the state of the art significantly on the very complex RoboCup Keepaway domain.

Keywords: Hierarchical reinforcement learning · HAM
RoboCup Keepaway

1 Introduction

Reinforcement learning (RL) tackles the problem of learning a rewarding behavior in an unknown environment via trial-and-error [18]. Recent advances in RL have led to great success on problems that pose significant challenges [12,15]. However, standard "flat" RL algorithms often learn slowly in environments requiring complex behaviors, due to the curses of dimensionality and history. *Hierarchical reinforcement learning* (HRL) aims to scale RL by incorporating prior knowledge about the structure of good policies into the algorithms [5]. Popular HRL solutions include the *options* theory [19], the *hierarchies of abstract machines* (HAMs) framework [1,14], and the *MAXQ* approach [7]. One of the major advantages of HRL approaches is the possibility of exploiting *temporal abstraction* and *hierarchical control*, where macro-actions following their own polices until termination.

In this paper, we focus on building intelligent agents that play the game of RoboCup Keepaway via hierarchical reinforcement learning. RoboCup Keepaway

© Springer Nature Switzerland AG 2018
H. Akiyama et al. (Eds.): RoboCup 2017, LNAI 11175, pp. 190–203, 2018.
https://doi.org/10.1007/978-3-030-00308-1_16

is a sub-task of the RoboCup soccer simulation 2D challenge [10,17]. It has been widely used as a machine learning benchmark [17], which presents significant challenges to machine learning methods, including continuous state and action spaces, multiple agents, and long and variable delays in the effects of actions. In RoboCup Keepaway, one team of keepers merely seeks to keep control of the ball for as long as possible. Following the idea of IIAMs, we write a partial policy as a HAM from the perspective of a single keeper, run multiple instances of the HAM, and use reinforcement learning to learn the optimal completion of the resulting joint HAM. We further apply the idea of HAMQ-INT [3], a novel HRL algorithm that identifies and exploits internal transitions within a HAM for efficient learning, to recursively shortcircuit the computation of Q values whenever applicable. We empirically confirm that HAMQ-INT outperforms the state of the art significantly on the benchmark RoboCup Keepaway domain. The main contribution of this paper is that we apply HAMQ-INT successfully to the RoboCup Keepaway domain, which, to the best of our knowledge, is the first application of the HAM framework to a very complex domain.

The remainder of the paper is organized as follows. Section 2 introduces some related work. Section 3 briefly reviews some background on RoboCup Keepaway and the HAM framework. Section 4 presents a concurrent HAM approach to RoboCup Keepaway. Section 5 presents the proposed HAMQ-INT algorithms. Section 6 describes the empirical result, and Sect. 7 concludes with discussion of future work.

2   Related Work

Stone et al. [16] develop a linear SARSA algorithm for RoboCup Keepaway following the options theory where the agent learns to select over a given set of low-level options. Along with some standard ball-controlling options, such as **Pass**() and **Hold**(), the keeper is also given a **GetOpen**() option which encodes the moving strategy when it is not controlling the ball. In their algorithm, each keeper learns separately assuming that other keepers and takers are part of the environment. In the experiment, we adopt their approach and develop an Option algorithm as one of the baselines. Kalyanakrishnan et al. [8] extend RoboCup Keepaway to Half Field Offense involving more agents and more complex behaviors. The authors notice that the Option algorithm has very sparse learning updates since each keeper is learning separately. They propose an inter-agent communication mechanism to facilitate information sharing among the agents and enable more frequent and reliable learning updates. In fact, since all the players begin with the same initial Q function and make the same updates, their action-value functions will always be alike, thereby reducing an essentially distributed problem to one of centralized control. In the experiment, we develop a concurrent-Option algorithm as an extension of this idea, where a global Q function is shared and maintained among all learners. Kalyanakrishnan et al. [9] extend the Option algorithm by including a specific learning component of the **GetOpen**() option. Their approach learns the option-selection policy over the ball-controlling options and the **GetOpen**() option iteratively: when one component is learning, the other one is kept unchanged. In contrast, our methods learn the two components simultaneously in a unified hierarchical reinforcement learning framework. Bai *et al.* [4] develop a MAXQ-based hierarchical planning algorithm for RoboCup domain. In this paper, we focus on hierarchical reinforcement learning instead.

3   Background

In this section, we review some background on the RoboCup Keepaway task, reinforcement learning and the general HAM framework.

Fig. 1. A 3 vs. 2 instance of RoboCup Keepaway.

3.1   RoboCup Keepaway

In RoboCup Keepaway, a team of keepers tries to maintain the ball possession within a limited field, while a team of takers tries to take the ball. Figure 1 shows an instance of Keepaway with 3 keepers and 2 takers. The system has continuous state and action spaces. A state encodes positions and velocities for the ball and all players. At each time step (within 100 ms), a player can execute a parametrized primitive action, such as turn(*angle*), dash(*power*) or kick(*power*, *angle*), where the turn action changes the body angle of the player, the dash action gives an acceleration to the player, and the kick action gives an acceleration to the ball if the ball is within the maximal kickable area of the player. All primitive actions are exposed to noises. Each episode begins with the ball and all players at fixed positions, and ends if any taker kicks the ball, or the ball is out of the field. The cumulative reward for the keepers is the total number of time steps for an episode. Instead of learning to select between primitive actions, the players are provided with a set of programmed options/skills including: (1) **Stay**() remaining stationary at the current position; (2) **Move**(d, v) dashing towards direction d with speed v; (3) **Intercept**() intercepting the ball; (4) **Pass**(k, v) passing the ball to teammate k with speed v; and (5) **Hold**() remaining stationary while keeping the ball kickable. The takers are assumed to follow fixed policies. The goal in RoboCup Keepaway is then to learn best-response policies for keepers on top of the provided low-level skills.

3.2 Reinforcement Learning with Hierarchies of Machines

Reinforcement Learning. *Reinforcement learning* (RL) usually tackles the problem of learning a rewarding behavior in an unknown environment modeled as a *Markov decision process* (MDP). Formally, an MDP is a tuple $\langle S, A, T, R, \gamma \rangle$, where S and A are the state and action spaces, $T(s'|s, a)$ and $R(s, a)$ are the transition and reward functions, and γ is a discount factor [6]. The goal for an MDP is to find an *optimal policy* $\pi^* : S \rightarrow A$ that maximizes the expected cumulative reward. In the setting of reinforcement learning, an agent learns an optimal policy by interacting with its environment. A Q learning agent achieves this by performing Q update, once it reaches state s' with reward r after executing action a in state s:

$$Q(s,a) \leftarrow (1 - \alpha)Q(s,a) + \alpha \left(r + \gamma \max_{a'} Q(s', a') \right), \tag{1}$$

where α is a learning rate. *Semi Markov decision processes* (SMDPs) allow for actions that take multiple time steps to terminate. The transition function for an SMDP has the form $T(s', N|s, a)$, where N is the number of time steps that action a takes. Similarly, the Q update rule for a SMDP is:

$$Q(s,a) \leftarrow (1 - \alpha)Q(s,a) + \alpha \left(r + \gamma^\tau \max_{a'} Q(s', a') \right), \tag{2}$$

where τ is number of time steps elapsed after executing action a in state s and before reaching state s', and r is the cumulative reward in-between.

The HAM Approach. The idea of HAM is to encode a partial policy for an agent as a set of hierarchical finite state machines with unspecified choice states, and use RL to learn its optimal completion. We adopt a different definition of HAM, allowing arbitrary call graph, despite the original definition of Parr and Russell [14] which requires that the call graph is a tree. Formally, a HAM $\mathcal{H} = \{\mathcal{N}_0, \mathcal{N}_1, \dots\}$ consists of a set of Moore machines $\mathcal{N}_i$ [13], where $\mathcal{N}_0$ is the root machine which serves as the starting point of the agent. A machine $\mathcal{N}$ is a tuple $\langle M, \Sigma, \Lambda, \delta, \mu \rangle$, where M is the set of machine states, Σ is the input alphabet which corresponds to the environment state space S, Λ is the output alphabet, δ is the machine transition function with $\delta(m, s)$ being the next machine state given machine state $m \in M$ and environment state $s \in S$, and μ is the machine output function with $\mu(m) \in \Lambda$ being the output of machine state $m \in M$. There are 5 types of machine states: **start** states are the entries of running machines; **action** states execute an action in the environment; **choose** states nondeterministically select the next machine states; **call** states invoke the execution of other machines; and, **stop** states end current machines and return control to calling machines. A machine $\mathcal{N}$ has uniquely one **start** state

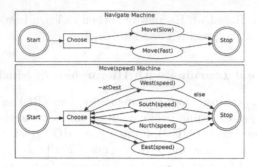

Fig. 2. An example of a HAM for a mobile robot.

```
Run (𝒩 : machine, z : stack, s : environment state) :
z.Push (𝒩)
m ← 𝒩.start
while m ≠ 𝒩.stop do
    if Type (m) = action then
    |   s ← Execute (μ(m))
    else if Type (m) = call then
    |   s ← Run (μ(m), z, s, π)
    if Type (m) = choose then
    |   z.Push (m)
    |   m ← Choose (z, s, μ(m))
    └   z.Pop ()
    else
    └   m ← δ(m, s)
z.Pop ()
return s
```

Algorithm 1: Running a HAM.

and one **stop** state, referred as $\mathcal{N}.start$ and $\mathcal{N}.stop$ respectively. For **start** and **stop** states, the outputs are not defined; for **action** states, the outputs are the associated primitive actions; for **call** states, the outputs are the next machines to run; and, for **choose** states, the outputs are the sets of possible choices, where each choice corresponds to a next machine state. For an example, see Fig. 2, which shows a HAM for a mobile robot navigating in a grid map. The Navigate machine has a choice state, at which it has to choose between Move(Fast) and Move(Slow). The Move(*speed*) machine has to select repeatedly between East, West, South and North with specified *speed* parameter until the robot is at its destination.

To run a HAM $\mathcal{H}$, a run-time stack (or stack for short) is needed. Each frame of this stack stores run-time information such as the active machine, its machine state, the parameters passing to this machine and the values of local variables used by this machine. Algorithm 1 gives the pseudo-code for running a HAM, where the **Execute** function executes an action in the environment and

```
Navigate(s : environment state):
speed ← Choose₁ (Slow, Fast)
s ← Move (s, speed)
return s

Move (s : environment state, speed : parameter):
while not s.atDest() do
    a ← Choose₂ (West, South, North, East)
    s ← Execute (a, speed)
return s
```

Algorithm 2: A HAM in pseudo-code for a mobile robot.

returns the next environment state, and the **Choose** function picks the next machine state given the updated stack z, the current environment state s and the set of available choices $\mu(m)$. Let $\mathcal{Z}$ be the space of all possible stacks given HAM $\mathcal{H}$. It has been shown that an agent running a HAM $\mathcal{H}$ over an MDP $\mathcal{M}$ yields a joint SMDP $\mathcal{H} \circ \mathcal{M}$ defined over the joint space of S and $\mathcal{Z}$. The only actions of $\mathcal{H} \circ \mathcal{M}$ are the choices allowed at choice points. A choice point is a joint state (s, z) with $z.\textbf{Top}()$ being a **choose** state. This is an SMDP because once a choice is made at a choice point, the system—the composition of $\mathcal{H}$ and $\mathcal{M}$—runs automatically until the next choice point is reached. The policy of this SMDP implements exactly the **Choose** function in Algorithm 1. An optimal policy of this SMDP corresponds to an optimal completion of the input HAM, which can be found by applying a HAMQ algorithm [14]. HAMQ keeps track of the previous choice point (s, z), the choice made c and the cumulative reward r thereafter. Whenever it enters into a new choice point (s', z'), it performs the SMDP Q update as follows:

$$Q(s, z, c) \leftarrow (1 - \alpha)Q(s, z, c) + \alpha \left(r + \gamma^\tau \max_{c'} Q(s', z', c') \right),$$

where τ is the number of steps between the two choice points.

As suggested by the language of ALisp [2], a HAM can be equivalently converted into a piece of code in modern programming languages, with *call-and-return* semantics and built-in routines for explicitly updating stacks, executing actions and getting new environment states. The execution of a HAM can then be simulated by running the code itself. This conversion is important, as it provides a much more efficient way of designing and running a HAM. For example, the HAM shown in Fig. 2 is equivalent to the pseudo-code in Algorithm 2, where a machine becomes a function. Here, **Execute** is the macro executing an action with specified parameters and returning the next environment state; the **Choose** macro extends the **Choose** function from Algorithm 1 to choose among not only a set of machine states, but also a set of parameters for the next machine. Bookkeeping codes for maintaining the stack are omitted for simplicity. Marthi *et al.* show that [11] multiple HAMs can be ran concurrently to form a joint HAM, and the same reinforcement learning technique (namely the HAMQ algorithm) can be applied to learn the optimal completion of the

```
Keeper (s : environment state):
while not s.Terminate() do
    if s.BallKickable() then
    |   m ← Choose₁ (Pass, Hold); s ← Run (m, s)
    else if s.FastestToBall() then
    |   s ← Intercept (s)
    else
    |   m ← Choose₂ (Stay, Move); s ← Run (m, s)
return s

Pass (s : environment state):
k ← Choose₃ (1, 2, . . . ); v ← Choose₄ (Normal, Fast)
while s.BallKickable() do
    |   s ← Run (Pass, k, v)
return s

Hold (s : environment state):
s ← Run (Hold)
return s

Intercept (s : environment state):
s ← Run (Intercept)
return s

Stay (s : environment state):
i ← s.TmControlBall()
while i = s.TmControlBall() do
    |   s ← Run (Stay)
return s

Move (s : environment state):
d ← Choose₅ (0°, 90°, 180°, 270°); v ← Choose₆ (Normal, Fast)
i ← s.TmControlBall()
while i = s.TmControlBall() do
    |   v ← Run (Move, d, v)
return s
```

Algorithm 3: The HAM for RoboCup Keepaway.

resulting joint HAM provided with appropriate synchronization semantics among the concurrently running HAMs.

4   The HAM Approach to RoboCup Keepaway

We develop the partial policy represented as a HAM from the perspective of a single keeper, and run multiple instances of this HAM concurrently for each keeper to form a joint policy for all keepers following the proposal of [11]. To run multiple HAMs concurrently, they have to be synchronized, such that if any machine is at its **choose** state, the other machines have to wait; if multiple machines are at their **choose** states, a joint choice is made instead of independent choice for each machine. For this purpose, players have to share their learned value functions and the selected joint choice. A joint Q update is developed to learn the joint choice selection policy as an optimal completion of the resulting joint HAM. Algorithm 3 shows the HAM written in pseudo-code for a single keeper. Here, **Keeper** is the root machine. The **Run** macro runs a machine or an option with specified parameters. **BallKickable**, **FastestToBall**, **TmControlBall** are predicates used to determine the transition inside a machine. It is worth noting that the **Move** machine only considers 4 directions, with direction $0°$ being the direction towards the ball, and so on.

5 Efficient Learning by Leveraging Internal Transitions

In this section, we introduce the concept of internal transition, and develop a hierarchical reinforcement learning algorithm that automatically identifies and exploits internal transitions for efficient learning, following the idea of Bai *et al.* [3].

5.1 Internal Transitions Within HAMs

It has been observed that a HAM with deep hierarchical structure, where there are many calls from a parent machine to one of its child machines over the hierarchy, induces many internal transitions. An internal transition is a transition over the joint state space, where only the run-time stack changes but the environment state does not. Internal transitions always come with zero rewards and deterministic outcomes in the resulting SMDP. Take the HAM for RoboCup Keepaway in Algorithm 3 as an example, there are many internal transitions within this single HAM. For example, when the **Pass** machine is selected at the choice point **Choose$_1$** of the **Keeper** machine, the next 2 consecutive choice points must be **Choose$_3$** and **Choose$_4$** within the **Pass** machine. When multiple HAMs are executing concurrently according to the concurrent schema shown in [11], there are even more internal transitions in the resulting joint HAM. For example, in a scenario of the 3 vs. 2 Keepaway game, where only keeper 1 can kick the ball, suppose the joint machine state is [**Choose$_1$, Choose$_2$, Choose$_2$**] with each element being the machine state of a HAM. If the joint choice made is [**Pass, Move, Stay**], then the next 2 consecutive machine states must be [**Choose$_3$, Choose$_5$, Stay**] and [**Choose$_4$, Choose$_6$, Stay**].

In general, the transition function of the resulting SMDP induced by running a HAM has the form $T(s', z', \tau | s, z, c) \in [0, 1]$, where (s, z) is the current choice point, c is the choice made, (s', z') is the next choice point, and τ is the number of time steps. Given a HAM with a deep hierarchy of machines, it is usually the case that there is no real actions executed between two consecutive choice points, therefore the number of time steps and the cumulative reward in-between are essentially zero. We call this kind of transition an internal transition, because the machine state changes but the environment state does not. Formally, a transition is a tuple $\langle s, z, c, r, s', z' \rangle$ with r being the cumulative reward. For an internal transition, we must have $s' = s$ and $r = 0$. In addition, because the dynamics of the HAM after a choice has been made and before an action is executed is deterministic by design, the next choice point (s, z') of an internal transition is deterministically conditioned only on $\langle s, z, c \rangle$. Let $\rho(s, z, c)$ be the $\mathcal{Z}$ component of the next choice point. If $\langle s, z, c \rangle$ leads to an internal transition, we must have $T(s, \rho(s, z, c), 0 | s, z, c) = 1$. Therefore, we have

$$\begin{aligned} Q(s, z, c) &= V(s, \rho(s, z, c)) \\ &= \max_{c'} Q(s, \rho(s, z, c), c'). \end{aligned} \tag{3}$$

So, we can store the rules of internal transition as $\langle s, z, c, z' \rangle$ tuples, where $z' = \rho(s, z, c)$. They can be used to recursively compute Q values according to Eq. 3 when applicable. The size of the set of stored rules can be further reduced, because the machine transition function δ of a HAM is usually determined by a set of predicates defined over environment state s, rather than the exact values of all state variables. For example, the machine transition function of machine Move(*speed*) in Fig. 2 depends only on the value of atDest(s) for any state s. Suppose $\langle s_1, z, c \rangle$ leads to an internal transition with (s_1, z') being the next choice point. Let the set of predicates used to determine the trajectory in terms of active machines and machine states from z.**Top**() to z'.**Top**() be $\mathcal{P} = \{P_1, P_2, \dots\}$. Let the value of $\mathcal{P}$ given state s be $\mathcal{P}(s) = \{P_1(s), P_2(s), \dots\}$. It can be concluded that the transition trajectory induced by $\mathcal{P}$ depends only on $\mathcal{P}(s_1)$, after choice c is made at choice point (s_1, z). On the other hand, if the set of predicates $\mathcal{P}$ over state s_2 ($s_2 \neq s_1$) has the same value as of state s_1, namely $\mathcal{P}(s_2) = \mathcal{P}(s_1)$, and the same choice c is made at choice point (s_2, z), then the followed transition trajectory before reaching the next choice point must also be the same as of $\langle s_1, z, c \rangle$. In other words, $\langle s_2, z, c \rangle$ leads to an internal transition such that $\rho(s_1, z, c) = \rho(s_2, z, c)$.

Thus, the rule of internal transition $\langle s_1, z, c, z' \rangle$ can be equivalently stored and retrieved as $\langle \mathcal{P}, \mathcal{P}(s_1), z, c, z' \rangle$, which automatically applies to $\langle s_2, z, c, z' \rangle$, if $\mathcal{P}(s_2) = \mathcal{P}(s_1)$. Here, z' is the stack of the next choice point such that $z' = \rho(s_1, z, c) = \rho(s_2, z, c)$. The size of the joint space of encountered predicates and their values is determined by the HAM itself, which is typically much smaller than the size of the state space. For example, for a problem with continuous state space (such as the RoboCup Keepaway domain we considered), this joint space is still limited. In summary, we can have an efficient way of storing and retrieving the rules of internal transition by keeping track of the predicates evaluated between two choice points.

5.2 The HAMQ-INT Algorithm

The main idea of HAMQ-INT is to identify and take advantage of internal transitions within a HAM. For this purpose, HAMQ-INT automatically keeps track of the predicates that are evaluated between two choice points, stores the discovered rules of internal transition based on predicates and the corresponding values, and uses the learned rules to shortcircuit the computation of Q values

---

QUpdate (s' : *state*, z' : *stack*, r : *reward*, t' : *current time*, $\mathcal{P}$: *evaluated predicates*):
if $t' = t$ then
$\quad \llcorner \ \rho[\mathcal{P}, \mathcal{P}(s), z, c] \leftarrow z'$
else
$\quad \llcorner$ **QTable** $(s, z, c) \leftarrow (1 - \alpha)$ **QTable** $(s, z, c) + \alpha(r + \gamma^{t'-t} \max_{c'} \mathbf{Q}(s', z', c'))$
$(t, s, z) \leftarrow (t', s', z')$

$\mathbf{Q}$ (s : *state*, z : *stack*, c : *choice*):
if $\exists \mathcal{P}$ *s.t.* $\langle \mathcal{P}, \mathcal{P}(s), z, c \rangle \in \rho.\mathbf{Keys}()$ then
$\quad | \quad q \leftarrow -\infty$
$\quad | \quad z' \leftarrow \rho[\mathcal{P}, \mathcal{P}(s), z, c]$
$\quad | \quad$ for $c' \in \mu(z.\mathbf{Top}())$ do
$\quad | \quad \quad \llcorner \ q \leftarrow \max(q, \mathbf{Q}(s, z', c'))$
$\quad \llcorner$ return q
else
$\quad \llcorner$ return **QTable** (s, z, c)

Algorithm 4: The HAMQ-INT algorithm.

whenever it is possible. To detect internal transitions, a global environment time t is maintained. It is incremented by one only when there is an action executed in the environment. When the agent enters a choice point (s', z') after having made a choice c at choice point (s, z), and finds that t is not incremented since the previous choice point, it must be the case that $s' = s$ and $\langle s, z, c \rangle$ leads to an internal transition. Let $\mathcal{P}$ be the set of predicates that have been evaluated between these two choice points. Then a new rule of internal transition $\langle \mathcal{P}, \mathcal{P}(s), z, c, z' \rangle$ is found. The agent can conclude that for any state x, if $\mathcal{P}(x) = \mathcal{P}(s)$, then $\langle x, z, c \rangle$ leads to an internal transition as well. In the implementation, the agent uses a hash table ρ to store the learned rules, such that $\rho[\mathcal{P}, \mathcal{P}(s), z, c] = z'$, if $\langle \mathcal{P}, \mathcal{P}(s), z, c, z' \rangle$ is a rule of internal transition. One thing to note is that, because z' is deterministically conditioned on $\langle \mathcal{P}, \mathcal{P}(s), z, c \rangle$ for an internal transition, the value of $\rho[\mathcal{P}, \mathcal{P}(s), z, c]$ will not be changed after it has been updated for the first time.

When the agent needs to evaluate a Q function, say $Q(s, z, c)$, and finds that $\langle s, z, c \rangle$ leads to an internal transition according to the current learned rules, Eq. 3 is used to decompose $Q(s, z, c)$ into the Q values of the next choice points, which are evaluated recursively in the same way, essentially leading to a tree of exact Bellman backups. In fact, only the terminal Q values of this tree needs to be learned, enabling efficient learning for the agent. Algorithm 4 gives the pseudo-code of the HAMQ-INT algorithm. Here, the **QTable** function returns the stored Q value as request. It can be implemented in either tabular or function approximation ways. The **Q** function evaluates the Q value of (s, z, c) tuple. It first checks whether (s, z, c) subjects to any learned internal transition rule. This is done by checking whether there exists an encountered set of predicates $\mathcal{P}$, such that $\langle \mathcal{P}, \mathcal{P}(s), z, c \rangle \in \rho.\mathbf{Keys}()$. The uniqueness of transition trajectory for an internal transition ensures that there will be at most one such $\mathcal{P}$. If there is such $\mathcal{P}$, **Q** uses the retrieved rule to recursively decompose the requested Q value according to Eq. 3; otherwise, it simply returns the stored Q value by querying `QTable`.

The **QUpdate** function performs the SMDP Q update. It is called once the agent enters a new choice point. The caller has to keep track of the current state s', the current stack z', the evaluated predicates $\mathcal{P}$ on state since the previous choice point and the cumulative reward r in-between. If the current time t' equals to the time t of the previous choice point, it must be the case that $\langle s, z, c, 0, s, z' \rangle$ is an internal transition. Thus, a new rule $\langle \mathcal{P}, \mathcal{P}(s), z, c \rangle$ is learned, and the ρ table is updated accordingly. If $t' \neq t$, meaning there are some actions executed in the environment, it simply performs the Q update. Finally, it uses the current (t', s', z') tuple to update the (global) previous (t, s, z) tuple, so the function will be prepared for the next call.

6 Experiment

We compare concurrent-HAMQ-INT, concurrent-HAMQ, concurrent-Option, Option and Random algorithms. The Option algorithm is adopted from [16], where the agent learns an option-selection policy over **Hold**() and **Pass**(k, v) options if it can kick the ball, otherwise it follows a fixed policy: if it is the fastest one to intercept the ball, it intercepts; otherwise, it follows a **GetOpen**() option. The **GetOpen**() option, which enables the agent to move to an open area in the field, is manually programmed beforehand. In the original Option learning algorithm, each agent learns independently. We argue that this setting is problematic, since it actually incorrectly assumes that other keepers are stationary. We extend Option to concurrent-Option, by sharing the learned value functions and the option selected. The HAM algorithms are not provided with the **GetOpen**() option. Instead, they have to learn their own versions of **GetOpen**() by selecting from **Stay** and **Move** machines. Each taker follows the same fixed policy: it always tries to intercept the ball. The Random algorithm is a non-learning version of Option, which selects available options randomly.

The SARSA(λ)-learning rule with a linear function approximator is used to implement the SMDP Q update for all learning algorithms. A state is represented as a vector of 15 features consisting of some distances and angles calculated from the state, which is then encoded as a huge binary vector following the *tile coding* technique. The resulting binary vector has approximately 50,000 bits but is constrained to have only with 480 ones. For HAMQ approaches, a dynamically calculated hash value of the run-time stack is used as its index. The learning rate α and the eligibility decaying rate λ are set to be 0.125 and 0.5 respectively. Figure 3a and b show the experiment result on a 3 vs. 2 instance of RoboCup Keepaway evaluated over training time and number of episodes respectively. The data points are averaged using a moving window with size of 1000 episodes. The training time is accounted from the perspective of the simulated world where a step/cycle takes exactly 100 ms. Provided with the same training time, algorithms with better learning performance will result to less episodes, since they learn to reliably control the ball very soon. It can be

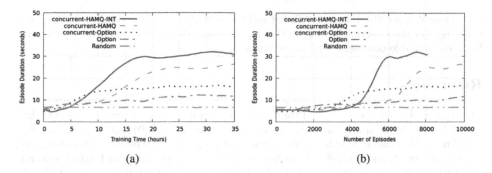

(a)   (b)

Fig. 3. Experimental result on a 3 vs. 2 instance of RoboCup Keepaway evaluated over (a) training time and (b) number of episodes. Two short videos showing the initial and converged policies of HAMQ-INT can be found at links 1 and 2 respectively.

seen from the result that concurrent-Option outperforms Option significantly, concurrent-HAMQ outperforms concurrent-Option after about 15 h of training, and concurrent-HAMQ-INT has the best performance. We expect the reason to be (1) significantly less number of Q values have to be learned because many of them are recursively decomposed into the combinations of other Q values following the Bellman backup tree induced by recursively applying the learned internal transition rules; and (2) one learned abstract internal transition rule from one transition can be applied to unlimited number of other states in the case of continuous state space.

7   Conclusions

In this paper, we present a concurrent hierarchical reinforcement learning approach to the benchmark RoboCup Keepaway domain. We apply the idea of HAMQ-INT that automatically discovers and exploits internal transitions within a HAM for efficient learning. We empirically confirm that the concurrent HAM approaches outperform the state of the art significantly on RoboCup Keepaway. In future work, we would like to apply this idea to the full RoboCup soccer simulation game and other challenging domains that require very complex behaviors. The way we taking advantage of internal transitions within a HAM can be seen as leveraging some prior knowledge of the transition model of a reinforcement learning problem, which happens to be deterministic. We would also like to extend this internal transition idea to more general reinforcement learning problems, where models are partially known in advance.

Acknowledgments. Funding for this research was provided by ONR under contract N00014-12-1-0609, and by DARPA under contract N66001-15-2-4048. Opinions, findings, and conclusion or recommendations expressed in this material are those of the authors and do not necessarily reflect the view of the funding agencies. The authors would like to thank the WrightEagle soccer simulation team (particularly, Changjie

Fan, Feng Wu, Ke Shi, Haochong Zhang and Guanghui Lu) for contributing to the base code used in the experiment. The authors would also thank the anonymous reviewers for their valuable comments and suggestions.

References

1. Andre, D., Russell, S.J.: Programmable reinforcement learning agents. In: Advances in Neural Information Processing Systems, pp. 1019–1025 (2001)
2. Andre, D., Russell, S.J.: State abstraction for programmable reinforcement learning agents. In: Proceedings of the 8th National Conference on Artificial Intelligence and 14th Conference on Innovative Applications of Artificial Intelligence, pp. 119–125 (2002)
3. Bai, A., Russell, S.J.: Efficient reinforcement learning with hierarchies of machines by leveraging internal transitions. In: Proceedings of the Twenty-Fifth International Joint Conference on Artificial Intelligence, IJCAI 2017, Melbourne, Australia, 19–25 August 2017
4. Bai, A., Wu, F., Chen, X.: Online planning for large Markov decision processes with hierarchical decomposition. ACM Trans. Intell. Syst. Technol. 6(4), 45 (2015)
5. Barto, A., Mahadevan, S.: Recent advances in hierarchical reinforcement learning. Discret. Event Dyn. Syst. 13, 341–379 (2003)
6. Bellman, R.: Dynamic Programming. Princeton University Press, Princeton (1957)
7. Dietterich, T.G.: Hierarchical reinforcement learning with the MAXQ value function decomposition. J. Mach. Learn. Res. 13(1), 63 (1999)
8. Kalyanakrishnan, S., Liu, Y., Stone, P.: Half field offense in RoboCup soccer: a multiagent reinforcement learning case study. In: Lakemeyer, G., Sklar, E., Sorrenti, D.G., Takahashi, T. (eds.) RoboCup 2006. LNCS (LNAI), vol. 4434, pp. 72–85. Springer, Heidelberg (2007). https://doi.org/10.1007/978-3-540-74024-7_7
9. Kalyanakrishnan, S., Stone, P.: Learning complementary multiagent behaviors: a case study. In: Baltes, J., Lagoudakis, M.G., Naruse, T., Ghidary, S.S. (eds.) RoboCup 2009. LNCS (LNAI), vol. 5949, pp. 153–165. Springer, Heidelberg (2010). https://doi.org/10.1007/978-3-642-11876-0_14
10. Kitano, H., et al.: The RoboCup synthetic agent challenge 97. In: Kitano, H. (ed.) RoboCup 1997. LNCS, vol. 1395, pp. 62–73. Springer, Heidelberg (1998). https://doi.org/10.1007/3-540-64473-3_49
11. Marthi, B., Russell, S.J., Latham, D., Guestrin, C.: Concurrent hierarchical reinforcement learning. In: IJCAI, pp. 779–785 (2005)
12. Mnih, V., et al.: Human-level control through deep reinforcement learning. Nature 518(7540), 529–533 (2015)
13. Moore, E.F.: Gedanken-experiments on sequential machines. Automata Stud. 34, 129–153 (1956)
14. Parr, R., Russell, S.: Reinforcement learning with hierarchies of machines. In: Advances in Neural Information Processing Systems, vol. 10 (1998)
15. Silver, D., et al.: Mastering the game of go with deep neural networks and tree search. Nature 529(7587), 484–489 (2016)
16. Stone, P., Sutton, R., Kuhlmann, G.: Reinforcement learning for robocup soccer keepaway. Adapt. Behav. 13(3), 165–188 (2005)
17. Stone, P., Kuhlmann, G., Taylor, M.E., Liu, Y.: Keepaway soccer: from machine learning testbed to benchmark. In: Bredenfeld, A., Jacoff, A., Noda, I., Takahashi, Y. (eds.) RoboCup 2005. LNCS (LNAI), vol. 4020, pp. 93–105. Springer, Heidelberg (2006). https://doi.org/10.1007/11780519_9

18. Sutton, R.S., Barto, A.G.: Reinforcement Learning: An Introduction, vol. 1. MIT Press, Cambridge (1998)
19. Sutton, R., Precup, D., Singh, S.: Between MDPs and semi-MDPs: a framework for temporal abstraction in reinforcement learning. Artif. Intell. **112**(1), 181–211 (1999)

Vision-Based Orientation Detection
of Humanoid Soccer Robots

Andre Mühlenbrock and Tim Laue[✉]

Universität Bremen, Fachbereich 3 – Mathematik und Informatik, Postfach 330 440,
28334 Bremen, Germany
{muehlenb,tlaue}@informatik.uni-bremen.de

Abstract. Knowing the positions of the other players on a football pitch
is a crucial aspect for playing successfully. However, knowing not only
the position but also the orientation of another player provides certain
tactical advantages. In this paper, we present a vision-based approach
for determining the orientation of humanoid NAO robots over short and
medium distances. It is based on the idea of analyzing the alignment of
other robots' foot sides. In a series of experiments, we demonstrate that
the approach is able to perform robust and precise orientation detection
in different scenarios.

1 Introduction

Without knowing the positions of other robots, at least in the immediate vicinity,
playing soccer in a reasonable manner is barely possible, as collisions and losing
possession of the ball will occur frequently. This is why almost all participants
across all RoboCup leagues employ some sort of obstacle or robot detection to
perform path planning and to support decision making. However, on higher tactical levels, the orientation of opponent robots becomes more and more important. Similar to humans, humanoid robots cannot move in all directions with
the same speed. For most robots, moving forward is predominant, requiring an
initial rotational movement towards the walk target. Thus, the time to reach a
certain position on the field, for instance to intercept a pass, always depends on
the initial orientation. Furthermore, humanoid soccer robots have a limited field
of view and cannot perceive what is happening behind them, often not even by
turning the head. These limitations in motion and perception imply that considering the opponent's orientation in decision making, for instance when choosing
the dribble direction or the next pass target, provides a tactical advantage as it
contributes to reducing the risk of interference by opponents.

In this paper, we present an approach to solve the first step towards such kind
of tactics: detecting the orientation of robots in sensor data. As we use the NAO
robot as platform, the approach is vision-based, processing data from the two
NAO cameras. Furthermore, as we base our work on the B-Human framework
[9], several already existing preprocessing steps are facilitated, including basic
robot detection. Our new approach uses the alignment of robot feet to compute

H. Akiyama et al. (Eds.): RoboCup 2017, LNAI 11175, pp. 204–215, 2018.
https://doi.org/10.1007/978-3-030-00308-1_17

orientations, as this feature turns out to be quite robust, in contrast to a robot's upper body, which might have a complex appearance due to moving arms and a jersey of almost arbitrary style. The major benefits of our approach are its ability to determine orientations even over distances of more than two meters, which is necessary as robots might walk quite fast, as well as its computational efficiency, which is important as the available computing time has always to be shared with many other components.

The remainder of this paper is organized as follows: First, Sect. 2 discusses related approaches to determine the position and orientation of soccer robots. Afterwards, necessary preliminary works for the orientation detection are presented in Sect. 3, followed by a description of our approach in Sect. 4. An evaluation of the accuracy and the performance of our approach is presented in Sect. 5. Finally, the paper concludes in Sect. 6.

2   Related Work

Early works in the RoboCup Standard Platform did not only ignore any orientation of other robots but also the robot appearance at all. Using AIBO robots, [4] as well as [6] only considered gaps in the perceived field's surface as areas that should be avoided. Algorithms for explicitly detecting other NAO robots have been presented by [2,8]. The latter approach also included the determination of the team the detected robot is playing for. This information was used to build a team-wide model of the opponents, as described in [5].

The RoboCup robot league that currently has the most advanced tactical plays is probably the Small Size League. In this league, orientation information is important as the robots' kick devices are always at the front part. However, through having external cameras over the field and standardized colored patterns (that encode position, identity, and orientation) on top of all robots, the detection process is quite simple and is solved by the standardized vision system [12].

A general approach to determine the orientation of objects is template matching. In a preprocessing step, a specific amount of images, containing objects with different orientations, must be analyzed for their features (like color gradients and normals) and saved as templates. To determine the orientation of an input image, its features must be compared with the templates. The orientation of the most similar template will be returned. However, template matching approaches require a lot of computing time. For instance, the software *Linemod* [3] has an average execution time of 119 ms on a 2,3 GHz Intel CPU. There is also a related approach which was tested in the Sony Four-Legged League using SIFT descriptors. The tested implementation has an average execution time of 300 ms on a 576 MHz CPU [7]. In [11], a decision tree learning approach that considered the alignment of the distinctive AIBO robot jerseys patches was described.

One recent work in the RoboCup Standard Platform League is based on a deep neural network which gets the brightness values of pixels of a robot region as input and returns a two dimensional direction vector [10]. The average error is declared with approximately $8°$ and the execution time is approximately 0.23 ms

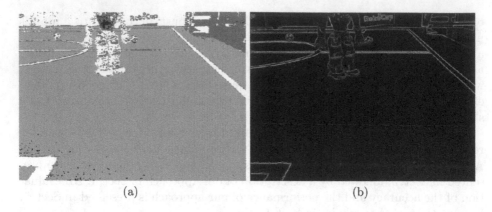

(a)   (b)

Fig. 1. (a) A color classified image and (b) a contrast-normalized Sobel image from the upper camera of a NAO. (Color figure online)

per robot region. However, it is not clear if this approach also works for moving robots and over which distances the result can be reproduced.

3   Preliminary Works

The approach presented in this paper does not work on plain images but on already preprocessed data. In addition, the basic task of detecting a robot in an image is also carried out by a different component.

In the B-Human framework [9], there are two different preprocessed images that are created from the original camera images. Both can be used for orientation detection. The first one is a color classified image, in which pixels are just classified as black, white, green, or no color (see Fig. 1a). As a first step, classifying a pixel's color is done by applying a threshold to its saturation to classify this pixel as whether colored or non-colored. For the distinction of black and white, there is just another threshold applied to the luminance. Finally, for green, there is a range defined regarding the hue. Due to recent changes in the setup of the Standard Platform League, no more color classes are needed. Robot jersey colors can be chosen arbitrarily and are thus not part of the color classification process.

The second image is the contrast-normalized Sobel image (see Fig. 1b). This is an image in which the pixels represent vectors whose lengths indicate how heavy the pixels' colors change and whose directions show the changing direction. In general, the contrast-normalized Sobel image offers a higher quality in finding silhouettes than the color classified image.

The B-Human framework already contains different implementations for robot detection. The one that has been used for this paper subsamples the color classified image along vertical lines and merges line parts that are not green within union find data structures. Field lines and balls are filtered out by size and shape so that only potential robot regions remain. These regions are used

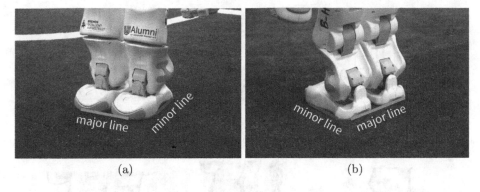

(a)   (b)

Fig. 2. Illustration of the major line and minor line definition on a (a) forward-facing and a (b) backward-facing robot.

for the orientation determination described in this paper. Please note that our approach is in no way limited to this particular player perception software.

4   The Orientation Detection Approach

The approach consists of two steps which both analyze the region around a previously recognized robot's feet. First, we search for two lines – the so-called *major line* and *minor line* – in this region. These two lines already allow calculating an orientation in the range of $[-90°, 90°)$. To obtain the complete orientation in the range of $[-180°, 180°)$, we determine whether the robot is facing forwards or backwards by analyzing two areas in the color classified image over the feet. Both steps turn out to work quite reliably. However, by focussing on the feet, the approach is not able to handle lying robots or robots that have a ball directly at their feet.

4.1   Determining Major Line and Minor Line

To determine the orientation of a robot region, we have defined two lines for which we are searching in the image. This can be done in the contrast-normalized Sobel image as well as in the color classified image. The major line is defined from toe to toe and from heel to heel while the minor line is defined as a side line of a foot. An example is shown in Fig. 2.

To find these lines, we have created the lower silhouette of the feet by scanning the image upwards for each pixel on the lower robot region border. In the contrast-normalized Sobel image, a pixel on the silhouette is found when it exceeds a length threshold. When the color classified image is used, a pixel on the silhouette is found when it is not green and more than two subsequent pixels are also not green. After we created the lower silhouette of the feet, we use *Andrew's Monoton Chain Algorithm* [1] to determine the lower convex hull.

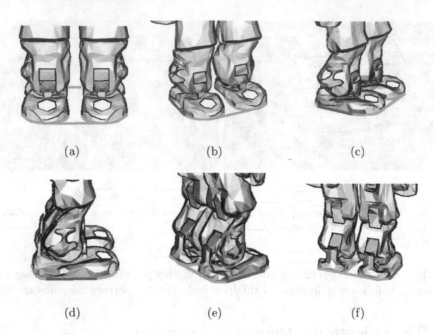

(a)   (b)   (c)

(d)   (e)   (f)

Fig. 3. Illustration of the major line (orange) and minor line (blue) on differently rotated robots. The silhouette is green. It is evident that there is always a greater sum of jumps on the silhouette in the range of the major line than on the silhouette in the range of the minor line. (Color figure online)

Looking at the longest three edges with a specific minimum length of the lower convex hull, it is evident that two of these are the major line and the minor line.

At this point, we have found at maximum three lines and have just to determine which of these lines are the major line and the minor line. For distinction, we calculate the sum of all jumps of neighboring pixels in the silhouette, which have a certain minimum length (the current, experimentally determined length is 2.4 pixels). The idea is that the major line has the greater sum of jumps because there is a gap between both feet (see Fig. 3). More precisely, there are three cases:

- Just one long line: In this case, the robot must have an orientation of approx. $0°$, $90°$, $-90°$ or $-180°$ and the line is parallel to the x-axis, since in all other cases there would be a second long line. When the sum of jumps is zero, we know that the recognized line is the minor line. If the sum of jumps is much larger than zero, we know that the line is the major line (see Fig. 3a/d).
- Two long lines: In this case, the line with the greater sum of jumps is the major line and the line with the smaller sum of jumps is the minor line (see Fig. 3b/c/e/f).
- Three long lines: This is just a special case which can occur with the NAO's feet and an orientation of nearly $180°$. In this case, the line with the lowest

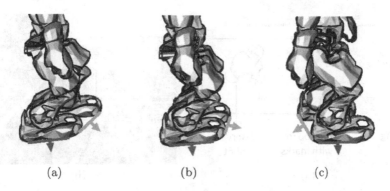

(a)   (b)   (c)

Fig. 4. Variation of major line (orange) and minor line (blue) in a walking sequence. (Color figure online)

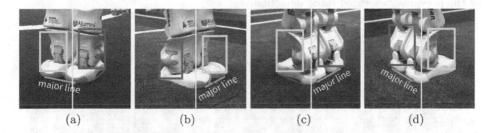

(a)   (b)   (c)   (d)

Fig. 5. Location of the major line (orange) and the area that contains more green pixels (yellow). (a/b) The major line and the yellow marked area are on the same side when the robot is facing forwards and (c/d) they are on a different side when the robot is facing backwards. (Color figure online)

sum of jumps is the minor line and the line that has the lowest mid point in the image is the major line.

If both lines have been found, we initially assume that the robot is facing forwards. To calculate the orientation, we transform the major line and minor line from image coordinates in field coordinates and define a vector v parallel to the transformated minor line and calculate the normal vector n to the transformated major line which is directed towards the observing robot. If $v \cdot n \leq 0$, we mirror the vector v so it is directed also towards the observing robot. Now we use the vector v to calculate the orientation $\alpha := atan2(-v_y, -v_x)$.

The reason for not simply using the normal vector n of the major line is that the major line obviously has a higher deviation when the robot is walking (see Fig. 4). If we just found the major line, we simply set $\alpha := 0°$ and add a flag that indicates that there is no information whether the robot is facing forwards or backwards, so the opposite orientation would be also plausible. When we just found the minor line, we set $\alpha := 90°$ and add the same flag, so that we know that the orientation is $90°$ or $-90°$.

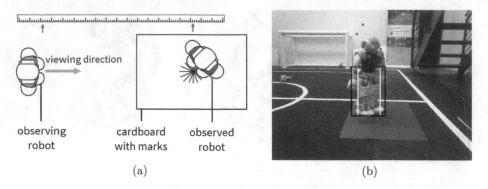

(a)   (b)

Fig. 6. (a) First experimental setup and (b) an image made by the upper camera of the observing robot. The rectangles indicate the inner and outer robot areas identified by the previously executed robot detection.

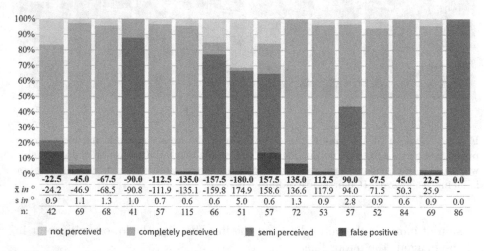

	-22.5	-45.0	-67.5	-90.0	-112.5	-135.0	-157.5	-180.0	157.5	135.0	112.5	90.0	67.5	45.0	22.5	0.0
x̄ in °	-24.2	-46.9	-68.5	-90.8	-111.9	-135.1	-159.8	174.9	158.6	136.6	117.9	94.0	71.5	50.3	25.9	-
s in °	0.9	1.1	1.3	1.0	0.7	0.6	0.6	5.0	0.6	1.3	0.9	2.8	0.9	0.6	0.9	0.0
n:	42	69	68	41	57	115	66	51	57	72	53	57	52	84	69	86

      ■ not perceived   ■ completely perceived   ■ semi perceived   ■ false positive

Fig. 7. Results of the first experiment with a distance of 120 cm. The contrast-normalized Sobel image was used here. $\bar{x}$ is the arithmetic mean, s is the standard deviation, and n is the number of evaluated perceptions.

4.2 Determining the Facing Direction of a Recognized Robot

Finally, we have to determine whether the recognized robot is facing forwards or facing backwards. To do this, we span two rectangles starting in the most left and the most right point of the silhouette (see Fig. 5a/b), and determine which of the two areas contains more green pixels.

When the area that contains more green pixels is on the same side as the major line, we know that the robot is facing forwards. When the area with more green pixels is on the opposite side, the robot is facing backwards (see Fig. 5c/d). If we detect that the robot is facing backwards, we just have to add $180°$ or $-180°$ to the previously computed orientation α.

5   Evaluation

To evaluate our approach, we performed a number of experiments, differing in the distance between the robots as well as in the robot motions. In all setups, we created two silhouettes in each robot region, the first by the contrast-normalized Sobel image and the second by the color classified image. This allows us to directly compare the results of the contrast-normalized Sobel image and the color classified image. In the following, we will present two of our experimental setups.

5.1   First Experimental Setup: Standing Robots

In the first experimental setup, the observed robot was placed in a distance of 60 cm, 120 cm, 180 cm, and 240 cm to the observing robot and was turned in 22.5°-steps around its axis for each distance. For accuracy, we used a cardboard with barely visible marks every 22.5°. Both robots were just standing still. The setup is depicted in Fig. 6.

In the evaluation, the returned orientation is classified as *completely perceived* when it does not deviate from the original orientation by more than ±11.25° (i. e. more than half of a step). When the algorithm was not able to determine the facing direction but the returned orientation is within the range of tolerance, it is classified as *semi perceived*. The returned orientation is classified as a *false positive* when it deviates by more than ±11.25°. The category *not perceived* means that the orientation detection was not successful. The arithmetic mean $\bar{x}$ is calculated over all completely perceived orientations while the standard deviation s is calculated over all completely and semi perceived orientations. The count of evaluated frames n differs from orientation to orientation.

In a nutshell, the results were extremly precise with the contrast-normalized Sobel image. The average false positive rate with 0.3 % at 60 cm, 2.5 % at 120 cm (see Fig. 7 for details), and 2.3 % at 180 cm is extremely low and the standard deviation is in nearly all distances up to 180 cm lower than 4° in nearly all cases. Only at a distance of 240 cm, the results were significantly worse.

5.2   Second Experimental Setup: Walking Observed Robot

In the second experimental setup we made, the observing robot is just standing again while the observed robot is walking in eight different directions with a speed of approximately 12 cm/s in the first execution and with a speed of approximtely 20 cm/s in the second execution (see Fig. 8).

In a preprocessing step of the evaluation, we estimated the ground truth orientation by calculating the rounded average of all returned orientations except for a few runaway values because we did not use the cardbord for exact positioning and had no ground truth tracking system available. The returned orientation is classified as completely perceived or semi perceived when it does not deviate from the expected orientation by more than (a) ±22.5° in the first execution

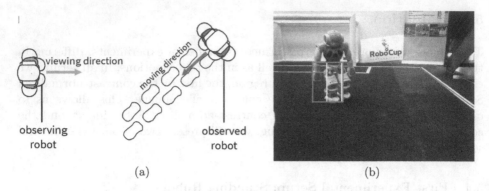

(a)   (b)

Fig. 8. (a) Second experimental setup and (b) an image made by the upper camera of the observing robot. The rectangles indicate the inner and outer robot areas identified by the previously executed robot detection.

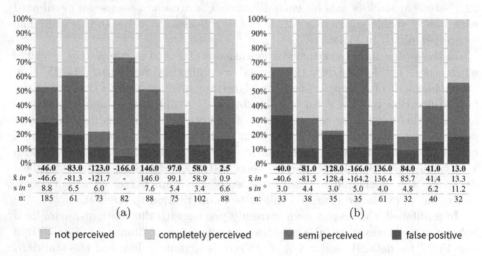

| | not perceived | | completely perceived | | semi perceived | | false positive |

Fig. 9. Results of the second experiment. The walking speed is (a) approximately 12 cm/s in the first execution and (b) approximately 20 cm/s in the second execution. The contrast-normalized Sobel image was used here. $\bar{x}$ is the arithmetic mean, s is the standard deviation, and n is the number of evaluated perceptions.

and (b) $\pm 15°$ in the second execution. We chose a higher tolerance in the first execution as the robot turned slightly while walking.

In some further experiments, the observing robot was also moving (shaking body and turning head) while the observed robot stands or was also moving. In these situations, the standard deviation only increases by approximately 5° while the perceiving rate was just slightly affected.

In summary, the results are good. The ratio of false positives to correctly perceived orientations is in the range of $\frac{3}{50}$ to $\frac{1}{3}$ depending on the orientation. In most cases, the reason for the incorrect perception was the wrong assignment of major and minor lines, so the returned orientation differs about 90°.

The standard deviation is in the range of 3.0° to 11.2° depending on the orientation. With the use of a downstream modeling component, it seems to be possible to use the orientation information returned by this algorithm to make decisions. Extended results are shown in Fig. 9.

5.3 Performance

We measured the execution time of single code sections as well as of the total orientation detection code as a function of the distance to the observed robot. We expected that the execution time is shorter at a higher distance, as the analyzed image region that contains the robot feet is smaller. The measurement was done just with standing robots but one can assume that there will not be a great difference to walking robots. The algorithm was processed by a NAO.

At a distance of 60 cm, the approach required the longest execution time with 0.53 ms. The scanning of the silhouette consumes the most time with 0.37 ms in the contrast-normalized Sobel image. It is noticeable that the scanning of the silhouette in the color-classified image takes only 0.13 ms. This is caused by some operations which are done for every pixel in the contrast-normalized Sobel image while the pixels can be read directly from the color-classified image.

The function of the total execution time in Fig. 10 decreases at longer distances. To also reduce the execution time in a short distance a bit, we could reduce the sampling rate for the silhouette. As we have seen in the evaluation, this should not take a great impact on the quality of the result.

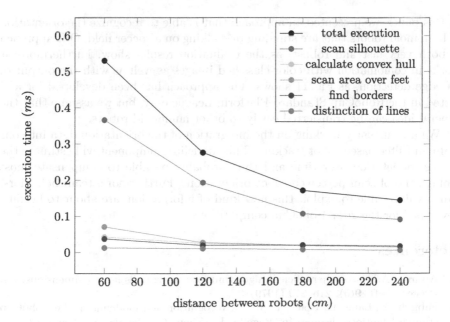

Fig. 10. Average execution time as a function of the distance to the observed robot. The contrast-normalized Sobel image was used for this experiment.

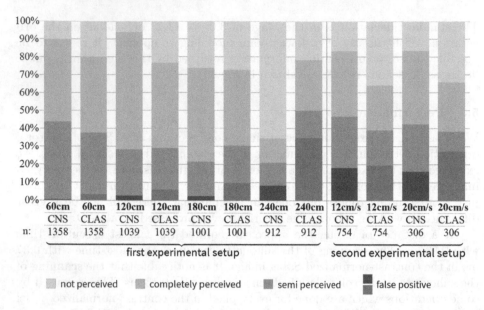

Fig. 11. Combined results of the first and second experimental setup. In addition to the silhouette, which is calculated by using the contrast-normalized Sobel image (CNS), we also calculated a second silhouette with the color classified image (CLAS).

6   Conclusion and Future Work

In this paper, we presented an approach that is able to recognize the orientation of humanoid robots that are standing or walking on a soccer field. Our approach is both very fast and robust, as the evaluation results show. Furthermore, it works in combination with color-classified images as well as with the output of an edge detection, as Fig. 11 shows. The approach has been developed for and tested in the RoboCup Standard Platform League only, but we assume that the general idea can be transferred easily to other humanoid robots.

We are currently working on the integration of the orientation data into our Kalman Filter-based robot tracking. This modeling component will estimate the robots' orientation over time and thus probably be able to compensate most ambiguities of semi perceived robot orientations. Furthermore, team behaviors, which will be able to exploit this new kind of information, are about to become developed for the 2017 RoboCup competitions.

References

1. Andrew, A.M.: Another efficient algorithm for convex hulls in two dimensions. Inf. Process. Lett. **9**(5), 216–219 (1979)
2. Fabisch, A., Laue, T., Röfer, T.: Robot recognition and modeling in the RoboCup standard platform league. In: Pagello, E., Zhou, C., Behnke, S., Menegatti, E., Röfer, T., Stone, P. (eds.) Proceedings of the Fifth Workshop on Humanoid Soccer Robots in Conjunction with the 2010 IEEE-RAS International Conference on Humanoid Robots, Nashville, TN, USA (2010)

3. Hinterstoisser, S., et al.: Model based training, detection and pose estimation of texture-less 3D objects in heavily cluttered scenes. In: Lee, K.M., Matsushita, Y., Rehg, J.M., Hu, Z. (eds.) ACCV 2012. LNCS, vol. 7724, pp. 548–562. Springer, Heidelberg (2013). https://doi.org/10.1007/978-3-642-37331-2_42

4. Hoffmann, J., Jüngel, M., Lötzsch, M.: A vision based system for goal-directed obstacle avoidance. In: Nardi, D., Riedmiller, M., Sammut, C., Santos-Victor, J. (eds.) RoboCup 2004. LNCS (LNAI), vol. 3276, pp. 418–425. Springer, Heidelberg (2005). https://doi.org/10.1007/978-3-540-32256-6_35

5. Laue, T., Röfer, T., Gillmann, K., Wenk, F., Graf, C., Kastner, T.: B-human 2011 – eliminating game delays. In: Röfer, T., Mayer, N.M., Savage, J., Saranlı, U. (eds.) RoboCup 2011. LNCS (LNAI), vol. 7416, pp. 25–36. Springer, Heidelberg (2012). https://doi.org/10.1007/978-3-642-32060-6_3

6. Lenser, S., Veloso, M.: Visual sonar: fast obstacle avoidance using monocular vision. In: Proceedings of the 2003 IEEE/RSJ International Conference on Intelligent Robots and Systems (IROS 2003), Las Vegas, USA, vol. 1, pp. 886–891 (2003)

7. Loncomilla, P., Ruiz-del-Solar, J.: Gaze direction determination of opponents and teammates in robot soccer. In: Bredenfeld, A., Jacoff, A., Noda, I., Takahashi, Y. (eds.) RoboCup 2005. LNCS (LNAI), vol. 4020, pp. 230–242. Springer, Heidelberg (2006). https://doi.org/10.1007/11780519_21

8. Metzler, S., Nieuwenhuisen, M., Behnke, S.: Learning visual obstacle detection using color histogram features. In: Röfer, T., Mayer, N.M., Savage, J., Saranlı, U. (eds.) RoboCup 2011. LNCS (LNAI), vol. 7416, pp. 149–161. Springer, Heidelberg (2012). https://doi.org/10.1007/978-3-642-32060-6_13

9. Röfer, T., et ail.: B-Human team report and code release 2016 (2016). https:// github.com/bhuman/BHumanCodeRelease/blob/master/CodeRelease2016.pdf

10. Tilgner, R., et al.: Sparse feature learning for visual robot angle estimation (2013). http://www.tzi.de/spl/pub/Website/Challenges2013/HTWK.pdf

11. Wilking, D., Röfer, T.: Realtime object recognition using decision tree learning. In: Nardi, D., Riedmiller, M., Sammut, C., Santos-Victor, J. (eds.) RoboCup 2004. LNCS (LNAI), vol. 3276, pp. 556–563. Springer, Heidelberg (2005). https://doi. org/10.1007/978-3-540-32256-6_52

12. Zickler, S., Laue, T., Birbach, O., Wongphati, M., Veloso, M.: SSL-vision: the shared vision system for the RoboCup small size league. In: Baltes, J., Lagoudakis, M.G., Naruse, T., Ghidary, S.S. (eds.) RoboCup 2009. LNCS (LNAI), vol. 5949, pp. 425–436. Springer, Heidelberg (2010). https://doi.org/10.1007/978-3-642-11876-0_37

Situation-Dependent Utility in Extended Behavior Networks

Matthias Hofmann[✉] and Thorben Seeland[✉]

Robotics Research Institute, TU Dortmund University, 44221 Dortmund, Germany
{matthias.hofmann,thorben.seeland}@tu-dortmund.de

Abstract. In this paper, we present a modification of extended behavior networks that enables an agent to learn the relationship between world states and undertaken actions. To this end, we introduce a situation-dependent utility value that is based on the observation of effects after the execution of an action. The utility values serve as bases of multi-dimensional interpolation functions, and supports the revised and extended action selection mechanism to take better actions over time. The evaluation shows that our approach improves action selection. We assess the performance of our system in the RoboCup domain using simulation.

1 Introduction and Related Work

Action selection is an important and well-addressed topic in autonomous robotics, esp. in the RoboCup domain. The simulation leagues are a suitable playground to investigate the performance of high-level behavior. Extended behavior networks provide a powerful and flexible framework for organizing and managing behaviors [1–3]. Our approach addresses two outstanding weaknesses of extended behavior networks: First, we provide a notion of learning to extended behavior networks, and second, we add knowledge of truth values of propositions over time to the network so that it is able to adapt itself to changing environmental conditions.

There is plethora of other methods that have been used for action selection in the robot soccer domain. For instance, a case-based approach has been applied to robot soccer for coordinated action selection [4]. A vision-based approach in combination with fuzzy reasoning has been investigated in [5]. Decision-tree learning was employed in the simulation league [6].

The remainder of the paper is structured as follows: We outline the main concepts of Extended Behavior Networks along with our changes in Sect. 2. We assess the performance and capabilities of the system in Sect. 3. We conclude the paper in Sect. 4.

2 Extended Behavior Networks

This section briefly describes the main concepts of prior versions of extended behavior networks. Therefore, Subsects. 2.1 and 2.2 are based on the work of

© Springer Nature Switzerland AG 2018
H. Akiyama et al. (Eds.): RoboCup 2017, LNAI 11175, pp. 216–227, 2018.
https://doi.org/10.1007/978-3-030-00308-1_18

Dorer [1]. Subsection 2.3 covers our changes to the existing system, introducing the concept of a situation-dependent utility value for effects of actions.

2.1 Notations and Conventions

For further reading of the paper, we define the following sets, relations, and operations.

1. S is the set of world states, $s \in S$.
2. P^+ is a set of atoms.
3. P is the set of atoms, and negated atoms P^+.
4. $L^\wedge$ is a language over P with logical $\wedge$.
5. L is a language over P with logical operations $\wedge$ and $\vee$.
6. Let $\tau : P^+ \times S \to [0 \ldots 1]$ the fuzzy value of an atom in relation to the world state, with $\tau(\neg p, s) = 1 - \tau(p, s)$, $\tau(p \wedge q, s) = \tau(p, s) \otimes \tau(q, s)$, $\tau(p \vee q, s) = \tau(p, s) \oplus \tau(q, s)$. $\otimes$ is a continuous t-Norm, and $\oplus$ a continuous t-Conorm [7,8]. Furthermore, $p, q \in P^+$.
7. Let def $: L \to Pot(P^+)$, and for $l \in L$, def(l) the set of all in l used atoms.

2.2 Extended Behavior Networks

Extended Behavior Networks consists of three basic components: Literals, (competence) modules, and goals. A literal a proposition that receives a (fuzzy) truth value by a function t with respect to the current world state s of the robot. Extended behavior networks utilize literals to formulate conditions for goals and modules, e.g. whether a specific goal has reached. A module contains preconditions Pre, a specific behavior b, and postconditions $Post$. In the course of this paper, b is also called an action. $Post$ consists of effects Eff_j, and a probability ex_j for the effect to become true. A goal comprises a target condition $GCon$. Moreover, there are a static and a situation-dependent importance (ι, r) of the goal, and a relevance condition $(RCon)$. Additionally, there is a set of parameters for extended behavior networks:

1. $\gamma \in [0..1]$ controls the influence of activation of modules.
2. $\delta \in [0..1]$ controls the influence of inhibition of modules.
3. $\beta \in [0..1]$ the inertia of activation across activation cycles.
4. $\theta \in [0..a]$ the activation threshold that a module has to exceed to be selected for execution, with a as the upper bound for a module's activation.
5. $\Delta\theta \in [0..\theta]$ the threshold decay.

The action selection mechanism distributes activation over the network. It is called revised and extended action selection mechanism (REASM) based on Maes [9], and consists of the following steps:

1. Calculate the executability e for each module.
2. Calculate the activation a^n for each module in the current execution cycle $n \in \{0, 1, \ldots\}$.

3. Combine activation and executability by a nondecreasing function $h : \mathbb{R} \times [0,1] \to \mathbb{R}$. The value $h(a^n, e)$ is called execution value.
4. If the maximum value $h(a_k^n, e_k)$ of a module k is greater than a threshold value $\theta > 0$, the behavior of module k is executed.
5. If the maximum value of $h(a_k^n, e_k)$ is smaller than θ, θ is decreased by $\Delta\theta$, and n incremented. The mechanism continues with the second step.

For activation spreading, the following rules apply:

1. A module k receives activation $a_{kg_i}^n{}'$ from goal g_i by the effect Eff_j, iff $Eff_j \in \text{def}(GCon_{g_i})$.
2. A module k receives negative activation $a_{kg_i}^n{}''$, iff $\neg Eff_j \in \text{def}(GCon_{g_i})$.
3. A module k receives activation $a_{kg_i}^n{}'''$ from goal g_i by a successor $succ$, iff $Eff_j \in \text{def}(Pre_{succ})$.
4. A module k receives negative activation $a_{kg_i}^n{}''''$ by the goal g_i by a successor $conf$, iff $\neg Eff_j \in \text{def}(Pre_{conf})$.
5. The activation of a module from goals is

$$a_{kg_i}^n = \text{absmax}\left(a_{kg_i}^n{}', a_{kg_i}^n{}'', a_{kg_i}^n{}''', a_{kg_i}^n{}''''\right),$$

6. and the overall activation of the module is

$$a_k^n = \beta a_k^{n-1} + \sum_i a_{kg_i}^n.$$

2.3   Introducing Situation-Dependent Utility

Prior versions of extended behavior networks [1,3] utilize fixed expectation (probability) values ex_j for each effect Eff_j in module k. However, determining ex_j is a difficult task, and is either done by optimization, or manually set by the behavior designer. This requires domain knowledge and experience. Additionally, ex_j is a generalization. Thus, modeling situation-dependency in prior versions of extended behavior networks would require the definition of additional competence modules that model relations between preconditions that are not part of the executability, and effects for each situation. Therefore, the number of competence modules could greatly increase. Although the executability of a module k depends on the world state, the effect of an action that is taken by the agent may greatly rely on the game situation as well. The original version of extended behavior networks does not take this relevant aspect into account.

   From a technical perspective, we replace the current probability of an effect to become true, ex_j by a situation-dependent rating value function $ex_j^*(s)$ that express the utility of an action at time t with respect to the world state s. Formally, we define for each effect Eff_j^* a function such that $ex_j^*(s) = \tau^*(Eff_j^*, s)$. In contrast to $\tau(Eff_j, s)$, $\tau^*(Eff_j^*, s)$ estimates the expectation value for each literal of the effects of each module with respect to $\tau(Eff_j, s)$ for all p in Pre. This means that only the subset of the world state is deemed relevant for the effect according to Pre, is used. Figure 1 summarizes the changes in the competence modules of the extended behavior networks.

Module k
$Pre \in \mathcal{L}^\wedge$ (Precondition)
$e = \tau(Pre, s)$ (Executability)
b (Behavior)
$Post = (Eff, ex)$ (Postcondition)
$Eff = \bigwedge_j Eff_j \in \mathcal{L}^\wedge, Eff_j \subset \mathcal{P}$ (Effect)
$ex_j = P(Eff_j)$ (Static Expectation)
a_k^n (Activation by Goals)
$h(a_k^n, e)$ (Utility)

Modul k^*
$Pre \in \mathcal{L}^\wedge$ (Precondition)
$e = \tau(Pre, s)$ (Executability)
b (Behavior)
$Post = (Eff^*, \tau^*)$ (Postcondition)
$Eff^* \subseteq \mathcal{P}, Eff_j^* \in def(Eff^*)$ (Effect)
$ex_j^*(s) = \tau_j^*(Eff_j^*, s)$ (Situation-dependent Effect Eff_j^*)
a_k^n (Activation by Goals)
$h(a_k^n, c)$ (Utility)

Fig. 1. We compare module k in its prior version shown in [1] with the new module k^*. Here, we replace ex_j with the function τ^*.

The definition of τ^* depends on the one hand on the observation of the effect itself, and on a relevance function r which takes the influence of the time t into account. This way, we observe the effect of the action over a period and calculate the value. Figure 2 exemplifies an observation function while Fig. 3 shows an example of a relevance function r. In this particular example, we assume that a soccer agent passes the ball to a team member. We observe that the ball rolls too far. Altogether, the utility value $\tau_{Pass}^*(BallNearTeammate, s)$ is calculated by using $\tau_B = \tau(BallNearTeammate, s)$:

$$\tau_{Pass}^*(BallNearTeammate, s) = \frac{\sum \tau_B(t) \cdot r(t)}{\sum r(t)} \tag{1}$$

Since we know the preconditions that are relevant for the current action, and the corresponding utility values, we need a mathematical method to keep this knowledge for reuse and update. Hence, we choose interpolation functions to save the relationship between preconditions (the game situation), actions, and the corresponding utility. This way, we are able to improve the knowledge of an agent over time by recording and rating the effects on each action in many situations. Moreover, after a training phase, unseen game situations can be assessed based on experience of previously seen game situations, and their utilities of actions. Finally, we are able to revise the knowledge of an agent by updating the system if something in the environment of the agent changes. To

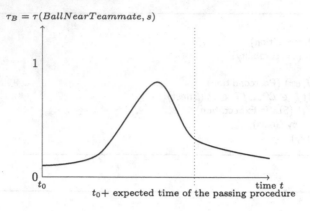

Fig. 2. We calculate $\tau^*_{Pass}(BallNearTeammate, s)$ by observing the effect of the action over time.

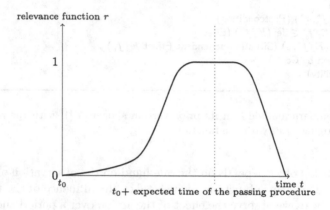

Fig. 3. We utilize the relevance function r for weighting the influence of t.

this end, outdated bases[1] can be removed from the agent's knowledge, and bases that are close to each other can be merged to a single base. The usage of the aforementioned aspects depend on the application, and are part of the design choices of the behavior engineer.

In this paper, we utilize radial basis functions based on Lowe [10]:

$$s_{RBF}(\underline{x}) = \sum_{j=1}^{m} \lambda_j \phi(\|\underline{x} - \underline{y_j}\|), \underline{x} \in \mathbb{R}^n. \tag{2}$$

The radial basis functions determine the weights λ_i by combining conditions of the interpolation with the interpolation function s_{RBF}. We solve the following equation for the application of radial basis functions:

---

[1] Base means a supporting point of the function.

$$\begin{pmatrix} f_1 \\ \vdots \\ f_m \end{pmatrix} = \begin{pmatrix} A_{11} & \cdots & A_{1m} \\ \vdots & \ddots & \vdots \\ A_{m1} & \cdots & A_{mm} \end{pmatrix} \cdot \begin{pmatrix} \lambda_1 \\ \vdots \\ \lambda_m \end{pmatrix} \tag{3}$$

with

$$A_{ij} = \phi(\|\underline{x}_i - \underline{y}_j\|). \tag{4}$$

Radial basis functions offer different types of interpolation functions ϕ. The most popular ones are the Gaussian ($\phi(r) = e^{-0.5\frac{r^2}{r_0^2}}$), multi-square ($\phi(r) = \sqrt{r^2 + r_0^2}$), and the thin-splate ($\phi(r) = r^2 \cdot \log(\frac{r}{r_0})$) method by Dunchon [11].

We implemented the radial basis interpolar based on Burkardt [12][2]. Equation 3 is solved by singular-value decomposition according to [13].

3 Evaluation

The evaluation exclusively addresses our changes to extended behavior networks. For evaluation, it is required to repeat the shown experiments many times in order to acquire knowledge about the utility of actions in the extended behavior network. Moreover, robotics has to deal with many uncertainties that may influence the results of the experiments. Therefore, it is in our case beneficial to use ground truth data in order to validate the concepts of our work. Due to the aforementioned reasons, it is very difficult to evaluate the system on robotic hardware. Therefore, we opted for an evaluation of the system with the Sim-Robot simulator based on the 2016 version of the B-Human framework [14][3].

This section is structured as follows: First, we describe the different types of extended behavior networks that are used in evaluation (see Subsect. 3.1). Second, we illustrate the initialization process, and two experimental setups (see Subsect. 3.2). Finally, the results are presented in Subsect. 3.3.

3.1 Types and Instances of the Extended Behavior Network

In this section, we describe the instance of the extended behavior network that we use for evaluation. First, we define the following literals:

- *angleToBall*: Describes the relative angle of the robot to the ball. The fuzzy value is 0 when the agent is heading the opposite direction of the ball, and vice versa.
- *ballValidity*: Confidence of the ball position on the field.
- *distanceToBall*: Distance of the robot to the ball. To define the fuzzy variable, we use the Euclidian, and a maximum distance that results into 0.
- *ballInsideGoal*: Becomes true if a goal was scored.

---

[2] Source code: https://people.sc.fsu.edu/~jburkardt/cpp_src/rbf_interp_nd/rbf_interp_nd.html.

[3] https://www.b-human.de/downloads/publications/2016/coderelease2016.pdf.

- *ballPosition*: Models whether the ball is in favorable position on the field and depends on relative positions to the own and opposite goal.
- *ballPossession*: Models whether a team is in ball possession.
- *danger*: Models whether an opponent blocks the ball.
- *passFreeTo#* Models whether the way to the team member is free for passing.
- *goodPassDistanceTo#*: Expresses whether the team member is in a good position for receiving a pass depending on the distance to the passing agent.
- *matePositionOf#*: Expresses whether the team member is in a favorable position on the field. This corresponds to the rating of the ball position on the field.
- *shotFree*: Models whether the way to the goal is free for kicking.
- *goodShotDistance*: Models whether the distance to the opponent goal is suitable for kicking.

The goals of the extended behavior networks are outlined in Table 1 while the modules are shown in Table 2. The parameters of the radial basis functions, and extended behavior networks are listed in Table 3. We choose the settings according to our initial experience with the system.

Table 1. Goals of the extended behavior network.

Goal 1	
$GCon$:	$\neg danger \wedge ballPossession$
$RCon$:	$\neg ballPossession$
ι:	0.8
Goal 2	
$GCon$:	$\neg danger \wedge ballPossession$
$RCon$:	$\neg ballPosition \vee danger \vee \neg ballPossession$
ι:	0.8
Goal 3	
$GCon$:	$ballInsideGoal$
$RCon$:	$trueValue$
ι:	1

While the structure of the extended behavior network is the same for all experiments, we define three different types of extended behavior networks: The first type is an instance of an *extended behavior network without our modifications*, i.e. with fixed ex_j. The second type is an extended behavior network with *situation-dependent utility values and offline training*. The third type is an*extended behavior network with situation-dependent utilities, and online adaptation*. This is simply done by constantly adding and revising the knowledge that has previously been acquired with the interpolation function.

Table 2. Modules of the extended behavior network.

shoot	
Pre:	$shotFree \land angleToBall \land ballValidity \land distanceToBall \land goodShotDistance$
Post	
Eff:	$ballInsideGoal \land ballPosition \land danger \land \neg distanceToBall$
(ex_j):	$(0.8, 0.8, 0.5, 0.6)$
dribble	
Pre:	$angleToBall \land ballValidity \land distanceToBall$
Post	
Eff:	$angleToBall \land ballValidity \land distanceToBall \land \neg danger \land ballPosition$
(ex_j):	$(0.6, 0.6, 0.6, 0.6, 0.7)$
passTo#	
Pre:	$passFreeTo\# \land goodPassDistanceTo\# \land matePositionOf\#$
Post	
Eff:	$ballPossession \land \neg danger \land ballPosition$
(ex_j):	$(0.8, 0.5, 0.7)$

Table 3. Strategy parameters of the extended behavior networks and the radial basis interpolation method.

Radial basis function interpolation	
$maxSupportPoints$	50
$minDistance$	0.05
Extended behavior network	
$h(a, e)$	$a \cdot e$
γ	0.7
δ	0.6
β	0.0
θ	0.3
$\Delta\theta$	0.1

3.2 Experiments

Before we start with evaluation, it is required to initialize the extended behavior networks with situation-dependent utilities. This is done as follows: We create 20 scenes, where 5 robots and the ball is being placed on predefined, but varying positions per scene onto the simulated SPL[4] field. The setup consists of one robot which is using an extended behavior network, and taking actions. Moreover, there are two team members, and two opponent players, which are fixed in their positions not doing anything. The agent executes ten times each of the actions

---

[4] Standard Platform League.

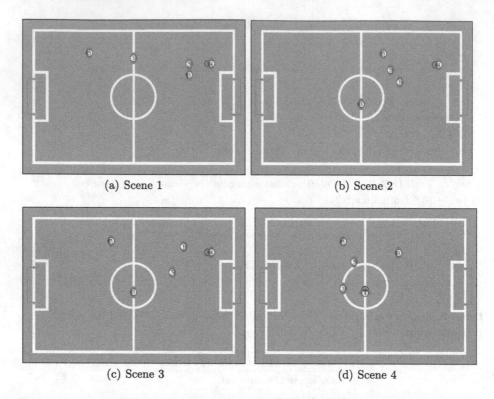

(a) Scene 1   (b) Scene 2

(c) Scene 3   (d) Scene 4

Fig. 4. Scenes used for evaluation. One team composes of the robots red 1 and red 5, the other team consists of robots blue 3, blue 4, and blue 5. (Color figure online)

on each scene. The observed utility and precondition values are recorded for later validation in the experiments.

Experiment 1 validates the system with respect to the initial conditions. To this end, we use scenes number 1 to 3 (see Fig. 4). In a first step, we determine the optimal action for each scene. This way, each possible action (*dribble*, *passTo3*, *passTo5* and *shoot*) is executed ten times on scenes 1 to 3. We record the fuzzy values of each literal of the postconditions, and calculate a and h. We use the average of these values for assessment. The best actions of each scene serve as a reference for comparison for the various extended behavior network types that have been previously trained. This way, we count how often the extended behavior network is able to conduct the optimal action. By using the aforementioned procedure, we find the best actions for scene 1 is *passTo3*, for scene 2 *passTo5*, and for scene 3 *shoot*.

In *experiment 2*, we change the environment by significantly increasing the ground friction in the simulation. As in the first experiment, we use scenes 1 and 2 again, but use scene 4 instead of scene 3 (see Fig. 4). Due to the higher friction, the ball is not able to reach the goal after kicking it. The further steps

Table 4. Number of taking the best action grouped by experiment and type of the extended behavior network.

	Experiment 1			Experiment 2		
	Scene 1	Scene 2	Scene 3	Scene 1	Scene 2	Scene 4
Unchanged EBN (10 attempts per scene)						
Fixed	0	0	10	0	0	0
Situation-dependent estimation with interpolation (10 attempts per scene)						
Gaussian (0.0)	5	10	2	5	9	9
Gaussian (0.5)	0	6	10	0	9	3
Gaussian (1.0)	0	0	10	0	0	0
Multiquad. (0.0)	1	0	10	0	6	7
Multiquad. (0.5)	0	1	10	0	2	2
Multiquad. (1.0)	0	0	10	0	0	0
Thin-plate-spline (0.0)	2	8	1	3	0	1
Thin-plate-spline (0.5)	1	0	10	0	0	1
Thin-plate-spline (1.0)	0	1	10	0	2	2
Situation-dependent, adaptive estimation with interpolation (30 attempts per scene)						
Gaussian (0.0)	29	30	0	27	30	30
Gaussian (0.5)	0	11	30	0	30	0
Gaussian (1.0)	0	0	30	0	0	0
Multiquad. (0.0)	0	0	30	0	0	0
Multiquad. (0.5)	0	0	30	0	30	30
Multiquad. (1.0)	0	0	30	0	0	1
Thin-plate-spline (0.0)	14	30	0	24	28	28
Thin-plate-spline (0.5)	0	0	28	3	1	0
Thin-plate-spline (1.0)	0	0	30	0	30	30

are the same as in experiment 1. The best action for scene 1 is *passTo3* and for scene 2 and scene 4 *passTo5*.

The adaptive, situation-dependent version of the extended behavior network is executed 30 times in each experiment in order to check convergence. The other types of the extended behavior networks are executed ten times.

3.3   Results

The following Table 4 lists the performance of each interpolation method in comparison to each type of extended behavior networks in both experimental setups with different initial parameters. Each interpolation method is by default initialized pessimistically (0.0), neutral (0.5), or optimistically (1.0) before the knowledge about actions and their effects are being introduced.

It is cognizable that the type and initialization of the interpolation methods play a key role in the performance of selecting the best action in the particular scenes. By trend, interpolation method works better if they are initialized neutral

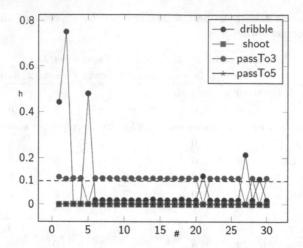

Fig. 5. Exemplification of the convergence of the adaptive, situation-dependent utility extended behavior network. The graph refers to exeperiment 2, scene 1. The interpolation method is thin-splate spline, and pessimistically. The optimal action is passTo3.

or optimistically. Moreover, the interpolation methods should ideally respect the interval [0..1]. Naturally, the performance of the approach depends on the number of scenes that are being used for training the situation-dependent extended behavior networks.

It can be seen that the best performance is achieved with the Gaussian interpolation method. With respect to the situation-dependent, adaptive version of the extended behavior network, the system was able to select the best actions despite scene 3 in experiment 1. It has to be mentioned that the performance of the extended behavior network with fixed expectation values depends on chosen values. The parameters used in Table 2 are based on own experiences and trials. Finding the best action for most of the scenes with fixed expectation values would require a parameter optimization procedure.

Figure 5 shows an example of the convergence capability of the situation-dependent, adaptive extended behavior network. The graph shows very fast convergence towards the optimal action in experiment 2 in scene 1. The result is consistent with the fact that the system was able to select the best action in this scene 24 times by using thin-splate interpolation and pessimistic initialization.

4   Conclusion and Future Work

In this paper, we have shown a modification to extended behavior networks by Dorer. We exchanged static expectation values by situation-dependent utility functions for the effects of actions. Our evaluation shows first promising results, and suggests the application of the adaptive, situation-dependent version of extended behavior networks.

For future work, we will integrate other kinds of interpolation methods. Interesting approaches are Shephard's interpolation [15], and the nearest-neighbor interpolation. Another topic is the application of our work to the entire decision making of a simulated soccer robot. This would make it possible to observe the effects of the behavior over entire games, and consequently, makes it possible to compare the performance of various methods on a game result basis. Finally, a lot of data can be recorded to serve as an input for training networks. We will also work towards an application of the proposed method on robotic hardware.

References

1. Dorer, K.: Behavior networks for continuous domains using situation-dependent motivations. In: IJCAI, vol. 99, pp. 1233–1238. Citeseer (1999)
2. Dorer, K.: Motivation, Handlungskontrolle und Zielmanagement in autonomen Agenten. Ph.D. thesis, Albert-Ludwigs-Universität Freiburg, Freiburg (1999)
3. Dorer, K.: Extended behavior networks for behavior selection in dynamic and continuous domains. In: Proceedings of the ECAI Workshop Agents in Dynamic Domains, Valencia, Spain. Citeseer (2004)
4. Ros, R., Arcos, J.L., de Mantaras, R.L., Veloso, M.: A case-based approach for coordinated action selection in robot soccer. Artif. Intell. **173**(9), 1014–1039 (2009)
5. Wu, C., Lee, T.: A fuzzy mechanism for action selection of soccer robots. J. Intell. Robot. Syst. **39**(1), 57–70 (2004)
6. Konur, S., Ferrein, A., Ferrein, E., Lakemeyer, G.: Learning decision trees for action selection in soccer agents. In: Proceedings of Workshop on Agents in Dynamic and Real-Time Environments (2004)
7. Zadeh, L.A.: Fuzzy logic and approximate reasoning. Synthese **30**(3 4), 407–428 (1975)
8. Gerla, G.: Fuzzy Logic: Mathematical Tools for Approximate Reasoning, vol. 11. Springer, Heidelberg (2013)
9. Maes, P.: The dynamics of action selection. In: Proceedings of the 11th International Joint Conference on Artificial Intelligence - Volume 2, IJCAI 1989, pp. 991–997. Morgan Kaufmann Publishers Inc., San Francisco (1989)
10. Lowe, D., Broomhead, D.: Multivariable functional interpolation and adaptive networks. Complex syst. **2**, 321–355 (1988)
11. Duchon, J.: Splines minimizing rotation-invariant semi-norms in sobolev spaces. In: Schempp, W., Zeller, K. (eds.) Constructive theory of functions of several variables. LNM, vol. 571, pp. 85–100. Springer, Heidelberg (1977). https://doi.org/10.1007/BFb0086566
12. Press, W.H.: Numerical Recipes 3rd Edition: The Art of Scientific Computing. Cambridge University Press, Cambridge (2007)
13. Liesen, J., Mehrmann, V.: Die singulärwertzerlegung. In: Liesen, J., Mehrmann, V. (eds.) Lineare Algebra, pp. 313–321. Springer, Wiesbaden (2015). https://doi.org/10.1007/978-3-658-06610-9_19
14. Laue, T., Spiess, K., Röfer, T.: SimRobot – a general physical robot simulator and its application in RoboCup. In: Bredenfeld, A., Jacoff, A., Noda, I., Takahashi, Y. (eds.) RoboCup 2005. LNCS (LNAI), vol. 4020, pp. 173–183. Springer, Heidelberg (2006). https://doi.org/10.1007/11780519_16
15. Gordon, W.J., Wixom, J.A.: Shepard's method of "Metric Interpolation" to bivariate and multivariate interpolation. Math. Comput. **32**, 253–264 (1978)

A Robust Algorithm: Find an Unknown Person via Referring Grounding

Xiping Wang, Feng Wu$^{(\boxtimes)}$, Dongcai Lu, and Xiaoping Chen

Multi-Agent Systems Lab, School of Computer Science and Technology,
University of Science and Technology of China, Hefei 230027, Anhui, China
{wxiping,ludc}@mail.ustc.edu.cn, {wufeng02,xpchen}@ustc.edu.cn

Abstract. We propose a simple but robust method to recognize an unknown person described in natural language. In this case, a robot is given a verbal description about a person whom the robot is required to recognize. This task is challenging since humans and robots have significantly mismatched perceptual capabilities (e.g., recognizing the color of a coat). Without assuming that all linguistic descriptions and perceptual data are correct, we use a probabilistic model to ground the target person. In particular, the acceptability of color descriptions is modeled based on visual similarity and the confusion matrix of the color classifier which make the system more robust to illumination. Two groups of experiments were conducted. Our experimental results demonstrate that our system is robust to both perception and description errors.

1 Introduction

Human-robot collaboration is still a challenging task, especially for service robots. In RoboCup@Home competition, there are many tasks related to humans, e.g., giving a drink to a person, following a man, guiding a woman, etc. In many cases, it is highly likely that the target person in the instructions is described ambiguously. Usually in the completion, a robot is required to find an unknown person through recognizing some special motions of the person, such as waving hand. A very common situation is that there are several people who may be the target person, e.g., when customs coming to a restaurant or guests visiting your house. Face recognition cannot be used in this scene because it needs to remember the person's face in advance. Robots need some simple but effective and intuitional features to identify the person.

Natural language is a flexible modality for human-robot interaction [3,13]. It is a natural way to identify a person by giving some visual feature descriptions through natural language. A referring expression is a linguistic product used to discriminate a specific object from the rest of the world. The robot needs to identify referents in the environment that are specified by its human partner. The ability to ground referring expressions is important for conversational agents aimed at real-world interaction. With the ability of grounding referring expressions to objects in the environment, robots can accomplish more complex tasks

H. Akiyama et al. (Eds.): RoboCup 2017, LNAI 11175, pp. 228–240, 2018.
https://doi.org/10.1007/978-3-030-00308-1_19

through human-robot collaboration. Kunze et al. [10] proposed an approach for searching for objects on the basis of Qualitative Spatial Relations (QSRs). Huo et al. [9] use natural spatial language to control a robot performing a fetch task in an indoor environment. Similarly, this paper aims to help the robot to recognize an unknown person via referring grounding. Two kinds of cues are used. They are QSRs and color.

Imagine such a scenario. Bill invited some friends come to his house. Lucy is one of the guests. Bill is busy in preparing for dinner and he may tell the robot: "bring ice tea to Lucy from the fridge. She sits beside the cupboard in the drawing-room and wears a red coat". The example sentences above contain two kinds of features about Lucy, color and spatial relations. Grounding the meaning of the descriptive words in natural language by mapping them to its perception will enable the robot to identify the specific physical person referred to. Actually, the robot may encounter some uncertainties. First, humans and robots have mismatched capabilities of perceiving the shared environment [12]. That is to say, the perceived results of the robot may be different from that of the human being. The robot is required to give an assessment of the acceptability of the information given by people based on its perception. There are two situations that may occur when evaluating the acceptability of a speaker's description about color. At first, there is ambiguity in naming colors even for people. One thinks a coat is orange, others may think it is yellow. Secondly, due to many scene accidental events such as unknown illuminant, presence of shadows and camera configuration, such as exposure, white balance, etc. people and color classifier often give different predications as to an object. For example, when illuminant becomes dark, the color classifier tends to judge the blue object as grey. However, blue and gray are not as visually similar as orange and yellow. Secondly, different from still objects, humans are likely to move which result in the previous spatial relation description becoming wrong. Furthermore, due to the limitations of perceptual algorithms, sensing results are not totally reliable. In the cases, the robot must select correct descriptions based on some strategy.

To tackle those problems above, we propose a set of computational mechanisms that correspond to the most commonly used descriptive strategies to evaluate the compatibilities between the referring expressions and numeric attribute values from robot's perception. The acceptability of color expression is evaluated both from visual similarity and the confusion matrix of the color classifier. Based on these mechanisms, we use a probabilistic model to determine the criteria for selecting the correct combination from all the descriptions to uniquely identify the referent. We tested the system under various conditions. Experiments show that even in the case that color classification is incorrect or the target person is mis-detected, our system can give the correct or approximate correct grounding results. Two groups of experiments are designed under different illuminations. The results indicate that the system is robust both to the perception errors and description errors. Note that our algorithm can be incorporated with other methods for more complex robot decision-making and planning [1,21]. In the following sections, we first give a brief discussion of the related work and then give an overview of our system and describe our probabilistic model and word grounding module. Then we designed two groups of experiments that correspond to several typical situations that may occur in reality to evaluate the robustness of our method. Finally, we conclude with our contribution and future work.

2   Related Work

There are two main problems during situated dialog. The speaker will encounter the problem of Referring Expression Generation (REG) when he intends to describe one object. Given Referring Expressions (REs), the listener needs to ground these REs to figure out the referent. The problem in this paper belongs to the latter. Computational approaches for referring grounding often consist of two key components [7].

The first component which can be called word grounding models [11] addresses formalisms that connect linguistic terms to the numerical features captured in the robot's representation of the perceived environment. In this paper, word grounding modules give assessment of the acceptability of QSRs and color expression. There are many lectures that focus on searching task using QSRs by relating an unknown object to a known object which can be called landmark [9,10]. The landmark in [11,12] also can be unknown objects. This makes the problem more complex. The robot need to grounding multi referents. However, for a service robot, it has already constructed a 2D map of the house in advance. The position of the stationary furniture (i.e., bookshelf, cupboards) which does not tend to move in everyday usage is known for the robot. It is easy and effective to select these furniture as landmark.

Different from QSRs, it is more complicated to describe color for machines due to scene accidental events. Therefore it is hard to evaluate the acceptability of color description. In [17], a perceptually based color-naming metric was designed to measure the compatibility between a color name and an arbitrary numeric color values in different color spaces (RGB and HSV). Based on this metric, [15] proposed to evaluate the acceptability of color description based on the deviation from its prototype in HSL space. This method can handle the visual similarity between similar colors such as yellow and orange. But it ignores the effects of scene accidental events such as illuminant. Although none of the color classifiers can solve the illuminant problem, the trend of error can be predicted. We can test the classifier on a large data set and obtain its confusion matrix. If 20% ground truth with a blue label are mistaken for gray, when the speaker described a coat as blue but the classifier predicted it as grey, the acceptability of blue should be enlarged even though blue and gray is not similar in color space. So we evaluate the acceptability of color expression based on the similarity in color space and the confusion matrix of the color classifier.

The second component extracts all the linguistic terms from referring expressions and combines their grounding models together to identify referents. Gorniak and Roy [7] address the interpretation of combinatory spatial REs with incremental filters, filter out a set of potential referents of each property using perceptual data. This is computationally efficient. However, these methods are based on the assumption that all these referring expressions and perceptual data are correct. When grounding a person, the assumption is not established due to the uncertainties discussed previously. Mast et al. [16] propose a probabilistic framework base on the discriminatory power (DP) to measure how likely expressions as a whole are to distinguish the target object from the distracter object for REG. In this paper, we choose this as a criterion to select correct expressions from all the descriptions then ground the target person. At the same time, the grounding results can be adjusted with the feedback of the human partner.

3   A Probabilistic Framework for Referring Grounding

3.1   System Overview

The setup of our experimental system is shown in Fig. 1(b). It is a simplified map of the dining-room in our lab. The robot is represented by a black dot. People in the room are represented by squares with respective colors. The robot is ordered to find Lucy whom it has never seen. It can ask people in the scene about the characteristics of Lucy until it confirms who is Lucy. The overall architecture is shown in Fig. 1(a). Through human-robot dialog, two kinds of cues, spatial relations and colors are supplied to a robot. As all the spatial relation (e.g., nearby, far from), landmarks (e.g. dining-table, TV) and color (e.g., red, grey) are known both for the robot and the speaker, we can find relationship prepositions and corresponding accusatives and color nouns in sentences by keyword matching. The robot perceives the surrounding environment and obtains the coordinates of people and their clothes colors. All the information is forwarded to word grounding module which evaluates the compatibilities between the word expressions from the dialog and the numeric attribute values or labels from perception. The probabilistic model will select the expressions that best match the robot's perception and figure out the referent.

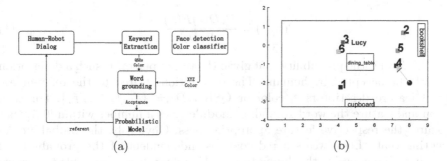

(a)   (b)

Fig. 1. (a) The overall architecture. (b) An example scene. (Color figure online)

3.2   Perception

Microsoft Kinect is used to obtain aligned RGB-D images. 2D laser scanners is used for localization and navigation. First a 2D occupancy grid map [5,8] is generated from the laser scanning results and odometry data. We annotate the different structures such as rooms, doors, furniture and other interested objects according to their semantic information in the grid map. The map constructed the world coordinate system of the home environment. The depth image is transformed into the world coordinate frame via tf [6]. We use HAAR [20] face detector to detect human face area in the RGB image. The corresponding area in the depth image is segmented to obtain human's location in world coordinate. It can be inferred that the area below the face area with the distance of equal height of the face corresponds to the human clothes. In order to reduce the influence of illumination, we use grey world [2] to correct color cast to a certain degree. A fuzzy color model which is learned from uncalibrated data obtained from "Google Image" in [19] is used as the color classifier.

3.3   Probabilistic Model

Suppose during the conversation, the speaker (No. 4 in Fig. 1(b)) uses three sentences to describe Lucy to the robot. "Lucy stands beside the dining-table in a blue coat.", "She is far from the cupboard.", "She is beside the bookshelf." It is obvious that the first sentence and the last sentence are contradictory. The robot has to find one strategy to figure out which one is credible. The characteristics described in the first two sentences clearly distinguish No. 3 from others. The characteristic described in the last sentence is unable to distinguish between No. 2 and No. 5. As a listener, the robot is more convinced that the No. 3 who is beside the dining-table in a blue coat is Lucy rather than the ones beside the bookshelf, as the discriminatory power (DP) of this description combination is greater. DP can be modeled by a probabilistic model $P(x|D)$ which means given a description D and a person x, the probability that the listener identifies the goal person x correctly. $P(x|D)$ can be formulated in the Bayesian framework:

$$P(x|D) = \frac{P(D|x)P(x)}{P(D)} \tag{1}$$

where $P(D|x)$ is the probability that given the target person x, such a description D would be accepted by humans. The description related to the referent are sets of feature descriptors f_i(color or QSR). $D := \{f_1, f_2, \ldots, f_n\}$. For each person and feature the word grounding module gives a number within $[0, 1]$ that measures the respective feature appropriateness. Obviously, the probability of accepting that "Lucy wears a red coat" is independent of the probability of accepting "She is beside the dining-table". Therefore, it is reasonable to assume that the acceptability of different features is stochastically independent.

$$P(D|x) = P(f_1|x) \cdot P(f_2|x) \cdot \ldots \cdot P(f_n|x) \tag{2}$$

$P(D)$ gives the probability that the description D suits an arbitrarily chosen person in the scene. Suppose there are M individuals in the scene. $P(X_i)$ is the probability of randomly choosing the person X_i in the scene. For simplicity, $P(X_i) = 1/M$. If multiple people in the scene suit the description D, the probability of correctly identifying the referent will reduce. Therefore, the following formula can be obtained.

$$P(D) = 1/M \sum_{i=1}^{M} P(D|X_i) \tag{3}$$

If the target person x exists, that is $x \in X$ (he has been detected by the robot), DP of the combination of the descriptions associated with him is certainly maximal. Based on these, the strategy for the robot to identify the credible descriptions can be obtained.

$$(D^*, x^*) = arg\ maxP(X_i|D) \tag{4}$$

D^* and x^* stand for the correct description combination for the referent and the person most likely to be the referent respectively. However, it is impossible to ensure that the robot can detect all the people in the scene. If No. 3 in Fig. 1(b) has not been detected by the robot, the optimal solution will be meaningless. Under this circumstance, the acceptability of the correct description will be very low. Worse still, in the presence of incorrect descriptions, it is difficult for the robot to be aware of its mis-detection. Suppose the robot infers that No. 6 is Lucy. After the robot says out its grounding result, according to conversation habits in general, the speaker will describe Lucy again to distinguish Lucy from No. 6. The correct descriptions will be repeated. It is sure that the repeated descriptions are credible. If the acceptability of this description is too low (below a threshold), the robot will realize that its grounding result is wrong and it hasn't detected Lucy. Then the robot will perceive the surrounding environment again. What's more, another hint can be obtained from the speaker's feedback, there is no need to perceive the whole environment again. The position where Lucy most likely stands can be inferred from the QSRs. We sample the unoccupied pose P_u in the map and consider the pose p^* which satisfies formula 5 as the position where the referent most likely stands. $QSRs^*$ is the combination of spatial relation expressions which is most consistent with speaker's feedback.

$$(QSRs^*, p^*) = arg\ maxP(P_u|QSRs) \tag{5}$$

3.4 Word Grounding Module

Functionally, word grounding module evaluates the compatibilities between the word expressions from the dialog and the numeric attribute value from sensors. Theoretically, this is the problem of designing membership functions for fuzzy concepts. There are several membership function generation techniques, such as methods based on subjective perception, heuristic methods, methods based on

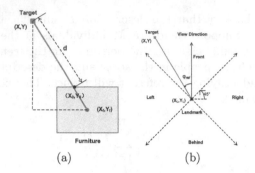

Fig. 2. (a) The distance between the target person and the furniture. The furniture is represented by a rectangle.(b) The relative angle of the target with respect to the landmark and the partition of the four directional relations. (Color figure online)

clustering, etc. [4] As for QSRs, we use the heuristic method which is designed based on rules to generate the membership functions for different spatial relations expressions. As for the color expressions, a method similar to clustering is used to design membership functions. Assume the face detector gives the coordinates of a person is (X, Y, Z) and color classifier predicts his clothes as C_M. The relationship prepositions and corresponding landmarks and color nouns extracted from the sentences is f_i, l_i and C_H. The position of the furniture (X_f, Y_f) can be obtained from the grid map. The minimum applicability for all descriptions in this paper is set to 0.5.

Qualitative Spatial Relation. QSRs consist of distance relations {nearby, beside, between, far from} and directional relations {left of, right of, front of, behind}. As to the directional relations, the landmark only can be the robot or the speaker. The distance d between the goal person and the furniture is shown in Fig. 2(a). $d = \sqrt{(X - X_0)^2 + (Y - Y_0)^2}$. The membership functions for the three binary relation (beside, nearby, far from) of the distance relations are designed in triangular shapes (Fig. 3(a)). When the distance d is close, the membership grade of beside is the highest; when d is far, the membership grade of far-from is the highest; otherwise, when d is moderate, the membership grade of nearby is the highest. The ternary relation (between) can be represented as the combination of two binary relations.

The four directional relations are showed in Fig. 2(b). Robot and speaker define the reference axis (view direction) which partitions the surrounding space. Then, the spatial relation is defined by the partition in which people lie with respect to the reference axis. Given the view direction $V = (x, y)$, to determine the partition, we calculate the relative angle φ_{rel}:

$$\varphi_{rel} = \tan^{-1} \frac{Y - Y_L}{X - X_L} - \tan^{-1} \frac{y}{x} \tag{6}$$

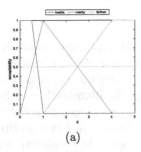 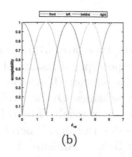 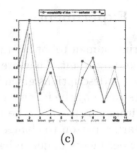

(a)   (b)   (c)

Fig. 3. (a) The applicability of each distance relation along d. (b) The applicability of each directional relation within the interval $[0, 2\pi]$. (c) The acceptability of blue for different colors predicted by the classifier. (Color figure online)

The membership functions for the four directional relations are designed as cosine curve shapes. For example, the membership function for FrontOf is:

$$P(f_i = \text{FrontOf}|x) = max(cos(\varphi_{rel} - cnt_i), 0) \tag{7}$$

cnt_i for directional relations FrontOf, LeftOf, Behind, RightOf, is 0, 0.5π, π, and 1.5π respectively. From Fig. 2(b), it is intuitive that the greater the deviation from cnt_i, the smaller the possibility to accept the description f_i. The applicability of each directional relation within $[0, 2\pi]$ is show in Fig. 3(b).

Color. Most computer vision works consider the eleven basic color terms of the English language: black, blue, brown, grey, green, orange, pink, purple, red, white, and yellow [18]. The visual similarity between C_H and C_M can be evaluated as the distance of their prototypes in HSV space. Color classifier can not be perfectly fit with human visual perception. The color classifier is likely to confuse some color pairs when under different illuminants. This results in its prediction differing from human's judgment. This also can be another evidence for their similarity. Therefore, the acceptability between C_H and C_M can be evaluated by the linear sum of their similarity in HSV $S(C_H, C_M)$ and the probability of confusing C_H with C_M $confusion(C_H, C_M)$ which is shown in formula 8.

$$P(C_H|C_M) = \alpha \cdot S(C_H, C_M) + \beta \cdot confusion(C_H, C_M) \tag{8}$$

where α and β is normalized coefficients. We test the color classifier on the eBay data set [19] and get its confusion matrix. Reference to the method of clustering in HSV space in [14, p. 2], we get the similarity matrix. The acceptability of blue for different colors predicted by the classifier is shown in Fig. 3(c). The red line is the possibility of confusing blue with different colors. The classifier is most likely to confuse blue with grey and purple. The green line shows the similarity in HSV. Even though the similarity between blue and grey is lower than 0.5, due to the high possibility of confusing blue with grey, the acceptability of blue is improved above the minimum acceptability. This improves the tolerance of our system to classifier errors and make it more robust to scene accidental events.

4   Experiments

During human-robot interaction, there are two factors that have influence on the grounding result. They are the perceptual results of computer vision algorithms and the descriptions given by its partner. Therefore, we verify the robustness of the system by the following two schemes. One is to change the illumination of the environment to affect the perception result. The other is to change the speaker or target person to change the descriptions. Therefore, we designed two groups of experiments under different light conditions. Under each light condition, for each of the speakers who have been detected by the robot, the robot is required to ground different target persons.

The setup of our experimental system is shown in Fig. 4(a). There are 7 people in the room. They are marked A~G. In the first group, all fluorescent lamps in the room are open. In the other, one lamp is turned off. The robot perceived the whole room. The detection results under bright and dim illuminations are shown in Fig. 4(c) and (d). The robot uses natural language to describe its grounding results and display it in rviz to ensure its partner can understand it. We did 66 ($6 \cdot 6 + 5 \cdot 6$) experiments in total. Three examples are shown in Tables 1, 2 and 3. At the left of the tables is the detection results by the robot. People detected by the robot are represented by squares. In the first

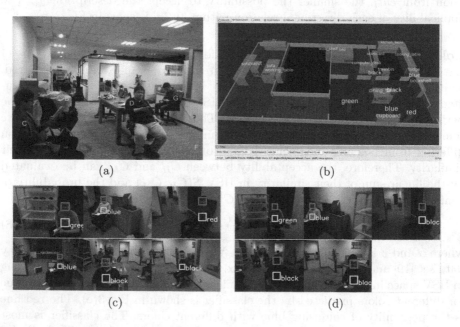

(a)   (b)

(c)   (d)

Fig. 4. (a) The setup of our experiments. (b) The world model of the robot. The detection results of people are shown in cylinders. The color of the one who it thinks to be the target person will turn red. Otherwise, it keeps blue. The detection results under bright and dim illumination are shown in (c) and (d) respectively. (Color figure online)

Table 1. Ground Peter

Speaker: D Ground Peter(F in Fig 4(a))	Dialog
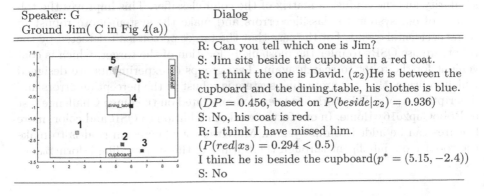	R: Can you tell which one is Peter? S: He wears a pink coat. (The robot misidentified blue as pink) R: I think the one is Peter. (x_3) He is nearby the cupboard and nearby the dining-table, his clothes is red. ($DP = 0.2755$, based on $P(pink\|x_3) = 0.6567$) S: No, he sits beside the bookshelf. R: I think this one is Peter. (x_4) He is beside the bookshelf. His clothes is blue. ($DP = 0.9989$, $P(beside\|x_4) = 0.917 > 0.5$) S: Yes

Table 2. Ground David who hasn't been detected

Speaker: D Ground David(E in Fig 4(a))	Dialog
	R: Can you tell which one is David? S: He sits beside the dining-table in an orange coat. R: I think the one is David. (x_3) He is nearby the cupboard and nearby the dining-table, his clothes is red. ($DP = 0.483$, based on $P(orange\|x_3) = 0.599$) S: No, he sits behind me and his coat is orange. R: I think I have missed him. ($DP = 0.444$, $P(orange\|x_6) = 0.293 < 0.5$) I think he is beside the dining-table($p^* = (3.95, -0.90)$) S: Yes

Table 3. Ground Jim whose color is misidentified

Speaker: G Ground Jim(C in Fig 4(a))	Dialog
	R: Can you tell which one is Jim? S: Jim sits beside the cupboard in a red coat. R: I think the one is David. (x_2)He is between the cupboard and the dining-table, his clothes is blue. ($DP = 0.456$, based on $P(beside\|x_2) = 0.936$) S: No, his coat is red. R: I think I have missed him. ($P(red\|x_3) = 0.294 < 0.5$) I think he is beside the cupboard($p^* = (5.15, -2.4)$) S: No

Table 4. The error rate of the overall system

Face detection error	21.4% (3/14)
Color classification error	27.3% (3/11)
Description error	18.9% (56/297)
Grounding error	12.1% (8/66)

example (under bright illuminations), the robot is required to ground Peter (F in Fig. 5(a)) who has been detected and his color has been predicted correctly. But during the conversation, the robot misidentified blue as pink. As red is most similar to pink, the robot thinks x_3 is Peter. After the speaker supplements more cues, according to the principle of maximum DP, the robot thinks x_4 is Peter. In the second example (under bright illuminations), the robot is required to ground David who hasn't been detected by the robot is shown in Table 2. Even though David has not been detected, according to QSRs, the robot calculates the most probable position where David exists. Therefore, this is a successful grounding. An example of unsuccessful grounding Jim who has been detected but whose color is misidentified is shown in Table 3. The error rate of the overall system is shown in Table 4. The description error is caused by speech misidentification or man-made mistakes. The grounding error is lower than the perception error and description error. It demonstrates that our grounding system is robust to the perception errors and description errors.

5   Conclusion

In this paper, we consider to help a robot recognize an unknown person through the descriptions consisting of spatial relations and coat color. We use a probabilistic model to model DP. The person described by the user can be grounded based on the criterion of maximizing DP. We use a word grounding module to evaluate the compatibility between the word expressions and the numeric attribute values. The acceptability of color descriptions is modeled base on visual similarity and the confusion matrix of the color classifier. This improves the tolerance of our system to classifier errors and make the system more robust to scene accidental events. For the case that the target person isn't detected by the robot, we use QSRs to infer the most likely location of the target, which is convenient for the robot to search again. Two groups of experiments are designed which indicates that our grounding system is robust to the perception errors and description errors. This work has been demonstrated on the Open Challenge test in RoboCup2016@Home. In our future work, in addition to QSR and color, more features can be added to our system. Moreover, our long-term goal is to make the robot more intelligent through the full use of the surrounding information.

Acknowledgments. This work was supported in part by National Natural Science Foundation of China (No. 61603368), the Youth Innovation Promotion Association of CAS (No. 2015373), and Natural Science Foundation of Anhui Province (No. 1608085QF134).

References

1. Bai, A., Wu, F., Chen, X.: Online planning for large Markov decision processes with hierarchical decomposition. ACM Trans. Intell. Syst. Technol. **6**(4), Article no. 45 (2015)
2. Buchsbaum, G.: A spatial processor model for object colour perception. J. Frankl. Inst. **310**(1), 1–26 (1980)
3. Chen, Y., Wu, F., Shuai, W., Wang, N., Chen, R., Chen, X.: Kejia robot - an attractive shopping mall guider. In: Proceedings of the 7th International Conference on Social Robotics, pp. 145–154 (2015)
4. Deschrijver, G., Kerre, E.E.: On the relationship between some extensions of fuzzy set theory. Fuzzy Sets Syst. **133**(2), 227–235 (2003)
5. Elfes, A.: Using occupancy grids for mobile robot perception and navigation. Computer **22**(6), 46–57 (1989)
6. Foote, T.: tf: the transform library. In: Proceedings of TePRA, pp. 1–6. IEEE (2013)
7. Gorniak, P., Roy, D.: Grounded semantic composition for visual scenes. J. Artif. Intell. Res. **21**, 429–470 (2004)
8. Grisetti, G., Stachniss, C., Burgard, W.: Improved techniques for grid mapping with Rao-Blackwellized particle filters. IEEE Trans. Robot. **23**(1), 34–46 (2007)
9. Huo, Z., Alexenko, T., Skubic, M.: Using spatial language to drive a robot for an indoor environment fetch task. In: Proceedings of IROS, pp. 1361–1366. IEEE (2014)
10. Kunze, L., Doreswamy, K.K., Hawes, N.: Using qualitative spatial relations for indirect object search. In: Proceedings of ICRA, pp. 163–168. IEEE (2014)
11. Liu, C., Chai, J.Y.: Learning to mediate perceptual differences in situated human-robot dialogue. In: Proceedings of AAAI, pp. 2288–2294 (2015)
12. Liu, C., Fang, R., Chai, J.Y.: Towards mediating shared perceptual basis in situated dialogue. In: Proceedings of Meeting of the Special Interest Group on Discourse and Dialogue, pp. 140–149 (2012)
13. Lu, D., Zhou, Y., Wu, F., Zhang, Z., Chen, X.: Integrating answer set programming with semantic dictionaries for robot task planning. In: Proceedings of the 26th International Joint Conference on Artificial Intelligence (2017)
14. Lu, Y., Gao, W., Liu, J.: Color matching for colored fiber blends based on the fuzzy c-mean cluster in HSV color space. In: Proceedings of FSKD, pp. 452–455 (2010)
15. Mast, V., Falomir, Z., Wolter, D.: Probabilistic reference and grounding with PRAGR for dialogues with robots. J. Exp. Theor. Artif. Intell. **28**(5), 889–911 (2016)
16. Mast, V., Wolter, D.: A probabilistic framework for object descriptions in indoor route instructions. In: International Conference on Spatial Information Theory, pp. 185–204 (2013)
17. Mojsilovic, A.: A computational model for color naming and describing color composition of images. IEEE Trans. Image Process. **14**(5), 690–699 (2005)

18. Van De Weijer, J., Khan, F.S.: An overview of color name applications in computer vision. In: Workshop on Computational Color Imaging (2015)
19. Van De Weijer, J., Schmid, C., Verbeek, J., Larlus, D.: Learning color names for real-world applications. IEEE Trans. Image Process. **18**(7), 1512–1523 (2009)
20. Viola, P., Jones, M.: Rapid object detection using a boosted cascade of simple features. In: Proceedings of CVPR (2001)
21. Wu, F., Ramchurn, S., Chen, X.: Coordinating human-UAV teams in disaster response. In: Proceedings of the 25th International Joint Conference on Artificial Intelligence, pp. 524–530 (2016)

Online Opponent Formation Identification
Based on Position Information

Takuya Fukushima[1](✉), Tomoharu Nakashima[1], and Hidehisa Akiyama[2]

[1] Osaka Prefecture University, Osaka, Japan
takuya.fukushima@edu.osakafu-u.ac.jp,
tomoharu.nakashima@kis.osakafu-u.ac.jp
[2] Fukuoka University, Fukuoka, Japan
akym@fukuoka-u.ac.jp

Abstract. The aim of this paper is to propose a method for identifying the opponent formation type in an online manner during a game. To do so, opponent teams were clustered according to the position of their players. Each cluster is investigated to determine the difficulty for our team to defeat such a strategy. Then, an identification model is used online to determine if the opponent team adopts such a strategy or not. Furthermore, we also investigate how quickly the opponent formation can be identified. Through a series of computational experiments, it is shown that the model can identify opponent formation quickly and accurately. Therefore, we show the effectiveness of the identification model to switch our strategy.

Keywords: Soccer simulation · Team strategy · Machine learning
Log analysis · Online identification

1 Introduction

In the domain of RoboCup 2D soccer simulation league, various strategies are implemented by teams to win the competition. For this purpose, it is important for the teams to determine the opponent strategy. Researches are conducted with various objectives such as training optimal decision models for individual players, predicting opponent's behavior to make decisions [1], taking the strategy that is the most suited against opponent teams [2], as well as improving players' behavior like pass and dribble [3,4]. One of the essential tasks in the development of a team in this league is to design an effective strategy. Since there is no perfect strategy, it is difficult to win against all teams with only one strategy. Therefore, to outperform a particular opponent team it is important to adopt the right counter-strategy against it. In order to select the most effective strategy, it is necessary for the team to have a set of strategies. Furthermore, the sooner the opponent team's strategy is identified, the sooner the team can adapt its strategy in order to increase its chance to win the game.

We proposed a model that determines the best player formation for corner-kick situations [2]. The model in [2] consists of two modules, learner and selector.

© Springer Nature Switzerland AG 2018
H. Akiyama et al. (Eds.): RoboCup 2017, LNAI 11175, pp. 241–251, 2018.
https://doi.org/10.1007/978-3-030-00308-1_20

The learner analyzes opponent team distributions obtained by applying hierarchical clustering and estimates the performance of our strategies against each cluster of opponents by using Bayesian estimator. The selector returns the best strategy to apply according to the estimations done by the learner part. It was shown that it is effective to change strategies by using only positional information of opponents. However, soccer games does not only consist in corner-kicks, thus such a method should be extended to any kind of game mode.

In this paper, we develop a new learner and focus on the method for identifying opponent teams' strategies. The strategy of the opponent team cannot be known right after the game starts. Thus, the identification of the opponent strategy must be done online during the game. This work assumes that strategies are expressed by opponent players' position. First, opponent teams are clustered according to the position of their players and each cluster is investigated to determine the difficulty for our team to defeat such a strategy. Then, an identification model is used online during a game to identify the strategy type (i.e., strategy cluster) of the current opponent team. The effectiveness of the proposed identification model is examined through a series of computational experiments, in order to verify the relationship between elapsed time and identification rate.

2   Related Work

In the research community of the RoboCup Soccer Simulation 2D, various works that focus on the analysis of opponent teams by using a coach agent have been proposed. For example, Gregory et al. [5] developed a coach agent that learns offensive and defensive advices by using decision trees. Ramin et al. [6] researched the coach development by using rule-based expert systems and decision-making trees. The coach learns to predict agent behavior and automatically generates advices to improve team's performance. Mazda et al. [7] also researched opponent modeling for prediction two-layered case based reasoning.

Additionally, the relationship between strategy and positioning was well investigated in [8]. For the strategy representation, some methods that focus on player positioning have been proposed. For example, Visser et al. [9] proposed a system for recognizing opponent's formations and then applying a counter formation. Luis et al. [10] proposed a method to change the players positioning according to the strategy of the team. In addition, Akiyama and Noda [11] proposed a player positioning method based on Delaunay Triangulation built from a set of ball coordinates. Other analysis of opponent team's strategy was proposed as Riley and Veloso [12] where they proposed a method for identifying the opponent team by recording the positions, passes and dribbles of opponent players. Faria et al. [13] proposed a formation classification method by using players and ball coordinates. However, the proposed method is not accurate enough and requires a large computation time amount. Therefore, a light and highly accurate method is required to perform strategy adaptation during a game.

3   Formation Identification

In this paper, we define a team strategy as the player's positioning during a game. It is assumed in this paper that opponent teams do not change their strategy during a game. In order to identify the strategy of the opponent team, it is necessary to recognize the features of the formation. In this section, we first describe how the formation's features are extracted. Then, we describe the method used to identify the strategy type of the opponent team.

3.1   Data Extraction Based on Opponent Position Information

To use players' position as the inputs of the learning model requires to consider their uniform numbers. Thus, the order of the players would be a problem in the construction of the model. To cope with this issue, an opponent formation is numerically expressed by discretizing the soccer field by a grid as shown in Fig. 1. Then, the number of players present in each cell is counted. The value of each cell is used as the input of the learning model. The value in each cell shows the number of opponent players at a certain cycle, and the results are integrated. Then, the average value is computed by dividing the integration obtained so far by the number of observed cycles. This set of the average values is used as input data of our identification model. For example, if the field is discretized by a grid of size 6×4, opponent formation is expressed by a 24-dimensional vector.

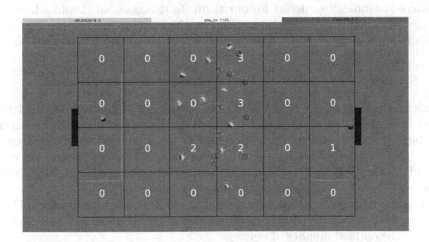

Fig. 1. Discretization of the soccer field by a grid of size 6×4.

3.2   Formation Identification Model

To investigate the effectiveness of the identification model, we compare the performance of three different supervised-learning-based classification methods: Neural Network (NN), Support Vector Machine (SVM) and Random Forest

(RF). Regardless the model used, the vector obtained in the previous section is used as input of the classification and each input is labeled by the corresponding opponent's formation. The methods used for labeling and generation of training data are explained in the following section.

4   Labeling Training Data

Opponent teams are assumed to try to counter our basic gameplay. Opponent teams' strategies are categorized according to the weaknesses of our formations. Training data are labeled according to this categorization. In this section, we first explain the criterion used to make the decision of changing our strategy or not. Secondly, we describe the opponent's strategy classification method and the labeling of training data.

4.1   Weaknesses Identification

In this work, our current strategy is considered as weak if our team has the ball for a large amount of consecutive steps during the game but fails to score a goal. In such a case, out team should change its strategy.

In order to identify such a situation, we define a weakness indicator. It is calculated from a lot of game logs for each opponent teams. Opponent teams for which the average value is equal to or larger than a particular threshold are considered as difficult to defeat for our team. In this case, we should adapt our strategy against this set of opponents. The method used to compute such a value is detailed in Sect. 5.

4.2   Strategy-Type Labeling Based on Opponent Positioning

In order to investigate the typical defensive formations, opponents teams determined from the previous section were clustered. To do so, a Gaussian mixture distribution is used, and its hyper-parameters are optimized using the Expectation Maximization (EM) algorithm. The optimal number of clusters is determined by using Calinski-Harabasz index [14]. The index is defined as the ratio of the within-cluster dispersion to the between-cluster dispersion.

Training data are labeled according to the different resulting clusters. These data are used to train the classification model where the number of labels conforms to the optimal number of clusters.

5   Experiments

Training data are labeled according to the different resulting clusters as described in Sect. 4. These data are used to train the classification model where the number of labels conforms to the optimal number of clusters. At first, we investigate the optimal number of clusters and classify the typical defensive formations of opponent teams. In a second experiment we identify the formation used by each opponent teams according to the locations of their players, in order to determine the most appropriate strategy in each situation. At the same time, we verify how many cycles are enough to identify the opponents' formations. For this purpose, we experiment with various numbers of elapsed steps in order to check the accuracy rate. The effect of the grid size on the accuracy rate is also investigated.

5.1   Clustering Process

In this first experiment, we classify the formation of opponent teams considered as difficult to defeat for our team and for which we should reconsider our strategy. We define a weakness indicator as in (1), where $p(k)$ is the ball possession time of our team and $g(k)$ is the score at the game k.

$$value(k) = d(g(k)) \cdot p(k),$$ (1)

$$d(x) = \begin{cases} 1 & (x = 0), \\ 0 & (x \geq 1). \end{cases}$$ (2)

The ball possession rate is estimated from the game logs. The team is considered to possess the ball if two consecutive kicks are done by players of the same team.

By determining the optimal number of clusters, we examine the number of distinct formation. Game logs were generated by making our team playing 200 games against various opponent teams. In the following, we made our team, HELIOS [15], playing against eleven opponent teams: CYRUS2014 [16], Info-Graphics [17], HERMES2015, Gliders2016 [18], FURY [19], HERMES2016 [20], MarliK2016 [21], Ziziphus [22], FRA-UNIted [23], WrightEagle [24] and Ri-one [25] that participated in the RoboCup competitions between 2014 and 2016. These teams are selected by using the weakness indicator. In this experiment, only the game logs of the first half were used. We tried to determine various different numbers of clusters varying between 2 and 10. The number of clusters with the highest Calinski-Harabasz index was selected as the optimal number of clusters. The formations of the opponent teams were expressed by discretizing the field by a grid of size 30×20. Thus, an opponent formation is represented by a 600-dimensional vector.

The experimental results are shown in Fig. 2. From the result, three or four clusters seem to be the optimal number. When the number of clusters is set to three, as shown in the Fig. 3, teams are categorized into two typical defensive strategies plus one strategy considered as normal. Such Fig. 3 above teams (like CYRUS2014, HERMES2015, FURY and Ziziphus) whose the defensive strategy consists in gathering all the players in front of the goal. The second defensive strategy we determined is employed by teams like InfoGraphics (Fig. 3 below) that aligns vertically its players to prevent the other team to perform passes going through the defense.

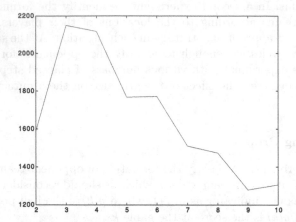

Fig. 2. Variation of the Calinsky-Harabasz index according to the number of clusters.

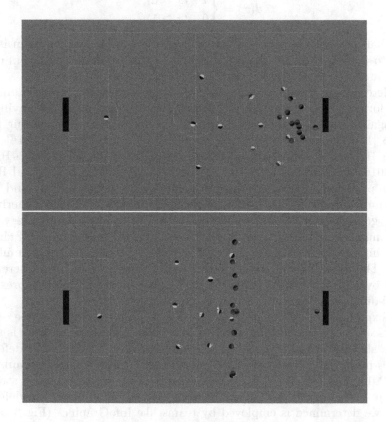

Fig. 3. Typical defensive formations. Top:"wall", bottom:"line".

When the number of clusters is set to four, a new type of defensive strategy (Gliders2016) looking likes the straight line strategy explained previously in addition to the results observed from the three clusters. The difference between InfoGraphics and Gliders2016 is that Gliders2016 is aggressive when holding balls, whereas InfoGraphics is passive. Therefore, InfoGraphics and Gliders2016 are treated as the same formation, and the optimum number of clusters is 3.

Let us call the formation depicted in the top of Fig. 3 as "wall", the formation depicted in the bottom of Fig. 3 as "line", and the other formation as "normal". We decide to change our strategy against "wall" and "line" formation teams. It should be noted that WrightEagle is classified as "normal". The aim of the proposed method are to find "wall" defense teams, thus the result that WrightEagle is classified as "normal" corresponds to our expectations.

5.2   Formation Identification

In this section, according to the results obtained in the previous experiment, the type of opponent teams' formations are identified according to their player formations. In order to verify if the proposed method can be used online, we investigated the relationship between amount of time spent to observe the opponent team and the accuracy rate of the classification model. We also investigated the influence of the grid size on the accuracy rate.

Based on the results of the first experiment, we trained different models used to recognize three classes. Fields are used five different discretization of the soccer field: 6×4, 12×8, 15×10, 24×16, 30×20. We made our team, Helios, play 19 games against teams who participated in RoboCup 2016, CYRUS2014, InfoGraphics, HERMES2015 and WrightEagle. We focused only on the first half of each game log. CYRUS2014 and InfoGraphics participated in RoboCup2014. HERMES2015 and WrightEagle participated in RoboCup 2015. Among the wall teams, CYRUS2014 and FURY change strategies according to goal difference. For this reason, we only used game data in which Helios did not score any goal against these two teams. For each class, we extracted position information from about 3000 logs and treated them as training data. Table 1 summarizes

Table 1. Opponent teams' formation labels.

Opponent team	Label
CYRUS2014	Wall
HERMES2015	Wall
FURY	Wall
Ziziphus	Wall
InfoGraphics	Line
Gliders2016	Line
others	Normal

Table 2. Hyper-parameters used for the classifiers.

Classifier	Parameter	Setting
NN	Activation function	Logistic function
	Optimization algorithm	L-BFGS method
	Structure	3 layers
	Number of neurons in Input layer	The number of grid
	Number of neurons in Output layer	3 neurons
	L2 penalty	0.0001
	Tolerance	0.0001
SVM	Kernel	Linear
	Penalty	1.0
	Tolerance	0.0001
RF	Criterion	Gini index
	Number of trees	10
	Sampling	bootstrap

the resulting labels. To do so, we performed the classification by testing three different classification models, a NN, a SVM and a RF. The hyper-parameters we employed for each model are summarized in Table 2.

The experimental results are depicted in the Figs. 4, 5, 6, 7 and 8. Each figure depicts the results according to a particular discretization of the soccer field. As shown in Figs. 4, 5, 6, 7 and 8 the models accuracy's convergence start from around 1500 cycles regardless the grid size. When the number of cycles is sufficiently large, the accuracy rates of each classifier are similar. Regarding NN and SVM, the accuracy rate is proportional to the number of grids, and it is high even for short amount of time spent to analyze the opponent formation. From

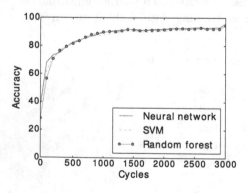
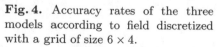

Fig. 4. Accuracy rates of the three models according to field discretized with a grid of size 6 × 4.

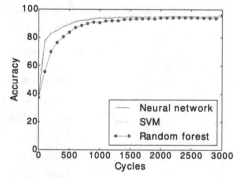

Fig. 5. Accuracy rates of the three models according to field discretized with a grid of size 12 × 8.

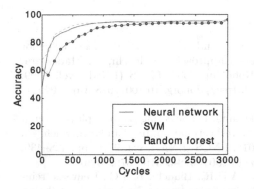

Fig. 6. Accuracy rates of the three models according to field discretized with a grid of size 15×10.

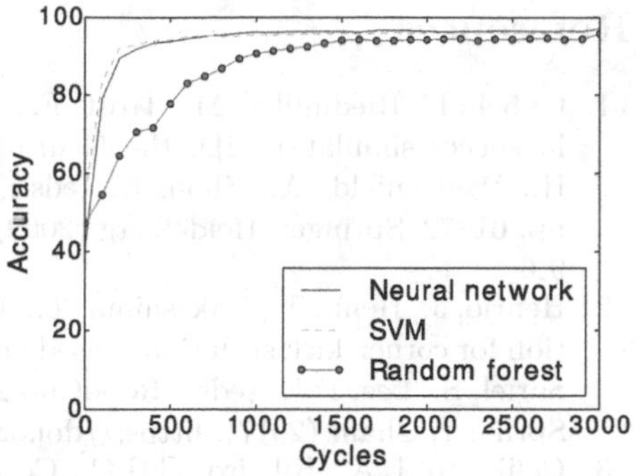

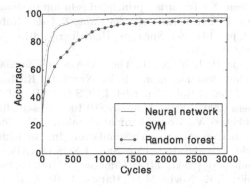

Fig. 7. Accuracy rates of the three models according to field discretized with a grid of size 24×16.

Fig. 8. Accuracy rates of the three models according to field discretized with a grid of size 30×20.

this results, we can state that the larger the grid is, the sooner the opponent formation can be identified.

On the other hand, with RF, when the number of cycles is small, the accuracy rate is low compared with NN and SVM.

6   Conclusion

In this paper, we proposed a method to identify opponent strategies online according to their player formations. The proposed method decides whether our current strategy should be changed or not by using opponent position information. If the opponent strategy can be figured out, it is possible to employ a more suited strategy to increase the chance to outperform the opponent. For this purpose, opponent formation was classified, and three identification models were constructed by using machine learning methods. Future works include surveying the classification rate for unknown teams. We will also investigate which strategy is effective against opponent teams.

References

1. Gabel, T., Riedmiller, M., Trost, F.: A case study on improving defense behavior in soccer simulation 2D: the NeuroHassle approach. In: Iocchi, L., Matsubara, H., Weitzenfeld, A., Zhou, C. (eds.) RoboCup 2008. LNCS (LNAI), vol. 5399, pp. 61–72. Springer, Heidelberg (2009). https://doi.org/10.1007/978-3-642-02921-9_6

2. Henrio, J., Henn, T., Nakashima, T., Akiyama, H.: Selecting the best player formation for corner-kick situations based on Bayes' estimation. In: Behnke, S., Sheh, R., Sarıel, S., Lee, D.D. (eds.) RoboCup 2016. LNCS (LNAI), vol. 9776, pp. 428–439. Springer, Cham (2017). https://doi.org/10.1007/978-3-319-68792-6_36

3. Celiberto, L.A., Ribeiro, C.H.C., Costa, A.H.R., Bianchi, R.A.C.: Heuristic reinforcement learning applied to RoboCup simulation agents. In: Visser, U., Ribeiro, F., Ohashi, T., Dellaert, F. (eds.) RoboCup 2007. LNCS (LNAI), vol. 5001, pp. 220–227. Springer, Heidelberg (2008). https://doi.org/10.1007/978-3-540-68847-1_19

4. Bai, A., Wu, F., Chen, X.: Towards a principled solution to simulated robot soccer. In: Chen, X., Stone, P., Sucar, L.E., van der Zant, T. (eds.) RoboCup 2012. LNCS (LNAI), vol. 7500, pp. 141–153. Springer, Heidelberg (2013). https://doi.org/10.1007/978-3-642-39250-4_14

5. Kuhlmann, G., Stone, P., Lallinger, J.: The UT Austin Villa 2003 champion simulator coach: a machine learning approach. In: Nardi, D., Riedmiller, M., Sammut, C., Santos-Victor, J. (eds.) RoboCup 2004. LNCS (LNAI), vol. 3276, pp. 636–644. Springer, Heidelberg (2005). https://doi.org/10.1007/978-3-540-32256-6_61

6. Fathzadeh, R., Mokhtari, V., Mousakhani, M., Shahri, A.M.: Coaching with expert system towards RoboCup soccer coach simulation. In: Bredenfeld, A., Jacoff, A., Noda, I., Takahashi, Y. (eds.) RoboCup 2005. LNCS (LNAI), vol. 4020, pp. 488–495. Springer, Heidelberg (2006). https://doi.org/10.1007/11780519_45

7. Ahmadi, M., Lamjiri, A.K., Nevisi, M.M., Habibi, J., Badie, K.: Using a two-layered case-based reasoning for prediction in soccer coach. In: Proceedings of the International Conference on Machine Learning; Models, Technologies and Applications, MLMTA 2003, pp. 181–185 (2003)

8. Pourmehr, S., Dadkhah, C.: An overview on opponent modeling in RoboCup soccer simulation 2D. In: Röfer, T., Mayer, N.M., Savage, J., Saranlı, U. (eds.) RoboCup 2011. LNCS (LNAI), vol. 7416, pp. 402–414. Springer, Heidelberg (2012). https://doi.org/10.1007/978-3-642-32060-6_34

9. Visser, U., Drücker, C., Hübner, S., Schmidt, E., Weland, H.-G.: Recognizing formations in opponent teams. In: Stone, P., Balch, T., Kraetzschmar, G. (eds.) RoboCup 2000. LNCS (LNAI), vol. 2019, pp. 391–396. Springer, Heidelberg (2001). https://doi.org/10.1007/3-540-45324-5_44

10. Reis, L.P., Lau, N., Oliveira, E.C.: Situation based strategic positioning for coordinating a team of homogeneous agents. In: Hannebauer, M., Wendler, J., Pagello, E. (eds.) BRSDMAS 2000. LNCS (LNAI), vol. 2103, pp. 175–197. Springer, Heidelberg (2001). https://doi.org/10.1007/3-540-44568-4_11

11. Akiyama, H., Noda, I.: Multi-agent positioning mechanism in the dynamic environment. In: Visser, U., Ribeiro, F., Ohashi, T., Dellaert, F. (eds.) RoboCup 2007. LNCS (LNAI), vol. 5001, pp. 377–384. Springer, Heidelberg (2008). https://doi.org/10.1007/978-3-540-68847-1_38

12. Riley, P., Veloso, M.: On behavior classification in adversarial environments. In: Proceedings of the 5th Distributed Autonomous Robotic Systems, pp. 371–380 (2000)

13. Faria, B.M., Reis, L.P., Lau, N., Castillo, G.: Machine learning algorithms applied to the classification of robotic soccer formations and opponent teams. In: Proceedings of the IEEE Cybernetics and Intelligent Systems, pp. 344–349 (2010)
14. Calinski, T., Harabasz, J.: A dendrite method for cluster analysis. Commun. Stat. **3**(1), 1–27 (1974)
15. Akiyama, H., et al.: HELIOS2016: team description paper. In: RoboCup2016, Leipzig, Germany, 6 p. (2016)
16. Khayami, R., et al.: CYRUS 2D simulation team description paper 2014. In: RoboCup2014, João Pessoa, Brazil, 6 p. (2014)
17. Pritam, S.: "Infographics" team: selecting control parameters via maximal Fisher information. In: RoboCup2014, João Pessoa, Brazil, 4 p. (2014)
18. Prokopenko, M., Wang, P., Obst, O., Jauregui, V.: Gliders 2016: integrating multi-agent approaches to tactical diversity. In: RoboCup2016, Leipzig, Germany, 6 p. (2016)
19. Darijani, A., Mostaejeran, A., Jamali, M.R., Sayareh, A., Salehi, M.J., Barahimi, B.: FURY 2D simulation team description paper 2016. In: RoboCup2016, Leipzig, Germany, 6 p. (2016)
20. Javan, M., Ramezanzadeh, A., Kashi, M., Mohamadi, S.E., Pashaeehir, A.: HERMES: soccer 2D simulation team description paper 2016. In: RoboCup2016, Leipzig, Germany, 6 p. (2016)
21. Nozari, N., et al.: MarliK 2016 team description paper. In: RoboCup2016, Leipzig, Germany, 5 p. (2016)
22. Pour, M.S., Ghasemi, A., Kalajooyeranjbar, K., Kalajooyeranjbar, K., Chaposhloo, M., Firoozbakht, M.: Ziziphus team description paper. In: RoboCup2016, Leipzig, Germany, 5 p. (2016)
23. Javan, M., Ramezanzadeh, A., Kashi, M., Mohamadi, S.E., Pashaeehir, A.: FRA-UNIted - team description 2016. In: RoboCup2016, Leipzig, Germany, 6 p. (2016)
24. Li, X., Chen, R., Chen, X.: WrightEagle 2D soccer simulation team description 2015. In: RoboCup2015, Hefei, China, 5 p. (2015)
25. Asai, K., et al.: RoboCup 2016–2D soccer simulation league team description Ri-one (Japan). In: RoboCup2016, Leipzig, Germany, 6 p. (2016)

Motion Detection in the Presence of Egomotion Using the Fourier-Mellin Transform

Santosh Thoduka[(✉)], Frederik Hegger, Gerhard K. Kraetzschmar, and Paul G. Plöger

Department of Computer Science, Bonn-Rhein-Sieg University of Applied Sciences, Grantham-Allee 20, 53757 Sankt Augustin, Germany
{santosh.thoduka,frederik.hegger,gerhardk.kraetzschmar, paulg.ploger}@h-brs.de

Abstract. Vision-based motion detection, an important skill for an autonomous mobile robot operating in dynamic environments, is particularly challenging when the robot's camera is in motion. In this paper, we use a Fourier-Mellin transform-based image registration method to compensate for camera motion before applying temporal differencing for motion detection. The approach is evaluated online as well as offline on a set of sequences recorded with a Care-O-bot 3, and compared with a feature-based method for image registration. In comparison to the feature-based method, our method performs better both in terms of robustness of the registration and the false discovery rate.

Keywords: Motion detection · Mobile robots
Egomotion compensation · Fourier-Mellin transform

1 Introduction

Autonomous mobile robots are expected to operate in dynamic environments with other agents such as humans, robots, pets etc. This is especially true for service robots that work in a home environment, such as in RoboCup@Home, and for outdoor robots that need to navigate through traffic and pedestrians. Moving objects in such environments can add to the complexity of certain tasks such as navigation, scene understanding and action monitoring; however, motion can also be an important cue for interpreting the environment and understanding the effects of actions.

While motion can be detected by infrared sensors, radars etc., vision-based motion detection is a practical and cheap solution for robots, and is a well-studied field, especially in the context of video surveillance systems. For a stationary camera, the methods used in video surveillance systems can be directly applied and used for detecting motion. However, robots often need to detect motion while they are in motion (egomotion); in such cases methods that rely on a static

© Springer Nature Switzerland AG 2018
H. Akiyama et al. (Eds.): RoboCup 2017, LNAI 11175, pp. 252–264, 2018.
https://doi.org/10.1007/978-3-030-00308-1_21

camera cannot be used directly because from the point of view of the robot, the entire image of the scene appears to be moving as the robot is moving.

Consider the two images in Fig. 1, which includes forward motion of the camera and a falling toy. As humans, our attention is naturally drawn to the toy even when we are moving, since it provides us with a visually salient stimulus [1, p. 41]. However, from a 2D image perspective, the entire scene has changed; the red arrows indicate the direction of apparent motion in the image due to camera motion and the green arrow indicates the direction of motion of the toy. The apparent motion of the scene follows a pattern, while the motion of the toy can be seen as an anomaly in this pattern (i.e. it is contrary to the expected egomotion-induced optical flow), and hence an indicator for the robot that some action is required. Detecting this motion is a challenging task for a robot as it involves being able to distinguish between global changes in the scene caused to its own motion and local changes due to the movement of other objects.

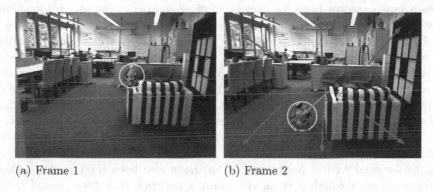

(a) Frame 1   (b) Frame 2

Fig. 1. Camera motion and independent motion (yellow circle) between frames. (Color figure online)

This paper tackles the problem of using 2D vision methods for detecting independent motions in the environment when the observer (a robot) *is also moving* through the environment. We approach this problem by combining existing methods: the Fourier-Mellin transform (FMT) [2] for compensating camera motion and temporal differencing for motion detection. The algorithm is able to run close to real-time on a robot.

The paper is structured as follows: Sect. 2 discusses related work, Sect. 3 explains the proposed approach, Sect. 4 discusses the results, along with a comparison to a feature-based method, and finally conclusions and future work are discussed in Sect. 5.

2   Related Work

The majority of the literature regarding motion detection considers scenes from a static camera, with some approaches allowing for slight camera motions; however, there has been an increase in vision-related work with camera motion due to the importance of autonomous driving and driver assistance systems [3].

For static cameras, methods such as background subtraction, temporal differencing and optical flow are well known for motion detection. However, none of these methods, used in isolation, are applicable for moving cameras since the majority of the changes in the scene would be caused by camera motion. Some methods [4–6] compensate for camera motion before applying differencing or optical flow to detect motion. Camera motion is typically compensated by first calculating optical flow or tracking features between frames, followed by selection of inlier vectors that best describe the dominant motion. The transformation estimated using the inlier vectors is then used to align the frames, minimizing the differences between the two frames due to camera motion.

Badino et al. [6] estimate 6D egomotion using optical flow calculated from stereo cameras. The computed egomotion is used to compensate the flow vectors such that only moving objects have large vectors. Kim et al. [7] use the Lukas-Kanade tracker both for camera motion compensation and for continuously updating a background model, and subsequently use background subtraction for motion detection. Meier et al. [8] use inertial-optical flow for egomotion and object motion estimation. Tracked features are classified as outliers and inliers based on whether they agree with the global motion seen in the image. The authors use the outliers specifically to detect and characterize the motion of independently moving objects. Kumar et al. [9] use machine learning to predict optical flow statistics (mean and covariance) given the head and eye velocities of the iCub robot. Moving objects are detected by comparing their flow vectors to the learned statistics.

Convolutional Neural Networks (CNNs) have also been used for compensation egomotion: Tokmakov et al. [10] train a network that uses ground truth optical flow to detect independently moving objects from a moving camera. Rezazadegan et al. [11] perform action recognition on moving cameras by first centering the person of interest. Agrawal et al. [12] compute the transformation between sequential images due to camera motion by using a Top-CNN which receives input from two identical Base-CNNs (one for each image).

A common theme in the related work is the use of optical flow or feature tracking methods, which rely on detecting good features. Apart from the work by Kumar et al. [9], there are no published results of extensive evaluation in different scenes or with varying parameters. Additionally, the hardware, frame rate, image size are often not reported, making it difficult to determine whether the methods can be run on a mobile robot.

Adjacent fields, such as visual odometry and structure-from-motion, essentially try to solve a similar problem: that of estimating camera motion. Most approaches in these fields also rely on detecting and tracking good features, but other methods have also been explored. For example, FMT has been used for visual odometry [13, 14] and found to be equally good or better than optical flow methods. The advantage of Fourier-based methods is that they are not dependent on finding good features and are robust to some lighting changes and frequency-dependent noise. The FMT approach calculates the similarity transform, which is a simplification of the affine and perspective transforms, which also makes it a better candidate for running on a robot with limited resources. We assume, as in other related work, that moving objects constitute less than half the image; i.e. the apparent motion of the scene due to camera motion is the dominant motion.

3   Approach

Since it has already been successfully used in visual odometry, we decided to use FMT to compensate camera motion. Additionally, in order to avoid calculation of features and optical flow, we then use temporal differencing for detecting independent motions. Our approach is based on a vision pipeline that has two stages: (1) FMT is used to compute the transform between consecutive frames, which is then used to align them, hence compensating camera motion. (2) Temporal differencing is performed on the aligned frames to detect moving objects.

I. Image registration using FMT: Image registration is the process of transforming an image to geometrically align it with a reference image. FMT was first used for image registration by Reddy et al. [2]. It is an extension of the phase correlation method and can simultaneously retrieve the rotation, scale and translation between images; i.e. it estimates the similarity transform for a given pair of images. The steps of the method can be seen in Fig. 2.

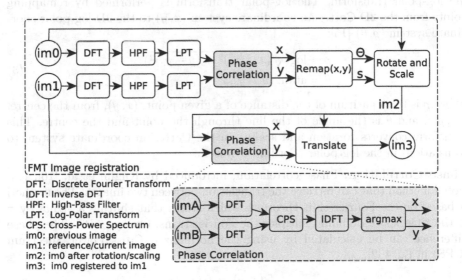

Fig. 2. Top: FMT image registration pipeline. Bottom: Phase correlation block which is used twice in the registration pipeline.

FMT-based image registration itself is a two-step process; the first step estimates the rotation and scale and the second estimates the translation. In both steps, phase correlation is used to find the translation between two images. In the first step, the input images to the phase correlation step are the log-polar transforms of the discrete Fourier transforms of the grayscale images ($im0$ and $im1$) to be registered. The estimated shift in the log-polar images (x, y) is converted into rotation θ and scale s and used to transform $im0$.

This transformed image $im2$ and the reference image $im1$ are the inputs to the second phase correlation step. The estimated translation from the second phase correlation step is used to transform $im2$ again. This resultant image $im3$ is now registered with the reference image $im1$.

Fourier-Mellin Transform: The FMT of a function $f(r, \theta)$ is given by [13]:

$$M_f(\boldsymbol{u}, v) = \frac{1}{2\pi} \int_0^\infty \int_0^{2\pi} f(r, \theta) \boldsymbol{r^{-ju}} e^{-jv\theta} d\theta \frac{d\boldsymbol{r}}{\boldsymbol{r}} \tag{1}$$

where the elements in bold are the Mellin transform parameters and the remaining ones are the Fourier transform parameters.

By substituting $r = e^\rho$, the FMT can be expressed as just a Fourier transformation [13]:

$$M_f(u, v) = \frac{1}{2\pi} \int_{-\infty}^\infty \int_0^{2\pi} f(e^\rho, \theta) e^{-ju\rho} e^{-jv\theta} d\theta d\rho \tag{2}$$

Log-Polar Transform: In practice, the variable substitution is realized using the log-polar transform. The log-polar transform is performed by remapping points from the 2D Cartesian coordinate system (x, y) to the 2D log-polar coordinate system (ρ, θ) [15]:

$$\begin{aligned} \rho &= \log(\sqrt{(x - x_c)^2 + (y - y_c)^2}) \\ \theta &= \operatorname{atan2}(y - y_c, x - x_c) \end{aligned} \tag{3}$$

where ρ is the logarithm of the distance of a given point, (x, y), from the centre, (x_c, y_c), and θ is the angle of the line through the point and the centre. This transform converts rotation and scaling in the Cartesian coordinate system to translations in the log-polar coordinate system.

Phase Correlation: Phase correlation, introduced by Kuglin et al. [16], is a global method that can retrieve the translation between two images. The method is based on the Fourier shift theorem, which states that shifting a signal by τ in the time/space domain multiples the Fourier transform by $e^{-j\omega\tau}$. The phase difference can be calculated by using the normalized Cross Power Spectrum (CPS) in Eq. 4 [2],

$$\begin{aligned} f_2(x, y) &= f_1(x - t_x, y - t_y) \\ F_2(\xi, \eta) &= e^{-j2\pi(\xi t_x + \eta t_y)} F_1(\xi, \eta) \\ CPS = e^{-j2\pi(\xi t_x + \eta t_y)} &= \frac{F_1(\xi, \eta) F_2^*(\xi, \eta)}{|F_1(\xi, \eta) F_2(\xi, \eta)|} \end{aligned} \tag{4}$$

where F_1 and F_2 are the Fourier transforms of f_1 and f_2, and ξ and η are the spatial frequencies in x and y.

The term $e^{-j2\pi(\xi t_x + \eta t_y)}$ is equivalent to the Fourier transform of a shifted Dirac delta function; hence, if we take the inverse Fourier transform of CPS, the result is a signal with a peak at (t_x, t_y). By finding the location of the peak we retrieve the translation between the two images.

Rotation Ambiguity: Since the Fourier magnitude plots are conjugate symmetric, there is an ambiguity in the recovered rotation. If the calculated rotation angle is θ, the actual rotation of the image could be θ or $\theta + \pi$. For this application, we assume that consecutive frames are never rotated by more than π radians and hence do not perform an extra step to resolve the ambiguity.

High-pass Filtering: During the phase-correlation step, apart from the peak at the actual rotation angle, there are additional peaks at multiples of 90°. Sometimes the peak at 0° is higher than the peak at the required rotation angle. Both [17] and [2] suggest applying a high-pass filter in the Fourier domain to prevent the false peak at 0°.

II. Motion Detection Using Temporal Differencing: We use temporal differencing for motion detection, and additional operations, such as thresholding, edge masking and clustering of contours, are used to eventually output a set of bounding boxes representing independently moving objects in the scene (see Fig. 3). Temporal differencing is performed by taking the absolute difference of the pixel intensities between the registered frame $im3$ and the current frame $im1$. A binary threshold is applied on the difference image with intensities above the threshold being set to 255 (white) and those below being set to 0 (black), hence selecting pixels where a large difference is seen.

Fig. 3. Motion detection pipeline

Edge Mask: Edges are regions in the image where there are discontinuities in the pixel intensities. If the images are imprecisely registered, the edges might not overlap exactly with each other. This will result in large values in the difference image and will likely be present in the thresholded image (such as the stripes of the sofa in Fig. 4b). In order to remove the edges (false detections), we construct an edge mask from the thresholded image by first applying Canny edge detection to the thresholded image and fitting contours to them. Oriented rectangles are then fit to the contours and are classified as edges if the aspect ratio is very high or very low. The rectangles which are classified as edges are then masked out as seen in Fig. 4c. It is also worth noting that this process causes some degradation in the detection of the moving stuffed toy as well; this is discussed further in the evaluation.

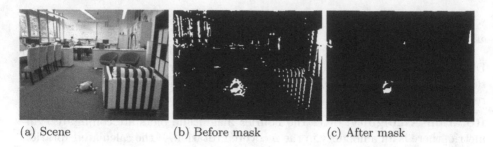

(a) Scene   (b) Before mask   (c) After mask

Fig. 4. Edge mask on a scene with egomotion and independent motion

Clustering: In order to separate the resultant threshold image into a set of regions, we cluster the white pixels based on their distance from each other. This is done by first finding contours, and then applying Euclidean clustering on the contour points.

Small clusters are discarded and bounding boxes are fit to each cluster. Some bounding boxes are ignored if the ratio of white to black pixels is low. The intermediate outputs from the motion detection pipeline can be seen in Fig. 5.

Fig. 5. The main steps of the motion detection pipeline: **Top:** previous, current and registered frame. **Bottom:** thresholded image, edge-masked image, bounding box of clustered contour points

Runtime: An open-source Python implementation of the FMT image registration method[1] was found to be too slow for our application (1.6 Hz). Our C++

---

[1] https://github.com/matejak/imreg_dft.

port[2] is able to process 320×240 images at 14.5 Hz on an Intel Core i3, 1.7 GHz processor, while the overall motion detection pipeline runs at 11 Hz.

4   Evaluation

For evaluation, we collected fifteen image sequences and annotated them with ground truth (GT) bounding boxes of moving objects. A Care-O-bot-3 with a head-mounted ASUS Xtion Pro 3D camera was used for recording the sequences. All sequences involve robot egomotion (linear: 0–0.3 m/s, angular: 0–0.3 rad/s) and the set of moving objects in the scene includes humans, doors and a stuffed toy. The experiments are run on the recorded sequences, but the algorithm is able to run on the robot as well with a ROS (Robot Operating System) wrapper.

In [18], the authors discuss evaluation methods and metrics for motion detection algorithms, suggesting the following for object-based metrics:

– True Positive (TP): "A detected foreground blob which overlaps a GT bounding box, where the area of overlap is greater than a proportion Ω_b of the blob area and greater than a proportion Ω_g of the GT box area."
– False Negative (FN): "A GT bounding box not overlapped by any detected object."
– False Positive (FP): "A detected foreground object which does not overlap a GT bounding box."

We use these definitions and choose $\Omega_b = \Omega_g = 0.5$. We regard a single GT object that is overlapped by multiple detected bounding boxes as a true positive (given that the total overlap proportion criteria holds). Since the definitions have been modified, $TP + FN$ does not equal the number of GT objects (as is usually the case). A TP in this case is an object that has been reliably detected, whereas a FN is an object that has not been detected at all. This gives us two ways of interpreting the results: one which considers objects reliably detected (true positive rate, TPR), and one which considers objects not detected at all (false negative rate, FNR). These two metrics and the false discovery rate, FDR, are defined as:

$$TPR = \frac{N_{TP}}{N_{gt}}, FNR = \frac{N_{FN}}{N_{gt}}, FDR = \frac{N_{FP}}{N_d} \tag{5}$$

where N_{TP}, N_{FN}, N_{FP}, N_{gt} and N_d are the number of true positives, false negatives, false positives, ground truth objects and detected objects.

4.1   Experiments

Six sequences are chosen for the first two experiments since they cover both translational and rotational robot motion, and different types of object motions.

---

[2] https://github.com/sthoduka/fmt_motion_detection.

Experiment 1: Frame Rate. For this experiment, the frame rate of the camera is kept constant at 30 Hz, but, by skipping frames, the effective frame rate of the algorithm is altered. This results in larger differences between frames (due to motion) at slower frame rates without additional effects like motion blur. As seen in Fig. 6, the frame rate has a large impact on the performance, most significantly when halving the frame rate to 15 Hz. Although in most cases 6 Hz results in the best TPR, the FDR also rises significantly at this frame rate. The object-level annotation is also a cause of the poor performance at higher frame rates: at 30 Hz, the small motions of parts of objects are detected instead of the motion of the entire object, which is observable at lower frame rates. Overall, this result suggests that the frame rate of the algorithm should be dynamically altered based on the speed of the robot and expected speed of the objects.

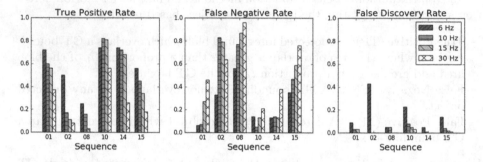

Fig. 6. Impact of altering time between consecutive frames

Experiment 2: Edge Mask. In general, applying the edge mask to the thresholded image reduces both the TPR and FDR, as seen in Fig. 7. Depending on the application, reducing the false detection rate to nearly zero at the expense of a decrease in true positive rate can be an acceptable compromise.

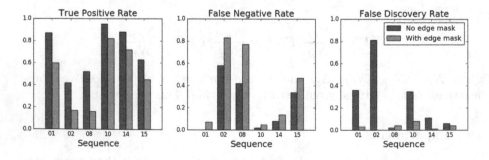

Fig. 7. Impact of applying an edge mask on the difference image

Comparison with a Feature-Based Approach. Here, we compare the results of the FMT method to a feature-based method. The monocular camera code from LIBVISO2 [19] is used for feature extraction and matching and the inlier vectors are used to estimate an affine transformation between consecutive frames. This affine transform is used to register the frames, after which the temporal differencing pipeline is used for motion detection. For both methods, we use the same parameters for temporal differencing, use frames of size 320×240, and skip every two frames (10 Hz effective frame rate). The experiments are run on a PC with an Intel Core i3, 1.7 GHz processor and 4 GB of RAM. The results of the comparison are seen in Table 1[3].

Table 1. Detection rates for the FMT and feature-based methods

Sequence	FMT			Feature-based		
	TPR	FNR	FDR	TPR	FNR	FDR
01	0.6	0.07	**0.03**	0.47	0.1	**0.24**
02	**0.17**	**0.83**	0.0	**0.25**	**0.75**	0.0
03	0.38	0.59	0.07	0.31	0.5	0.0
04	0.38	0.37	0.05	0.33	0.45	0.02
05	0.3	0.29	0.09	0.23	0.46	0.1
06	0.5	0.39	**0.0**	0.48	0.41	**0.11**
07	0.59	0.29	**0.09**	0.62	0.28	**0.18**
08	**0.16**	**0.77**	0.04	**0.06**	**0.8**	0.15
09	0.29	0.52	0.0	0.3	0.5	0.03
10	0.82	0.05	**0.08**	0.79	0.07	**0.19**
11	0.46	0.12	**0.04**	0.38	0.12	**0.14**
12	0.48	0.52	0.0	0.45	0.48	0.0
13	**0.03**	**0.95**	0.0	**0.03**	**0.95**	0.0
14	0.72	0.14	0.01	0.74	0.13	0.04
15	0.45	0.47	0.04	0.41	0.52	0.05

The TPR and FNR are comparable for the two methods; the sequences where the motions are far away or short and quick tend to have low TPR and high FNR in both cases. The reason for the higher FDR for the feature-based method is evident from Fig. 8, which shows the x and y translations for sequence 10. The sequence consists of the robot rotating to the left at a constant speed (0.3 rad/s), with some people moving in the scene. The FMT method shows a relatively constant translation in x and no translation in y, whereas the feature-based method is a lot noisier, with some large spikes; these spikes most likely account for the increased FDR. Similar behaviour was seen in the other sequences as

---

[3] All output videos can be found here: https://www.youtube.com/playlist?list=PL1r Zfrn4gV_jc-Y3FdsEujE6RfWYi20gy.

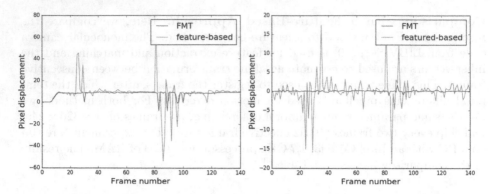

Fig. 8. Pixel translations for sequence 10 along the x-axis (left) and y-axis (right) for the FMT and feature-based methods.

well. The FMT method is able to run at about 11 Hz, while the feature-based method runs at 12 Hz, with comparable CPU and memory usage. This suggests that the FMT method is more robust while using the same amount of resources.

5   Conclusions and Future Work

In this paper, we combined existing approaches for independent motion detection from a moving camera. The Fourier-Mellin-based image registration method was used for egomotion compensation and temporal differencing for motion detection. Unlike other methods, FMT does not rely on the detection of good features, which is one of its advantages. For the set of sequences evaluated, a frame rate of 10–15 Hz was found to be ideal for the detection rate; at 30 Hz, motions between frames are sometimes too small to be detected. The algorithm processes frames at 11 Hz, which allows it to be run close to real-time on a robot within the range of the ideal frame rate. In comparison to a feature-based method, it performs better in terms of robustness of the registration and the false discovery rate. A more systematic evaluation is required to determine the limits on object and camera motion speed, depth variance of the scene and depth of the moving objects. Dynamically varying the frame rate based on the speed of the robot and applying the motion detection output to a task of the robot, such as safe navigation or turning towards a waving person, is future work.

Acknowledgements. We gratefully acknowledge the continued support by the b-it Bonn-Aachen International Center for Information Technology and the Bonn-Rhein-Sieg University of Applied Sciences. We also thank Alex, Argentina and Deebul for proof-reading the paper.

References

1. Frintrop, S.: VOCUS: A Visual Attention System for Object Detection and Goal-Directed Search. LNCS (LNAI), vol. 3899. Springer, Heidelberg (2006). https://doi.org/10.1007/11682110
2. Reddy, B.S., Chatterji, B.N.: An FFT-based technique for translation, rotation, and scale-invariant image registration. IEEE Trans. Image Process. **5**(8), 1266–1271 (1996)
3. Gehrig, S., Franke, U.: Stereovision for ADAS. In: Winner, H., Hakuli, S., Lotz, F., Singer, C. (eds.) Handbook of Driver Assistance Systems, pp. 495–524. Springer, Cham (2016). https://doi.org/10.1007/978-3-319-12352-3_22
4. Kim, J., Ye, G., Kim, D.: Moving object detection under free-moving camera. In: 2010 IEEE International Conference on Image Processing, pp. 4669–4672. IEEE (2010)
5. Hariyono, J., Hoang, V.-D., Jo, K.-H.: Moving object localization using optical flow for pedestrian detection from a moving vehicle. Sci. World J. **2014** (2014)
6. Badino, H., Franke, U., Rabe, C., Gehrig, S.: Stereo vision-based detection of moving objects under strong camera motion. In: Proceedings of the First International Conference on Computer Vision Theory and Applications, pp. 253–260 (2006)
7. Kim, S.W., Yun, K., Yi, K.M., Kim, S.J., Choi, J.Y.: Detection of moving objects with a moving camera using non-panoramic background model. Mach. Vis. Appl. **24**(5), 1015–1028 (2013)
8. Meier, D., Brockers, R., Matthies, L., Siegwart, R., Weiss, S.: Detection and characterization of moving objects with aerial vehicles using inertial-optical flow. In: 2015 IEEE/RSJ International Conference on Intelligent Robots and Systems (IROS), pp. 2473–2480. IEEE (2015)
9. Kumar, S., Odone, F., Noceti, N., Natale, L.: Object segmentation using independent motion detection. In: 2015 IEEE-RAS 15th International Conference on Humanoid Robots (Humanoids), pp. 94–100. IEEE (2015)
10. Tokmakov, P., Alahari, K., Schmid, C.: Learning Motion Patterns in Videos. CoRR, vol. abs/1612.07217 (2016)
11. Rezazadegan, F., Shirazi, S., Upcroft, B., Milford, M.: Action Recognition: From Static Datasets to Moving Robots. CoRR, vol. abs/1701.04925 (2017)
12. Agrawal, P., Carreira, J., Malik, J.: Learning to see by moving. In: Proceedings of the IEEE International Conference on Computer Vision, pp. 37–45 (2015)
13. Kazik, T., Göktoğan, A.H.: Visual odometry based on the Fourier-Mellin transform for a rover using a monocular ground-facing camera. In: 2011 IEEE International Conference on Mechatronics (ICM), pp. 469–474. IEEE (2011)
14. Goecke, R., Asthana, A., Pettersson, N., Petersson, L.: Visual vehicle egomotion estimation using the Fourier-Mellin transform. In: 2007 IEEE Intelligent Vehicles Symposium, pp. 450–455. IEEE (2007)
15. Sarvaiya, J.N., Patnaik, S., Bombaywala, S.: Image registration using log-polar transform and phase correlation. In: TENCON 2009-2009 IEEE Region 10 Conference, pp. 1–5. IEEE (2009)
16. Kuglin, C.D., Hines, D.C.: The phase correlation image alignment method. In: Proceeding of IEEE International Conference on Cybernetics and Society, pp. 163–165 (1975)
17. Stone, H.S., Tao, B., McGuire, M.: Analysis of image registration noise due to rotationally dependent aliasing. J. Vis. Commun. Image Represent. **14**(2), 114–135 (2003)

18. Lazarevic-McManus, N., Renno, J., Makris, D., Jones, G.: Designing evaluation methodologies: the case of motion detection. In: Proceedings of 9th IEEE International Workshop on PETS, pp. 23–30 (2006)
19. Geiger, A., Ziegler, J., Stiller, C.: StereoScan: dense 3D reconstruction in real-time. In: Intelligent Vehicles Symposium (IV) (2011)

A Review on Locomotion Systems
for RoboCup Rescue League Robots

João Oliveira[✉], Leonardo Farçoni, Adam Pinto, Rafael Lang, Ivan Silva,
and Roseli Romero

Warthog Robotics, São Carlos School of Engineering and Institute of Mathematics
and Computer Science, University of São Paulo, São Carlos, SP, Brazil
{joao.montanha,leonardo.farconi,adam.moreira,rafael.lang}@wr.sc.usp.br,
insilva@sc.usp.br, rafrance@icmc.usp.br

Abstract. A research paper was conducted in the Warthog Robotics
group to gather information about robotic locomotion systems and some
hybrid implementations on these designs. The purpose is to develop a
new prototype to compete in the RoboCup Rescue League using the
acquired data. This paper describes three fundamental locomotion systems (wheeled, tracked and legged) presenting a comparison to analyze
their advantages and disadvantages. The presented hybrid and transformable locomotion systems have tracks and an actuator, such as wheels,
legs or arms attached to its structure, and the capability to adjust its
own tracks in different scenarios. A comparison was made regarding the
needs of the competition, having systems recommended to each one of
the relevant tasks in the scenarios proposed by the league.

Keywords: Locomotion systems · Rescue robot
Tracked locomotion · Hybrid locomotion · Fundamental locomotion

1 Introduction

Mobile robots are being constantly developed to substitute humans in rescue
tasks, and therefore preventing people in hazardous environments. The RoboCup
Rescue Robot League[1] collaborates with this evolution by encouraging research
teams to compete in a simulated disaster area, resembling a post earthquake or
tsunami scenario, with their developed robots, which need to be able to overcome
obstacles and uneven terrains to find and rescue fictitious victims.

This research addresses the differences between wheeled, legged and tracked
locomotion as well as their combinations and applications as an initial study
for a future RoboCup Rescue League robot project for the Warthog Robotics
research group from the University of São Paulo, Brazil.

This paper is organized as follows: Sect. 2 describes each fundamental locomotion system by itself, while Sect. 3 introduce some robot implementations of
these systems combined in different ways, which are compared in Sect. 4 regarding a rescue scenario, and Sect. 5 concludes this research paper.

---

[1] http://wiki.robocup.org/Robot_League.

© Springer Nature Switzerland AG 2018
H. Akiyama et al. (Eds.): RoboCup 2017, LNAI 11175, pp. 265–276, 2018.
https://doi.org/10.1007/978-3-030-00308-1_22

2   Differences Between Singular Locomotion Systems

In a dynamic environment, the locomotion system chosen for a robot needs to be well planned, since each locomotion system has its own advantages and disadvantages regarding energy consumption, mobility, speed and complexity. Considering that the robots mentioned in this paper have hybrid locomotion systems, it is important to be familiar with each individual configuration to determine which is better for each scenario.

2.1   Wheeled

The wheeled mechanism usually has advantages when running on smooth surfaces, where it can move at high speeds and with good performance in turning flexibility, while being simple to control and consuming less energy than a tracked mechanism [1,2], thus being highly recommended for flat surfaces. However, the mobility of the wheeled mechanism in uneven terrain is limited by the diameter of its wheels [2], which is a problem considering how chaotic a rescue scenario usually is, therefore it is not recommended for rough terrain.

Using wheels to overcome obstacles such as steps and stairs is not recommended as the wheel radius has to be greater than the obstacle height. For climbing and descending slopes, the slippage of the surface needs to be considerate, but in general wheels can be used for this task. Regarding gaps, wheels are highly not recommended as they need to be in contact with the ground to produce movement, and the contact length is minimal when compared to the tracked one.

2.2   Tracked

An alternative to overcome obstacles is the use of tracks for locomotion, war tanks are a good example of this. A robot using tracked locomotion can move robustly on rough terrain [3] due to its high adaptability to terrain conditions when compared to the wheeled locomotion [1], being highly recommended for this purpose even though it consumes more energy and moves at lower speeds [4,5], which is not payed off on flat surfaces. The track adds stability to the robot, decreases terrain pressure, has a simple control system, a prominent off-road mobility and allows the robot to climb higher steps than the wheeled does [6], being recommended when overcoming both steps and stairs. While on slopes, its friction assists on a stable movement, and on gaps the tracks rely on the size of the robot and its center of mass to avoid falling over.

The tracked locomotion can be divided into two categories according to its configuration: the fixed ones (F-track mechanism) and the transformable ones (T-track mechanism). The T-track mechanism was developed to fix the turning inflexibility and high power consumption presented in the F-track by adjusting itself to each soil and optimizing the track contact length with the ground [4].

2.3 Legged

A legged based locomotion is unstable and more complex to be controlled when compared to the previous ones [2]. Despite these disadvantages, legs can assist on high climbing (high steps and steep slopes) and on overcoming larger gaps than tracked or wheeled robots can, due to the ability to extend its legs to become body supports on the other side of the gap [3]. This characteristic allows legged robots to outperform wheeled and tracked robots in scenarios where there are abrupt discontinuities such as rescues in fallen buildings [1], therefore being highly recommended to overcoming both step and gap. The other important tasks for a rescue robot can also be performed by this mechanism in some way, even though there are options with less complex systems.

2.4 Comparison

The information displayed in this section is summarized in Table 1, where each one of the fundamental locomotion systems is rated for a series of tasks for a RoboCup Rescue League robot based on previous competitions and the scenarios shown in each one. The criteria used for this recommendations considers the ability to execute the task based on the literature and the geometric model of the robots, without considering its implementation or complexity. For example, the legged system has the ability to execute all theses tasks, but it has a high complexity and difficult implementation. The wheeled system can execute theses tasks as well, though the radius needs to be much larger than the tracked and legged actuators.

Table 1. Singular locomotion systems compared in relevant tasks for a RoboCup Rescue League competitor robot. Each system was evaluated as *highly not recommended* (HNR), *not recommended* (NR), *recommended* (R) and *highly recommended* (HR).

Tasks	Wheeled	Tracked	Legged
Overpassing a gap	HNR	NR	HR
Going through a step	NR	R	HR
Overcoming stairs	NR	R	R
Climbing and descending slopes	R	R	R
Moving on rough terrain	NR	HR	R
Moving on flat surface	HR	NR	R

3 Existing Hybrid Locomotion Systems

To expand the work field, some robots adopt two or more fundamental locomotion systems together, as can be seen on upcoming subsections. In this section, existing robots that use hybrid systems are studied individually regarding its characteristics and solutions for overcoming the challenges given in the competition.

3.1   MOBIT - The All-in-One Robot

The MOBIT robot is designed to be compact, light, robust and energy-efficient by exploring the advantages of each locomotion system on each terrain condition [1], guaranteed by its capability to operate on wheeled, tracked and legged mode.

MOBIT has four independent legs attached to its body that can rotate 360° with tracks along the legs length, which add versatility due to its degrees of freedom. Thereby, numerous locomotion modes are possible, as seen in Fig. 1, where wheeled, tracked and legged mode are shown [1].

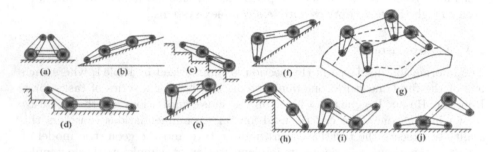

Fig. 1. Possible locomotion modes of MOBIT: (a) wheeled mode; (b) and (c) possible stances to climb ladders and slopes in tracked mode; (d) initial stance when starting to climb a ladder; (e) and (f) stances to overcome steeper slopes by pushing the robot's center of gravity to a stable region; (g) legged mode; (h), (i) and (j) example of other modes that can be achieved with MOBIT [1].

A series of experiments conducted by Duan et al. [1] showed that the robot could reach 8.5 km/h in wheeled mode opposed to the expected 10 km/h that were not achieved due to power supply weight. These experiments also mentioned the differences between stances shown in Figs. 1(b) and (c), which lay in its turning characteristic, because of their different structure and kinematics modules. Another relevant characteristic that was verified is the robot's capability of lifting itself up and moving in legged mode despite its weight that can reach up to 35 Kg.

The ability to climb stairs, to traverse steps and to recover after tipped over were also verified - the robot was able to overcome a 410 mm high step by using its tracked arms; a step greater than the length of the tracks (only 350 mm).

3.2   Quadruped Tracked Robot with Manipulative Legs

Developed by Fujita et al. [3], the robot has two tracks and four legs that are capable of not only assisting movement, but also manipulating objects and obstacles. The number of legs could be six or more to guarantee a more stable gait, but its mobility would be affected by the weight increase and energy consumption [3].

Regarding the robot's mobility, it can move in track movement at a 500 mm/s maximum speed; overcome large gaps that would be impossible for a tracked-only robot to overcome; and its legs can assist at climbing high steps and steep slopes. The capability to overcome gaps is deeply studied by Fujita et al. [3] along with the manipulation process to lift boards and retrieve objects, as seen in Fig. 2(b).

The results in Fujita et al. [3] experiment show that the locomotion speed over a gap is 150 mm/s and the robot can run over up to 300 mm: 2.5 times the result of a tracked-only robot and 77% of the robot length. The robot was capable to lift a 900 mm board weighting 1 Kg laid obliquely on an object which was 500 mm high, retrieving successfully a target object of 115 g.

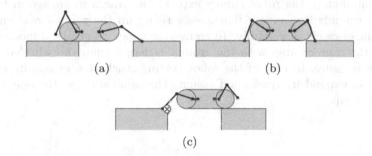

(c)

Fig. 2. A quadruped tracked robot overcoming a substantial gap. Extract from [3].

3.3 Wheel-Track Mobile Robot with Retractable Track

Considering both the adaptability of a tracked locomotion system to different soils, and the efficiency of a wheeled one, a retractable track locomotion system was envisioned by Guo et al. [2]. This transformable wheel-track works by expanding and retracting its track for tracked and wheeled modes, respectively, thus creating the need for a track made of a material with low elastic modulus. Adopting a transformable mechanism instead of a hybrid system that switches between locomotion modes saves weight and space [2].

The wheel-track unit is composed of two rotating gear rings that mesh with the track to transmit large force on tracked mode. In wheeled mode, the gear rings engage with parts of the track teeth to rotate together. It also has a sub-arm capable of assisting the robot in tracked mode to overcome high obstacles.

Analyses of the step-climbing ability of the robot were conducted, in which it was able to overcome obstacles that were no more than 80 mm high in wheeled mode, needing to change to tracked mode to climb higher obstacles with the assistance of a sub-arm located on the robot, being able to overcome a 240 mm obstacle. For comparison, the radius of the gear ring was 165 mm and the sub-arm length was 450 mm [2]. In regard to the soil differences, although the tracked mode presents a higher traction apart, the difference is relatively small on soils with low cohesion, such as snow and dry land, while in high cohesion soils, such as sand and clay, the track's traction is bigger than the wheel's.

A second generation of the robot was developed with improvements on the track and tests were conducted in grass and clay [6]. In wheeled mode at low speeds the robot was capable of running without slipping (no more than 0.3 m/s). With torque increase, the robot slips proportionally to the torque. For tracked mode, the adhesive force is large enough to avoid slips. The Wheel-Track Transformation Robot (WTTR), as it is called [5], works in a similar way, but with an sub-arm as an extra support mechanism used to climb steps, as shown in Fig. 3. Hu et al. [5] also mentions locomotion strategies to overcome obstacles that can be faced in a scenario formed by disasters: climbing a step, traversing a gap and escaping a groove.

To climb a step, the robot simply expands its tracks to engage in tracked mode and extends its support that assists rising up the robot's rear end and crossing the obstacle successfully. To transverse a gap, the tracked mode is also useful as the contact area with the ground is larger than the wheeled mode, decreasing pressure. In case of the robot getting stuck at a groove in wheeled mode, it can expand its tracks and assume the same state as the one used to transverse a gap.

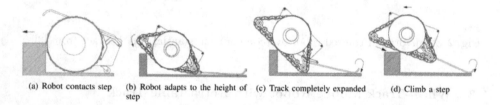

(a) Robot contacts step   (b) Robot adapts to the height of   (c) Track completely expanded   (d) Climb a step
                                step

Fig. 3. Wheel-Track Transformation Robot (WTTR) process of climbing a step [5].

3.4   Transformable Wheel-Track in NEZA-I and Amoeba-III

The NEZA-I [4] and Amoeba-III [7] are similar projects conducted by the same authors and can be analyzed together as they both have the same locomotion system - a self-adaptive mobile mechanism with two symmetric transformable wheel-track (TWT) units that make changing locomotion mode and transforming the track configuration feasible, as it is illustrated in Fig. 4. This adaptation occurs autonomously by the constraint force information, which improves the efficiency of the motors and simplifies the operation.

On flat and rough terrain, the robot contacts the ground by wheel and track, which can be considered as an imaginary wheel due to it being tangent to the ground. This minimizes the contact length, providing turning flexibility and saving energy. When in track mode, only the tracks are used for locomotion, which can be adjusted and therefore can change the locomotion posture to overcome different obstacles.

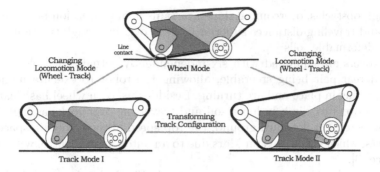

Fig. 4. The NEZA-I and Amoeba-III scheme to change locomotion mode and transform its track configuration [7].

3.5   Tracked Robot with Manipulative Arm

Tracked robots that have manipulative arms often have problems to move under short heights and to perform when flipped over. Considering this, Ben-Tzvi et al. [8] developed and studied a tracked mobile robot with manipulative arms integrated to its base so that the robot becomes sturdy and capable of moving and using the arm on both sides.

Beyond the basic actions that a manipulative arm can perform, this arm specifically was designed to be able to assist locomotion in a similar way that the sub-arms described in Subsect. 3.3 do, as shown in Fig. 5. The arm is composed of two parts that are linked and represented by orange and blue colors in this figure, with the blue one being the innermost one.

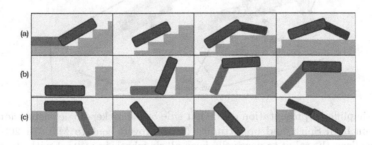

Fig. 5. The track robot with manipulative arms in four different situations which the arm can be used to assist locomotion: (a) climbing stairs; (b) climbing a step; (c) descending a step [8].

3.6   Rocker-Bogie Suspension

Developed by NASA[2] and used on two identical rovers sent to Mars in 2004, this mobility system was designed to meet some requirements, such as traversing

---

[2] https://trs.jpl.nasa.gov/handle/2014/38435.

25 cm high obstacles, overcoming sloped terrains in any variation between 0 and 20° tilt and traveling distances superior to 1 km over hard high traction terrains and soft deformable soils [9].

The rovers are equipped with six independently actuated wheels, with the front and rear pair being steerable, allowing the robot to execute maneuvers such as turning in place and arc turning. Besides this, each wheel has cleats that assist the rovers to climb in loose soil and traversing over rocks as high as the wheel diameter. On flat hard ground, the top speed of these robotic spacecrafts is 4.6 cm/s, which is not used on Mars due to an autonomous control with hazard avoidance [9].

The rocker-bogie suspension is represented in Fig. 6, showing only the left side of the structure. The six wheels are connected to the body of the rover with this mechanical configuration with a differential mechanism attaching the left and right sides that enables the robot to passively keep all of the wheels in contact with the ground even on severely uneven terrains, keeping the wheels pressure on the ground balanced, avoiding sinking in soft soil due to excessive pressure. Furthermore, all six wheels being in contact with the ground can help the movement when climbing hard uneven terrain, maximizing the vehicle's motive force capability by actuating each wheel independently. This suspension is also capable of absorbing significant energy from driving loads and, with the center of mass being near the pivot point of the suspension, the rovers can withstand a tilt of 45° in any direction without overturning.

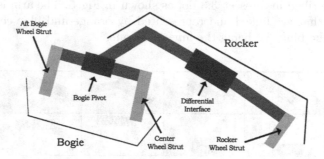

Fig. 6. A simplified representation of the left side of the rocker-bogie suspension structure used on both Spirit and opportunity NASA rovers sent to Mars in 2004. This suspension allows the robot to passivelly keep all six wheels in contact with the ground. Detailed structure is available in reference [9].

Tests were conducted by Lindemann et al. [9] in slopes with angles between 0 and 20° at different orientations in two different surfaces: one being a high friction mat with obstacles up to 25 cm high and the other one being the same mat with dry loose sand on top. On the first one, the robot was able to climb over obstacles up to 15 cm high on all slopes, and up to 20 cm high on slopes with angles between 10 and 15° without excessive wheel slippage. In the soft soil, the rover sinks down between 1 and 2 cm, increasing to as much as 12 cm while traversing obstacles over 15 cm high, increasing the energy consumption due to soil work. The fact that Spirit was working on Mars until March 22, 2010 and Oppotunity is still working (last update was on March 21, 2017)[3] also validates the efficiency of this mechanism.

3.7   Mecanum Wheels

Although a wheeled robot isn't suitable for a disaster environment such as the proposed by the Robocup Rescue League, it is interesting to notice the possibilities that mecanum wheels can add to an hybrid project (such as the legged-wheeled hybrid studied by Fujiya et al. [10]), considering that the omni-direction feature can save time and space to perform maneuveurs. Figure 7 shows how the primitive moves can be achieved in a four wheeled robot, although it is possible to use only three, which could cause the robot to tip over more often [11].

Besides the inability to work in irregular surfaces, as any wheeled locomotion system generally is, the mecanum wheel has some problems regarding slippery areas due to slippage [12] and moving in rough terrains that can cause sand or dirt to pile up on the side of the wheels, preventing the robot to move laterally. This latter problem can be solved by modifying the angle of each roller and by using a combination of two wheels where it would be used only one, as seen on [13].

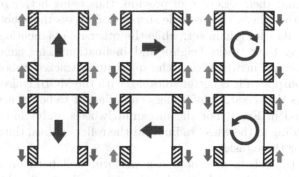

Fig. 7. Primitive moves for a mecanum wheeled robot with four wheels. If all wheels go to the same direction, the robot goes forward or backwards (first column of the diagram). If only the diagonals do so, the robot goes left or right (second column). Otherwise, if each side of the robot goes to one direction, as shown in the third column, the robot rotates [14].

4   Comparison Between Locomotion Systems

For comparing the locomotion systems studied in this paper, it is necessary to create comparison parameters. Considering that the objective comprises of

---

[3] https://mars.nasa.gov/mer/mission/status.html.

satisfying the Robocup Rescue League challenges, the required capabilities are: overpassing gaps; going through steps; overcoming stairs; climbing and descending slopes; moving on rough terrain and on flat surfaces.

Overcoming wide gaps requires that the robot have a support on the opposite side of the gap, otherwise it will fall down when its center of gravity exceeds the edge of its current platform [3]. Following this thought, the quadruped tracked robot, as seen in Fig. 2(b), has advantages over the others, as it is the only one to have proper legs for this purpose, thus being highly recommended for this task. The MOBIT is also recommended to this task, as it can use its tracks as legs for this purpose, however it doesn't have the same flexibility. For the transformable wheel-track robot with retractable track, the gap must be shorter than the size of the robot itself, which then can expand its tracks to escape a groove and is not recommended for this task solely, even though it is a solution to an eventual stick. The other two robots left can overcome gaps only if the condition of the center of gravity not exceeding the edge is matched, therefore not being recommended when facing wide gaps [3]. The rocker-bogie and mecanum wheel are not suitable for this task, as the wheels need to be in contact with the ground to produce movement, therefore they are highly not recommended for this task alone.

Regarding steps, all robots presented in this paper can perform well and are recommended for this task, but in different ways and heights, which is severely influenced by the robot height as well. Robots like the quadruped tracked and the one with manipulative arm (Fig. 5) can easily overcome obstacles due to the assistance that their legs or arm provide, thus being better solutions than the others. For the others, rocker-bogie suspension allows the robot to overcome steps as high as its wheel diameter, while the other robots mentioned surmount this by adjusting their tracks heights and inclination. The same principle is used to climb stairs, in which case the quadruped tracked robot can use its tracks for this purpose if it is better suitable, with the MOBIT also being highly recommended as the versatility of its legs can adapt it to better accomplish this task as displayed in Fig. 1. For the mecanum wheels, only thin steps can be surpassed according to the wheel radius and the rollers radius, thus being highly not indicated for those tasks.

For slopes, the robots presented can perform well both on climbing and descending, as the track can be used to improve adhesion to the ground and the rocker-bogie was approved in tests for slopes tilted up to 20°. The mecanum wheels can be used to descend a slope, but many things need to be taken into consideration for the mechanism to ascend a slope, such as inclination and slippery, thus being not recommended when overcoming slopes is important [15].

The robots can operate well in rough and uneven terrain using its tracks as supports, being the ones with some kind of support, such as MOBIT, the quadruped tracked and the tracked arm highly recommended as they can easily overcome eventual sticks. Even though, for flat surfaces wheeled mechanisms are highly recommended due to reduced contact surface (reducing friction), thus increasing speed and saving energy. Rocker-bogie is highly recommended for both cases, as it is designed to work properly on rough terrain even though it uses wheels, which has been proven as rovers working on Mars use this mechanism. It is important to notice that, even though the mecanum wheel enables the robot to easily move in any direction as seen in Fig. 7, it consumes more energy than a normal wheel as the movement of a mecanum wheel sometimes isn't completely used to move the robot to the same direction. The tracked with arm is not recommended to work on flat surface as it does not have a mechanism to reduce the contact area with the ground, while the other robots have. This discussion is summed up on Table 2, in which the robots are classified for each required capability.

Table 2. Recommended locomotion systems for each specific task: Overpassing a gap (I), going through a step (II), overcoming stairs (III), climbing and descending a slope (IV), moving on rough terrain (V) and moving on flat surface (VI). Each system was evaluated as *highly not recommended* (HNR), *not recommended* (NR), *recommended* (R) and *highly recommended* (HR).

Tasks	MOBIT	Quadruped tracked	WTTR	NEZA-I and Amoeba-III	Tracked w/Arm	Rocker-Bogie	Mecanum wheels
I	R	HR	NR	NR	NR	HNR	HNR
II	R	HR	R	R	HR	R	HNR
III	HR	HR	R	R	HR	R	HNR
IV	R	R	R	R	R	R	NR
V	HR	HR	R	R	HR	HR	HNR
VI	HR	R	R	R	NR	HR	HR

5 Conclusion

In chaotic environments, such as the proposed in the RoboCup Rescue League, versatility is a key feature to success. Robots that combine the three locomotion systems mentioned in this paper can adjust themselves to benefit from the advantages of these architectures and avoid the disadvantages by switching systems.

To guarantee a good range of mobilities, a track-legged hybrid was suggested, as this combination adds the capability to move in rough and irregular terrains while overcoming obstacles, steps and gaps. Although the wheeled locomotion is not mandatory for this environment, it delivers speed and saves energy when compared to the tracked one, while being easier to control and more stable than the legged system, so it can be useful if it is possible to implement wheels in the project. Therefore, the quadruped tracked robot and the MOBIT have recommended mobility architectures for a rescue environment.

Future work in this field will include other locomotion systems, such as hexapod robots, hopping mechanisms and softrobotics actuators[4].

---

[4] https://softroboticstoolkit.com/actuators.

References

1. Duan, X., Huang, Q., Rahman, N., Li, J.: MOBIT, a small wheel-track-leg mobile robot. In: The Sixth World Congress on Intelligent Control and Automation, WCICA 2006, vol. 2, pp. 9159–9163. IEEE (2006)
2. Guo, W., Jiang, S., Zong, C., Gao, X.: Development of a transformable wheel-track mobile robot and obstacle-crossing mode selection. In: 2014 IEEE International Conference on Mechatronics and Automation (ICMA), pp. 1703–1708. IEEE (2014)
3. Fujita, T., Sasaki, T., Tsuchiya, Y.: Hybrid motions by a quadruped tracked mobile robot. In: 2015 IEEE International Symposium on Safety, Security, and Rescue Robotics (SSRR), pp. 1–6. IEEE (2015)
4. Li, Z., Ma, S., Li, B., Wang, M., Wang, Y.: Design and basic experiments of a transformable wheel-track robot with self-adaptive mobile mechanism. In: 2010 IEEE/RSJ International Conference on Intelligent Robots and Systems (IROS), pp. 1334–1339. IEEE (2010)
5. Hu, J., Peng, A., Ou, Y., Jiang, G.: On study of a wheel-track transformation robot. In: 2015 IEEE International Conference on Robotics and Biomimetics (ROBIO), pp. 2460–2465. IEEE (2015)
6. Guo, W., Di Teng, Y.L., Gao, X.: Analysis of terrain interaction with a wheel-track robot. In: 2015 IEEE International Conference on Robotics and Biomimetics (ROBIO), pp. 1852–1857. IEEE (2015)
7. Li, Z., Ma, S., Li, B., Wang, M., Wang, Y.: Kinematics analysis of a transformable wheel-track robot with self-adaptive mobile mechanism. In: 2010 International Conference on Mechatronics and Automation (ICMA), pp. 1537–1542. IEEE (2010)
8. Ben-Tzvi, P., Goldenberg, A.A., Zu, J.W.: Design, simulations and optimization of a tracked mobile robot manipulator with hybrid locomotion and manipulation capabilities. In: IEEE International Conference on Robotics and Automation, ICRA 2008, pp. 2307–2312. IEEE (2008)
9. Lindemann, R.A., Voorhees, C.J.: Mars exploration rover mobility assembly design, test and performance. In: 2005 IEEE International Conference on Systems, Man and Cybernetics, vol. 1, pp. 450–455. IEEE (2005)
10. Fujiya, T., Mikami, S., Nakamura, T., Hama, K.: Locomotion method of a rescue robot with multi-legs and Omni-directional wheels. In: 2014 13th International Conference on Control Automation Robotics & Vision (ICARCV), pp. 1627–1630. IEEE (2014)
11. Dickerson, S.L., Lapin, B.D.: Control of an Omni-directional robotic vehicle with Mecanum wheels. In: Proceedings of National Telesystems Conference, NTC 1991, vol. 1, pp. 323–328. IEEE (1991)
12. Popovici, C., Mândru, D., Ardelean, I.: Design and development of an autonomous Omni-directional mobile robot with Mecanum wheels. In: IEEE International Conference on Automation, Quality and Testing (2014)
13. Ramirez-Serrano, A., Kuzyk, R.: Modified Mecanum wheels for traversing rough terrains. In: 2010 Sixth International Conference on Autonomic and Autonomous Systems, pp. 97–103. IEEE (2010)
14. Xie, L., Herberger, W., Xu, W., Stol, K.A.: Experimental validation of energy consumption model for the four-wheeled Omni-directional Mecanum robots for energy-optimal motion control. In: IEEE 14th International Workshop on Advanced Motion Control (AMC), pp. 565–572. IEEE (2016)
15. Shimada, A., Yajima, S., Viboonchaicheep, P., Samura, K.: Mecanum-wheel vehicle systems based on position corrective control. In: 31st Annual Conference of IEEE on Industrial Electronics Society, IECON 2005, 6-pp. IEEE (2005)

Skills, Tactics and Plays for Distributed Multi-robot Control in Adversarial Environments

Lotte de Koning[1]($\boxtimes$), Juan Pablo Mendoza[2], Manuela Veloso[2], and René van de Molengraft[1]

[1] Departement of Mechanical Engineering, Eindhoven University of Technology, Eindhoven, The Netherlands
c.k.m.d.koning@student.tue.nl, m.j.g.v.d.Molengraft@tue.nl
[2] School of Computer Science, Carnegie Mellon University, Pittsburgh, USA
jpmendoza@ri.cmu.edu, mmv@cs.cmu.edu

Abstract. This work presents a pioneering collaboration between two robot soccer teams from different RoboCup leagues, the Small Size League (SSL) and the Middle Size League (MSL). In the SSL, research is focused on fast-paced and advanced team play for a centrally-controlled multi-robot team. MSL, on the other hand, focuses on controlling a distributed multi-robot team. The goal of cooperation between these two leagues is to apply teamwork techniques from the SSL, which have been researched and improved for years, in the MSL. In particular, the Skills Tactics and Plays (STP) team coordination architecture, developed for centralized multi-robot team, is studied and integrated into the distributed team in order to improve the level of team play. The STP architecture enables more sophisticated team play in the MSL team by providing a framework for team strategy adaptation as a function of the state of the game. Voting-based approaches are proposed to overcome the challenge of adapting the STP architecture to a distributed system. Empirical evaluation of STP in the MSL team shows a significant improvement in offensive game play when distinguishing several offensive game states and applying appropriate offensive plays.

Keywords: Robot soccer · Multi-robot system
Distributed coordination · Team plan execution

1 Introduction

RoboCup is an international robot soccer organization, founded to promote research in robotics and artificial intelligence. The ultimate goal of RoboCup is to beat, by 2050, the winner of the most recent human soccer World Cup with a team of fully autonomous humanoid robot soccer players, complying with the official rules of FIFA. To accomplish this goal, teams compete annually in various soccer leagues, each of which focuses on the different challenges of robot soccer.

© Springer Nature Switzerland AG 2018
H. Akiyama et al. (Eds.): RoboCup 2017, LNAI 11175, pp. 277–289, 2018.
https://doi.org/10.1007/978-3-030-00308-1_23

This work is related to two of those soccer competitions: Small Size League[1] (SSL) and Middle Size League[2] (MSL) (Fig. 1). SSL is specialized in fast-paced and advanced team play within a central coordinated multi-robot team. In MSL on the other hand, research focuses on coordination of a distributed multi-robot team. Both teams operate in adversarial environments. In order to reach the RoboCup goal, research and accomplishments of the different leagues should be brought together. This work presents a co-operation between the SSL team CMDragons from the Carnegie Mellon University in Pittsburgh (United States) and the MSL team Tech United from Eindhoven University of Technology (the Netherlands).

Much research [3,8,9,12] has been done on team planning of centrally coordinated multi-robot teams. However, when the number of robots in the system increases, computations exponentially increase in complexity. Distributed multi-robot systems are a solution to this computation problem [11], as each individual robot computes its tasks. As high-level team planning is the same for both centrally coordinated and distributed multi-robot systems, the research on team planning in centrally coordinated systems can be beneficially used in distributed systems. This work presents an integration of a planning algorithm designed for a centrally coordinated multi-robot team into a distributed multi-robot team.

The case study used for this work is the RoboCup environment. Towards the RoboCup goal of beating a human soccer team, the number of robots in the team will increase to 11, therefore a distributed solution is desired [11]. The advanced planning strategies developed by the SSL over the past years [1,2,6], can be used in the distributed teams, such as the MSL. For this work, the Skills, Tactics and Plays (STP) planning algorithm [2], developed by the CMDragons team for small size soccer robots, is integrated into the Tech United middle size robots to increase the level of team play in Tech United attacks. Compared to planning algorithms designed for multi-robot teams [3,8,9,12], the STP architecture is specifically designed to control an autonomous multi-robot team in a dynamic environment with the presence of adversary's. The architecture contains predefined team plans, the plays, which are chosen during game play based on the world state. The tactics and skills associated with a play define the single robot behaviour during the execution of a play.

This paper presents the approach and challenges of integrating an architecture developed for a centralized multi-robot team into a distributed multi-robot team. In particular, a distributed team of robots, with differences in their estimated state of the world, needs to agree on a team plan and role assignments in a fair way. To overcome this problem, voting systems are considered to determine which play to use, as well as their optimal role assignment [4,5,7]. The new algorithm in the Tech United MSL team is evaluated with simulations and show that using the SSL approach can significantly improve the level of team play.

The remainder of the paper is organized as follows: Sect. 2 presents briefly the current Tech United strategy; Sect. 3 explains the Skill, Tactics and Play

---

[1] http://wiki.robocup.org/wiki/Small_Size_League.
[2] http://wiki.robocup.org/wiki/Middle_Size_League.

(STP) architecture designed by the CMDragrons team; Sect. 4 describes the integration of STP in the Tech United software and finally; Sect. 5 gives the simulation results which show the improvement of the Tech United's offense; the paper is concluded in Sect. 6.

(a) Small Size League at RoboCup European Open 2016, Eindhoven, the Netherland

(b) Middle Size League at RoboCup 2015, Hefei, China

Fig. 1. Both competitions at RoboCup tournaments

2 Tech United MSL Strategy

For this study STP is used to integrate offensive plays into the Tech United team. The current Tech United offensive strategy assigns roles to the active robots, which include specific tasks. The goalkeeper defends the goal, two defenders position between the ball and their own goal, and two attackers execute an attack on adversary's half. Two attacker roles are distinguished: the Attacker-Main is the role that manipulates the ball and the AttackerAssist positions on the adversary's half to potentially receive the ball. Roles execute tasks which involve decision making and selecting skills to complete the task.

This current implementation does not allow the team to easily change strategies shortly before a game or add new strategies to the software. Using the STP architecture, this will be possible.

3 Skill Tactics Play Algorithm

The Skills, Tactics and Plays (STP) architecture was designed by CMDragons to coordinate a centralized team of autonomous robots to achieve long-term goals [2]. This architecture enables simple specification of team plans as plays, which are then executed individually by each robot through tactics and skills. STP enables the team to adapt their team strategy as a function of the state of the game, resulting in highly versatile teamwork. This section describes each component of STP and how the CMDragons team uses STP for team planning.

3.1 STP Components

Skills. At the most basic level, each robot is capable of performing a certain set of low-level skills. Skills are base behaviors that can be parameterized to achieve various goals. In the domain of robot soccer, these skills include navigating safely and quickly to a specific target location, shooting the ball with a specified velocity, and intercepting a moving ball, among others. Skills alone do not encode goal-oriented behavior, but are used in a set of skills to achieve goals.

Tactics. Tactics are goal-oriented behaviors that each individual robot performs to carry out a team plan. These behaviors may be composed of skills, organized to work cohesively towards achieving a goal. In the CMDragons team, tactics are implemented as finite state machines that control the flow of the different skills that make up a tactic.

Each role has a specific set of tactics to perform. Some of the most prominent tactics in the CMDragons team include the Goalkeeper to block shots from the adversary, Defenders to prevent the adversaries from passing and shooting, the AttackerMain to manipulate the ball to score goals on the adversary, and AttackerAssists to position themselves to receive a pass from the AttackerMain. Tactics, like skills, may be parametrized. For example, the AttackerAssist may restrict their search for a good pass location to a specific region of the field.

Plays. In STP, team strategy is encoded into a playbook, made up of a set of plays. A play is a team plan specified as a list of roles that the team of robots must fulfill. Each role, within the context of STP, is defined as a sequence of tactics to be completed sequentially. Additionally, plays specify applicability conditions: *preconditions* specify the set of game states under which a play should be considered for selection, while *invariants* specify the set of game states under which the team does not need to abort this play and select a new one.

Table 1 shows a slightly simplified example of a play in the CMDragons playbook. This play is applicable when all preconditions match the world state: the ball is in the adversary's half of the field (their_side), and there are no opponents on our half of the field (!opp_our_side), and our team has possession of the ball (offense). Furthermore, if this play is selected for execution, it will remain in execution until either the invariants become false, – i.e., the ball moves to our side of the field (their_side becomes false) or the opponent team gains possession of the ball (!defense becomes false), or all the robots have finished performing their role.

3.2 STP Procedure

During each step of execution, the team selects a joint plan, optimally assigns roles to each robot, and then each robot individually executes its role. This section describes this procedure, with an emphasis on the team components.

Table 1. An example of a play

PRECOND their_side && !opp_our_side && offense
INVARIANT their_side && !defense
NUMROBOTS 1 6
ROLE 0
Goalkeeper
ROLE 1
AttackerMain
ROLE 2
Defender
ROLE 3
AttackerAssist front_center
ROLE 4
AttackerAssist front_left
ROLE 5
AttackerAssist front_right

Play Selection. First, the team's central intelligence decides whether the play that was last used is still applicable. That is, it checks if the last play's invariants are still true, and if at least one of the robots has not yet finished its role. If these are both true, no new play is selected; if it is false, a new play is selected from the set of plays whose preconditions hold. If there are multiple plays whose preconditions hold, a play among the set is chosen randomly, with potentially different probabilities for each play.

Optimal Role Assignment. Once a play has been selected, each of the roles in the play is assigned to a robot in the team. Given N active robots $\mathcal{P} = \{\rho_0, \rho_1, \ldots, \rho_N\}$, STP optimally assigns the first N roles $R = \{r_0, r_1, \ldots, r_N\}$ to them optimally, based on a cost function $C : \mathcal{P} \times R \to \mathbb{R}$. In the CMDragons, this cost function $C(\rho_i, r_j)$ is an estimate of the time that it would take robot ρ_i to complete role r_j. To do this, a cost matrix $\mathcal{C}$ of size $N \times N$ is created, such that the entry at row i and column j corresponds to the computed cost $C(\rho_i, r_j)$. From this cost matrix, algorithms such as the Hungarian algorithm [10] can be used to find the assignment from roles to robots that minimizes the total cost. It is important to note that the costs in matrix $\mathcal{C}$ are computed from the centrally-estimated state of the world, common to all the robots in the team.

    The optimal role assignment computation used by the CMDragons is similar to the approach of Tech United, the only difference are the costs. Where the SSL team uses time, the MSL team uses distances. Assuming constant speed during repositioning we can consider time and distance to be equivalent.

Individual Role Execution. After STP distributes the roles of the selected play to each of the robots, they proceed to individually execute their assigned tactic. In

SSL, this step also occurs in a centralized controller, with only the final motion command being sent to each individual physical robot. However, the computation of each tactic happens in parallel, with only very limited communication between robots at this stage.

3.3 STP in Distributed Team

The bulk of the problem of adapting the STP architecture to the MSL lies in the previous two steps: play selection and optimal role assignment. In SSL both steps are performed by a central controller, in MSL however, each robot computes strategy individually. Therefore, the play selection and role assignment is done in five separate computations. To execute a team plan towards a common goal, it is important for the team to agree on the selected play and role assignment. Section 4 discusses in detail the integration of this joint play selection and role assignment in MSL.

4   Integration of STP in MSL

The integration of STP involves four main components from the Tech United software: (i) communication (ii) the game state evaluation, (iii) the role assignment and (iv) the tactics execution. Figure 2 is an overview of the strategy components needed for the STP integration. Highlighted are the new designed components, the playbooks with plays, the play selection algorithm and the tactics, and the re-used and extended components, communication, game state evaluation and role assignment. This section explains each component in more detail.

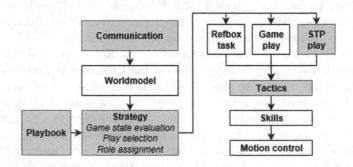

Fig. 2. Three main components for STP: playbook, strategy, play execution.

4.1 Overview STP Algorithm in MSL

Algorithm 1 shows the complete STP integration algorithm. First the world state is evaluated on the preconditions and based on those preconditions a play may be selected (lines 1–2). If a play is selected, the play roles are assigned to the active robots using the role assignment (lines 4–5). In the execution part, first the robot checks whether its team mates are still executing the same play, to ensure all robots execute the same team plan. In addition, the invariants are checked whether those are still true (lines 7–10). If one of those is false, the robot will abort the play and updates its play status to NOT_IN_PROGRESS. Finally, the robot uses the *play_selected* variable from the play selection, and the play status to determine whether a play or the default game play will be executed (lines 12–19). Default game play refers to the strategy as explained in Sect. 2.

Algorithm 1. Algorithm executing a play

1: world.Precond ← evaluateWorldState()
2: *play_selected* ← playSelection(world.Precond)
3:
4: **if** (*play_selected*) **then**
5:     *assignedRoles* ← RoleAssignment(*play_selected*)
6:
7: **if** (PLAY_IN_PROGRESS) **then**
8:     *peerInProgress* ← checkPlayStatePeers()
9:     **if** (!*peerInProgress* **OR** !play.invariants) **then**
10:         PLAY_NOT_IN_PROGRESS
11:
12: **if** (PLAY_NOT_IN_PROGRESS) **then**
13:     **if** (*play_selected*) **then**
14:         execute_play(*assignedRoles*)
15:         PLAY_IN_PROGRESS
16:     **else**
17:         execute_default_play()
18: **else if** (PLAY_IN_PROGRESS) **then**
19:     execute_play(*assignedRoles*)

4.2 Plays and Playbooks

A play P is a predefined team plan which executes a sequence of tactics T_i per robot. The playbook contains a selection of N plays: $\{P_0, P_1, ..., P_N\}$, this selection can specifically be chosen before a game, dependent on the opponent. During a game, one playbook is used. The active play is selected based on the world state. One of the two designed plays for this work, is given by Table 2. The play set-up is similar to the set-up designed by the CMDragons (Table 1). Preconditions and invariants are defined as world state conditions such as ball possession (ourBall), ball location (ballZone) and number of active opponents. Furthermore, the set of roles R is given with several parameters. First the type of role, which includes the sequence of tactics $\{T_1, T_2, ..., T_N\}$. Secondly, a target position, which is used for role assignment. The sequence of the N roles given by the play $R = \{r_1, r_2, ..., r_N\}$ indicates the priority of each role when assigning roles to the set of robots $\mathcal{P}$. In this case, the AttackerMain is the most important role and the Defender the least important. Section 4.4 discusses this role assignment. Finally, in this play role 1 and 2, the two AttackerAssist roles, are assigned to a specific zone in the field. While positioning during the play execution, the role is bounded to this zone. Figure 3 shows the specified zones and target positions for the roles.

Table 2. An offensive play designed for MSL with three offensive robots and one defensive robot

---

AttackWithThree

PRECOND ourBall && ballZone1 && 4
INVARIANTS ourBall
role[0]
    Goalkeeper
    GOAL
role[1]
    AttackerMain
    BALL_POS
role[2]
    AttackerAssist
    PENALTYAREA_CORNER_LEFT
    ZONE_A
role[3]
    AttackerAssist
    PENALTYAREA_CORNER_RIGHT
    ZONE_B
role[4]
    Defender
    {0, -CIRCLERADIUS}

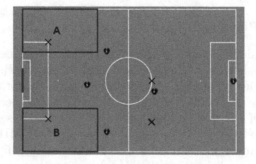

Fig. 3. Target positions for roles are indicated with a cross. The AttackerAssist roles are bounded for positioning to zone A and B.

4.3   Play Selection

For selection of a play from the playbook $\{p_1, p_2, ..., p_N\}$, first the game state is evaluated. The game state is evaluated for all preconditions of the plays, such as the number of opponents and the ball location in field. Each robot evaluates these preconditions individually based on the shared worldmodel.

Where in SSL play selection is done by one coordinator, the play selection in a distributed system is done by each robot individually. The robot compares the game state conditions with the preconditions in the plays. In this work, the playbook consists of two plays in addition to the default play. If no preconditions match the world state conditions, default game play is executed. When the world state conditions do match the preconditions, the matching play is selected. To successfully execute a team plan, it is relevant that the team agrees on executing the same play. Therefore, each robot communicates the selected play with peers such that robots can individually determine whether its chosen play is correct. Each robot gathers the communicated selected plays in one list and sorts the selected plays. From this sorted list, the most common play is found (the mode). This play is feasible if the play is chosen by more than half of the number of active robots. If the mode is not feasible, no play will be selected and default game play is executed. If the mode is feasible, each robot will select the mode as the selected play.

4.4   Distributed Role Assignment

Once the optimal play has been selected given the state of the world, the roles for that play must be filled by the different robots. This is done following the current role assignment algorithm used by Tech United. The role assignment is based on the distance of the current robot position $x(\rho_i)$ to the fixed role position of the selected refbox task $x(r_j)$. Depending on the number of active robots N, N roles are assigned based on priority $R = \{r_1, r_2, ..., r_N\}$. Each robot computes a cost matrix C with the distances from each robot ρ_i to role r_j: $C : \mathcal{P} \times R \to \mathbb{R}$. Then, computations are done to determine the optimal role assignment where the total to be travelled distance by the robots from current position to role position is minimal: $C\left(\sum \rho_i \in \mathcal{P}[C^i]\right)$. To ensure all robots have the same role assignment, such that all roles are begin executed, all robots communicate their optimal role assignment. Currently, from these role assignment calculations, the role assignment of the active robot with lowest ID is used to divide the roles optimally.

4.5   Tactics Execution

To execute the selected play, a sequence of tactics is performed by each role. Algorithm 2 shows an example of the tactics to be performed by the Attacker-Main role. A tactic may involve decision making, – e.g., choosing a pass receiver as shown in the example. To complete the tactic, a set of skills is selected using the function doAction. Tactic transitions take place either after finishing a tactic, – e.g., when the AttackerMain possesses the ball the role transits into the give_pass state, or when a peer robot completes a certain tactic, – e.g., when the AttackerMain possesses the ball, the AttackerAssist roles transits to the receive_pass tactic. Therefore, communication is also required while executing tactics.

Algorithm 2. Sequence of tactics to be executed by the AttackMain.

1: **switch** AttackerMain.tactic **do**
2:     **case** intercept_ball
3:         doAction(intercept_ball)
4:     **case** give_pass
5:         *pass_receiver* ← choosePassReceiver()
6:         doAction(shoot_at_target, *pass_receiver*)
7:     **case** wait_to_end_play
8:         *target* ← findOptimalPosition()
9:         doAction(go_to_target, *target*)

---

5   Simulations and Results

The integration of STP in the Tech United software is empirically evaluated with simulations. Two offensive plays were integrated, each for different world state, where the ball location precondition differs. Figure 4a show these ball locations. Play 1 will be executed when the ball is located in zone 1. Play 2 when the ball is located in zone 2. For all other ball locations, regular offensive game play, as explained in Sect. 2, is executed. The simulations are attacks from one of these zones with 4 robots: one goalkeeper and the first three roles defined by the play. These attackers are the black robots in Fig. 4a. The attacks are performed against two defenders, the red robots in the Figure. The results of 60 attacks using the STP integration, are compared to the results of 60 attacks playing without STP.

5.1   Results

The difference in the attack using STP and not using STP is shown in Fig. 4. The black robots are the attacking robots, the two red robots the defenders and the ball is orange and located in zone 1. The two defenders defend in between the ball and home goal. They follow the ball and try to block and intercept passes from the attackers. Figure 4b shows the positioning before the attackers are in ball possession. The AttackerMain (AM) intercepts the ball while the AttackerAssist (AA) roles are positioning within their assigned zone. The target positions for the AA roles are indicated with the blue cross, the red cross indicates the target position of the AM. The difference with the attack without using STP, as shown in Fig. 4c, is that two robots are positioning on the adversary's half. In Fig. 4c

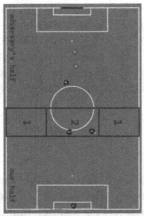 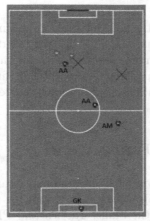 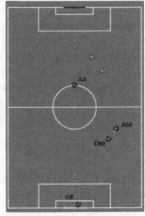

(a) For ball in zone 1, play 1 is executed, for ball in zone 2, play 2 is executed. For all other situations, regular game play is executed. Black robots: attackers, red robots: defenders.

(b) Attack with STP: AM intercepts the ball (target red cross), AA's position in given zone (target blue cross).

(c) Attack without STP: AM intercepts the ball, AA positioning on opponent half, DM positioning on own half.

Fig. 4. Simulations of attacks using STP and not using STP. Black robots are attackers, red robots defenders.

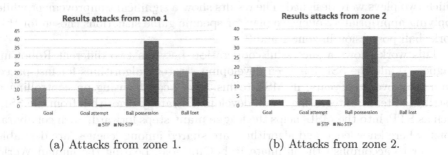

(a) Attacks from zone 1.

(b) Attacks from zone 2.

Fig. 5. Comparison of 60 attacks between a team using STP and a team not using STP. Graph shows results after max. 4 passes starting in the zone: goal, goal attempt, ball possession or the ball was lost.

can be seen that the AM intercepts the ball, while only one AA is positioning on adversary's half and the DefenderMain (DM) on their own half.

The results of the attacks from the two zones are given in Fig. 5. Attacks were performed from each of the given zones (Fig. 4a). When the attacking team made four passes, the attack was rated as ball possession for the team. If the attack finished before these four passes, the attack results either in a goal, a goal attempt or the ball was lost. For both plays the similar conclusions can be drawn.

The total number of lost balls, either a failed pass or an interception by the opponent, is equal for both the STP integration and no STP integration. Therefore, it can be concluded that the STP integration does not have an influence on this parameter. Furthermore, attacking without the plays, resulted mostly in ball possession for the team, the attackers did not find the chance to shoot at goal. Using the STP integration on the other hand results in significantly more goals and goal attempts.

6   Conclusions and Future Work

This paper presented a novel effort in adapting team-level strategy from the centrally-controlled Small Size League of RoboCup to the distributed Middle Size League. In particular, the Skills, Tactics and Plays (STP) team-planning architecture was successfully integrated in the Tech United team. The main challenges for this integration were the agreement on a common team plan to execute and optimally assign the team plan roles to the active robots. Voting-based approaches were used to overcome these challenges. Each robot individually selects a play and computes the costs for optimal role assignment. Both are communicated among all robots. The most common selected play is chosen by each robot and role assignment is computed based on an averaged cost matrix. Both methods are proven to be robust by the performed simulations.

Simulations with and without the STP integration were performed. Three robots performed attacks against to adversary's for game state situations for which two plays were designed. The results show a significant improvement while applying appropriately-offensive play for specific game situations chosen for this work: ball possession in zone 1 and 2.

This work shows a successful cooperation between two different RoboCup leagues. While the SSL has been developing strategy algorithms for fast-paced team play over the years, in MSL teams have been focusing on controlling a distributed team. Integrating a well-developed strategy algorithm from the SSL, such as STP, into the MSL, helps the league many steps forward. Such collaborations, where knowledge and algorithms are shared among leagues, are desirable in order to accomplish the ultimate RoboCup goal: beating the human World Cup winner of 2050 with a fully autonomous humanoid robot soccer team.

References

1. Biswas, J., Mendoza, J.P., Zhu, D., Choi, B., Klee, S.D., Veloso, M.M.: Opponent-driven planning and execution for pass, attack, and defense in a multi-robot soccer team. In: Proceedings of AAMAS 2014, the Thirteenth International Joint Conference on Autonomous Agents and Multi-Agent Systems (2014)
2. Browning, B., Bruce, B., Bowling, M., Veloso, M.: STP: skills, tactics and plays for multi-robot control in adversarial environments. Proc. Inst. Mech. Eng. Part I: J. Syst. Control Eng. **219**(1), 33–52 (2004)

3. Brumitt, B., Stentz, A.: Dynamic mission planning for multiple mobile robots. In: Proceedings of the IEEE International Conference on Robotics and Automation, vol. 3, pp. 2396–2401 (1996)
4. Castelpietra, C., Iocchi, L., Nardi, D., Piaggio, M., Scalzo, A., Sgorbissa, A.: Coordination among heterogeneous robotic soccer players. In: Proceedings of the IEEE/RSJ International Conference on Intelligent Robots and Systems, (IROS 2000), vol. 2, pp. 1385–1390. IEEE (2000)
5. Farinelli, A., Scerri, P., Tambe, M.: Building large-scale robot systems: distributed role assignment in dynamic, uncertain domains. In: Proceedings of Workshop on Representations and Approaches for Time-Critical Decentralized Resource, Role and Task Allocation, vol. 102 (2003)
6. Galindo, C., Fernández-Madrigal, J.A., González, J., Saffiotti, A.: Robot task planning using semantic maps. Rob. Auton. Syst. **56**(11), 955–966 (2008)
7. Hunsberger, L., Grosz, B.J.: A combinatorial auction for collaborative planning. In: Proceedings of Fourth International Conference on MultiAgent Systems, pp. 151–158. IEEE (2000)
8. Janssen, R.: Centralized learning and planning: for cognitive robots operating in human domains (2014)
9. Jensen, R.M., Veloso, M.M.: OBDD-based universal planning: specifying and solving planning problems for synchronized agents in non-deterministic domains. In: Wooldridge, M.J., Veloso, M. (eds.) Artificial Intelligence Today. LNCS (LNAI), vol. 1600, pp. 213–248. Springer, Heidelberg (1999). https://doi.org/10.1007/3-540-48317-9_9
10. Kuhn, H.W.: The Hungarian method for the assignment problem. In: Naval Research Logistics, pp. 83–97. IEEE (2006)
11. Parker, L.E.: Designing control laws for cooperative agent teams. In: Proceedings of the IEEE International Conference on Robotics and Automation, pp. 582–587 (1993)
12. Svestka, P., Overmars, M.: Coordinated path planning for multiple robots. Rob. Auton. Syst. **7**, 83–124 (1997)

Modelling a Solenoid's Valve Movement

Arthur Demarchi$^{(\boxtimes)}$, Leonardo Farçoni, Adam Pinto, Rafael Lang,
Roseli Romero, and Ivan Silva

Warthog Robotics, São Carlos School of Engineering,
Institute of Mathematics and Computer Science,
University of São Paulo, São Carlos, SP, Brazil
{arthur.demarchi,leonardo.farconi,adam.moreira,
rafael.lang}@wr.sc.usp.br, rafrance@icmc.usp.br, insilva@sc.usp.br

Abstract. Solenoid Valves are broadly used as electromechanical actuators when robustness and strength are needed. More specifically, in the Warthog Robotics group project WRMagic, the solenoid is used as an impact generator to impulse a rigid body. The literature recommends to deeply understand the plunger's movement in response to the applied voltage in the coil terminals for applications of this magnitude. This paper models a solenoid system using it's own magnetic field closed circuit and the model is implemented in Simulink for various input voltage cases.

Keywords: Model · Solenoid · Valve · Simulink

1 Introduction

Solenoids are actuators comprised of a helical coil wrapped around a ferromagnetic core. This core can either be fixed, being used mainly to generate a concentrated electromagnetic field, or free to move in the coil axis. This property of creating force in the presence of electrical current is considered an electromechanical energy conversion, which makes the solenoid useful for many applications such as dialysis machines [1], MRIs [2,3], Washing Machines [4], Electrical lockers [5], pressurizers [6], controlled brakes [7] in the automotive industry, Solenoid Valves, a switch that control the flux of fluids in hydraulic systems [8], and finally in the Smallsize [9] and MiddleSize [10] Soccer Leagues of Robocup as a "kicking tool".

This paper was conceived at the "Centro de Robótica Aplicada da Universidade de São Paulo" (CROB), as a study of the research group Warthog Robotics, with the goal of defining the theoretical ground to improve the WRMagic Project (Smallsize) [11] and to develop other projects in soccer and rescue RoboCup categories [12]. The WRMagic is an autonomous football robot that uses a solenoid as actuator to impulse a rigid object, that simulates a kick or pass on a football game. Even though the literature on solenoids is large, studies are focused primarily on industrial [13] and research applications. Their emphasis, therefore, is on limited empirical or simplified models related to Superconducting

© Springer Nature Switzerland AG 2018
H. Akiyama et al. (Eds.): RoboCup 2017, LNAI 11175, pp. 290–301, 2018.
https://doi.org/10.1007/978-3-030-00308-1_24

applications [14–16], solenoid's fabrication [14,17,18], physical characteristics [17,19,20], maximum force [21], shape [16], inductance [22,23], self-capacitance [24], hysteresis characteristics [25,26], robustness [27] and others which do not completely fulfill our purposes. Our solenoids, therefore, are produced based, with adaptations, on another model exposed by us on [28] and some practical knowledge since that model is only valid for simple finite coils, not physical solenoids.

In this research we aim to obtain a complete model of a real generic solenoid so as to relate all variables, from materials to geometry, that influence on the core's movement. Such complete model will give us the ability to choose the best solenoid configuration for different applications in our projects, as also to develop better control algorithms for them.

This paper is organized as follow: in the introduction, some concepts will be presented, then, using those concepts in the second section the algebraic deduction will be exposed. After that, in the third section, the Simulink's model construction is explained and finally the results of said simulation are displayed in graphs, that are on the fourth section. The last section is a conclusion based on said accumulated data.

1.1   Solenoid Valve Functioning

It's well known, by the application of Ampere's law, that a union of turns when energized by current generate a magnetic field on it's interior, being this field approximately parallel to the surface of turns [29]:

$$\oint_C B.dl = \mu_0.I \tag{1}$$

where B is the Magnetic Field, dl is an element of the Any Closed Curve (C), μ_0 is the magnetic permeability and I is the total electrical current in the surface enclosed by the Curve.

When a ferromagnetic material is positioned at the coil axis edge, and there's electrical current through the coil, a magnetic field is concentrated in the interior of the material creating a magnetic force in the coil axis and pulling the material to the center of the coil, therefore if the magnetic force is controlled via the electric current injection it is possible to create an actuator as in Fig. 1(a).

1.2   Solving Magnetic Circuits

Solving a magnetic circuit can be a difficult task. However Fitzgerald [30] proposes the following hypothesis allow the calculation of a magnetic circuit by an equivalent electric circuit:

- The inductance outside does not influence on the final magnitude of the field
- There is no spreading of the magnetic field in the gaps of the solenoid.
- All the magnetic field is confined in the closed magnetic circuit.

- The magnetic permeability of the gap is practically equal to the void's.
- The Displacement terms of the Maxwell's equations are insignificant.
- The Magnetic inductance of the magnetic field strength (H) in the magnetic field flux (B) is insignificant in every point of the system.
- The Magnetic inductance can be considered Homogeneous.

Based on those assumptions, the magnetic circuit can be solved by considering the system static at each time step. Therefore the dynamic characteristics will be derived based on Newton's law and on application of static magnetic calculation at each instant. This makes it possible to approximate, the magnetic circuit to an equivalent one-dimensional electric circuit that can be analyzed using basic circuit theory. This equivalent electric circuit obeys the following rules:

1. As said in the first hypothesis, the passage of magnetic flux (equivalent to current) exists only in the ferromagnetic material and the gap.
2. The reluctance is substituted by analogue resistors.
3. Coils are substituted by voltage sources, being its voltage equivalent to the number of turns times their electric Current.

2   Model Deduction

2.1   Algebraic Approach

To model the solenoid's plunger, it will be used the concepts exposed in Sect. 1.2 and the basics of newtonian mechanics. The problem will be approached with two basic equations: the electrical and the mechanical, that is, the equation that rules the voltage in the coil's terminals and the equation of force balance in the coil axis. The first equation is represented as follows:

$$V = \frac{\partial \lambda_{(x,i)}}{\partial t} + R.i_{(t)} \tag{2}$$

being the voltage on the coil equal to the Ohm's law $R.i_{(t)}$ plus the Voltage from Len's Law $\frac{\partial \lambda_{(x,i)}}{\partial t}$. And the second approach:

$$F_{res} = F_{mag} + F_{hooke} + P_x - F_\mu - F_{vis} \tag{3}$$

the sum of forces on the coil axis which contains the magnetic force, Hooke's force, a component of weight, friction and viscosity force. Also, the magnetic permeability will be considered constant to any given magnetic flux.

2.2   Magnetic Circuit Analysis

As the Solenoid's Resistance is a constant and the current function is not trivial to describe, the analysis begins with the description offlux linkage [λ]:

$$\lambda_{(x,i)} = N.\varPhi \tag{4}$$

where N represents the number of turns in the coil and Φ represents the Magnetic Flux.

The magnetic flux is a variable which depends on the magnetic circuit, formed in this case by the coil, plunger, iron core magnetic path and gap. When transformed into to a electric circuit, the magnetic circuit of the Fig. 1(a) can be displayed as in Fig. 1(b), in which $\Re_1$ and $\Re_3$ are the reluctance of the effective path traveled by the flux in the iron core and $\Re_2$ is the sum of the reluctance of the plunger and gap. Its possible to simplify the circuit in Fig. 1(b) applying the relation of parallelism between $\Re_1$ and $\Re_3$ which results in $\Re_{ic}$, the iron core reluctance. Its also interesting for the analysis to separate $\Re_2$ in the sum of $\Re_0$ and $\Re_{pl}$ resulting in a new circuit, represented by Fig. 1(c).

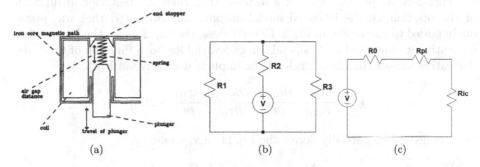

(a)   (b)   (c)

Fig. 1. Typical representations of a solenoid valve: (a) physical component, extracted from [31], (b) equivalent electrical circuit and (c) simplified equivalent electrical circuit

Therefore, based on the relation 5, that determines the reluctance [30]:

$$\Re = \frac{l}{\mu_r.\mu_0.A} \tag{5}$$

the following equations are defined:

$$\Re_{ic} = \frac{l_{ic}}{\mu_{ic}.\mu_0.A_{pl}} \tag{6}$$

$$\Re_{pl} = \frac{x_{(t)} + l_{pl}}{\mu_{pl}.\mu_0.A_{pl}} \tag{7}$$

$$\Re_0 = \frac{l_0 - x_{(t)}}{\mu_0.A_{ic}} \tag{8}$$

To relate the linkage flux and the reluctance its possible to pursue the path:

$$N.i_{(t)} = \Re_n.\Phi$$
$$N.i_{(t)} = (\Re_{ic} + \Re_{pl} + \Re_0).\Phi$$
$$N^2.i_{(t)} = (\Re_{ic} + \Re_{pl} + \Re_0).\Phi.N$$
$$N^2.i_{(t)} = (\Re_{ic} + \Re_{pl} + \Re_0).\lambda$$

$$\lambda_{(x,i)} = \frac{N^2.i_{(t)}}{\mathfrak{R}_{ic} + \mathfrak{R}_{pl} + \mathfrak{R}_0} \tag{9}$$

As represented on Fig. 1(a), A_{pl} is identical to A_0. It's possible to simplify these formulas and sum the total reluctance:

$$\Sigma\mathfrak{R} = \frac{l_{ic}.A_0.\mu_{pl} + l_{pl}.A_{ic}.\mu_{ic} + l_0.A_{ic}.\mu_{ic}.\mu_{pl} + x_{(t)}.(A_{ic}.\mu_{ic} - A_{ic}.\mu_{ic}.\mu_{pl})}{A_{ic}.A_0.\mu_0.\mu_{pl}.\mu_{ic}} \tag{10}$$

Which finally results in the linkage flux in the form of:

$$\lambda_{(x,i)} = \frac{A_{ic}.A_0.\mu_0.\mu_{pl}.\mu_{ic}.N^2.i_{(t)}}{l_{ic}.A_0.\mu_{pl} + l_{pl}.A_{ic}.\mu_{ic} + l_0.A_{ic}.\mu_{ic}.\mu_{pl} + x_{(t)}.A_{ic}.\mu_{ic}.(1 - \mu_{pl})} \tag{11}$$

Therefore its possible to find a formula that rules λ's behavior in function of the position(x), the intended model output, and current(i) that was previously added to the model in Eq. 2. Nevertheless, the Eq. 2 needs the linkage flux derivative in time, and as λ depends on two variables both function of time, the derivative follows the chain's rule of the implicit derivative in Eq. 2.

$$V = \frac{\partial\lambda_{(x,i)}}{\partial i_{(t)}}.\frac{\partial i_{(t)}}{\partial t} + \frac{\partial\lambda_{(x,i)}}{\partial x_{(t)}}.\frac{\partial x_{(t)}}{\partial t} + R.i_{(t)} \tag{12}$$

So it is needed to partially derive the Eq. 11 in $x_{(t)}$ and $i_{(t)}$.

$$\frac{\partial\lambda_{(x,i)}}{\partial x_{(t)}} = \frac{-N^2.\mu_{fr}^2.\mu_{vl}.\mu_0.A_{fr}^2.A_0.(1 - \mu_{vl}).i_{(t)}}{(l_{fr}.A_0.\mu_{vl} + l_{vl}.A_{fr}.\mu_{fr} + l_0.A_{fr}.\mu_{fr}.\mu_{vl} + x_{(t)}A_{fr}.\mu_{fr}.(1 - \mu_{vl}))^2} \tag{13}$$

$$\frac{\partial\lambda_{(x,i)}}{\partial i_{(t)}} = \frac{A_{fr}.A_0.\mu_0.\mu_{vl}.\mu_{fr}.N^2}{l_{fr}.A_0.\mu_{vl} + l_{vl}.A_{fr}.\mu_{fr} + l_0.A_{fr}.\mu_{fr}.\mu_{vl} + x_{(t)}.A_{fr}.\mu_{fr}.(1 - \mu_{vl})} \tag{14}$$

The equation above seems to be complicated, however, it is possible to simplify the visualization with some new definitions of global constants.

$$k_{t1} = A_{fr}.A_0.\mu_0.\mu_{pl}.\mu_{ic}.N^2 \tag{15}$$

$$k_{t2} = A_{ic}.\mu_{ic}.(1 - \mu_{pl}) \tag{16}$$

$$k_{t3} = l_{ic}.A_0.\mu_{pl} + l_{pl}.A_{ic}.\mu_{ic} + l_0.A_{ic}.\mu_{ic}.\mu_{pl} \tag{17}$$

Replacing the Eqs. 15, 16 and 17 in 13 and 14. Then, replacing the result of this procedure in the Eq. 12 it's finally viable to visualize the first differential equation of this model:

$$V = \frac{k_{t1}.\frac{\partial i_{(t)}}{\partial t}}{x_{(t)}.k_{t2} + k_{t3}} - \frac{k_{t1}.k_{t2}.i_{(t)}.\frac{\partial x_{(t)}}{\partial t}}{(x_{(t)}.k_{t2} + k_{t3})^2} + R.i_{(t)} \tag{18}$$

2.3   Mechanical System Analysis

The objective of this section is to study the equation exposed in Sect. 2.1 and rewrite it in function of our output variables $i_{(t)}$ and $x_{(t)}$. Firstly, from the Eq. 3

each term can be expanded in:

$$F_{res} = m.\frac{\partial^2 x_{(t)}}{\partial^2 t} \qquad\qquad F_{hooke} = -K.x_{(t)} \qquad\qquad F_\mu = m.g.Cos(\theta).\mu_\mu$$

$$F_{mag} = \frac{\partial W'_{(x_{(t)},i_{(t)})}}{\partial x} \qquad\qquad P_x = m.g.Sen(\theta) \qquad\qquad F = \beta.\frac{\partial x_{(t)}}{\partial t}$$

In those equations its possible to visualize that the only variable that differs from our output is $W'_{(x_{(t)},i_{(t)})}$, therefore it is needed to deepen in its study. To accomplish that, the following relation [31], will be used.

$$W'_{(x_{(t)},i_{(t)})} = \int_0^{i_{(t)}} \lambda_{(x_{(t)},i_{(t)})}.di \tag{19}$$

Therefore

$$F_{mag} = \int_0^{i_{(t)}} \frac{\partial \lambda_{(x_{(t)},i_{(t)})}}{\partial x_{(t)}}.di \tag{20}$$

Reminding that $\frac{\partial \lambda_{(x_{(t)},i_{(t)})}}{\partial x_{(t)}}$ is already defined by Eq. 13.

$$F_{mag} = -\frac{k_{t1}.k_{t2}.i_{(t)}^2}{2.(k_{t2}.x_{(t)} + k_{t3})^2} \tag{21}$$

to simplify the Differential Equation it will be used a new global constant k_{t4}:

$$k_{t4} = m.g.Sen(\theta) + m.g.Cos(\theta).\mu_\mu \tag{22}$$

Lastly, replacing all forces and the constant k_{t4} in the Eq. 3:

$$m.\frac{\partial^2 x_{(t)}}{\partial^2 t} = -\frac{k_{t1}.k_{t2}.i_{(t)}^2}{2.(k_{t2}.x_{(t)} + k_{t3})^2} - K.x_{(t)} - k_{t4} - \beta.\frac{\partial x_{(t)}}{\partial t} \tag{23}$$

2.4   Final Differential Equations

With the equations achieved it's unlikely that a algebraic solution will be found, but a numeric solution is needed. Then, the Differential Equations must be rearranged in a way that facilitates the construction of a flowchart in the Simulink Application, of the software Matlab.

$$\frac{\partial i_{(t)}}{\partial t} = (\frac{x_{(t)}.k_{t2} + k_{t3}}{k_{t1}})(\frac{k_{t1}.k_{t2}.i_{(t)}.\frac{\partial x_{(t)}}{\partial t}}{(x_{(t)}.k_{t2} + k_{t3})^2} - R.i_{(t)} + V) \tag{24}$$

$$\frac{\partial^2 x_{(t)}}{\partial^2 t} = (-\beta.\frac{\partial x_{(t)}}{\partial t} - K.x_{(t)} - k_{t4} - \frac{k_{t1}.k_{t2}.i_{(t)}^2}{2.(k_{t2}.x_{(t)} + k_{t3})^2}).\frac{1}{m} \tag{25}$$

3   Simulation

By the Differential Eqs. 24 and 25 the flowchart in the following figures was build. Figure 3 shows the dependencies of each output and also how the input proprieties are transformed into the global constants defined in section 2. Figures 4(b), (c) and (d) show how the constants and variables interact to form the Current Differential Equation. Finally the Fig. 5(a) and (b) form the Differential Equation that rules the valve's movement (Fig. 2).

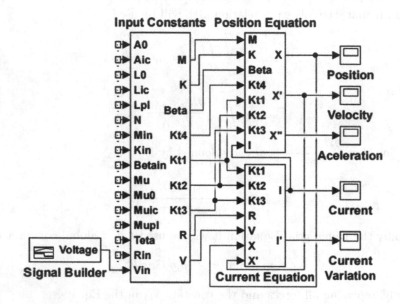

Fig. 2. Superficial visualization of simulink

4   Results

Running the model drew in Sect. 3 for the inputs:

- $A_0 = 0.0005\,m^2$
- $A_{fr} = 0.00005\,m^2$
- $L_0 = 0.0010\,m$
- $L_{ic} = 0.5000\,m$

- $L_{pl} = 0.1000\,m$
- $N = 1000.0\,Turns$
- $M = 0.1000\,kg$
- $K = 1.0000\,\frac{N}{m}$

- $\beta = 10.000\,Nsm^{-1}$
- $\mu_{atr} = 0.0000\,u.a$
- $\mu_0 = 0.4000\pi\mu\frac{H}{m}$
- $\mu_{fr} = 1000.0\,\frac{H}{m}$

- $\mu_{pl} = 1000.0\,\frac{H}{m}$
- $\theta = 0.0000°$
- $R = 0.0800\Omega$
- $V = V_{(t)}$

Where all the geometrical values, and the number of turns, were taken from measures of a real solenoid. The resistance was calculated based on the wires dimensions and the magnetic permissiveness are based on the greatness of normal ferromagnetic material such as iron. The friction coefficient is considered null because of the position in which the solenoid is being analyzed in Fig. 1(a). $V_{(t)}$ is a Decreasing ramp that varies in initial value from 10,000V to 220,00V for each output graph, and has it's final value at 0,0100s as 0V. This should simulate

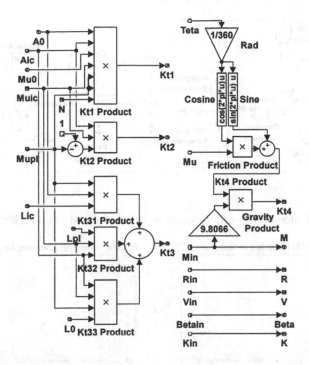

Fig. 3. Input constants to global constants transformation

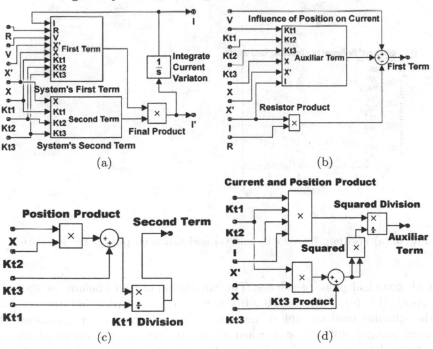

Fig. 4. Current differential equation: (a) model and the terms of the current equation: (b) first term, (c) second term and (d) auxiliary term for the first term

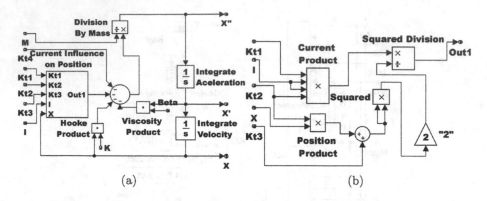

Fig. 5. Differential position equation: (a) model and (b) auxiliary term

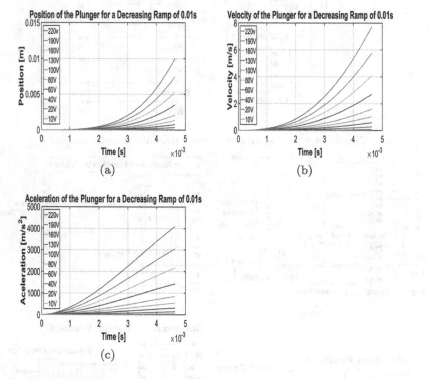

Fig. 6. (a) Position, (b) velocity and (c) aceleration outputs of the simulation

a quick non-ideal pulse of voltage. The Simulation outputs behave as shown in Figs. 6(a), (b), (c), 7(a) and (b). It's seen in those graphs that the response to the stimulus tend to explode into instability, which was expected since the solenoid plunger will only stop when it's middle reaches the center of the coil but the model assumes, in Eqs. 7 and 8, that the plunger has infinite length and is pursuing a infinite path.

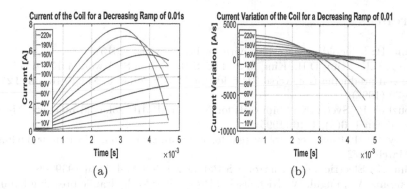

Fig. 7. (a) Current and (b) current variation outputs of the simulation

In those graphs, for any variable, the increasing voltage inputs generated ten outputs similar in form and characteristics, and so we must conclude that the Simulink model can be used as a tool to anticipate any solenoid behavior. Although it is impossible to confirm this without the proper validation, all indicates that the flowchart model can be used to develop new solenoids for our projects, if those don't disobey any of the hypothesis in this paper and also have a limited small path to cross.

5   Conclusion

Although the literature about this type of model is not as extensive as one would expect, in this paper we achieved the objective to model the solenoid's plunger motion. Unfortunately this model can only work for the small amount of time that takes for the plunger to achieve the final point of its direct path in the spring direction, which means, the simulation is only valid for the time where $x_{(t)} < L_0$. It is also not considered the variation of the magnetic permeability which can lead to a unfaithfully result if the ferromagnetic material is on its saturated state.

As future works, we plan to overcome the model constraints by changing our approach in the magnetic circuit analysis, its intended to integrate the magnetic field for each point in space, via Biot Savart law, to later find the function that determines exactly how the flux behaves inside the solenoid, and then, find the magnetic force and the coil voltage with said function. But, although our current approach have it's constraints, it is already a useful tool to analyze solenoids with small, limited, position variations. Its also, in our plans to validate this, and the next model, with data acquired from real solenoids in controlled experiments.

References

1. Gant, P.: Solenoid valves evolve with medical devices (2015)
2. Jeong, E.K., Kim, D.H., Kim, M.J., Lee, S.H., Suh, J.S., Kwon, Y.K.: A solenoid-like coil producing transverse RF fields for MR imaging. J. Magn. Reson. **127**(1), 73–79 (1997)
3. Konzbul, P., Sveda, K.: Shim coils for NMR and MRI solenoid magnets. Measur. Sci. Technol. **6**(8), 1116 (1995)
4. Athey, S.: Hydraulic control system for a washing machine. US Patent 3,646,948, 7 March 1972
5. John, K.: Electric locker control. US Patent 2,153,088, 4 April 1939
6. Shanping, W., Fugui, W., Nicholls, C.: Pressurizer for hydraulic breaking hammer. CN Patent 2,888,072, 11 April 2007
7. Branciforte, M., Meli, A., Muscato, G., Porto, D.: Ann and non-integer order modeling of abs solenoid valves. IEEE Trans. Control Syst. Technol. **19**(3), 628–635 (2011)
8. Ribeiro, M.: Válvulas de Controle e Segurança, 5th edn. Tek, São Paulo (1999)
9. Adachi, Y., Kusakabe, H., et al.: Robodragons 2016 extended team description (2016)
10. Bachmann, D., Belsch, E., et al.: Carpe noctem cassel team description 2016 (2016)
11. Small Size League Technical Committee: Laws of the RoboCup small size league 2016 (2016)
12. RoboCupRescue Robot League: Robocup rescue rulebook
13. Nagy, L., Szabó, T., Jakab, E.: Electro-dynamical modeling of a solenoid switch of starter motors. Proc. Eng. **48**, 445–452 (2012)
14. Moriyama, H., Mitsui, H., Ohmori, J., Mine, S., Nishijima, S., Okada, T.: Design and fabrication of highly stabilized close-packed superconducting solenoid. IEEE Trans. Magn. **32**(4), 3028–3031 (1996)
15. Kaiho, K., Namba, T., Ohara, T., Koyama, K.: Optimization of superconducting solenoid. Cryogenics **16**(10), 587–588 (1976)
16. Byun, J.K., Park, I.H., Nah, W., Lee, J.H., Kang, J.: Comparison of shape and topology optimization methods for hts solenoid design. IEEE Trans. Appl. Supercond. **14**(2), 1842–1845 (2004)
17. Song, C.W., Lee, S.Y.: Design of a solenoid actuator with a magnetic plunger for miniaturized segment robots. Appl. Sci. **5**(3), 595–607 (2015)
18. Wang, L., et al.: Design and construction of a prototype solenoid coil for mice coupling magnets. IEEE Trans. Appl. Supercond. **20**(3), 373–376 (2010)
19. Olivares-Galvan, J., Campero-Littlewood, E., Escarela-Perez, R., Magdaleno-Adame, S., Blanco-Brisset, E.: Coil systems to generate uniform magnetic field volumes. In: COMSOL Conference 2010 Boston-United States: COMSOL (2010)
20. Tai, C.M., Liao, C.N.: A physical model of solenoid inductors on silicon substrates. IEEE Trans. Microwave Theory Techn. **55**(12), 2579–2585 (2007)
21. Sung, B.J., Lee, E.W., Lee, J.G.: A design method of solenoid actuator using empirical design coefficients and optimization technique. In: IEEE International Electric Machines and Drives Conference, IEMDC 2007, vol. 1, pp. 279–284. IEEE (2007)
22. Kumar, G.R., Chaddah, P.: Optimization of superconducting solenoid magnet geometries for minimum inductance. Cryogenics **27**(5), 229–236 (1987)
23. Wheeler, H.A.: Inductance chart for solenoid coil. Proc. IRE **38**(12), 1398–1400 (1950)

24. Knight, D.W.: The self-resonance and self-capacitance of solenoid coils (2010). http://www.g3ynh.info/zdocs
25. Sheng, C., Hai, N.L., Cheng, Y.X., Bao-Lin, T.P.: Proportional solenoid valve flow hysteresis modeling based on PSO algorithm. In: 2013 Third International Conference on Instrumentation, Measurement, Computer, Communication and Control (IMCCC), pp. 1064–1067. IEEE (2013)
26. Ruderman, M., Gadyuchko, A.: Phenomenological modeling and measurement of proportional solenoid with stroke-dependent magnetic hysteresis characteristics. In: 2013 IEEE International Conference on Mechatronics (ICM), pp. 180–185. IEEE (2013)
27. Badcock, R., Bumby, C., Jiang, Z., Long, N.: Solenoid winding using YBCO roebel cable. Phys. Proc. **36**, 1159–1164 (2012)
28. Montes, R.S., Santos, P.H.N., Lang, R.G., Silva, I.N.: Modelagem dinâmica da geração de força axial de um solenoide. In: Modelagem dinâmica da geração de força axial de um solenoide, 21 SIICUSP, pp. 1–3, October 2013
29. Buck, W.: Eletromagnetismo. McGraw Hill, Brasil (1998)
30. Fitzgerald Jr., A., Kinsley, C.: Electric Machinery, 3rd edn. Bookman, New Delhi (1979)
31. Cheung, N., Lim, K., Rahman, M.: Modelling a linear and limited travel solenoid. In: Proceedings of the International Conference on Industrial Electronics, Control, and Instrumentation, IECON 1993, pp. 1567–1572. IEEE (1993)

The NAO Backpack: An Open-Hardware Add-on for Fast Software Development with the NAO Robot

Matías Mattamala, Gonzalo Olave$^{(\boxtimes)}$, Clayder González,
Nicolás Hasbún, and Javier Ruiz-del-Solar

Department of Electrical Engineering, Universidad de Chile Advanced Mining
Technology Center (AMTC), Av. Tupper 2007, Santiago, Chile
{mmattamala, golave, jruizd}@ing.uchile.cl

Abstract. We present an open-source accessory for the NAO robot, which enables to test computationally demanding algorithms in an external platform while preserving robot's autonomy and mobility. The platform has the form of a backpack, which can be 3D printed and replicated, and holds an ODROID XU4 board to process algorithms externally with ROS compatibility. We provide also a software bridge between the B-Human's framework and ROS to have access to the robot's sensors close to real-time. We tested the platform in several robotics applications such as data logging, visual SLAM, and robot vision with deep learning techniques. The CAD model, hardware specifications and software are available online for the benefit of the community.

Keywords: NAO robot · SPL · ODROID XU-4 · ROS

1 Why Would the NAO Need a Backpack?

Let us start with a short story: *some weeks ago, Arya, one of the NAO robots in our lab, became tired of always having the same behaviors and applying the same logic for all her problems, recognizing lines, blobs and other robots using the same old-fashioned algorithms. After some hours reflecting on it, she horrified realized that it was impossible for her to figure out other computer vision paradigms; moreover, she had become aware of her own existence and physical limitations. There was knowledge beyond its restricted understanding, solutions unreachable for its limited capabilities.* This story, despite fictional, hides a real issue in the Standard Platform League (SPL): Developments are limited by the constraints of the standard platform itself [1]. Softbank's NAO robot currently used in the SPL presents several advantages over other humanoid platforms - for instance, the number of degrees of freedom or its price-, but possess strong limitations in terms of processing power, having only a single physical core (2 virtual). This issue demands the use of custom frameworks heavily optimized for the platform in order to be used in *real-time*[1] applications such as robot-soccer.

---

[1] In the robot soccer domain, we understand as *real-time* tasks that can be processed in a frequency close to camera rate, i.e. 15–30 Hz.

© Springer Nature Switzerland AG 2018
H. Akiyama et al. (Eds.): RoboCup 2017, LNAI 11175, pp. 302–311, 2018.
https://doi.org/10.1007/978-3-030-00308-1_25

Hence, huge advances and software solutions from the robotics community, mainly developed within the widely-used ROS framework, are not easily transferable or applicable in the robot soccer domain. Analogously, it is difficult for the SPL community to provide solutions for the other robotics communities apart of efficient algorithms to solve domain-specific problems.

In this work, we face the previous issue by presenting a new open-hardware accessory for the NAO which allows us to test algorithms in a powerful, ROS-compatible platform, as well as to anticipate future developments for the league: The **NAO Backpack**. This device lets the NAO robot carry more powerful hardware - an ODROID XU4- while preserving autonomy and mobility, avoiding the issues of using external hardware via Wi-Fi (high latency) or long Ethernet cables that limits the robot's movements, allowing to test algorithms in a realistic setup.

Here we provide the guidelines to reproduce the NAO backpack, its physical design and software involved. In Sect. 2 we first show a brief review of commercial and open-source accessories for the NAO. In Sect. 3 we describe the hardware and software components of the NAO backpack. In Sect. 4 we show some applications of the backpack for real-time dataset recording, visual SLAM and deep learning. Finally, in Sect. 5, we finish by covering some future backpack improvements and challenges for the community.

2 A Brief Review of NAO Accessories

To the best of our knowledge, the range of accessories for the NAO robot is very limited. There are a few commercial products available, but mainly focused on extending its *exteroceptive* capabilities or facilitating its use in human environments. Some of them are listed as follows:

- Aldebaran Robotics' Laser Head [3]: An official but discontinued Hokuyo laser rangefinder for mapping applications.
- Robots Lab's NAO Car [4]: A NAO-sized BMW Z4 electric car with laser mapping capabilities
- Robots Lab's Docking station [5]: A fancy-looking seating to charge the NAO. We also revised some of the most popular 3D printing projects websites (GrabCAD, Thingiverse and Autodesk 123D) looking for NAO projects, and we found the following:
- NAO Helmet for Microsoft Kinect [6]: A 3D printed helmet for a Kinect model.
- NAO Helmet for Asus Xtion [7]: 3D printed helmet for the Asus RGB-D sensor.
- NAO Bag for ODROID U3 [8]: This project designed by K. Chatzilygeroudis is comparable to ours, so we discuss the differences below.

The Chatzilygeroudis' NAO Bag was designed to be attached on top of the current battery cover; however, there are no specifications about power supply, connectivity, or benchmarking. This bag was after used by Canzobre et al. [9], who improved the discussion by providing references about similar works, as well as providing comparisons between different CPUs (ODROID XU3 and U3), and commercially available power supplies. They also propose different mounting configurations to hold both the CPU and the batteries, and showed an application of robot mapping with RGB-D sensors.

This work has several similitudes to ours, but the differences are significant. On the contrary to Canzobre et al. whose mounting designs are not openly available, we provide a full open backpack design, to be fabricated easily with current rapid prototyping tools; our design can carry both the external processing units as well as the battery, and works as a replacement for the battery cover. Despite not providing comparisons with different processing units and power supplies, we propose a set of tested components and provide the physical parameters of the backpack for that configuration, such as the mass, center of mass and inertia. Furthermore, we also provide software bridges to communicate a NAO running the B-Human (BH) framework, widely used in the SPL [2], with the backpack. The bridge allows us to exploit the efficiency of the BH software while taking advantage of the ROS community developments.

In Summary, Few Accessories are Available for the NAO Nowadays. the Expensive Price for Home Users as Well as the no Hardware Modification Rule of the SPL [1] Can Explain Part of This Situation. Some Previous Attempts to Extend the Processing Capabilities of the NAO Have Been Tried Before, but Most of Them Have Prevailed Closed Within Research Communities. With This Work, We Hope to Contribute to Spread These Ideas as Well as to Motivate Discussions About the Current Limitations in the SPL.

3 The NAO Backpack

3.1 Mechanical Design

We wanted the backpack to be easily attached and detached from the robot, so we base the design on the plastic rear cover of the battery maintaining the through holes for the screws to fit in and hold the backpack. Since we are concerned about autonomy, a hard requirement was to fit the ODROID XU4, a 2-cell LiPo battery, and a voltage regulator. For more details refer the next section.

Center of Mass and Inertia. For our purposes, it is mandatory to give inertial information about the backpack's physical parameters to generate the appropriate matrices for calculating the dynamic movements of the Nao robot, in both simulated and real tests. The units of the *inertial matrix I_0, mass M_0* and *center of mass C_0* are all in MKS system, calculated with respect to the coordinate system showed in the Fig. 1b. All these parameters were computed by considering the real distribution of components in the backpack.

$$I_0 = \begin{pmatrix} 5.66e^{-4} & 3.74e^{-6} & -2.13e^{-4} \\ 3.74e^{-6} & 6.46e^{-4} & -9.76e^{-6} \\ -2.13e^{-4} & -9.76e^{-6} & 8.17e^{-5} \end{pmatrix} \quad M_0 = 0.2074 \quad C_0 = \begin{pmatrix} -0.0197 \\ 0 \\ 0.052 \end{pmatrix}$$

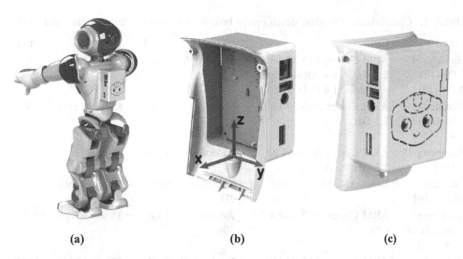

(a)   (b)   (c)

Fig. 1. A render of the backpack's CAD model. (a) Full NAO wearing the backpack. (b) Interior view with the ODROID XU4 with coordinate system. (c) External view, showing some ports and ventilation holes.

Construction Aspects. Because one objective of the backpack is to be open hardware, we use 3D printing for its construction. The printer we used is the XYZ DaVinci Jr 1.0 [10], with 0.1 mm resolution in the Z axis for the details of the fitting parts, 2 layers for the outside shell, and for infill 10% is recommended. An impact resistance test is still needed to ensure the reliability of the backpack and to ensure continuous operation of the robot.

Stability and Mobility. Given the addition of the backpack to the robot, we expect changes in its stability and mobility; in fact, the center of mass of the torso link moves about 15 mm backwards. We tested the basic gait implemented in the B-Human framework on the NAO - previously modifying the inertial configuration of the robot with the new mass and center of mass-, and there were no significant differences with the original gait.

3.2 Hardware and Software

The backpack's hardware mainly consists of a development board plus the electronics to power it autonomously.

ODROID XU4. In this version of the NAO backpack, we choose a Hardkernel ODROID XU4 as main computation board. Despite existing several other alternatives in the market, we preferred this because its relation performance/price as well as the successful experience shown by the aerial robotics community [11, 12]. In addition, XU4 support eMMC modules that surpass considerably a SD-UHS card performance, an ideal feature for robotics applications. A comparison between different boards can be found in Table 1.

Table 1. Comparison of modern development boards that support Ubuntu Linux and ROS.

Board	CPU	GPU	RAM	Size	Price
Hardkernel ODROID XU4 [13]	ARM Cortex-A15 32-bit 2 GHz × 4 + ARM Cortex-A7 32-bit 1.4 GHz × 4	Mali-T628 MP6	2 Gb	83 × 58 mm	$59
Hardkernel ODROID C2 [14]	ARM Cortex A53 64-bit 1.5 GHz × 4	Mali 450	2 Gb	85 × 56 mm	$46
Raspberry Pi 3 [15]	ARM Cortex A-53 64-bit 1.2 GHz × 4	VideoCore IV	1 Gb	85 × 49 mm	$35
BeagleBone Black [16]	Sitara AM335 × 1 GHz × 1	SGX530 3D	512 Mb	86 × 53 mm	$45
Qualcomm DragonBoard 410c [17]	ARM Cortex A53 64-bit 1.2 Ghz	Adreno 306	1 Gb	85 × 54 mm	$75
Nvidia Jetson TK1 [18]	ARM Cortex-A15 32-bit × 4	Kepler 192 cores	2 Gb	127 × 127 mm	$192
Nvidia Jetson TX1 (module) [19]	ARM Cortex-A57 64-bit × 4	Maxwell 256 cores	4 Gb	87 × 50 mm	$304

Battery. Despite the battery available in the NAO kit nominally provides 60 min of active use, in robot soccer we have noticed a performance below this time close to 30 min. ODROID XU4 board requires a 5 V/4A power supply, so we chose a suitable battery to power the ODROID during a time comparable to the NAO while playing. We selected a standard 2-Cell 1000mAh LiPo battery plus an UBEC 5 V/3A to power the board. Since we are not connecting any other device than a Wi-Fi dongle for specific applications, these specifications are enough for our purposes.

Connectivity with the Robot. The NAO V5 robot has one USB port as well as Ethernet Gigabit and Wi-Fi 802.11 a/b/g/n connectivity [20]. We are interested in high throughput applications such as image streaming from the robot to the backpack at frame-rate, so we selected the Ethernet connection.

3.3   Software Architecture

As we stated before, our software architecture is focused in communicating the B-Human framework currently used in the NAO with ROS. A general overview of our approach is presented in Fig. 2.

NAO Software: Backpack Communication Modules. On the NAO side, we use the B-Human framework (BH) [21], which we review briefly. This basically provides two threads: The *Cognition* thread that runs at 30 Hz and performs image processing, modeling, localization and decision making; the *Motion* thread reads joints and IMU data, estimates the torso state and computes the robot gait. Each task performed by a thread is named *module*, whilst the information a module provides is called

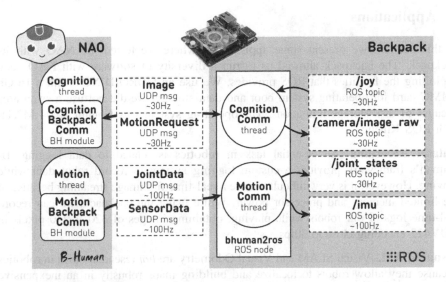

Fig. 2. The NAO Backpack's B-Human-to-ROS communication overview with some examples of nodes running on ROS.

representation. We implemented a module in both *Cognition* and *Motion* (*CognitionBackpackComm* and *MotionBackpackComm*) that transmit selected representations from each thread via UDP communication. Data is serialized with BH's libraries, packed and send through different ports to distinguish the source.

In general, all *Motion* data is sent in single packets because it size is below the maximum allowed by the network. However, a critical situation can occur in *Cognition* while sending images because their size is over the maximum; in that case, we send an initial packet with the expected image size, then we fragment and send the image packets sequentially.

Backpack Software: bhuman2ros Bridge. On the Odroid XU4, we implemented a ROS node *bhuman2ros* that works as a *driver* for the incoming NAO data. The node launches two threads, *CognitionComm* and *MotionComm*, which wait and publish information obtained from *Cognition* and *Motion* respectively, to the corresponding ROS topics. For instance, the BH's *Image* representation is published in ROS as a *sensor_msgs/Image* message in a/*camera/image_raw* topic.

Image packets reception faces similar issues than mentioned before while sending them. Since we fragment the image and UDP connection is unreliable, packets can be lost or delayed between the NAO and the ODROID; here we choose a naïve policy of dropping the current image if we receive the initial packet of the next one. In practice, this policy and the direct wire connection between both boards allows us to have a continuous streaming, publishing ROS messages close to sensor rate.

In addition, we implemented a simple joystick mapper in the *CognitionComm* that subscribes the/*joy* topic. Joystick commands are translated into BH's *MotionRequest* representations used for gait orders, serialized and send back to NAO using the same approach as used in the Backpack modules.

4 Applications

In this section, we present some applications where we tested the NAO with its backpack. The backpack allowed us to run a diversity of software with NAO data, exploiting the facilities that ROS provides. We use an ODROID XU4 with a 16 Gb eMMC card for operating system boot and data storage; we did not use a swap area because of disk storage limitations. The operating system was Ubuntu 16.04 MATE with ROS Kinetic.

Dataset Recording. An essential task in robotics is related to data logging. B-Human's framework provides a custom logging system to record robot data while playing. However, it is very difficult to save a real-time full image streaming because of the limited memory and processor power. While using the backpack, we can record real-time logs of our robots while playing, obtaining images of 320×240 pixels in YUV422 encoding close to 30fps.

Visual SLAM. Visual SLAM and Visual Odometry are *hot* research topics in robotics because they allow robots to localize and building maps robustly in an inexpensive way. Nowadays, several open-source systems are available, being ORB-SLAM2 [22], LSD-SLAM [23], SVO [11] and DSO [24] the most popular one. We tested ORB-SLAM2 in the backpack following the official instructions for compiling and execution, being able to run the system at 12fps with images of 640×480 pixels without disabling functionalities, while displaying the GUI via VNC through Ethernet connection.

Deep Learning Applications. SegNet [25] and Faster R-CNN [26] are two popular deep networks for semantic segmentation and object detection respectively, so we wanted to test the feasibility of running these algorithms with NAO data. We build the libraries following the official instructions of each package before checking appropriate linking of ARM-based libraries during compilation and disabling GPU features. For SegNet we use caffe-SegNet [27] with pretrained models already included in the repository, particularly we tested the *SegNet SUN low resolution* architecture trained for indoor scenes with 37 different classes; other complex architectures were not tested because of memory issues (this might be possible by adding a swap space). We implemented a ROS node to subscribe and resize the images to fit the 224×224 input of SegNet, to measure the inference time and to display the output.

Faster R-CNN was tested in a similar manner. We use the Python implementation from the author [28] with a *Zeigler and Fergus 5-layer (ZF-5)* architecture pretrained with the PASCAL VOC Challenge 2007 dataset; there is an option to try a VGG16 architecture but it was unable to run because of memory as well. We also implemented a test node but since this network resizes the input images automatically we just measure the inference time and displayed output images on demand.

It is important to mention that we also tried some optimizations to improve the inference time. We noticed that changes in the numeric libraries can have a huge impact on performance since they can exploit multi-core parallelism in the ODROID. For instance, changing ATLAS libraries by OpenBLAS can improve performance by almost 50%. Some results are shown in Tables 2 and 3:

Table 2. Average processing time results for SegNet SUN low resolution (224×224 pixels) with different numeric libraries and scenes.

Class	ATLAS	OpenBLAS
Bathroom	26.48 s	13.48 s
Rest space	24.71 s	13.54 s
Living room	24.95 s	13.67 s
Library	25.06 s	13.46 s

Table 3. Average processing time results for Faster R-CNN (ZF-5) with different numeric libraries and input image size.

Size (pixels)	ATLAS	OpenBLAS
200×150	6.05 s	2.92 s
500×375	16.14 s	8.03 s
800×600	20.83 s	11.60 s

5 Summary and Future Perspectives

We finish by summarizing the advantages of the NAO Backpack for the SPL, as well as providing guidelines for further developments with this platform, that we hope will help further developments of the league. The 3D printable file of the backpack and the software and hardware specifications to replicate the functionalities of the backpack, will be made available online after this paper is accepted in the symposium.

What we have today with this contribution:

- **Replicability of the platform:** By providing the CAD models as well as the software bridges, we hope that many teams will take advantage of this platform to improve their own research.
- **Testing of popular algorithms in robot soccer domain:** Since the Backpack runs ROS, we can test algorithms already developed within this framework. Hence, both new and old algorithms that are usually prohibitive with the current hardware can be evaluated *without pain* in the robot soccer problem.
- **Collaboration in a *common tongue*:** ROS provides many tools and is supported by a huge community worldwide. By having access to tools such as *rosbag* or *Rviz*, we can record and share real-time recorded datasets of our robots, which can accelerate the development and collaboration in the league.

On the other hand, we foresee the following improvements to our platform:

- **Hardware Upgrades:** The ODROID XU4 is one of the powerful CPU development boards available in the market and widely used in aerial robotics because of its balance between computational power and weight. However, it is not the best choice for computer vision applications since they require high levels of parallelism, such as deep learning. Modern small boards with GPUs, such as the NVIDIA Jetson TX1 would suit better for these applications; it would be interesting to work in new backpacks with GPU support.
- **New bridges for different frameworks:** We covered the problem for the B-Human's framework because of its popularity, and since the ROS bridges already exist for NaoQi [29]. However, to reach compatibility across all the SPL teams, we need ROS bridges for the UPenn's Lua-based framework, UNSW's, Leipzig's, Austin Villa's, and many others.

6 Supplementary Material

The NAO backpack package is freely distributed in the UChile Robotics GitHub; this provides the CAD models, list of components, and instructions to run the backpack and NAO software: https://github.com/uchile-robotics/nao-backpack.

Acknowledgments. We thank the B-Human SPL Team for sharing their code-release, providing the communication libraries and data structures used in this project, as well as the ROS developers and community for their efforts to unify robotics developments. This research was partially funded by FONDECYT Project 1161500.

References

1. RoboCup Technical Committee: RoboCup Standard Platform League (NAO) Rule Book (2017). http://www.tzi.de/spl/pub/Website/Downloads/Rules2017.pdf
2. Röfer, T., Laue, T.: On B-Human's code releases in the standard platform league – software architecture and impact. In: Behnke, S., Veloso, M., Visser, A., Xiong, R. (eds.) RoboCup 2013. LNCS (LNAI), vol. 8371, pp. 648–655. Springer, Heidelberg (2014). https://doi.org/10.1007/978-3-662-44468-9_61
3. Aldebaran Robotics: Laser Head (2017). http://doc.aldebaran.com/114/family/robots/laser.html
4. RobotLab: NAO robot car (2017). http://www.robotlab.com/store/car
5. RobotLab: NAO Docking Station (2017). http://www.robotlab.com/store/nao-docking-station
6. NAO Kinect Helmet. https://grabcad.com/library/naokinecthelmet-1
7. NAO Xtion Helmet. https://grabcad.com/library/naoxtionhelmet-1
8. NAO Bag for Odroid U3. http://www.thingiverse.com/thing:343727
9. Canzobre, D.S., Regueiro, C.V., Calvo-Varela, L., Iglesias, R.: Integration of 3-D perception and autonomous computation on a nao humanoid robot. Robot 2015: Second Iberian Robotics Conference. AISC, vol. 417, pp. 161–173. Springer, Cham (2016). https://doi.org/10.1007/978-3-319-27146-0_13
10. XYZ Printing DaVinci Jr 1.0. http://us.xyzprinting.com/us_en/Product/da-Vinci-1.0-Junior
11. Forster, C., Pizzoli, M., and Scaramuzza, D.: SVO: fast semi-direct monocular visual odometry. In: IEEE International Conference on Robotics and Automation (2014)
12. Giusti, A., et al.: A machine learning approach to visual perception of forest trails for mobile robots. IEEE Robot. Autom. Lett. **1**, 661–667 (2015)
13. Hardkernel: ODROID XU4 (2017). http://www.hardkernel.com/main/products/prdt_info.php?g_code=G143452239825
14. Hardkernel: Odroid C2 (2017). http://www.hardkernel.com/main/products/prdt_info.php?g_code=G145457216438&tab_idx=1
15. Raspberry Foundation: Raspberry Pi 3 (2017). https://www.raspberrypi.org/products/raspberry-pi-3-model-b/
16. Beagleboard: Beagleboard Black (2017). https://beagleboard.org/black
17. Qualcomm: Dragonboard 410c (2017). https://developer.qualcomm.com/hardware/dragonboard-410c
18. Nvidia: Jetson TK1 (2017). http://www.nvidia.com/object/jetson-tk1-embedded-dev-kit.html

19. Nvidia: Jetson TX1(2017). http://www.nvidia.com/object/embedded-systems-dev-kits-modules.html
20. Softbank Robotics: NAO Connectivity. http://doc.aldebaran.com/2-1/family/robots/connectivity_nao.html
21. Röfer, T., et al.: B-Human Team Report and Code Release 2014 (2014)
22. Mur-Artal, R., Tardós, J.D.: ORB-SLAM2: An Open-Source SLAM System for Monocular, Stereo and RGB-D Cameras. arXiv (2016)
23. Engel, J., Schöps, T., Cremers, D.: LSD-SLAM: large-scale direct monocular SLAM. In: Fleet, D., Pajdla, T., Schiele, B., Tuytelaars, T. (eds.) ECCV 2014. LNCS, vol. 8690, pp. 834–849. Springer, Cham (2014). https://doi.org/10.1007/978-3-319-10605-2_54
24. Engel, J., Koltun, V., Cremers, D.: DSO: Direct Sparse Odometry. arXiv (2016)
25. Badrinarayanan, V., Kendall, A., Cipolla, R.: SegNet: A Deep Convolutional Encoder-Decoder Architecture for Image Segmentation. arXiv (2015)
26. Ren, S., He, K., Girshick, R., Sun, J.: Faster R-CNN: Towards Real-Time Object Detection with Region Proposal Networks. arXiv (2015)
27. Kendall, A.: Implementation of Caffe-SegNet (GitHub). https://github.com/alexgkendall/caffe-segnet
28. Girshick, R.: Python implementation of faster R-CNN (Github). https://github.com/rbgirshick/py-faster-rcnn
29. Aldebaran NAO ROS stack (2017). http://wiki.ros.org/nao

Model-Based Fall Detection and Fall Prevention for Humanoid Robots

Thomas Muender[1] and Thomas Röfer[1,2(✉)]

[1] Universität Bremen, Fachbereich 3 – Mathematik und Informatik,
Postfach 330 440, 28334 Bremen, Germany
thomas.muender@uni-bremen.de
[2] Cyber-Physical Systems, Deutsches Forschungszentrum für Künstliche Intelligenz,
Enrique-Schmidt-Str. 5, 28359 Bremen, Germany
thomas.roefer@dfki.de

Abstract. Fall detection and fall prevention are crucial for humanoid robots when operating in natural environments. Early fall detection is important to have sufficient time for making a stabilizing movement. Existing approaches mostly analyze the sensor data to detect an ongoing fall. In this paper, we use a physical model of the robot to detect whether the measured sensor data indicates a fall in the near future. A trajectory for the foot is calculated to compensate the rotational velocity and acceleration of the fall. In an evaluation with the humanoid robot NAO, we demonstrate that falls can be detected significantly earlier than with traditional sensor classification with little false-positive detections during staggering. Falls due to small to medium impacts can be prevented.

1 Introduction

Humanoid robots are inherently unstable due to their small footprint compared to the height of their center of mass (CoM) [24]. This is a problem widely encountered in locomotion generation for robots such as humanoid walking and kicking. Even though there are many improvements in fall prevention and controlled walking [7,26] robots are still at risk to fall due to obstacles, impacts, or uneven/soft ground.

In order to prevent a humanoid robot from falling, two steps are necessary: First, the fall has to be detected. Fall detection must be fast in order to have sufficient time left to perform a counter-action. Furthermore it has to be robust to false-positive detections to prevent the robot from initiating a counter action when it is not necessary. To this time, fall detection is mostly achieved using a form of sensor classification. In contrast to other existing methods, the approach presented in this paper does not only classify sensor data to detect an ongoing fall, but it rather determines whether the sensor data can lead to a fall in the near future. A physical model is used to simulate the effect of the forces acting on the robot. The model can be used to calculate whether the robot will be in

H. Akiyama et al. (Eds.): RoboCup 2017, LNAI 11175, pp. 312–324, 2018.
https://doi.org/10.1007/978-3-030-00308-1_26

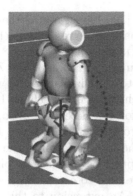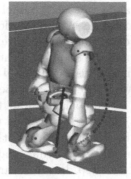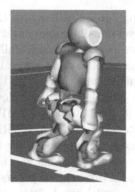

Fig. 1. Stepping motion to prevent a fall using the SSIP model. (Color figure online)

a stable or an unstable state. In case of an unstable state, the model calculates how the robot will fall. This can be used to prevent the robot from falling over.

The main contribution of this paper is the development of a physical model for a humanoid robot capable of describing the robot during a fall. We extend the commonly used inverted pendulum model by a stand space and body dynamics of the robot. Analyzing the common approach to use linearization for the non-linear inverted pendulum shows that it is not feasible to describe a falling motion. Therefore, we use an iterative model to simulate the dynamics of the robot. This model is used to detect imminent falls and perform a counter motion. We demonstrate that a fall can be detected significantly earlier in comparison to traditional sensor classification methods. Falls due to small to medium impacts to the robot can mostly be prevented using a lunge.

The paper is organized as follows: In Sect. 2, we analyze related work, followed by the development of the physical model and functions in order to detect and prevent a fall in Sect. 3. In Sect. 4, the evaluation of the developed approach is described. A comprehensive discussion of the results is given in Sect. 5, followed by the conclusion in Sect. 6.

2   Related Work

Fall detection is reliant on sensors such as inertia sensors and pressure sensors. A classification of the sensor data into stable states and unstable states is a common approach used in several works [16,18]. Such approaches are very robust but detect falls rather late. A related approach by Höhn et al. uses pattern recognition on the sensor data to detect specific patterns only present during a fall [8]. Other approaches use a model to predict the expected sensor values. The deviation between the expected sensor values and the real sensor values is used for fall detection. Renner and Behnke model the expected sensor data using sinusoidal functions [15]. In order to detect falls during layered motions, Tay *et al.* [20] use interpolated sensor models based on body angles. Also machine learning can be utilized for training a sensor model [10]. Latest approaches use two-level classification neural networks in combination with regression to achieve high levels of accuracy in fall detection and posture monitoring [1].

A general concept to evaluate the stability of humanoid robots is the Zero-Moment-Point (ZMP) [21]. The ZMP is widely used to stabilize humanoid walking [7] and kicking [22]. However, Renner and Behnke [15] as well as Höhn et al. [8] evaluated the ZMP as not being suited for fall detection. Also, the Foot-Rotation Indicator (FRI) [6], was not applied to fall detection yet.

A common approach for the fall prevention is the integration into the generation of the walking motion [2,7]. Dynamic adaptations of the gait phases leading to different step sizes and step durations are able to compensate small impacts and irregularities such as an uneven floor. An extension to this approach is the calculation of a specific point for the foot placement. The Capture Point (CP) [14] and the Foot-Placement-Estimator (FPE) [23] both rely on this approach. Most of these approaches use an inverted pendulum model as a basis. Zhao et al. [27] argue that this model does not model important dynamics of the hip and the ankle as well as the ground reaction force. They developed a hip-ankle and bent-knee strategy to deal with instabilities [11]. A combination of both strategies with machine-learned weights is used by Yi et al. [25].

Mao et al. argue that the Capture Point approach is not feasible for practical use. They developed a continuous step controller [13] that counters the instability with a series of steps. In order to deal with uneven ground, Lee and Goswami [12] developed a moment-based controller that uses the ground reaction force and the center of pressure minimizing the torque on the foot. An extension is the reactive stepping controller [26] modeling the robot as a turning wheel. In contrast to the CP and FPE, a specific target point for the foot can be calculated and it is not necessary to continuously update the target point to a position further away from the origin. This is especially helpful performing a controlled motion on a pre-calculated trajectory.

3   Approach

In order to prevent a humanoid robot from falling, a fall detection method is required, capable of robustly detecting a fall as early as possible. This is necessary to have enough time left to perform a counter-motion. All related work uses some kind of classification of sensor data in order to detect specific patterns only present during a fall. These approaches only detect a fall when it is already in progress. Analyzing a falling motion of a humanoid robot, multiple stages can be identified. An event that brings the robot into instability accelerates the upper body of the robot. The stand space (convex hull of the foot/feet on the ground) generates a counteracting force reducing the acceleration of the upper body. In this first stage, it is not clear whether the robot will only stagger or fall down. If the upper body acceleration is too strong, the robot will fall. Otherwise it will only stagger, which should not be detected as a fall. Therefore, all other approaches do not classify this stage as falling, because it is not clear yet whether a fall will happen or not.

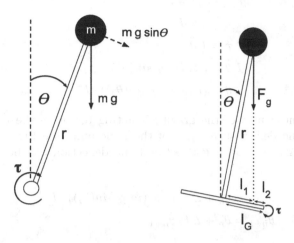

Fig. 2. Schematics for the inverted pendulum model (left) and the extended Stand Space Inverted Pendulum model (right).

To detect a fall as early as possible, it is already necessary to evaluate whether a fall will happen later on in this first stage. In order to make a statement whether the measured sensor data will lead to a fall in the future, it is necessary to calculate how they will effect the robot. This task is done using a physical model of the robot applying the measured accelerations and velocities. The Linear Inverted Pendulum model (LIP) models the movement of the robot's CoM as a 3-dimensional linear inverted pendulum [9], see Fig. 2. An inverted pendulum is suited to describe a falling robot as falling is a rotational motion around the edge of the foot. However, the simplified LIP model is not suited to model the robot during a fall for two reasons: First, the stand space of the foot, which generates a counteracting force to the fall, is not considered. In addition, all forces generated by the joints of the robot are also not integrated into this model. Second, the non-linear pendulum equations cannot be calculated directly. Therefore, they are linearized in this model. Linearization is done by the assumption that either $sin(\alpha) \approx \alpha$ for small values of α or the height of the pendulum mass from the ground is constant [7]. When generating upright motions such as walking, these assumptions can be made. In the case of modeling a fall however, they are not valid. As linearization is not an option and precise modeling is necessary, we develop an iterative model using a numerical approximation of the non-linear differential equation with the Euler integration.

3.1 Stand Space Inverted Pendulum Model (SSIP)

In order to design an iterative inverted pendulum model, we develop a function for the angular acceleration $\ddot{\theta} \in \mathbb{R}^3$ of the CoM. Such a function can be defined using the torque $\tau \in \mathbb{R}^3$ acting on the base of the pendulum. It uses the vector $r \in \mathbb{R}^3$ of the lever arm of force, the linear force $F \in \mathbb{R}^3$ produced by the mass m, and the gravity $g \in \mathbb{R}^3$ as well as the inertia tensor $I \in \mathbb{R}^{3x3}$.

$$\tau = r \times F \tag{1}$$

$$\tau = I \, \ddot{\theta} \tag{2}$$

$$I \, \ddot{\theta} = r \times (m \, g \, sin(\theta)) \tag{3}$$

$$\ddot{\theta} = (r \times (m \, g \, sin(\theta))) \cdot I^{-1} \tag{4}$$

Only the tangential part of the gravity is acting to rotate the mass, which is dependent on the deflection $\theta \in \mathbb{R}^3$ of the pendulum, see Fig. 2. An iterative term for the angular velocity $\dot{\theta} \in \mathbb{R}^3$ and the deflection can be defined using Euler integration.

$$\dot{\theta}_{n+1} = \dot{\theta}_n + \triangle t \cdot (r \times (m \, g \, sin(\theta))) \cdot I^{-1} \tag{5}$$

$$\theta_{n+1} = \theta_n + \triangle t \cdot \dot{\theta}_{n+1} \tag{6}$$

Iterating Eqs. 5 and 6 with a small $\triangle t$ give a precise approximation of the rotational motion of the pendulum. However, this model cannot assert whether the robot will fall anyway. Therefore, we integrate the stand space of the robot given by its feet. The pendulum has a plate attached to the bottom and the point of rotation moves to the edge of this plate, see Fig. 2. The plate generates a stabilizing torque counteracting the tangential part of the gravity which is responsible for the angular motion of the pendulum and the respective fall of the robot. We can define this counteracting torque τ_{stand} using the vector from the origin of the foot to the point of rotation on the edge of the foot $l \in \mathbb{R}^3$ and the gravity. But the lever arm of force l is dependent on the deflection of the pendulum.

$$\tau_{stand} = (l_G - l_1) \times g \tag{7}$$

$$\tau_{net} = \sum_i \tau_i \tag{8}$$

$$\ddot{\theta} = (\tau_{fall} + \tau_{stand}) \cdot I^{-1} \tag{9}$$

The length between the projection of the gravitational force into the stand space and the edge of the stand space defines the acting part of the the stabilizing torque's lever arm of force, l_2. Using the length r and the deflection of the pendulum, we can calculate the inactive part l_1. By subtracting l_1 from the whole length of the stand space in the direction of the fall, we can obtain the acting part l_2, see Eq. 7.

Utilizing the fact that the net torque can be defined as the sum of all individual torques acting around an axis, see Eq. 8, we can sum up the stabilizing torque and the one responsible for the fall and integrate them into Eq. 9.

This extended model could already give an indication whether the robot will fall, when initialized with the measured sensor data and then iterated. But the robot might perform a motion while getting into instability. Such motion generates an additional torque that can amplify or counteract the falling motion. Therefore the torque generated by the motion of all joints of the robot in respect to the rotation point at the edge of the foot has to be calculated.

The inverse rigid body dynamics [5] describes the problem of calculating the torques based on the kinematics (motion) of a body and the body's inertial properties. A model of the robot's rigid body given by the mass and moment of inertia of all body parts and how they are connected is needed. In addition with the generalized angular positions (q), velocities ($\dot{q}$), and accelerations ($\ddot{q}$) of all joints, the inverse dynamics can be defined as $\tau = ID(model, q, \dot{q}, \ddot{q})$. In order to calculate the inverse dynamics, the recursive Newton-Euler algorithm is used in this work.

$$\ddot{\theta} = (\tau_{fall} + \tau_{stand} + \sum_{i \in N} \tau_i) \cdot I^{-1} \tag{10}$$

$$\dot{\theta}_{n+1} = \dot{\theta}_n + \triangle t \cdot (\tau_{fall} + \tau_{stand} + \sum_{i \in N} \tau_i) \cdot I^{-1} \tag{11}$$

The obtained torques for each joint i around the axis orthogonal to the fall direction can be summed up and added to Eq. 9, resulting in Eq. 10. The sum of torques around the fall axis can be used to calculate the complete rotational acceleration acting on the robot. This can be used to form the final iterative model (Eq. 11) using Eqs. 5 and 6.

Initializing this model with the measured angle and angular velocity of the robot and iterating it will either provide an upright stabilizing pendulum motion or a rotational pendulum motion. We can decide whether the robot will fall directly based on this simulation. When the Stand Space Inverted Pendulum model will fall, also the robot will fall down approximately following the simulated motion.

3.2 Fall Prevention

In order to prevent the robot from falling, one or more steps are necessary [19]. Orienting towards a human model, a dedicated long-range step is most promising. Performing such a step requires one foot to keep contact to the ground, and one to perform the stepping motion. Deciding which foot performs which task is dependent on the direction of the fall and the current position of the feet. If one foot is already in mid-air, it is used to perform the step. If both feet are on or close to the ground, the foot in the direction of the fall has to keep contact with the ground as the point of rotation is at its edge.

Such a step should meet two requirements in order to prevent the fall. The rotational acceleration as well as the rotational velocity have to be compensated to stop the rotational motion of the fall. Regarding the first requirement, we can refer to the inverted pendulum model, see Fig. 2. The rotational acceleration is caused by the tangential part of gravity, which depends on the deflection of the pendulum. It is no longer accelerated if the base is positioned directly under the CoM. This can be achieved by placing the stepping foot directly under the CoM, which will then become the base of the pendulum.

Calculating the target position for the foot can be done using the motion of the robot's CoM over time calculated by the model. For convenience, we can define the iterative SSIP model as a closed function $\theta_t = SSIP(\theta_0, \dot{\theta}_0, t)$. This can be used to calculate the position of the CoM $\mathcal{P}$ at time t using the Rodrigues formula $Rot()$ [3] and the CoM in upright position CoM_0, see Eq. 12.

$$\mathcal{P}(t) = Rot(SSIP(\theta_0, \dot{\theta}_0, t)) \cdot CoM_0 \tag{12}$$

$$\mathcal{T}(t) = T_{POR \to Robot} \cdot \begin{bmatrix} \mathcal{P}(t)_x \\ \mathcal{P}(t)_y \\ footheight \end{bmatrix} \tag{13}$$

Equation 12 gives us the position of the CoM at time t with respect to the point of rotation (POR). As we know the point of rotation at the edge of the foot, we can transform the function into the robot coordinate system in order to actuate the joints using inverse kinematics [16]. As the foot should be positioned on the ground with its sole, the height of the last joint from the sole $footheight$ is used as the z-coordinate.

In addition to the rotational acceleration, the rotational velocity has to be compensated as well. We could actuate a joint in the opposite direction using the acceleration to compensate the velocity. But as motors often cannot be actuated precisely, this could cause another instability. Therefore we propose a different strategy: If the CoM has a deflection in the opposite direction of the fall when the stepping foot makes contact with the ground, the acceleration caused by the deflected pendulum and the rotational velocity of the fall can cancel each other out. This leaves the question of how much the pendulum has to be deflected in order to compensate the rotational velocity completely and coming to a stop in the upright position.

Making the simplifying assumption that the falling motion started in an almost upright position of the CoM, we already know which deflection is necessary to compensate the velocity. It is the current state of the pendulum in the opposing direction. Such a deflection could be achieved by doubling the distance of the target position of the foot from the POR. But when the stepping foot makes contact with the ground, its stand space will also compensate a part of the velocity. We do not have to calculate how much rotational velocity it will compensate, but rather how much we can reduce the deflection while still being in a stable state. As the projection of the gravitational force acting on the CoM has to be within the stand space, see Sect. 3.1 and Fig. 2, in order to still be stable, we can calculate the deflection using $tan^{-1}\frac{l_G}{r}$.

$$\mathcal{D}(t) = Rot(SSIP(\theta_0, \dot{\theta}_0, t) - tan^{-1}\frac{l_G}{r}) \cdot CoM_0 \tag{14}$$

$$\mathcal{T}(t) = T_{POR \to Robot} \cdot \begin{bmatrix} \mathcal{D}(t)_x + \mathcal{P}(t)_x \\ \mathcal{D}(t)_y + \mathcal{P}(t)_y \\ footheight \end{bmatrix} \tag{15}$$

Instead of doubling the distance between the POR and the target position, we can define a second function for the target position integrating the deflection that will be compensated by the stand space, see Eq. 14. By adding up both

Fig. 3. Experimental setup

target positions before transforming them into the robot's coordinate system, we can achieve a target position for the foot that will compensate both rotational acceleration and velocity, see Eq. 15.

A trajectory for the stepping foot can be computed using the function $\mathcal{T}(t)$ from Eq. 15. Figure 1 visualizes the trajectory with the reachable poses in green and non-reachable parts in red. In order to keep the robot stable on the foot after the step, an additional closed-loop PID controller for the hip and knee joints is used. A controlled transition into the stand is used to bring the robot back into a standard operation state.

4   Evaluation

A series of experiments was performed to evaluate the method developed. The algorithms described were implemented for the humanoid robot NAO [17] using the B-Human code release [16]. All experiments used this robot and shared the same setup (cf. Fig. 3). A controlled impact to the upper body of the robot was generated using a padded weight of 800 g attached to a cord of 1m, which was fixated above the robot. The weight was deflected to different angles to produce impacts with varying strength. For each deflection set, impacts from four sides (left, right, front, and back side of the robot) were tested with five repetitions each. For the evaluation of the fall detection, two types of experiments were performed: A general functionality test (a) evaluating the correct detection of the state the robot is in. The second experiment (b) compared a traditional sensor classification method used by the team B-Human [16] with the method presented in this paper. For the fall prevention, an additional functionality test (c) was done. The results of all experiments can be reviewed in Tables 1, 2 and 3. All experiments were performed with an impact of different strength indicated by the displacement of the pendulum and from the different directions front (f), back (b), left (l), and right (r).

For the functionality test of the fall detection (cf. Table 1), four different impacts with increasing strength (two led to staggering, two led to a fall) were

Table 1. Results of the fall detection functionality experiment (5 trials each).

Impact	Walking (trivial)				Small, no fall				Medium, no fall				Strong, fall				Very strong, fall			
Impact direction	f	b	l	r	f	b	l	r	f	b	l	r	f	b	l	r	f	b	l	r
Detection rate in %	100	100	100	100	100	100	100	100	0	20	60	40	100	100	100	100	100	100	100	100

Table 2. Results of the fall detection comparative experiment (5 trials each)

impact	45° (strong impact, fall)				60° (very strong impact, fall)			
impact direction	f	b	l	r	f	b	l	r
traditional sensor classification ($\varnothing\pm\sigma$ in ms)	625.2 ± 11.1	729.2 ± 15.5	639.2 ± 8.1	636.2 ± 5.4	667.2 ± 8.7	355.0 ± 17.6	349.0 ± 12.3	338.3 ± 12.4
model-based fall detection ($\varnothing\pm\sigma$ in ms)	153.0 ± 5.9	201.4 ± 7.0	226.8 ± 6.7	228.6 ± 4.9	100.8 ± 4.9	104.6 ± 4.7	126.0 ± 5.8	111.8 ± 5.7
mean difference in ms	472.2	527.8	412.4	408.0	266.4	248.4	223.0	226.5

tested in addition to the trivial case of normal walk without an impact. 80 passes were performed in total. In the cases of trivial walking and staggering due to small impacts, the state was correctly classified as stable. Also the cases that led to a fall due to strong and very strong impacts were correctly classified as a fall. Only in the case of strong staggering due to a medium impact, the detection rate dropped to a value between 60% and 0%.

The comparative experiment for the fall detection was performed with two types of impacts (45° and 60° weight deflection), both led to a fall. The time between the impact and the detection of a fall was measured. The results are presented in Table 2. For all eight types of impacts (four sides times two different strengths, 40 passes in total), the method presented in this paper was able to detect the fall significantly earlier (t-Test with $p < 0.001$). This resulted in earlier detection between 408 ms to 527 ms for the strong impacts and between 223 ms to 266 ms for very strong impacts.

The evaluation of the fall prevention was performed with three different strengths of impact (45°, 55° and 65° weight deflection). All impacts would have led to a fall without a counter-motion. Table 3 shows the results for all 60 passes of the experiment with the rate of successfully achieved fall preventions. For a weight deflection of 45°, the fall could be prevented for almost all passes (18 of 20). With increasing strength of impacts, the successful fall preventions dropped to 7 of 20 for the deflection of 55° and to 3 of 20 for the deflection of 65°. It is to note that impacts from the front, which led to a backwards fall of the robot, could be generally prevented much less than from the other sides whereas impacts from the sides could be prevented better.

Table 3. Results of the fall prevention functionality experiment (5 trials each)

Impact	45°				55°				65°			
Impact direction	f	b	l	r	f	b	l	r	f	b	l	r
Fall prevention rate in %	60	100	100	100	0	20	60	60	0	0	40	20

5   Discussion

The approach developed in this paper uses a physical model of the humanoid robot in order to calculate the effects of sensor data towards the future motion of the robot and if this motion represents a fall. We argued that this approach should be able to detect a fall earlier than traditional classification of sensor data. The results of the comparative study (b) confirm this assumption, detecting a fall between a quarter to half a second earlier than the method used by the team B-Human in the RoboCup. It is to note that this is a comparison to a single specific approach and the findings cannot be generalized without further evaluation. However, Renner and Behnke [15] define the forewarning time as a criterion in their evaluation. The forewarning time is the duration between fall detection and the robot's body reaching 25° deviation from the upright posture. This deviation is also the criterion detecting forward and backward falling in the B-Human system. Therefore, the *mean difference* values from Table 2 are comparable to the forewarning times reported by Renner and Behnke. The times their method achieved is 500–600 ms, but under the assumption that the robot is executing a regular walk movement, which is exploited by their approach. In addition, most of their attempts would not have brought the robot to a fall even without a fall prevention, so they were definitely not comparable to the *very strong impact* category here, where the advantage of the new approach over the old one is smaller.

The functionality evaluation (a) revealed that when the NAO is heavily staggering (medium impact) but not falling, this approach falsely detects a fall. These false positive detections most likely originate from deviations between the model and the NAO robot. Hardware limitations of the NAO such as imprecise inertia and joint angle sensors and strong joint play in the leg joints are likely to produce a deviation from the model. Furthermore, the NAO does only provide joint angle measurements, but not the joint velocities and accelerations needed to calculate the inverse dynamics used in our model. Joint velocities and accelerations are therefore calculated by a motor model [4] and only give approximated values. These reasons indicate why false-positive measurements are likely.

The results from the evaluation of the fall prevention (c) show a distinct drop in the rate of successful fall preventions between 45° and 55° weight deflection. In the first case almost all falls could be prevented whereas in the latter less than half of all passes were successful. This can be explained by the fact that the leg motors of the NAO are too slow to reach the position necessary to prevent the fall. During the experiments, we observed that the leg which should be at least positioned under the CoM was not able to reach this position before the fall was no longer preventable. We argue that the rate of successful fall prevention could be improved for strong pushes using a hardware platform with superior motors for the leg joints. In general, pushes from the front could be prevented worse than others. This relates to the fact that the actuation limits of the NAO's legs are more restricted to the back than to the front. Overall, falls to the side could be prevented better, which affiliates to the moment of inertia of the robot. Rotation to the front and back are more accelerated than to the sides.

Concluding our findings, the presented approach is capable of detecting fall earlier than the method we compared to and prevent falls in limitation to the capabilities of the hardware. The main limiting factor is the hardware of the NAO that was used for the evaluation. In future work, we would like to generalize our findings using a superior hardware platform. In addition, we could model the robot in more detail if sufficient computation power is accessible to iterate the model, potentially further improving the results.

6   Conclusion

This paper presents a novel approach for fall detection and prevention for humanoid robots. We developed an iterative model based on the inverted pendulum and extended it with a stand space and the body dynamics of the robot. The model is used to simulate the effects of acting forces on the robot measured by sensors. If the simulated motion represents a fall, a counter-motion is performed. The trajectory for this motion is also based on the future states of the robot's CoM calculated by the model. We demonstrate that this method can detect a fall significantly earlier than traditional methods. The practical use is limited by the hardware of the robot, but this approach is promising for robots with accurate sensors and precise joints. With improved computational power, a more precise model can be used to potentially obtain even better results.

References

1. Abeyruwan, S.W., Sarkar, D., Sikder, F., Visser, U.: Semi-automatic extraction of training examples from sensor readings for fall detection and posture monitoring. IEEE Sens. J. **16**(13), 5406–5415 (2016)
2. Adiwahono, A.H., Chew, C.M., Huang, W., Dau, V.H.: Humanoid robot push recovery through walking phase modification. In: 2010 IEEE Conference on Robotics Automation and Mechatronics (RAM), pp. 569–574. IEEE (2010)
3. Altmann, S.L.: Rotations, Quaternions, and Double Groups (1986)
4. Böckmann, A., Laue, T.: Kick motions for the NAO robot using dynamic movement primitives. In: Behnke, S., Sheh, R., Sarıel, S., Lee, D.D. (eds.) RoboCup 2016. LNCS (LNAI), vol. 9776, pp. 33–44. Springer, Cham (2017). https://doi.org/10. 1007/978-3-319-68792-6_3
5. Featherstone, R.: Inverse Dynamics. In: Featherstone, R. (ed.) Rigid Body Dynamics Algorithms. Springer, Heidelberg (2014)
6. Goswami, A.: Postural stability of biped robots and the foot-rotation indicator (FRI) point. Int. J. Robot. Res. **18**(6), 523–533 (1999)
7. Graf, C., Röfer, T.: A center of mass observing 3D-LIPM gait for the RoboCup standard platform league humanoid. In: Röfer, T., Mayer, N.M., Savage, J., Saranlı, U. (eds.) RoboCup 2011. LNCS (LNAI), vol. 7416, pp. 102–113. Springer, Heidelberg (2012). https://doi.org/10.1007/978-3-642-32060-6_9
8. Höhn, O., Gačnik, J., Gerth, W.: Detection and classification of posture instabilities of bipedal robots. In: Tokhi, M.O., Virk, G.S., Hossain, M.A. (eds.) Climbing and Walking Robots, pp. 409–416. Springer, Heidelberg (2006). https://doi.org/ 10.1007/3-540-26415-9_49

9. Kajita, S., Kanehiro, F., Kaneko, K., Fujiwara, K., Yokoi, K., Hirukawa, H.: A realtime pattern generator for biped walking. In: Proceedings of the 2002 IEEE International Conference on Robotics and Automation (ICRA 2002), Washington, D.C., USA, pp. 31–37 (2002)

10. Kalyanakrishnan, S., Goswami, A.: Learning to predict humanoid fall. Int. J. Humanoid Robot. 8(02), 245–273 (2011)

11. Kiemel, S.: Balance maintenance of a humanoid robot using the hip-ankle strategy. Ph.D. thesis, TU Delft, Delft University of Technology (2012)

12. Lee, S.H., Goswami, A.: Ground reaction force control at each foot: a momentum-based humanoid balance controller for non-level and non-stationary ground. In: 2010 IEEE/RSJ International Conference on Intelligent Robots and Systems (IROS), pp. 3157–3162. IEEE (2010)

13. Mao, W., Kim, J.J., Lee, J.J.: Continuous steps toward humanoid push recovery. In: IEEE International Conference on Automation and Logistics, ICAL 2009, pp. 7–12. IEEE (2009)

14. Pratt, J., Carff, J., Drakunov, S., Goswami, A.: Capture point: a step toward humanoid push recovery. In: 2006 6th IEEE-RAS International Conference on Humanoid Robots, pp. 200–207. IEEE (2006)

15. Renner, R., Behnke, S.: Instability detection and fall avoidance for a humanoid using attitude sensors and reflexes. In: 2006 IEEE/RSJ International Conference on Intelligent Robots and Systems, pp. 2967–2973. IEEE (2006)

16. Röfer, T., et al.: B-human team report and code release 2016 (2016). https://github.com/bhuman/BHumanCodeRelease

17. Aldebaran Robotics: NAO Documentation (2016). http://doc.aldebaran.com. Accessed 12 Aug 2018

18. Ruiz-del Solar, J., Moya, J., Parra-Tsunekawa, I.: Fall detection and management in biped humanoid robots. In: 2010 IEEE International Conference on Robotics and Automation (ICRA), pp. 3323–3328. IEEE (2010)

19. Stephens, B.: Push recovery control for force-controlled humanoid robots. Ph.D. thesis, Carnegie Mellon University Pittsburgh, Pennsylvania USA (2011)

20. Tay, J., Chen, I.-M., Veloso, M.: Fall prediction for new sequences of motions. In: Hsieh, M.A., Khatib, O., Kumar, V. (eds.) Experimental Robotics. STAR, vol. 109, pp. 849–864. Springer, Cham (2016). https://doi.org/10.1007/978-3-319-23778-7_56

21. Vukobratović, M., Borovac, B.: Zero-moment point-thirty five years of its life. Int. J. Humanoid Robot. 1(01), 157–173 (2004)

22. Wenk, F., Röfer, T.: Online generated kick motions for the NAO balanced using inverse dynamics. In: Behnke, S., Veloso, M., Visser, A., Xiong, R. (eds.) RoboCup 2013. LNCS (LNAI), vol. 8371, pp. 25–36. Springer, Heidelberg (2014). https://doi.org/10.1007/978-3-662-44468-9_3

23. Wight, D.L., Kubica, E.G., Wang, D.W.: Introduction of the foot placement estimator: a dynamic measure of balance for bipedal robotics. J. Comput. Nonlinear Dyn. 3(1), 011009 (2008)

24. Winter, D.A.: Human balance and posture control during standing and walking. Gait Posture 3(4), 193–214 (1995)

25. Yi, S.J., Zhang, B.T., Hong, D., Lee, D.D.: Learning full body push recovery control for small humanoid robots. In: 2011 IEEE International Conference on Robotics and Automation (ICRA), pp. 2047–2052. IEEE (2011)

26. Yun, S.K., Goswami, A.: Momentum-based reactive stepping controller on level and non-level ground for humanoid robot push recovery. In: 2011 IEEE/RSJ International Conference on Intelligent Robots and Systems (IROS), pp. 3943–3950. IEEE (2011)
27. Zhao, J., Schutz, S., Berns, K.: Biologically motivated push recovery strategies for a 3D bipedal robot walking in complex environments. In: 2013 IEEE International Conference on Robotics and Biomimetics (ROBIO), pp. 1258–1263. IEEE (2013)

RoboCup 2D Soccer Simulation League: Evaluation Challenges

Mikhail Prokopenko[1](✉), Peter Wang[2], Sebastian Marian[3], Aijun Bai[4],
Xiao Li[5], and Xiaoping Chen[5]

[1] Complex Systems Research Group, Faculty of Engineering and IT,
The University of Sydney, Sydney, NSW 2006, Australia
`mikhail.prokopenko@sydney.edu.au`
[2] Data Mining, CSIRO Data61, PO Box 76, Epping, NSW 1710, Australia
[3] Compa-IT, Sibiu, Romania
[4] Department of Electrical Engineering and Computer Sciences,
University of California Berkeley, Berkeley, USA
[5] Multi-Agent Systems Lab, School of Computer Science and Technology,
University of Science and Technology of China, Hefei, China

Abstract. We summarise the results of RoboCup 2D Soccer Simulation League in 2016 (Leipzig), including the main competition and the evaluation round. The evaluation round held in Leipzig confirmed the strength of RoboCup-2015 champion (WrightEagle, i.e. WE2015) in the League, with only eventual finalists of 2016 competition capable of defeating WE2015. An extended, post-Leipzig, round-robin tournament which included the top 8 teams of 2016, as well as WE2015, with over 1000 games played for each pair, placed WE2015 third behind the champion team (Gliders2016) and the runner-up (HELIOS2016). This establishes WE2015 as a stable benchmark for the 2D Simulation League. We then contrast two ranking methods and suggest two options for future evaluation challenges. The first one, "The Champions Simulation League", is proposed to include 6 previous champions, directly competing against each other in a round-robin tournament, with the view to systematically trace the advancements in the League. The second proposal, "The Global Challenge", is aimed to increase the realism of the environmental conditions during the simulated games, by simulating specific features of different participating countries.

1 Introduction

The International RoboCup Federation's Millennium challenge sets an inspirational target that by mid-21st century, a team of fully autonomous humanoid soccer players shall win the soccer game, complying with the official rule of the FIFA, against the winner of the most recent World Cup [1]. In pursuit of this goal, the RoboCup Federation has introduced multiple leagues, with both physical robots and simulation agents, which have developed different measures of their progress over the years. The main mode, of course, is running competitions at the national, regional and world cup levels. In addition, however,

© Springer Nature Switzerland AG 2018
H. Akiyama et al. (Eds.): RoboCup 2017, LNAI 11175, pp. 325–337, 2018.
https://doi.org/10.1007/978-3-030-00308-1_27

various leagues have included specific evaluation challenges which not only complement the competitions, but also advance the scientific and technological base of RoboCup and Artificial Intelligence in general. Typically, a challenge introduces some new features into the standard competition environment, and then evaluates how the teams perform under the new circumstances.

For example, during an evaluation round of RoboCup 2001 the rules of the soccer simulator were modified in such a way that "dashing on the upper half of the field resulted in only half of normal speed for all the players" [2]. This modification was not announced in advance, and while the changed conditions were obvious to human spectators, none of the simulation agents could diagnose the problem [2].

A specific technical challenge was presented by the so-called Keepaway problem [3], when one team (the "keepers") attempt to keep the ball away from the other team (the "takers") for as long as possible.

Later on, the focus of evaluation in RoboCup 2D Soccer Simulation League shifted from changing the physics of the simulation or the tactics of the game, to studying the diverse "eco-system" of the League itself, which has grown to include multiple teams. The Simulated Soccer Internet League (SSIL) was designed to allow a continual evaluation of the participating teams during the time between annual RoboCup events: pre-registered teams could upload their binaries to a server on which games were played automatically [4]. The SSIL was used at some stage as a qualification pathway to the annual RoboCup, but this practice was discontinued due to verification problems.

Several other challenges and technical innovations introduced in Soccer Simulation Leagues (both 2D and 3D), including heterogeneous players, stamina capacity model, and tackles, are described in [5]. This study further pointed out the importance of the online game analysis and online adaptation.

More recently, a series of "drop-in player challenges" was introduced by [6] in order to investigate how real or simulated robots from teams from around the world can cooperate with a variety of unknown teammates. In each evaluation game, robots/agents are drawn from the participating teams and combined to form a new team, in the hope that the agents would be able to quickly adapt to meaningfully play together without pre-coordination. The "drop-in" challenge was adopted by RoboCup Standard Platform League (SPL) and both RoboCup Soccer Simulation Leagues, 2D and 3D. In all the considered leagues, the study observed "a trend for agents that perform better at standard team soccer to also perform better at the drop-in player challenge" [6].

At RoboCup-2016 in Leipzig, several soccer and rescue leagues increased realism of the competition by holding their competitions outdoors. In the SPL, a separate competition was successfully held not on the customary green carpet but rather on an artificial turf, under diverse natural lighting conditions. Similarly, Middle Size Soccer League also successfully implemented a Technical Challenge under these difficult conditions, while the Humanoid League used artificial turf and real soccer balls[1].

---

[1] http://robocup2016.org/press-releases/leipzig-best-place-for-robots-and-friends/
452749.

In this paper, we describe the latest evaluation challenge, introduced by RoboCup 2D Soccer Simulation League [7,8] in 2016, in order to trace the progress of the overall League. Furthermore, we describe two possibilities for future challenges: one intended to systematically trace the advancements in the League ("The Champions Simulation League"), and the other aimed to increase the realism of the environmental conditions during the simulated games ("The Global Challenge").

2   Methodology and Results

2.1   Actual Competition

The RoboCup-2016 Soccer Simulation 2D League included 18 teams from 9 countries: Australia, Brazil, China, Egypt, Germany, Iran, Japan, Portugal and Romania. The last group stage was a round-robin tournament for top 8 teams. It was followed by the two-game semi-final round, a single-game final, and 3 more playoffs between third and fourth, fifth and sixth, and seventh and eighth places.

In the two-game semi-final round, HELIOS2016 (Japan) [9] defeated team Ri-one (Japan) [10], 3:0 and 4:0, while Gliders2016 (Australia) [11,12] defeated team CSU_Yunlu (China) [13], winning both games with the same score 2:1.

The single-game final between HELIOS2016 and Gliders2016 went into the extra time, and ended with Gliders2016 winning 2:1.

The third place was taken by team Ri-one which won against CSU_Yunlu 3:0.

Oxsy (Romania) [14] took the fifth place, winning 4:0 against Shiraz (Iran) [15]; and MT2016 (China) [16] became seventh, winning against FURY (Iran) [17] on penalties 4:2. The final ranking of RoboCup-2016 (Leipzig, Germany) is shown in the left column of Table 1.

2.2   Ranking Estimation

Using the ranking estimation methodology established by [18,19], we conducted an 8-team round-robin tournament for top 8 teams from RoboCup-2016. The estimation process used the released binaries of top RoboCup-2016 teams[2], where all 28 pairs of teams play approximately 4000 games against one another. The following *discrete* scheme was used for discrete point calculation:

- Firstly, the average score between each pair of teams (across all 4000 games) is rounded to the nearest integer (e.g. "1.2 : 0.5"is rounded to "1 : 1").
- Next, points are allocated for each pairing based on these rounded results: 3 for a win, 1 for a draw and 0 for a loss.
- Teams are then ranked by the sum of the points received against each opponent. The total goal difference of the rounded scores is used as a tie-breaker.

The final ranking r^d under this scheme is presented in Table 1.

---

[2]   https://chaosscripting.net/files/competitions/RoboCup/WorldCup/2016/2DSim/
    binaries/.

Table 1. Round-robin results (average goals scored and points allocated with the discrete scheme) for the top 8 teams from RoboCup 2016, ordered according to their final actual competition rank, $\mathbf{r^a}$. The scores are determined by calculating the average number of goals scored over approximately 4000 games rounded to the nearest integer, then awarding 3 points for a win, 1 point for a draw and 0 points for a loss. The resultant ranking is marked with $\mathbf{r^d}$.

	Gliders	HELIOS	Ri-one	CSU_Yunlu	Oxsy	Shiraz	MT2016	FURY	Goals	Points	r^d
Gliders		0.3 : 0.4	2.8 : 0.3	1.9 : 0.3	0.7 : 0.8	3.8 : 0.4	5.0 : 0.0	2.5 : 0.2	18 : 1	17	1
HELIOS	0.4 : 0.3		1.8 : 0.1	3.0 : 0.2	1.2 : 0.5	4.3 : 0.3	3.6 : 0.0	2.5 : 0.0	17 : 1	17	2
Ri-one	0.3 : 2.8	0.1 : 1.8		1.1 : 1.1	0.2 : 1.8	0.6 : 0.5	0.4 : 0.0	0.6 : 0.5	3 : 10	4	6
CSU_Yunlu	0.3 : 1.9	0.2 : 3.0	1.1 : 1.1		0.5 : 1.2	2.0 : 0.7	1.4 : 0.0	1.2 : 0.4	6 : 8	11	4
Oxsy	0.8 : 0.7	0.5 : 1.2	1.8 : 0.2	1.2 : 0.5		3.5 : 0.5	4.4 : 0.0	3.0 : 0.1	16 : 4	15	3
Shiraz	0.4 : 3.8	0.3 : 4.3	0.5 : 0.6	0.7 : 2.0	0.5 : 3.5		0.5 : 0.1	0.8 : 1.0	5 : 16	5	5
MT2016	0.0 : 5.0	0.0 : 3.6	0.0 : 0.4	0.0 : 1.4	0.0 : 4.4	0.1 : 0.5		0.0 : 0.0	0 : 15	2	8
FURY	0.2 : 2.5	0.0 : 2.5	0.5 : 0.6	0.4 : 1.2	0.1 : 3.0	1.0 : 0.8	0.0 : 0.0		2 : 12	3	7

In order to capture the overall difference between any two rankings $\mathbf{r^a}$ and $\mathbf{r^b}$, the L_1 distance is utilised [18]:

$$d_1(\mathbf{r^a}, \mathbf{r^b}) = \|\mathbf{r^a} - \mathbf{r^b}\|_1 = \sum_{i=1}^{n} |r_i^a - r_i^b|, \tag{1}$$

where i is the index of the i-th team in each ranking, $1 \leq i \leq 8$.

The distance between the actual ranking $\mathbf{r^a}$ and the estimated ranking $\mathbf{r^d}$ is

$$d_1(\mathbf{r^a}, \mathbf{r^d}) = |1-1| + |2-2| + |3-6| + |4-4| + |5-3| + |6-5| + |7-8| + |8-7| = 8.$$

The top two teams were fairly close in their performance (confirmed by the final game, which needed extra time). Similarly the 7th and 8th teams were similar in strength too (not surprisingly their playoff ended up with penalties). The main discrepancy between the actual and estimated results is due to performances of two teams: Oxsy (whose rank is estimated as third, while the actual rank was only fifth) and Ri-one (which finished the competition as third, while its average rank is estimated to be sixth).

2.3   A Critique of the Continuous Ranking Scheme

There exists another ranking method: *continuous* scheme [18, 19]:

- Teams are ranked by the sum of average points obtained against each opponent across all 4000 games.
- The total goal difference of the non-rounded scores is used as a tie-breaker.

Both schemes, discrete and continuous, were introduced in order to evaluate different competition formats, using the top 8 teams of 2012 and 2013 [18, 19]. However, over the years it has become apparent that the continuous scheme suffers from two major drawbacks, violating the balance of points (3 for a win, 1 for a draw and 0 for a loss) and overestimating the points for draws and losses. Specifically, under the continuous scheme:

1. There is a bias to attribute more points to draws with higher scores.
2. There is a bias to reduce the advantage of the three-points-for-a-win standard.

1. Let us consider two opposite scenarios: (i) two teams A and B of equal strengths, denoted $A \Leftrightarrow B$, but with a stronger defensive capability, play N games resulting in the average $0 : 0$ score; and (ii) two teams X and Y of equal strengths $X \Leftrightarrow Y$, but with a stronger attacking capability, play N games resulting in the average $q : q$ score, where $q > 0$ is sufficiently large, e.g., $q = 3$. In the first pair, the scores of individual games, which may or may not be draws, do not diverge much from $0 : 0$, as the teams are defensive. And so the actual drawn scores $0 : 0$ dominate among the results, with large outliers $k : 0$ or $0 : k$, for $k > 0$ being relatively rare. Thus, the continuous points p attained by teams A and B stay close to 1.0, for example, $p_A \approx p_B \approx 1.2$.

In the second pair, the scores of individual games, which again may or may not be draws, diverge more from the average $q : q$, due to a higher variability of possible high scores. Consequently, the proportion of actual draws among N games is much smaller in comparison to the first pair, and the large outliers $k : 0$ or $0 : k$, even for $k > q$, are more numerous. As a result, the teams X and Y exchange wins and losses more often than teams A and B, acquiring more points for their respective wins. This yields the continuous points p_X and p_Y significantly higher than 1.0, for example, $p_X \approx p_Y \approx 1.4$, creating a general bias to attribute more points to the drawn contests with higher scores: $p_A \approx p_B < p_X \approx p_Y$. A typical sample of 10,000 scores $q_1 : q_2$, where both q_1 and q_2 are normally distributed around the same mean q, with the standard deviation $\sigma = 1.0$, results in the following continuous points $p_{\Leftrightarrow}(q)$ for different draws around q: $p_{\Leftrightarrow}(0) = 1.23$ for draws $0.38 : 0.38$, $p_{\Leftrightarrow}(1) = 1.33$ for draws $1.07 : 1.08$, $p_{\Leftrightarrow}(2) = 1.36$ for draws $1.99 : 2.00$, and $p_{\Leftrightarrow}(3) = 1.38$ for draws $3.02 : 3.00$.

While the higher scoring teams may be expected to get an advantage at a tie-breaker stage, getting more continuous points for the same outcome is obviously an unfair bias. The discrete scheme does not suffer from this drawback as the average scores are converted into the identical discrete points immediately, i.e., $p_A = p_B = p_X = p_Y = 1.0$.

It is easy to see that the lower bound for the continuous points shared by any two teams of equal strength is $\inf_{\Leftrightarrow} = 1.0$ (attainable only if all N games are drawn), while the upper bound is $\sup_{\Leftrightarrow} = 1.5$ (attained in the extreme case when all N games are non-draws, with wins and losses split equally). Consequently, under the continuous scheme, the points attributed to equal teams drawing on average, are overestimated, being somewhere between the lower and upper bounds: $\inf_{\Leftrightarrow} < p < \sup_{\Leftrightarrow}$, while the expected result (one point) sits only at exactly the lower bound.

2. The "three-points-for-a-win" standard which was widely adopted since FIFA 1994 World Cup finals "places additional value on wins with respect to draws such that teams with a higher number of wins may rank higher in tables

than teams with a lower number of wins but more draws"[3]. To illustrate the second drawback of the continuous scheme we will contrast two scenarios, comparing the combined points of two drawn contests against the combination of one-won and one-lost contests.

Firstly, we consider a case when team Q is paired with teams U and Z, such that $Q \Leftrightarrow U$ and $Q \Leftrightarrow Z$. We do not expect transitivity, and so $U \Leftrightarrow Z$ is not assumed. The continuous points for team Q resulting from these two iterated match-ups, both drawn, could vary between these lower bound $(\inf_{\Leftrightarrow,\Leftrightarrow})$ and upper bound $(\sup_{\Leftrightarrow,\Leftrightarrow})$:

$$\inf_{\Leftrightarrow,\Leftrightarrow} = \inf_{\Leftrightarrow} + \inf_{\Leftrightarrow} = 2.0$$

$$\sup_{\Leftrightarrow,\Leftrightarrow} = \sup_{\Leftrightarrow} + \sup_{\Leftrightarrow} = 3.0$$

Typically the combined points vary around the level of $p_Q \approx 2.6$, which is an overestimation of the ideal outcome by more than half-a-point.

Secondly, we consider a scenario with team R matched-up against teams V and W, with team V being weaker than R, denoted $R \Rightarrow V$, while the team W is stronger than R, denoted $R \Leftarrow W$. The relative strength of V and W is not important for our comparison. The continuous points that team R attains from the first pair, against the weaker opponent V, are bounded by $\inf_{\Rightarrow} = 1.5$ (just a slight over-performance) and $\sup_{\Rightarrow} = 3.0$ (the total dominance with all N games won):

$$1.5 = \inf_{\Rightarrow} < p_R < \sup_{\Rightarrow} = 3.0 \ .$$

In practice, the stronger team rarely drops below $p_R \approx 2.0$ points. In the second pair, team R is weaker, and its continuous points are bounded by $\inf_{\Leftarrow} = 0.0$ (the total inferiority with all N games lost) and $\sup_{\Leftarrow} = 1.5$ (getting almost to an equal standing):

$$0.0 = \inf_{\Leftarrow} < p_R < \sup_{\Leftarrow} = 1.5 \ .$$

In practice, the weaker team rarely reaches beyond $p_R \approx 1.0$ points. A typical sample of 10,000 scores $q_1 : q_2$, where q_1 and q_2 are normally distributed around the means q and 0.0 respectively, with the standard deviation $\sigma = 1.0$, results in the following continuous points $p_{\Rightarrow}(q)$ for different won contests around q: $p_{\Rightarrow}(1) = 2.31$ for wins $1.07 : 0.38$, $p_{\Rightarrow}(2) = 2.75$ for wins $2.00 : 0.38$, and $p_{\Rightarrow}(3) = 2.94$ for wins $2.97 : 0.38$. Correspondingly, the continuous points $p(q)$ for the respective lost contests sampled under the same distribution are overestimated above 0.0 as follows: $p_{\Leftarrow}(1) = 0.32$, $p_{\Leftarrow}(2) = 0.13$, and $p_{\Leftarrow}(3) = 0.04$.

The combined continuous points for team R after these match-ups, one won and one lost, could vary between the lower bound of and the upper bound of

$$\inf_{\Rightarrow,\Leftarrow} = \inf_{\Rightarrow} + \inf_{\Leftarrow} = 1.5$$

$$\sup_{\Rightarrow,\Leftarrow} = \sup_{\Rightarrow} + \sup_{\Leftarrow} = 4.5$$

---

[3] https://en.wikipedia.org/wiki/Three_points_for_a_win.

In practice, $2.0 < p_R < 4.0$. That is, the combined continuous points of a win and a loss typically vary around $p_R \approx 3.0$, which is an appropriate outcome.

Contrasting the possible bounded intervals and typical outcomes of two contests (two draws versus one win and one loss) immediately highlights that the continuous points do not differentiate these scenarios sufficiently well. The intention of the three-points-for-a-win standard was precisely to preference the one-win-and-one-loss scenario over the two-draws scenario, $p_{\Rightarrow,\Leftarrow} = 3 > p_{\Leftrightarrow,\Leftrightarrow} = 2$. In other words, team Q with two drawn contests should achieve a lower rank than team R with a won and a lost contest, with the difference being the cost of a single drawn game. The continuous scheme fails in this regard, by producing, on average, less than half-a-point difference, $p_{\Rightarrow,\Leftarrow} \approx 3.0 > p_{\Leftrightarrow,\Leftrightarrow} \approx 2.6$. In fact, it is quite conceivable that $p_{\Rightarrow,\Leftarrow}$ could happen to be less than $p_{\Leftrightarrow,\Leftrightarrow}$ under the continuous scheme in some cases, as $\inf_{\Rightarrow,\Leftarrow} < \sup_{\Leftrightarrow,\Leftrightarrow}$. In other words, one hard-won contest, e.g. $p_{\Rightarrow}(1) = 2.31$, coupled with a serious loss, e.g., $p_{\Leftarrow}(3) = 0.04$ could earn less points (e.g., $p_{\Rightarrow,\Leftarrow} \approx 2.35$) than two high-scoring draws, e.g. $p_{\Leftrightarrow}(3) = 1.38$ (resulting in $p_{\Leftrightarrow,\Leftrightarrow} \approx 2.76$)—definitely, something not intended by the three-points-for-a-win standard.

Again, the discrete scheme easily overcomes this drawback as the average scores are converted into the appropriate discrete points for each contest (3 for a win, 1 for a draw and 0 for a loss), and combined only afterwards.

The two problems identified for the continuous scheme may amplify over many match-ups in a 8-teams round-robin, especially when there are many teams of similar strength (which is the case in the Simulation League in recent years). The biases become even more pronounced in the absence of transitivity in teams' relative strengths. In light of these concerns, we suggest that some recent works employing the continuous scheme, e.g. [20], would benefit from re-evaluation.

2.4   Evaluation Round

The 2016 competition also included an evaluation round, where all 18 participating teams played one game each against the champion of RoboCup-2015, team WrightEagle (China), i.e., WE2015 [21]. Only two teams, the eventual finalists Gliders2016 and HELIOS2016, managed to win against the previous year champion, with Gliders defeating WrightEagle 1:0, and HELIOS2016 producing the top score 2:1.

We extended this evaluation over 1000 games, again playing WE2015 against the top 8 teams from RoboCup-2016. Table 2 summarises the evaluation for RoboCup-2016: both actual scores obtained in Leipzig and the averages over 1000 games.

The evaluation round confirmed the strength of RoboCup-2015 champion in the League. It is evident that WE2015, if entered in 2016, would likely have achieved third rank. To confirm this conjecture we combined the estimation results presented in Table 1 with the estimates of WE2015 scores from Table 2, summarised in Table 3.

Table 2. Evaluation round results for the top 8 teams playing against WE2015. Top row: actual scores obtained at RoboCup-2016 in Leipzig; bottom row: average scores over 1000 games.

	Gliders2016	HELIOS2016	Ri-one	CSU_Yunlu	Oxsy	Shiraz2016	MT2016	FURY
WE2015	0 : 1	1 : 2	7 : 1	2 : 0	4 : 1	3 : 2	4 : 0	11 : 2
WE2015	1.4 : 1.8	1.3 : 1.7	5.0 : 0.5	2.7 : 0.5	3.5 : 1.3	4.0 : 0.8	5.9 : 0.0	4.8 : 0.4

Table 3. Evaluation round-robin results (average goals scored and points allocated with discrete scheme), combined for the top 8 teams from RoboCup 2016 and the RoboCup-2015 champion (WE2015). The resultant evaluation ranking is marked with r^e.

	Gliders	HELIOS	WE2015	Ri-one	CSU_Yunlu	Oxsy	Shiraz	MT2016	FURY	Goals	Points	r^e
Gliders		0.3 : 0.4	1.8 : 1.4	2.8 : 0.3	1.9 : 0.3	0.7 : 0.8	3.8 : 0.4	5.0 : 0.0	2.5 : 0.2	20 : 2	20	1
HELIOS	0.4 : 0.3		1.7 : 1.3	1.8 : 0.1	3.0 : 0.2	1.2 : 0.5	4.3 : 0.3	3.6 : 0.0	2.5 : 0.0	19 : 2	20	2
WE2015	1.4 : 1.8	1.3 : 1.7		5.0 : 0.5	2.7 : 0.5	3.5 : 1.3	4.0 : 0.8	5.9 : 0.0	4.8 : 0.4	29 : 8	18	3
Ri-one	0.3 : 2.8	0.1 : 1.8	0.5 : 5.0		1.1 : 1.1	0.2 : 1.8	0.6 : 0.5	0.4 : 0.0	0.6 : 0.5	4 : 15	4	7
CSU_Yunlu	0.3 : 1.9	0.2 : 3.0	0.5 : 2.7	1.1 : 1.1		0.5 : 1.2	2.0 : 0.7	1.4 : 0.0	1.2 : 0.4	7 : 11	11	5
Oxsy	0.8 : 0.7	0.5 : 1.2	1.3 : 3.5	1.8 : 0.2	1.2 : 0.5		3.5 : 0.5	4.4 : 0.0	3.0 : 0.1	17 : 8	15	4
Shiraz	0.4 : 3.8	0.3 : 4.3	0.8 : 4.0	0.5 : 0.6	0.7 : 2.0	0.5 : 3.5		0.5 : 0.1	0.8 : 1.0	6 : 20	5	6
MT2016	0.0 : 5.0	0.0 : 3.6	0.0 : 5.9	0.0 : 0.4	0.0 : 1.4	0.0 : 4.4	0.1 : 0.5		0.0 : 0.0	0 : 21	2	9
FURY	0.2 : 2.5	0.0 : 2.5	0.4 : 4.8	0.5 : 0.6	0.4 : 1.2	0.1 : 3.0	1.0 : 0.8	0.0 : 0.0		2 : 17	3	8

3   Proposed Challenges

3.1   Champions Simulation League

In order to trace the progress of the League over time it is interesting to compare performance of several previous champions, directly competing against each other in a round-robin tournament. For example, we evaluated relative performance of six champions of RoboCup-2011 to RoboCup-2016: WrightEagle (WE2011 [22,23], WE2013 [24,25], WE2014 [26], WE2015 [21]), HELIOS2012 [27] and Gliders2016 [11,12].

The round-robin results over 1000 games, presented in Table 4, confirmed the progress of the League over the last six years, with the resultant ranking r^l completely concurring with the chronological ranking r^t, i.e., $d_1(r^l, r^t) = 0$.

3.2   Global Challenge

Another proposal suggests to pit together the best teams from each of the top 6 or 8 participating countries (for example, in 2016 it would have been Australia, Brazil, China, Egypt, Germany, Iran, Japan, Romania), with two "home-and-away" games between opponents. There can be 14 games for a home-and-away single-elimination round with 8 teams; or 30 games for a home-and-away double round-robin with 6 teams. The "Global Challenge" will be distinguished from the

Table 4. Champions Simulation League round-robin results (average goals scored and points allocated with discrete scheme), for six champions of RoboCup 2011 to 2016. To distinguish WE2015 and WE2014 results, non-rounded scores were used as a tie-breaker. The resultant league ranking with discrete point allocation scheme is marked with r^1.

	Gliders2016	WE2015	WE2014	WE2013	HELIOS2012	WE2011	Goals	Points	r^1
Gliders2016		1.8 : 1.4	1.8 : 1.3	1.7 : 0.9	1.2 : 0.1	2.0 : 1.0	9 : 4	15	1
WE2015	1.4 : 1.8		2.5 : 2.5	3.0 : 2.5	2.2 : 0.9	4.0 : 2.9	13 : 12	8	2
WE2014	1.3 : 1.8	2.5 : 2.5		2.8 : 2.6	2.3 : 0.8	3.9 : 3.0	13 : 12	8	3
WE2013	0.9 : 1.7	2.5 : 3.0	2.6 : 2.8		1.9 : 0.9	2.9 : 3.2	12 : 12	6	4
HELIOS2012	0.1 : 1.2	0.9 : 2.2	0.8 : 2.3	0.9 : 1.9		2.6 : 1.8	6 : 9	3	5
WE2011	1.0 : 2.0	2.9 : 4.0	3.0 : 3.9	3.2 : 2.9	1.8 : 2.6		12 : 16	1	6

main competition by playing the games with different parameters, for example, higher noise, or even with random player(s) disconnecting. In other words, the Global Challenge will focus on resilience of the teams in the face of unexpected conditions.

In each game, the home side would choose a hidden parameter to vary, in order to represent some features of their country (like high altitude in Bolivia or long-distance travel to Australia). These parameters will not be known to the opposition, but would be the same for both teams in that game.

The full list of possible hidden server parameters may include a significant number (currently, the number of server parameters is 27) and the set of change-able parameters will be agreed in advance. The global challenge mode will be selected via a new parameter, for example, server::global_challenge_mode, introduced in the simulation server (server.conf). When the global_challenge_mode parameter is set to true, the server will permit the left side coach (the home side) to send a command like this: (change_player_param (param_1 value) (param_2 value)... (param_N value)).

For example, if the home side chooses to simulate some bad weather conditions or a soggy pitch, these server parameters can be changed: ball_accel_max, ball_decay, ball_rand, ball_speed_max, catch_probability, inertia_moment, kick_rand, player_rand.

Exploiting their own strong points, and possibly trying to exploit some weak points of the opponent, the home side could change some of the available parameters in a way that creates an advantage. While the adjusted environment will be applied equally to the both teams, the task of the left side coach (the home team) will be to optimise the choice of the adjusted parameters to maximise the home side advantage.

4   Conclusion

We summarised the results of RoboCup-2016 competition in the 2D Soccer Simulation League, including the main competition and the evaluation round.

The evaluation round confirmed the strength of RoboCup-2015 champion (WrightEagle, i.e. WE2015) in the League, with only eventual finalists of 2016 (Gliders2016 and HELIOS2016) capable of winning against WE2015. After the RoboCup-2016, we extended this evaluation, over 1000 games for each pair, in a multi-game round-robin tournament which included the top 8 teams of 2016, as well as WE2015. The round-robin results confirmed that WE2015 would take third place, behind the champion team (Gliders2016) and the runner-up (HELIOS2016). This establishes WE2015 as a stable benchmark for the 2D Simulation League. In doing so we offered a critique of a particular ranking method (the *continuous* scheme), arguing that the *discrete* scheme is more appropriate.

We then followed with proposing two options to develop the evaluation challenge further. The first such possibility introduces "The Champions Simulation League", comprising several previous champions, directly competing against each other in a round-robin tournament. "The Champions Simulation League" can systematically trace the advancements in the League, measuring the progress of each new champion over its predecessors. We evaluated The Champions Simulation League with the champions from 2011 to 2016, producing a ranking which completely concurs with the chronological order, and confirming a steady progress in the League. Arguably, simulation leagues are the only ones in RoboCup where such an evaluation is possible, given the obvious constraints and difficulties with running such a tournament in robotic leagues.

Tracing such advances is especially important because different champion teams usually employ different approaches, often achieving a high degree of specialisation in a sub-field of AI, for example, automated hierarchical planning developed by WrightEagle [21,23,24,26,28], opponent modelling studied by HELIOS [27], and human-based evolutionary computation adopted by Gliders [11,12]. Many more research areas are likely to contribute towards improving the League, and several general research directions are recognised as particularly promising: nature-inspired collective intelligence [29–31], embodied intelligence [32–35], information theory of distributed cognitive systems [36–41], guided self-organisation [42–44], and deep learning [45–47].

The other proposed evaluation challenge ("The Global Challenge") aims to model environmental conditions during the games by simulating specific features of different participating countries, such as climate, infrastructure, travel distance, etc. This, arguably, may increase the realism of the simulated competition, making another small step toward the ultimate Millennium challenge.

Acknowledgments. A majority of RoboCup 2D Soccer Simulation teams, including the 2016 champion team, Gliders2016, are based on the well-developed code base *agent2d* [48], release of which has greatly benefited the RoboCup 2D Simulation community. Several teams, including WrightEagle and Oxsy, are independent of *agent2d*.

References

1. Burkhard, H.D., Duhaut, D., Fujita, M., Lima, P., Murphy, R., Rojas, R.: The road to RoboCup 2050. IEEE Robot. Autom. Mag. **9**(2), 31–38 (2002)
2. Obst, O.: Using model-based diagnosis to build hypotheses about spatial environments. In: Polani, D., Browning, B., Bonarini, A., Yoshida, K. (eds.) RoboCup 2003. LNCS (LNAI), vol. 3020, pp. 518–525. Springer, Heidelberg (2004). https://doi.org/10.1007/978-3-540-25940-4_47
3. Stone, P., Kuhlmann, G., Taylor, M.E., Liu, Y.: Keepaway soccer: from machine learning testbed to benchmark. In: Bredenfeld, A., Jacoff, A., Noda, I., Takahashi, Y. (eds.) RoboCup 2005. LNCS (LNAI), vol. 4020, pp. 93–105. Springer, Heidelberg (2006). https://doi.org/10.1007/11780519_9
4. Obst, O.: Simulation league – league summary. In: Kaminka, G.A., Lima, P.U., Rojas, R. (eds.) RoboCup 2002. LNCS (LNAI), vol. 2752, pp. 443–452. Springer, Heidelberg (2003). https://doi.org/10.1007/978-3-540-45135-8_40
5. Akiyama, H., Dorer, K., Lau, N.: On the progress of soccer simulation leagues. In: Bianchi, R.A.C., Akin, H.L., Ramamoorthy, S., Sugiura, K. (eds.) RoboCup 2014. LNCS (LNAI), vol. 8992, pp. 599–610. Springer, Cham (2015). https://doi.org/10.1007/978-3-319-18615-3_49
6. MacAlpine, P., Genter, K., Barrett, S., Stone, P.: The RoboCup 2013 drop-in player challenges: a testbed for ad hoc teamwork. In: Proceedings of the 2014 International Conference on Autonomous Agents and Multi-agent Systems, AAMAS 2014, pp. 1461–1462. International Foundation for Autonomous Agents and Multiagent Systems (2014)
7. Kitano, H., et al.: The RoboCup synthetic agent challenge 97. In: Kitano, H. (ed.) RoboCup 1997. LNCS, vol. 1395, pp. 62–73. Springer, Heidelberg (1998). https://doi.org/10.1007/3-540-64473-3_49
8. Noda, I., Stone, P.: The RoboCup soccer server and CMUnited clients: implemented infrastructure for MAS research. Auton. Agents Multi-agent Syst. **7**(12), 101–120 (2003)
9. Akiyama, H., et al.: HELIOS2016: team description paper. In: RoboCup 2016 Symposium and Competitions: Team Description Papers, Leipzig, Germany, July 2016
10. Asai, K., et al.: RoboCup 2016–2D soccer simulation league team description Ri-one (Japan). In: RoboCup 2016 Symposium and Competitions: Team Description Papers, Leipzig, Germany, July 2016
11. Prokopenko, M., Wang, P., Obst, O., Jaurgeui, V.: Gliders 2016: integrating multi-agent approaches to tactical diversity. In: RoboCup 2016 Symposium and Competitions: Team Description Papers, Leipzig, Germany, July 2016
12. Prokopenko, M., Wang, P.: Disruptive innovations in RoboCup 2D soccer simulation league: from cyberoos'98 to Gliders2016. In: Behnke, S., Sheh, R., Sariel, S., Lee, D.D. (eds.) RoboCup 2016. LNCS (LNAI), vol. 9776, pp. 529–541. Springer, Cham (2017). https://doi.org/10.1007/978-3-319-68792-6_44
13. Li, P., Ma, X., Jiang, F., Zhang, X., Peng, J.: CSU_Yunlu 2D soccer simulation team description paper 2016. In: RoboCup 2016 Symposium and Competitions: Team Description Papers, Leipzig, Germany, July 2016
14. Marian, S., Luca, D., Sarac, B., Cotarlea, O.: OXSY 2016 team description. In: RoboCup 2016 Symposium and Competitions: Team Description Papers, Leipzig, Germany, July 2016

15. Asali, E., et al.: Shiraz soccer 2D simulation team description paper 2016. In: RoboCup 2016 Symposium and Competitions: Team Description Papers, Leipzig, Germany, July 2016

16. Zhang, L., Yao, B., Chen, S., Lv, G.: MT2016 RoboCup simulation 2D team description. In: RoboCup 2016 Symposium and Competitions: Team Description Papers, Leipzig, Germany, July 2016

17. Darijani, A., Mostaejeran, A., Jamali, M.R., Sayareh, A., Salehi, M.J., Barahimi, B.: FURY 2D simulation team description paper 2016. In: RoboCup 2016 Symposium and Competitions: Team Description Papers, Leipzig, Germany, July 2016

18. Budden, D., Wang, P., Obst, O., Prokopenko, M.: Simulation leagues: analysis of competition formats. In: Bianchi, R.A.C., Akin, H.L., Ramamoorthy, S., Sugiura, K. (eds.) RoboCup 2014. LNCS (LNAI), vol. 8992, pp. 183–194. Springer, Cham (2015). https://doi.org/10.1007/978-3-319-18615-3_15

19. Budden, D.M., Wang, P., Obst, O., Prokopenko, M.: RoboCup simulation leagues: enabling replicable and robust investigation of complex robotic systems. IEEE Robot. Autom. Mag. **22**(3), 140–146 (2015)

20. Gabel, T., Falkenberg, E., Godehardt, E.: Progress in RoboCup revisited: the state of soccer simulation 2D. In: Behnke, S., Lee, D.D., Sariel, S., Sheh, R. (eds.) RoboCup 2016: Robot Soccer World Cup XX. LNAI. Springer, Berlin (2016)

21. Li, X., Chen, R., Chen, X.: WrightEagle 2D soccer simulation team description 2015. In: RoboCup 2015 Symposium and Competitions: Team Description Papers, Hefei, China, July 2015

22. Bai, A., Lu, G., Zhang, H., Chen, X.: WrightEagle 2D soccer simulation team description 2011. In: RoboCup 2011 Symposium and Competitions: Team Description Papers, Istanbul, Turkey, July 2011

23. Bai, A., Chen, X., MacAlpine, P., Urieli, D., Barrett, S., Stone, P.: WrightEagle and UT Austin villa: RoboCup 2011 simulation league champions. In: Röfer, T., Mayer, N.M., Savage, J., Saranlı, U. (eds.) RoboCup 2011. LNCS (LNAI), vol. 7416, pp. 1–12. Springer, Heidelberg (2012). https://doi.org/10.1007/978-3-642-32060-6_1

24. Zhang, H., Jiang, M., Dai, H., Bai, A., Chen, X.: WrightEagle 2D soccer simulation team description 2013. In: RoboCup 2013 Symposium and Competitions: Team Description Papers, Eindhoven, The Netherlands, June 2013

25. Zhang, H., Chen, X.: The decision-making framework of wrighteagle, the RoboCup 2013 soccer simulation 2D league champion team. In: Behnke, S., Veloso, M., Visser, A., Xiong, R. (eds.) RoboCup 2013. LNCS (LNAI), vol. 8371, pp. 114–124. Springer, Heidelberg (2014). https://doi.org/10.1007/978-3-662-44468-9_11

26. Zhang, H., Lu, G., Chen, R., Li, X., Chen, X.: WrightEagle 2D soccer simulation team description 2014. In: RoboCup 2014 Symposium and Competitions: Team Description Papers, Joao Pessoa, Brazil, July 2014

27. Akiyama, H., Shimora, H., Nakashima, T., Narimoto, Y., Yamashita, K.: HELIOS2012: team description paper. In: RoboCup 2012 Symposium and Competitions: Team Description Papers, Mexico City, Mexico, June 2012

28. Bai, A., Wu, F., Chen, X.: Online planning for large Markov decision processes with hierarchical decomposition. ACM Trans. Intell. Syst. Technol. **6**(4), 45:1–45:28 (2015)

29. Sayama, H.: Guiding designs of self-organizing swarms: interactive and automated approaches. In: Prokopenko, M. (ed.) Guided Self-Organization: Inception. ECC, vol. 9, pp. 365–387. Springer, Heidelberg (2014). https://doi.org/10.1007/978-3-642-53734-9_13

30. Nallaperuma, S., Wagner, M., Neumann, F.: Analyzing the effects of instance features and algorithm parameters for maxmin ant system and the traveling salesperson problem. Front. Robot. AI **2**, 18 (2015)
31. Hamann, H., et al.: Hybrid societies: challenges and perspectives in the design of collective behavior in self-organizing systems. Front. Robot. AI **3**, 14 (2016)
32. Pfeifer, R., Bongard, J.C.: How the Body Shapes the Way We Think: A New View of Intelligence. The MIT Press, Cambridge (2006)
33. Polani, D., Sporns, O., Lungarella, M.: How information and embodiment shape intelligent information processing. In: Lungarella, M., Iida, F., Bongard, J., Pfeifer, R. (eds.) 50 Years of Artificial Intelligence. LNCS (LNAI), vol. 4850, pp. 99–111. Springer, Heidelberg (2007). https://doi.org/10.1007/978-3-540-77296-5_10
34. Der, R.: On the role of embodiment for self-organizing robots: behavior as broken symmetry. In: Prokopenko, M. (ed.) Guided Self-Organization: Inception. ECC, vol. 9, pp. 193–221. Springer, Heidelberg (2014). https://doi.org/10.1007/978-3-642-53734-9_7
35. Ghazi-Zahedi, K., Haeufle, D.F.B., Montfar, G., Schmitt, S., Ay, N.: Evaluating morphological computation in muscle and dc-motor driven models of hopping movements. Front. Robot. AI **3**, 42 (2016)
36. Ay, N., Bertschinger, N., Der, R., Guttler, F., Olbrich, E.: Predictive information and explorative behavior of autonomous robots. Eur. Phys. J. B-Condens. Matter **63**(11), 329–339 (2008)
37. Tishby, N., Polani, D.: Information theory of decisions and actions. In: Cutsuridis, V., Hussain, A., Taylor, J.G. (eds.) Perception-Action Cycle: Models, Architectures, and Hardware, pp. 601–636. Springer, New York (2011)
38. Cliff, O.M., Lizier, J.T., Wang, X.R., Wang, P., Obst, O., Prokopenko, M.: Towards quantifying interaction networks in a football match. In: Behnke, S., Veloso, M., Visser, A., Xiong, R. (eds.) RoboCup 2013. LNCS (LNAI), vol. 8371, pp. 1–12. Springer, Heidelberg (2014). https://doi.org/10.1007/978-3-662-44468-9_1
39. Lizier, J.T., Prokopenko, M., Zomaya, A.Y.: A framework for the local information dynamics of distributed computation in complex systems. In: Prokopenko, M. (ed.) Guided Self-Organization: Inception. ECC, vol. 9, pp. 115–158. Springer, Heidelberg (2014). https://doi.org/10.1007/978-3-642-53734-9_5
40. Cliff, O.M., Prokopenko, M., Fitch, R.: An information criterion for inferring coupling of distributed dynamical systems. Front. Robot. AI **3**, 71 (2016)
41. Cliff, O.M., Lizier, J.T., Wang, P., Wang, X.R., Obst, O., Prokopenko, M.: Quantifying long-range interactions and coherent structure in multi-agent dynamics. Artif. Life **23**(1), 34–57 (2017)
42. Prokopenko, M.: Guided self-organization. HFSP J. **3**(5), 287–289 (2009)
43. Der, R., Martius, G.: The Playful Machine - Theoretical Foundation and Practical Realization of Self-Organizing Robots. Springer, Heidelberg (2012). https://doi.org/10.1007/978-3-642-20253-7
44. Prokopenko, M.: Guided Self-Organization: Inception. Springer, Berlin (2014). https://doi.org/10.1007/978-3-642-53734-9
45. Bengio, Y., Courville, A., Vincent, P.: Representation learning: a review and new perspectives. IEEE Trans. Pattern Anal. Mach. Intell. **35**(8), 1798–1828 (2013)
46. Schmidhuber, J.: Deep learning in neural networks: an overview. Neural Netw. **61**, 85–117 (2015)
47. Greenwald, H.S., Oertel, C.K.: Future directions in machine learning. Front. Robot. AI **3**, 79 (2017)
48. Akiyama, H.: Agent2D Base Code (2010). http://www.rctools.sourceforge.jp

Humanoid Robot Detection Using Deep Learning: A Speed-Accuracy Tradeoff

Mohammad Javadi[1], Sina Mokhtarzadeh Azar[2], Sajjad Azami[2],
Saeed Shiry Ghidary[2], Soroush Sadeghnejad[1(✉)], and Jacky Baltes[3]

[1] Bio-Inspired System Design Lab, Amirkabir University of Technology
(Tehran Polytechnic), No. 424, Hafez Avenue, P. O. Box 15875-4413, Tehran, Iran
s.sadeghnejad@aut.ac.ir
[2] Cognitive Robotics Lab, Amirkabir University of Technology (Tehran Polytechnic),
No. 424, Hafez Avenue, P. O. Box 15875-4413, Tehran, Iran
[3] Department of Electrical Engineering, National Taiwan Normal University,
162 Heping E Road Sec. 1, Taipei 10610, Taiwan

Abstract. Recent advances in computer vision have made the detection of landmarks on the soccer field easier for teams. However, the detection of other robots is also a critical capability that has not garnered much attention in the RoboCup community so far. This problem is well represented in different RoboCup Soccer and Rescue Robot Leagues. In this paper, we compare several two-stage detection systems based on various Convolutional Neural Networks (CNN) and highlight their speed-accuracy trade off. The approach performs edge based image segmentation in order to reduce the search space and then a CNN validates the detection in the second stage. We use images of different humanoid robots to train and test three different CNN architectures. A part of these images was gathered by our team and will be publicly available. Our experiments demonstrate the strong adaptability of deeper CNNs. These models, trained on a limited set of robots, are able to successfully distinguish an unseen kind of humanoid robot from non-robot regions.

Keywords: Robot detection · Robot vision · Humanoid robots
Deep learning · Convolutional neural networks · Image segmentation

1 Introduction

The RoboCup federation's ambitious goal for 2050 was stated in 1997: a team of fully autonomous humanoid robot soccer players shall win the soccer game against the winner of the World Cup [1,13]. In order to reach this purpose, researchers are working on multidisciplinary problems to solve various challenges of creating such intelligent systems. Also, annual RoboCup competitions within different leagues make incremental steps toward this big goal [2]. A crucial part of these systems is extracting information from visual data, i.e., computer vision.

M. Javadi, S. M. Azar and S. Azami—Contributed equally to this work.

© Springer Nature Switzerland AG 2018
H. Akiyama et al. (Eds.): RoboCup 2017, LNAI 11175, pp. 338–349, 2018.
https://doi.org/10.1007/978-3-030-00308-1_28

A lot of literature has been published on robot vision. Some of them were focusing on mutual identification of robots and more generally, robot body detection. This becomes vital in disaster situations like rescue robots where robots may want to identify each other using camera feed alone, but is also important in soccer where a player must be able to identify teammates and opponents. Humanoid robot teams, in RoboCup Soccer Leagues, must recognize landmarks on the field, e.g., field lines and the goal posts, for localization. But in this paper, we focus on body detection of other robots to present and compare different robust detection systems to detect and classify robot bodies in realistic and complex environments.

Our proposed systems are set to use deep learning methods for validating the results of image segmentation approaches and are expected to stay accurate in different light conditions. Results of this work have been evaluated and tested on three different hardware ranging from a mini computer used by our humanoid robots to a high-speed powerful server equipped with GPU. This leads to a comparison between accuracy and computation speed which is important for robots since there is always a limited computational power available.

The main contributions of this paper are:

1. Using and evaluating three Convolutional Neural Networks with different parameters and iterations to create robust body detection systems for humanoid robots.
2. Using different hardware to provide a speed-accuracy trade off since heterogeneous robots are going to use the system in realistic scenarios.
3. Two step procedure for body detection using image segmentation and CNN.
4. A novel data set of three different humanoid robots captured in realistic conditions and positions from the upper camera of robot in action.
5. Presenting experimental evidence that the proposed system can be used in action by robots in real life scenarios.

The rest of the paper consists of 6 sections: Sect. 2 presents an overview of methods and approaches in object recognition of robots and Deep Learning classification. Section 3 explains our method in detail. Section 4 contains information about the used dataset, experimental result and evaluation metrics are reported in detail in Sects. 5 and 6. Finally, in Sect. 7, we provide a summary of the work, conclusions and directions for the future work.

2 Related Works

To deal with the vision problem for 2050, the team of robots needs to understand the environment at least as the human team understands it. Limited dynamic range of cameras, changes in color due to brightness, and distortions due to motion make it impossible to create a robust system which classifies robot bodies using raw color information only. In this section, we briefly review the previous works on image segmentation and robot detection. For image segmentation, despite the fact that color segmentation is common in RoboCup Soccer Leagues

[3], Ma et al. [4] presented an approach as the "edge flow" which facilitates the integration of color and texture for this purpose. Fan et al. [5] integrated the results of color-edge extraction and SRG (seeded region growing) to provide homogeneous image regions with accurate and closed boundaries. On the other hand, Ren et al. [6] presented Region Proposal Networks (RPNs) that simultaneously predicts the object bounds and objectness scores at each position. In the case of robot detection and object recognition, Sabe et al. [7] focused on obstacle detection by plane extraction from data captured by stereo vision. In another work, Farazi et al. [8] used color segmentation of the black color range for obstacle detection. They also implemented a robot detector using a HOG feature descriptor in the form of a cascade classifier for detection of the igus® Humanoid Open Platform [9]. Arenas et al. [10] used a nested cascade of boosted classifiers for detection of Aibo robot and humanoid robots. Shangari et al. [11] evaluated combinations of cascade classifier with Histograms of Oriented Gradients, Local Binary Patterns, and Haar-like features for Humanoid robots detection and believed LBP feature is more useful than the others. Albani et al. [12] used a Deep Learning approach for NAO robot detection in the RoboCup Standard Platform League (SPL). Here, we show that this approach can be extended to deal with different types of robots and be used in other RoboCup leagues.

3   Proposed Approach

Figure 1 shows an overview of our system. A wide-angle YUV422 image is the input of our system. A human first trains the system by selecting seed pixels to create a look up table for color classification. This table is a mapping from YUV color space to a set of specific colors and assigns a class label (green, black, white or unknown) to each pixel.

To use edge based image segmentation and Hough Transform algorithms, we compute a binary image which describes edge intensity of each pixel in a given raw image. A gray-scale image is generated by extraction of the Y channel. Afterward, we compute the Scharr gradient operator (explained in [19]) on the gray-scale image which results in the desired binary image. The new images compared to the camera image can be seen in Fig. 2.

3.1   Segmentation and Bounding Box Extraction

Reduction of the search space can increase the performance of the whole system, both in terms of time and accuracy. In order to find regions of interests (ROI), first a vertical scan line runs inside the binary image to find pixels with high edge intensity [19]. These edge spots build ROI boundaries and have the potential to construct the same shape. Then, based on two different approaches we find related spots and connect them to build the boundary of the objects, like a ball, the lines, the goals and the obstacles. The first approach is Euclidean distance of selected spots in the X and Y directions, and the second one is the size and the color of the area around them that can help identify which object the spots

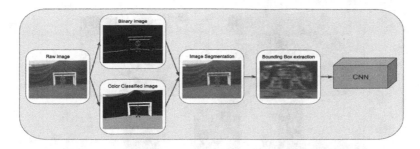

Fig. 1. Overview of our system. (Color figure online)

Fig. 2. Left: system input in RGB format. Middle: color classified image. Right: binary image. (Color figure online)

belong to. For example, in the case of obstacle detection, after perception of the black area around two adjacent spots inside the big green space and due to the fact that robots should have black foot in the RoboCup humanoid league, it can be concluded that considered boundary and it's edge spots belongs to the robot feet. To extract the proposed region for a robot, our algorithm moves from the region of the detected feet to left and right until a continues green region according to a threshold is being detected. Then, we crop a rectangle from left most points to right most points in the X axis and from foot to horizontal line (computed from robot structure) in the Y axis. Regions inside other bigger bounding boxes are omitted from the set of proposed regions (see Fig. 3).

3.2 Validation

As shown in Fig. 3, regions extracted in the previous section may contain false positives. Similar to work in [12], we have a validation step in which a CNN is used to omit irrelevant outputs from detected regions. Three different architectures were used in our work, namely LeNet, SqueezeNet and GoogLeNet [21]. These models were chosen because of their computational efficiency. The training of deep CNNs requires a lot of data and computational power. Preparing this amount of training data for every specific task is very time consuming and even may not be possible in some domains. Furthermore, not every one has access to high end GPUs to train these models. To solve this problem, pretrained networks on other datasets with different tasks are fine-tuned on a new relatively small

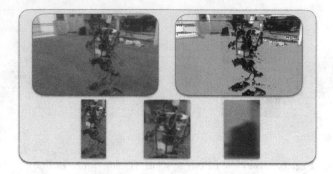

Fig. 3. Top left: input image. Top right: color classified image. Edge spots are blue colored, related spots are connected with red lines. Bottom left: true positive robot region. Bottom middle: proposed region is inside the bottom left region and will be ignored. Bottom right: false positive robot region. (Color figure online)

dataset for a new task. Here we fine-tune SqueezeNet and GoogLeNet architectures that are pretrained on the Imagenet Dataset, for our validation task.

3.3 CNN Architectures

A brief overview of all three architectures is in Fig. 4. First architecture we used is a variant of the LeNet architecture [17]. The main difference is the number of output filters in first convolution, second convolution and first fully connected layer which are set to 20, 50 and 500 respectively. Also one fully connected layer is deleted. GoogLeNet is the second architecture used in this work. This model is a deep Convolutional Neural Network which makes use of layers called Inception modules [14]. The most recent architecture that focuses on decreasing model parameters is the work of Iandola et al. [16]. In a similar approach to [14], fire modules are used to construct the model. In their work the same level of accuracy as AlexNet [21] is achieved with 50x fewer parameters. This model is both fast and accurate which makes it a good choice to run on humanoid robots.

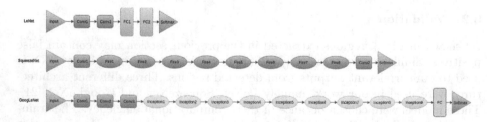

Fig. 4. View of three architectures with convolution and fully connected layers visible only. Depth of an architecture is the count of convolution and FC layers. Fire and Inception modules has depth of 2 convolutions. Therefore LeNet, SqueezeNet and GoogLeNet have depths of 4, 18 and 22 respectively.

4 Dataset Description

To train our models we gathered some images from three different robots (Fig. 5) inside a soccer field. 500 images of each robot were selected. Additionally, 500 images from SPQR NAO Image dataset [12] were chosen randomly. We also used 2000 random nonrobot images from their dataset. This 2000 robot and 2000 nonrobot images were used as our dataset. We make images of our humanoid robots publicly available and encourage others to add images of their robots to help gather a larger dataset of different kinds of humanoids for future research.

Fig. 5. Sample images of the used dataset. The left one is a sample image of ARASH. In middle we have DARWIN and the right one is KIARASH.

5 Implementation Details for CNNs

Our implementation is based on Caffe [15]. Training parameters are mainly the same as in original papers. Details are presented in Table 1. We trained LeNet from scratch. GoogLeNet and SqueezeNet were fine-tuned. SqueezeNet v1.1 was chosen from different versions of SqueezeNet because of less computation.

6 Experimental Results

In our validation step, we aim to distinguish between robot and non-robot regions. Therefore the problem is being modeled as a binary classification problem. Different experiments were conducted to evaluate performance of all three models. First, the robot and non-robot images were shuffled separately and 66% of each were chosen for training, the rest were chosen for the test set. Due to randomness in training procedure, each model was trained 5 times and average accuracy of those models on the test set is reported. According to the presented results in Table 2, all models perform well in this dataset (LeNet a bit lower than the other two). Also, the variance of accuracies in all architectures is reasonably low.

Time needed for every forward pass of all three architectures is reported in Table 3. Our measurements were on two different GPUs (GTX 980 with 2048 Cuda cores and GT 620 m with 96 Cuda cores), a general purpose laptop CPU

Table 1. Training parameters details. Batch size for SqueezeNet and GoogLeNet were limited due to lack of memory. Learning Rate is multiplied by gamma every stepsize.

	LeNet	SqueezeNet	GoogLeNet
Iteration	8000	2000	2000
Batch size	256	64	32
Base learning rate	0.001	0.001	0.0001
Learning rate policy	Step	Step	Step
Step size	1000	500	500
Gamma	0.1	0.1	0.1
Momentum	0.9	0.9	0.9

Table 2. Average and maximum accuracy of 5 models of each architecture on the test set. Images of all robots in train and test set.

	Average accuracy	Max accuracy
LeNet	94.83	97.94
GoogLeNet	99.90	100
SqueezeNet	100	100

Table 3. Average test time of every architecture on different platforms.

	GTX980 (ms)	GT620 m (ms)	Core i5 2.50 GHz (ms)	Celeron dual Core 1.10 GHz (ms)
LeNet	0.25	0.76	2.36	4.17
GoogLeNet	6.97	48.77	602.73	1754.03
SqueezeNet	2.13	16.63	48.55	173.33

and a humanoid robot CPU. As expected, LeNet is faster than deeper architectures by a large margin. SqueezeNet is faster than GoogLeNet and runs in a reasonable time on Humanoid robot's system. Time for a forward pass of GoogLeNet increases dramatically when using a CPU only.

We set two other experiments to compare the efficiency of the three architectures in a more difficult situation. First, all Images of ARASH were being separated from other robots and were given as a test set. 500 random non-robot images were also being added to the test set. Trained models on images from other three robots showed promising results on test set (see Table 4). Same experiment was conducted using the Robotis OP robot. This time average accuracy of LeNet decreased about 20% (see Table 5). Other two deeper models were still performing well on test set. We can see that SqueezeNet and GoogLeNet can be trained on Images of limited types of robots and distinguish between unseen new robot and non-robot regions. This is closer to capabilities of human vision (we can distinguish between robot and non-robot by seeing samples from two or three kinds of robots). Due to high variance of LeNet on this experiment, we

Table 4. Average and maximum accuracy of 5 models of each architecture on test set. No images of ARASH in training set.

	Average accuracy	Max accuracy
LeNet	97.56	98.9
GoogLeNet	99.4	99.8
SqueezeNet	99.3	99.3

Table 5. Average and maximum accuracy of 5 models of each architecture on test set. No images of Darwin in training set.

	Average accuracy	Max accuracy
LeNet	76.4	97.3
GoogLeNet	99.4	100
SqueezeNet	100	100

would like to report a 95% normal-based Confidence Interval of accuracy, which is equal to (56.4, 96.4).

To further evaluate discriminative power of models we changed the problem to a multiclass classification problem. Five classes of non-robot, Arash, Robotis-OP, kiarash and NAO were considered. 500 images from every class were chosen. We used 60% of data for training and other 40% for testing the models. Base Learning rate for GoogLeNet was set to 0.00001. Average accuracy of models in Table 6 shows that increasing difficulty of the problem by increasing number of classes lowers the accuracy of weaker models. GoogLeNet's discriminative power can be higher than SqueezeNet if proper amount of data is available. Here, due to low amount of data and higher number of parameters in GoogLeNet relative to SqueezeNet the former shows poor performance relative to latter. Generally, due to superior performance of SqueezeNet in speed and accuracy, this model is a good choice for difficult classification tasks in a humanoid robot.

Table 6. Average and maximum accuracy of 5 models of each architecture on test set in multiclass problem.

	Average accuracy	Max accuracy
LeNet	54.06	58.80
GoogLeNet	86.46	89.00
SqueezeNet	98.60	98.60

For more precise comparison, confusion matrices of multiclass experiment are reported below in formula 1, 2 and 3 noted as CM. Also, precision, recall, and f1-score are reported in Tables 7, 8 and 9, respectively.

$$CM_{GoogLeNet} = \begin{array}{c} \\ nonrobot \\ ARASH \\ DARWIN \\ KIARASH \\ NAO \end{array} \overset{\displaystyle nonrobot \ ARASH \ DARWIN \ KIARASH \ NAO}{\begin{bmatrix} 186 & 4 & 2 & 4 & 4 \\ 0 & 132 & 0 & 16 & 52 \\ 3 & 4 & 188 & 4 & 1 \\ 0 & 5 & 20 & 174 & 1 \\ 1 & 0 & 2 & 11 & 186 \end{bmatrix}} \qquad (1)$$

$$CM_{SqueezeNet} = \begin{array}{c} \\ nonrobot \\ ARASH \\ DARWIN \\ KIARASH \\ NAO \end{array} \overset{\displaystyle nonrobot \ ARASH \ DARWIN \ KIARASH \ NAO}{\begin{bmatrix} 200 & 0 & 0 & 0 & 0 \\ 0 & 186 & 0 & 1 & 13 \\ 0 & 0 & 200 & 0 & 0 \\ 0 & 0 & 0 & 200 & 0 \\ 0 & 0 & 0 & 0 & 200 \end{bmatrix}} \qquad (2)$$

$$CM_{LeNet} = \begin{array}{c} \\ nonrobot \\ ARASH \\ DARWIN \\ KIARASH \\ NAO \end{array} \overset{\displaystyle nonrobot \ ARASH \ DARWIN \ KIARASH \ NAO}{\begin{bmatrix} 49 & 3 & 144 & 4 & 0 \\ 0 & 129 & 4 & 67 & 0 \\ 0 & 0 & 195 & 5 & 0 \\ 0 & 5 & 2 & 193 & 0 \\ 1 & 7 & 128 & 64 & 0 \end{bmatrix}} \qquad (3)$$

Table 7. Evaluation results for GoogLeNet.

Class	Precision	Recall	F1-score	Support
nonrobot	0.98	0.93	0.95	200
ARASH	0.91	0.66	0.77	200
DARWIN	0.89	0.94	0.91	200
KIARASH	0.83	0.87	0.85	200
NAO	0.76	0.93	0.84	200
Avg/Total	0.87	0.87	0.86	1000

Table 8. Evaluation results for SqueezeNet.

Class	Precision	Recall	F1-score	Support
nonrobot	1.00	1.00	1.00	200
ARASH	1.00	0.93	0.96	200
DARWIN	1.00	1.00	1.00	200
KIARASH	1.00	1.00	1.00	200
NAO	0.94	1.00	0.97	200
Avg/Total	0.99	0.99	0.99	1000

Table 9. Evaluation results for LeNet.

Class	Precision	Recall	F1-score	Support
nonrobot	0.98	0.24	0.39	200
ARASH	0.90	0.65	0.75	200
DARWIN	0.41	0.97	0.58	200
KIARASH	0.58	0.96	0.72	200
NAO	0.00	0.00	0.00	200
Avg/Total	0.57	0.56	0.48	1000

7   Conclusion

In this study, we presented and tested various real time two-stage vision systems for humanoid robot body detection with promising results. Our pipeline performs a preprocessing stage to reduce search space and a CNN validates the results of ROI detection. The variety of structures and colors in humanoid robots (unlike standard platforms) demands more flexible detection systems than using color segmentation alone, so it makes sense to use edge based image segmentation. Also, this approach performs well in different lighting conditions in the context of time and accuracy. For validation step, we used three different CNNs and tested each on three different hardware, comparison of these systems lets us choose the proper system regarding our application and available computational power. Also, a novel dataset of humanoid body images is published with this project. All the images and sample codes are available on project's repository under https://github.com/AUTManLab/HumanoidBodyDetection. As future works, we are planning to develop a fast and complete humanoid body classifier using a more customized CNN architecture.

Acknowledgements. This research is supported by a grant to Jacky Baltes from the "Center of Learning Technology for Chinese" and the "Aim for the Top University Project" of the National Taiwan Normal University (NTNU) in Taipei, Taiwan. The research is also supported through a grant to Jacky Baltes by the Ministry of Education, Taiwan, and Ministry of Science and Technology, Taiwan, under Grants no. MOST 105-2218-E-003 -001 -MY2.

References

1. Gerndt, R., Seifert, D., Baltes, J.H., Sadeghnejad, S., Behnke, S.: Humanoid robots in soccer: robots versus humans in RoboCup 2050. IEEE Robot. Autom. Mag. **22**(3), 147–154 (2015)
2. Baltes, J., Sadeghnejad, S., Seifert, D., Behnke, S.: RoboCup humanoid league rule developments 2002–2014 and future perspectives. In: Bianchi, R.A.C., Akin, H.L., Ramamoorthy, S., Sugiura, K. (eds.) RoboCup 2014. LNCS (LNAI), vol. 8992, pp. 649–660. Springer, Cham (2015). https://doi.org/10.1007/978-3-319-18615-3_53

3. Rőfer, T., et al.: B-Human team report and code release 2013 (2013). http://www.b-human.de/downloads/publications/2013.CodeRelease2013.pdf

4. Ma, W.Y., Manjunath, B.S.: EdgeFlow: a technique for boundary detection and image segmentation. IEEE Trans. Image Process. **9**(8), 1375–88 (2000)

5. Fan, J., Yau, D.K., Elmagarmid, A.K., Aref, W.G.: Automatic image segmentation by integrating color-edge extraction and seeded region growing. IEEE Trans. Image Process. **10**(10), 1454–66 (2001)

6. Ren S, He K, Girshick R, Sun J. Faster R-CNN: towards real-time object detection with region proposal networks. In: Advances in Neural Information Processing Systems, pp. 91–99 (2015)

7. Sabe, K., Fukuchi, M., Gutmann, J.S., Ohashi, T., Kawamoto, K., Yoshigahara, T.: Obstacle avoidance and path planning for humanoid robots using stereo vision. In: 2004 IEEE International Conference on Robotics And Automation, 2002 Proceedings, ICRA 2004, vol. 1, pp. 592–597. IEEE, April 2004

8. Farazi, H., Allgeuer, P., Behnkem, S.: A monocular vision system for playing soccer in low color information environments. In: Proceedings of 10th Workshop on Humanoid Soccer Robots, IEEE-RAS International Conference on Humanoid Robots, Seoul, Korea (2015)

9. Farazi, H, Behnke, S.: Real-time visual tracking and identification for a team of homogeneous humanoid robots. In: Proceedings of 20th RoboCup International Symposium, Leipzig, Germany, July 2016

10. Arenas, M., Ruiz-del-Solar, J., Verschae, R.: Detection of AIBO and humanoid robots using cascades of boosted classifiers. In: Visser, U., Ribeiro, F., Ohashi, T., Dellaert, F. (eds.) RoboCup 2007. LNCS (LNAI), vol. 5001, pp. 449–456. Springer, Heidelberg (2008). https://doi.org/10.1007/978-3-540-68847-1_47

11. Shangari, T.A., Shams, V., Azari, B., Shamshirdar, F., Baltes, J., Sadeghnejad, S.: Inter-humanoid robot interaction with emphasis on detection: a comparison study. Knowl. Eng. Rev. 32 (2017)

12. Albani, D., Youssef, A., Suriani, V., Nardi, D., Bloisi, D.D.: A deep learning approach for object recognition with NAO soccer robots. In: Behnke, S., Sheh, R., Sarıel, S., Lee, D.D. (eds.) RoboCup 2016. LNCS (LNAI), vol. 9776, pp. 392–403. Springer, Cham (2017). https://doi.org/10.1007/978-3-319-68792-6_33

13. Shangari, T.A., Shamshirdar, F., Heydari, M.H., Sadeghnejad, S., Baltes, J., Bahrami, M.: AUT-UofM humanoid teensize joint team; a new step toward 2050's humanoid league long term RoadMap. In: Kim, J.-H., Yang, W., Jo, J., Sincak, P., Myung, H. (eds.) Robot Intelligence Technology and Applications 3. AISC, vol. 345, pp. 483–494. Springer, Cham (2015). https://doi.org/10.1007/978-3-319-16841-8_44

14. Szegedy, C., et al.: Going deeper with convolutions. In: Proceedings of the IEEE Conference on Computer Vision and Pattern Recognition, pp. 1–9 (2015)

15. Jia, Y., et al.: Caffe: convolutional architecture for fast feature embedding. In: Proceedings of the 22nd ACM International Conference on Multimedia, 3 November 2014, pp. 675–678. ACM (2014)

16. Iandola, F.N., Han, S., Moskewicz, M.W., Ashraf, K., Dally, W.J., Keutzer, K.: SqueezeNet: alexNet-level accuracy with 50x fewer parameters and <0.5 MB model size. arXiv preprint arXiv:1602.07360 24 February 2016

17. LeCun, Y., Bottou, L., Bengio, Y., Haffner, P.: Gradient-based learning applied to document recognition. Proc. IEEE **86**(11), 2278–324 (1998)

18. Jiang, X., Bunke, H.: Edge detection in range images based on scan line approximation. Comput. Vis. Image Underst. **73**(2), 183–99 (1999)

19. Levkine, G.: Prewitt, Sobel and Scharr gradient 5×5 convolution matrices. Image Process. Artic. Second. Draft. (2012)
20. Deng, J., Dong, W., Socher, R., Li, L.J., Li, K., Fei-Fei, L.: Imagenet: a large-scale hierarchical image database. In: 2009 IEEE Conference on Computer Vision and Pattern Recognition, CVPR 2009, pp. 248–255. IEEE, 20 June 2009
21. Krizhevsky, A., Sutskever, I., Hinton, G.E.: Imagenet classification with deep convolutional neural networks. In: Advances in Neural Information Processing Systems, pp. 1097–1105 (2012)

Recognition of Grasp Points for Clothes Manipulation Under Unconstrained Conditions

Luz María Martínez[✉] and Javier Ruiz-del-Solar

Advanced Mining Technology Center and Department of Electrical Engineering,
Universidad de Chile, Santiago, Chile
{luz.martinez,javier.ruizdelsolar}@amtc.cl

Abstract. In this work a system for recognizing grasp points in RGB-D images is proposed. This system is intended to be used by a domestic robot when deploying clothes lying at a random position on a table. By taking into consideration that the grasp points are usually near key parts of clothing, such as the waist of pants or the neck of a shirt. The proposed system attempts to detect these key parts first, using a local multivariate contour that adapts its shape accordingly. Then, the proposed system applies the Vessel Enhancement filter to identify wrinkles in the clothes, allowing to compute a roughness index for the clothes. Finally, by mixing (i) the key part contours and (ii) the roughness information obtained by the vessel filter, the system is able to recognize grasp points for unfolding a piece of clothing. The recognition system is validated using realistic RGB-D images of different cloth types.

Keywords: Clothing recognition · Depth image · Grasp points
Wrinkle analysis

1 Introduction

The development of service robotics has had an explosive increase during the last decade. In particular, new opportunities have been opened for the development of domestic robots, whose aim is to assist humans in daily, repetitive, or boring home tasks. One of these tasks is the handling of clothes, with the final goal of washing, ironing, folding, and storing the clothes according to the user's preference. When clothes are manipulated under unconstrained conditions, one of the key aspects to be solved is the determination of the grasp points to be used by the domestic robot.

In order to address this task, we propose a system for recognizing grasp points in RGB-D images, which is intended to be used by a domestic robot when deploying clothes lying at a random position on a table. By taking into consideration that the grasp points are usually placed near key clothes parts, such as the waist of pants or the neck in a shirt. The proposed system attempts to detect first these key regions using a local multivariate contour [3] that adapts its shape

© Springer Nature Switzerland AG 2018
H. Akiyama et al. (Eds.): RoboCup 2017, LNAI 11175, pp. 350–362, 2018.
https://doi.org/10.1007/978-3-030-00308-1_29

accordingly. Then, the proposed system applies the Vessel Enhancement filter [2] to identify wrinkles in clothing. Although this filter was originally designed to detect blood vessels on medical images based on their tubular geometric structure, in this work it is applied over the depth images in order to highlight the tubular shape of the wrinkles. Which allows us to compute a roughness index for the clothes. Then, by combining (i) the contours of the key parts and (ii) the roughness information obtained by the vessel filter, the system is able to recognize grasp points for unfolding a piece of clothing, which does not require having previously stored these points. We postulate that this approach obtains a better representation, than classical approaches based on the analysis of sliding windows or rectangular regions around a point of interest.

The proposed system can be of interest for researchers working in the development of similar systems (e.g. RoboCup @HOME and Amazon Picking Challenge teams), for their later integration in domestic service robots. The system is validated using realistic RGB-D images of different clothing types obtained from the Clothing Dataset [14,16].

This paper is organized as follows. Section 2 presents some related work. Section 3 presents the proposed grasp detection system, and Sect. 4 shows the system evaluatation. Finally, discussion and conclusions are given in Sect. 5.

2   Related Work

There are many challenges associated with the manipulation of deformable objects, such as clothing. There are also different strategies to find the best way to grasp such objects. Some researchers prefer a two stage process, where the first task is to classify the object and then apply a pose recognition method [7–9].

Depending on the classification result, a proper garment pose recognition algorithm is applied. One approach is to use a *Dense* SIFT descriptor over depth images, obtaining invariance to rotation and scale, as an input to a *Basis Kernel function* (RBK) SVM on the first stage, and a *Linear Kernel function* SVM [7,8] on the second. Another approach is to perform classification on both stages by means of a *deep Convolutional Neural Networks* (CNN) [9].

With the arrival of cheaper depth sensors, some reliable methods have been developed based on depth data. Particularly when dealing with a garment over a table; the following approaches have been proposed based on 3D descriptors: *Geodesic-Depth Histogram* (GDH) [13], *Fast Point Feature Histogram* (FPFH) [22][23], *Heat Kernel Signature* (HKS) [15] and *Fast Integral Normal 3D* (FINDDD) [11]. However, once the piece of clothing hangs from a robot's gripper, it is common to take advantage of the classification and pose recognition procedure to identify optimal grasping points, which the robot can use to unfold the garment properly and efficiently.

Wrinkles are considered an important piece of information when working with clothes for the purpose of recognition, unfolding, or ironing. The "wrinkledness" measure has been widely used in state of the art algorithms, that use entropy measures to analyze how much of the surrounding area of a point has normals aligned in the same orientation, i.e. a flat surface or a combination of a few flat surfaces [12]. A more advanced analysis of wrinkles has also been carried out, aiming to identify their shape and topology using a size based classification procedure, which requires detecting the length, width and height of each wrinkle [21].

Trying to identify two grasping points for the robot to hold every garment class and ease its manipulation over a table, is an interesting problem. As a case of study, one approach developed to grasp a hand towel is to drag one hand along a towel border from a random point, until reaching a corner. Then, the other gripper repeats the process looking for an opposite corner [4–6,19,20]. Another approach is to train a *Hough Forest* for each garment class, where images are manually labeled with relevant grasping points [1].

3   Grasp Point Detections System

Taking into consideration that the grasp points are usually near key clothing parts, such as the waist of pants or the neck in a shirt. We detect this key regions using a local multivariate contour [3] that adapts its shape accordingly, and the Vessel Enhancement filter [2] to identify wrinkles in clothing. This filter was designed to detect blood vessels on medical images, based on their tubular geometric structure; but when used in clothing depth images, it highlights the tubular shape of the wrinkles, allowing for the computation of a roughness index of the item. Combining the key part contours and the roughness information obtained by the vessel filter, we propose a system able to compute grasp points for unfolding a piece of clothing, which does not require having previously stored these points.

The proposed system is divided in three main parts: *Garment Key Part Recognition*, *Wrinkle Analysis* and the method that combines the previous steps called *Grasp Point Detections*. Figure 1 shows a general block diagram of the proposed system.

3.1   Garment Key Part Recognition

The garment key part recognition it is based in VFH descriptors in a selected region performing a matching with k-nearest neighborhood. In this section a training phase is carried out by marking the region where the key part was observed on each image. Then a test phase where we search this key part in the image.

The VFH descriptor method [18] computes a global descriptor, which is formed by a histogram of the normal components of the object's surface. The histogram captures the shape of the object, and the viewpoint from which the point cloud is taken. First, the angles α, ϕ and θ are computed for each point based on its normal and the normal of the point cloud's centroid c_i. The viewpoint-dependent component of the descriptor is a histogram of the angles between the vector $p_c - p_v$ and each normal point. The other component is a Fast Point Feature Histogram (FPFH) [17] estimated for the centroid of the point cloud,

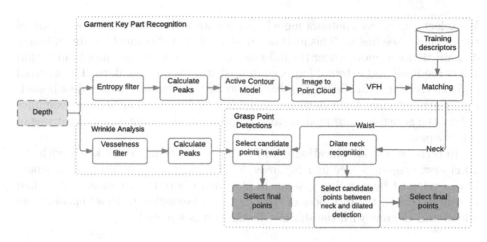

Fig. 1. Diagram of the grasp points detection system.

and an additional histogram of the distances of the points in the cloud to the cloud's centroid. The VFH descriptor is a compound histogram representing four different angular distributions of surface normals. In this work, the PCL implementation [10] is used, where each of those four histograms has 45 bins and the viewpoint-dependent component has 128 bins, totaling 308 bins.

In the recognition phase (Algorithm 1) the local maximums of the entropy filter image are considered as candidates points for contour evaluation in search of the key part of the clothing (see line 3).

Algorithm 1. Garment parts recognition

---

1 **Function** RecognitionGarmentPart(*img*)
    Input : Depth image to evaluate
    Output: Label of the garment part recognition
2   entropy = entropyFilter(*img*)
3   points = getPeaks(entropy)
4   listLabel = []
5   **for** *p in points* **do**
6   localRegion = getLocalRegion(*p, img*)
7   pcloud = *img2pointcloud*(*localRegion*)
8   normals = *getNormals*(*pcloud*)
9   vfh = *getVFHdescriptor*(*normals*)
10   neight, dist = knn.findNearest(vfh, 10)
11   listLabel.append(selectLabel(neight, dist))
12   **end**
13   **return** selectLabels(points, listLabel)

For contour evaluation, that is the selection of the contour of the part of the garment to be detected, we evaluated: edge detections and segmentation (Felenszwabs's, SLIC, Quickshift, Compact watershed, and Region Adjacency Graph).

We select the active contours models [3], for its adaptation to the key part of the clothing (see line 6). This method consists of curves defined within an image domain that can move under the influence of internal forces coming from within the curve itself and external forces computed from the image data. The internal and external forces are defined so that the snake will conform to an object boundary or other desired features within an image. In Fig. 2 we can see two examples of how the active contour models were adapted starting from a point that was in the key part.

In terms of the classification used for the recognition, we use k-NN with the 10 closest neighbors (see line 10), over VFH descriptors (see lines 6–9), where it was selected by a voting system. In the case where two or more classes had the same voting, the distances of the neighbors belonging to those classes were added and the one with the shortest distance was selected.

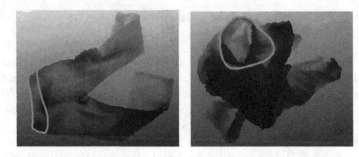

Fig. 2. Left: countour in waist pant. Right: countour in neck shirt.

3.2   Wrinkle Analysis

The classical approach for the wrinkle analysis is based on an entropy filter, which measures how much of the surrounding area of the point has normals aligned in the same orientation i.e. a flat surface or a combination of a few flat surfaces [12].

The entropy measure is computed using a local descriptor based on the surface normals of a 3D point cloud. In particular, we use the inclination and azimuth angles in the spherical coordinates representation of the normal vectors:

$$(\phi, \theta) = \arccos\left(\frac{z}{r}\right), \arctan\left(\frac{y}{x}\right) \tag{1}$$

$$r = \sqrt{x^2 + y^2 + z^2} \tag{2}$$

Where ϕ is the inclination and θ is the azimuth, (x, y, z) are the 3D point coordinates, and r is the radius in spherical. Then, the distribution model is created in a bi-dimensional histogram with the inclination and azimuth values in a local region around each point (64×64 bins), and its entropy is computed as:

$$H(X) = -\sum_{i=1}^{n} p(x_i) \log p(x_i) \tag{3}$$

This work proposes to exploit the geometric structure of clothes contours on depth images, by means of the Multiscale Vessel Enhancement Filter (MVEF) proposed by Frangi et al. This filter was originally designed to detect blood vessels on medical images, which have a tubular-like geometric structure [2].

The filter is applied to grayscale images and is based on a local *vesselness* measure, which is obtained by a second order approximation of the point and its neighborhood. The three lower Hessian eigenvalues are used to geometrically model the region by an ellipsoid, whose shape and orientation are defined by the eigenvalues and the related eigenvectors. Depending on the eigenvalue magnitudes, the filter can discriminate the region into plate, line and tubular-like structures. Furthermore, the author discusses the high noise and background suppression capabilities of the filter, in relation to the objective tubular structures.

In this work, depth images are used as the filter input, avoiding the complexity associated with highly textured cloth pieces, which can generate false positives. The filter highlights the tubular shape of the wrinkles and the folds generated by the clothes in the depth image. In order to account for patterns of different sizes, the filter strategy is to apply the described process at multiple scale levels, choosing the maximum local vesselness measure as the candidates points to grasp (Fig. 3).

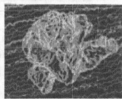

Fig. 3. Left: input depth image. Center: entropy filter. Right: vessel filter

3.3 Grasp Point Detections

Taking the information from the detection of the key part and the local maxima on the wrinkles image, the grasp points are extracted in the following ways depending on the detected class:

- *T-Shirt and Shirt (Algorithm 2):* First, the local maximum points of the vessel filter image are obtained as candidate points (see line 2). Then, a morphological dilation is applied to the mask representing the neck and only those points that are within the dilated outline were filtered. To select between them, lines are created between all pairs of candidate points, selecting the one which passed closer to the contour center of the neck (see lines 4–13).

- *Pants (Algorithm 3):* First, the local maximum points of the vessel filter image are obtained as candidate points (see line 2). Then, the pair of points of the waist detection contour that are further away are searched. To select the grasp points, we looked for the ones closer to the previous points while lying within the contour (see lines 4–13).

Algorithm 2. Select Grasp Points : T-Shirt and Shirt

---

1 **Function** selectPointsNeck(*mask, points*)
2 | *center_point* = getCenterPoint(mask) ;
3 | mask2 = dilate(mask);
4 | filteredPoints = points in mask2 and not in mask ;
5 | min_dist = -1 ;
6 | **for** *p1 in filteredPoints* **do**
7 | **for** *p2 in filteredPoints* **do**
8 | *straight_line* = getStraightLine(*p1, p2*);
9 | dist = distancePoint2Line(*center_point, straight_line*) ;
10 | **if** *dist < min_dist or min_fist == -1* **then**
11 | pointA, pointB = p1, p2 ;
12 | **end**
13 | **end**
14 | **end**
15 | **return** pointA, pointB;

Algorithm 3. Select Grasp Points : Pant

    Input   : Mask of the garment part detection and the local maxima
               points of the wrinkle analysis with the vessel filter
    Output: Two grasp points
1 **Function** selectPointsWaist()
2 | *pe*1, *pe*2 = getExtremePoint(mask)
3 | min_dist = -1
4 | **for** *p1 in filteredPoints* **do**
5 | **for** *p2 in filteredPoints* **do**
6 | *d1* = getEuclideanDist(*p1, pe*1) + getEuclideanDist(*p2, pe*2)
7 | *d2* = getEuclideanDist(*p1, pe*2) + getEuclideanDist(*p2, pe*1)
8 | *dist* = min(*d1, d2*)
9 | **if** *dist < min_dist or min_fist == -1* **then**
10 | pointA, pointB = p1, p2
11 | **end**
12 | **end**
13 | **end**
14 | **return** pointA, pointB;

4   Evaluation

4.1   Setup and Methodology

This work was evaluated using the Clothing Dataset [14,16], which consists of depth pointcloud images of common deformable clothing pieces laying on a table. Meaningful clothing parts are manually annotated with polygons. The data was recorded using a Kinect 3D camera, which provides 640 × 480 pixels color images and pointclouds in PCD v.7 format. The dataset also provides segmentation masks for foreground-background segmentation. We only considered 3 classes among the 6 available on the dataset: Pants, Shirt, T-Shirt.

Two parts of the proposed system were evaluated using the Clothing Dataset: garment key part recognition and grasp point detections. In the garment key part recognition process we used 100 images of each class, 300 in total; using 60% of them for training, and 40% for the testing phase. In the grasp point detections we used 40 images of each class, 120 in total, where the key parts were correctly identified and at least a single grasp point is visible.

4.2   Results

Garment Parts recognition

The results of the detection of the key parts of clothing can be observed in the confusion matrix in Table 1. In the table, a low detection rate is observed in the Neck T-Shirt class mainly because of the similarity it has with the Waist Pant class by its semicircular shape. Unlike Shirt class has a different shape and gets to get 74% recognition.

In the key parts recognition of all classes analyzed only the 24% is remained as no-detection. These detections are because a Voxel Grid filter is applied to the point cloud which reduces the number of points, but these points are not enough to continue with the algorithm. However in most cases works well, but in others the selected parameters eliminate too many points.

Table 1. Garment Parts recognition confusion matrix. Classes: neck shirt (NS), neck t-shirt (NTS), waist pant (W), no detection (ND).

	NS	NTS	W	ND
NS	**74%**	2%	0%	24%
NTS	5%	**29%**	26%	40%
W	5%	25%	**60%**	10%

Grasp Points Detections

In the implementation a rectangular region of length 51 was generated around the detected points and the selected points in the ground truth. Using the metric Intersection over Union (IoU) to measure the accuracy of the grasp points detections defined with the Eq. 4.

$$IoU = Intersection/Union \tag{4}$$

Table 2 shows the average of the IoU metrics for the 120 images. Where all classes of the IoU average of best located point have a similar detection rate, but the T-Shirt class results get worse considering both points. This may mean that the selected images of the t-shirt class have the second point more occluded in proportion than the other classes.

Table 2. IoU results for the points grasp detections.

	Pant	Shirt	T-Shirt
Mean all points	0.34	0.28	0.07
Mean best point	0.65	0.57	0.54

In the best point calculation is considering only the most accurate detected point of both points, as the average exceeds 0.5 of IoU, confirmed that at least one of the grasp points could serve to get unfold the clothes. In the particular results of each key part, the same proportions can be observed, i.e. the best detection results of grip points is in the Pant class, then in Shirt and finally T-Shirt.

However, only those detections with an IoU greater than 50% were considered correct. Obtaining the following results in the detection of 1 and 2 points.

Table 3. Recall of the points grasp detections.

	1 point	2 points
Shirt	55%	33%
T-Shirt	48%	29%
Pant	63%	43%

In Table 3 it can be seen that at least one of the grasp points results close to or greater than 50% detection. This may be because in the selected images of the database, the key part of the clothing class and at least one of the grab points are always visible, but the second point may be hidden. In these cases, it is difficult for the system to detect a point near the ground truth.

In the Tables 2 and 3, the results of 1 point and best point detection are close enough, it can be considered that at least the 55% in the Shirt class, the 48% in the T-Shirt class and the 63% in the Pant class of the best point have a useful fit.

In the Fig. 4 it is possible to observe the results of the detection of grasp points and the images of the different steps of the algorithm in images of different classes.

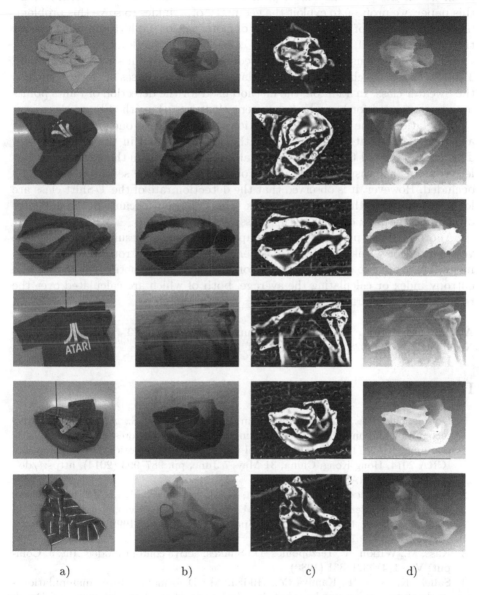

a)   b)   c)   d)

Fig. 4. Results of the algorithm. (a) RGB image, (b) depth image with the detected boundary of the key part marked in blue, (c) wrinkle analysis with the vessel filter and the local maxima points in red, and (d) detected grasp points in red. (Color figure online)

5   Discussion and Conclusions

Grasp point detection is a complex problem because of its high dimensionality, given by all the positions that a piece of clothing can take when wrinkled. In this paper, we propose to exploit the geometry of wrinkles to solve this problem, based on the class of the detected part of clothing: for T-Shirt and Shirt classes the neck is searched, while the waist is considered for the Pant class.

The algorithm used the same procedure to detect points on the Shirt and T-shirt classes, which could be extrapolated to similar classes of clothes, such as the Sweater class. In addition, the method used for the detection of Pants points may be expanded for lower body garment classes, such as the Shorts class.

In relation to the grasp point detection results, at least one of the points has a high detection rate with respect to the points marked in the ground truth. This can be related to the selected database images, where the key part and at least one of the grasp points is always observed, while the second point can be occluded. However, it is observed that the detection rate of the T-Shirt class are lower compared to the other two classes. This can occur because of the difficulty of defining the neck contour in this class.

Another of the proposals of this paper is to use the resulting image of the vessel filter for wrinkle analysis, in order to calculate the "roughness" of a garment. There are two options proposed for calculating this metric, calculating the entropy index or calculating the average, both of which are calculated over the total area of the garment.

Acknowledgments. This work was funded by CONICYT- PCHA/Doctorado Nacional/2014-21140280 and FONDECYT Project 1161500.

References

1. Doumanoglou, A., Kargakos, A., Kim, T., Malassiotis, S.: Autonomous active recognition and unfolding of clothes using random decision forests and probabilistic planning. In: 2014 IEEE International Conference on Robotics and Automation, ICRA 2014, Hong Kong, China, 31 May–7 June, pp. 987–993 (2014). https://doi.org/10.1109/ICRA.2014.6906974
2. Frangi, A.F., Niessen, W.J., Vincken, K.L., Viergever, M.A.: Multiscale vessel enhancement filtering. In: Wells, W.M., Colchester, A., Delp, S. (eds.) MICCAI 1998. LNCS, vol. 1496, pp. 130–137. Springer, Heidelberg (1998). https://doi.org/10.1007/BFb0056195
3. Kass, M., Witkin, A., Terzopoulos, D.: Snakes: active contour models. Int. J. Comput. Vis. 1(4), 321–331 (1988)
4. Salleh, K., Seki, H., Kamiya, Y., Hikizu, M.: Deformable object manipulation - study on passive tracing by robot. In: Student Conference on Research and Development - SCOReD 5 (2007)
5. Salleh, K., Seki, H., Kamiya, Y., Hikizu, M.: Inchworm robot grippers in clothes manipulation - optimizing the tracing algorithm. In: International Conference on Intelligent and Advanced Systems (ICIAS), pp. 1051–1055 (2007)

6. Sahari, K.S.M., Seki, H., Kamiya, Y., Hikizu, M.: Real-time path planning tracing of deformable object by robot. Int. J. Smart Sens. Intell. Syst. **3**(3) (2010)
7. Li, Y., Chen, C.F., Allen, P.K.: Recognition of deformable object category and pose. In: Proceedings of the IEEE International Conference on Robotics and Automation (ICRA) (2014)
8. Li, Y., Xu, D., Yue, Y., Wang, Y., Chang, S.F., Grinspun, E., Allen, P.K.: Regrasping and unfolding of garments using predictive thin shell modeling. In: Proceedings of the IEEE International Conference on Robotics and Automation (ICRA) (2015)
9. Mariolis, I., Peleka, G., Kargakos, A., Malassiotis, S.: Pose and category recognition of highly deformable objects using deep learning. In: ICAR, pp. 655–662. IEEE (2015). http://dblp.uni-trier.de/db/conf/icar/icar2015.html#MariolisPKM15
10. PCL: Point cloud library 1.7. http://www.pointclouds.org
11. Ramisa, A., Alenya, G., Moreno-Noguer, F., Torras, C.: FINDDD: a fast 3D descriptor to characterize textiles for robot manipulation. In: Proceedings of the International Conference on Intelligent Robots and Systems (IROS), pp. 824–830 (2013)
12. Ramisa, A., Alenyá, G., Moreno-Noguer, F., Torras, C.: Determining where to grasp cloth using depth information. In: FernÃąndez, C., Geffner, H., Manyá, F. (eds.) CCIA. Frontiers in Artificial Intelligence and Applications, vol. 232, pp. 199–207. IOS Press (2011). http://dblp.uni-trier.de/db/conf/ccia/ccia2011.html#RamisaAMT11
13. Ramisa, A., Alenyá, G., Moreno-Noguer, F., Torras, C.: Using depth and appearance features for informed robot grasping of highly wrinkled clothes. In: ICRA, pp. 1703–1708. IEEE (2012). http://dblp.uni-trier.de/db/conf/icra/icra2012.html#RamisaAMT12
14. Ramisa, A., Alenyá, G., Moreno-Noguer, F., Torras, C.: Learning RGB-D descriptors of garment parts for informed robot grasping. Eng Appl. Artif. Intell. **35**, 246–258 (2014). http://www.sciencedirect.com/science/article/pii/S0952197761400147X
15. Ramisa, A., Alenyá, G., Moreno-Noguer, F., Torras, C.: Learning RGB-D descriptors of garment parts for informed robot grasping. Eng. Appl. Artif. Intell. **35**(Complete), 246–258 (2014)
16. Ramisa, A., Alenyá, G., Moreno-Noguer, F., Torras, C.: A 3D descriptor to detect task-oriented grasping points in clothing. Pattern Recogn. **60**, 936–948 (2016). http://www.sciencedirect.com/science/article/pii/S0031320316301558
17. Rusu, R.B., Blodow, N., Beetz, M.: Fast point feature histograms (FPFH) for 3D registration. In: Proceedings of the 2009 IEEE International Conference on Robotics and Automation, ICRA 2010, pp. 1848–1853. IEEE Press, Piscataway (2009). http://dl.acm.org/citation.cfm?id=1703435.1703733
18. Rusu, R.B., Bradski, G.R., Thibaux, R., Hsu, J.M.: Fast 3D recognition and pose using the viewpoint feature histogram. In: IROS, pp. 2155–2162. IEEE (2010). http://dblp.uni-trier.de/db/conf/iros/iros2010.html#RusuBTH10
19. Sahari, K.S.M., Seki, H., Kamiya, Y., Hikizu, M.: Clothes manipulation by robot grippers with roller fingertips. Adv. Robot. **24**(1–2), 139–158 (2010). http://dblp.uni-trier.de/db/journals/ar/ar24.html#SahariSKH10
20. Salleh, K., Seki, H., Kamiya, Y., Hikizu, M.: Inchworm robot grippers for clothes manipulation. Artif. Life Robot. **12**(1–2), 142–147 (2008). https://doi.org/10.1007/s10015-007-0456-6

21. Sun, L., Aragon-Camarasa, G., Rogers, S., Siebert, J.P.: Accurate garment surface analysis using an active stereo robot head with application to dual-arm flattening. In: ICRA, pp. 185–192. IEEE (2015). http://dblp.uni-trier.de/db/conf/icra/icra2015.html#SunARS15
22. Willimon, B., Walker, I.D., Birchfield, S.: Classification of clothing using midlevel layers. ISRN Robot. (2013)
23. Willimon, B., Walker, I.D., Birchfield, S.: A new approach to clothing classification using mid-level layers. In: ICRA, pp. 4271–4278. IEEE (2013). http://dblp.uni-trier.de/db/conf/icra/icra2013.html#WillimonWB13a

Interactive Machine Learning Applied to Dribble a Ball in Soccer with Biped Robots

Carlos Celemin[1]([✉]) [iD], Rodrigo Perez[1] [iD], Javier Ruiz-del-Solar[1] [iD],
and Manuela Veloso[2] [iD]

[1] Advanced Mining Technology Center and Department of Electrical Engineering,
Universidad de Chile, Santiago, Chile
{carlos.celemin,rodrigo.perez.d,jruiz}@ing.uchile.cl
[2] Computer Science Department, Carnegie Mellon University, 5000 Forbes Avenue,
Pittsburgh, PA 15213, USA
veloso@cmu.edu

Abstract. An Interactive Machine Learning (IML) approach for training a dribbling engine for humanoid biped robots in RoboCup competitions (Standard Platform League) is presented. The proposed dribbling approach solves two decision problems: the determination of the dribbling direction and the calculation of the walking velocities required for pushing the ball toward the desired direction. Moreover, the prediction of the position of moving balls is used for improving the dribbling performance, when it is needed to intercept a moving ball. A combination of batch and incremental learning is used for shaping the policies of the dribbling controller. Results obtained from previous RoboCup competitions, and also from specific experiments, validate the proposed methods.

Keywords: Robot soccer · Learning from demonstration · Robot behavior
Human feedback

1 Introduction

In RoboCup soccer competitions, dribbling a ball is an important behavior needed for either defensive or offensive playing. The challenge for a dribbling engine of a robot is to navigate through the field and to avoid opponents, while keeping the ball possession; i.e. the robot needs to push the ball to a target, but the path of the ball is also controlled.

Most of the works reporting dribbling mechanisms are in the context of the wheeled robots [1, 2], and simulation leagues [3, 4]. For humanoid biped robots, most of the decision making systems developed for dribbling are a combination of walking and kicking behaviors, like the Finite State Machine (FSM) presented in [5] that is refined with human feedback. The same strategy of dribbling is used in [6], where a complex system of kicks is developed. Therefore, the robot walks toward the ball and according to the situation, the most convenient kick is selected, i.e. the system is mostly supported on the potential of the kicks. In contrast, in [7] is presented a system of In-walk kicks that is combined with a very efficient gait. However, there are some other approaches that do not divide the dribbling process between walking and kicking at all. For instance,

© Springer Nature Switzerland AG 2018
H. Akiyama et al. (Eds.): RoboCup 2017, LNAI 11175, pp. 363–375, 2018.
https://doi.org/10.1007/978-3-030-00308-1_30

[8] introduced a method for a gait that plans the steps of the walk for performing kicks while walking. A RL and prior knowledge based strategy that pushes the ball without kicks is presented in [9], it simply executes the task by walking against the ball. Our first work related to dribbling with humanoid robots was based on the same concept for pushing the ball [10]; a controller computes the velocity requests for the walking engine; in that case the agent was trained with RL and a Genetic Algorithm. In [10] is proposed to split the behavior into two simpler subtasks: A*lignment* for positioning the robot in front of the ball and the target; and *Ball-pushing* for walking against the ball with the appropriate velocity in order to keep its possession. In [11], the learning process of our system was improved using Interactive Machine Learning (IML). We proposed COACH, an interactive framework that allows users to provide corrective feedback to a policy, while this is being executed. In that work, COACH was used for training the sub-task *Ball-Pushing*. The results showed that the human advice during execution lets the learning process to attain best performances in less time than the RL scheme proposed in [10].

IML methods in general, and COACH [11] in particular, allow non-expert users without deep knowledge of the system properties, to train and adapt systems to specific requirements. This characteristic is important in situations where final users need to adapt a system to new conditions. For instance, in the context of RoboCup teams, wherein students join the project for short time periods, they work and focus on specific problems, but sometimes it is required to change the behavior of external systems developed by members who are no longer in the team. With this concern, we focused on applying IML strategies that allow tuning the dribbling system by users who do not know exactly how the decision-making system internally works.

In this work the methodology applied for training our last version of the dribbling engine, based mostly on IML, is introduced. This new system does not split the dribbling behavior in two sub-tasks, but faces the dribbling problem by addressing two main decisions: "how to push the ball? and "where to push the ball?". This last aspect was not considered in our former works [10, 11], because in those works the dribbling direction was always towards the opponent's goal. The proposed dribbling system controls the walking velocities for pushing the ball to a specific target, but the dribbling direction while navigating considers the ball's and opponents' relative positions. The system is also able to take into account the fact that a ball is moving, and to predict its position for better approaching it.

The work is organized as follows: In Sect. 2, the modules that compose the proposed dribbling engine are described. In Sect. 3, the IML approaches used for training the dribbling modules are introduced. The proposed methodology is validated in Sect. 4, using results collected during official RoboCup competition, but also with experiments that test each proposed module. Finally, in Sect. 5 conclusions of this work are drawn.

2 Dribbling Strategy

As already mentioned, the dribbling task is split in two decision problems: *where to dribble?*, which is related to decide the direction where the ball is pushed; and *how to dribble?*, which is concerned to the computation of velocity requests necessary for walking against the ball properly, pushing it towards the desired direction.

2.1 Dribbling Controller

This module is the responsible of solving the second decision problem mentioned in the previous paragraph. The controller computes the velocity requests to the walking engine in order to push the ball in the direction computed by the module that decides where to dribble, i.e. the linear velocities v_x, v_y and the rotation velocity v_θ. The state space is represented with the angles and distances shown in Fig. 1, where ρ is the robot-ball distance, γ is the robot-ball angle, and φ is the dribbling direction-robot complementary angle. In Fig. 1 the dribbling direction is the angle between the ball and the opponent goal, but in other cases it could be a different direction (e.g. due to obstacles). The angles γ and φ have to be zero for the robot to be aligned to the ball and target, and the distance ρ has to be low in order to keep possession of the ball.

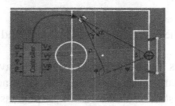

Fig. 1. Variables observed by the robot.

The assumption taken in this controller is very intuitive. It is supposed that each velocity axis is in charge of decreasing one of the variables γ, φ, and ρ. For instance, if the robot rotates with v_θ proportionally to the angle γ, the robot would be aligned to the ball. If simultaneously the sideward velocity v_y is proportional to the angle φ, the robot would walk by a circle centered in the ball position until it is aligned to the ball and the target; when the robot is aligned, it can walk against the ball with velocity v_x proportional to the distance ρ in order to walk faster when it is far, and slower when it is near for pushing to a close distance. In [10] was discussed a simple linear proportional controller based on the previous description, but in order to walk more effective paths, that work proposed to use a Takagi-Sugeno Fuzzy System as non-linear approximation for mapping from states to velocities, keeping the same assumption but with state dependent gains for the proportional controller.

2.2 Dribbling Direction Computation

The system described before had the target fixed in the center of the opponent's goal, and the direction to dribble was always towards that target. Another system is required to compute different directions in order to dribble towards the goal, but avoiding collisions and decreasing the risk of pushing the ball out from the field. Then, this system is related with the problem *where to dribble?* Since the robot can detect the opponents with its camera, it is possible to have a map of obstacles. However, differently to other leagues, in the SPL it is a very challenging problem to model and predict the behavior of the opponent team in this adversarial environment. Therefore, in our UChile Robotics Team, the opponents' positions are tracked but are assumed static for navigation purposes. Due to this assumption, and that there is no prediction of the future states, the navigation problem with the dribbling is not tackled with long term path planning approaches, rather, the strategy is to compute the dribbling direction in every time step, based on the updated state of the environment (i.e. the positions of the other robots and the ball).

The dribbling is not a typical navigation problem, since it has to be controlled the robot and ball positions, taking into account that the ball is moved with a very constrained strategy. Moreover, in our approach, the trajectory to go and push the ball is defined by the controller; and a high-level system computes the direction that the ball has to follow. Our proposal is inspired by the potential fields [12, 13] methods in which there are attracting and repulsive objects, whose forces depend on the distances. Nevertheless, this application has some specific characteristics that make necessary two considerations:

1. The attractive force of the opponent goal is constant, and does not decrease with the distance.
2. The opponents and posts are obstacles that need to be avoided. The repulsive force works when the robot starts dribbling far from any obstacle. However, it is possible that a dribbling episode starts with the ball in the possession of an opponent, i.e. the ball can be just beside the feet of the opponent. In those cases, the direction that minimizes the possibility of collision is an angle orthogonal to the line between the opponent and the ball.

In Fig. 2 are depicted some examples to show why is better to push the ball perpendicularly to the opponent when the ball is in the opponent's possession. The blue arrow is the direction to dribble with minimum probability of collision with the opponent (red jersey), taking into account that the goal is in the right hand side of the picture. In Fig. 2(a) the ball is beside the opponent; the trajectories red and yellow are likely to make a collision with the opponent before and after pushing the ball respectively. The red and gray directions can be the result of combining the attraction of the goal and the repulsive force of the obstacle. The gray path could be the case when the goal is very far and its force has low incidence whereas the obstacle has a high repulsive force. The result is a dangerous movement that definitely would end up with a punishment for our robot. In Fig. 2(b) the ball is very close to the opponent but behind it. In that case the repulsive force and the attraction of the goal in the right hand side of the picture would sum to the gray direction, which would end up with the robot dribbling by the path of the same color, which is also dangerous. On the other hand, the blue direction is the safest to take possession of the ball and keep dribbling to the goal in the right.

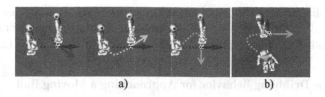

Fig. 2. Ball dribbling paths when the ball is close to the opponent (blue path is desired). (Color figure online)

With the previous considerations it is proposed a system that computes a sum of weighted candidate angles to dribble. Each candidate angle is related to an object of interest in the field. These objects are: the center of the opponent's goal, the goalposts, the final line of the field, and every opponent-robot in the field. The weights of each angle are obtained as the product between two factors: an importance weight k_o associated to each kind of object, and a distance measure between the object and the ball. The distance measure is calculated with the Euclidean distance evaluated in a Gaussian kernel, and then its values are in the range [0–1]; being this value close to one if the object is very near to the ball. The weight of the candidate angle to the goal depends only on its importance weight k_g, as shown in (1).

The candidate angles to dribble depend on each object: for the final line the candidate direction is an angle orthogonal to the line with direction to the own side of the team. This is for minimizing the risk of pushing the ball out of the field when it is very close to the line. The candidate direction of the opponent goal is the angle between the ball and the goal; this is the only attracting object. As described before the obstacles (opponent robots and goalposts) have candidate directions, which are perpendicular to the obstacle-ball line. Since there are two possible orthogonal angles, the chosen candidate is the one that has lower difference with the opponent's goal direction. The linear combination of the angles is normalized by the weights, for computing the dribbling direction D:

$$D = \frac{a_g k_g + \sum_{o=1}^{No} a_o w_o}{k_g + \sum_{o=1}^{No} w_o} = \frac{a_g k_g + \sum_{o=1}^{No} a_o k_o \exp\left(-\frac{d_o^2}{2\sigma_o^2}\right)}{k_g + \sum_{o=1}^{No} k_o \exp\left(-\frac{d_o^2}{2\sigma_o^2}\right)}$$

(1)

where a_g is the angle of the ball to the opponent goal, k_g is the constant importance weight associated to the goal, a_o is the dribbling candidate angle associated to the o-*th* interest object in the field, w_o is the distance dependent weight associated to each interest object. This is computed with the importance weight k_o and the Gaussian distance that takes the Euclidean distance d_o between the ball and the object o, and has an associated standard deviation σ_o to each type of object that defines a security distance, where the object has more influence on the dribbling direction.

With this direction D, the dribbling controller of Sect. 2.1 computes the walking velocities based on the variables depicted in Fig. 1, but the angle φ is computed with respect to D rather than the angle between the ball and the center of the target.

2.3 Using the Dribbling Behavior for Approaching a Moving Ball

The dribbling controller is always used when the robot is attacking even without having possession of the ball, e.g. when the robot is trying to "steal" the ball from an opponent or intercepting a pass done by either a teammate or an opponent. In order to address this challenge properly, the robot should move to a predicted position of the moving ball, like human players do.

Thus, the strategy applied in this work is to keep the described structure of the dribbling controller, and to track a predicted position of the ball instead of the actual one; the robot predicts the trajectory of the ball and evaluates if at certain point it is possible to intercept it. In case it is possible, then the robot moves to that position. Alternatively, the robot can move to a position that is close to the predicted final position of the ball.

3   Interactive Training of the Dribbling Engine

As it was explained in Sect. 1, it is necessary to make this system easily trainable by non-experts, since it can be required to change the parameters of the system during the competition before a game. For instance, when the walking engine is modified, the dribbling controller needs to be tuned again. The same happens when the team's strategy needs to be fixed for facing the characteristics of a specific opponent team. Interactive approaches are used for letting the users to adapt the dribbling controller module and the dribbling direction computation module easily using incremental and batch learning. Although the dribbling engine works by combining the dribbling controller and the dribbling direction computation modules, both are trained independently for the ease of the process. Then, for training the dribbling controller the direction to dribble is set always toward the opponent goal. For training the dribbling direction computation module, demonstrations can be provided using static game situations, without the need of running the dribbling controller (Sect. 3.2).

3.1   Incremental Learning for the Dribbling Controller

In [11] COACH was used for training policies with corrective feedback provided by human teachers during execution time. This feedback is a binary advice of how the executed continuous action has to be modified (increased or decreased). Then, using Stochastic Gradient Descent (SGD) the framework updates the policy; therefore the next time step the policy has a new set of parameters. In [11] the framework was presented for shaping approximations based on linear models of radial features. However, those principles can be applied to different types of approximation like the fuzzy model used in this problem. In Algorithm 1 is described how COACH works. More details can be seen in [11].

The users may have an insight of how an action can be modified for obtaining a better performance, but he/she hardly knows precisely the magnitude of the required correction. With the previous assumption, COACH updates the policy setting a constant error magnitude e, whereas its sign is given from the feedback binary signal.

For training a policy, lines 4-11 of Algorithm 1 are executed every time step during execution: first the agent observes the world (line 4), then the policy is computed and the action executed (lines 5–6), it checks if there is human advice: h has a value of 1 if the teacher says "increase the action", -1 for "decrease the action" and 0 if there is not feedback. If there is feedback, the error assumption is computed (line 10) and the SGD update of the policy is carried out taking into account specific considerations of the used approximation model. This framework is applied while the user sets the environment with several varied conditions of ball and robot initial positions, then provide feedback in order to shape the policy for achieving a desired behavior.

Algorithm 1: Basic Structure of COACH (simple framework).

```
1:    e ← constant  // error magnitude
2:    α ← constant  // learning parameters
3:    while true do
4:        s̄ ← getStateVec()
5:        a = P(s̄)
6:        TakeAction( P(s̄) )
7:        wait for next time step
8:        h ← gethumanCorrectiveAdvice()
9:        if h=! 0
10:           error ← h · e
11:           updatePolicyModel(α, error, s̄)
12:       end if
13:   end while
```

3.2 Training of the Dribbling Direction Computation Module

In the dribbling direction model expressed by (1) it is necessary to tune the parameters k_o for all the interest objects mentioned in Subsect. 2.2, and their deviations σ_o, which define the distance where each object o-th has more influence. The procedure for training the module consists in two alternative stages (the second one is optional): first, a batch learning process based on a dataset of instances demonstrated by the user is executed. Then, if the user considers necessary a local update, a second stage of tuning is carried out based on corrective feedback provided incrementally by the user with COACH (Algorithm 1 is applied). The second stage of tuning is not required when the user is satisfied by the resulting model of the batch learning process.

Batch Stage. It is collected a dataset of several static game situations wherein the user selects the desired direction to dribble. An interface shows an inactive scenario and allows the user to change the positions of the ball, and the opponent robots, but also to set the desired dribbling direction. Then, the positions (input) and direction (output) are attached as an instance of the demonstrations dataset. In other words, for gathering the direction demonstrations it is not necessary to have the dribbling controller running, and this can be done without active robots. With the dataset of situations and decisions, it is performed an optimization process for obtaining a set of parameters that fits the model to the data based on a Genetic Algorithm; in this case a set of parameters is represented by an individual that is evaluated by the fitness function selected for this problem and discussed below.

For selecting an appropriate fitness functions it must be taken into account that human teacher demonstrations can include instances that are noisy, inconsistent or ambiguous [14, 15]. For instance, in this context users can provide instances with different directions to dribble for similar states. The inconsistent data can be considered as outliers in the demonstrations set that do not need to be fitted with the model. However, with the typical mean square error (MSE) that takes into account only second order statistics and that is used in regressions, it is assumed Gaussianity in the error distribution. Then, the shortcoming of this is that, the outliers can have a large impact in the process of matching the model to the demonstrations.

Some works have used information-theoretic measures to face similar problems. For example [16] applies the minimization of the error entropy (MEE), which is equivalent to minimize the distance between the PDF of the desired data and the model output. This helps to fit the model to most of the data, and drops the importance of outliers that are far from the PDF, which contribute to have a high MSE. For this reason we selected as fitness function the MEE criterion described in [16].

Incremental Stage. After the batch stage, or if the user considers to fix the system's behavior for a specific situation, the user sets the particular ball and opponent positions with the interface used for collecting the demonstrations, and provides corrective feedback in the angles domain. While the advice is provided, COACH updates the model's parameters of (1) using SGD, with the derivatives of the model with respect to the parameter p_o, which can be k_o or σ_o in (2), where h is the human advice for increasing or decreasing the action, and η is the step size.

$$\Delta p_o = \eta h \frac{\partial D}{\partial p_o} \tag{2}$$

4   Experiments and Results

In participations to RoboCup competitions, the developed dribbling engine has had an important role as our (UChile Robotics Team) main attack strategy, but also in the defensive plays. Since most of the scored goals (GF) were derived from dribbling plays (65% in RoboCup 2016), we compare in Fig. 3 the average scored and allowed goals per match in the last 3 participations respecting the performance of 2013, when the team did not have a dribbling behavior. In RoboCup 2014, we used our first dribbling approach [10], and the average number of GF increased in 50%, while the allowed (GA) was reduced by 15%. In RoboCup 2015 and 2016 the dribbling strategy used was the presented in this work, except for the prediction strategy for approaching moving balls.

For those years the average of GF raised in ~120%, while the percentage of the GA decreased in about 55%. Data of these results is available online[1].

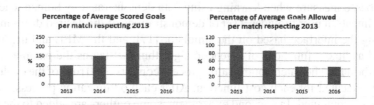

Fig. 3. Percentage of average goals per match compared to the performance of 2013.

Experiments were carried out for evaluating the performance of the different modules of the dribbling controller, and presented in the next sub sections. Some illustrations of the proposed system are shown in the video[2].

4.1 Dribbling Without Ball Interception

The performance of the dribbling controller trained with the approach described in [10], and used in the RoboCup 2014 competitions, is compared with the dribbling controller described in this work, and used in the RoboCup 2015 and 2016 competitions. The comparison is done in terms of time to dribble to a target, time that the robot lost ball possession while dribbling because it pushes the ball very far, and distance required to dribble to a target (the shorter the better). Several static scenarios with different initial ball and robot positions were run to dribble with the controllers obtained with both approaches. In Fig. 4 is shown the increase obtained in these performance indices when the dribbling controller presented in this work is used. As it can be observed, the proposed dribbling controller and its learning method obtains a policy that reduces 12% the time for dribbling from the initial point to the target, reduces in 50% the periods of time that the ball possession is lost, and also reduces to the half the additional walked distance with respect to the length of the line given by the connection of the points initial robot position-initial ball position-target position, in order to push the ball.

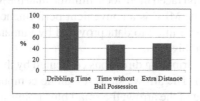

Fig. 4. Performance indices of the dribbling learned with the proposed strategy with respect to the original scheme.

---

[1] http://www.tzi.de/spl/bin/view/Website/WebHome.
[2] https://youtu.be/Oc9dMag4RFw.

4.2 Dribbling Direction Computation

This section presents experiments intended to show why it is more convenient to use an Entropy-based measure when learning using data demonstrated by human teachers. In the experiments, a user provides a set of demonstrations of the desired dribbling directions using the interface based on the simulator [17], and the MEE and the MSE are compared as fitness functions of a genetic algorithm that learns the parameters of (1) that fit to the data. The batch optimization process consists of 30 runs of the evolutionary algorithm executed for each cost function. After each optimization process, both cost functions are computed. In a second experiment, some outliers are added to the original dataset, ambiguous directions are associated to instances that represent similar situations of inputs already contained in the original set. The best performance of each experiment is presented along with the mean and standard deviation.

In Table 1, the results of the experiments with the original data demonstrated by the user show that when the optimization minimizes the MEE, it obtains even lower indices of MSE with respect to the achieved by the optimizer that minimizes the squared error. In the second experiment, the error metrics are increased as expected, but the same trend of the first experiment is obtained with wider differences, since in almost all the optimization runs using MEE as objective function, the found parameter sets computed lower MSE indices than the best of the obtained solutions from the optimization processes using the MSE cost function.

Table 1. Results of the batch learning for the dribbling direction module

Dataset:		Mean Square Error			Entropy Error		
	Fitness Function	Min	Mean	Std	Min	Mean	Std
Demonstrated	MSE	0.0245	0.0275	0.0028	0.0295	0.0370	0.0072
	MEE	0.0215	0.0248	0.0024	0.0231	0.0307	0.0057
Dataset:		Square Error			Entropy Error		
Demonstrated	Fitness Function	Min	Mean	Std	Min	Mean	Std
+	MSE	0.1132	0.1144	0.0011	0.0835	0.0873	0.0033
Outliers	MEE	0.1064	0.1082	0.0013	0.0794	0.0845	0.0037

The MSE fitness function faced more local minima than the MEE, and outliers played an important role on it. The MEE is a convenient performance metric for these cases wherein a model needs to be fitted to data provided by human users that time to time could be inconsistent or ambiguous.

In Fig. 5 are shown the dribbling directions computed by the system trained with the original dataset in part (a). The arrows show the angle computed to dribble if the ball position is at the beginning of the arrow; the small blue points are the positions of opponent robots.

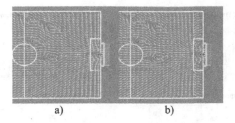

a)   b)

Fig. 5. Response of the dribbling direction computation system. (a) After the Batch Learning. (b) after local update with incremental learning using COACH

As a proof of concept of the incremental stage, a second experiment was executed for modifying the resulting policy of the batch process that used the original database of the previous experiment. In this case, the dribbling direction strategy is modified incrementally with COACH only for the specific cases when the ball is close to the final line, specifically between the corners and the goalposts, in order to make the robot to dribble more towards the front of the goal than dribbling from the side directly to the goal. This can be more convenient because in front of the goal there are more probabilities to score a goal after a kick. In part (b) of Fig. 5 it is shown the response of the same system after tuning it, it is possible to see that the final line now has more influence for rejecting the ball to the own side. This change of strategy was executed for some specific situations, while the behavior keeps the same performances for the rest of the situations.
Ball Interception

The strategy of intercepting the ball was validated in five different scenarios where the robot was standing in the middle of the field, and the ball was thrown from the opponent's goal to the other side of the field. Each scenario had an initial ball position and velocity, and the robot had to intercept the ball and start to dribble toward the opponent goal. The proposed strategy of going to the predicted ball position and the previous strategy of going to the current position without prediction were compared; ten executions per scenario were run for computing the average performance. The episodes were stopped when the robot got possession of the ball and was aligned to the target. The evaluation indices were the duration of the episode, and the final distance between the ball and the target, since this distance would be larger in the cases in which the robot does not intercept the ball at all. As it can be observed in Fig. 6, in most of the cases the time decreased between 5 to 40% when using ball prediction. In cases like the first experiment, wherein the robot lasts almost the same time to intercept the ball with both approaches, the distance of the ball to the target was smaller at the end of the episode when the ball prediction was used; i.e. for that case, it takes the same time to intercept the ball using both systems, but with the approach based on the ball prediction, the robot intercepts the ball in a better position because the decision was: "trying to anticipate the ball movement".

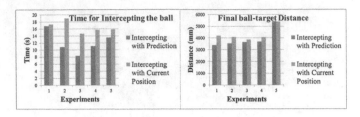

Fig. 6. Performance indices for five cases of ball interception

5   Conclusions

This work presented the dribbling strategy and its learning approach that has led to UChile Robotics Team to compete and qualify to the semifinals stage during RoboCup 2015 and 2016. The paper presents some comparative results obtained in the competitions, but also experiments that quantify the benefits of the training methods for developing the complete dribbling policy.

The reported experiments confirm that IML approaches are an excellent alternative to solve decision problems in which there is not enough capacity and observability to model the environment, and to compute a plan to achieve a goal. IML techniques benefit from the knowledge that users have about the problem, which can be shared with the agents easily, without the need of coding that knowledge.

Moreover, the results of the process for learning the dribbling direction module showed that using the EEM metric as cost function is useful in contexts where human teachers provide demonstrations that can be contaminated with ambiguous data. Additionally, it was shown that COACH makes possible to adjust the dribbling direction module behavior for specific game situations, without the necessity of gathering a new set of demonstrations and executing the batch process.

References

1. Li, X., Zell, A.: Nonlinear predictive control of an omnidirectional robot dribbling a rolling ball. In: Proceedings of IEEE International Conference Robotics Automation, pp. 1678–1683 (2008)
2. Riedmiller, M., Hafner, R., Lange, S., Lauer, M.: Learning to dribble on a real robot by success and failure. In: Proceedings of IEEE International Conference Robotics Automation, pp. 2207–2208 (2008)
3. Carvalho, A., Oliveira, R.: Reinforcement learning for the soccer dribbling task. In: 2011 IEEE Conference Computational Intelligence Games, CIG 2011, pp. 95–101 (2011)
4. Macalpine, P., Depinet, M., Stone, P.: UT Austin Villa 2014: RoboCup 3D simulation league champion via overlapping layered learning. In: Proceedings of Twenty-Ninth AAAI Conference Artificial. Intelligence, pp. 1–7 (2015)
5. Meriçli, Ç., Veloso, M., Akin, H.: Task refinement for autonomous robots using complementary corrective human feedback. Int. J. Adv. Robot. Syst. **8**, 68–79 (2011)
6. Barrett, S., Genter, K., Hester, T., Quinlan, M., Stone, P.: Controlled kicking under uncertainty. In: The Fifth Workshop on Humanoid Soccer Robots at Humanoids (2010)

7. Laue, T., Röfer, T., Gillmann, K., Wenk, F., Graf, C., Kastner, T.: B-human 2011 – eliminating game delays. In: Röfer, T., Mayer, N.M., Savage, J., Saranlı, U. (eds.) RoboCup 2011. LNCS (LNAI), vol. 7416, pp. 25–36. Springer, Heidelberg (2012). https://doi.org/10.1007/978-3-642-32060-6_3

8. Alcaraz-Jiménez, J.J., Herrero-Pérez, D., Martinez-Barberá, H., Alcaraz, J., Herrero, D., Mart, H.: A closed-loop dribbling gait for the standard platform league. In: Workshop on Humanoid Soccer Robots of the IEEE-RAS International Conference on Humanoid Robots (Humanoids) (2011)

9. Latzke, T., Behnke, S., Bennewitz, M.: Imitative reinforcement learning for soccer playing robots. In: Lakemeyer, G., Sklar, E., Sorrenti, Domenico G., Takahashi, T. (eds.) RoboCup 2006. LNCS (LNAI), vol. 4434, pp. 47–58. Springer, Heidelberg (2007). https://doi.org/10.1007/978-3-540-74024-7_5

10. Leottau, L., Celemin, C., Ruiz-del-Solar, J.: Ball dribbling for humanoid biped robots: a reinforcement learning and fuzzy control approach. In: Bianchi, Reinaldo A.C., Akin, H.Levent, Ramamoorthy, S., Sugiura, K. (eds.) RoboCup 2014. LNCS (LNAI), vol. 8992, pp. 549–561. Springer, Cham (2015). https://doi.org/10.1007/978-3-319-18615-3_45

11. Celemin, C., Ruiz-del-Solar, J.: Interactive learning of continuous actions from corrective advice communicated by humans. In: Almeida, L., Ji, J., Steinbauer, G., Luke, S. (eds.) RoboCup 2015. LNCS (LNAI), vol. 9513, pp. 16–27. Springer, Cham (2015). https://doi.org/10.1007/978-3-319-29339-4_2

12. Damas, Bruno D., Lima, Pedro U., Custódio, Luis M.: A modified potential fields method for robot navigation applied to dribbling in robotic soccer. In: Kaminka, Gal A., Lima, Pedro U., Rojas, R. (eds.) RoboCup 2002. LNCS (LNAI), vol. 2752, pp. 65–77. Springer, Heidelberg (2003). https://doi.org/10.1007/978-3-540-45135-8_6

13. Tang, L., Liu, Y., Qiu, Y., Gu, G., Feng, X.: The strategy of dribbling based on artificial potential field. In: 2010 3rd International Conference Advanced Computer Theory Engineering, vol. 2, pp. 307–311 (2010)

14. Argall, B.D., Chernova, S., Veloso, M., Browning, B.: A survey of robot learning from demonstration. Rob. Auton. Syst. 57, 469–483 (2009)

15. Chernova, S., Thomaz, A.L.: Robot learning from human teachers. Synth. Lect. Artif. Intell. Mach. Learn. 8, 1–121 (2014)

16. Erdogmus, D., Principe, J.C.: An error-entropy minimization algorithm for supervised training of nonlinear adaptive systems. IEEE Trans. Signal Process. 50, 1780–1786 (2002)

17. Laue, T., Spiess, K., Röfer, T.: SimRobot – a general physical robot simulator and its application in robocup. In: Bredenfeld, A., Jacoff, A., Noda, I., Takahashi, Y. (eds.) RoboCup 2005. LNCS (LNAI), vol. 4020, pp. 173–183. Springer, Heidelberg (2006). https://doi.org/10.1007/11780519_16

Collision-Detection
for RoboCup@Work-Competitions

Sebastian Zug, Martin Seidel, Jonathan Beckhaus, and Nico Winkelsträter[✉]

Otto-von-Guericke University, Magdeburg, Germany
{Zug,maseidel}@ovgu.de,
{beckhaus,winkelst}@st.ovgu.de

Abstract. The RobotCup@Work league is motivated by industrial scenarios where objects has to be automatically transported between different working positions. During these operations the rules prohibit and
penalize collisions of robots with the arena. Human referees distributed
around the arena are responsible for identifying occurred collisions and
for their annotation. If a robot moves parts of the arena, a collision is
obvious. But, a slight contact is hard to recognize, since not all referees
do have a permanent line of sight to the robot and distraction, caused
by the surrounding, fatigue, or personal perception are human factors
that might affect the outcome of a run. A majority vote might smooth
the results, but it is an unsatisfactory solution in debatable situations.

We describe the evaluation of a proof-of-concept implementation for
a distributed collision detection, based on a network of acceleration sensors. We investigated different configurations - a single device mounted
directly on the robot, an instrumented arena and a combination of both
approaches. The paper summarizes a first evaluation based on a proof-
of-concept implementation.

Keywords: RoboCup · RoboCup@Work · Collision-Detection

1 Introduction

1.1 Motivation

The RoboCup RoboCup@Work league[1] (short @Work) is one of the youngest
competition in the RoboCup family. It is inspired by industrial mobile manipulation scenarios comprises separate runs. Each of them addresses different aspects
of mapping, navigation, and manipulation capabilities for transporting assembly parts from one working place to another. At the begin of each run the robot
receives an automatically generated list of transportation tasks from the refbox[2] [10]. A local planner is responsible to calculate an optimal task execution

---

[1] RoboCup@Work website: http://www.robocupatwork.org/.

[2] The referee-box or shorten refbox is a software controlling robot competitions. Its
capabilities varies per competition and reaches from time keeping, task generation,
and scoring. https://github.com/robocup-at-work/at_work_central_factory_hub.

© Springer Nature Switzerland AG 2018
H. Akiyama et al. (Eds.): RoboCup 2017, LNAI 11175, pp. 376–384, 2018.
https://doi.org/10.1007/978-3-030-00308-1_31

(a)   **(b)**

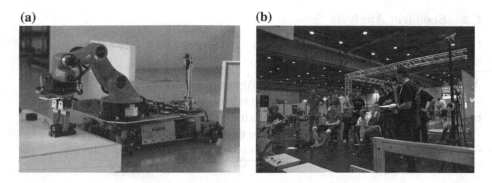

Fig. 1. (a) @Work robot of the robOTTO team while grasping an object. (b) @Work referees monitoring a run during WorldCup in Leipzig 2016.

sequence and to start its implementation. After reaching the selected working desk, the robot has to recognize the correct objects and to grasp them, as visible in Fig. 1a. Afterwards the robot has to transport and place the objects to the corresponding desk or into an object-specific cavity. From run to run the complexity increases permanently by varying the types and numbers of manipulation objects, additional obstacles, and positions of forbidden areas.

At the end of each run the number of correctly picked and placed objects and the execution time is mapped on a score. Dropping an object or any contact with the environment during the navigation phase [8] generate penalties. Currently, human referees are responsible to detect the occurrence of a collision. During a run, they are distributed around the arena, monitor the competition and log their observations manually. These logs are aggregated and evaluated after the run. Based on our experience, intermediate results would be helpful for teams to decide whether to restart a bad run within the remaining time or to let it continue. Especially for debatable situations this is not implementable without stopping a run's execution followed by a discussion of the referees. But, this procedure would disturb the atmosphere and the attractiveness of the competition. Another reason against the current concept is the number of referees necessary to monitor the whole arena. Many teams complain the required effort, one participant is permanently blocked due to the referee service.

Even in real sport events it is debated to replace impartial referees to some aspects. In [4] for instance the authors showed that the decision can be biased by such simple factors as the colours of the sportswear (blue/red). An automatic referee systems for sport or robotic competitions could guarantee a transparent and objective evaluation as well as an intuitive just-in-time presentation of received information. Correspondingly, most of the leagues already integrate automated referee systems. Especially the teams with a football background apply goal line referees based on vision systems. We therefore propose an on-line collision detection, which is based on an external sensor system that directly interacts with the referee box. This paper describes the challenges and presents a proof-of-concept implementation.

1.2   Scenario Analysis

In a first step we summarize our @Work experiences and define a list of assumptions and requirements:

A1. The setup has to cover heterogeneous robots. The @Work League allows participants to design an individual robot system. Most groups use customized Kuka youBots, but, currently founded, new teams started to design their systems from scratch. Hence, we have to develop our collision detection systems that does not rely on any interface (power supply, communication media, assembly points) on the robot.

A2. We have no access on robot's state. We want to receive a high degree of acceptance for our collision detection system. Consequently, it is not intended to define an API which has to be implemented by the teams providing robot data as position, path, velocity information.

A3. The characteristics of the floor is unpredictable. The arena of the @Work league stands directly on the floor. Its material and characteristics vary for each event in general and changes locally caused by a heterogeneous surface as well as by supply shafts and openings too.

A4. People might touch the arena elements while watching the runs. During a run, all participants are next to the arena observing the robot. It is possible that elements are touched or at worst moved in this exciting situation.

A5. The setup of the arena ($\approx 9 \times 6$ m) is changed at every competition. The structure of the arena is redesigned for each competition. The entire length of the arena elements is approximately 25 m in combination with desks of different height and an rotating round table. The needed flexibility limits the applicability of global sensing systems such as tactile sensors. Additionally, the size of the arena makes it difficult to cover the whole setup with only one sensor.

2   Development of a Collision Detection System

2.1   Definition of an Appropriate Sensor System

The assumptions A1 to A5 specify the preconditions of a sensing system suitable to recognize contact and collision situations. In contrast to other implementations of automated referee systems embedded in RoboCup competitions (Middle Size League [3], Standard Platform League [9] or Small Size League [12]) we cannot apply common RGB or RGB-D sensor systems. The only (slightly similar) approach is discussed in the Standard Platform League whose organizers intend to detect unsporting behaviour (specific collision of two robots) automatically this year [11]. Based on our assumptions (A5), it is not possible to implement a camera based localization system offering the required spatial resolution for detecting collisions in a large scale, highly dynamic environment as the @Work arena. During the last German Open we had the opportunity to evaluate an

OptiTrack system covering the whole arena[3]. The system worked fine as a reference positioning system but it is not able to identify a permitted interaction of a robot and a arena element correctly.

An alternative sensing element are mechanical or tactile sensors [6]. But these sensor types are not applicable for our scenario due to the length of the arena contour (A5) and the unpredictable structure of the robots (A1). All teams mounted laser scanner on the front and backside of the robot. Hence, a spontaneous integration of a bumper system to the robot or a complete coverage of all arena parts by a tactile skin is not possible. Additionally, the occurrence of a sensor ring would change robot's geometry and consequently disturb in path planning and execution algorithms (A1, A2).

Consequently, we evaluated the implementation of an Inertial Measurement Unit (IMU). While evaluating acceleration and rotational speed values, it can be positioned flexibly at the robot. The literature describes the usage of inertial force/torque sensors or accelerometers. Both are used either for mobile robots [7] or in manipulators [1]. As described in the mentioned papers, these sensors demand a complex sensor data processing strategy classifying disturbances and actual collisions in a reliable way [2].

2.2 Experimental Setup

Based on this decision we evaluated 3 concepts for mounting the acceleration sensors - an individual one tagged onto the robot, a distributed system of n sensors mounted to the arena and a combined setup exchanging the detection results. The evaluation was done in our laboratory with a robot of the robOTTO team.

We designed a test setup that combines two Arduino Mega ADK equipped with a MPU9250[4] sensor. Figure 2 depicts the robot on the left

Fig. 2. Experimental setup integrating to accelerometers and a bumper array

side, with an IMU measurement unit mounted on top of it. An array of bumpers in front generated the ground truth signal. The IMU tagged to the arena element is visible in front. All sensor systems were connected to one PC recording all data.

2.3 Robot Centric Solution

While moving the robot in a straight line to the instrumented arena part we recorded the acceleration values (vector norm of horizontal parts) and the

---

[3] Provided by the European Robotics League (ERL).
[4] https://www.invensense.com/products/motion-tracking/9-axis/mpu-9250/.

bumper outputs for two different scenarios (collision with an arena segment, free movement and braking till stop) with speeds between 0.1 and 0.7 m/s. Figure 3 illustrates the bad signal to noise ratio caused by the vibrations of the youBot's omnidirectional wheels. As visible in all diagrams, this effect is correlated with the speed of the robot. For the further development it is remarkable that the peaks, caused by a collision with the table at low speed (upper diagram on the left side), are much smaller than the acceleration amplitude of a free run (lower diagram on the right side). The dashed red line represents the point in time, when one of the bumpers was activated. Each bumper shows a specific immersion depth before it becomes conductive. Consequently, we have to consider a jitter when evaluating the quality of the local collision detectors.

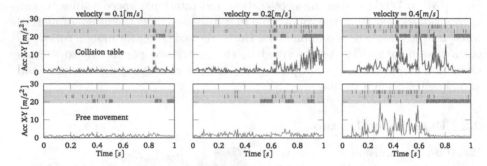

Fig. 3. Acceleration amplitudes for collision and free run situations. The red line shows the occurrence of a collision measured by the bumpers front of the robot

Due to the characteristics of the signal the motion detection capabilities of the MPU 9250 or static threshold for acceleration as described in [5] could not be applied. We implemented three different detection algorithms those results are marked within the gray bars in Fig. 3:

1. a simple gradient base approach comparing the current deviation of the signal with a static threshold ($\Delta acc > 2.0 \, \text{m/s}^2$),
2. a statistical evaluation of the quantiles of the last 25 samples related to the actual measurement and
3. a T-test for the means of historic ($n = 100$) and a current sample set ($n = 10$).

The second approach generates a constant number of false positives in each case, while the count of faulty classifications increases for the gradient filter significantly for higher velocities. The T-test provides a reliable but delayed detection result for lower velocities but shows weakness for higher speed levels. It is important to realize, that the evaluation was done off-line. Due to the needed computational performance, the second and the third detection algorithms cannot provide the result within the refresh period of 5 ms. A more powerful hardware would help to cope with this problem.

A combination of the first two filters detected all collisions successfully, but generated a huge amount of false positives too. An improved filter mechanism or a fusion of multiple methods would improve the quality of the classification. A conjunction of our filter outputs reduces false positives by half. However, despite all efforts, this output does not fulfil our requirements.

Result 1: *The correct identification of collisions requires a multi-detector strategy. It is difficult to configure these algorithms so that they generates a reliable output for the whole spectrum of velocities.*

Arena Centric Solution We intend to stabilize the detection quality by additional measurements aggregated at the arena elements. In a first research series we analysed the characteristic pattern of a collision and the stability of these measurements. Figure 4 shows outputs for collisions with different speeds. The significant change of the signal caused by a collision, enables a precise detection of a collision situation. The IMU includes a digital signal processor called Motion Processor that fuses acceleration and gyroscope data It offers motion detection that can be configured flexibly according to signal amplitudes and patterns. In our case, we defined a acceleration threshold based on a noise analysis of the used sensor.

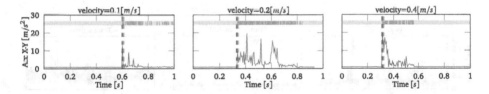

Fig. 4. Acceleration amplitudes measured at the table according to the velocity of the robot

Figure 4 depicts the outputs for different speed levels. The line illustrates the cumulative acceleration occurring in horizontal direction in case of a collision with the robot. All critical situations were correctly detected, we could not recognise any false positives or false negatives.

Result 2: *The collision detection units integrated in the wall elements are able to identify even slight touches with low velocities. The execution effort is very limited, due to the fact, that the filter is implemented in hardware inside the sensor.*

Combined Solution Beside the successful results of the arena centric solution we have to consider probably occurring external disturbances effecting the arena elements (A4). Visitors or participants may disturb the walls or desks during a run. Hence, we intended to combine the collision signals from both origins. This configuration was evaluated off-line due to the demanded computational power for analysing the robot based data sets.

We evaluated unreliable detector outputs from robot signals and filtered them by recognized collisions of the arena sensor. Due to the unreliable output of the robot based detectors we generate a huge amount of fault positives on this side, but still miss collisions for very low velocities. Hence, the validity of the common result was much lower; this result does not justify the additional efforts.

Result 3: *The combined result of the detector output is not suitable to identify external disturbances, especially if the robot touches an arena element with a low velocity (< 0.1 cm/s).*

3   Evaluation at RoboCup

Until now the evaluation was done in the laboratory. During the German Open 2017 we had the opportunity to extend experiments on three other @Work robots. We changed the setup in three points. Firstly, the measurement unit was glued (instead of screwed) on a arbitrary free position on robot's surface. Secondly, the bumper array was replaced by a video system as the ground truth sensor. Lastly, the algorithm implemented for the arena IMU was improved and includes an automated offset calibration and parameter definition now.

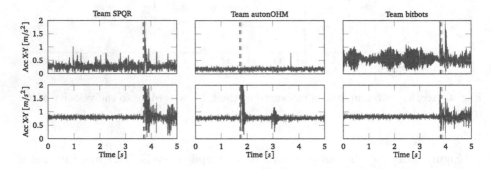

Fig. 5. Exemplary outputs of the IMU measurement units for low speed collisions $0.05 m/s$ and $5s$, The upper line depicts the acceleration data from the robots, the lower the measurements from the arena element.

During the investigations we focused on velocities smaller than 0.1 m/s; in all other cases the preliminary experiments generated perfect matches. Figure 5 depicts the new results for three robots hitting the arena element with a speed of 0.05 m/s.

All robots show an individual pattern of acceleration data. Based on their mechanical structure and the assembly point of the IMU, it ranges from a constant noise level (team autonOHM) up to a time correlated oscillation (team bitbots). These measurements confirm our Result 2 and illustrate that it is not possible to find a common filter strategy and an optimal sensor position without a series of preliminary investigations. This cannot be provided during the competition. Consequently, the damping effect in case of team autonOHM avoids a correct detection of the collision (marked by the red line) at all!

In contrast, the reimplementation of the detector provided perfect results from the instrumented arena for all evaluated velocity levels (0.03 m and 0.05 m). Besides, we did not receive any side effect by humans or other robots moving close to the arena.

4 Future Work

The current proof-of-concept implementation of the instrumented arena hast to be enhanced in different directions. We have to investigate an optimal dissemination of the sensing elements on the arena elements. Additionally, the sensor hardware has to be enhanced by an communication interface (wired / non-wired) and to be integrated into the refbox. A first multiple device test is planned during RoboCup 2017 in Nagoya.

References

1. Cho, C.N., Kim, J.H., Lee, S.D., Song, J.B.: Collision detection and reaction on 7 dof service robot arm using residual observer. J. Mech. Sci. Technol. **26**(4), 1197–1203 (2012)
2. Cho, C.N., Song, J.B.: Collision detection algorithm robust to model uncertainty. Int. J. Control., Autom. Syst. **11**(4), 776–781 (2013)
3. Dias, A., Almeida, J., Martins, A., Silva, E.: Real-time visual ground-truth system for indoor robotic applications. In: Sanches, J.M., Micó, L., Cardoso, J.S. (eds.) IbPRIA 2013. LNCS, vol. 7887, pp. 304–313. Springer, Heidelberg (2013). https://doi.org/10.1007/978-3-642-38628-2_36
4. Feltman, R., Elliot, A.J.: The influence of red on perceptions of relative dominance and threat in a competitive context. J. Sport. Exerc. Psychol. **33**(2), 308–314 (2011)
5. He, F., Du, Z., Sun, L., Lin, R.: Collision signal processing and response in an autonomous mobile robot. Neural Parallel Sci. Comput. **15**(3), 319 (2007)
6. Kerpa, O., Weiss, K., Worn, H.: Development of a flexible tactile sensor system for a humanoid robot. In: Proceeding of Intelligent Robots and Systems 2003 (IROS 2003), IEEE/RSJ International Conference on 2003, vol. 1, pp. 1–6. IEEE (2003)
7. Kim, K.S., Llado, T., Sentis, L.: Full-body collision detection and reaction with omnidirectional mobile platforms: a step towards safe human-robot interaction. Auton. Robot. **40**(2), 325–341 (2016)
8. Kraetzschmar, G.K., Hochgeschwender, N., Nowak, W., Hegger, F., Schneider, S., Dwiputra, R., Berghofer, J., Bischoff, R.: RoboCup@Work: competing for the factory of the future. In: Bianchi, R.A.C., Akin, H.L., Ramamoorthy, S., Sugiura, K. (eds.) RoboCup 2014. LNCS (LNAI), vol. 8992, pp. 171–182. Springer, Cham (2015). https://doi.org/10.1007/978-3-319-18615-3_14
9. Nezhad, M.S.R., Ghiasvand, O.A.: Ground-truth localisation system for humanoid soccer robots using RGB-D camera. Int. J. Comput. Vis. Robot. **7**(3), 285–301 (2017)

10. Niemueller, T., Zug, S., Schneider, S., Karras, U.: Knowledge-based instrumentation and control for competitive industry-inspired robotic domains. KI-Künstliche Intell. **30**(3), 289–299 (2016)
11. Weitzenfeld, A., Biswas, J., Akar, M., Sukvichai, K.: RoboCup small-size league: past, present and future. In: Bianchi, R.A.C., Akin, H.L., Ramamoorthy, S., Sugiura, K. (eds.) RoboCup 2014. LNCS (LNAI), vol. 8992, pp. 611–623. Springer, Cham (2015). https://doi.org/10.1007/978-3-319-18615-3_50
12. Zhu, D., Veloso, M.: Event-based automated refereeing for robot soccer. Auton. Robot. **41**(7), 1–23 (2016)

An Omni-Directional Kick Engine
for Humanoid Robots with Parameter
Optimization

Pedro Pena$^{(\boxtimes)}$, Joseph Masterjohn, and Ubbo Visser

Department of Computer Science, University of Miami, 1365 Memorial Drive,
Coral Gables, FL 33146, USA
{pedro,joe,visser}@cs.miami.edu

Abstract. Incorporating a dynamic kick engine that is both fast and effective is pivotal to be competitive in one of the world's biggest AI and robotics initiative: RoboCup. Using the NAO robot as a testbed, we developed a dynamic kick engine that can generate a kick trajectory with an arbitrary direction without prior input or knowledge of the parameters of the kick. The trajectories are generated using cubic splines (two degree three polynomials with a via-point). The trajectories are executed while the robot is dynamically balancing on one foot. When the robot swings the leg for the kick motion, unprecedented forces might be applied on the robot. To compensate for these forces, we developed a Zero Moment Point (ZMP) based preview controller that minimizes the ZMP error. Although a variety of kick engines have been implemented by others, there are only a few papers on how kick engine parameters have been optimized to give an effective kick or even a kick that minimizes energy consumption and time. Parameters such as kick configuration, limit of the robot, or shape of the polynomial can be optimized. We propose an optimization framework based on the Webots simulator to optimize these parameters. Experiments of the physical robot show promising results.

1 Introduction

Generating dynamic motions on a robot without explicitly programming the motion is a difficult task and a fairly new research area. Kick engines such as [1,2,8,10,13,15] have been developed for the NAO robot and although they are dynamic, there are static values incorporated into the kicks such as retraction points, foot position from floor, hip/ankle pitch and hip/ankle roll ratio, and shapes of trajectories. These values are usually derived from empirical observations and are not guaranteed to be optimal values. The difficulty of the task is to optimize parameters on the physical robot because the robot is limited by hardware, energy consumption, and most importantly real time execution. Hence, the robot cannot run for thousands or millions of iterations to get a good set of parameters. Other dynamic kick engines such as [16] developed a kick engine for the THOR-MANG from Robotis that generate static kick motions. Lengagneua

© Springer Nature Switzerland AG 2018
H. Akiyama et al. (Eds.): RoboCup 2017, LNAI 11175, pp. 385–397, 2018.
https://doi.org/10.1007/978-3-030-00308-1_32

et al. [7] have developed a kick engine that incorporates optimization offline and a re-planning step when the kick is executed but do not optimize on the physical robot or use a simulation software that takes into account hardware properties of the robot. We propose a new kick engine for the NAO robot that can dynamically balance on one foot using a Zero Moment Point (ZMP) based preview controller while also generating kick trajectories using cubic splines. The values of the kick trajectories are optimized in the Webots Simulator to get a good set of parameter values. The overview of the control frame work is presented in Fig. 1.

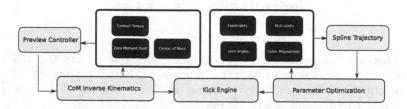

Fig. 1. Overview of the control framework for the kick engine

The major components of the control framework are preview controller, spline trajectory, center of mass (CoM) inverse kinematics, and parameter optimization. The paper is organized as follows: we discuss relevant work in the next section and describe the ZMP based preview controller in Sect. 3. Section 4 describes how to move the center of mass to the desired position, and Sect. 5 describes how the kick trajectory is generated. The model optimization on the kick is discussed in Sect. 6, and our experiments and results are explained in Sect. 7, followed by the conclusion in Sect. 8.

2   Related Work

Wenk et al. [13] developed a kick engine that generates online kick motions using trajectories generated by Bézier curves, but in order to create such motions, the humanoid robot has to dynamically balance on one foot so it can handle any force generated by the kick. In order to find these forces, Wenk et al. used inverse dynamics to calculate the ZMP. Inverse dynamics can be computed such that given the acceleration, we work out the forces. The Inverse Dynamics problem was solved using a variation of the Recursive Newton Euler Algorithm (RNEA). For the kick trajectories the authors used Bézier curves that are continuously differentiable to generate a kick.

Böckmann et al. [2] provided a mass spring damper model to model motor behavior, and modified the ZMP equation to account for this behavior to get the actual motor position rather than a believed state. The authors also adapted Dynamic Motion Primitives (DMP) to generate kick trajectories. Kick trajectories are usually generated from Bézier curves or via-point kick trajectories, but here the authors used a PD controller with a forcing term in the transformation system to control the shape of the trajectory.

Sung et al. [11] used full body motion planning and via-point representation to generate joint angle trajectories. These trajectories are generated using five degree polynomials and via points are specified to constrain the swing trajectory. For the balancing the authors also used ZMP. In order to create efficient full body motion trajectories the author used optimization techniques such as Semi-Infinite Programming (SIP) to specify constraints such as minimal energy and torque. The optimization also dealt with joint redundancy.

Yi et al. [16] used THOR-OP (Tactical Hazardous Operations Robot - Open Platform) full sized humanoid robot to generate kick and walk motions for the AdultSize League in RoboCup 2014. The robot had a hybrid walking controller that used two types of controllers: ZMP preview controller and a ZMP based reactive controller. The ZMP based reactive controller used techniques such as Central Pattern Generators to create motions that require less computation than the ZMP preview controller. The kick motions generated were handled by the hybrid walking controller to create smooth transitions between the dynamic walk and strong kick.

The kick engine of Xu et al. [15] is separated into four phases: preparation, retraction, execution, and wrap-up phase. The authors use a grid space to find the kick that maximizes the distance in the retraction point and minimizes the angle between the direction of the foot and the direction of the ball. The maximum distance of the retraction point of the foot is assumed to create the greatest impulse. The stabilization of the robot is done with a Body Inclination Control that controls the torso angle to maintain the center of mass in the support polygon. The authors also found the reachable space through experimentation. The kick engine was experimented on the NAO robot.

Although these approaches use a dynamic kick engine that utilizes a controller for balancing and generate kicks online or offline, they all lack a framework that uses model optimization to find kicks under certain constrains such as strongest kick or fastest kick. In our approach, we use a controller for balancing and cubic splines for kick trajectory and then we use optimization to find a good set of parameters for the kick. Next, we will discuss each component of the kick engine.

3   ZMP Based Preview Controller

This section describes how the robot stabilizes on the supporting foot. A ZMP based Preview Controller is used to keep the Zero Moment Point (*ZMP*) in the support polygon. The first section describes the definition of ZMP and how it is derived. The following section will illustrate how the Preview Controller uses the ZMP to stabilize the robot (Figs. 2 and 3).

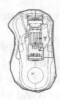 

Fig. 2. Support polygon   **Fig. 3.** ZMP location

3.1 Zero Moment Point

In order for the humanoid robot to balance, it has to maintain contact with the ground. When the robot is at rest, the Center of Mass (CoM) has to be inside the support polygon. The CoM is defined by:

$$CoM = \frac{m_j \mathbf{c}_j}{M} \tag{1}$$

where $(m_j, \mathbf{c}_j)$ is the weight and position vector respectfully of the jth link, and $M = \sum m_j$. The support polygon is the area touched by the robot and the ground. When the robot is kicking, the area touched by the robot in the ground is the supporting foot. The support polygon is the convex hull of the foot touching the ground and it is defined by

$$CoS = \left\{ \sum \alpha_j \mathbf{p}_j | \alpha_j \geq 0, \sum \alpha_j = 1, \mathbf{p}_j \in S(j = 1, ..., N) \right\}$$

where $S(j = 1, ..., N)$ is the set of edges of the supporting foot. When the robot is at rest, the CoM criterion is enough to stabilize the robot, but if the robot is in motion, the CoM might leave the support polygon. In that case, we can use another criterion to verify the supporting foot still has contact with the ground.

The dynamic criterion for the robot to maintain contact with the ground is the Zero Moment Point (*ZMP*) [12]. In order to correctly balance the robot, roboticists use ZMP to keep the robot from falling. The ZMP is the point where the robot's contact point with the ground does not generate a moment about the y and x axis. This is defined by

$$ZMP = \{p_o \times f + \tau = 0 | \tau_x, \tau_y = 0\}. \tag{2}$$

Therefore the robot does not rotate about these axes and tip over. Notice that the ZMP criterion does not say anything about the moment about the z axis. This rotation is allowed in the ZMP but it does not fall but rotate about the z axis. In order to derive the ZMP, the x and y components of (2) need to be solved and approximated by discretized points:

$$ZMP_{approx.} = \{(p_i - p_o) \times f_i + \tau_i = 0 | \tau_{ix}, \tau_{iy} = 0\}.$$

Therefore,

$$p_x = \frac{\sum_{i=1}^{N} -\tau_{iy} - (p_{iz} - p_z)f_{ix} + p_{ix}f_{iz}}{\sum_{i=1}^{N} f_{iz}} \ and \tag{3}$$

$$p_y = \frac{\sum_{i=1}^{N} \tau_{ix} - (p_{iz} - p_z)f_{iy} + p_{iy}f_{iz}}{\sum_{i=1}^{N} f_{iz}}. \tag{4}$$

This is a very simple model, the full dynamics of the physical world can not be captured. Hence, a Kalman filter was used to add noise to the model. The measurement model used for the Kalman filter was the foot sensors from the NAO robot. The data from the foot sensors were used to solve for (3) and (4). The foot sensors give us values for the normal ground force exerted at the contact points. Therefore all the terms in (3) and (4) except f_{iz} are zero, resulting in

$$p_x = \frac{\sum_{i=1}^{N} p_{ix}f_{iz}}{\sum_{i=1}^{N} f_{iz}} \quad p_y = \frac{\sum_{i=1}^{N} p_{iy}f_{iz}}{\sum_{i=1}^{N} f_{iz}}. \tag{5}$$

The NAO robot has four sensors in the each foot, and it can be used to measure the magnitude of the force. Using (5) and the magnitude and position of each sensor, the empirical ZMP can be computed. For the belief model of the Kalman filter, we use (2) and we approximate the ZMP using a linear inverted pendulum [3,5]. The dynamics of the inverted pendulum is well understood in physics and it is used to model the dynamics of balancing for the humanoid robot. The top of the pendulum is assumed to be the CoM of the robot and the bottom part is assumed to be negligible. Therefore, we need to assume that the legs of the robot do not weigh much compared to the center of mass of the robot. Therefore, the linear and angular momentum of the center of mass is

$$\mathcal{P} = M\dot{c} \quad \mathcal{L} = c \times M\dot{c} \tag{6}$$

To compute the approximated ZMP, we use (2) and (6) and get,

$$p_x = \frac{(z-p_z)\ddot{x}}{\ddot{z}+g} \quad p_y = \frac{(z-p_z)\ddot{y}}{\ddot{z}+g} \tag{7}$$

With a belief and measurement model, we can get a close approximation to the ZMP. We can now use a controller that will control the ZMP to maintain it in the polygon of the supporting foot. This will be discussed in the next section.

3.2 Preview Controller

The ZMP Preview Controller is based on the cart table model and it is a closed-loop system [3,4,6]. This model assumes that given the cart on the table, the Center of Pressure (*CoP*) (foot of the table) is affected, and in turn, affects the stability of the table (ZMP is affected). The ZMP Preview Controller is based on future ZMP positions of the robot. Since the robot is not walking, it is assumed that the robot will have the same future preview gains. This is an important simplification because it helps with the computation time. The Preview Controller uses a Linear Quadratic Regulator (*LQR*) to find the optimal values of the gains,

$$J = \sum_{j=1}^{\infty} \left\{ Q(p_j^{ref} - p_j)^2 + Ru^2j \right\}$$

where R and Q are weights. The LQR tries to solve a Riccati differential equation for the optimal values,

$$\mathbf{P} = \mathbf{A}^T \mathbf{P} \mathbf{A} + \mathbf{c}^T Q \mathbf{c} - \mathbf{A}^T \mathbf{P} \mathbf{b} (R + \mathbf{b}^T \mathbf{P} \mathbf{b})^{-1} \mathbf{b}^T \mathbf{P} \mathbf{A}$$

where,

$$\mathbf{A} = \begin{bmatrix} 1 & \delta t & \delta t^2/2 \\ 0 & 1 & \delta t \\ 0 & 0 & 1 \end{bmatrix}, \quad \mathbf{b} = \begin{bmatrix} \delta t^3/6 \\ \delta t^2/2 \\ \delta t \end{bmatrix}, \quad \mathbf{c} = \begin{bmatrix} 1 & 0 & -z/g \end{bmatrix}$$

and tries to minimize the cost function $\mathbf{J}$ by using the input and $\mathbf{K}$ such that,

$$u_k = -\mathbf{K} x_k + \begin{bmatrix} f_1 & f_2 & \cdots & f_N \end{bmatrix} \begin{bmatrix} p_{k+1}^{ref} \\ \vdots \\ p_{k+N}^{ref} \end{bmatrix}$$

where

$$\mathbf{K} = (R + \mathbf{b}^T \mathbf{P} \mathbf{b})^{-1} \mathbf{b}^T \mathbf{P} \mathbf{A}$$
$$f_i = (R + \mathbf{b}^T \mathbf{P} \mathbf{b})^{-1} \mathbf{b}^T (\mathbf{A} - \mathbf{b} \mathbf{K})^{T*(i-1)} \mathbf{c}^T Q$$

This calculation is only done once and it is used for the Preview Controller. When all the optimal values have been calculated, the state transition equation can be used to compute the next CoM position, velocity and acceleration,

$$\mathbf{x_{k+1}} = \mathbf{A} \mathbf{x_k} + \mathbf{b} u_k$$

It is important to note that $p^{ref} = \left\{ p_{k+1}^{ref}, \cdots p_{k+N}^{ref} \right\}$ will always be the same because p^{ref} will always be in the supporting foot of the kick and it will not move. Therefore, it will save computation time since p^{ref} is a constant when computing u_k. When u_k is computed and we find the next CoM, then we need to move the CoM to next position. This will be discussed in the next section.

4   Analytical Approximation for Inverse Kinematics

In order to move the CoM to the position that was given by the Preview Controller, an analytical approximation using Inverse Kinematics can be used to move the joints to the correct position. Since the Center of Mass is not directly actuated by a specific joint, an analytical approximation can be used. The position of the CoM can be affected by the leg joints. Let's assume the CoM is above the leg joints, then we can approximate the CoM using the hip joints and ankle joints. In the frontal plane, the CoM can be affected by the hip and ankle roll. If we approximate the joints and the CoM using a two-link arm [9], then we can use an analytical solution to move the CoM. The first link of the arm is the ankle roll joint to the hip roll joint. The second arm is the hip roll joint to the center of mass. The link of the first and second arm are revolute joints, and the end effector which is the CoM does not have a joint. The length of the first

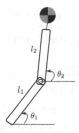

Fig. 4. An approximation of the center of mass kinematic for Inverse Kinematic model. l_1 is the length from the ankle to the hip and l_2 is the length from the hip to the center of mass. This is approximation is done to the frontal plane and saggital plane. The hip pitch ($\theta_{2,pitch}$), hip roll ($\theta_{2,roll}$), ankle pitch ($\theta_{1,pitch}$) and ankle roll ($\theta_{1,roll}$) are adjusted according to the Inverse Kinematic model.

arm is the distance from the ankle roll to the hip roll, l_1 and the length of the second arm, l_2, is the distance from the hip roll to the CoM. In the frontal plane, we want our end-effector to get to (y, z). y is the difference between the next CoM's y position and the current CoM's y position. z is the plane that CoM is constrained on. Now, that the problem is defined, we can use these values to get the two angles we need, but we first need to get the range from the first link to the next CoM position in the frontal plane, (y, z) (Fig. 4),

$$r = \sqrt{(y - \alpha_{ankle,y}) + (z - \alpha_{ankle,z})} \tag{8}$$

With r, the second angle, θ_2, can be found. But before computing θ_2, we need to find the angle α that corresponds to the angle formed by l_1, l_2, and r. Therefore, we can use the cosine law to get the following,

$$\alpha = \cos^{-1} \frac{l_1^2 + l_2^2 - r^2}{2l_1l_2}, \quad \theta_2 = \alpha \pm \pi \tag{9}$$

Therefore there are two solutions for θ_2 but only one can give us the correct solution because of the balancing constraint placed on the robot. Hence the correct solution is as follows

$$\theta_2 = \begin{cases} \alpha - \pi, & \text{if right kick} \\ \alpha + \pi, & \text{else left kick} \end{cases}$$

To compute θ_1, the angle opposite of l_2, β, needs to be calculated first. To calculate β, the law of cosines can be reused and we end up with,

$$\beta = \cos^{-1} \frac{r^2 + l_1^2 - l_2^2}{2l_1r}, \tag{10}$$

β gives the angle in the triangle, but the θ_1 is the angle between y-axis and l_1. To get this angle, the bearing of the first link to the the next CoM position is needed,

$$\arctan 2(z, y), \quad \theta_1 = \arctan 2(z, y) \pm \beta \tag{11}$$

There are also two solutions for θ_1, and a condition is given to decide which on to use,

$$\theta_1 = \begin{cases} \arctan 2(z, y) - \beta, & \text{if right kick} \\ \arctan 2(z, y) + \beta, & \text{else left kick} \end{cases}$$

The same needs to be do in the sagittal plane. The only difference in the sagittal plane, is that instead of hip and ankle roll, hip and ankle pitch will be used, and the trigonometric solution is done for point (x, z). When both calculations are done for the frontal and saggital plane, the current CoM position can now be inferred from these four joint angles.

5   Kick Trajectory Using Cubic Spline

In order to generate kick trajectory, the most trivial case is to change the leg joint angles until a desired kick configuration has been reached. This is tedious work and will be suboptimal since the joint space is very large. Another approach is to use optimization to find key-frame values, but this only works for a set of kicks and it is not dynamic enough to create any kick trajectory. Therefore, a more efficient solution is to generate motions using polynomials [14]. Polynomials are a great solution in robot motion because they can be configured to generate smooth curves. To generate a polynomial for the kick motion requires constraints such that the motion generated by the polynomial does not conflict with any unwanted configuration. The polynomials will not be used in the joint space, but rather will be used to determine the next position of the swinging foot. When the position of the foot is determined by the cubic polynomial, the Inverse Kinematic module will provide the angles for the foot position requested. For the kick motion, two cubic polynomials are generated. The point where the two polynomials meet is called the via-point. The purpose of this point will be discussed later. The cubic polynomial is as follows,

$$\alpha_1(t) = a_{13}t^3 + a_{12}t^2 + a_{11}t + a_{10} \quad \alpha_2(t) = a_{23}t^3 + a_{22}t^2 + a_{21}t + a_{20}$$

In order to generate an arbitrary motion, specific constraints need to be put upon the polynomials. Since there are two cubic polynomials (i.e. 8 coefficients/degrees of freedom), there are 8 constraints. The first constraint is the point of the first polynomial at $t = 0$. At $t = 0$, the kick motion will swing the leg back. This is called the retraction point. This is the point farthest from the ball. The second constraint is that the velocity of the first point at $t = 0$ which is zero. The third constraint is the position of the via-point where both cubic polynomials meet. The via-point is used to determine the height of the kick trajectory. It is also a very important point because it is where both polynomials meet. Hence, both polynomials need to have the same position at this point and their velocities need to match. Moreover, the acceleration at the via point for both polynomials need to also match. This guarantees a smooth trajectory with

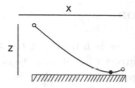

Fig. 5. These two polynomials are generated for a front kick. Since the front kick does not vary on the y-plane, it is two dimensional in the x and z plane. The white circles are the beginning and end points of the kick respectively. The black circle is the via-point that constraints the height of the polynomial. The first polynomial is from the first white circle to the black circle, and the second polynomial is from the black circle to the last white circle.

C^2 continuity. The last two constraints define the position and velocity of the second cubic spline at $t = t_f$. The constraints are summarized as follows (Fig. 5),

$$
\begin{aligned}
\alpha_1(0) &= [x_0, y_0, z_0] && \text{(retraction point)} \\
\dot{\alpha}_1(0) &= [0, 0, 0] \\
\alpha_1(t_{via}) &= [x_{t_{via}}, y_{t_{via}}, h_{floor}] && \text{(constraint on foot from floor)} \\
\alpha_2(0) &= [x_{t_{via}}, y_{t_{via}}, h_{floor}] && \text{(constraint on foot from floor)} \\
\dot{\alpha}_1(t_{via}) &= \dot{\alpha}_2(0) \\
\ddot{\alpha}_1(t_{via}) &= \ddot{\alpha}_2(0) \\
\alpha_2(t_f) &= [x_f, y_f, z_f] && \text{(contact point)} \\
\dot{\alpha}_2(t_f) &= [0, 0, 0]
\end{aligned}
$$

Moreover, as shown above, the constraints are defined as vectors because there needs to be polynomials for the x, y, and z plane. The six cubic polynomials (two for each plane) will form a parametric curve in $\mathbb{R}^3$. To solve the coefficients of the polynomials we solve the following system which was created by inputting the constraint in the polynomial and rearranging terms,

$$
\begin{bmatrix}
1 & t_{via} & 0 & 0 & 0 \\
0 & 0 & 1 & t_f & t_f^2 \\
0 & 0 & 1 & 2t_f & 3t_f^2 \\
2t_{via} & 3t_{via}^2 & -1 & 0 & 0 \\
2 & 6t_{via} & 0 & -2 & 0
\end{bmatrix}
\begin{bmatrix}
a_{12} \\
a_{13} \\
a_{21} \\
a_{22} \\
a_{23}
\end{bmatrix}
=
\begin{bmatrix}
\frac{\alpha_1(t_{via}) - \alpha_1(0)}{t_{via}^2} \\
\frac{\alpha_2(t_f) - \alpha_2(t_{via})}{t_{via}^2} \\
0 \\
0 \\
0
\end{bmatrix}
\tag{12}
$$

As seen in (12), a_{10}, a_{11}, and a_{20} do not need to be a part of the system of equations because their answer is trivial:

$$
\alpha_1(0) = a_{10} \quad \dot{\alpha}_1(0) = a_{11} \quad \alpha_2(0) = a_{20}
$$

Solving (12), gives us the coefficients for our polynomials, but we still are missing one step. Before we begin solving (12), we need to determine the optimal via point position. This is discussed in Sect. 6.

6   Model Optimization

Generating a good parameter set is important to attain a good kick. Although these values can be found empirically, it is a tedious task. We therefore used the Covariance Matrix Adaptation Evolution Strategy (*CMA-ES*) for model optimization. The values were optimized and visualized in Webots, which can be seen as the standard simulation software for NAOqi. The first parameter set optimized was the time length of the kick and the speed towards the via point. The second run on the model optimization was done on the time length of the kick, the speed of the via point, and the via point location in the x, y, z plane. Although this gave good results, the via point was moved equally proportionally in 3D space, which resulted in a polynomial where the cubic and quadratic components were negligible in the specified interval of t. Therefore for the last optimization run, the via point was moved disproportional in the x, y, and z plane to generate curves in 3D space.

Table 1. Optimization results. The time column is the duration of the kick. The percent column shows the percent of the time spent on the first polynomial. X, Y, and Z Via is the Via point in 3D space.

Run	Dimensions	Distance (meters)	Num. Eval.	Time (ms)	Percent	X Via	Y Via	Z Via
Seed	0	2.008	0	1180	0.5	0.5	0.5	0.5
1	2	2.124	6516	853	0.46	0.5	0.5	0.5
2	3	2.230	10633	1316	0.53	0.49	0.49	0.49
3	5	2.696	320	2273	0.77	0.1	0.42	0.44

Although we got promising results from the optimization, we believe we can get better results for the optimization by increasing the dimension of the optimization. As you can see in Table 1, as we include more parameters, there is an increase in the distance of the optimal kick as well as a decrease in the number of generations until convergence. The additional parameters that can be added are: kick limit configuration (exploring a set of limits on the polynomials that can generate a good kick), end points of the polynomial, and the time it takes to get to the retraction point.

7   Experiments

For the validation of our approach, various kicks were generated and data for the balancing and spline trajectory generation was recorded. Figure 6(a) shows the ZMP reference point for a right front kick was 0.03 for x and 0.052 for y for all preview reference points in the preview controller. Although the x and y ZMP values varies around the reference points, the error is less than 1 cm which is less than the radius of the foot or support polygon. Furthermore, the small error accumulated is due to the simplification of the inverse kinematic model, but it still gives a good approximation to the CoM position. The CoM position in Fig. 6(b) is very close to the ZMP value because when the robot is balancing on one foot, it does not generate a force in the x or y axis. This can be verified in Fig. 6(c), which is very close to zero. The graph in Fig. 6(c) is bounded between -1.5×10^{-4} and 2×10^{-4}. Hence, the difference between the estimated ZMP and the estimated CoM is negligible within working levels of precision. Although we might be tempted to control the CoM alone and disregard ZMP because they coincide, we need to notice that if a force is applied to the robot by another robot, it will generate a force in the x or y axis, which in turn might make the CoM leave the support polygon, but we can still use the ZMP criterion to stabilize the robot. In Fig. 6(d) and (e), the polynomials in the x, y, and z plane have been generated and projected in 3D space. The blue polynomial is the first polynomial and the orange polynomial is the second polynomial generated, and the union is the via point. As can be observed, the polynomials are very close to a straight line. This is due to the configuration limit of the robot. Since the robot operates in a very small space, the coefficients of the polynomials are very small (less than 1). Therefore, the quadratic and cubic terms are negligible and the linear term is dominant. In order to get better shapes for the kick trajectories, we used CMA-ES optimization to generate shapes by moving the via point from being halfway. The configuration limit of the kick trajectory can be visualized in 6(f). A video of the kick engine can be found at: https://www.youtube.com/watch?v=4fmuqI_CpQw.

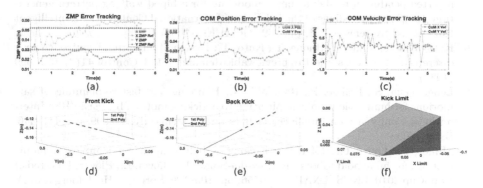

Fig. 6. (a) The ZMP error between the reference point and the actual ZMP. (b) The position of the center of mass in x and y. (c) The center of mass velocity. (d)–(e) The dashed polynomial is generated first. (d) The front kick trajectory in 3D space. (e) The back kick trajectory in 3D space. (f) The kick limit of the NAO in 3D space.

8 Conclusion

We have developed and implemented a dynamic kick engine that dynamically balances using a ZMP based preview controller. The preview controller is given the center of mass position based of the error in the ZMP. In order to move the center of mass to the correct position, we use a simplified model that consists of a two link arm. The end effector of the arm is denoted as the center of mass. The kick trajectory is generated using cubic splines. The knot in the cubic splines is called the via point, and it is used to control the shape of the polynomial. The kick was optimized using a simulation software called Webots. On Webots, we optimized the via point position, the speed to the via point, and the time duration of the kick. The optimization attained optimal set of parameters without having to experiment on the robot to find them. These values were used on the physical robot to verify results.

References

1. Becht, I., de Jonge, M., Pronk, R.: A dynamic kick for the NAO robot. Project Report, July 2012
2. Böckmann, A., Laue, T.: Kick motions for the NAO robot using dynamic movement primitives. arXiv preprint arXiv:1606.00600 (2016)
3. Kajita, S., Hirukawa, H., Harada, K., Yokoi, K.: Introduction to Humanoid Robotics, vol. 101. Springer, Heidelberg (2014). https://doi.org/10.1007/978-3-642-54536-8
4. Kajita, S., et al.: Biped walking pattern generation by using preview control of zero-moment point. In: Proceedings of the IEEE International Conference on Robotics and Automation, ICRA 2003, vol. 2, pp. 1620–1626. IEEE (2003)
5. Kajita, S., Kanehiro, F., Kaneko, K., Yokoi, K., Hirukawa, H.: The 3D linear inverted pendulum model: a simple modeling for a biped walking pattern generation. In: 2001 Proceedings of the IEEE/RSJ International Conference on Intelligent Robots and Systems, vol. 1, pp. 239–246. IEEE (2001)
6. Katayama, T., Ohki, T., Inoue, T., Kato, T.: Design of an optimal controller for a discrete-time system subject to previewable demand. Int. J. Control **41**(3), 677–699 (1985)
7. Lengagneua, S., Fraisse, P., Ramdani, N.: Planning and fast re-planning of safe motions for humanoid robots: application to a kicking motion. In: IEEE/RSJ International Conference on Intelligent Robots and Systems, IROS 2009, pp. 441–446. IEEE (2009)
8. Müller, J., Laue, T., Röfer, T.: Kicking a ball – modeling complex dynamic motions for humanoid robots. In: Ruiz-del-Solar, J., Chown, E., Plöger, P.G. (eds.) RoboCup 2010. LNCS (LNAI), vol. 6556, pp. 109–120. Springer, Heidelberg (2011). https://doi.org/10.1007/978-3-642-20217-9_10
9. Murray, R.M., Li, Z., Sastry, S.S., Sastry, S.S.: A Mathematical Introduction to Robotic Manipulation. CRC Press, Boca Raton (1994)
10. Strom, J., Slavov, G., Chown, E.: Omnidirectional walking using ZMP and Preview control for the NAO humanoid robot. In: Baltes, J., Lagoudakis, M.G., Naruse, T., Ghidary, S.S. (eds.) RoboCup 2009. LNCS (LNAI), vol. 5949, pp. 378–389. Springer, Heidelberg (2010). https://doi.org/10.1007/978-3-642-11876-0_33
11. Sung, C.H., Kagawa, T., Uno, Y.: Planning of kicking motion with via-point representation for humanoid robots. In: 2011 8th International Conference on Ubiquitous Robots and Ambient Intelligence (URAI), pp. 337–342. IEEE (2011)
12. Vukobratović, M., Borovac, B.: Zero-moment point-thirty five years of its life. Int. J. Humanoid Robot. **1**(01), 157–173 (2004)

13. Wenk, F., Röfer, T.: Online generated kick motions for the NAO balanced using inverse dynamics. In: Behnke, S., Veloso, M., Visser, A., Xiong, R. (eds.) RoboCup 2013. LNCS (LNAI), vol. 8371, pp. 25–36. Springer, Heidelberg (2014). https://doi.org/10.1007/978-3-662-44468-9_3
14. Williams, R.L.: Simplified robotics joint-space trajectory generation with a via point using a single polynomial. J. Robot. (2013)
15. Xu, Y., Mellmann, H.: Adaptive motion control: dynamic kick for a humanoid robot. In: Dillmann, R., Beyerer, J., Hanebeck, U.D., Schultz, T. (eds.) KI 2010. LNCS (LNAI), vol. 6359, pp. 392–399. Springer, Heidelberg (2010). https://doi.org/10.1007/978-3-642-16111-7_45
16. Yi, S.J., McGill, S., He, Q., Hong, D., Lee, D.: Walk and kick motion generation for a general purpose full sized humanoid robot. In: Workshop on Humanoid Soccer Robots, IEEE-RAS International Conference on Humanoid Robots (Humanoids). IEEE (2014)

A Benchmark Data Set and Evaluation of Deep Learning Architectures for Ball Detection in the RoboCup SPL

Simon O'Keeffe[✉] [iD] and Rudi Villing [iD]

Department of Electronic Engineering, Maynooth University, Maynooth, Ireland
`simon.okeeffe.2010@mumail.ie`, `rudi.villing@nuim.ie`

Abstract. This paper presents a benchmark data set for evaluating ball detection algorithms in the RoboCup Soccer Standard Platform League. We created a labelled data set of images with and without ball derived from vision log files recorded by multiple NAO robots in various lighting conditions. The data set contains 5209 labelled ball image regions and 10924 non-ball regions. Non-ball image regions all contain features that had been classified as a potential ball candidate by an existing ball detector. The data set was used to train and evaluate 252 different Deep Convolutional Neural Network (CNN) architectures for ball detection. In order to control computational requirements, this evaluation focused on networks with 2–5 layers that could feasibly run in the vision and cognition cycle of a NAO robot using two cameras at full frame rate (2×30 Hz). The results show that the classification performance of the networks is quite insensitive to the details of the network design including input image size, number of layers and number of outputs at each layer. In an effort to reduce the computational requirements of CNNs we evaluated XNOR-Net architectures which quantize the weights and activations of a neural network to binary values. We examined XNOR-Nets corresponding to the real-valued CNNs we had already tested in order to quantify the effect on classification metrics. The results indicate that ball classification performance degrades by 12% on average when changing from real-valued CNN to corresponding XNOR-Net.

Keywords: Convolution neural network · Deep learning · Ball detection XNOR-Net

1 Introduction

In the RoboCup Soccer Standard Platform League (SPL), ball detection has frequently relied on hand-crafted heuristic approaches that rely on colour with some shape constraints. The Softbank Robotics NAO robots that are used in the SPL have limited computational resources and this is a principal reason why heuristic vision processing approaches have been used to date.

In 2016, rule changes led to a change of the standard ball from an orange street hockey ball to a 10 cm foam ball with the 32 panel black and white pattern typical of a traditional soccer ball. The principal challenge of this new ball is that it does not have

© Springer Nature Switzerland AG 2018
H. Akiyama et al. (Eds.): RoboCup 2017, LNAI 11175, pp. 398–409, 2018.
https://doi.org/10.1007/978-3-030-00308-1_33

a unique colour on the field of play and for that reason colour alone cannot be used to detect it. Furthermore the ball can be difficult to distinguish from parts of other robots or when partly occluding field objects such as lines, goal posts, and robots. In general, heuristic based vision processing approaches need to deal with many different conditions identified through domain expertise and trial and error testing. Our own team's heuristic based ball detection was found to regularly require the addition of extra conditions, tended to produce many false positives, and suffered from a limited ball detection range (when compared to the previous orange ball detector). In 2017, the SPL rules have been changed to permit play in natural and variable light conditions and this further challenges the heuristic based approach.

Given the difficulties associated with heuristic based ball detection, a more sophisticated approach is required that is more robust and less dependent on colour and uniform lighting. Deep Convolutional Neural Networks (CNNs) are recognised as the state of the art for object recognition [1] and we expect that such state of the art approaches should outperform the heuristic based algorithms that we and other teams have used to date. Given a suitable dataset, a Deep Neural Network (of which CNNs are but one possibility) can learn features of the ball that are robust to lighting changes, occulusion and distractor conditions, and movement by the robot or the ball. Therefore the first contribution of this paper is to publish an extensive labelled data set of ball images that may be used for training and subsequent test of Deep Neural Networks and other machine learning techniques.

One of the key factors that has enabled the advancement of Deep Neural Networks (DNNs) has been the use of Graphical Processing Units (GPUs), with speed-ups on the order of 10 to 30-fold in comparison to CPU only processing [2]. However, DNN approaches are much less typical with low power embedded systems that do not have a GPU due to the computational requirements. Therefore our second contribution is an evaluation of multiple Deep CNN architectures that may be feasibly implemented on the NAO robot and similar low power embedded systems. This evaluation focuses on the classification metrics of the networks and the inference time per image.

There are a number of approaches that may be used to reduce the computational requirements of Deep CNNs and these are described under related work. Our third contribution is a specific evaluation of XNOR-Net [3], a particularly promising approach for reducing computation and speeding up inference that quantizes both the network weights and activations to binary values.

The remainder of this paper is organized as follows: Sect. 2 presents some related work and motivates the evaluation of XNOR-Net. Section 3 describes the approach taken to the dataset. Our network design approach is presented in Sect. 4. Section 5 contains our results and discussion. Finally Sect. 6 presents our conclusion and future work.

2   Related Work

Most of the computation performed during training and application of DNNs results from the multiplication of real-valued weights by real-valued activation values. Several approaches have been proposed to improve the computational efficiency of the network at both training and inference time.

Shallow networks have been used to estimate deep networks. First Reference 4 showed that a large enough hidden layer of sigmoid units can approximate any decision boundary. However for vision and speech processing, shallow networks generally can't compete with deep models [5].

Pre-trained deep networks can be compressed by pruning redundant weights in a trained network to reduce the size of the network at inference time. Early methods for pruning a network included weight decay [6], Optimal Brain Damage [7], and Optimal Brain Surgeon [8]. More recent approached to pruning included Deep Compression [9], which reduces the storage and energy required to run inference on large networks so they can be deployed on mobile devices. Deep compression does this by removing redundant connections and quantizing weights so that multiple connections share the same weight, and then use Huffman coding to compress the weights.

Designing compact blocks that use fewer parameters at each layer of a deep network can help to save memory and computational costs. Replacing the fully connected layer with global average pooling was examined in the Network in Network architecture [10], GoogLenet [11], and Residual-Net [12], which have achieved state-of-the-art results on several benchmarks. The bottleneck structure (which uses 1×1 convolutions) in Residual-Net has been proposed to reduce the number of parameters and improve speed.

High precision parameters are not very important in achieving high performance in deep networks [13] and many approaches have proposed quantizing parameters to reduce the size of the network. The authors in [13] proposed to quantize the weights of fully connected layers in a deep network by vector quantization techniques. They showed that simply thresholding the weight values at zero decreases the top-1 accuracy on ILSVRC2012 by less than 10%. Other work examined using ternary weights with the weights restricted to $+1/0/-1$ [14] and networks that used ternary weights and 3-bits activations [15].

Several researchers have gone a step beyond the above quantization approaches to network binarization. Initially, the performance of highly quantized or binarized networks were believed to be very poor due to the destructive property of binary quantization [16]. However, this was later shown not to be the case. BinaryConnect [17] trains a DNN with binary weights during forward and backward propagations, but retains the precision of the stored weights in which gradients are accumulated. The authors found that BinaryConnect acted as a regularizer and obtained near state-of-the-art results on MNIST, CIFAR-10 and SVHN. BinaryNet [18] was proposed as an extension of BinaryConnect. In BinaryNet both weights and activations are binarized, constrained to either $+1$ or -1. If all operands of the convolutions are binary, then the convolutions can be estimated by XNOR and bit counting operations. This quantization can also applies to the fully connected layers. Again, this approach achieved nearly state-of-the-art results on the MNIST, CIFAR-10 and SVHN datasets. XNOR-Net is another method that binarizes the weights and activations in a network [3]. XNOR-Net differs from BinaryNet in the binarization and the network structure. XNOR-Net was found to outperform BinaryNet on large datasets (e.g. ImageNet).

3 General Approach and Data Set

As a low power embedded processor, the Intel Atom processor of the NAO robot does not have the compute power needed to execute standard DNN techniques applied to the entire full resolution camera image at camera frame rate (usually 30 frames per second). Therefore we assume a general vision pipeline in which a ball candidate region proposal algorithm first scans the image for ball candidates using some unspecified but computationally efficient technique (that may be heuristic based or not). We then assume that one or a subset of proposed ball candidate regions are tested using a DNN to determine which candidate (if any) best represents a ball.

To ensure a data set that is suitable for training and testing the DNN component of this pipeline while maximizing flexibility for future developments the requirements for a benchmark data set are as follows. The data should provide full images with labelled region coordinates that specify ball and non-ball candidate regions (patches). In addition, the data set should contain a wide variety of candidates (with and without ball) that span the space of conditions under which a ball must be detected.

Our final data set comprises 6564 unique 640 × 480 images and it is available for download at https://www.roboeireann.ie/research/SPLBallDataset.zip. From this set of images, 5209 ball patches (candidate regions which contain a ball) and 10924 non-ball patches (candidate regions which do not contain a ball) are extracted.

The data set is divided into training, validation and test sets such that 70% is used for training, 15% for validation, and the remaining 15% for test. The ball patch data includes candidates that were close (less than 3 m away) and far away from the robot (3–8 m away). It includes candidates that were in free space on the field and candidates that were near, partially occluding or, if appropriate, partially occluded by various distractors (penalty spots, field lines and intersections, and robot parts). The data set includes ball candidates where the robot and ball were both static and where the robot, ball, or both were moving. Finally, the data includes ball candidates on various pitch surfaces, some of which were under artificial light and others under natural light. The non-ball patches include field lines and intersections, robot parts, goal parts, shoes, feet, and hands. A selection of ball and non-ball patches can be seen in Fig. 1.

Fig. 1. Example of ball and non-ball patches extracted from full images in the dataset

The dataset was prepared from vision log files collected at RoboCup and in our laboratory. In all, 31 log files were used. All log files were captured from NAO V4 and

NAO V5 robots. The logs were captured from 9 different robots and the logs include a mix of top camera and bottom camera. Bottom camera images were captured natively at 640 × 480 pixels resolution whereas top camera images were captured at 1280 × 960 pixels resolution and then decimated to 640 × 480. Images used YUV format.

The ball pixels were manually labelled in images extracted from five of the log files. The remaining log files were first processed through our existing heuristic based ball detector. Using this approach, each image was always labelled with a non-ball patch location, that is, the location of a candidate considered but ultimately rejected as a ball. In addition the same image was labelled with a ball patch location if our existing ball detector accepted one of the ball candidates it had processed. The patches associated with each image were inspected afterwards and manually re-classified as ball or non-ball as needed. This ensured that the data set was not negatively affected by weaknesses (primarily false positives) in our existing ball detector.

Ball patches in the source images varied from 12 × 12 pixels (the minimum size we permitted) up to 158 × 158 pixels. The luminance (Y) channel of each ball and non-ball patch was extracted and resized to a standard size for later training and test of DNNs. We used sizes of 12 × 12, 20 × 20, and 32 × 32 for reasons explained in Sect. 4.1. Resizing was performed using the computationally efficient nearest-neighbor algorithm since that is likely to be used in the vision pipeline on the NAO robot.

Simply extracting all ball and non-ball patches from consecutive image frames in each log file can result in excessively correlated patches in the case that neither the robot nor the ball is moving. To eliminate such correlation we included a ball or non-ball patch from a given log file in the data set only if the mean absolute difference between its pixels and those of the previously included patch exceeded a threshold of 10 luminance points per pixel. This threshold was determined empirically by examining the mean absolute difference of patches from consecutive frames throughout the data set. This process eliminated 43.2% of the ball and non-ball patches due to correlation.

Many ball-patches that had already been included in the data set were based on a bounding box that cropped the ball tightly and excluded extraneous information as a consequence. However, it may not always be possible for the ball candidate proposal algorithm to achieve this. Therefore, we augmented the data set by creating variants of ball and non-ball patches that were more loosely cropped (and where the ball was smaller in the patch as a consequence). To do this, we went back to the patches in the images prior to resizing to standard patch sizes. The original bounding box around each patch was first scaled by value between 1.1 and 1.5 chosen at random. The bounding box was then translated by a random value between −0.33 to 0.33 times its new edge length in the horizontal direction and similarly translated by a random value in the vertical direction. If the original bounding box for a patch was at the border of the image it was excluded from augmentation. The data set after augmentation contains 89% more patches, consisting of 5209 ball and 10924 non-ball patches.

4   Deep CNN Evaluation Design

The evaluation was designed to evaluate the performance of a large number of Deep CNN networks that could be expected to execute quickly enough on the NAO robot. If images from both cameras in a NAO robot are processed at their maximum rate then there is a time budget of approximately 16.7 ms available to process each image and perform any necessary perception and cognition activities. Therefore, a Deep CNN that will be used in the vision pipeline can consume only a portion of that time budget. The shorter the inference time, the more likely it is that the network can be applied to multiple candidate patches rather than just one, so this makes it attractive to identify network architectures which can make inference as quickly as possible while maintaining accuracy.

We used the Caffe framework to develop and test our network architecture [19]. Caffe is a deep learning framework that facilitates rapid testing of different network architectures because the network architectures are specified by configuration files. In addition, Caffe can switch between using CPU and GPU depending on the host platform which allows for fast training on a machine with a GPU with subsequent deployment to another system having only a CPU, such as the NAO robot, for inference testing.

4.1   Network Design

There are a number of parameters that can be used to specify a network. One of the most fundamental of these is the size of the input image patch. Our existing heuristic based ball detector performs worst with balls that are more than 3 m from the robot. With a 640 × 480 pixel image the ball diameter at 3 m from the robot is approximately 20 pixels. This decreases to 12 pixels between 5 m and 6 m and to 7–8 pixels at 8 m from the robot. This suggested that patch sizes between 8 and 20 pixels square could be appropriate. We are aware of two other RoboCup SPL teams that have considered Deep CNNs for ball detection. Nao-Team HTWK reported a network that uses 20 × 20 pixel input patches [20] while UT Austin Villa's code release 2016 [21] used somewhat larger 32 × 32 pixel patches.

These input patch sizes are similar in size to those of the well-studied LeNet architecture [22] which used 32 × 32 pixel patches. LeNet was one of the first convolutional networks and operated on the MNIST dataset of hand-written digits. The authors presented many different variants of LeNet with the most successful consisting of 2 convolutional layers followed by 2 fully connected layers, with 20 outputs in the first layer, 50 outputs in the second layer, 500 in the third layer and 10 outputs for the final layer for each of the 10 digits. It used 5 × 5 convolution kernels.

More recent work on CNNs such as VGGNet [23] and GoogLeNet [11] has introduced smaller kernel sizes. Smaller kernels have the advantage of capturing more detail yet they can be stacked up to capture wider receptive fields (e.g. two 3 × 3 kernels in different layers together have a receptive field of 5 × 5). For this reason we evaluated designs with various kernel sizes. Network in Network [10] introduced the idea of 1 × 1 convolution kernels. Such a kernel can be used to reduce the number of parameters in the network and may be used as a convolutional layer in the network, where it is known as a bottleneck, or to replace the fully connected layers that are often placed at the end of a CNN (coupled with average pooling). Our evaluation included network designs that replaced fully connected layers with 1×1 convolutional layers.

Batch Normalization [24] layers normalize the input batch by its mean and variance. This technique was introduced to overcome internal covariate shift where the distribution of each layer's inputs changes during training as the parameters of the previous layers change. The authors found that Batch Normalization speeds up training time, achieving the same accuracy with 14 times fewer training steps as well being more robust to high learning rates and parameter initialization. Rectified Linear Units (ReLUs) [25] are now commonplace in many state-of-the-art deep neural networks. ReLUs are used over the sigmoid function as they have a reduced likelihood of vanishing gradient. The constant gradient of ReLUs results in faster learning.

In our Deep CNN designs, a convolutional block consists of convolution, Batch Normalisation, ReLU activation and max pooling in that order. The last three of these operations are optional and we tested networks both with and without these operations.

The Nao-Team HTWK network is similar to LeNet but with fewer outputs at each layer. It comprises two convolutional layers using 5×5 kernels and max pooling followed by two fully connected layers. We included four variations of the HTWK network as the authors did not specify whether or not Batch Normalization or ReLU activations were used. We also included the UT Austin Villa network which is a shallower network featuring just one convolution layer using 7×7 kernels and one fully connected layer. In total we evaluated these 252 designs based on the parameter options in Table 1.

Table 1. Deep CNN design parameters.

Design parameter	Values tested
Layers	2 layer networks: 1 conv layer and 1 FC or 1×1 conv layer 4 layer networks: 2 conv layers and 2 FC or 1×1 conv layers; 3 conv layers and 1 FC or 1×1 conv layers 5 layer networks: 3 conv layers and 2 FC or 1×1 conv layers
Convolutional layers	
Kernel size	$1 \times 1, 3 \times 3, 5 \times 5, 7 \times 7$ (7×7 only applied to 32×32 input patch)
Kernel dilation	1 or 2
Stride	1, 2, or 4
Output channels (kernels)	6, 8, 10 or 12
Pooling	None, Max pooling, or Average Pooling (Average pooling used only for the final 1×1 convolution layer)
Activation	None or ReLU
Batch normalization	Yes or no
Fully connected layers	
Layer outputs	16, 32, or 48
Activation	ReLU

4.2   XNOR-Net

The XNOR-Net architecture binarizes activations and kernel weights within a network so that the multiplications and additions in a convolution may be replaced by XNOR and bit counting (pop count) operations. A key element required to successfully train an XNOR-Net is the block structure of a convolutional layer which is different to block structure in a typical real-valued CNN in order to reduce the loss of information [3]. The modified convolution block for XNOR-Net therefore consists of the following blocks in the order specified: Batch Normalization, Binary Activation, Binary Convolution, and finally pooling.

The authors of XNOR-Net claim a dramatic 58× speedup when using XNOR based convolution in comparison to a normal real-valued convolution. This number does depend on the number of input channels and the kernel size and for our networks the number would be smaller (e.g. for 12 channels and 3 × 3 kernels the theoretically predicted speedup would be 40×). Achieving this speedup in practice is challenging but the method is attractive and for this reason we evaluate the impact of the XNOR-Net quantization on classification metrics for a subset of networks.

5   Results and Discussion

5.1   Real Valued Network Precision and Recall

Figure 2 summarizes the precision and recall classification metrics for all real-valued networks tested on the test set. It is clear that the recall performance is relatively insensitive to the network design parameters in the networks under test ($M = 97.2\%$, $SD = 1.5\%$). The precision performance is somewhat more variable. In a RoboCup setting, false positive ball detections are often more harmful than false negatives since they may lead to poor autonomous behavior decisions. Among the real-valued CNNs under test, thirty-two had a precision greater than 99%. A common feature of the networks with precision less than 90% was that none used ReLU activation or batch normalization. (This is relevant to XNOR-Net designs as binarized networks are inherently incompatible with ReLU activation.)

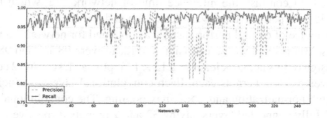

Fig. 2. Precision and recall for all real valued CNNs. Networks 0–65 use 12 × 12 input images, networks 66–241 use 20 × 20 input images, and the remainder use 32 × 32 input images. For each input dimension, the networks are sorted in ascending order by number of multiplications.

The network with the best overall classification performance measured by F_1 score (number 222) obtained 98.9% recall and 99.4% precision using a 5 layer network. With this data set, the HTWK network with ReLU and normalization (number 206) demonstrated 96.1% precision and 98.6% recall, the HTWK network without ReLU and normalization (number 204) scored a lower 92.4% precision with 96.6% recall, and UT Austin Villa's network (number 242) achieved 96.7% precision and 95.9% recall.

Inference times for the same networks when executed on the NAO robot are presented in Fig. 3. These were only measured for real-valued networks since the unoptimized XNOR-Net implementation used in this work performed floating point multiplications internally and provided no speed up. There is very little correlation between classification performance in Fig. 2 and inference time in Fig. 3 ($\rho = 0.13$). This suggests that, for ball detection, choosing a more complex network with a longer inference time is unlikely to be of much benefit. The networks for each input dimension are presented in order of the number of multiplications. The spikes in inference time correspond to networks with a larger number of weighted layers and smaller convolution kernels. The convolutions in the Caffe framework are performed using BLAS matrix multiplication, as such a large number of multiplications can be combined into one matrix multiplication. Therefore more BLAS calls with fewer multiplications per call will be slower.

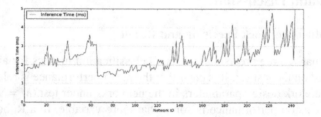

Fig. 3. Inference time on the NAO for all real valued networks evaluated (0–65 use 12×12 input images, 66–241 use 20×20 input images, and the remainder use 32×32 input images). Inference times larger than 5 ms are not shown in the figure.

On the other hand, although network 66 produced the fastest inference time of 1.4 ms, its balance of F_1 score performance and inference time was in the bottom 18% of all networks tested. In contrast, the inference time of network 222, which had the best overall classification performance, was rather long at 4.8 ms.

The best balance of overall performance was obtained for network 16 whose inference time was 2.05 ms and whose precision and recall were 98.1% and 98.0% respectively. The design of this network features a 12×12 input patch size and 2 convolutional layers with twelve 3×3 kernels each. Each convolutional layer also included ReLU activation, batch normalization and 2×2 max pooling. The convolutional layers were followed by 2 fully connected layers having 32 and 2 outputs respectively.

For comparison, the inference times of the HTWK network with ReLU and normalization (number 206), HTWK network without ReLU and normalization (number 204), and UT Austin Villa network (number 242) were 2.7 ms, 2.2 ms, and 2.3 ms respectively.

5.2   XNOR-Net Performance

The classification statistics of a small number of XNOR-Net designs corresponding to real-valued networks already tested were also evaluated. In general XNOR-Net designs exhibited greater sensitivity to the training parameters chosen and often failed to converge or had poor performance when training parameters derived from the equivalent real-valued networks were used.

Figure 4 indicates that XNOR-Nets have degraded classification performance compared to equivalent real-valued CNNs, as expected, and attain average scores that are almost 12% lower. In general more complex networks with more weights in hidden layers were more robust to the destructive effect of binary quantization. XNOR-Nets use binary activation rather than ReLU activation and it is possible that this is a contributor to the poor performance as the lack of ReLU activation was associated with the worst precision statistics for real-valued networks.

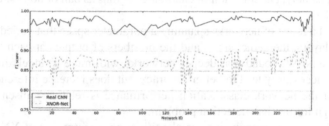

Fig. 4. Comparison of F_1 score for real-valued networks and corresponding XNOR-Net designs.

5.3   Recall Performance for Different Ball Detection Scenarios

We examined the recall performance of all networks in more detail by examining the recall for different subsets of test images that were grouped by ball detection scenario. The scenarios examined were ball far away (more than 3 m), ball in free space, ball moving, ball in natural light, ball on or near a line, and ball occluding, occluded by, or near a robot.

Figure 5 summarizes the results and shows that performance was quite consistent across the scenarios. Nevertheless, moving balls or balls in natural light or far away provide the biggest detection challenges to the networks. Somewhat surprisingly, the scenarios that provide the greatest challenge to our existing heuristic based ball detection, namely ball on line and ball on robot, are handled very well by the majority of networks.

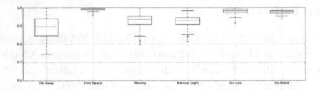

Fig. 5. Recall performance of all real-valued networks across different ball detection scenarios.

6 Conclusion and Future Work

This work presented a data set for benchmarking ball detection in RoboCup soccer. Full images with labelled ball and non-ball regions have been published so that the entire vision pipeline may be tested, but in this work we focused on one particular aspect of that pipeline, namely, classification of candidate regions as ball or non-ball using Deep CNNs.

We trained a range of networks spanning a parameter space that varied the number of weighted layers, the kernel sizes, and the numbers of outputs at each layer among other parameters. We found that deeper networks with more channels in the hidden layers do not necessarily lead to better accuracy but does increase inference time. We conclude that the network classification performance is relatively insensitive to the network design for this ball detection problem.

This work focused on analyzing the classification performance of XNOR-Net and did not use an optimized implementation that could benefit from the binary weights and activations. We found that XNOR-Net architectures had an F_1 score that was 12% lower than the corresponding real valued network on average. The theoretically predicted speed up (by replacing real multiplications with binary XNOR) for our CNN layers is between 29× and 40×. This speed up could allow more image patches to be evaluated within the available time budget on the robot or to enable substantially more complex networks to be feasibly executed. If more image patches can be evaluated during each cycle, then this work could extend to classifying additional field objects such as robots and goal posts to the architecture. For this reason we intend to examine the feasibility of a sufficiently optimized implementation on the Intel Atom processor as part of our future work.

Acknowledgements. The authors would like to acknowledge the valuable inclusion of labelled images in the data set from the final year project work of Robert McCraith. The authors would like to gratefully acknowledge funding provided by the Irish Research Council under their Government of Ireland Postgraduate Scholarship 2013.

References

1. Krizhevsky, A., Sutskever, I., Hinton, G.E.: Imagenet classification with deep convolutional neural networks. In: Advances in Neural Information Processing Systems, pp. 1097–1105 (2012)

2. Raina, R., Madhavan, A., Ng, A.Y.: Large-scale deep unsupervised learning using graphics processors. In: Proceedings of the 26th Annual International Conference on Machine Learning, pp. 873–880 (2009)
3. Rastegari, M., Ordonez, V., Redmon, J., Farhadi, A.: XNOR-Net: ImageNet classification using binary convolutional neural networks. arXiv preprint arXiv:1603.05279 (2016)
4. Cybenko, G.: Approximation by superpositions of a sigmoidal function. Math. Control., Signals, Syst. (MCSS) **2**, 303–314 (1989)
5. Seide, F., Li, G., Yu, D.: Conversational speech transcription using context-dependent deep neural networks. In: Interspeech, pp. 437–440 (2011)
6. Hanson, S.J., Pratt, L.: Comparing biases for minimal network construction with back-propagation. Adv. Neural. Inf. Process. Syst. **1**, 177–185 (1989)
7. LeCun, Y., Denker, J.S., Solla, S.A., Howard, R.E., Jackel, L.D.: Optimal brain damage. In: NIPs, pp. 598–605 (1989)
8. Hassibi, B., Stork, D.G.: Others: second order derivatives for network pruning: optimal brain surgeon. In: Advances in Neural Information Processing Systems, pp. 164–164 (1993)
9. Han, S., Mao, H., Dally, W.J.: Deep compression: compressing deep neural networks with pruning, trained quantization and huffman coding. arXiv preprint arXiv:1510.00149 (2015)
10. Lin, M., Chen, Q., Yan, S.: Network in network. arXiv preprint arXiv:1312.4400 (2013)
11. Szegedy, C., et al.: Going deeper with convolutions. In: Proceedings of the IEEE Conference on Computer Vision and Pattern Recognition, pp. 1–9 (2015)
12. He, K., Zhang, X., Ren, S., Sun, J.: Deep residual learning for image recognition. Proceedings of the IEEE Conference on Computer Vision and Pattern Recognition. pp. 770–778 (2016)
13. Gong, Y., Liu, L., Yang, M., Bourdev, L.: Compressing deep convolutional networks using vector quantization. arXiv preprint arXiv:1412.6115 (2014)
14. Arora, S., Bhaskara, A., Ge, R., Ma, T.: Provable Bounds for Learning Some Deep Representations. ICML. pp. 584–592 (2014)
15. Hwang, K., Sung, W.: Fixed-point feedforward deep neural network design using weights +1, 0, and −1. In: Signal Processing Systems (SiPS), IEEE Workshop on 2014, pp. 1–6 (2014)
16. Courbariaux, M., Bengio, Y., David, J.-P.: Training deep neural networks with low precision multiplications. arXiv preprint arXiv:1412.7024 (2014)
17. Courbariaux, M., Bengio, Y., David, J.-P.: Binaryconnect: training deep neural networks with binary weights during propagations. In: Advances in Neural Information Processing Systems, pp. 3123–3131 (2015)
18. Courbariaux, M., Hubara, I., Soudry, D., El-Yaniv, R., Bengio, Y.: Binarized neural networks: training deep neural networks with weights and activations constrained to +1 or −1. arXiv preprint arXiv:1602.02830 (2016)
19. Jia, Y., et al.: Caffe: convolutional architecture for fast feature embedding. In: Proceedings of the 22nd ACM International Conference on Multimedia, pp. 675–678 (2014)
20. HTWK, N.-T.: Team Research Report. http://robocup.imn.htwk-leipzig.de/documents/TRR_2016.pdf?lang=en. (2016)
21. UT Austin Villa Code Release. https://github.com/LARG/spl-release (2016)
22. LeCun, Y., Bottou, L., Bengio, Y., Haffner, P.: Gradient-based learning applied to document recognition. Proc. IEEE **86**, 2278–2324 (1998)
23. Simonyan, K., Zisserman, A.: Very deep convolutional networks for large-scale image recognition. arXiv preprint arXiv:1409.1556 (2014)
24. Ioffe, S., Szegedy, C.: Batch normalization: accelerating deep network training by reducing internal covariate shift. arXiv preprint arXiv:1502.03167 (2015)
25. Nair, V., Hinton, G.E.: Rectified linear units improve restricted boltzmann machines. In: Proceedings of 27th International Conference on Machine Learning (2010)

Champion Papers

SRC: RoboCup 2017 Small Size League Champion

Ren Wei[✉], Wenhui Ma, Zongjie Yu, Wei Huang, and Shenghao Shan

Fubot Shanghai Robotics Technology Co. LTD, Shanghai, People's Republic of China
ninjawei@fubot.cn

Abstract. In this paper, we present our robot's hardware overview, software framework and free-kick strategy. The free-kick tactic plays a key role during the competition. This strategy is based on reinforcement learning and we design a hierarchical structure with MAXQ decomposition, aiming to train the central server to select a best strategy from the predefined routines. Moreover, we ad-just the strategy intentionally before the final. Our team won the first place in the SSL and we hope our effort can contribute to the RoboCup artificial intelligent progress.

Keywords: RoboCup · SSL · MAXQ · Free-kick · Reinforcement learning

1 Introduction

As a famous international robot event, RoboCup appeals to numerous robot enthusiasts and researchers around the world. The small size league (SSL) is one of the oldest leagues in RoboCup and consists of 28 teams this year. A SSL game takes place between two teams of six robots each. Each robot must conform to the specified dimensions: the robot must fit within a 180 mm diameter circle and must be no higher than 15 cm. The robots play soccer with an orange golf ball on a green carpeted field that is 9 m long by 6 m wide. All objects on the field are tracked by a standardized vision system that processes the data provided by four cameras that are attached to a camera bar located 4 m above the playing surface. Off-field computers for each team are used for the processing required for coordination and control of the robots. Communication is wireless and uses dedicated commercial radio transmitter/receiver.

We introduce the hardware overview and software framework in this paper. The software framework has a plugin system which brings extensibility. For the high level strategy, our energy is focused on the free-kick because we want to find a more intelligent and controllable one. Controllable means that we hope our team can switch strategy in case that the opponent change their strategy in next game. The intelligent and the controllable are not contradictory. Many research also indicate the importance of free-kick [1, 3].

In recent years, many applications about reinforcement learning have sprung up, for instance, the AI used in the StarCraft and DotA. These applications require the cooperation between agents and the RoboCup is a perfect testbed for the research of reinforcement learning for its simplified multi-agents environment and explicit goal. In this

© Springer Nature Switzerland AG 2018
H. Akiyama et al. (Eds.): RoboCup 2017, LNAI 11175, pp. 413–422, 2018.
https://doi.org/10.1007/978-3-030-00308-1_34

context comes our free-kick strategy and the empirical result in the RoboCup 2017 indicates that our strategy has out-standing performances.

The remainder of this paper is organized as follows. Section 2 describes the overview of the robot's hardware. Section 3 presents the details of robotics framework we used. Section 4 introduces the markov decision process (MDP) and the MAXQ method in the Sect. 4.1, then illustrates the application in our free-kick strategy. The Sect. 5 shows the result. Finally, Sect. 6 concludes the paper and points out some future work.

2   Hardware

In this part, we describe the overview of the robot mechanic design. The controller board is shown in Fig. 1 and the mechanical structure is in Fig. 2.

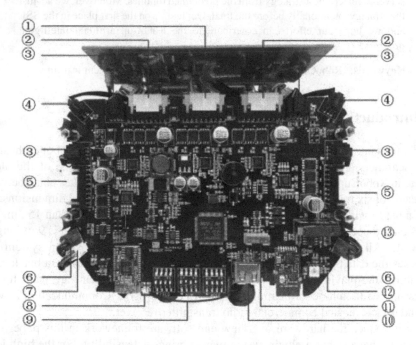

Fig. 1. Controller board overview

Our CPU is STM32F407VET6. The main components are:

(1) Colored LED interface
(2) Motor Controller interface
(3) Encoder interface
(4) Infrared interface
(5) Motor interface
(6) Speaker interface
(7) LED screen interface
(8) Mode setting switcher

(9) Bluetooth indicator
(10) Debug interface
(11) Joystick indicator
(12) Booster switcher

Fig. 2. Mechanical structure

(1) LED screen
(2) Charge status indicator
(3) Kicker mechanism
(4) Bluetooth Speaker
(5) Battery
(6) Universal wheel
(7) Power button
(8) Energy-storage capacitor

3 Software Framework

RoboKit is a robotics framework developed by us, as shown in Fig. 3. It contains plugin system, communication mechanism, event system, service system, parameter server, network protocol, logging system and Lua Script bindings etc. We develop it with C++ and Lua, so it is a cross platform framework (working on windows, Linux, MacOS etc.). For SSL, we developed some plugins based on this framework, such as vision-plugin, skill-plugin, strategy-plugin etc. Vision-plugin contains multi-camera fusion, speed filter and trajectory prediction. Skill-plugin contains all of the basic action such as kick, intercept, chase, chip etc. And strategy-plugin contains defense and attack system.

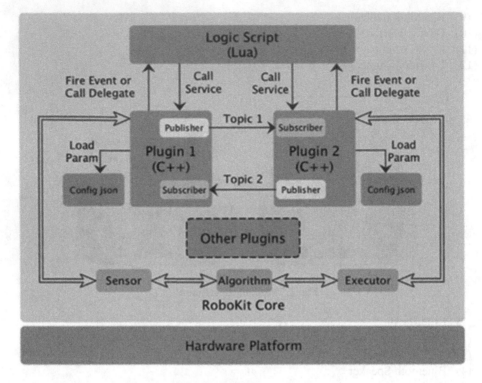

Fig. 3. RoboKit structure

4   Reinforcement Learning

Reinforcement learning has become an important method in RoboCup. Stone, Veloso [3, 4, 12], Bai [2], Riedmiller [13] et al. have done a lot of work on the online learning, SMDP Sarsa (λ) and MAXQ-OP for robots planning.

Free-kick plays a significant role in the offense, while the opponents' formation of defense are relatively not so changeable. Our free-kick strategy is inspired from that a free-kick can also be treated as a MDP and the robot can learn to select the best free-kick tactics from a certain number of pre-defined scripts. For the learning process, we also implement the MAXQ method to handle the large state space.

In this chapter we will first briefly introduce the MDP and MAXQ, further details can be found here [9]. Then, we will show how to implement this method in our free-kick strategy, involving the MDP modeling and the sub-task structure construction.

4.1   MAXQ Decomposition

The MAXQ technique decomposes a markov decision process M into several sub-processes hierarchically, denoted by $\{M_i, i = 0, 1, \dots, n\}$. Each sub-process M_i is also a MDP and defined as $\langle S_i, T_i, A_i, R_i \rangle$, where S_i and T_i are the active state and termination set of M_i respectively. When the active state transit to a state among T_i, the M_i is solved. A_i is a set of actions which can be performed by M or the subtask M_i. $R_i(s'|s, a)$ is the pseudo-reward function for transitions from active states to termination sets, indicating the upper sub-task's preference for action a during the transition from the state s' to the state s. If the termination state is not the expected one, a negative reward would be given to avoid M_i generating this termination state [9]

$$Q_i^*(s, a) = V^*(a, s) + C_i^*(s, a) \tag{1}$$

Where $Q_i^*(s, a)$ is the expected value by firstly performing action M_i at state s, and then following policy π until the M_i terminates. $V^\pi(a, s)$ is a projected value function of hierarchical policy π for sub-task in state s, defined as the expected value after executing policy π at state s, until M_i terminates.

$$V^*(i, s) = \begin{cases} R(s, i) & \text{if } M_i \text{ is primitive} \\ max_{a \in A_i} Q_i^*(s, a) & \text{otherwise} \end{cases} \tag{2}$$

$C_i^*(s, a)$ is the completion function for policy π that estimates the cumulative reward after executing the action M_a, defined as:

$$C_i^*(s, a) = \sum_{s', N} \gamma^N P(s', N|s, a) V^*(i, s') \tag{3}$$

The online planning solution is explained in [2], and here we list the main algorithms.

```
Algorithm 1. OnlinePlanning ()
Input: an MDP model with its MAXQ hierarchical structure
Output: the accumulated reward r after reaching a goal
r ← 0
s ← GetInitState()
r ← r + InitialAction(a₀, s)
while s ∉ G₀
do
    ⟨v, aₚ⟩ ← EvaluateState(0, s, [0,0,··· ,0])
    r ← r + ExecuteAction(aₚ, s)
    GetNextState()
return r
```

Here we set an initial action update before the system start updating. The initial action enable us to modify the strategy according to the opponent's defense formation.

```
Algorithm 2. EvaluateState(i,s,d)
Input: subtask M_i, state s and depth array d
Output: ⟨V*(i,s),a_p*⟩
if M_i is primitive then return ⟨R(s,M_i),M_i⟩
else if s ∉ S_i and s ∉ G_i then return ⟨-∞,nil⟩
else if s ∈ G_i then return ⟨0,nil⟩
else if d[i] ≥ D[i] then return ⟨HeuristicValue(i,s),nil⟩
else
      ⟨v*,a_p*⟩ ← ⟨-∞,nil⟩
      for M_k ∈ Subtasks(M_i) do
        if M_k is primitive or s ∉ G_k then
            ⟨v,a_p⟩ ← EvaluateState(k,s,d)
            v ← v + EvaluateCompletion(i,s,k,d)
            if v > v*
                ⟨v*,a_p*⟩ ← ⟨v,a_p⟩
      end
return ⟨v*,a_p*⟩
```

Algorithm 2 summarizes the major procedures of evaluating a subtask. The procedure uses an AND-OR tree and a depth-first search method. The recursion will end when:

(1) the subtask is a primitive action;
(2) the state is a goal state or a state outside the scope of this subtask;
(3) a certain depth is reached.

```
Algorithm 3. EvaluateCompletion (i,s,a,d)
Input: subtask M_i, state s, action M_a and depth array d
Output: estimated C*(i,s,d)
G̃_a ← ImportanceSampling(G_a,D_a)
v ← 0
for s' ∈ G̃_a do
  d' ← d;
  d'[i] ← d'[i] + 1
  v ← v + 1/G̃_a EvaluateState(i,s',d')
end
return v
```

Algorithm 3 shows a recursive procedure to estimate the completion function, where $\tilde{G}_a$ is a set of sampled states drawn from prior distribution D_a using importance sampling techniques.

4.2   Application in Free-Kick

Now we utilize the techniques we mentioned in our free-kick strategy. First we should model the free-kick as a MDP, specifying the state, action, transition and reward functions.

State. As usual, the teammates and opponents are treated as the observations of environment. The state vector's length is fixed, containing 5 teammates and 6 opponents.

Action. For the free-kick, the actions includes kick, turn and dash. They are in the continuous action space.

Transition. We predefined 60 scripts which tell agent the behavior of team-mates. These scripts are chosen randomly. For the opponents, we simply assume them moving or kicking (if kickable) randomly. The basic atomic actions is modeled from the dynamics.

Reward Function. The reward function considers not only the ball scored, which may cause the forward search process terminates without rewards for a long period. Considering a free-kick, a satisfying serve should never be intercepted by the opponents, so if the ball pass through the opponents, we give a positive reward. Similarly, we design several rewards function for different sub-tasks.

Next, we implement MAXQ to decompose the state space. Our free-kick MAXQ hierarchy is constructed as follows:

Primitive Actions. We define three low-level primitive actions for the free-kick process: the kick, turn and dash. Each primitive action has a reward of −1 so that the policy reach the goal fast.

Subtasks. The kickTo aims to kick the ball to a direction with a proper velocity, while the moveTo is designed to move the robot to some locations. To a higher level, there are Lob, Pass, Dribble, Shoot, Position and Formation behaviors where:

(1) Lob is to kick the ball in the air to lands behind the opponents;
(2) Pass is to give the ball to a teammate.
(3) Dribble is to carry the ball for some distance.
(4) Shoot is to kick the ball to score.
(5) Position is to maintain the formation in the free-kick.

Free-Kick. The root of the process will evaluate which sub-task should the place kicker should take.

Our hierarchy structure is shown in Fig. 4. Note that some sub-tasks need parameters and they are represented by a parenthesis.

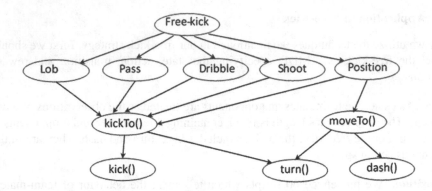

Fig. 4. Hierarchical structure of free-kick

5 Performance Evaluation

To evaluate the strategy's performance, we filter out the defense frames from the log files of teams in RoboCup 2016. Then we summarize each team's defense strategy and write a simulator to defend against our team.

For each team, we run 200 free-kick attacks. Tables 1 and 2 shows the test results. Compare to the primitive free-kick strategy, our new strategy has a higher rate to score from a free-kick and that's what we expected.

Table 1. Training result against log files of RoboCup 2016 above: Free-kick with primitive routine below: Free-kick using RL

Opponent	Free-kicks	Goals	Score rate
KIKS	200	14	7.0%
RoboFEI	200	0	0.0%
STOx's	200	25	12.5%
Parsian	200	7	3.5%
ER-force	200	18	9.0%
Opponent	Free-kicks	Goals	Score rate
KIKS	200	35	17.5%
RoboFEI	200	52	26.0%
STOx's	200	48	24.0%
Parsian	200	22	11.0%
ER-force	200	69	34.5%

In the RoboCup 2017, the strategy is tested. Note that the mechanism is not idealize, some teamwork fails frequently. Still, it can be seen from the Tables 2 and 3 that our team outperforms other teams.

Table 2. RoboCup 2017 round robin result

Opponent (round robin)	Score
KIKS	1:0
RoboFEI	9:0
ER-force	1:0

Table 3. RoboCup 2017 result of Elimination

Opponent (elimination)	Score
STOx's	1:0

Before the Final, we got the log file of other teams and modified the strategy by specifying the initial action of place kicker (i.e. the kicker would directly pass the ball to teammates for the Parsian's defense robot is not so close) after analyzing the defense routine of opponents. The test result is in Table 4.

Table 4. Test result before final

Opponent (log simulated)	Free-kicks	Goals	Score Rate
Parsian	200	61	30.5%
ER-force	200	47	23.5%

During the final, our robots' shoot speed broke the restriction frequently and one robot was sent off. Luckily, our team wins with a narrow margin (Table 5).

Table 5. Final result

Opponent (final)	Score
Parsian	4:1
ER-force	2:1

6 Conclusion

This paper presents our robot's hardware and software framework. We implement the reinforcement learning in our free-kick tactic. Based on the related work, we divide the free-kick into some sub-tasks and write some hand-made routines for the learning process. The results of the competition prove the efficiency of our strategy. In the meantime, we find that some generated policies are missions impossible, which never been followed by robots fully. Therefore, we need to consider more constraints and the mechanical needs to be more flexible. Our contribution lies in the realization of reinforcement learning in the SSL, which is a first step from simulation to reality. In the future, we plan to imply more artificial intelligent technologies in SSL and make efforts to the competition between human and robots in RoboCup 2050.

References

1. Mendoza, J.P., Simmons, R.G., Veloso, M.M.: Online learning of robot soccer free kick plans using a bandit approach. In: ICAPS, pp. 504–508, June 2016
2. Bai, A., Wu, F., Chen, X.: Towards a principled solution to simulated robot soccer. In: Chen, X., Stone, P., Sucar, L.E., van der Zant, T. (eds.) RoboCup 2012. LNCS (LNAI), vol. 7500, pp. 141–153. Springer, Heidelberg (2013). https://doi.org/10.1007/978-3-642-39250-4_14
3. Mendoza, J.P., Biswas, J., Zhu, D., Wang, R., Cooksey, P., Klee, S., Veloso, M.: CMDragons 2015: coordinated offense and defense of the SSL champions. In: Almeida, L., Ji, J., Steinbauer, G., Luke, S. (eds.) RoboCup 2015. LNCS (LNAI), vol. 9513, pp. 106–117. Springer, Cham (2015). https://doi.org/10.1007/978-3-319-29339-4_9
4. Stone, P., Sutton, R., Kuhlmann, G.: Reinforcement learning for robocup soccer keepaway. Adapt. Behav. **13**(3), 165–188 (2005)
5. Kalyanakrishnan, S., Liu, Y., Stone, P.: Half field offense in robocup soccer: a multiagent reinforcement learning case study. In: Lakemeyer, G., Sklar, E., Sorrenti, Domenico G., Takahashi, T. (eds.) RoboCup 2006. LNCS (LNAI), vol. 4434, pp. 72–85. Springer, Heidelberg (2007). https://doi.org/10.1007/978-3-540-74024-7_7
6. Thrun, S., Burgard, W., Fox, D.: Probabilistic Robotics, vol. 1. MIT press, Cambridge (2005)
7. Bruce, J., Veloso, M.: Real-time randomized path planning for robot navigation. In: IEEE/RSJ International Conference on Intelligent Robots and Systems, vol. 3, pp. 2383–2388. IEEE (2002)
8. Ye, Y., Zhao, Y., Wang, Q., Dai, X., Feng, Y., Chen, X.: SRC team description paper for RoboCup 2017 (2017)
9. Dietterich, T.G.: Hierarchical reinforcement learning with the MAXQ value function decomposition. J. Mach. Learn. Res. **13**(1), 63 (1999)
10. Ren, C., Ma, S.: Dynamic modeling and analysis of an omnidirectional mobile robot. In: Intelligent Robots and Systems (IROS), pp. 4860–4865 (2013)
11. Kober, J., Mülling, K., Krömer, O., Lampert, C.H., Schölkopf, B., Peters, J.: Movement templates for learning of hitting and batting. In: IEEE International Conference on Robotics and Automation, pp. 1–6 (2010)
12. Stone, P.: Layered Learning in Multi-agent Systems: A Winning Approach to Robotic Soccer. The MIT press, Cambridge (2000)
13. Gabel, T., Riedmiller, M.: On progress in RoboCup: the simulation league showcase. In: Ruiz-del-Solar, J., Chown, E., Plöger, P.G. (eds.) RoboCup 2010. LNCS (LNAI), vol. 6556, pp. 36–47. Springer, Heidelberg (2011). https://doi.org/10.1007/978-3-642-20217-9_4

Rhoban Football Club: RoboCup Humanoid Kid-Size 2017 Champion Team Paper

Julien Allali, Rémi Fabre, Loic Gondry, Ludovic Hofer$^{(\boxtimes)}$, Olivier Ly,
Steve N'Guyen, Grégoire Passault, Antoine Pirrone, and Quentin Rouxel

Rhoban Football Club Team, LaBRI, University of Bordeaux, Bordeaux, France
`{lhofer,quentin.rouxel}@labri.fr`

Abstract. In 2017, Rhoban Football Club reached the first place of the Kid-Size soccer competition for the second time, and was awarded best humanoid by the jury (https://www.robocuphumanoid.org/hl-2017/results/.). Capitalizing over the hardware design and software basis from previous participations, we improved both robustness and overall behaviors of our humanoid robots. An interesting milestone reached is the opportunistic pass ability; since such an high-level team play behavior can only work after solving underlying difficulties like having a good field localization, robust and reliable detection of vision features, a repeatable locomotion with odometry etc. This paper describes the most meaningful improvements accomplished over this year along with perspectives of future work.

1 Introduction

During the 2017 competition, Rhoban humanoid robots scored 41 goals. 2 goals were scored against Rhoban, in both cases by our own robots because of a technical bug with our localization system that was fixed during the competition. Indeed, the banishment of magnetic compass[1] in 2017 makes it more likely to observe this kind of failure. We also scored the highest number of points during the drop-in games, which was a new challenge mixing different teams in the 2017 edition. This was a great opportunity for teams to get ready for real game situations. In this paper, we present the main modifications we added to both software and hardware since RoboCup 2016.

2 Hardware

Like every team, Rhoban continuously tries to improve its robots by observing new problems each year at the RoboCup and trying to fix it for the next year. In 2017 our new *Sigmaban 2* robots are 68 cm tall with Dynamixel MX106 on

---

[1] https://www.robocuphumanoid.org/materials/rules/.

© Springer Nature Switzerland AG 2018
H. Akiyama et al. (Eds.): RoboCup 2017, LNAI 11175, pp. 423–434, 2018.
https://doi.org/10.1007/978-3-030-00308-1_35

the legs, which has proven an efficient and robust compromise between our now old MX64 based 58 cm tall Sigmaban and the various taller prototypes (90 cm in 2015, 80 cm in 2016). The mechanical parts of the robots are now entirely machined and screwed aluminium rather than bent for a better precision. Some other significant improvement have been made this year and are described below.

2.1   Feet Pressure and Load Cells

Sensing pressures under the feet is one of the specificities of our small humanoid robots, as explained in the 2016 champion paper [1] and open-source project[2].

In 2017, we switched to a more robust, full Wheatstone bridge, 40 kg rated, off the shelf load cells. These load cells are smaller than the previous ones and are able to handle higher forces because they are made of 3 mm thick steel. To improve the solidity of our robots, and to avoid exposing the load cells and especially the strain gauges below the feet, we also switched to another hardware fixation, as depicted on Fig. 1. The load cells are now on the top of the feet plate and the deformation is transmitted through the plate, using a nylon ring to reduce frictions.

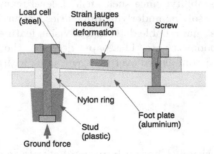

Fig. 1. Fixation of load cells on the feet plate for RoboCup 2017. An exaggerated deformation is represented to understand how the measurement is done.

2.2   Hot-Swap

We designed an hot-swap power board that offers the possibility to switch the batteries without any transition phase where the robot computer is not powered. To achieve this, the new battery is plugged before the old one is unplugged and a *single pole, double throw* switch is used to change which battery powers the motors. Two diodes allow the batteries to be simultaneous power sources of the computer, regardless of the switch position. This system is more efficient than the hard reset that was needed during the half-time break in previous years.

---

[2] https://github.com/Rhoban/ForceFoot.

2.3   Open-Sourcing Dynamixel Board

Our Dynamixel board, which includes three parallel USART buses to reduce the low-level delays that was already introduced in 2016 [1] is now available as an open-source project[3].

2.4   Head Protection

In previous years, 3D-printed camera protections were used. This year, the protections were cut into the same aluminum used for the robot's body. This turned out to be a strong downgrade. When a collision occurs with the head of the robot, 3D-printed protections bend, effectively absorbing a portion of the impact. With the aluminum protections, most of the impact is directly transmitted to the motors' shafts. Rotational offsets up to 6° were commonly observed on the head pitch servomotors after a fall and having the head's shaft completely severed became a common issue.

3   Motion

3.1   Walk Engine

From 2014 to 2016, all of our robots were relying on the open-source *IKWalk* engine presented in [15]. For this 2017 edition of the RoboCup competition, this walk engine has been improved to a new version, *QuinticWalk*[4], leading to a smoother and stabler motion. This new walk engine follows the same principles as the old one but with many details updated.

As introduced by [2], the movement is open loop and does not use any ZMP criterion or dynamics modeling. The shapes of target trajectories are built geometrically from a set of parameters in the Cartesian space. All target joint positions are then computed through an inverse kinematics of the legs of the robot. These parameters are manually tuned on the physical humanoid robot (trials and errors) until a fast and balanced motion is achieved. The main changes are the following:

- The trajectories are represented by using 5th order polynomial splines. This splines allow for continuous accelerations. Hence, the computed theoretical torques generated by the motion at each joint are also continuous, as well as the ZMP trajectory on the ground.
- Acceleration continuity is ensured during omnidirectional walk as well as parameter update (in a way similar as done in [9]).
- Instead of expressing the target trajectories with respect to the moving frame of the *trunk*, all Cartesian positions and orientations (12 degrees of freedom)

---

[3] https://github.com/Rhoban/DXLBoard.
[4] Source code available at: https://github.com/RhobanProject/Model/tree/master/QuinticWalk.

are expressed with respect to the support foot, fixed on the ground. The overall motion is easier to define but the discontinuity of the representation has to be handle at the support swap.

– The handling of the double support phase is implemented. A low frequency and stable gait can be achieved with the right set of parameter values.

– On the walk startup, the trunk begin to oscillate during an half cycle before the legs in order to initialize the dynamics of weight swigging of the robot.

As a result, the displacement of the robot is qualitatively far stabler, especially on our bigger robots. For example, the lateral steps do not trigger constantly the stabilization module anymore (see [12]) which was required to prevent the robot from falling.

However, the effects of the Runge phenomenon can be observed on some parts of the trajectories. The current implementation could be improved by replacing the polynomial splines by the optimal bang-bang jerk control developed by [4].

4   Vision

Our main vision system has been completely changed in 2017. The method we used before was mainly based on multiple hand-tailored OpenCV filtering, but for our purpose, this "standard" method has reached its limits in terms of complexity, robustness and maintainability. The new vision pipeline is much simpler and requires much less hand tuning. Moreover, it also appeared to be quite robust to the environments changes in luminosity and color.

Regions of interest (ROI) for the ball and the goal posts are extracted from the full image, using the robot's state (ground plane projection on the camera plane) and a kernel convolution on an Integral Image filter. These ROIs are then classified by a Convolutional Neural Network, see Fig. 2.

(a) Score of ROI for goal posts   (b) Result of goal posts detection

Fig. 2. Score of ROI for goal posts

4.1   Identification of ROI by Integral Images

The first step of ball and goal post detection is to identify ROI which are likely to contain them. The ROI are squares and their size is computed according to the robot model. A ROI is supposed to measure twice the size of the ball, due to perspectives, the size might vary inside the image.

The score of a ROI is computed based on white and green densities inside the region. Local densities can be obtained at a low computational cost based on integral images, see [5]. For the ball, the density of white at the center of the region should be higher than the average density in the whole region, on the other hand, the density of green in the center of region should be lower than in the whole region. The same pattern applies for goal post detection, but the region which has to contain a high density of white is the top center of the region. A visualization of the score function is shown for the goal posts in Fig. 2a. Positive scores are shown in red and negative scores in black. Note that if a region of interest should exceed the margin of the image, then its score is zero.

In order to ensure a satisfying frame rate, a maximum of 4 ROI per frame are classified by each neural network. Selection is based on scores and intersection of ROI is forbidden.

4.2   Classification

Convolutional Neural Networks (ConvNet) have become the state of the art methods in various computer vision tasks [10]. Several off-the-shelf very powerful architectures are available such as [13,14] but unfortunately none were usable in the very limited embedded computers of our robots. We thus designed our custom ConvNet using a c++ library with no external dependencies[5]. The aim of the approach was to design a minimal architecture able to classify ball and goal post patches with at least 95% accuracy.

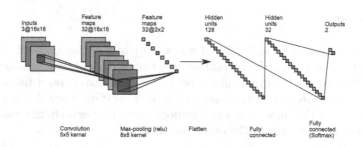

Fig. 3. Architecture of the reduced ConvNet used for ball classification in the RoboCup 2017

---

[5] https://github.com/tiny-dnn/tiny-dnn.

After some hand-tuning we obtained a quite small network (cf. Fig. 3) able to classify small $16 \times 16 \times 3$ patches with good results (cf. Table 1).

Table 1. Learning results for ball and posts classification.

	nb training/validation	Learning rate	Accuracy
Ball	7400/1500	0.013	96.8%
Posts	13500/2500	0.0425	96.92%

This architecture was used both for ball and goal post classification, with the small difference that the goal network has only 16 feature maps.

4.3   Logging and Image Tagging

One key functionality to this system is the ability to quickly obtain a large quantity of labeled data. To do so, patches extracted from ROIs were uploaded on an online tagging tool[6] accessible to the public. Tagging was made simple with a responsive "*Google ReCaptcha*" style interface. This tool was used by several supporters from outside the team and allowed to get thousands of labeled patches in a matter of a few hours, thus freeing precious time to the team members. In order to ensure the quality of the tagging from non expert users, a consensus based approach on the label was implemented (a patch is considered correctly labeled if it was tagged more than N times and if more than $X\%$ of the tag were consistent). Moreover, new users were first required to correctly label a set of images previously labeled by the team members. To date, approximately 10000 patches of balls and 4000 of goal posts were positively labeled. Finally, a slight gamification of the system was added through a leaderboard in order to motivate users. The project is open source[7] and the data are available once registered.

5   Strategy

Last year, our strategy to kick the ball was simply to face the center of the goals. However, this is not a satisfying solution for several reasons. For instance, when the ball is located on the corners of the field, it is better to center it before trying to score a goal. Moreover, depending on the ball location, the tolerance on the orientation is not the same, it is more important to face exactly the goals when we are near than if we are in the other half field.

5.1   Kick Model

In order to be able to optimize the kick decisions, we started by establishing a model of the noise on the kick based on real-world data. We used a simple model

---

[6] http://rhoban.com/tagger/.

[7] https://www.github.com/rhoban/tagger.

where the kick distance r and the kick direction θ are sampled from Gaussian distributions.

$$r \sim N(\mu_r, \sigma_r)$$
$$\theta \sim N(\mu_\theta, \sigma_\theta) \tag{1}$$

5.2   Value Iteration for the Kick Strategy

Choosing the decision and the type of kick is modeled as a Markov decision problem, MDP for short.

The current state $s \in S$ can be any position of the ball on the field using discrete grid (for instance every 20 cm), or also *out* or *goal* if the ball goes out of the field or scores a goal. The possible actions $a \in A$ are tuples (k, θ) of the selected kick k (forward kick or lateral kick) and kick orientations θ, which are also discrete (for instance every 5°).

We can then build a model of the stochastic transition function, using random samples, as depicted on Fig. 4. This model is actually the estimation of $P(s'|s, a)$, i.e. the probability of reaching the state s' knowing that we were in the state s and we applied the action a.

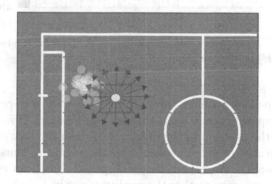

Fig. 4. The transition function is approximated using random sampling for each possible state s and action a.

We then use the value iteration algorithm [3] with the following iterative method:

$$V(s) = \max_a \left[\sum_{s' \in s} P(s'|s, a)(R(s, s') + V(s')) \right]$$
$$V(goal) = 0 \tag{2}$$
$$V(out) = -1000$$

Where $R(s, s')$ is the reward for getting in state s' from state s. In our case, we choose the reward to be the negative number of seconds required to walk from the position of state s to the state s'. Thus, the value of $V(s)$ can here be understood as the (negative) time required to score a goal for the better possible sequence of kicks.

We update the values of each state iteratively until one complete iteration did not changed the value of any state.

The action a that maximizes $V(s)$ for each $s \in S$ is then the kick and orientation that should be used depending on where the ball is located on the field. Moreover, we can also select several actions that produce similar values, using a tolerance threshold. This is an interesting information since it can be used to know how accurate we need to be when trying to approach the ball. Figure 5 shows an example of result obtained.

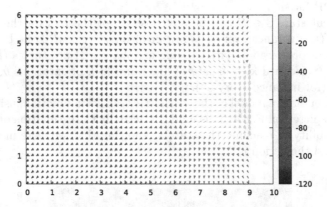

Fig. 5. The values of $V(s)$ (using color gradient) on the field for the better kicks (using a tolerance) for each position on the field (Color figure online)

Approaching the kick problem through MDP allowed us to provide satisfying policies without requiring heavy hand-tuning of parameters. However, in order to take into account the position of the other robots into the kick decision process, it would be necessary to add dimensions to the problem, thus leading to the curse of dimensionality. We expect to use approach based on continuous state and action MDP to improve further the quality of our kick decision policies. This approach has already been successful for reducing the time require to reach a satisfying position for kicking [8].

5.3   Team Play

All robots share some information about their state, including their position estimation, the estimation of where the ball is on the field, their game state (for instance if they are playing, fallen or penalized).

A kicker score, which is an estimation of the time that would be required for the robot to reach the ball and the value $V(s)$ depending on the ball position is also shared to choose which robot will handle the ball and kick it. This robot shares the estimation of the position of the ball after its next shoot, using the mean μ of the kick model. We achieved opportunistic passes this way. Indeed, the robots were trying to walk where the ball *would be* in the future, after the next kick of the robot currently handling the ball.

In the future, this might be achieved in a better way, taking in account the positions of other robots to adjust the kick. From a technical point of view, we are also considering electing a virtual team "captain", that would take the decision for the whole strategy, which would considerably simplify the organization of team play.

5.4   Camera Model Calibration

In the current state of the competition, robots still fall frequently. The deformation that is caused on the mechanical parts has been a recurrent issue since the geometric model of the robot is constantly used in the vision pipeline. For example to compute the Cartesian egocentric distance between the robot and the detected ball on the ground. A dismountable, low cost calibration setup was designed specifically for calibration. The markers on the setup are detected with an off-the-shelf algorithm [6] by the robot whose cleats are used to ensure an accurate position on the ground. A dance-like motion was implemented so that the tags are seen from a multitude of perspectives.

A hundred samples, containing the joint positions of the robot and the measured coordinates of the tags in pixel space, are downloaded from the robot. Since the actual positions of the tags are known, an error can be calculated for each tag of each measure using the direct kinematics of the robot.

A black box optimization algorithm [7] is used to minimize a function of the errors, the inputs of the optimization being angular offsets in the camera joint (pitch, roll, yaw), in the neck joint (roll, yaw), in the IMU joint (pitch, roll) and a parameter that quantifies the measure noise in pixel space. 25% of the samples are used for cross-validation.

During the 2017 RoboCup, almost every robot was calibrated between matches. Offsets of more than $3°$ were often found in-between.

6   Development and Workflow

6.1   Build System and Architecture

One of the main issue about software architecture is managing the dependencies with third party libraries, and also with our own different packages. We switched to catkin, which is a build system used by the ROS community [11]. We also developed custom scripts to be able to manage all our many repositories, which helps us to install and update automatically all the dependencies when installing the development environment on a new system.

Since the robots have the same architecture (x86 64 bits) than our computers, we can deploy directly the binaries on it without actually cross-compilation. Some flags are just provided to avoid using extended instructions like SSE4 unavailable on the robots.

In the future, we plan to switch to Intel NUC7i5BNK as main computer, which would provide better overall CPU performances.

6.2   Behavior Viewer

A considerable portion of our strategy is implemented using finite state machine representations. Even if this is a convenient tool to represent the behaviour of the robot, increasing the number of possible states and transitions makes it quadratically harder to validate all possible game scenarios. For instance, free kicks or yellow and red cards that were introduced in the 2017 rules made these states machines more complex.

In order to test our strategy, to reproduce a game situation and check how the robot behaves, a simulated mode has been implemented in our software. From a kinematics simulation (no physics), robot's state and environment are faked. We designed a tool called the *Behavior Viewer* (Fig. 6) which is used to setup and easily reproduce any wanted scenario by mocking the robot position, the ball and also some obstacles. Note that the exact same behaviour code is running in the fake environment and in our robots during actual games, including the referee instructions listening.

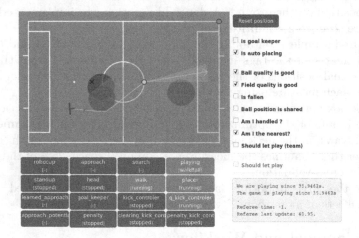

Fig. 6. An example of situation in the Behavior Viewer involving a robot playing with the ball, obstacles, trajectory and vision cone.

6.3   Monitoring and Replay

In addition of previously explained off-line testing process, it is also important to be able to monitor what is happening during the game and to investigate on the logs. Our online monitoring system, which captures the UDP packets that are used by our robots for strategy communication and produces a visualization, now also captures images from a webcam and logs everything so that we can replay a full game step by step. We can also synchronize the robot timestamped log files to have even more accurate data. Figure 7 is an example of the result.

This system was extensively used for testing games and produces better unbiased opinions about what is needed to be fixed or improved.

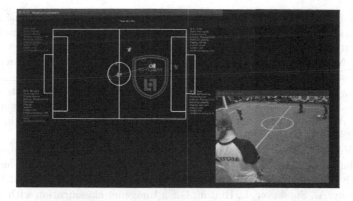

Fig. 7. Monitoring both the state of our robots and the images with full replay ability after the games

7   Conclusion

We now have full monitoring logs from all of the RoboCup games of this year. We plan to use them as an objective tool to define what are the priorities in order to improve the game on our robots.

An early version of other robots detection and obstacle avoidance was implemented. However this detection is still difficult, mainly because opponent robot appearances are unknown and building a training dataset is hard during the competition. Sharing images among teams maybe one of the possible solutions.

Tackling this problem would really improve the quality of the games. First because we would like the robots to be able to avoid from colliding each other in the future, but also use this information to compute more sophisticated strategy. Free kicks are also a good rule-tool for the referees to encourage detecting robots by penalizing the robots colliding each other.

References

1. Allali, J., et al.: Rhoban football club: RoboCup humanoid kid-size 2016 champion team paper. In: Behnke, S., Sheh, R., Sariel, S., Lee, D.D. (eds.) RoboCup 2016. LNCS (LNAI), vol. 9776, pp. 491–502. Springer, Cham (2017). https://doi.org/10.1007/978-3-319-68792-6_41
2. Behnke, S.: Online trajectory generation for omnidirectional biped walking. In: 2006 IEEE International Conference on Robotics and Automation (ICRA 2006), pp. 1597–1603. IEEE (2006)
3. Bellman, R.: A markovian decision process. J. Math. Mech. 679–684 (1957)
4. Broquere, X., Sidobre, D., Herrera-Aguilar, I.: Soft motion trajectory planner for service manipulator robot. In: 2008 IEEE/RSJ International Conference on Intelligent Robots and Systems (IROS 2008), pp. 2808–2813. IEEE (2008)
5. Crow, F.C.: Summed-area tables for texture mapping. ACM SIGGRAPH Comput. Graph. **18**(3), 207–212 (1984)

6. Garrido-Jurado, S., Muñoz-Salinas, R., Madrid-Cuevas, F.J., Marín-Jiménez, M.J.: Automatic generation and detection of highly reliable fiducial markers under occlusion. Pattern Recogn. **47**(6), 2280–2292 (2014)
7. Hansen, N., Ostermeier, A.: Completely derandomized self-adaptation in evolution strategies. Evol. comput. **9**(2), 159–195 (2001)
8. Hofer, L., Rouxel, Q.: An operational method toward efficient walk control policies for humanoid robots. In: Proceedings of the Twenty-Seventh International Conference on Automated Planning and Scheduling, ICAPS 2017, Pittsburgh, Pennsylvania, USA, 18–23 June 2017, pp. 489–497 (2017)
9. Hugel, V., Jouandeau, N.: Walking patterns for real time path planning simulation of humanoids. In: 2012 IEEE International Symposium on Robot and Human Interactive Communication (RO-MAN 2012), pp. 424–430. IEEE, RO-MAN (2012)
10. Krizhevsky, A., Sutskever, I., Hinton, G.E.: Imagenet classification with deep convolutional neural networks. In: Advances in Neural Information Processing Systems, pp. 1097–1105 (2012)
11. O'Kane, J.M.: A Gentle Introduction to ROS (2014)
12. Passault, G., Rouxel, Q., Hofer, L., N'Guyen, S., Ly, O.: Low-cost force sensors for small size humanoid robot (video contribution). In: 2015 IEEE-RAS International Conference on Humanoid Robots (Humanoids 2015), pp. 1148–1148. IEEE (2015). https://youtu.be/_d7Phe0qois
13. Redmon, J., Divvala, S., Girshick, R., Farhadi, A.: You only look once: unified, real-time object detection. In: Proceedings of the IEEE Conference on Computer Vision and Pattern Recognition, pp. 779–788 (2016)
14. Ren, S., He, K., Girshick, R., Sun, J.: Faster R-CNN: towards real-time object detection with region proposal networks. In: Advances in neural information processing systems, pp. 91–99 (2015)
15. Rouxel, Q., Passault, G., Hofer, L., N'Guyen, S., Ly, O.: Rhoban hardware and software open source contributions for robocup humanoids. In: Proceedings of 10th Workshop on Humanoid Soccer Robots at IEEE-RAS International Conference on Humanoid Robots (2015)

Advanced Soccer Skills and Team Play of RoboCup 2017 TeenSize Winner NimbRo

Diego Rodriguez(✉), Hafez Farazi, Philipp Allgeuer, Dmytro Pavlichenko,
Grzegorz Ficht, André Brandenburger, Johannes Kürsch, and Sven Behnke

Autonomous Intelligent Systems, Computer Science,
University of Bonn, Bonn, Germany
{rodriguez,farazi,pallgeuer,pavlichenko,ficht,behnke}@ais.uni-bonn.de,
http://ais.uni-bonn.de

Abstract. In order to pursue the vision of the RoboCup Humanoid League of beating the soccer world champion by 2050, new rules and competitions are added or modified each year fostering novel technological advances. In 2017, the number of players in the TeenSize class soccer games was increase to 3 vs. 3, which allowed for more team play strategies. Improvements in individual skills were also demanded through a set of technical challenges. This paper presents the latest individual skills and team play developments used in RoboCup 2017 that lead our team Nimbro winning the 2017 TeenSize soccer tournament, the technical challenges, and the drop-in games.

1 Introduction

Every year the RoboCup Humanoid League raises its bar in its competitions. This year, the league increased the allowed number of players in the TeenSize soccer games to 3 vs. 3, which encourages the development of more complex team play strategies. At the same time, a new competition called *Drop-in games* was introduced in which a team is composed of robots from different institutes or universities. This paper presents our recent developments to address these modifications and shows their performance in the competition. Our robots won all TeenSize 2017 competitions: the soccer tournament, the Drop-in games and the technical challenges. In RoboCup 2017 we used our fully open-source 3D printed platform, the igus® Humanoid Open Platform [1]. Moreover, we upgraded one of our classic robots, Dynaped, so that it is able to get up from the prone and supine lying positions in order to be rule-compliant. Both platforms are shown in Fig. 1, along with the human members of our team NimbRo. We released a video of the competition 2017 highlights[1].

---

[1] RoboCup 2017 NimbRo TeenSize highlights video: https://youtu.be/6ldHWWH feBc.

© Springer Nature Switzerland AG 2018
H. Akiyama et al. (Eds.): RoboCup 2017, LNAI 11175, pp. 435–447, 2018.
https://doi.org/10.1007/978-3-030-00308-1_36

Fig. 1. Left: the igus® Humanoid Open Platform robot. Middle: the team NimbRo. Right: the upgraded Dynaped robot for RoboCup 2017.

2   Robot Platforms

Igus Humanoid Open Platform. Over the last four years, the igus® Humanoid Open Platform [1] (Fig. 1 left) has been developed as an open-source hardware and software project. Thanks to its 3D printed exoskeleton, the 92 cm tall robot weights only 6.6 kg. The platform incorporates an Intel Core i7-5500U CPU running a 64-bit Ubuntu OS, and a Robotis CM730 microcontroller board, which electrically interfaces with its Robotis Dynamixel MX actuators. The CM730 also incorporates 3-axis accelerometer and gyroscope sensors, for a total of 6 axes of inertial measurement. For visual perception, the robot is equipped with a Logitech C905 USB camera fitted with a wide-angle lens. The robot software is based on the ROS middleware, and is a continuous evolution of the ROS software that was written for the NimbRo-OP [2].

Dynaped. Dynaped has been playing since RoboCup 2009 for team NimbRo. Its original design had 14 degrees of freedom (DOF): 5 DoF per leg, 1 DoF per arm, and 2 DoF in the neck. Dynaped is distinguished by its effective use of parallel kinematics coupled with high torque, provided by pairs of EX-106 actuators in the roll joints of the hip and ankle, and pitch joints in the knee. All other DoFs are driven by single actuators. The torso is constructed entirely of aluminum and consists of a cylindrical tube and a rectangular cage that holds the electronics. Similar to the igus® Humanoid Open Platform, Dynaped is equipped with an Intel Core i7-5500U CPU, a CM740 controller board (newer version of CM730), and a USB camera with a wide-angle lens. Dynaped used the same software components as the igus® Humanoid Open Platform such as perception, bipedal walking, team communication, soccer behaviors, among others, thanks to their modularity and robustness. Dynaped's competition performance and hardware design, contributed to NimbRo winning the Louis Vuitton Best Humanoid Award in both 2010 and 2012 [3].

In order to be allowed to play in RoboCup 2017, Dynaped needed to be upgraded. Having only 1 DOF per arm, Dynaped was not able to get up either from prone or supine lying position. We included thus an additional DOF in each arm, namely a pitch elbow. Both the arm and the forearm are made from carbon fiber and reinforced against torsion with aluminum bars (Fig. 1 right).

3   Software Design

3.1   Visual Perception

As part of the preprocessing, we convert the RGB images to the HSV space because of its intuitive nature and handful separation of brightness and chromatic information. To compensate the high distortion coming from the wide-angle lenses, we use the pinhole camera model to compensate radial and tangential distortion. Using this distortion model, once the object of interest is identified, we project it into egocentric world coordinates. For calibrating the pose of the camera, we use the Nelder-Mead method [4] to minimize the reprojection error of detected field lines.

Ball Detection. We utilize a histogram of oriented gradients (HOG) descriptor in a cascade classifier trained using AdaBoost with positive and negative samples. Because of the computational cost of using sliding windows [5] we use the descriptor only on those candidates that are preselected based on shape, size, and colour.

Line Detection. On artificial grass, the painted field lines are not clearly white; thus an edge detector followed by probabilistic Hough line detection are implemented. Line segments are filtered to avoid false positives. Finally, the remaining similar line segments are merged to produce fewer larger lines. The shorter line segments are used for detecting the field circle, while the remaining lines are passed to the localization method. Figure 2 shows an example of the output of the object detection. For more details, please refer to [6].

Localization on the Soccer Field. We propose a multi-hypothesis model to estimate the three-dimensional robot pose (x, y, θ) on the field. We mainly use integrated gyroscope values as the source of orientation information and treat the heading initialization a classification problem making use of the specific possible locations where the robot can be placed according to the rules, namely, at the touch-line in the robot's own half facing the field, or near the center circle and goal area facing the opponent goal. We start four instances of our localization module with different initial hypothesis locations. For each instance, we handle the unknown data association of ambiguous landmarks, such as goal posts and T-junctions. Over time, we try to update the location of the hypothesis towards an estimated position. We update the location based on a probabilistic model

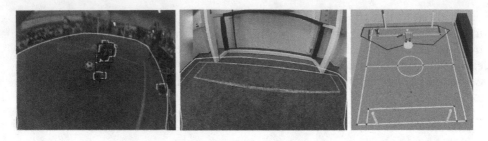

Fig. 2. Left: Image with ball (magenta circle), obstacles (black square) and field boundary (yellow lines) detections on RoboCup 2017. Middle: one input image for our localization method. Right: visualization of the localization of the robot in Rviz. (Color figure online)

of landmark observations involving mainly lines and goal posts [6]. The inputs to the probabilistic model come from the vision module and dead-reckoning odometry data. Finally, the hypothesis with the highest probability prevails and the others are deleted. A sample output of the localization is shown in Fig. 2.

3.2 Bipedal Walking

The gait of our robots is formulated in three different spaces: joint space, inverse (Cartesian) space and abstract space. The last one is a convenient formulation for humanoid robots for balancing and walking presented in [7]. The central pattern generator based gait is an extension of our previous work [8]. Starting from a halt pose defined in the abstract space, the central pattern adds waveforms features like leg lifting, leg swinging, arm swinging, among others. The resulting abstract configuration is then transformed to the inverse space where more motion components are added. The result is finally converted into joint space to command the actuators. Several feedback mechanisms have been implemented on top of the open-loop gait that help to stabilize the robot [9]. Each of these mechanisms acts as a PID-feedback controlling the fused angle deviations of the robot by adding corrective actions to the central pattern generated waveforms. The fused angles are an intuitive representation of orientations that offer benefits over Euler angles for balance [10]. These mechanisms, illustrated in Fig. 3, include arm angle, hip angle, continuous foot angle, support foot angle and CoM shifting. The step timing is computed using our capture step framework [11], based on the lateral CoM state [9].

3.3 Soccer Behaviors

Based on the visual perception of the game state, including ball detections, obstacle detections, and the estimated pose of the robot on the field, our robots must decide on and execute a strategy for playing soccer. This primarily involves localizing the ball and scoring a goal while avoiding obstacles, but also extends to team communications, team play, and coordination of the game using the

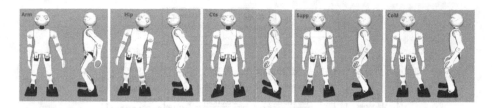

Fig. 3. Corrective actions in the sagittal and lateral planes, from left to right: arm angle, hip angle, continuous foot angle, support foot angle, and CoM shifting actions. The actions have been exaggerated for clearer illustration.

information from the RoboCup Humanoid league game controller. A custom two-layered hierarchical finite state machine (FSM) has been implemented for this purpose and runs in a separate behaviors node. The lower of these two layers is referred to as the Behavior FSM, and is responsible for implementing low-level skills such as searching for the ball, going to the ball, dribbling and kicking. The upper layer is referred to as the Game FSM, and builds on the skills implemented in the lower layer to implement game behaviors such as default ball handling, which attempts to kick or dribble a ball into goals, and positioning, which is used for the auto-positioning setup phase during a kickoff. In general, the game states combine groups or sequences of skills to execute certain soccer game state-specific behaviors.

3.4 Team Play

Teams participating in the TeenSize class in RoboCup 2017 can be composed by a maximum of three robots: one goalkeeper and two field players. We define dynamic *Player Tasks* which are frequently reassigned during the game. This task tells the robot what it is supposed to do according to its own state in the field and the state of its teammates. We define the following tasks: Attack, Defend, KeepGoal, ChangeTask and WaitClearOut. In addition, we define a task manager which is in charge of the safe assignment of these tasks. Each of this tasks is associated with a respective state of the game FSM (Fig. 4).

Attack Task. A robot with this task, known as *striker*, has active interaction with the ball. In possession of the ball, the robot will try to score either by kicking directly or by dribbling to get a better position for kicking the ball. The robot will also reach the ball and search for the ball in case the robot does not possess it. Searching for the ball, the robot goes first to the place where the ball was last seen. It turns on the spot and if the ball location is still unknown, it will go to the penalty marks, first to the closest and then to the furthest one. Reaching the ball means to place the robot behind the ball so it can kick or dribble. When approaching the ball, the robot does consider the ball as an obstacle in order to avoid undesired hits.

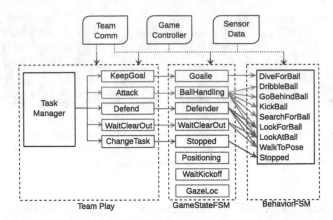

Fig. 4. Based on sensor data, the game controller and the team communication, the task manager assigns a task to each robot. Each task is associated to a state of the Game FSM, which triggers a sequence of behaviors in a lower-level Behavior FSM.

Defend Task. The *defender* robot is not supposed to have contact with the ball but to be ready to change its task and approach the ball if necessary. Its position is defined by a vector coming from the middle of its own goal towards the position of the ball. The magnitude of this vector is defined proportional to the distance of the ball to the own goal and saturated in order to avoid collisions with team members. In case the ball is not visible, this magnitude is calculated using the pose of the striker. In this manner, the robot is able: (i) to block opposite direct shots, (ii) to be ready for one-vs-one fights, and (iii) to get possession of the ball in case the previous striker is taken out of the match. With respect to the orientation, the robot tries to look in the direction of the ball. Figure 5 shows the pose of the defender for different ball locations. In order to avoid collisions with other teammates, the initial shortest path (straight line) is modified such that any teammate in between the path is surrounded (Fig. 6).

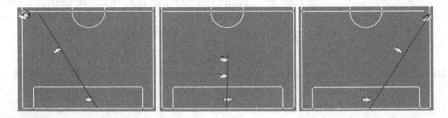

Fig. 5. Different poses that the defender might have according to the ball pose. On the middle the minimum distance between field players is shown in red. (Color figure online)

KeepGoal Task. The behavior of this task mainly depends on the proximity of the ball, of the opponents, and of the teammates to the own goal. Because

Fig. 6. Collision avoidance between field players. The defender considers the pose of the striker and surrounds it.

the other teammates have to coordinate their behaviors according to what the goalkeeper is doing, the decision if the goalkeeper has to clear out the ball is managed by the task manager. When the goalkeeper receives the signal to clear out the ball, it goes to the ball and hits it in direction of the opposite goal. It can also get a signal to dive including the diving direction. On the other hand, if the task manager decides that the goalkeeper does not need to clear out the ball, the robot will only move laterally on the same horizontal level of the ball position.

WaitClearOut. Different to the FIFA rules, the RoboCup Humanoid League has a special rule that prohibits more than one robot to be in the own area for more than 10 s. For this reason, when the ball is the own goal area, an additional coordination between team members is required. When a robot announces that it will clear out the ball from the own goal area, a *WaitClearOut* task reassignment occurs. In this task, the robots go closer to the ball without entering the own goal area to avoid the illegal defense. The path is planned such that the robot will not block the shot from an other robot clearing out the ball. In addition, the target pose in this task is assigned such that two robots will not collide with each other (Fig. 7).

The task manager of each robot determines the desired task and triggers special events that have to be coordinated. The desired task depends on each role. A goalkeeper only has assigned the task *KeepGoal*, while a field player can alternate between *Attack*, *Defend*, *ChangeTask* and *WaitClearOut*. In order to handle possible noise or very fast alternating data that could lead to a continuous task change, the request is only made once the decision is confirmed for a defined number of consecutive cycles. This voting system is persistent for all decisions taken by the task manager. If there is only one field player in the match, it will be assigned to *Attack*. The robot with the task of *Defend* can request a task change to the striker, but not vice versa. If the defender estimates that it is the closest to the ball, it will request a task change. When a striker leaves the field, because of a service or a penalization, it announces its egress such that a task assignment can be done immediately.

Fig. 7. Ball clear out by the goalkeeper. The yellow line represents the planned path, while the surrounded red cross refers to the instantaneous 2D target pose. Note that the robots always look at the ball. The figure at the rightmost shows the game after the clear out. (Color figure online)

Clearing out the ball by the goalie is a special event to be handled by the task manager because it implies task changes of the field players. In this case, the rest of the field players change to the *WaitClearOut* task, that place them in a strategic position once the ball has been cleared out. The decision of clearing out the ball by the goalie depends mostly on the ball location. The field is divided in three regions (Fig. 8). The first region is the goal area with an additional outer tolerance. In goal area, the goalie gets the highest priority, and when it is asked to clear out the ball, the field players set their task to *WaitClearOut*. The second region limits the possible areas where the goalkeeper can clear out the ball. If the ball is further away, the goalie just waits for its teammates. In this region, however, the goalie only chases the ball to clear it out if there is no teammate close to the own goal, i.e., if there is no teammate between our goal and the presence line (Fig. 8). In the third region, the goalkeeper takes a more passive role and gazes at the ball to be ready for diving.

The task assignment is based on an asynchronous request-and-response system that ensures that there is only one robot actively interacting with the ball. This prohibits, for example, that two robots try to kick the ball simultaneously which could lead to team self-collisions. The request for a task reassignment depends on the state of the robot and its teammates. This state comprises current task, ball distance, ball visibility, ball possession, ball location, current robot pose, if the robot is active and if the robot is not fallen. This information is estimated using the team communication data broadcast at a rate of 8 Hz. Only recent

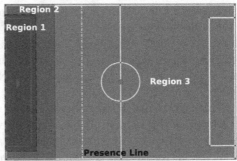

Fig. 8. Areas determining goalkeeper ball clearing behavior. In Region 1, goalkeeper needs to clear out the ball. In Region 3, the robot is remains in its goal. In Region 2, the goalkeeper clears out the ball if there is no field player between the own goal and the presence line (yellow dotted line). (Color figure online)

data (received in the last 5 s) is, however, considered because of possible hardware failures or communication errors.

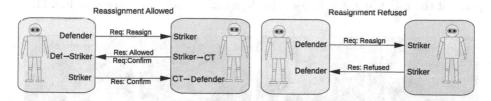

Fig. 9. Task assignment. A defender sends a request to change task. If the request is accepted, the striker is assigned to ChangeTask. It requests a confirmation, and the defender changes its task. If the request is refused, both robots keep their current tasks.

For task reassignment, the robot with the *Attack* task has a higher priority over *Defend*, i.e., a defending robot can only change its task if it is allowed by the current striker. When the defender finds itself in a better position to possess the ball, it requests to change tasks. If the striker also determines that its teammate is in a more convenient position, the striker changes its task to *ChangeTask* and sends back a response. The requester changes correspondingly its task and sends a confirmation such that the robot with task *ChangeTask* can change to the new task. On the other hand, if the original striker finds that it is in a better position to possess the ball, it sends back a negative response and no task reassignment takes place (Fig. 9).

The team play strategies presented here were used in the RoboCup2017 competition. Figure 10 shows official matches in which the striker and defender roles can be distinguished.

Fig. 10. Team play in RoboCup 2017.

3.5   Landing Motions

In a match during the competition, the robot might fall even with a robust and fine-tuned gait. The actions of our opponent can lead to difficult situations as happened in RoboCup 2016 [12]. This implies that the robot needs to know how to land. We designed landing motions that are activated when the robot would face an inevitable fall situation either in forward or backward direction. The aim of these motions is to protect the hardware of the robot from impacts in delicate parts of the robot, e.g. the knees. The designed motions are shown in Fig. 11.

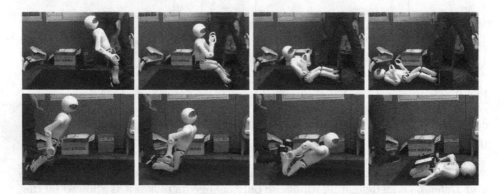

Fig. 11. Landing Motions in forward and backward direction.

3.6 Human-Robot Interfaces

To configure and calibrate the robots, a web application system is used with the robot PC as the web server. Even over a poor quality wireless network, the connection is robust by making use of the client-server architecture of web applications and the highly developed underlying web protocols. In addition, most of the processing is carried out by the client, resulting in a low computational cost for the robot. The web application allows the user: to start, to stop, to monitor ROS nodes, to display status information, to dynamically reconfigure the robot, and to visualize the processed vision, amongst others.

4   Game Performance

In RoboCup 2017, our robots scored 37 goals in 12 matches and did not receive any goal. 27 goals were scored during seven games of the TeenSize tournament and the remaining 10 goals were scored in five Drop-in games. This proved the robustness of the methods presented in this paper. Our robots won all the matches in the TeenSize tournament including the final 2:0 vs. HuroEvolutionTN (Taiwan). In the Drop-in games, the individual skills were tested and our robots have obtained 21 points in total, having a margin of 19 points to the team in second place.

5   Technical Challenges

In RoboCup 2017 there were four technical challenges. They were designed to evaluate specific capabilities of robots in isolation, separately from the regular games. In this section we briefly describe our strategies for these challenges.

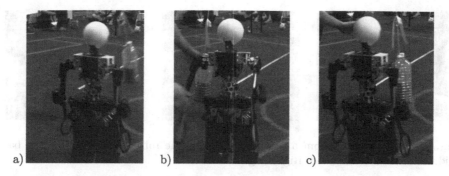

Fig. 12. Dynaped withstanding a push from the front. (a) Before impact. (b) Immediately after impact. One can see that the robot is unstable. (c) Stable posture is recovered.

Push Recovery. In this challenge, the robot is pushed from the front and from the back. The goal is to withstand the impact and recover a stable posture. In RoboCup 2017, Dynaped successfully completed this challenge, withstanding the push from a 1.5 kg pendulum which was retracted by 55 cm (Fig. 12).

High Jump. In this challenge, the task is to jump as high as possible and remain in the air as long as possible. In order to perform this task, a jumping motion was designed using our keyframe editor. In RoboCup 2017, one of ours igus® Humanoid Open Platform robot successfully performed a jump of height 4.5 cm, remaining 0.192 s in the air and stand stable afterwards.

High Kick. The goal of this challenge is to kick the ball over the obstacle into the goal. In order to complete this challenge and overcome as high an obstacle as possible, a modified foot was used by one of our igus® Humanoid Open Platform robots for kicking. The foot had a smooth concave shape which allowed it to scoop the ball effectively and, hence, kick it upwards, overcoming the obstacle. In RoboCup 2017, our robot was able to complete this challenge with a height of 8 cm. The execution of a high kick over a 21 cm obstacle, recorded during testing in our lab, is shown in Fig. 13.

Fig. 13. Robot performing a high kick over a 21 cm obstacle. (a) The ball is being scooped by the foot. (b) The ball is kicked upwards. (c) The ball overcame the obstacle.

Fig. 14. Robot scoring from a moving ball. Left: the robot is waiting for the ball. Middle: the kick is executed. Right: a goal is scored.

Goal Kick from Moving Ball. The task of this challenge is to score a goal by kicking the moving ball into the goal. The ball is rolling along the goal area line. We solved this task as follows: first, we shift all weight onto one of the legs while having the other leg lifted and ready to kick; then, we estimate the velocity of the rolling ball and hence, time of arrival thereof to the kicking region; and, finally, we perform the kick according to the previous estimate. Following this strategy our robot was able to successfully complete this challenge. Our robot, performing this task during tests in our lab, is shown in Fig. 14.

6   Conclusions

In this paper, we presented the methods and approaches that lead us to win all possible competitions in the TeenSize class for the RoboCup 2017 Humanoids League in Nagoya: the soccer tournament, the Drop-in games, and the technical challenges. We presented individual skills regarding the perception and the bipedal gait, and their application in the technical challenges. Additionally, team skills were also extensively explained.

Acknowledgements. This work was partially funded by grant BE 2556/13 of German Research Foundation.

References

1. Allgeuer, P., Farazi, H., Schreiber, M., Behnke, S.: Child-sized 3D Printed igus humanoid open platform. In: Proceedings of 15th IEEE-RAS International Conference on Humanoid Robots (Humanoids) (2015)
2. Allgeuer, P., Schwarz, M., Pastrana, J., Schueller, S., Missura, M., Behnke, S.: A ROS-based software framework for the NimbRo-OP humanoid open platform. In: 8th Workshop on Humanoid Soccer Robots, International Conference on Humanoid Robots (2013)
3. Missura, M., Münstermann, C., Mauelshagen, M., Schreiber, M., Behnke, S.: RoboCup 2012 best humanoid award winner NimbRo TeenSize. In: Chen, X., Stone, P., Sucar, L.E., van der Zant, T. (eds.) RoboCup 2012. LNCS (LNAI), vol. 7500, pp. 89–93. Springer, Heidelberg (2013). https://doi.org/10.1007/978-3-642-39250-4_9

4. Nelder, J.A., Mead, R.: A simplex method for function minimization. Comput. J. **7**(4), 308–313 (1965)
5. Dalal, N., Triggs, B.: Object detection using histograms of oriented gradients. In: Pascal VOC Workshop, ECCV (2006)
6. Farazi, H., Allgeuer, P., Behnke, S.: A monocular vision system for playing soccer in low color information environments. In: 10th Workshop on Humanoid Soccer Robots, IEEE-RAS International Conference on Humanoid Robots (2015)
7. Behnke, S.: Online trajectory generation for omnidirectional biped walking. In: Proceedings of 2006 IEEE International Conference on Robotics and Automation (ICRA) (2006)
8. Missura, M., Behnke, S.: Self-stable omnidirectional walking with compliant joints. In: 8th Workshop on Humanoid Soccer Robots, Humanoids Conference (2013)
9. Allgeuer, P., Behnke, S.: Omnidirectional bipedal walking with direct fused angle feedback mechanisms. In: Proceedings of 16th IEEE-RAS International Conference on Humanoid Robots (Humanoids) (2016)
10. Allgeuer, P., Behnke, S.: Fused angles: a representation of body orientation for balance. In: International Conference on Intelligent Robots and Systems (IROS) (2015)
11. Missura, M., Behnke, S.: Walking with capture steps. In: IEEE-RAS International Conference on Humanoid Robots, pp. 526–526 (2014)
12. Farazi, H., et al.: RoboCup 2016 humanoid teensize winner nimbro: robust visual perception and soccer behaviors. In: Behnke, S., Sheh, R., Sariel, S., Lee, D.D. (eds.) RoboCup 2016. LNCS (LNAI), vol. 9776, pp. 478–490. Springer, Cham (2017). https://doi.org/10.1007/978-3-319-68792-6_40

Grown-Up NimbRo Robots Winning RoboCup 2017 Humanoid AdultSize Soccer Competitions

Grzegorz Ficht$^{(\boxtimes)}$, Dmytro Pavlichenko, Philipp Allgeuer, Hafez Farazi,
Diego Rodriguez, André Brandenburger, Johannes Kürsch, Michael Schreiber,
and Sven Behnke

Autonomous Intelligent Systems, Computer Science,
University of Bonn, Bonn, Germany
{ficht,pavlichenko,pallgeuer,rodriguez,behnke}@ais.uni-bonn.de,
http://ais.uni-bonn.de

Abstract. The ongoing evolution of the RoboCup Humanoid League led in 2017 to the introduction of one vs. one soccer games for the AdultSize robots, which motived our team NimbRo to enter this category. In this paper, we present the mechatronic design of our upgraded robot Copedo and the newly developed NimbRo-OP2, which received the RoboCup Design Award. We also describe improved approaches to visual perception of the game situation, including compassless localization on a soccer field with symmetric appearance, and the generation of soccer behaviors. At RoboCup 2017 in Nagoya, our robots played very well, winning the AdultSize soccer tournament with high scores. Our robots also won the technical challenges and we present the developed solutions.

1 Introduction

With the ongoing evolution of its rules, RoboCup Humanoid League, competition each year is becoming more realistic and closer to playing games against human soccer players. In 2017, for the first time, AdultSize class robots were playing one vs. one matches, which meant bringing the soccer game to a larger scale, along with all of its inherent difficulties. In previous years, our team NimbRo has competed in the Humanoid League within the KidSize, and more recently, the TeenSize classes [1–4].

In order to compete in the AdultSize category, it was necessary to procure hardware that is not only in compliance with the new set of rules, but also performs well under the conditions that a robot may face during the competition. For that purpose, we have prepared two robots capable of play: Copedo and NimbRo-OP2 (Fig. 1). Our robust hardware played a major role in our success, where over the span of five games in the soccer tournament and a set of technical challenges, our robots secured victory in both, without the need for repairs or maintenance. We describe the mechanic design of our robots in Sect. 2, and our approach for the technical challenges in Sect. 5.

© Springer Nature Switzerland AG 2018
H. Akiyama et al. (Eds.): RoboCup 2017, LNAI 11175, pp. 448–460, 2018.
https://doi.org/10.1007/978-3-030-00308-1_37

Fig. 1. Left: our AdultSize Robots Copedo and the NimbRo-OP2. Right: the NimbRo team at RoboCup 2017 in Nagoya, Japan.

Our open-source software is advanced with each RoboCup, with many modules being added and existing ones being improved. With the introduction of identically looking field halves in 2015 and the ban on magnetometers in 2017, localisation has become much more difficult. The approach we used for breaking the symmetry and localising in these conditions, as well as how we combine this information with our ball position estimate to plan further actions are described in Sect. 3.

2   Mechanic Robot Design

2.1   Copedo

Copedo was constructed to compete at RoboCup 2012 in Mexico and played in the TeenSize class until 2015. Initially, Copedo was 114 cm tall and had a weight of 8 kg [2]. To comply with the AdultSize class rules, our robot was extended to be 131 cm tall and 10.1 kg in weight. The upgrade of Copedo was based on another one of our robots—Dynaped, as it was upgraded in 2016 [4]. Copedo has been fitted with new electronics and onboard PC to use our open source ROS-based framework just like Dynaped, and our other robots. Copedo is constructed from milled carbon fiber parts that are assembled to rectangular shaped legs and flat arms. The torso is constructed entirely from aluminum and consists of a cylindrical tube and a rectangular cage that holds the main electronic components. During the upgrade process, the cylindrical tube was replaced with a longer one, while the cage was that of the NimbRo-OP. To comply with the vision system of our other robots, Copedo received a new 3D printed head, similar to the one used in the igus® Humanoid Open Platform [5]. The process and result of the hardware modifications can be seen in Fig. 2.

With a new head allowing for pan and tilt motions, Copedo has 14 actuated degrees of freedom (DoF). The hip roll, hip pitch, and knee DoF are driven by master-slave pairs of Robotis Dynamixel EX-106+ actuators. All other DoFs are driven by single actuators including EX-106+ actuators for ankle roll,

Fig. 2. Left: copedo before the upgrade. Middle: copedo after the upgrade. Right: copedo during the semi-finals at RoboCup 2017 in Nagoya.

EX-106+ actuators for hip yaw and RX-64 actuators for shoulder pitch, as well as the neck yaw and pitch. The robot has been fitted with cleats in the corners of its feet, to assist walking on artificial grass. More details on the robot's core mechanical design features can be found in [2].

Along with the necessary structural upgrade, Copedo has received a new Intel NUC computer with an Intel Core i7-7567U processor operating at a maximum frequency of 4.0 GHz. The PC is fitted with 4 GB of RAM and a 128 GB solid state disk. Available communication interfaces include USB 3.0, HDMI, Mini DisplayPort and Gigabit Ethernet. The PC is connected to a Robotis CM740 board, which communicates with all actuators on a RS485 star topology bus. The CM740 incorporates a 3-axis accelerometer and gyroscope for a total of 6 axes of inertial sensory data.

2.2 NimbRo-OP2

According to the requirements of the RoboCup 2017 Humanoid league, we developed a new platform: the NimbRo-OP2 [6]. Being almost 135 cm tall and only 18 kg in weight, the robot is able to participate in both TeenSize and AdultSize classes. The robot's exoskeleton was 3D printed with an industrial-grade SLS printer out of PA-12 nylon, which contributes greatly to its low weight. In terms of electronics, the robot uses the same Intel NUC in combination with the Robotis CM740 as Copedo. There also exists the possibility of further upgrading the unit, through the inclusion of standard VESA75 and VESA100 mounts.

The structure of the robot has been simplified as much as possible to maintain low complexity, but retain functionality that is required when playing soccer. The robot in its entirety uses 34 Dynamixel MX-106 actuators. The upper body kinematics consists of three serial chains—two arms and a neck connecting the head to the trunk. The neck consists of a yaw and a pitch joint, while the arms have two pitch and one roll joint. In the legs, we decided to use parallel

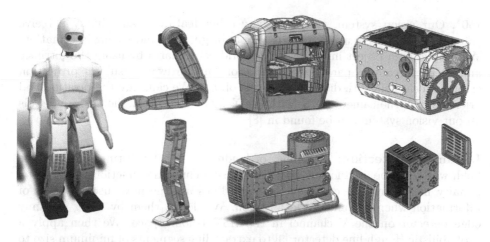

Fig. 3. Left: assembled NimbRo-OP2. Right: CAD visualisation of key robot components: extended and compressed parallel kinematics leg, cross section of the arm, rear view on the trunk, knee and ankle/hip joints.

kinematics along with external gearing to allow for more torque output, which is necessary for dynamic walking.

The design made use of our long experience with building humanoid robots. Creating a new robot is a complex and time-consuming process, of which manufacturing plays a big role. By taking advantage of the versatility of 3D printing, we were able to develop an affordable, customisable, highly-capable, adult-sized humanoid robot in little time. The whole design and manufacturing process took less than six months. A view of the finished robot and some of its key design features can be seen in Fig. 3.

Simplicity was one of the key points in creating the design. This is best shown when looking at the knee of the robot, which houses eight actuators with only three plastic parts, two of which are covers that are not critical for bearing the load. Upon removal of the covers, servos are easily accessible for any maintenance that might be needed. The servos themselves are exposed through strategic venting hole placement to help with cooling. Most of the parts in the design are symmetrical, meaning that a single part is used in multiple spots. This minimises the amount of spare parts needed for repairs, in case a part should break. This can be seen in the ankle and hip joints, the knee joints as well as the thigh and shank links.

3 Software Design

3.1 Visual Perception

Our humanoid robots perceive the environment through digital cameras. Each robot is equipped with one Logitech C905 camera, utilising a wide-angle lens with an infrared cut-off filter. In this configuration, its field-of-view is nearly

150°. Our vision system, amongst many other features, can reliably perceive game-relevant objects using texture, shape, brightness, and colour information. We project each object into egocentric world coordinates by using the intrinsic and extrinsic camera parameters. Variations in hardware result in projection errors, which scale with distance from the object. We calibrate the position and orientation of the camera frame with the Nelder-Mead [7] method. More details on our vision system can be found in [8].

Landmark Detection: A number of landmarks can be distinguished on the field, which can be used for localisation. These include line junctions, goal posts, penalty marks and the center circle. Field lines are the most useful source of information when it comes to localisation. We detect them by using a Canny edge detector on the V channel in the HSV colour space. We then apply a probabilistic Hough line detector [9] to extract line segments of minimum size to filter out white non-line objects. These segments are then connected to produce less, but longer lines, finally achieving a set of lines that correspond to field lines and the center circle. An example output of our vision system detecting selected objects can be seen in Fig. 4.

Fig. 4. Left: a captured image with detected ball (pink circle), field lines (light blue), field boundary (yellow lines), and goal post (dark blue lines). Right: visualisation of our obstacle detection. (Color figure online)

Localisation and Breaking the Symmetry: To solve the global localisation problem, our method relies on having a source of global yaw rotation of the robot. We used to utilise the compass sensor in previous years, but due to the magnetometer ban, introduced in the rules of the Humanoid League in 2017, we now use the integrated gyro measurements as the source for yaw orientation. In our case, gyro integration is a reliable source of orientation tracking, but it needs a global reference. In order to set the initial heading, we could either use manual initialisation or automatic initial orientation estimation. Although manual initialisation can be done once before the start of each game, it can fail during the match. Sometimes restarting the operating system of the robot is

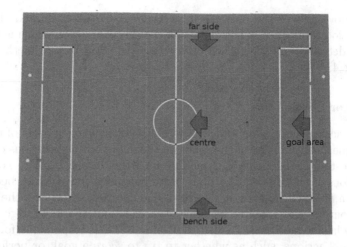

Fig. 5. Set of predefined positions the robot can start in.

unavoidable, which will force a reinitialisation of the heading. As a result, we reformulated the heading initialisation problem as a classification task.

According to the rules, there are a few predefined positions and orientations that the robot can start in or enter the game from. As shown in Fig. 5, the robot can start in four different positions. In two of the spots, it should face the opponent goal—near the center circle and goal area. The other two sets of locations are at the sideline in the robot's own half—facing the field. We employ a multi-hypothesis version of our localisation module, which is initialised with four instances of initial hypothetical locations. During a brief period at the beginning, the robot tries to find the most probable hypothesis among all running instances. This stops when either the process times out or the robot finds the best hypothesis. Finally, the vision module keeps the best instance and discards the rest. To make sure that the decision is correct, we double check the result based on the perceived landmarks like goalposts and the center circle.

Obstacle Detection: Obstacle detection is a crucial ability in the game, especially when the robot is handling the ball. In our software, obstacle detection is done mainly based on a model of colour distribution on the perceived robots. By having the minimum and maximum height of the robot in each size class, we roughly know what size to expect in each distance from the observer. We search for the respected bounding box size in each distance level and discard obstacle candidates that are not in the expected size range. After detecting each obstacle bounding box, we compare the colour histogram of each of the bounding boxes to the expected model of the obstacle, which are then labeled as either teammate, rival robot, or the referee. The detection history is then clustered in egocentric world coordinates and filtered based on the location of each cluster. Finally, to make the output robust against false negatives, we predict the expected movement of the obstacle in accordance to the estimated changes in the robot's location. Each of the clusters has a certainty level, which is increased when it is detected, and decreased otherwise. The effect of this method can be seen in Fig. 4.

3.2 Soccer Behaviours

Once the visual perception module has established the current state of the game, including the localised pose of the robot on the field and the positions of the ball and any obstacles, the behaviour module uses this information to control the soccer actions of the robot. Two finite state machines (FSM) have been implemented in a hierarchical fashion on top of one another, to process the available data and output the required walking velocities and motion triggers for the robot. The higher-level FSM, called the Game FSM, is responsible for deciding on game-level actions, such as whether to try to score a goal, or perform auto-positioning, or defend the goals. The lower-level FSM on the other hand, called the Behaviour FSM, implements fundamental soccer skills such as dribbling and kicking the ball, and walking to a localised ball position while avoiding obstacles.

Ball Approach: Approaching the ball is a fundamental skill on the level of the Behaviour FSM. The robot should walk as efficiently as possible to the required position behind the ball, without pushing the ball away. A circular halo is established around the ball, and the approach phase is divided into the near and far cases. In the far case, the robot only turns and walks forward, to maximise its speed and stability in covering ground, while in the near case, slower side-stepping is added to allow the robot to get around the ball efficiently. This is illustrated on the top left in Fig. 6.

Obstacle Avoidance: If an obstacle blocks the approach to the ball, obstacle avoidance is applied on the level of the Behaviour FSM. The robot is slowed down, yaw rotation is added to turn it away from the obstacle, and the linear velocity of the robot is rotated to limit the radial component of the velocity towards the obstacle (see top right in Fig. 6). The maximum allowed radial velocity is a function of the proximity of the obstacle, and can also be negative, pushing the robot away from the obstacle.

Obstacle Ball Handling: If an obstacle is close to the ball or blocks the path from the ball to the goals, obstacle ball handling is applied on the level of the Game FSM. This rotates the ball target away from obstructions, and if the ball target is no longer safely in goals, or the obstacle is too close to the ball, dribbling is enforced for safety, as shown on the bottom left in Fig. 6. The correct foot to dribble with is also enforced to avoid collisions with the obstacle as much as possible.

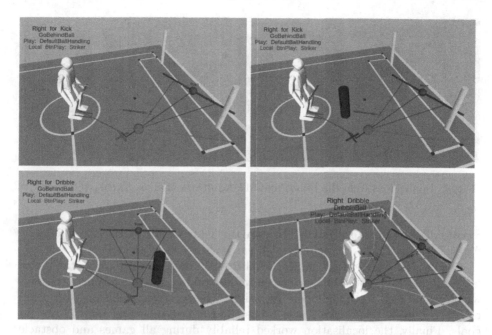

Fig. 6. Simulation screenshots showing the behaviour visualisations for the Go Behind Ball behaviour (top left), how this changes when an obstacle is blocking the ball (top right), when an obstacle is blocking the path from the ball to the goal (bottom left), and the dribble behaviour (bottom right).

Kicking and Dribbling: When the robot is behind the ball and aligned with the ball target, either the Kick or Dribble behaviours activate as required, and drive the ball towards the target. When Dribble activates (see bottom right in Fig. 6), a large variance of ball position is tolerated that allows dribbling to continue. The robot however consistently tries to correct for any misalignments in its dribble approach. If the dribble lock is lost, the ball approach is started once more.

4   Performance in Soccer Tournament

At RoboCup 2017, eight teams participated in the soccer tournament. Our robot NimbRo-OP2 played three round robin games vs. teams ZSTT (Taiwan & Korea), KIS (Japan), and CIT Brains (Japan). The robot scored very reliably, such that the three games were clearly won with a total score of 26:0. In semi-final, our robots NimbRo-OP2 and Copedo played vs. team IRC (IRC) and clearly won with a score of 9:0.

In the final, our robot NimbRo-OP2 faced the robot Sweaty (Germany). Sweaty had shown good walking and kicking capabilities during the competition. The two robots, fighting for the ball are shown in Fig. 7. Our robot had clear advantages in such fights, avoiding the opponent and maintaining balance while

Fig. 7. Impressions from the RoboCup 2017 AdultSize final vs. Sweaty (Germany).

Sweaty often lost balance and had to leave the field. NimbRo-OP2 scored reliably. After 7:0 at half time, the game ended early with a score of 11:1.

During the competition games, NimbRo-OP2 has shown a very stable and fast walk. It never lost its balance when walking in free space. The only occasions which would lead to the fall were situations when a strong collision with other robots occurred. The kicking was robust and strong, allowing us to score far goals. Finally, the localisation worked reliably during all games and obstacle avoidance allowed to win fights for the ball by dribbling it around the opponent, which was often the case in the finals.

5   Technical Challenges

In addition to the main competition, technical challenges test how well a robot can perform a specific task in isolation. At RoboCup 2017, four technical challenges were posed: Push Recovery, High Jump, High Kick, and Kick a Moving Ball. In this section we present our strategy for three technical challenges which were addressed for RoboCup 2017.

5.1   Push Recovery

The goal of this challenge is to withstand a strong push. An impact is applied to the robot on the level of the CoM by a pendulum. To define the impulse, the 3 kg weight is retracted by a distance d from the point of contact with the robot. The push is applied only from the front and from the back. The robot has to be walking on the spot during the whole challenge.

During the challenge we used the gait [10] completely unchanged from the configuration in the regular games. NimbRo-OP2 was able to successfully withstand a push with $d = 70$ cm. Our robot, recovering after the push is shown in Fig. 8.

Fig. 8. Our robots performing the technical challenge. Left, Middle: NimbRo-OP2 performing push recovery. Right: copedo performing the high jump.

5.2 High Jump

The goal of high jump is to jump as high as possible and remain airborne as long as possible. The challenge was performed using a predesigned jump motion, which was constructed with a keyframe editor. Execution of this motion on Copedo resulted in a partially successful trial. The robot jumped higher than 10 cm, but upon landing a stable posture was not held. Copedo performing the jump is depicted in Fig. 8.

5.3 Goal Kick from Moving Ball

This challenge requires a robot to score a goal by kicking a moving ball into the goal. The ball is rolled from a ramp along the goal area line. The difficulty is defined by the angle of the ramp, and the distance d_{ramp} from the endpoint of the ramp to the ball in its initial static position. We solved for this task is as follows:

1. Before the ball is released, execute a pre-kick motion. During this motion, the robot goes from a standard standing posture to a posture with one support leg. The other leg is lifted and folded in order to be ready for kicking.
2. Estimate the time t_{arrive} needed for the ball to arrive in the region where it can be kicked into the goal by the previously folded leg.
3. Execute the kicking motion when the ball is in the kick region according to the estimation from the previous step.

The motions described above are designed using our keyframe editor. In order to estimate the time needed for the ball to arrive in the kick region, we utilise the ball detection information obtained from the vision module, described in

Sect. 3.1. Ball observations arrive in real-time and are stored in a stack S, where $\forall s \in S : s = \langle p, r, t \rangle$, where p is a confidence of the detection, r is the estimated position of the ball, and t is a time stamp of the measurement. The position r is represented in a 2D coordinate frame which covers the surface of the playing field and has its origin at the position of the robot.

We estimate the velocity of the ball with the two latest measurements s_1, s_2 : $p_1, p_2 > p_{min} \lor t_2 - t_1 > \delta t$, where p_{min} is a predefined minimal confidence for the measurement, and $\delta t > 0$ is a predefined minimal time difference between two measurements. Given such measurements s_1 and s_2, we estimate the velocity v:

$$v = \frac{d(r_2, r_1)}{t_2 - t_1},\tag{1}$$

where $d(\cdot, \cdot)$ is the Euclidean distance. Each obtained estimate v is pushed into a double-ended queue V of maximum size N. We smooth the velocity by averaging over V:

$$v_{smooth} = \frac{1}{|V|} \sum_{i=1}^{N} V_i.\tag{2}$$

Finally, we estimate the time of arrival of the ball using the smoothed velocity and the most recent pair of measurements:

$$t_{arrive} = \frac{d(r_{kick}, r_2)}{v_{smooth}},\tag{3}$$

where r_{kick} is a predefined position of the ball which is optimal for performing the kick.

This simple strategy worked well for this challenge, because the ball moves with a velocity that is close to uniform. In addition, the region where the ball can be kicked into the goal is by far not limited to the position r_{kick}. That is why small deviations of the estimate t_{arrive} from the ground truth do not

Fig. 9. NimbRo-OP2 kicking a moving ball. Left: the robot is waiting for the ball in pre-kick posture with right leg prepared for a kick. Middle: the ball reached the target location and the kick is being performed. Right: goal successfully scored, stable posture is reached.

cause failures. At RoboCup 2017, we used the following parameters: $p_{min} = 0.5$, $\delta t = 0.1$ and $N = 3$. NimbRo-OP2 was able to score a goal from a moving ball with the largest possible d_{ramp}, as shown in Fig. 9.

6   Conclusions

In this paper, we described the mechatronic design of our robots and some of the perception and control approaches that led to our success in the Humanoid League AdultSize soccer competition and technical challenges. At RoboCup 2017, we participated in the AdultSize category for the first time and with very little time to prepare, we were able to produce two robots that were able to secure a victory in both competitions. Over a span of five soccer games we aggregated a total score of 46:1, conceding a single goal in the finals, and gathered 21 points from three technical challenges. A video showing the competition highlights is available online[1].

Our new robot NimbRo-OP2 was also awarded the RoboCup Design Award by Flower Robotics. The hardware of the NimbRo-OP2[2] as well as our software[3] were released open-source to GitHub with the hope that other teams and research groups benefit from our work.

Acknowledgements. This work was partially funded by grant BE 2556/13 of the German Research Foundation (DFG).

References

1. Lee, D.D., et al.: RoboCup 2011 humanoid league winners. In: Röfer, T., Mayer, N.M., Savage, J., Saranlı, U. (eds.) RoboCup 2011. LNCS (LNAI), vol. 7416, pp. 37–50. Springer, Heidelberg (2012). https://doi.org/10.1007/978-3-642-32060-6_4

2. Missura, M., Münstermann, C., Mauelshagen, M., Schreiber, M., Behnke, S.: RoboCup 2012 best humanoid award winner NimbRo TeenSize. In: Chen, X., Stone, P., Sucar, L.E., van der Zant, T. (eds.) RoboCup 2012. LNCS (LNAI), vol. 7500, pp. 89–93. Springer, Heidelberg (2013). https://doi.org/10.1007/978-3-642-39250-4_9

3. Missura, M., et al.: Learning to improve capture steps for disturbance rejection in humanoid soccer. In: Behnke, S., Veloso, M., Visser, A., Xiong, R. (eds.) RoboCup 2013. LNCS (LNAI), vol. 8371, pp. 56–67. Springer, Heidelberg (2014). https://doi.org/10.1007/978-3-662-44468-9_6

4. Farazi, H., et al.: RoboCup 2016 humanoid teensize winner NimbRo: robust visual perception and soccer behaviors. In: Behnke, S., Sheh, R., Sarıel, S., Lee, D.D. (eds.) RoboCup 2016. LNCS (LNAI), vol. 9776, pp. 478–490. Springer, Cham (2017). https://doi.org/10.1007/978-3-319-68792-6_40

---

[1] RoboCup 2017 NimbRo AdultSize highlights: https://youtu.be/RG2O5OwGdSg.

[2] Hardware: https://github.com/NimbRo/nimbro-op2.

[3] Software: https://github.com/AIS-Bonn/humanoid_op_ros.

5. Allgeuer, P., Farazi, H., Schreiber, M., Behnke, S.: Child-sized 3D printed igus humanoid open platform. In: Proceedings of 15th IEEE-RAS International Conference on Humanoid Robots (Humanoids) (2015)
6. Ficht, G., Allgeuer, P., Farazi, H., Behnke, S.: NimbRo-OP2: grown-up 3D printed open humanoid platform for research. In: Proceedings of 17th IEEE-RAS International Conference on Humanoid Robots (Humanoids) (2017)
7. Nelder, J.A., Mead, R.: A simplex method for function minimization. Comput. J. **7**(4), 308–313 (1965)
8. Farazi, H., Allgeuer, P., Behnke, S.: A monocular vision system for playing soccer in low color information environments. In: 10th Workshop on Humanoid Soccer Robots, IEEE-RAS International Conference on Humanoid Robots (2015)
9. Matas, J., Galambos, C., Kittler, J.: Robust detection of lines using the progressive probabilistic Hough transform. In: Vision and Image Understanding (2000)
10. Allgeuer, P., Behnke, S.: Omnidirectional bipedal walking with direct fused angle feedback mechanisms. In: Proceedings of 16th IEEE-RAS Internatioanl Conference on Humanoid Robots (Humanoids), (Cancún, Mexico) (2016)

B-Human 2017 – Team Tactics and Robot Skills in the Standard Platform League

Thomas Röfer[1,2]([✉]), Tim Laue[2], Arne Hasselbring[3], Jesse Richter-Klug[2],
and Enno Röhrig[2]

[1] Deutsches Forschungszentrum für Künstliche Intelligenz,
Cyber-Physical Systems, Enrique-Schmidt-Str. 5, 28359 Bremen, Germany
thomas.roefer@dfki.de
[2] Universität Bremen Fachbereich 3 – Mathematik und Informatik,
Postfach 330 440, 28334 Bremen, Germany
{tlaue,jesse,roehrig}@uni-bremen.de
[3] Hamburg University of Technology,
Am Schwarzenberg-Campus 3, 21073 Hamburg, Germany
arne.hasselbring@tuhh.de

Abstract. The team *B-Human* won the main competition and, together with the team *HULKs*, the Mixed Team Competition in the RoboCup Standard Platform League 2017. In this paper, we argue that in the current state of the league, the development of sophisticated robot behaviors makes a difference between the top teams, while other abilities such as perception, modeling, and motion have been solved to a similar degree by the different top teams. We describe our general tactical approaches for the main competition as well as for the Mixed Team competition. In addition and as an example for a behavior-related robot skill, we present our approach to realtime path planning for humanoid robots with limited processing power.

1 Introduction

B-Human is a joint RoboCup team of the University of Bremen and the German Research Center for Artificial Intelligence (DFKI). The team was founded in 2006 as a team in the Humanoid League, but switched to participating in the Standard Platform League in 2009. Since then, we participated in eight RoboCup German Open competitions, the RoboCup European Open, and nine RoboCups and only lost four official games. As a result, we won all German Open and European Open competitions, the RoboCups 2009, 2010, 2011, 2013, and 2016. This year, we won both the main competition and, together with the team HULKs as the team *B-HULKs*, the newly introduced mixed team competition. We also won the technical challenge, i.e., the penalty shootout competition.

This paper is organized as follows: Sect. 2 motivates the focus on behavior development in the Standard Platform League, followed by an explanation of the tactics currently employed by B-Human in Sect. 3. The adjustments made for the Mixed Team Competition are described in Sect. 4. Section 5 gives a detailed

© Springer Nature Switzerland AG 2018
H. Akiyama et al. (Eds.): RoboCup 2017, LNAI 11175, pp. 461–472, 2018.
https://doi.org/10.1007/978-3-030-00308-1_38

explanation of B-Human's path planner. Finally, Sect. 6 sums up this paper and names potential for future improvements.

2   The Importance of Robot Behaviors in the RoboCup Standard Platform League

The overall challenge of creating successful software for the RoboCup Standard Platform League can be seen as a set of major sub-challenges that have to be solved:

Vision. All major field elements need to be perceived reliably (i.e., without many false negatives and positives) over reasonable distance and with computational efficiency.

Modeling. To keep track of the own position, the position and velocity of the ball as well as of other robots on the field, modeling algorithms have to compute precise and stable state estimates.

Motion. A fast and robust walk, preferentially combined with a flexible and strong kick, is a necessity to perform competitively in the adversarial RoboCup scenario.

Behavior. To select the right actions, given the currently estimated state of the surrounding world, a flexible behavior is needed. Especially for playing in a team of five or more robots, many details, such as a stable role assignment, have to be addressed.

As in other RoboCup soccer leagues, the rules of the game are changed every year to make the overall problem harder and more similar to professional human football. Each year, these changes often only focus on one or two of the aforementioned areas. In recent years, major changes have been the introduction of white goals, the start of play by blowing a real whistle, the black and white ball (all affecting perception and modeling), arbitrary jersey designs (perception), and artificial grass (motion). All top teams have solved these challenges in a robust manner. There exist different solutions that each have certain advantages and disadvantages, but all can be considered to have an overall similar level of quality. For instance, for ball detection, there are pure model-based approaches such as the one used by B-Human [7] as well as many solutions that involve the training of a classifier such as the one by *UT Austin Villa* [3]. In general, when considering the implementations of the top teams, balls can be perceived over distances of several meters, robots can walk with decent velocity, and self-localization is precise and robust. Thus, further major improvements in these areas would not be any game changer.

One can notice that there have not been any major rule changes directly affecting the behavior. Furthermore, major properties of the overall setup – the size and design of the field as well as the number of robots – remained constant. There will probably some changes in 2018, e.g., the introduction of free kicks, but this has not finally be decided at the point of time when writing

Fig. 1. RoboCup 2017 final between B-Human (black jerseys, playing from left to right) and Nao-Team HTWK (blue jerseys, playing from right to left). The ball is in midfield and both teams distribute their robots over the field according to their respective tactical concepts. (Color figure online)

this paper. Thus, the current behaviors of all teams have evolved over multiple years. Furthermore, the behavior seems to be the one part that is missing in most code releases of the top teams, i.e., one can consider the actual implementations of low level behaviors such as ball handling and dribbling as well as the formulas and parameters for tactics such as roles and positioning as *secret*. In contrast, the formalism in which the behavior is specified is often known. Many teams, such as B-Human, use hierarchical finite state machines, e.g., using *CABSL* [5].

In summary, given similarly competitive solutions for most other tasks and a certain level of secrecy in behavior development, one could say that in the current Standard Platform League, the development of robot and team behaviors is a crucial aspect that makes a difference.

3   Current Tactics

When playing with five robots per team, the number of possible tactics and team formations is quite limited. When assigning the goalkeeper task to one specific robot and letting this robot stay within its own penalty area, as it is done by B-Human and almost all other teams, only four field players remain for specific tasks. It is common among the top teams to not assign fixed roles to field players but to perform a permanent task negotiation via wireless communication. When assigning roles, various information is taken into account by the B-Human robots, such as the information about a robot's maximum velocity, which is not very high compared to the size of the current field and which makes it necessary to maintain a reasonable coverage of the field throughout all game situations.

The current roles in normal games (that slightly differ from those used in the Mixed Team Competition, as described in Sect. 4) are: two defenders that dynamically adapt their positions depending on the current ball position, one striker that always approaches the ball, and one supporter that is mainly waiting in an offensive position to perform a rebound in case of a successful save of the opponent goalkeeper. A typical formation is depicted in Fig. 1.

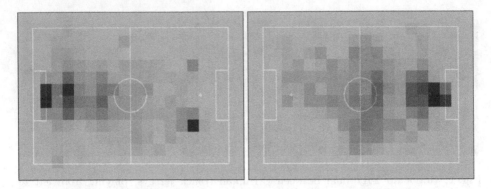

Fig. 2. Heatmaps of the whole teams of the two 2017 finalists: B-Human (left image, playing from left to right) and Nao-Team HTWK (right image, playing from right to left). The darker a square, the more time it has been occupied by a robot of the respective team. The figure has been created by using the *Team Communication Monitor* log files that are publicly available at the Standard Platform League's website [6].

This approach puts a focus on a strong defense and realizes offensive play by long distance shots – made possible by the kick implementation described in [4] – towards the opponent goal. Overall, this tactic appears to work well. At RoboCup 2017, B-Human was, on the one hand, the Champions Cup team that received the least goals (one goal in 116 min of play) and was, on the other hand, among the teams that scored the most goals (34 goals, only the *Nao Devils* scored more – 36 goals). Detailed results can be found on the league's website [6]. The heatmap in Fig. 2 shows a summary of the placement of the robots over the whole final game.

The 2017 final opponent, *Nao-Team HTWK*, which is one of the most successful teams in this league, has a different tactical approach: There is no offensive supporter waiting for long balls as the robots do not shoot in general. Instead, ball possession is gained in midfield, where three robots are placed, and the ball is dribbled towards the opponent goal. This is nicely reflected by the heatmap in Fig. 2. Although being quite different, this approach also led to a high number of scored goals (28) and only few received goals (5).

By comparing the different heatmaps of both teams, there is one noticeable issue: the corners of the opponent half are almost not occupied. This is in stark contrast to human soccer, where it is common to dribble towards the ground line and to pass cross the opponent's goal. It appears to be worth investigating to implement such behaviors in the future.

4   Mixed Team Competition

This year, the *Mixed Team Competition* was held for the first time, replacing the *Drop-In Competition*, which had been the Standard Platform League's testbed for multi-agent cooperation from 2014 until 2016 and which B-Human won twice.

For the first year of this new competition, each mixed team consisted of a pair of normal teams. This pairing remained fixed over the whole competition and had to be defined in advance, i.e., together with the teams' application for the main competition.

As we are convinced of the necessity of performing many full system tests under realistic conditions to achieve a high performance in a competition, we were looking for a partner team that we could meet several times for testing and coordination. Given these prerequisites, the HULKs have been the perfect partner. Their university is only about one hour away from Bremen and they were also strongly committed to the Mixed Team Competition.

As in this competition both members of a mixed team use their own soccer competition code base, only two major issues have to be resolved for playing together as a team: agreeing on a strategy for playing with six robots and speci-fying a standard communication protocol that extends the rather basic elements of the SPL standard message. To provide a real multiple-teams robot cooper-ation, the standard communication protocol was the only code shared between the two teams. The protocol is documented in the B-Human team report [7].

4.1 Strategy Agreements

Since the normal B-Human five-robot strategy has shown very good results in the past years (in comparison to the state-of-the-art team play in the Standard Platform League), the combined team agreed to use basically the same, but split the former support role (cf. "6.2.1 Roles and Tactic" in [7]).

However, as role names, we now used chess pieces:

King. The goalkeeper robot.
Queen. The ball-playing robot.
Rooks. Two robots that are positioned defensively, moving mainly horizontally in front of the goal.
Knight. A robot that is positioned offensively to help the Queen, jumping in when she looses the ball.
Bishop. A robot that is positioned far inside the opponent half to be able to receive a pass.

The general well-tried procedure is that every robot is calculating a role selection suggestion for itself and each connected teammate, but uses the role selection of the captain robot. The captain robot is determined by the lowest (not penalized) connected teammate number. The reason behind this procedure is to always have a suggestion available but inhibit the chance that the robots play with different role selections at the same time. Furthermore, we decided that all B-Human teammates have a smaller number than their HULKs colleagues to additionally support the selection robustness (because we reduce the possi-bility of switching between slightly different algorithms). True to the wish of maximizing the inter-team soccer play we force our robots to spread themselves over the field equally (by role selection). In fact, the full B-HULKs lineup had a

Fig. 3. An example scene of a possible B-HULKs match. B-HULKs robots wearing black (B-Human) or gray (HULKs) jerseys. From left-to-right they are currently performing the roles King, Rook, Rook, Knight, Queen, and Bishop.

B-Human robot with the role King, Rook, and Queen-or-else-Knight, completed with HULKs robots as Rook, Bishop, and Queen-or-else-Knight. Figure 3 shows an example of a standard positioning.

4.2   Collaborative Field Coverage

The black-and-white ball cannot be seen across the whole field and the field of view of the robot is not very wide. Therefore, if the ball is lost, it is searched for in a coordinated team effort. B-Human robots use a common model for the field coverage (cf. Fig. 4), which is gradually synchronized through team communication. Based on this, each robot will look at positions nearby, which have not been observed for a long time. To allow each individual robot to still create the model when playing together with HULKs robots, all teammates broadcast their estimated pose on the field, head posture, and all obstacles detected. Using this information together with an occlusion model (cf. Fig. 5), our robots add the field of view of the non-B-Human robots to their own coverage model, allowing them to search for the ball as if being in a B-Human-only team.

4.3   Additional Adjustments

For the positioning in the Ready state, i.e., preparing for a kickoff, the general method used by B-Human (cf. "6.2.6 Kickoff" in [7]) has been implemented by

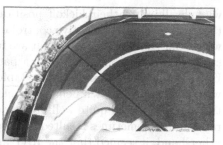

Fig. 4. An illustration of the common coverage model. The field is discretized into 12 × 18 areas. Green areas were observed recently, while red areas have not been observed for a longer time. (Color figure online)

Fig. 5. Occlusion of the field of view with an average head posture. Depending on the head posture, the occlusion caused by the own body differs by several square meters.

the HULKs. However, due to the special role assignment in Mixed Team games, the procedure needed to be slightly adjusted. Otherwise, it could have happened that two robots of the same team take defensive positions, which would cause instant position switching after kickoff because of their different roles (cf. Sect. 4.1). Therefore – in contrast to regular games – the role assignment is also active during the Ready state, and the Ready position selection checks each possible assignment for constraints that disallow certain role-position combinations.

Another piece of team play that has been coordinated between B-Human and the HULKs is the handling of balls near the King (i.e., the goalkeeper). In this case, the King communicates its intention to play the ball. The Queen would then get out of the way of the King.

In the area of modeling, the whistle and the obstacle model have been communicated between HULKs and B-Human robots to build a more complete world model.

4.4 Competition Results

During the competition, the B-HULKs played four games and won all of them, although the final win required an additional penalty shootout. As both teams have robust implementations of all basic abilities required, such as stable walking, ball recognition, and self-localization, all robots on the field were able to play together reliably according to the strategy described above. The robots from B-Human and the HULKs equally contributed to our success in this competition.

5 Path Planning

Implementing the different roles often requires robots to be able to walk from one position on the field to another one without bumping into other robots, e.g., when walking to their kickoff positions or when walking to a distant ball. In these cases, a purely reactive control can be disadvantageous, because it usually would not consider obstacles that are further away, which might result in getting stuck. Therefore, our robots use a path planner in these situations since 2011. Until 2014, it was based on the Rapidly-Exploring Random Tree approach [2] with re-planning in each behavior cycle, i.e., for each new image taken. Although the planner worked quite well, it had two major problems: On the one hand, the randomness sometimes resulted in suboptimal paths and in oscillations[1]. On the other hand, it seemed that the RRT approach is not really necessary for solving a 2-D planning problem, as the planner actually did. Thus, it was slower than it needed to be.

5.1 Approach

Therefore, it was replaced by a visibility-graph-based 2-D A* planner (cf. Fig. 6). The planner represents obstacles as circles on which they can be surrounded and the path between them as tangential straight lines. As a result, a path is always an alternating sequence of straight lines and circle segments. There are four connecting tangents between each pair of non-overlapping obstacle circles, only two between circles that overlap, and none if one circle contains the other (cf. Fig. 7). In addition, the current position of the robot and the target position are only points, not circles, which also influences the number of tangents. A robot can either walk in clockwise or in counter clockwise direction around an obstacle. It also always walks forward. This means that it has to leave a circle in the same direction it has entered it. In the path planning problem, this actually results in two nodes per obstacle circle, one for clockwise movement and one for counter clockwise movement, which are not directly connected.

With up to nine other robots on the field, four goal posts, the ball, and the optional requirement to avoid the own penalty area, the number of edges in the visibility graph can be quite high. Thus, the creation of the entire graph could be a very time-consuming task. Therefore, the planner creates the graph while planning, i.e., it only creates the outgoing edges from nodes that were already reached by the A* planning algorithm (cf. Fig. 6). Thereby, the A* heuristic (which is the Euclidean distance) not only speeds up the search, but it also reduces the number of nodes that are expanded. When a node is expanded, the tangents to all other *visible* nodes that have not been visited before are computed. *Visible* means that no closer obstacle circles intersect with the tangent, which would prevent traveling directly from one circle to another. To compute the visibility efficiently, a sweep line approach is used (cf. Fig. 8a). However, correctly ordering the circles by their distance would require quite a lot of bookkeeping, because of their different sizes and their possible intersections (cf. circle 5 in Fig. 8a). Instead, the sweepline is just ordered by the closest distances between circles and to check whether the endpoint of a tangent is reachable, the tangent is intersected with all circles in the sweepline the furthest point of which is closer

---

[1] Although the planner tried to keep each new plan close to the previous one.

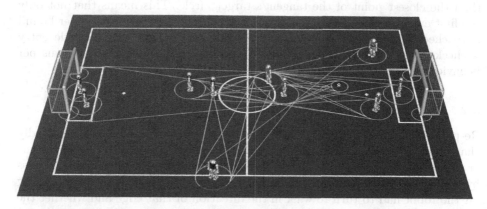

Fig. 6. Visualization of the planning process. The robot on the left of the center circle plans a path to a position suitable to kick the ball on the right towards the opponent goal. The obstacle circles and the edges expanded are shown in yellow. Sectors of the obstacle circles that are not traversable, either because they overlap with another circle or they are too close to the field border, are depicted in red. Barriers the robot is not allowed to cross, either to avoid walking through the goal net or because it should not enter its penalty area, are also shown in red. The shortest path determined is marked in green. (Color figure online)

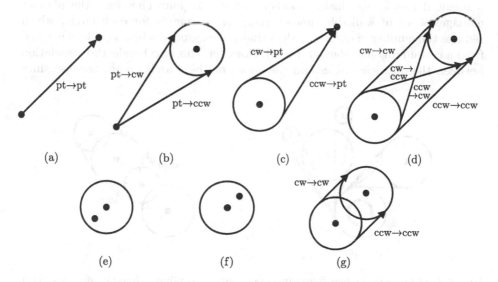

Fig. 7. Seven different combinations of nodes with the corresponding walking directions on the circles (point, clockwise, counter clockwise). (a) Point to point. (b) Point to circle. (c) Circle to point. (d) Circle to circle. (e, f) No tangents if point or smaller circle is inside other circle. (g) Circles overlap.

than the closest point of the tangent's target circle. This means that not only the first entry in the sweepline is checked, but all entries until the upper bound is reached. However, in most cases, this still means that only a single entry is checked. As a result, the planning process never took longer than 1 ms per behavior cycle in typical games.

5.2   Avoiding Oscillations

Re-planning in each behavior cycle bears the risk of oscillations, i.e., repeatedly changing the decision, for instance, to avoid the closest obstacle on either the left or the right side. The planner introduces some stability into the planning process by adding an extra distance to all outgoing edges of the start node based on how far the robot had to turn to walk in the direction of that edge and whether the first obstacle is passed on the same side again (no extra penalty) or not (extra penalty). Note that this does not violate the requirement of the A* algorithm [1] that the heuristic is not allowed to overestimate the remaining distance, because the heuristic is never used for the outgoing edges of the start node.

5.3   Overlapping Obstacle Circles

The planning process is a little bit more complex than it appears at first glance: As obstacles can overlap, ingoing and outgoing edges of the same circle are not necessarily connected, because the robot cannot walk on their connecting circle segment if this is also inside another obstacle region. Therefore, the planner manages a set of walkable (non-overlapping) segments for each circle, which reduces the number of outgoing edges that are expanded when a circle is reached from a certain ingoing edge (cf. Fig. 6). However, this also breaks the association between the obstacle circles and the nodes of the search graph, because since

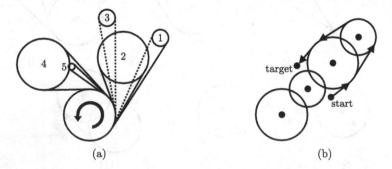

(a)   (b)

Fig. 8. (a) Computing edges from tangents using a sweepline ordered by distance (here for tangents starting in counter clockwise direction). All tangents are processed ordered by their direction. Right tangents enter a circle into the sweepline, left tangents remove a circle from the sweepline. The tangents with an endpoint that is the closest in that direction are kept (depicted as solid lines), all other tangents are removed (depicted as dotted lines). (b) An example for reaching the same circle twice.

some outgoing edges are unreachable from a certain ingoing one, the same circle can be reached again later through another ingoing edge that now opens up the connection to other outgoing edges (cf. Fig. 8b). To solve this problem, circles are cloned for each yet unreached segment, which makes the circle segments the actual nodes in the search graph. However, as the graph is created during the search process, this cloning also only happens on demand.

5.4 Forbidden Areas

There are two other extensions in the planning process. Another source for unreachable segments on obstacle circles is a virtual border around the field. In theory, the shortest path to a location could be to surround another robot outside of the carpet. The virtual border makes sure that no paths are planned that are closer to the edge of the carpet than it is safe (cf. Fig. 6). On demand, the planner can also activate lines surrounding the own penalty area to avoid entering it. The lines prevent passing obstacles on the inner side of the penalty area. In addition, edges of the visibility graph are not allowed to intersect with these lines. To give the planner still a chance to find a shortest path around the penalty area, four obstacle circles are placed on its corners in this mode. A similar approach is also used to prevent the robot from walking through the goal nets.

5.5 Avoiding Impossible Plans

In practice, it is possible that the robot should reach a position that the planner assumes to be unreachable. On the one hand, the start position or the target position could be inside obstacle circles. In these cases, the obstacle circles are "pushed away" from these locations in the direction they have to be moved the least to not overlap with the start/target position anymore before the planning is started[2]. For instance in Fig. 6, the obstacle circle surrounding the ball was slightly moved away to make the target position reachable.

On the other hand, due to localization errors, the start and target location could be on different sides of lines that should not be passed. In these cases, the closest line is "pushed away". For instance, if the robot is inside its penalty area although it should not be, this would move the closest border of the penalty area far enough inward so that the robot's start position appears to be outside for the planning process so that a solution can be found.

6 Conclusion and Future Work

For successfully playing robot soccer and winning the RoboCup, several sub-problems need to be solved. In this paper, we represented the hypothesis that in

---

[2] Note that when executing the plan, these situations are handled differently to avoid bumping into other robots.

the current state of the RoboCup Standard Platform League, the development of sophisticated robot behaviors makes a difference between the top teams, in contrast to other tasks such as perception or motion, which have converged to solutions of similar quality.

As examples, we described our general tactical approaches for the main competition as well as for the Mixed Team competition, which we also won together with the HULKs. Furthermore, as an example for robot skills, our realtime path planning approach has been presented.

As there are still many open issues, regarding team tactics as well as robot skills, that have not been solved yet by any team, one major focus for RoboCup 2018 will be on the further improvement of the robot behaviors. In addition, the Standard Platform League currently plans to introduce some major changes such as free kicks that will require even more behavior development.

References

1. Hart, P., Nilsson, N., Raphael, B.: A formal basis for the heuristic determination of minimum cost paths. IEEE Trans. Syst. Sci. Cybern. 4(2), 100–107 (1968)
2. LaValle, S.M.: Rapidly-exploring random trees: a new tool for path planning. Technical report TR 98–11, Computer Science Department, Iowa State University (1998)
3. Menashe, J., et al.: Fast and precise black and white ball detection for RoboCup soccer. In: RoboCup 2017: Robot World Cup XXI, Nagoya, Japan, July 2017
4. Müller, J., Laue, T., Röfer, T.: Kicking a ball – modeling complex dynamic motions for humanoid robots. In: Ruiz-del-Solar, J., Chown, E., Plöger, P.G. (eds.) RoboCup 2010. LNCS (LNAI), vol. 6556, pp. 109–120. Springer, Heidelberg (2011). https://doi.org/10.1007/978-3-642-20217-9_10
5. Röfer, T.: CABSL – C-based agent behavior specification language. In: Akiyama et al. (eds.) RoboCup 2017. LNAI, vol. 11175, pp. 135–142. Springer, Cham (2018). http://www.informatik.uni-bremen.de/kogrob/papers/RC-Roefer-18.pdf
6. RoboCup Federation: Website RoboCup Standard Platform League (2017). http://spl.robocup.org
7. Röfer, T.: B-human team report and code release 2017 (2017). http://www.b-human.de/downloads/publications/2017/coderelease2017.pdf

UT Austin Villa: RoboCup 2017 3D Simulation League Competition and Technical Challenges Champions

Patrick MacAlpine[(✉)] and Peter Stone

Department of Computer Science, The University of Texas at Austin, Austin, USA
{patmac,pstone}@cs.utexas.edu

Abstract. The UT Austin Villa team, from the University of Texas at Austin, won the 2017 RoboCup 3D Simulation League, winning all 23 games that the team played. During the course of the competition the team scored 171 goals without conceding any. Additionally, the team won the RoboCup 3D Simulation League technical challenge by winning each of a series of three league challenges: free, passing and scoring, and Gazebo running challenge. This paper describes the changes and improvements made to the team between 2016 and 2017 that allowed it to win both the main competition and each of the league technical challenges.

1 Introduction

UT Austin Villa won the 2017 RoboCup 3D Simulation League for the sixth time in the past seven years, having also won the competition in 2011 [1], 2012 [2], 2014 [3], 2015 [4], and 2016 [5] while finishing second in 2013. During the course of the competition the team scored 171 goals and conceded none along the way to winning all 23 games the team played. Many of the components of the 2017 UT Austin Villa agent were reused from the team's successful previous years' entries in the competition. This paper is not an attempt at a complete description of the 2017 UT Austin Villa agent, the base foundation of which is the team's 2011 championship agent fully described in a team technical report [6], but instead focuses on changes made in 2017 that helped the team repeat as champions.

In addition to winning the main RoboCup 3D Simulation League competition, UT Austin Villa also won the RoboCup 3D Simulation League technical challenge by winning each of the three league challenges: free, passing and scoring, and Gazebo running challenge. This paper also serves to document these challenges and the approaches used by UT Austin Villa when competing in the challenges.

The remainder of the paper is organized as follows. In Sect. 2 a description of the 3D simulation domain is given. Section 3 details the most important improvement to the 2017 UT Austin Villa team: fast walk kicks, while Sect. 4 analyzes the contribution of this improvement in addition to the overall performance of

© Springer Nature Switzerland AG 2018
H. Akiyama et al. (Eds.): RoboCup 2017, LNAI 11175, pp. 473–485, 2018.
https://doi.org/10.1007/978-3-030-00308-1_39

the team at the competition. Section 5 describes and analyzes the league challenges that were used to determine the winner of the technical challenge, and Sect. 6 concludes.

2   Domain Description

The RoboCup 3D simulation environment is based on SimSpark [7,8], a generic physical multiagent system simulator. SimSpark uses the Open Dynamics Engine (ODE) library for its realistic simulation of rigid body dynamics with collision detection and friction. ODE also provides support for the modeling of advanced motorized hinge joints used in the humanoid agents.

Games consist of 11 versus 11 agents playing two 5 min halves of soccer on a 30 × 20 m field. The robot agents in the simulation are modeled after the Aldebaran Nao robot, which has a height of about 57 cm, and a mass of 4.5 kg. Each robot has 22° of freedom: six in each leg, four in each arm, and two in the neck. In order to monitor and control its hinge joints, an agent is equipped with joint perceptors and effectors. Joint perceptors provide the agent with noise-free angular measurements every simulation cycle (20 ms), while joint effectors allow the agent to specify the speed/direction in which to move a joint.

Visual information about the environment is given to an agent every third simulation cycle (60 ms) through noisy measurements of the distance and angle to objects within a restricted vision cone (120°). Agents are also outfitted with noisy accelerometer and gyroscope perceptors, as well as force resistance perceptors on the sole of each foot. Additionally, agents can communicate with each other every other simulation cycle (40 ms) by sending 20 byte messages.

In addition to the standard Nao robot model, four additional variations of the standard model, known as heterogeneous types, are available for use. These variations from the standard model include changes in leg and arm length, hip width, and also the addition of toes to the robot's foot. Teams must use at least three different robot types, no more than seven agents of any one robot type, and no more than nine agents of any two robot types.

The main change for the 2017 RoboCup 3D Simulation League competition from previous years was the removal of crowding rules. Previously, too many players crowded around the ball caused players to be penalized and beamed to the sideline. Crowding rules were primarily enforced to decrease the number of collisions between robots as multiple collisions at the same time can slow down the simulator and potentially cause it to crash. With existing touching rules such that a player is beamed to the sideline if a group of three or more players are touching each other, and the addition in 2016 of charging fouls that penalize players for running into opponents, it was determined that crowding rules were no longer needed.

Figure 1 shows a visualization of the Nao robot and the soccer field during a game.

Fig. 1. A screenshot of the Nao humanoid robot (left), and a view of the soccer field during a 11 versus 11 game (right).

3   Fast Walk Kicks

Many components developed prior to 2017 contributed to the success of the UT Austin Villa team including dynamic role assignment [9], marking [10], and an optimization framework used to learn low level behaviors for walking and kicking via an overlapping layered learning approach [11]. This section discusses the development of a new and important component for 2017: fast walk kicks. Fast walk kicks refer to the ability of agents to approach the ball and quickly kick it without having to first come to a stop and enter a stable standing position. The amount of time it takes for agents to approach and kick the ball is an important consideration as kick attempts that take longer to perform give opponents a better chance to stop them from being executed.

The UT Austin Villa team specifies kicking motions through a periodic state machine with multiple key frames, where a key frame is a parameterized static pose of fixed joint positions. Figure 2 shows an example series of poses for a kicking motion. While some joint positions are specified by hand, a subset of values for joint positions are optimized using the CMA-ES [12] algorithm and overlapping layered learning [11] methodologies.

Prior to the 2017 competition all kicking motions performed by the UT Austin Villa team first required the agent to come to a stable standing position with both feet on the ground before kicking the ball. The team's fastest kicks took about 0.5 s to execute but only traveled a little over 5 m. Longer kicks, traveling as far as 20 m, were slower and could take up to 2 s to execute.

The UT Austin Villa team has noticed a couple trends when optimizing parameter values for kicks: policies with more parameters allow for longer kicks, and policies with more parameters allow for kicking motions with shorter durations that are quicker to execute without the robot becoming unstable and falling over. As adding more parameters to a policy increases the space of policies that can be represented, it is not surprising that policies with more parameters have

Fig. 2. Example of a fixed series of poses that make up a kicking motion.

allowed for kicks that can travel farther and be executed faster. However, adding more parameters to a kick can make learning slower and more difficult, and there is likely an upper limit on the number of parameters that can effectively be learned as CMA-ES does not scale well to thousands of parameters [13].

Given a desire to develop a kick with good distance that is very fast to execute, we decided to learn kicking motion parameters for every joint over 12 simulation cycles (24 ms)—such a kicking motion is thus learned over the entire range of possible poses for any kick less than 0.25 s in duration. We optimized ≈260 parameters for this kick across 1000 generation of CMA-ES using a population size of 300—previously we have used a CMA-ES population size of 150 when optimizing kicks consisting of ≈75 parameters, however we decided to double the size of the population due to the larger number of parameters being optimized. Initial parameter values were seeded with joint angles taken from a subset of poses used by our longest kick: joint angle values across a 12 simulation cycle window of the kick that include when the ball is struck by the foot. During learning we used the following fitness function that rewards the agent for the distance the ball is kicked, encourages accuracy by giving a Gaussian penalty for the difference/offset between the desired and actual angles that the ball travels, and promotes stability via a negative value if the agent falls over during kicking:

$$
fitness_{\text{kick}} = \begin{cases} -1 & : \text{Agent Fell} \\ \text{distBallTraveledForward} * e^{-\text{angleOffset}^2/360} & : \text{Otherwise} \end{cases}
$$

The resulting kick learned from this optimization takes 0.24 s to execute, travels close to 20 m in distance (nearly the same distance as our longest kicks that can take up to 2 s to execute), and provides a substantial increase in the team's performance—a performance analysis of using fast walk kicks is provided in Sect. 4.1.

As our learned kick takes less than 0.25 s to execute, the robot must begin the kicking motion starting from a walking position, and perform a "walk kick" due to there not being enough time for the robot to first assume a standing position before striking the ball. During walk kicks it is important that a robot has its non-kicking support leg on the ground before initiating a kicking motion as otherwise the robot will likely fall over. When attempting walk kicks, the UT Austin Villa agent will wait until its support leg is on the ground—as determined by a large enough force measured by the force resistance perceptor on the sole of the agent's support leg's foot—before beginning a kick. The magmaOffenburg team, who also developed a walk kick for this year's competition, similarly ensure that a robot's support leg is on the ground before attempting a kick [14].

4 Main Competition Results and Analysis

In winning the 2017 RoboCup competition UT Austin Villa finished with a perfect record of 23 wins and no losses[1]. During the competition the team scored 171 goals while conceding none. Despite finishing with a perfect record, the relatively few number of games played at the competition, coupled with the complex and stochastic environment of the RoboCup 3D simulator, make it difficult to determine UT Austin Villa being better than other teams by a statistically significant margin. At the end of the competition, however, all teams were required to release their binaries used during the competition. Results of UT Austin Villa playing 1000 games against each of the other twelve teams' released binaries from the competition are shown in Table 1.

Table 1. UT Austin Villa's released binary's performance when playing 1000 games against the released binaries of all other teams at RoboCup 2017. This includes place (the rank a team achieved at the 2017 competition), average goal difference (values in parentheses are the standard error), win-loss-tie record, and goals for/against.

Opponent	Place	Avg. goal diff.	Record (W-L-T)	Goals (F/A)
magmaOffenburg	2	3.756 (0.057)	983-0-17	3778/22
FUT-K	3	4.793 (0.056)	995-0-5	4823/30
AIUT3D	5	5.946 (0.054)	1000-0-0	5981/35
BahiaRT	6	6.677 (0.055)	1000-0-0	6677/0
FCPortugal	7	6.753 (0.062)	1000-0-0	6818/65
Nexus3D	11	7.486 (0.035)	1000-0-0	7486/0
KgpKubs	8	7.510 (0.057)	1000-0-0	7510/0
RoboCanes	4	7.801 (0.066)	1000-0-0	7806/5
HfutEngine3D	12	7.952 (0.049)	1000-0-0	7957/5
Miracle3D	10	8.404 (0.056)	1000-0-0	8404/0
ITAndroids	9	11.169 (0.057)	1000-0-0	11169/0
RIC-AASTMT	13	11.466 (0.051)	1000-0-0	11466/0

UT Austin Villa finished with at least an average goal difference greater than 3.75 goals against every opponent. Additionally, UT Austin Villa won all but

---

[1] Full tournament results can be found at https://www.robocup2017.org/file/results/0730/0730_soccer_simulation_3d.pdf.

22 games that ended in ties—no losses—out of the 12,000 that were played in Table 1 with a win percentage greater than 98% against all teams. These results show that UT Austin Villa winning the 2017 competition was far from a chance occurrence. The following subsection analyzes the contribution of fast walk kicks (described in Sect. 3) to the team's dominant performance.

4.1 Analysis of Fast Walk Kicks

To analyze the contribution of fast walk kicks (Sect. 3) to the UT Austin Villa team's performance, we played 1000 games between a version of the 2017 UT Austin Villa team with fast walk kicks turned off—and no other changes—against each of the RoboCup 2017 teams' released binaries. Results comparing the performance of the UT Austin Villa team with and without using fast walk kicks are shown in Table 2.

Table 2. Average goal difference achieved by versions of the UT Austin Villa team with and without fast walk kicks, and the gain in average goal difference by using fast walk kicks, when playing 1000 games against all teams at RoboCup 2017.

Opponent	Fast walk kicks	No fast walk kicks	Fast walk kicks gain
UTAustinVilla	0[a]	−0.557	0.557
magmaOffenburg	3.756	2.159	1.597
FUT-K	4.793	2.912	1.881
AIUT3D	5.946	4.824	1.122
BahiaRT	6.677	4.051	2.626
FCPortugal	6.753	4.701	2.052
Nexus3D	7.486	7.002	0.484
KgpKubs	7.510	5.532	1.978
RoboCanes	7.801	6.113	1.688
HfutEngine3D	7.952	6.827	1.125
Miracle3D	8.404	6.830	1.574
ITAndroids	11.169	10.294	0.875
RIC-AASTMT	11.466	10.526	0.940

[a]Games were not played, but assumed to be an average goal difference of 0 in expectation with self play.

Against all opponents the average goal difference was higher when using fast walk kicks, with the gain in average goal difference performance against each opponent averaging 1.423 goals. These results show that fast walk kicks provide a substantial improvement in game performance to the UT Austin Villa team.

4.2   Additional Tournament Competition Analysis

To further analyze the tournament competition, Table 3 shows the average goal difference for each team at RoboCup 2017 when playing 1000 games against all other teams at RoboCup 2017.

Table 3. Average goal difference for each team at RoboCup 2017 (rows) when playing 1000 games against the released binaries of all other teams at RoboCup 2017 (columns). Teams are ordered from most to least dominant in terms of winning (positive goal difference) and losing (negative goal difference).

	UTA	mag	FUT	FCP	AIUT	Rob	Bah	Kgp	Hfut	Mir	Nex	ITA	RIC
UTAustinVilla	—	3.756	4.793	6.753	5.946	7.801	6.677	7.510	7.952	8.404	7.486	11.169	11.466
magmaOffenburg	-3.756	—	0.058	1.698	1.441	2.692	2.593	2.863	3.627	5.340	4.088	4.760	6.210
FUT-K	-4.793	-0.058	—	1.621	1.989	2.077	2.165	2.603	4.151	4.986	5.297	5.313	6.597
FCPortugal	-6.753	-1.698	-1.621	—	0.325	0.695	1.031	1.735	2.388	3.991	2.950	4.287	5.352
AIUT3D	-5.946	-1.441	-1.989	-0.325	—	0.506	0.449	0.738	2.077	2.721	3.223	2.609	5.536
RoboCanes	-7.801	-2.692	-2.077	-0.695	-0.506	—	1.068	1.852	2.279	4.175	2.612	3.309	4.791
BahiaRT	-6.677	-2.593	-2.165	-1.031	-0.449	-1.068	—	0.393	1.005	1.437	1.448	1.645	3.120
KgpKubs	-7.510	-2.863	-2.603	-1.735	-0.738	-1.852	-0.393	—	0.974	1.115	0.638	1.664	3.027
HfutEngine3D	-7.952	-3.627	-4.151	-2.388	-2.077	-2.279	-1.005	-0.974	—	0.436	0.081	0.180	1.426
Miracle3D	-8.404	-5.340	-4.986	-3.991	-2.721	-4.175	-1.437	-1.115	-0.436	—	0.562	0.525	2.693
Nexus3D	-7.486	-4.088	-5.297	-2.950	-3.223	-2.612	-1.448	-0.638	-0.081	-0.562	—	0.179	1.691
ITAndroids	-11.109	-4.700	-5.313	-4.287	-2.609	-3.309	-1.645	-1.664	-0.180	-0.525	-0.179	—	1.889
RIC–AASTMT	-11.466	-6.210	-6.597	-5.352	-5.536	-4.791	-3.120	-3.027	-1.426	-2.693	-1.691	-1.889	—

It is interesting to note that the ordering of teams in terms of winning (positive goal difference) and losing (negative goal difference) is strictly dominant— every opponent that a team wins against also loses to every opponent that defeats that same team. Relative goal difference does not have this same property, however, as a team that does better against one opponent relative to another team does not always do better against a second opponent relative to that same team. UT Austin Villa is dominant in terms of relative goal difference, however, as UT Austin Villa has a higher goal difference against each opponent than all other teams against the same opponent.

5   Technical Challenges

For the fourth straight year there was an overall technical challenge consisting of three different league challenges: free, passing and scoring, and Gazebo running challenge. For each league challenge a team participated in points were awarded toward the overall technical challenge based on the following equation:

$$\text{points}(rank) = 25 - 20 * (rank - 1)/(numberOfParticipants - 1)$$

Table 4 shows the ranking and cumulative team point totals for the technical challenge as well as for each individual league challenge. UT Austin Villa earned the most points and won the technical challenge by taking first in each of the

Table 4. Overall ranking and points totals for each team participating in the RoboCup 2017 3D Simulation League technical challenge as well as ranks and points awarded for each of the individual league challenges that make up the technical challenge.

Team	Overall		Free		Passing and scoring		Gazebo running	
	Rank	Points	Rank	Points	Rank	Points	Rank	Points
UTAustinVilla	1	**75.00**	1	**25.00**	1	**25.00**	1	**25.00**
magmaOffenburg	2	43.00	3	11.67	4	13.00	2	18.33
AIUT3D	3	30.33	4	5.00	3	17.00	3–4	8.33
FCPortugal	4	29.33	—	—	2	21.00	3–4	8.33
BahiaRT	5	23.33	2	18.33	6	5.00	—	—
HfutEngine3D	6	9.00	—	—	5	9.00	—	—

league challenges. The following subsections detail UT Austin Villa's participation in each league challenge[2].

5.1 Free Challenge

During the free challenge, teams give a five minute presentation on a research topic related to their team. Each team in the league then ranks the top five presentations with the best receiving 5 votes and the 5th best receiving 1 vote. Additionally several respected research members of the RoboCup community outside the league vote, with their votes being counted double. The winner of the free challenge is the team that receives the most votes. Table 5 shows the results of the free challenge in which UT Austin Villa was awarded first place.

Table 5. Results of the free challenge.

Team	Votes
UTAustinVilla	**59**
BahiaRT	49
magmaOffenburg	46
AIUT3D	42

UT Austin Villa's free challenge submission[3] presented the team's fast walk kicks discussed in Sect. 3. Additionally, UT Austin Villa's free challenge submission divulged preliminary work on representing the policy of a kicking motion

---

[2] Videos of the passing and scoring challenge and the Gazebo running challenge can be found at http://www.cs.utexas.edu/~AustinVilla/sim/3dsimulation/# 2017challenges.

[3] Free challenge entry description available at http://www.cs.utexas.edu/~Austin Villa/sim/3dsimulation/AustinVilla3DSimulationFiles/2017/files/UTAustinVilla FreeChallenge2017.pdf.

as a neural network, and using deep learning [15] and the Trust Region Policy Optimization (TRPO) algorithm [16] to learn longer kicks. The BahiaRT team provided details about an optimization framework they created, the magmaOffenburg team talked about a 2D simulator they use for testing the strategy layer of their team, and the AIUT3D team introduced a motion editor for 3D Simulation League agents[4].

5.2 Passing and Scoring Challenge

In the course of the passing and scoring challenge[5], a group of four agents on one team attempts to pass the ball between themselves—such that each agent touches the ball at least once—before scoring a goal in as little time as possible. At the beginning of the challenge the ball is placed at the center of the field and the agents must start with at least a three meter distance, along the X axis, from each other. If the initial position of the agents does not comply with the rules, the team is awarded a score of 85. The challenge ends when a goal is scored, the ball leaves the field, or 80 s have passed. For each distinct agent kicking the ball—judged as the ball traveling freely for at least 2.5 m after being kicked, the score is reduced by one point. If a goal is scored, the score is reduced by one point. If the goal is scored after the ball has been kicked by all four players, the score is the time (in seconds) from the start of the trial until the scoring event. The objective of the challenge is to get as low a score as possible.

The starting position and strategy used by UT Austin Villa for the passing and scoring challenge is shown in Fig. 3. Whichever agent is closest to the ball passes the ball to a position about a meter in front of the next farthest agent from the goal as shown by the yellow arrows in Fig. 3. Once the ball has been sequentially passed forward between agents and the agent closest to the goal receives the ball, that agent kicks the ball in the goal as shown by the pink arrow in Fig. 3. When agents are not the closest agent to the ball they just stand in place.

Table 6 shows the results of the passing and scoring challenge where teams were ranked by the average score of a team's best (lowest) three out of four trials. UT Austin Villa won the challenge with an average score/time of less than 20. Each of UT Austin Villa's passing and scoring challenge trial scores were better than all the scores of other teams' trials.

5.3 Gazebo Running Challenge

Ongoing work within the RoboCup community is the development of a plugin[6] for the Gazebo [17] robotics simulator to support the RoboCup 3D Simulation

---

[4] https://github.com/AIUT3D/aiut3d-motion-editor.

[5] Details and framework for the passing and scoring challenge at https://github.com/ magmaOffenburg/magmaChallenge#passing-challenge.

[6] https://bitbucket.org/osrf/robocup3ds.

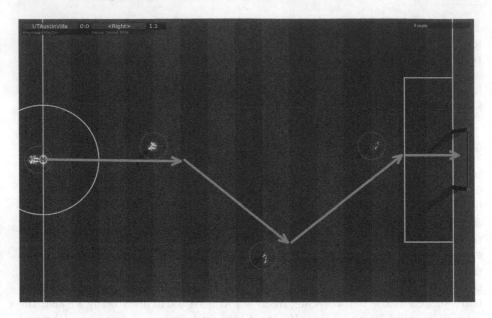

Fig. 3. Starting positions and strategy for the passing and scoring challenge. Yellow arrows represent passes between agents and the pink arrow represents a shot on goal. (Color figure online)

Table 6. Scores for each of the teams competing in the passing and scoring challenge.

Team	Trial 1	Trial 2	Trial 3	Trial 4	Average of best three trials
UTAustinVilla	**19.34**	**20.26**	**21.28**	**19.38**	**19.66**
FCPortugal	82.00	21.58	22.06	22.18	21.94
AIUT3D	31.26	53.66	33.98	35.98	33.74
magmaOffenburg	30.38	83.00	23.66	82.00	45.35
HfutEngine3D	35.58	84.00	82.00	83.00	66.86
BahiaRT	81.00	83.00	83.00	82.00	82.00

League. As such, a challenge[7] was held where robots attempt to walk forward as fast as possible for 20 s in the Gazebo simulator without falling. In preparation for the challenge UT Austin Villa optimized fast walking parameters for the team's omnidirectional walk engine [18] within the Gazebo simulator using the CMA-ES algorithm [12]. Walk engine parameters were optimized for 300 generations of CMA-ES with a population size of 150.

Results of the Gazebo running challenge are shown in Table 7. Each participating team performed four running attempts and were scored by the average forward walking speed across their three best attempts. UT Austin Villa won

---

[7] Framework for running the Gazebo running challenge at https://github.com/magmaOffenburg/magmaChallenge.

Table 7. Speed in meters per second for each of the teams competing in the Gazebo running challenge.

Team	Run 1	Run 2	Run 3	Run 4	Average of best three runs
UTAustinVilla	**1.176**	**1.210**	**1.159**	**1.179**	**1.188**
magmaOffenburg	0.354	0.365	0.417	0.256	0.379
AIUT3D	0.000	0.000	0.000	0.000	0.000
FCPortugal	0.000	0.000	0.000	0.000	0.000

the challenge with all of the team's runs having a speed of over 1.15 m/s. Each of UT Austin Villa's running attempt speeds were greater than all other teams' attempts. UT Austin Villa also won this same challenge at RoboCup 2016 [5].

6   Conclusion

UT Austin Villa won the 2017 RoboCup 3D Simulation League main competition as well as all technical league challenges[8]. Data taken using released binaries from the competition show that UT Austin Villa winning the competition was statistically significant. The 2017 UT Austin Villa team also improved dramatically from 2016 as it was able to beat the team's 2016 champion binary by an average of 1.339 ($\pm$0.039) goals across 1000 games.

In an effort to both make it easier for new teams to join the RoboCup 3D Simulation League, and also provide a resource that can be beneficial to existing teams, the UT Austin Villa team has released their base code [19][9]. This code release provides a fully functioning agent and good starting point for new teams to the RoboCup 3D Simulation League (it was used by six teams at the 2017 competition: AIUT3D, HfutEngine3D, KgpKubs, Miracle3D, Nexus3D, and RIC-AASTMT). Additionally the code release offers a foundational platform for conducting research in multiple areas including robotics, multiagent systems, and machine learning.

Acknowledgments. Thanks to members of the BahiaRT and magmaOffenburg teams for helping put together the passing and scoring challenge and the Gazebo running challenge. This work has taken place in the Learning Agents Research Group (LARG) at the Artificial Intelligence Laboratory, The University of Texas at Austin. LARG research is supported in part by NSF (IIS-1637736, IIS-1651089, IIS-1724157), Intel, Raytheon, and Lockheed Martin. Peter Stone serves on the Board of Directors of Cogitai, Inc. The terms of this arrangement have been reviewed and approved by the University of Texas at Austin in accordance with its policy on objectivity in research.

---

[8] More information about the UT Austin Villa team, as well as video highlights from the competition, can be found at the team's website: http://www.cs.utexas.edu/~AustinVilla/sim/3dsimulation/#2017.

[9] Code release at https://github.com/LARG/utaustinvilla3d.

References

1. MacAlpine, P., et al.: UT Austin Villa 2011: a champion agent in the RoboCup 3D soccer simulation competition. In: Proceedings of 11th International Conference on Autonomous Agents and Multiagent Systems (AAMAS 2012) (2012)
2. MacAlpine, P., Collins, N., Lopez-Mobilia, A., Stone, P.: UT Austin Villa: RoboCup 2012 3D simulation league champion. In: Chen, X., Stone, P., Sucar, L.E., van der Zant, T. (eds.) RoboCup 2012. LNCS (LNAI), vol. 7500, pp. 77–88. Springer, Heidelberg (2013). https://doi.org/10.1007/978-3-642-39250-4_8
3. MacAlpine, P., Depinet, M., Liang, J., Stone, P.: UT Austin Villa: RoboCup 2014 3D simulation league competition and technical challenge champions. In: Bianchi, R.A.C., Akin, H.L., Ramamoorthy, S., Sugiura, K. (eds.) RoboCup 2014. LNCS (LNAI), vol. 8992, pp. 33–46. Springer, Cham (2015). https://doi.org/10.1007/978-3-319-18615-3_3
4. MacAlpine, P., Hanna, J., Liang, J., Stone, P.: UT Austin Villa: RoboCup 2015 3D simulation league competition and technical challenges champions. In: Almeida, L., Ji, J., Steinbauer, G., Luke, S. (eds.) RoboCup 2015. LNCS (LNAI), vol. 9513, pp. 118–131. Springer, Cham (2015). https://doi.org/10.1007/978-3-319-29339-4_10
5. MacAlpine, P., Stone, P.: UT Austin Villa: RoboCup 2016 3D simulation league competition and technical challenges champions. In: Behnke, S., Sheh, R., Sarıel, S., Lee, D.D. (eds.) RoboCup 2016. LNCS (LNAI), vol. 9776, pp. 515–528. Springer, Cham (2017). https://doi.org/10.1007/978-3-319-68792-6_43
6. MacAlpine, P., et al.: UT Austin Villa 2011 3D simulation team report. Technical report AI11-10, The University of Texas at Austin, Departmet of Computer Science, AI Laboratory (2011)
7. Boedecker, J., Asada, M.: SimSpark-concepts and application in the RoboCup 3D soccer simulation league. In: SIMPAR 2008 Workshop on the Universe of RoboCup Simulators, pp. 174–181 (2008)
8. Xu, Y., Vatankhah, H.: SimSpark: an open source robot simulator developed by the RoboCup community. In: Behnke, S., Veloso, M., Visser, A., Xiong, R. (eds.) RoboCup 2013. LNCS (LNAI), vol. 8371, pp. 632–639. Springer, Heidelberg (2014). https://doi.org/10.1007/978-3-662-44468-9_59
9. MacAlpine, P., Price, E., Stone, P.: SCRAM: scalable collision-avoiding role assignment with minimal-makespan for formational positioning. In: Proceedings of the Twenty-Ninth AAAI Conference on Artificial Intelligence (AAAI 2015) (2015)
10. MacAlpine, P., Stone, P.: Prioritized role assignment for marking. In: Behnke, S., Sheh, R., Sarıel, S., Lee, D.D. (eds.) RoboCup 2016. LNCS (LNAI), vol. 9776, pp. 306–318. Springer, Cham (2017). https://doi.org/10.1007/978-3-319-68792-6_25
11. MacAlpine, P., Stone, P.: Overlapping layered learning. Artif. Intell. **254**, 21–43 (2018)
12. Hansen, N.: The CMA Evolution Strategy: A Tutorial (2009). http://www.lri.fr/~hansen/cmatutorial.pdf
13. Omidvar, M.N., Li, X.: A comparative study of CMA-ES on large scale global optimisation. In: Li, J. (ed.) AI 2010. LNCS (LNAI), vol. 6464, pp. 303–312. Springer, Heidelberg (2010). https://doi.org/10.1007/978-3-642-17432-2_31
14. Dorer, K.: Learning to use toes in a humanoid robot. In: RoboCup 2017. LNAI, vol. 11175, pp. 168–179. Springer, Cham (2018)
15. Bengio, Y., Goodfellow, I.J., Courville, A.: Deep learning. Nature **521**, 436–444 (2015)

16. Schulman, J., Levine, S., Abbeel, P., Jordan, M., Moritz, P.: Trust region policy optimization. In: Proceedings of the 32nd International Conference on Machine Learning (ICML 2015), pp. 1889–1897 (2015)
17. Koenig, N., Howard, A.: Design and use paradigms for gazebo, an open-source multi-robot simulator. In: Intelligent Robots and Systems (IROS) (2004)
18. MacAlpine, P., Barrett, S., Urieli, D., Vu, V., Stone, P.: Design and optimization of an omnidirectional humanoid walk: a winning approach at the RoboCup 2011 3D simulation competition. In: Proceedings of the Twenty-Sixth AAAI Conference on Artificial Intelligence (AAAI 2012) (2012)
19. MacAlpine, P., Stone, P.: UT Austin Villa RoboCup 3D simulation base code release. In: Behnke, S., Sheh, R., Sariel, S., Lee, D.D. (eds.) RoboCup 2016. LNCS (LNAI), vol. 9776, pp. 135–143. Springer, Cham (2017). https://doi.org/10.1007/978-3-319-68792-6_11

Enhancing Software and Hardware Reliability for a Successful Participation in the RoboCup Logistics League 2017

Till Hofmann[1]([✉]), Victor Mataré[2], Tobias Neumann[2], Sebastian Schönitz[3], Christoph Henke[3], Nicolas Limpert[2], Tim Niemueller[1], Alexander Ferrein[2], Sabina Jeschke[3], and Gerhard Lakemeyer[1]

[1] Knowledge-Based Systems Group, RWTH Aachen University, Aachen, Germany
hofmann@kbsg.rwth-aachen.de
[2] MASCOR Institute, FH Aachen University of Applied Sciences, Aachen, Germany
[3] Cybernetics Lab IMA/ZLW & IfU, RWTH Aachen University, Aachen, Germany

Abstract. In 2017, the RoboCup Logistics League (RCLL) has seen major changes to the playing field layout, which allows for more configuration variants that are now generated randomly and automatically, leading towards a more realistic smart factory scenario. The Carologistics team developed a new strategy for exploration and improved existing components with a particular focus on navigation and error handling in the behavior engine and high-level reasoning. We describe the major concepts of our approach with a focus on the improvements in comparison to last year, which enabled us to win the competition in 2017.

1 Introduction

The RoboCup Logistics League focuses on multi-robot coordination in an industrial smart factory environment. The domain presents interesting challenges for research in automated reasoning, planning, and scheduling.

The Carologistics team has participated in RoboCup 2012–2017 and in the RoboCup German Open 2013–2017, winning first place in both competitions from 2014 to 2017. Overall, our success is due to a stable middleware foundation, incremental refinement of components, and continuous recruitment of new talent.

In 2017, the league has seen a shift in focus towards the production phase. The exploration phase has been simplified, most notably by removing the requirement for teams to identify machines by means of a signal light code. The production phase in turn was extended in time and a new type of modular production system (MPS) was introduced. The size of the playing field was increased from $12\,\text{m} \times 6\,\text{m}$ to $14\,\text{m} \times 8\,\text{m}$, while the zone size was reduced. This increased the number of possible zones for MPS placement from 24 to 106. Unambiguous MPS positioning rules were formulated, so that the playing field layout can now be automatically generated by the Refbox. Point rewards have been re-balanced to reflect the increased emphasis on production instead of exploration.

© Springer Nature Switzerland AG 2018
H. Akiyama et al. (Eds.): RoboCup 2017, LNAI 11175, pp. 486–497, 2018.
https://doi.org/10.1007/978-3-030-00308-1_40

This paper is based on last year's edition [1], highlighting in particular how the Carologistics team adapted to the new challenges posed by the updated game logic. For a general description of the RCLL we refer to [2–5].

2   The Carologistics Platform

The standard robot platform of this league is the Robotino by Festo Didactic [6]. The Robotino is developed for research and education and features omnidirectional locomotion, a gyroscope and webcam, infrared distance sensors, and bumpers. The teams may equip the robot with additional sensors and computation devices as well as a gripper device for product handling. Our software is based on the Fawkes robotics framework [7], which integrates modules for all essential functional components.

2.1   Hardware System

Our current robot system is based on the Robotino 3. The modified Robotino used by the Carologistics RoboCup team is shown in Fig. 1. It features an additional webcam to identify machine markers, a RealSense depth camera to recognize the conveyor belt, and two Sick laser range finders.

We use a forward facing Sick TiM571 and a tilted backwards facing Sick TiM551 laser scanner for collision avoidance and self-localization. The TiM571 has a scanning range of 25 m (10 m for the TiM551) at a resolution of $1/3°$ (1° for the TiM551). An additional laptop increases the computation power and allows for more elaborate methods for self-localization, computer vision, and reasoning.

Several parts were custom-made for our robot platform. As described in detail in the next section, a custom-made gripper based on Festo fin-ray fingers and 3D-printed parts are used for product handling. The gripper is able to adjust for slight lateral and height offsets. The previously used servo motors have been replaced by stepper motors in order to increase positioning accuracy of the lateral axis. The motor is controlled with an additional Arduino board together with a motor shield. The acceleration of the motors follows an acceleration profile for smoothly increasing an decreasing the motor speed to avoid positioning errors. As no encoders are used, a micro switch for initializing the lateral axis position is used.

Fig. 1.   Carologistics Robotino 2017.

2.2   Mechanical Adaptations

To increase the agility of the robot, an additional back-facing laser scanner was added. As shown in Fig. 2 on the left, the laser is mounted just above the Robotino's computational unit under a slope of 12°, enabling it to perceive other robots' main body and not only the center pillar.

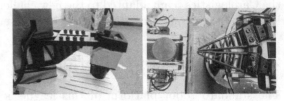

Fig. 2. Back-facing laser and new gripper

Another adaptation was made to the gripper system. Some of the grippers were damaged in past games and had to be replaced by the new version of Festo flex fingers, which required a newly designed mounting as shown in Fig. 2 on the right. The design consists of two easily separable parts. The first part is attached to the gripper while the second part is attached to the Dynamixel motor. Both parts are mounted together via a dovetail guide to enable quick replacement of a damaged gripper during a match.

2.3   Software Frameworks

The Fawkes robotics framework [7] serves as a central integration and coordination system. It implements a hybrid blackboard and messaging mechanism for inter-component communication, a vast library of primitives for I/O and data processing, and a flexible API for thead time-slicing and synchronization. Furthermore, it provides an adapter that allows us to integrate ROS nodes [8]. This has proven to be a great asset over time, given the continuous and rapid advancement of robotic technologies. It allows us to flexibly evaluate and integrate new technologies from the ROS ecosystem (cf. Sect. 3.1).

The overall software structure is inspired by the three-layer architecture [10] as shown in Fig. 3. It consists of a deliberative layer for high-level reasoning, a reactive execution layer for breaking down high-level commands and monitoring their execution, and a feedback control layer for hardware access and functional components.

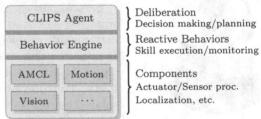

Fig. 3. Behavior layer separation [9]

3   Advances to Functional Software Components

3.1   Driving

To increase navigation flexibility we decided to change our navigation approach to the ROS Navigation Stack (navstack). It consists of several packages for local and global path planning, obstacle representations in an occupancy grid (occ-grid) and recovery behaviours to unstuck the robot. Apart from the very active maintaining community around the navstack, other benefits are the numerous options to further increase navigation performance with other ROS packages. One example for this is a ROS node we use to check the velocity commands computed by the move_base for validity. As we cannot guarantee that the local planner is real-time capable, we have to verify collision-free locomotion.

One of the key advantages of ROS is the ability to adapt to environmental challenges. If the robot has to take care of velocity constraints in certain areas, one could design a ROS node that provides a velocity veto functionality to overwrite motion commands or to set parameters for the navigation during runtime.

On top of the navstack we still make use of a global planner called Nav-Graph, which utilizes the MPS positions detected in exploration phase. This is directly implemented in Fawkes and simply sends new goal poses to the navstack throughout its own plan. The benefit here is that we can represent domain features within the NavGraph's environmental representation (e.g., MPS positions and/or highways which allow faster motion).

In particular we use the costmap_2d package as a representation of an occ-grid. This graph representation is used by the global and local planners managed by the move_base node[1], which loads a global and a local planner as plugins. move_base is responsible for receiving a desired goal and managing planning and motion execution as well as failure handling (Fig. 4).

The global planning is performed by a graph-based planning approach represented in the ROS package called global_planner[2]. This planner implements the A* search algorithm [11] to efficiently find paths within an occ-grid from start to goal. However, in practice we get a lot of navigation goals that are inside obstacles. By design, the global planner fails in this situation and thus we have to find a cell that is close to the desired goal. Finding this free cell is performed by an adoption of the potential field method [12]. This allows us to robustly find paths leading to a position close to an infeasible goal.

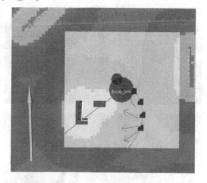

Fig. 4. move_base screenshot

Paths generated by the global planner are forwarded by the move_base to the local planner. For this we equip the teb_local_planner [13] (teb stands for "Timed Elastic Band") to achieve trajectories that are optimized w.r.t. execution time, obstacle distance and kinematic constraints. Kinematic constraints tell the local planner that we are moving with omnidirectional locomotion, thus we can save time in rotating to the final orientation of the final goal waypoint during motion.

---

[1] move_base wiki page at http://wiki.ros.org/move_base.

[2] http://wiki.ros.org/global_planner.

In unfortunate situations the navigation gets stuck (either the global planner does not find any valid path or the local planner can't find legal motion commands which do not lead to collisions). On a conceptual level, the move_base executes recovery behaviours in these situations. Our former navigation makes use of an escape behaviour (particularly another potential field) which we simply ported to be used as a recovery behaviour in the move_base.

3.2 Reactive Behavior

In previous work we have described the Lua-based Behavior Engine (BE) [14]. It serves as the reactive layer to interface between the low- and high-level systems (see Fig. 3). The BE provides a library of so-called *skills* that aggregate inter-component execution monitoring and reactive strategies into domain-related actions. Each skill describes a hybrid state machine (HSM), which can be conceived as a directed graph with nodes representing states for action execution, and/or monitoring of actuation, perception, and internal state. Edges denote jump conditions implemented as Boolean functions. For the active state of a state machine, all outgoing conditions are evaluated, typically at about 15 Hz. If a condition fires, the active state is changed to the target node of the edge. A table of variables holds information like the world model, for example storing numeric values for object positions. It remedies typical problems of state machines like fast growing number of states or variable data passing from one state to another. Skills are implemented using the light-weight, extensible scripting language Lua.

Fig. 5. Workpiece sits tilted on the rim (top), and is pushed down by moving the left finger individually (bottom).

One of the issues that continues to require substantial effort on the behavior layer is the MPS interaction. Since the current gripper design does not allow for sufficiently precise placement of workpieces on the conveyor belt, there is always a significant chance that workpieces may end up misaligned and tilted, with one edge sitting on the metal rim of the conveyor (Fig. 5 top). In this case, MPS processing (i.e. cap/ring mounting/removal) would likely fail and the processing step would be wasted. Fortunately, the MPS interaction has been changed in 2017 so that the conveyor belt will only start moving *after* a prepare-instruction has been sent to the MPS. Our gripper design with an independent servo for each finger thus allows us to give the workpiece a nudge on each side to make sure it slides off the rim and rests completely on the conveyor before the MPS operation is started (see Fig. 5 bottom).

4   High-Level Decision Making and Task Coordination

4.1   Exploration

Due to the much simplified exploration phase, the old exploration agent had to be rewritten. Since the number of zones has increased from 24 to 106, the deliberate zone-by-zone strategy used in previous years is not feasible any more. The responsible CLIPS agent code could be reduced from over 900 LoC to 580 LoC. The idea is to let all three robots roam the playing field on predefined routes while a RANSAC-based line detection algorithm scans for patterns that look like the straight wall panel of an MPS. From the pose of the detected line we can compute a reasonable hypothesis of where to look for the tag and position the robot accordingly. Once a tag has been found, its pose is discretized to multiples of 45° and reported to the refbox. Since the playing field is always symmetric, we can compute the pose of the opposite MPS according to the logic specified in the rulebook, which allows us to use machines of both teams for exploration. Progress is immediately shared between all robots to avoid duplicate effort and to allow each robot to compute a navigational graph on its own.

4.2   Reasoning and Planning

As in previous competitions, we use a distributed, local-scope, and incremental reasoning approach [9] implemented in the rule-based production system CLIPS [15]. As shown in Fig. 3, the CLIPS agent constitutes the decision making layer and builds on top of the behavior engine (cf., Sect. 3.2). We pursue the same general strategy as in previous years: Each agent acts on its own and synchronizes its world model with the other agents. A master agent ensures that the world models of all three agents are consistent. The master is determined dynamically through leader election. If the other agents cannot communicate with the master, a re-election is triggered. This ensures a consistent world model while dealing with robot and network failures in a robust way. Each agent follows an incremental strategy, i.e., in each step, it decides which step to take next based on its current world model. To avoid conflicts with the other robots, the currently selected next step is communicated to the other agents and a different step is selected if a conflict with another agent's strategy arises.

This year, we focused on improving the stability of the agent. In particular, we decided to focus on producing C0s (i.e., the product of lowest complexity) and implemented several recovery strategies, which allowed us to continue producing orders even in the event of a machine handling error. While the implemented monitoring strategies already improved error handling significantly in certain situations, we realized that a more principled approach is required to accomplish robust execution. Implementing such a principled execution monitoring strategy will be our goal for the next competitions.

5 Multi-robot Simulation in Gazebo

We have continued working on the *open simulation environment* [17] based on Gazebo (see Fig. 6). The simulation environment supports a full 3D physical simulation of an RCLL game including Referee Box (refbox), MPS placement and handling, and multi-robot communication. We see multiple advantages of such a simulation environment: For one, it lowers the burden for new teams, both in financial efforts and development requirements. A game setup including a full playing

Fig. 6. Simulation of the RCLL 2015 with MPS stations [16].

field, a set of MPSs, and three fully equipped robots has a high initial cost. Instead of buying a complete field, new teams can start developing in simulation and even compete in the simulation competition without buying any robot hardware, which may also increase the interest by non-robotic research communities (cf., next section). Additionally, the simulation environment allows for more rapid agent development. In a typical development cycle, all components of the lower and middle layer (see Fig. 3) must be working before the agent development can start, as the agent usually relies on all the lower-level components. With the simulation, we can replace challenging tasks such as picking and putting products with simulated actions that always succeed. This way, agent development can start much sooner. Third, a simulation environment allows for rapid test cycles. This supports more elaborate integration and regression tests, which is crucial for such complex systems. Using the simulation in a fully automated fashion even offers the possibility of fully automatic tests.

This year, we improved the performance of the simulation by simplifying the models used in Gazebo. We added support for the new storage stations, and enabled random MPS placements by the refbox.

5.1 Planning and Execution Competition at ICAPS

The Planning and Execution Competition for Logistics Robots in Simulation[3] (PExC) [2] was held for the first time at the 27th International Conference on Automated Planning and Scheduling (ICAPS) 2017. The goal of the competition is to improve the cooperation between the planning and the robotics communities. The motivation stems from the observation that even though robotics domains often serve as motivating example for planning research, planning techniques are rarely used in robotic applications in general, and in the RoboCup Logistics League in particular. Both communities may benefit from a closer cooperation. For the robotics community, planning may improve the performance significantly by enabling both, more product deliveries and the production of more

---

[3] More information is available at http://www.robocup-logistics.org/sim-comp.

complex products. For the planning community, the RCLL serves as an interesting application scenario with a medium complexity and additional challenges in terms of closely integrated planning and execution.

PExC is based on the RCLL rules of 2016. The competition focuses on production and the exploration phase is skipped. All games are played in simulation (cf., Sect. 5), which lowers the barrier for new participants, especially from the planning community, while providing a realistic test scenario with simulated physics [17]. All simulations ran in a local small-scale cluster based on Kubernetes, which allows to play a large number of games in an automated fashion.

While contributing to the design, organization, and implementation of the competition, the Carologistics team also participated with two different approaches. The first approach uses the Procedural Reasoning System (PRS) [18] with a centralized global strategy that uses a specific master agent that assigns tasks to all robots [19]. The second approach uses a (non-temporal) PDDL-based planner with macro actions [20] and postpones scheduling to be solved at run-time during execution.

6 League Advancements and Continued Involvement

Carologistics members are and have been active members of the Technical, Organizational, and Executive Committees and were involved in various changes that shaped the league, such as merging the two playing fields and using physical processing machines [4,5]. Furthermore, we are major contributors to the autonomous refbox [21] and to the open simulation environment described in Sect. 5. We have also been a driving factor in the establishment of the RoboCup Industrial umbrella league [4] and the cross-over challenge between the RCLL and RoboCup@Work league [22].

6.1 RCLL Referee Box and MPS Stations

The refbox was introduced in 2013 by the Carologistics team [5] as part of their work in the Technical Committee and has been maintained by the team since then. The goal of the refbox is to ease the work for referees by keeping track of the production state and by awarding points.

In 2017, significant changes to the refbox have been introduced. For one, the refbox has been adapted to the new playing field. The new rules of the field layout have been encoded into the refbox and an external field configuration generator developed by team GRIPS[4] has been integrated. This allows a random, automatic generation of playing fields during the game setup and eases the referees' tasks while increasing the automation in the league, and therefore increases the league's similarity to a smart factory.

Furthermore, significant work has been put into the communication between refbox and MPS. In past competitions, communication between the refbox and

---

[4] http://www.robocup.tugraz.at.

MPS was not very robust, which led to a number of game restarts due to a malfunctioning playing field. For this reason, a new communication method has been introduced and a first version has been implemented for the refbox. The goal is to switch to the new communication method for the 2018 competitions. With the new implementation, network failures will only lead to a delay in communication but will not affect the state of the MPSs nor the game.

6.2   Public Release of Full Software Stack

For eleven years we have developed the *Fawkes Robot Software Framework* [7]. Its development has been mainly driven for various RoboCup leagues [23]. It has been used in RoboCup@Home, MSL, SPL and has now been evolved for the RCLL, also shown in Fig. 7.

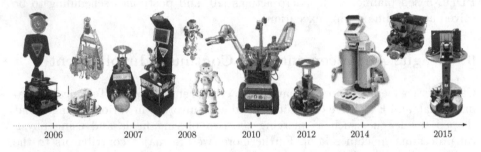

| 2006 | 2007 | 2008 | 2010 | 2012 | 2014 | 2015 |

Fig. 7. Robots running (parts of) Fawkes which were or are used for the development of the framework and its components [23].

While the domain-independent Fawkes framework is being developed in public, Carologistics was the first team in the RCLL to also release its full RCLL-specific stack[5].

6.3   RoboCup Technical Challenge

In the RCLL, each MPS has an Augmented Reality (AR) tag, which encodes a unique identifier in a 5×5 grid of black and white squares, and which can be used to identify the machine. However, with the goal to adapt to common industrial logistics scenarios, the Markerless Machine Recognition and Production challenge requires a machine recognition without using tags.

We solved this challenge by training a neural network which has a videostream as input and the likelihood of the machine types as output. We did this in a three step approach: Taking data, labeling data, and training the neural network.

---

[5] 2016 release: https://www.fawkesrobotics.org/projects/rcll2016-release/, release for 2017 is in preparation.

Most of our data was taken at the RoboCup German Open 2017. Using the Behavior Engine (cf., Sect. 3.2), we drove around each MPS and took pictures from different positions. We paid special attention to the diversity of the images: different light conditions, multiple backgrounds, and varying blurriness. We took a training set of 5000 images for each machine type. To label the images, we developed a program that allows for an interactive and convenient labeling.

Afterwards, we trained Google's pre-trained Inception-v3 model [24] and can usually recognize an MPS with one image. If a single image is not sufficient, we drive around the MPS until we are confident enough to report the machine type.

7   Conclusion

Following the major changes of 2015 and 2016, the year 2017 has been a year of stabilization both for the RCLL and for the Carologistics team. The team itself saw major shifts in personnel, with many long-time members phasing out and substantial recruitment of new talent. On a technical level, it became apparent that many core components have reached a state of relative maturity, while others have evolved into a degree of complexity that warrants a principled re-engineering.

One particular example is the CLIPS agent, which encodes a wealth of smart heuristics and recovery strategies. However, the codebase goes back to the 2012 version of the RCLL, and continuous ad-hoc fixes have grown the state model to a point where the control flow is difficult to understand and a principled error handling approach is no longer possible. Thus, one of the major challenges of next year's competition will be to design a more structured agent framework with a more sophisticated execution monitoring strategy.

Acknowledgments. The team members in 2017 are Christoph Gollok, Mostafa Gomaa, Daniel Habering, Christoph Henke, Till Hofmann, Daniel Künster, Nicolas Limpert, Victor Mataré, Tobias Neumann, Tim Niemueller, Sebastian Schönitz and Carsten Stoffels.

We gratefully acknowledge the financial support of *RWTH Aachen University* and *FH Aachen University of Applied Sciences*.

We thank the *Hans Hermann Voss-Stiftung* (http://www.hans-hermann-voss-stiftung. de/) for their financial support, as well as the *Festo Didactic SE* (https://www.festo-didactic.com) and *SICK Sensor Intelligence* (https://www.sick.com) for sponsoring our efforts by providing hardware and manufacturing support.

V. Mataré and T. Hofmann were supported by the DFG grants *FE-1077/4-1* and *GL-747/23-1* (respectively) on Constraint-based Transformations of Abstract Task Plans into Executable Actions for Autonomous Robots (http://gepris.dfg.de/gepris/ projekt/288705857?language=en).

T. Niemueller was supported by the German National Science Foundation (DFG) research unit *FOR 1513* on Hybrid Reasoning for Intelligent Systems (https://www. hybrid-reasoning.org).

References

1. Niemueller, T., et al.: Improvements for a robust production in the RoboCup logistics league 2016. In: Behnke, S., Sheh, R., Sarıel, S., Lee, D.D. (eds.) RoboCup 2016. LNCS (LNAI), vol. 9776, pp. 589–600. Springer, Cham (2017). https://doi.org/10.1007/978-3-319-68792-6_49
2. Niemueller, T., Karpas, E., Vaquero, T., Timmons, E.: Planning competition for logistics robots in simulation. In: WS on Planning and Robotics (PlanRob) at International Conference on Automated Planning and Scheduling (ICAPS), London, UK (2016)
3. Deppe, C., et al.: RoboCup Logistics League - Rules and Regulations (2017). http://www.robocup-logistics.org/rules
4. Niemueller, T., et al.: Proposal for advancements to the LLSF in 2014 and beyond. In: ICAR - 1st Workshop on Developments in RoboCup Leagues (2013)
5. Niemueller, T., Ewert, D., Reuter, S., Ferrein, A., Jeschke, S., Lakemeyer, G.: RoboCup logistics league sponsored by festo: a competitive factory automation testbed. In: Behnke, S., Veloso, M., Visser, A., Xiong, R. (eds.) RoboCup 2013. LNCS (LNAI), vol. 8371, pp. 336–347. Springer, Heidelberg (2014). https://doi.org/10.1007/978-3-662-44468-9_30
6. Karras, U., Pensky, D., Rojas, O.: Mobile robotics in education and research of logistics. In: IROS 2011 - Workshop on Metrics and Methodologies for Autonomous Robot Teams in Logistics (2011)
7. Niemueller, T., Ferrein, A., Beck, D., Lakemeyer, G.: Design principles of the component-based robot software framework fawkes. In: Ando, N., Balakirsky, S., Hemker, T., Reggiani, M., von Stryk, O. (eds.) SIMPAR 2010. LNCS (LNAI), vol. 6472, pp. 300–311. Springer, Heidelberg (2010). https://doi.org/10.1007/978-3-642-17319-6_29
8. Quigley, M., et al.: ROS: an open-source robot operating system. In: ICRA Workshop on Open Source Software (2009)
9. Niemueller, T., Lakemeyer, G., Ferrein, A.: Incremental task-level reasoning in a competitive factory automation scenario. In: Proceedings of AAAI Spring Symposium 2013 - Designing Intelligent Robots: Reintegrating AI (2013)
10. Gat, E.: Three-layer architectures. In: Kortenkamp, D., Bonasso, R.P., Murphy, R. (eds.) Artificial Intelligence and Mobile Robots, pp. 195–210. MIT Press (1998)
11. Russell, S., Norvig, P.: A Modern Approach. Artificial Intelligence, vol. 25, p. 27. Prentice-Hall, Englewood Cliffs (1995)
12. Barraquand, J., Langlois, B., Latombe, J.C.: Numerical potential field techniques for robot path planning. IEEE Trans. Syst. Man. Cybern. **22**(2), 224–241 (1992)
13. Rösmann, C., Feiten, W., Wösch, T., Hoffmann, F., Bertram, T.: Trajectory modification considering dynamic constraints of autonomous robots. In: Proceedings of ROBOTIK 2012 7th German Conference on Robotics, VDE, pp. 1–6 (2012)
14. Niemüller, T., Ferrein, A., Lakemeyer, G.: A lua-based behavior engine for controlling the humanoid robot nao. In: Baltes, J., Lagoudakis, M.G., Naruse, T., Ghidary, S.S. (eds.) RoboCup 2009. LNCS (LNAI), vol. 5949, pp. 240–251. Springer, Heidelberg (2010). https://doi.org/10.1007/978-3-642-11876-0_21
15. Wygant, R.M.: CLIPS: a powerful development and delivery expert system tool. Comput. Ind. Eng. **17**(1–4) (1989)
16. Niemueller, T., Lakemeyer, G., Ferrein, A.: The RoboCup logistics league as a benchmark for planning in robotics. In: 25th International Conference on Automated Planning and Scheduling (ICAPS) - WS on Planning in Robotics (2015)

17. Zwilling, F., Niemueller, T., Lakemeyer, G.: Simulation for the RoboCup logistics league with real-world environment agency and multi-level abstraction. In: Bianchi, R.A.C., Akin, H.L., Ramamoorthy, S., Sugiura, K. (eds.) RoboCup 2014. LNCS (LNAI), vol. 8992, pp. 220–232. Springer, Cham (2015). https://doi.org/10.1007/978-3-319-18615-3_18

18. Alami, R., Chatila, R., Fleury, S., Ghallab, M., Ingrand, F.: An architecture for autonomy. Int. J. Rob. Res. **17**(4) (1998)

19. Niemueller, T., et al.: Cyber-physical system intelligence. In: Jeschke, S., Brecher, C., Song, H., Rawat, D.B. (eds.) Industrial Internet of Things. SSWT, pp. 447–472. Springer, Cham (2017). https://doi.org/10.1007/978-3-319-42559-7_17

20. Hofmann, T., Niemueller, T., Lakemeyer, G.: Initial results on generating macro actions from a plan database for planning on autonomous mobile robots. In: Proceedings of the 27th International Conference on Automated Planning and Scheduling (ICAPS), Pittsburgh, PA, USA (2017)

21. Niemueller, T., Zug, S., Schneider, S., Karras, U.: Knowledge-based instrumentation and control for competitive industry-inspired robotic domains. KI - Künstliche Intelligenz **30**(289–299) (2016)

22. Zug, S., et al.: An integration challenge to bridge the gap among industry-inspired RoboCup leagues. In: Behnke, S., Sheh, R., Sariel, S., Lee, D.D. (eds.) RoboCup 2016. LNCS (LNAI), vol. 9776, pp. 157–168. Springer, Cham (2017). https://doi.org/10.1007/978-3-319-68792-6_13

23. Niemueller, T., Reuter, S., Ferrein, A.: Fawkes for the RoboCup logistics league. In: Almeida, L., Ji, J., Steinbauer, G., Luke, S. (eds.) RoboCup 2015. LNCS (LNAI), vol. 9513, pp. 365–373. Springer, Cham (2015). https://doi.org/10.1007/978-3-319-29339-4_31

24. Szegedy, C., Vanhoucke, V., Ioffe, S., Shlens, J., Wojna, Z.: Rethinking the inception architecture for computer vision. arXiv e-prints, December 2015

RoboCup@Work Winners 2017 Team AutonOHM

Jon Martin[✉], Helmut Engelhardt, Tobias Fink, Marco Masannek,
and Tobias Scholz

University of Applied Sciences Nuremberg Georg-Simon-Ohm,
Kesslerplatz 12, 90489 Nuremberg, Germany
{jon.martingarechana,engelhardthe57850,finkto51573,
masannekma61828,scholzto52032}@th-nuernberg.de
http://www.autonohm.de

Abstract. This paper presents the team AutonOHM which won the
RoboCup@Work competition in 2017. The tests to be performed during the RoboCup@Work 2017 competition are presented and a detailed
description of the team's hardware and software concepts are exposed.
Furthermore, improvements for future participations are discussed.

1 Introduction

The RoboCup@Work league, established in 2012, focuses on the use of mobile
manipulators and their integration with automation equipment for performing
industrial-relevant tasks [4]. After introducing the league and tests performed in
2017, we present our hardware and software approaches. This year we focused
on improving our gripper to grasp heavier objects and increasing the robustness
and velocity of the system by implementing more intelligent recovery behaviors
and reactions to sensor feedbacks.

Section 4 shows the team's hardware concept. In Sect. 5 the main software
modules such as the state machine, localization and object detection are presented. Finally, the conclusion provides a prospect to further work of team
AutonOHM (Sect. 7).

2 AutonOHM

The AutonOHM-@Work team at the University of Applied Sciences Nuremberg
Georg-Simon-Ohm was founded in September 2014. The team consists of Bachelor and Master students, supervised by a research assistant.

AutonOHM participated for the first time in the German Open 2015 tournament. In 2016 the team continued improving their system and competed in the
RoboCup@Work world championship in Leipzig and in the European Robotics
League in Bonn showing remarkable progress within the tournaments ranking
and the robot performance. In 2017 additional team members joint AutonOHM

© Springer Nature Switzerland AG 2018
H. Akiyama et al. (Eds.): RoboCup 2017, LNAI 11175, pp. 498–508, 2018.
https://doi.org/10.1007/978-3-030-00308-1_41

Fig. 1. Team AutonOHM in Nagoya after wining the RoboCup@Work competition

to improve the hardware and implement new functions on the robot. Thus new software approaches in the field of arm kinematics and grasping moving objects were developed. With the improvements of the former and new team members, team AutonOHM reached by a wide margin the 1st place in the German Open 2017 competition in Magdeburg. Even though the robot showed a great performance, many points were lost, as the current gripper was not able to grasp heavy and small objects.

Thanks to their new "German champions" title, the team received the economical support that allowed them to participate in the World Championship 2017 in Nagoya, Japan. To trespass their own result and take the chance to win at Nagoya, a new hardware approach of the gripper has been developed to overcome existing problems. This improvement allowed team AutonOHM (see Fig. 1) to grasp nearly every object without any problems. As a result, the World Championship has been won and the points of the German Open competition have been exceeded.

3   RoboCup@Work

In this section we introduce briefly the tests that have been performed during the 2017 RoboCup@Work world championship. For more detailed information see the last rulebook release in [3].

3.1   Tests

Basic Navigation Test: The purpose of the Basic Navigation Test (BNT) is to test the navigation capabilities of the robots in a goal-oriented, autonomous way. The arena is initially known and can be mapped during a set-up phase (see Fig. 3). The task specification, consist on a series of triples, each of which specifies a place, an orientation, and pause duration. The robots must reach and cover specific markers in a specified orientation and wait for the specified duration before facing the next task. In order to increase the complexity, dynamic unknown obstacles and yellow barrier tapes, which are not allowed to be crossed, are positioned in the arena (Fig. 2).

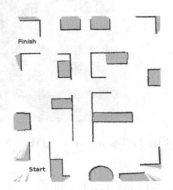

Fig. 2. The @Work arena during the RoboCup world cup in Nagoya (Color figure online)

Fig. 3. Map used for navigation

Basic Manipulation Test: The purpose of the Basic Manipulation Test (BMT) is to demonstrate basic manipulation capabilities by the robots, like grasping or placing an object. During the test, 5 objects have to be grasped and delivered from one workstation to another nearby workstation.

Basic Transportation Test: The purpose of the Basic Transportation Test (BTT) is to assess the ability of the robots for combined navigation and manipulation tasks. The robot receives the position of all available objects in the arena and a series of delivery position where some of the objects must be transported. The robot is free to plan its desired path to do this grasping and delivery tasks. This test is repeated three times with an increment of the difficulty and penalties during the competition. Also like in the BNT-Test, not previously known dynamic obstacles and yellow barrier tapes will limit the mobility of the robot during the task.

Precision Placement Test: The purpose of the Precision Placement Test (PPT) is to assess advance perception and manipulation abilities. The robot needs to detect object-specific cavities and introduce the grasped objects into them.

Rotating Table Test: The purpose of the Rotating Table Test (RTT) is to assess the robot's ability to detect and grasp moving objects which are placed on a rotating turntable.

Final: The final competition is a combination of all the above mentioned tests performed in a single round.

4   Hardware Description

We use the KUKA omni directional mobile platform youBot (Fig. 4), as it provides a hardware setup almost ready to take part in the competition. At the end effector of the manipulator, an Intel RealSense 3D SR300 camera has been mounted for detecting objects. This 3D camera has been chosen due to its ability to provide a 3D point cloud in short distances. Next to the camera, the standard gripper is replaced by an own developed, two-finger gripper. Basis is a motor mount for two Dynamixel servos provided by the team b-it-bots[1]. Two 3D printed fingers with soft rubber wheels are attached to the motors. The gripper allows grasping bigger, heavier and more complex objects than the standard YouBot gripper. Unfortunately we still have difficulties to grasp small and flat objects such as the distance tube.

Two laser scanners, one at the front and one at the back of the youBot platform, are used for localization, navigation and obstacle avoidance. The youBot's default Intel Atom computer has been replaced with an external Intel Core i7-4790K computer, providing more computing power for intensive tasks like 3D point cloud processing. Table 1 shows our hardware specifications.

Table 1. Hardware specifications

Fig. 4. KUKA youBot platform of the team AutonOHM.

PC 1	
CPU	Intel i7-4790K
RAM	16 GB DDR3
OS	Ubuntu 14.04
Gripper	
Type	3D printed, two-finger
Motors	Dynamixel AX-12A
Sensors	
Lidar Front	SICK TiM571
Lidar Back	SICK TiM571
Camera	Intel RealSense SR300

---

[1] https://github.com/mas-group.

5   Software Description

We use different open source software packages to compete in the contests. Image processing is handled with OpenCV library (2D image processing and object recognition) and PCL (3D image processing). For mapping and navigation we use gmapping and navigation-stack ROS-packages[2]. Additionally robot-pose-ekf package is used for fusing the data from the IMU and the wheel encoders, to provide more accurate data to the navigation and localization system.

The main packages we developed are further explained in the following sections. These include the state machine (Sect. 5.1), modules for global localization, localization in front of service areas (Sect. 5.2) and packages for object detection (Sect. 5.3) and manipulation (Sect. 5.4). As a new feature for the RoboCup 2017 German Open contest, we developed a module for grasping moving objects (Sect. 5.5).

Furthermore, there are other small packages including:

task_planner: After the task list is received from the referee box, the best route is calculated considering the maximum transport capacity and distances between the workstations.

youbot_inventory: With youbot_inventory it is possible to save and reuse destination locations, workstation heights and laser data.

5.1   Mission Planning

For the main control of the system, a state machine with a singleton pattern design has been developed (Fig. 5). In the initialization state, the robot receives the map, localizes itself on it and waits in "stateIdle" for new tasks to perform. These tasks are supplied by the referee box, processed by the task_planner node and sent to the state machine divided into a vector of smaller subtasks. The subtasks *Move*, *Wait*, *Grasp*, *Delivery*, *PreciseDelivery* and *RotatingTable* are now managed in the "stateNext".

The first step for each task is always to *Move* (navigate) to a specific position. Depending on the accuracy on the localization, the robot may execute a fine localization, which is explained in Sect. 5.2 and performed by the service_area_approach node. During a navigation test, once the location is reached, the robot needs to *Wait* on its position for a defined time before facing the next navigation goal. During the manipulation and transportation tasks, after the specific work station location is reached, the robot may look for specific object, container or cavity on the workstation. In case of a *Grasp* subtask, the exact pose of the desired object is identified. For *Delivering* an object, the robot may first need to recognize the exact pose of containers or cavities for *PreciseDelivery*. Once the desired pose is located, the arm manipulation is activated, whether for picking up and storing the object on the robot or for delivering it. The

---

[2] http://wiki.ros.org/.

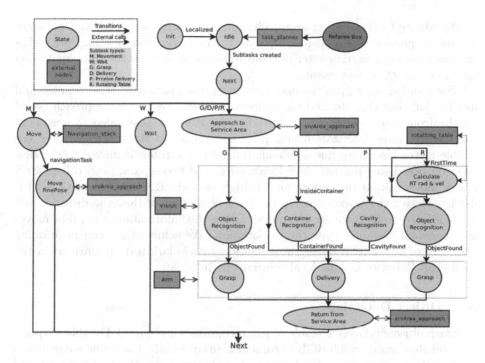

Fig. 5. State machine

vision and arm nodes are explained in Sects. 5.3 and 5.4 respectively. In case of a *RotatingTable* subtask, before searching for an object, a preprocessing approach must be performed. Here the velocity and the movement radius of the objects are calculated. The rotating table approach is explained in Sect. 5.5. Once the manipulation subtask is finished, the robot moves away from the service area and returns to the "stateNext" that will manage the following subtask to do.

Even if it is not shown in the image, most of the states have error handling behaviors that manage recovery actions in case a navigation goal is not reachable, an object cannot be found or a grasping was unsuccessful. It is very important to notice these failures and react to them by repeating the action or triggering planning modifications. If an object has not been grasped for example, it is not necessary to deliver it and therefore a task planner reconfiguration is required.

The state machine framework can be found on GitHub under our laboratory's repository[3].

5.2   Localization

For localization in the arena, we use our own particle filter algorithm. Its functionality is close to amcl localization, as described in [1,5]. The algorithm is capable of using two laser scanners and an omnidirectional movement model. Due

---

[3] https://github.com/autonohm/obviously.

to the Monte Carlo filtering approach, our localization is robust and accurate enough to provide useful positioning data to the navigation system. Positioning accuracy with our particle filter is about 6 cm, depending on the complexity and speed of the actual movement.

For more accurate positioning, such as approximation to service areas and moving left and right to find the objects on them, we use an approach based on the front laser scanner data. Initially, the robot is positioned by means of the particle filter localization and ROS navigation. If the service area is not visible in the laser scan due to its small height, the robot is moved to the destination pose using particle filter localization and two separate controllers for x and y movement. If the service area is high enough, RANSAC algorithm [2] is used to detect the workstation in the laser scan. Out of this, the distance and angle relative to the area are computed. Using this information, the robot moves in a constant distance along the workstation. We achieved a mean positioning accuracy of under 3 cm during a navigation benchmark tests performed in the European Robotics League local tournament in Milan.

5.3 Object Detection

To grasp objects reliably, a stable object recognition is required. For this purpose, an Intel RealSense SR300 RGB-D camera is used. Firstly, the robot navigates to a pregrasp position. Once the base reaches this position, the arm is positioned above the service area. Due to the limited field of view, the robot base moves right and left so all the objects in the workstation can be discovered. On each position, the plane of the service area is searched in the point cloud using the RANSAC algorithm. The detected points are then projected to the 2D RGB image and used as a mask to segment the objects in the 2D image. As all workstations have a white surface, the canny edge detector is used in order to find the concave border of the object in the segmented images for a more accurate result. To classify an object, the following features are extracted: length, width, area, circle

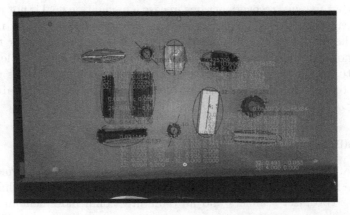

Fig. 6. Detected objects on a service area

factor, corners count and black area. With the help of a kNN classifier and the extracted features, the similarity to each previously trained item is calculated. With this information and the inventory information from the referee box, the best possible fitting combination for the detected object on the workstation is searched. To estimate the location of the object, its mass center is calculated. For the rotation of the object, the main axis of inertia is computed and used. The robot will now move in front of the elected object and activate the object recognition again to obtain a more accurate gripping pose (Fig. 6).

5.4   Object Manipulation

The Object Detection node publishes its result as a coordinate transformation represented in Fig. 7 as "target". The arm controller transforms the target's pose into the arm's workspace and calculates the corresponding joint angles with a self developed solution for the inverse kinematics: Starting with the TCP pointing orthogonally on the target position, the number of solutions is limited by the arm's specifications. Therefore, the 3D equations can be broken down to simple 2D calculations and the law of cosines.

After validating the results, the arm controller calls an interface function of the KUKA youbot drivers to set the target angles, which then move the joint motors with the internal control parameters.

To increase the precision in narrow environments and complex tasks such as grasping or precise placement, the steps between two positions can be interpolated for pseudo-linear movements. Currently the trajectory is followed point to point, but we are developing the trajectory generation for the driver interface to achieve smoother and also more precise motions.

The gripper interface is provided by a microcontroller board which connects the main computer with the two servo motors via serial connections. The communication protocol for the Dynamixels enables us to set predefined positions by

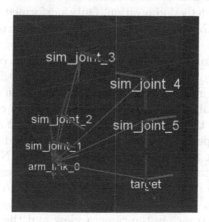

Fig. 7. Simulation of the inverse kinematics

Fig. 8. Robot in front of the rotating turntable waiting for objects

sending target angles and also to receive feedback data. With repeated gripper status checks, the arm controller is able to notice if objects are grasped or lost during motions and can therefore react accordingly.

5.5   Rotating Turntable

In this task, the robot needs to grasp three objects in motion, which are placed on a rotating turntable. Currently the direction of rotation of the table is fixed and the speed is set by the referees before this competition starts. Object position and orientation on the table can be chosen by the team themselves. The following algorithm considers various parameters such as the rotation speed, rotating direction and the pose of each object on the table.

The robot first navigates to the rotating turntable and extends the manipulator arm to an object detection position. Only performed once, a preprocessing approach is started to obtain the adjusted speed, the direction of rotation and object pose. At first, an object recognition of the first recognized item is executed to collect the 2D position of the circular path. With the collected data points, a RANSAC [2] based algorithm calculates the center and the radius of this path. Having all necessary circle properties, the robot is then able to estimate the rotation speed of the table. Since the pose of the objects can be selected by the team, all objects share the same radius. Therefore, the manipulator is extended to a search and grasp position, adjusted to the calculated results.

As an improvement for the World Championship in Nagoya, we attached a small RGB camera on top of the manipulator. With this extension, we were able to further improve the reliability of our algorithm and to reduce the execution time of the entire task. A simple background change algorithm is now applied to detect the object entrance in the camera view and the previously calculated velocity is used to close the gripper at the right time. With the implemented feedback of the gripper the robot recognizes, whether grasping was successful or has failed. In case of success, the object is placed on the robot and the manipulator then returns back to its previously search position to grasp the remaining objects. If the grasping fails, the manipulator stays in the position and waits for a new object recognition.

As the object pose on the table can be chosen by the teams and the rotation speed of the turntable is having a minor variance, we decided to place all objects on a defined radius. The manipulator pose was adjusted to this radius above the table. With usage of the background change recognition and a random delay for closing the gripper, we were able to grasp all objects. This simplification of our existing algorithm was used to be faster and to obtain more points in the competition (Fig. 8).

6 Results

(See Table 2).

Table 2. Results of the RoboCup@Work competition in 2017.

Place	Team	BNT	BMT	BTT1	BTT2	RTT	BTT3	PPT	Final	Total
1	AutonOHM	400	1118	700	850	1169	1071	600	450	6358
2	RobOTTO	350	700	450	700	1154	300	150	250	4054
3	LUHbots	200	1134	50	1304	0	0	150	625	3463
4	b-it-bots	350	700	0	0	225	0	225	650	2150
5	ARC@Work	38	300	0	0	0	0	0	0	338
6	RoboErectus	0	0	0	0	0	0	0	0	0
7	Starline	0	0	0	0	0	0	0	0	0
8	RED	0	0	0	0	0	0	0	0	0

7 Conclusion and Future Work

This paper described the participation of team AutonOHM in the RoboCup @work league. It provided detailed information of the hardware setup and software modules like localization, autonomy, image processing and object manipulation.

To win the RoboCup@Work world championship we improved our existing robot in different fields. With the new manipulator approach, we were able to save time, due to faster and more reliable arm movements. An additional RGB camera has been attached on the manipulator to update our existing rotating turntable algorithm and increase its reliability. Furthermore, minor corrections have been done in the navigation and object detection approaches to reduce the execution time of each task.

In order to further improve the robot's capabilities, our main priorities for the future are: Develop a new energy concept for a longer run-time of the youbot platform; Improve our log and recovery system by increasing the feedbacks from different sensors such as the gripper, laser scanners and camera. Finally, as the youbot has been discontinued, we started developing a new mobile platform that will be shorter for a better navigation performance and that integrates optimal place for the new energy concept and computer (NUC i7).

References

1. Dellaert, F., Fox, D., Burgard, W., Thrun, S.: Monte Carlo localization for mobile robots. In: Proceedings 1999 IEEE International Conference on Robotics and Automation (Cat. No.99CH36288C), vol. 2, pp. 1322–1328, May 1999
2. Fischler, M.A., Bolles, R.C.: Random sample consensus: a paradigm for model fitting with applications to image analysis and automated cartography. Commun. ACM 24(6), 381–395 (1981)
3. Hochgeschwender, N., et al.: Work Rulebook (2017)
4. Kraetzschmar, G.K.: RoboCup@Work: competing for the factory of the future. In: Bianchi, R.A.C., Akin, H.L., Ramamoorthy, S., Sugiura, K. (eds.) RoboCup 2014. LNCS (LNAI), vol. 8992, pp. 171–182. Springer, Cham (2015). https://doi.org/10.1007/978-3-319-18615-3_14
5. Thrun, S., Burgard, W., Fox, D.: Probablistic Robotics. Massachusetts Institute of Technology (2006)

homer@UniKoblenz: Winning Team of the RoboCup@Home Open Platform League 2017

Raphael Memmesheimer[(✉)], Vikor Seib, and Dietrich Paulus

Active Vision Group, Institute for Computational Visualistics,
University of Koblenz-Landau, 56070 Koblenz, Germany
{raphael,vseib,paulus}@uni-koblenz.de,
http://homer.uni-koblenz.de, http://agas.uni-koblenz.de

Abstract. In this paper we present the approaches that we used for this year's RoboCup@Home participation in the Open Platform League. A special focus was put on team collaboration by handing over objects between two robots of different teams that were not connected by network. The robots communicated using natural language (speech synthesis, speech recognition), a typical human-robot "interface" that was adapted to robot-robot interaction. Furthermore, we integrated new approaches for online tracking and learning of an operator, have shown a novel approach for teaching a robot new commands by describing them using natural language and a set of previously known commands. Parameters of these commands are still interchangeable. Finally, we integrated deep neural networks for person detection and recognition, human pose estimation, gender classification and object recognition.

Keywords: RoboCup@Home · RoboCup · Open Platform League
Domestic service robotics · homer@UniKoblenz

1 Introduction

In this year's RoboCup we participated in the RoboCup@Home Open Platform League. The team consisted of one supervisor and 6 students. Additionally, two more students were supporting the preparation. This year we participated successfully at the RoboCup World Cup where we achieved the first place. After the RoboCup World Cup in Hefei, China (2015) this is the second time that we achieved this title. Beside RoboCup competitions we also attend the European Robotics League and participated in the ICRA Mobile Manipulation Challenge.

For this year's participation we focused on cooperation between robots of different teams. We demonstrated this twice. Once at the RoboCup GermanOpen and once in RoboCup@Home Open Platform league, where robots of two different teams where handing over objects without an established network connection. This was achieved by using human-robot interaction interfaces and adapt

© Springer Nature Switzerland AG 2018
H. Akiyama et al. (Eds.): RoboCup 2017, LNAI 11175, pp. 509–520, 2018.
https://doi.org/10.1007/978-3-030-00308-1_42

them to robot-robot interaction. The robots were talking to each other using speech synthesis, recognizing objects via speech recognition and handing over objects using the same approach that humans are using to get objects handed over by a person. Furthermore, we created an approach for semantically mapping rooms without prior knowledge. We demonstrated this using an attention guided process, where the robot extracts the face pose of a person. The robot directed its view to the perceived direction and started finding furniture. The location was transmitted to an auxiliary robot to put an object on top of the recognized table.

This year we also improved our team's infrastructure by a continuous software integration and built our packages for a variety of processor architectures.

Section 2 gives a short overview of the RoboCup@Home competition. In Sect. 3 we present the robots that we used for this years participation. A special focus is put on the hardware changes that the robots have undergone. Section 4 describes the architecture and software approaches we are using. An overview of the current research topics is given in Sect. 5. Finally, Sect. 6 summarizes and concludes this paper.

2   RoboCup@Home

The RoboCup@Home league [1] aims at bringing robots into domestic environments and support people in daily scenarios.

The league has been separated into three sub-leagues, namely the Domestic Standard Platform league (DSPL), the Social Standard Platform League (SSPL) and the Open Platform League (OPL). The first two are based on standard platforms provided by commercial companies and aim at benchmarking teams on their integrated software on a common hardware platform. The extension possibilities of these platforms is limited. The Open Platform League is targeting teams that built their own robots or use robots that don't belong to one of the two standard platform leagues. The robots can be customized individually as long as they follow the definitions by the rulebook. The goal of the league is to follow one general rulebook for all sub-leagues. In comparison to the soccer league, where a global goal is defined and the rules are heavily influenced by the FIFA rules, in RoboCup@Home the rules are defined on an yearly basis. The competition is divided into three stages. The first stage aims at benchmarking basic functionalities like manipulating, speech understanding, finding, tracking and following persons, recognizing objects and navigation capabilities.

In the second stage the basic functionalities from the first stage are integrated to form more complex tasks. The robots have to e.g. set a table, serve in a restaurant at a random location without prior knowledge and help to carry and store groceries. In the finals the top two teams of each sub-league show a demonstration which should be interesting from a research and application perspective.

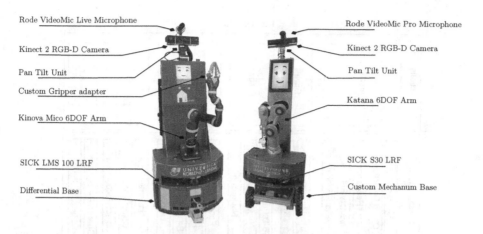

Rode VideoMic Live Microphone

Kinect 2 RGB-D Camera

Pan Tilt Unit

Custom Gripper adapter

Kinova Mico 6DOF Arm

SICK LMS 100 LRF

Differential Base

Rode VideoMic Pro Microphone

Kinect 2 RGB-D Camera

Pan Tilt Unit

Katana 6DOF Arm

SICK S30 LRF

Custom Mechanum Base

Fig. 1. The robots Lisa (left) and Marge (right). Lisa is our main robot, inspired by Marge as a successor. Both robots run the same software with minor exceptions the model descriptions and hardware interfaces.

3   Hardware

In 2017 we updated our two domestic robot platforms slightly (Fig. 1). We extended the sensor setup on our main robot's head. The sensor head's basis is 3d-printed and allows for modular extensions. In addition to the Microsoft Kinect 2 which has a slightly higher field of view in comparison to the Microsoft Kinect or the Asus Xtion, we mounted two Asus Xtion RGB-D cameras. One is facing forward, closely located to the Kinect 2 and is used on demand where the Kinect 2 fails to provide depth information (i.e. on black furniture). The second one is facing backwards in order to track persons during guiding. This has the benefit that the pan tilt unit does not need to turn around by 180 degree during following. We changed the directional microphone setup on our main robot. The Rode VideoMic Pro was replaced by a Rode VideoMic Go as the new microphone does not need an external battery and we found no drawbacks in the speech recognition results. For sound source localization we now interface the microphone array of the Kinect 2. Those four microphones allow us to localize sound sources in front of the camera. The power supply was changed to TB47S lithium ion batteries with 22.2 V and 99.9 Wh by DJI, usually used in drones. We use a pair of these in each robot. The batteries can be changed independently and therefore allow hot swapping. Further, the batteries can be transported on airplanes being the ideal choice for traveling with the robots. We use the Kinova Mico arm for mobile manipulation, but designed adapters for allowing interchangeable custom 3d-printed end-effector attachments. The original mechanics for controlling the end-effectors are still used. For gripping tasks we mount Festo Finrays at the attachments, but are flexible to use and design additional tools [2]. An Odroid C2 mini computer is used to interface the base control on our main robot and display the robotic face even when the main

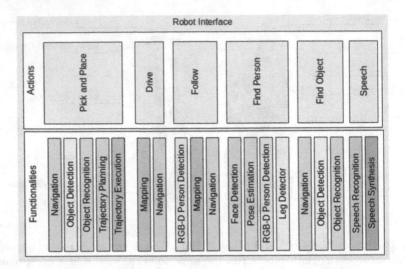

Fig. 2. Our robot architecture. The robot interface is used as a central interface for accessing the high level robot action (also behaviours) and is common for all our robots. The high level robot actions make use of the basic functionalities, these functionalities are reused in different actions. Similar color encode that the class of the functionality/action. Interesting is that actions like pick and place are relying on a variety of functionalities which reflect a high failure rate in the competition. (Color figure online)

computer is not running. The auxiliary robot is now also equipped with an 10 in. screen for supporting the human robot interaction with the robotic face.

4   Approaches

We now present briefly present our architecture and then give description on our algorithmic approaches (see Fig. 2 for a visual overview).

Architecture. ROS [3] Kinetic and Ubuntu 16.04 are building the basis of our architecture. On top of ROS, our developed software is focusing on an higher level representation that simplifies the development of demonstrations. Behaviors are modelled using the ROS actionlib and are interfaced by a robot API which is common for both robots. The behaviours can be executed on both robots by only adjusting the robot model representations.

Object Detection. For object detection we use a planar surface estimation and cluster objects above the planar surface. The robot tilts the RGB-D camera towards a possible object location. The gathered point cloud is then transformed into the robots coordinate frame where an up facing normal vector defines the search space for the planar surfaces. Points above the plane hypotheses are individually clustered each resulting in an object hypothesis. In an additional step those hypotheses are filtered to eliminate too small clusters and objects that can not be manipulated.

For obstacle avoidance we estimate planar surfaces on all axes in order to extract table tops, level and side walls of bookcases. These planar points are used for estimating a 3d grip map used for obstacle avoidance and has been found sufficient for the majority of manipulation tasks. In comparison to the use of the full point cloud as an input for the grid map estimation is the robustness against effects like speckles.

Object Recognition. From the filtered object hypotheses we extract an image patch that is passed to an object classification network. In contrast to previous attendances [4] we now use a pre-trained Inception [5] network where we fine tune the final layer. For training we created a dataset containing 4000 images with different perspectives around the object and at different camera heights of all official competition objects. We skipped further data augmentation as we found no major recognition improvements. The resulting training images have been shared before the competition days with all participating teams.

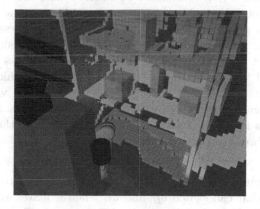

Fig. 3. The robot during the grasping process. The planar surfaces are extracted and a 3d gridmap is generated for obstacle avoidance.

Manipulation. MoveIt! [6] is used as a motion planning framework for manipulation tasks. The RRT-connect [7] algorithm is used for trajectory planning. Planar surfaces at the main axes are extracted and used for obstacle avoidance by an octree based 3d gridmap representation [8] (see Fig. 3). We evaluated and integrated different approaches for the manipulation task. First, we adjust the position of the robot in order to get a certain distance to the object. This allows us to increase the probability of a successful trajectory execution. Many trajectories can not be executed with required accuracy for the end-effector target pose. Therefore, we execute trajectories with target poses in front of the object where the end-effector is aligned upwards. The distance is then again adjusted by movements of the robot base. This approach has some disadvantages i.e., the robot needs enough space for the movements. A second approach samples possible grasp hypotheses around the object and checks if the estimated pose is executable. If the execution fails the next possible grasp pose is generated until a valid one is found. The second approach overcomes the need to adjust the robot's position.

Speech Recognition. For speech recognition we use a grammar based solution supported by an academic license for the VoCon speech recognition software by Nuance[1]. We combine continuous listening with a begin and end-of-speech detection to get good results even for complex commands. Recognition results below a certain threshold are rejected. The grammar generation is supported by the content of a semantic knowledge base that is also used for our general purpose architecture.

Speech Understanding. We propose a novel approach to teach a robot an unknown command by natural language assuming that the given instruction set is representable with a BNF grammar. To achieve this, first we define a broad BNF grammar containing a huge set of commands that the robot is able to execute. We use a grammar compiler [9] to generate a parser with the BNF grammar as input. In this parser we then connect the parser to actual robot actions and extract the parameters. In case the robot receives a command that was not connected to a robot action (that's what we call unknown command) the robot asks for further instructions. When you have a very broad set of robot actions you can create a high variety of new commands. Since we also can extract parameters for the unknown commands and replace them the command is applicable in a broad variety of situations.

Operator Following. We developed an integrated system to detect and track a single operator that can switch *off* and *on* when it leaves and (re-)enters the scene. Our method is based on a set-valued Bayes-optimal state estimator that integrates RGB-D detections and image-based classification to improve tracking results in severe clutter and under long-term occlusion. The classifier is trained in two stages: First, we train a deep convolutional neural network to obtain a feature representation for person re-identification. Then, we bootstrap an online classifier that discriminates the operator from remaining people on the output of the state-estimator. See Fig. 4 for an visual overview. The approach is applicable for following and guiding tasks.

Person Detection. For person detection we integrated multiple approaches for different sensors that can be optionally fused and used to verify measurements

---

[1] http://www.nuance.com/for-business/speech-recognition-solutions/vocon-hybrid/index.htm.

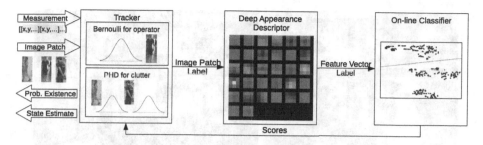

Fig. 4. Tracking Overview. A RFS Bernoulli single target tracker in cooperation with a deep appearance descriptor to re-identify and online classify the appearance of the tracked identity. Measurements, consisting of positional information and an additional image patch serve as input. The Bernoulli tracker estimates the existence probability and the likelihood of the measurement being the operator. Positive against negative appearances are contentiously trained. The online classifier returns scores of the patch being the operator.

Fig. 5. The gesture estimates visualized. The joint estimated are denoted by the red circles. The blue font states the classified gesture. p stands for pointing, w for waving, l for left, r for right and a for arm. Note that there are also joint estimated that have been extracted for the reflection in the door. (Color figure online)

of other sensors. A leg detector [10] is applied on the laser data. This yields high frequency, but error prone measurements. For finding persons in point clouds we follow an approach by Munaro et al. [11]. The most reliable detections are by a face detection approach [12], assuming that the persons are facing the camera. For gender estimation we then apply an approach by Levi et al. [13].

Gesture Recognition. Joints of persons are estimated using a convolutional pose machine [14,15]. Relations between the arm joints are then constrained by their angle relations to classify gestures like waving, pointing and a stop sign for both arms individually. The convolutional pose machine is able to extract all joint positions of all persons in one pass. The center of the person is projected to the robot frame by depth projection. Figure 5 gives an example visualization of the joint estimation and the corresponding estimated class labels of the gesture per person.

(A)   (B)

Fig. 6. Handing over objects as a team collaboration with team SocRob [16] in RoboCup German Open 2017 (A) and during the preparation with team Happy Mini [17] during RoboCup 2017 in Nagoya (B). There was no network connection between the robots.

Fig. 7. Handover between a person and a robot. The same approach is used for detecting a handover of a person to robot as we did for a robot to robot handover

Team Collaboration. A focus of our RoboCup@Home participation was a team to team collaboration. In RoboCup@Home German Open we collaborated with SocRob team and in this year's WorldCup we collaborated with Team Happy-Mini. We built on top of our approaches from 2015, where both of our robots where transferring tasks by natural language to each other. To be more precise, the speech synthesis of one robot was recognized by the speech recognition of the other robot. The robots were not connected by network. This year we transferred this approach to an inter-team collaboration and extended it by adapting an other human-robot interface to it successfully. In addition to the natural language communication we adapted the same approach for handing over objects from a human to a robot as we did for handing over objects between both robots.

Figure 6 show these same approaches in action between robots as well as between a person and a robot (Fig. 7).

5   Current Research

Imitation Learning. With the recent development in pose estimation algorithms it is now possible to develop approaches for imitation learning by visual observation that will passively observe human instructors and allow the reasoning to adapt the behaviour. Where in the past the human instructors need to be wired or marked using visual markers to extract the needed joints we can now extract them passively allowing the instructors to perform a task in a natural way and therefore do not affect the instructor [18].

The goal is to develop approaches that let the operator work as free as possible from any markers or unnatural interactions with the robot or observation system. We further reduce the components, therefore a mobile robot equipped with a visionary system and a manipulator will be sufficient to imitate the performed tasks as it would be done by another person.

The first step is extracting the human poses and set them into relations of further observations like detected objects and the general semantic knowledge of the robot.

These observations should be classified. The classes are represented by the robot behaviours. For instance we can classify a movement behaviour by observing the human pose and set it into relation with certain points of interest in the map. This yields a set of problems we want to address:

- action classification based on the robot observations and semantic representation
- developing an approach for the robot to estimate a next best view location for extracting as much meaningful information for the classification as possible
- a probabilistic representation that allows reasoning based on the input observations
- for more precise imitation learning tasks we try to analyze the human movements of the arm and hand in relation to recognized objects and adapt it to a robot arm that may is has different degrees of freedom.

The first step is the creation of a dataset that extends existing datasets on action classification. These datasets currently are focusing on simple actions like running, walking and kicking. We aim to create a dataset with focus on domestic indoor activities which includes next to the RGB-D camera stream also the knowledge of the robot about it's environment like the map and the points/regions of interest.

3D Shape Classification. Most of the robots in RoboCup@Home are equipped with 3D sensors (e.g. RGBD-cameras). One of the most used libraries for 3D data processing is the Point Cloud Library (PCL) [19]. The PCL offers many 3D descriptors, algorithms and useful data structures. Further, a complete object recognition pipeline [20] and an adaptation of Implicit Shape Models (ISM) to 3D data [21] is available. However, these two object classification methods in the PCL are either not flexible enough or do not provide sufficiently good results.

We are currently working on a 3D shape classification approach to overcome these limitations. For our own approach we take inspiration from Naive-Bayes Nearest Neighbor (NBNN) and combine it with the localized hough-voting scheme of ISM. We obtain a competitive 3D classification algorithm that combines the best of ISM and NBNN. The direct utilization of extracted features in training for the codebook makes our method learning-free (as NBNN and contrary to ISM that uses vector quantization). On the other hand the localized hough-voting of ISM allows to filter out erroneous feature correspondences and irrelevant side maxima. Our algorithm is competitive with standard approaches for 3D object classification on commonly used datasets.

Currently, we focus on several methods to estimate a descriptor's relevance during training to obtain a smaller, more descriptive codebook and omit redundancies. We achieve the goal of codebook cleaning without significant loss or even with an increase of classification performance. Further, we experiment with means of selecting relevant dimensions of a feature descriptor. We inspect the structure of the applied SHOT descriptor and identify less-significant descriptor dimensions that are left out after training. All of these is combined with a global verification approach to boost the classification performance. We plan to make the source code of our approach publicly available and thus to make a contribution to the PCL and boost the performance of open-source 3D classification software.

Affordances. To adequately fulfill its tasks a mobile robot needs to understand its environment. Object classification is a crucial capability when it comes to environment understanding. However, object classification by itself may not be sufficient as it only addresses the task of deciding what a specific object is. In many cases we also want to know *how* that specific object can be used by a robot or a human. The action possibilities offered by an object to a specific agent (e.g. human, robot) are called affordances [22].

Special requirements on service robots arise if considering that service robots share a common environment with humans. Domestic service robots even reside in environment specifically designed for humans. It is thus crucial for service robots to understand humans and their actions. In other words, in a human-centered environment with humans as agents, a robot needs to be aware of affordances for humans, but also of affordances for itself as the robot also forms an agent in that domestic environment. We have successfully shown how an agent representing a human is used to visually infer affordances for sitting and for lying down [23]. A robot equipped with such a notion of affordances is enabled to assist and guide people in a domestic environment.

We are additionally exploring another abstraction of the agent model concept. Instead of a human or robot we model a hand agent (which again can be a human hand or a robotic gripper). This agent model allows us to detect grasping affordances and to estimate suitable grasping poses for given objects. Together with the above mentioned object classification approach this grasping affordances estimation can be combined to form a complete processing pipeline for mobile manipulation. Further, imitation learning will be helpful to achieve more accurate results in grasping affordance estimation.

6 Summary and Outlook

In this paper we described the how the team is composed, gave a brief overview of RoboCup@Home, described the hardware changes in comparison to previous attendances. A major focus was set on the description of the software approaches. In the end we gave an insight on our current research topics.

We proposed an novel approach for speech understanding which we proved to be adaptable to unknown commands. In addition, we have shown a team-team collaboration without relying on network connection, but instead on interfaces that are also commonly used for human-robot interaction. Together with team SocRob and Happy Mini we have shown the first two robot-robot hand overs between robots from different teams in the league. In the final demonstration we have shown that the robot is able to localize moved furniture which could be used for later manipulation tasks. The localization was attentionally guided by view direction analysis of a person. In the future we aim for more application of our current research topics.

Acknowledgement. First we want to thank the participating students Niklas Yann Wettengel, Florian Polster, Lukas Buchhold, Malte Roosen, Moritz Löhne, Ivanna Myckhalchychyna and Daniel Müller. Thanks to Nuance Communications Inc. for supporting the team with an academic licence for speech recognition. Further we want to thank NVIDIA for the grant of a graphics card that has been used for training the operator re-identification and the object classification.

References

1. van Beek, L., Holz, D., Matamoros, M., Rascon, C., Wachsmuth, S.: Robocup@home 2017: Rules and regulations (2017). http://www.robocupathome. org/rules/2017_rulebook.pdf
2. Stückler, J., Behnke, S.: Adaptive tool-use strategies for anthropomorphic service robots. In: 2014 14th IEEE-RAS International Conference on Humanoid Robots (Humanoids), pp. 755–760. IEEE (2014)
3. Quigley, M., et al.: ROS: an open-source robot operating system. In: ICRA Workshop on Open Source Software (2009)
4. Seib, V., Kusenbach, M., Thierfelder, S., Paulus, D.: Object recognition using Hough-transform clustering of surf features. In: International Workshops on Electrical and Computer Engineering Subfields, pp. 176–183. Scientific Cooperations Publications (2014)
5. Szegedy, C., et al.: Going deeper with convolutions. In: IEEE Conference on Computer Vision and Pattern Recognition, CVPR 2015, Boston, MA, USA, 7–12 June 2015, pp. 1–9. IEEE Computer Society (2015) https://doi.org/10.1109/CVPR. 2015.7298594
6. Chitta, S., Sucan, I., Cousins, S.: Moveit![ros topics]. IEEE Rob. Autom. Mag. **19**(1), 18–19 (2012)

7. Kuffner, J.J., LaValle, S.M.: RRT-connect: an efficient approach to single-query path planning. In: IEEE International Conference on Proceedings of the Robotics and Automation, ICRA 2000, vol. 2, pp. 995–1001. IEEE (2000)

8. Hornung, A., Wurm, K.M., Bennewitz, M., Stachniss, C., Burgard, W.: OctoMap: an efficient probabilistic 3D mapping framework based on octrees. Auton. Rob. **34**(3), 189–206 (2013)

9. Ford, B.: Parsing expression grammars: a recognition-based syntactic foundation. In: Jones, N.D., Leroy, X. (eds.) Proceedings of the 31st ACM SIGPLAN-SIGACT Symposium on Principles of Programming Languages, POPL 2004, Venice, Italy, 14–16 January 2004, pp. 111–122. ACM (2004). https://doi.org/10.1145/964001.964011

10. Lu, D.V., Smart, W.D.: Towards more efficient navigation for robots and humans. In: IEEE/RSJ International Conference on Intelligent Robots and Systems (IROS), pp. 1707–1713. IEEE (2013)

11. Munaro, M., Menegatti, E.: Fast RGB-D people tracking for service robots. Auton. Rob. **37**(3), 227–242 (2014)

12. Zhang, K., Zhang, Z., Li, Z., Qiao, Y.: Joint face detection and alignment using multitask cascaded convolutional networks. IEEE Sig. Process. Lett. **23**(10), 1499–1503 (2016)

13. Levi, G., Hassner, T.: Emotion recognition in the wild via convolutional neural networks and mapped binary patterns. In: Proceedings of the 2015 ACM on International Conference on Multimodal Interaction, pp. 503–510. ACM (2015)

14. Cao, Z., Simon, T., Wei, S.-E., Sheikh, Y.: Realtime multi-person 2D pose estimation using part affinity fields. In: CVPR (2017)

15. Wei, S.-E., Ramakrishna, V., Kanade, T., Sheikh, Y.: Convolutional pose machines. In: CVPR (2016)

16. Ventura, R., et al.: Socrob@ home: team description paper for robocup@ home (2016)

17. Demura, K., et al.: Happy mini 2017 team description paper

18. Kuniyoshi, Y., Inaba, M., Inoue, H.: Learning by watching: extracting reusable task knowledge from visual observation of human performance. IEEE Trans. Rob. Autom. **10**(6), 799–822 (1994). https://doi.org/10.1109/70.338535

19. Rusu, R.B., Cousins, S.: 3D is here: point cloud library (PCL). In: 2011 IEEE International Conference on Robotics and Automation (ICRA), pp. 1–4. IEEE (2011)

20. Aldoma, A., et al.: Tutorial: point cloud library: three-dimensional object recognition and 6 DOF pose estimation. IEEE Rob. Autom. Mag. **19**(3), 80–91 (2012)

21. Knopp, J., Prasad, M., Willems, G., Timofte, R., Van Gool, L.: Hough transform and 3D SURF for robust three dimensional classification. In: Daniilidis, K., Maragos, P., Paragios, N. (eds.) ECCV 2010. LNCS, vol. 6316, pp. 589–602. Springer, Heidelberg (2010). https://doi.org/10.1007/978-3-642-15567-3_43

22. Gibson, J.J.: The Ecological Approach to Visual Perception. Routledge, Abingdon (1986)

23. Seib, V., Knauf, M., Paulus, D.: Affordance origami: unfolding agent models for hierarchical affordance prediction. In: Braz, J., et al. (eds.) VISIGRAPP 2016. CCIS, vol. 693, pp. 555–574. Springer, Cham (2017). https://doi.org/10.1007/978-3-319-64870-5_27

Author Index